CRACKNELL'S STATUTES

Constitutional and Administrative Law

Fourth Edition

D G CRACKNELL
LLB, of the Middle Temple, Barrister

OLD BAILEY PRESS

OLD BAILEY PRESS
at Holborn College, Woolwich Road,
Charlton, London, SE7 8LN

First published 1995
Fourth edition 2005

© D G Cracknell 2005

All Old Bailey Press publications enjoy copyright protection.

All rights reserved. No part of this publication may be reproduced or transmitted in any form or by any means, electronic, mechanical, photocopying, recording or otherwise, or stored in any retrieval system of any nature without either the written permission of the copyright holder, application for which should be made to the Old Bailey Press, or a licence permitting restricted copying in the United Kingdom issued by the Copyright Licensing Agency.

Any person who infringes the above in relation to this publication may be liable to criminal prosecution and civil claims for damages.

ISBN 1 85836 584 8

British Library Cataloguing-in-Publication.

A catalogue record for this book is available from the British Library.

Printed and bound in Great Britain.

CONTENTS

PREFACE

Preparing a collection of statutory material for students studying constitutional and administrative law presents particular problems. The absence of a written constitution leaves the editor with the task of selecting, from a mosaic of legislative measures, Acts that, by general consensus, possess some particular constitutional significance.

These problems are compounded by the fact that, unlike some of the other 'core' subjects, the range of issues falling within the constitutional and administrative law syllabus can vary widely from one institution to another.

In addition to updating the statutory provisions previously included, in the light of any repeals, insertions or substitutions, this edition includes, amongst others, the relevant provisions of the Anti-social Behaviour Act 2003, the European Parliamentary and Local Elections (Pilots) Act 2004 and the Asylum and Immigration (Treatment of Claimants, etc) Act 2004.

The extracts from statutes contained in this book incorporate provisions, and amendments to and substitutions within those provisions, which were in force on 1 February 2005. The source of any changes is recorded at the end of each statute.

Although they were not in force on 1 February, s26 of and Schedules 1 and 2 to the Asylum and Immigration (Treatment of Claimants, etc) Act 2004 (provisions relating to the new Asylum and Immigration Tribunal) have been covered since it is known that they will come into force on 4 April 2005.

Suggestions as to material which should be included in future editions would be gratefully received and carefully considered.

ALPHABETICAL TABLE OF STATUTES

MAGNA CARTA 1297

(25 Edw 1)

29 Imprisonment, etc, contrary to law

No freeman shall be taken or imprisoned, or be disseised of his freehold, or liberties, or free customs, or be outlawed, or exiled, or any other wise destroyed; nor will we not pass upon him, nor condemn him, but by lawful judgment of his peers, or by the law of the land. We will sell to no man, we will not deny or defer to any man either justice or right.

BILL OF RIGHTS 1688

(1 Will & Mar sess 2 c 2)

Whereas the lords spiritual and temporall and comons assembled at Westminster lawfully fully and freely representing all the estates of the people of this realme did upon the thirteenth day of February in the yeare of our Lord one thousand six hundred and eighty eight present unto their Majesties then called and known by the names and stile of William and Mary Prince and Princess of Orange being present in their proper persons a certaine declaration in writeing made by the said lords and comons in the words following viz

Whereas the late King James the Second by the assistance of diverse evill councillors judges and ministers imployed by him did endeavour to subvert and extirpate the Protestant religion and the lawes and liberties of this kingdome

By assumeing and exerciseing a power of dispensing with and suspending of lawes and the execution of lawes without consent of Parlyament.

By committing and prosecuting diverse worthy prelates for humbly petitioning to be excused from concurring to the said assumed power.

By issueing and causeing to be executed a commission under the great seale for erecting a court called the court of commissioners for ecclesiasticall causes.

By levying money for and to the use of the Crowne by pretence of prerogative for other time and in other manner then the same was granted by Parlyament.

By raising and keeping a standing army within this kingdome in time of peace without consent of Parlyament and quartering soldiers contrary to law.

By causing severall good subjects being protestants to be disarmed at the same time when papists were both armed and imployed contrary to law.

By vilating the freedome of election of members to serve in Parlyament.

By prosecutions in the Court of King's Bench for matters and causes cognizable onely in Parlyament and by diverse other arbitrary and illegall courses.

And whereas of late yeares partiall corrupt and unqualifyed persons have beene returned and served on juryes in tryalls and particularly diverse jurors in tryalls for high treason which were not freeholders.

And excessive baile hath beene required of persons committed in criminall cases to elude the benefitt of the lawes made for the liberty of the subjects.

And excessive fines have been imposed.

And illegall and cruell punishments inflicted.

And severall grants and promises made of fines and forfeitures before any conviction or judgement against the persons upon whome the same were to be levyed.

All which are utterly and directly contrary to the knowne lawes and statutes and freedom of this realme.

And whereas the said late King James the Second haveing abdicated the government and the throne being thereby vacant his Hignesse the Prince of Orange (whome it hath pleased Almighty God to make the glorious instrument of delivering this kingdome from popery and arbitrary power) did (by the advice of the lords spirituall and temporall and diverse principall persons of the commons) cause letters to be written to the lords spirituall and temporall being protestants and other letters to the several countyes cityes universities boroughs and cinque ports for the choosing of such persons to represent them as were of right to be sent to Parlyament to meete and sitt at Westminster upon the two and twentyeth day of January in this yeare one thousand six hundred eighty and eight in order to such an establishment as that their religion lawes and liberties might not againe be in danger of being subverted, upon which letters elections haveing beene accordingly made.

And thereupon the said lords spirituall and temporall and commons pursuant to their respective letters and elections being now assembled in a full and free representative of this nation takeing into their most serious consideration the best means for attaining the ends aforesaid doe in the first place (as their auncestors in like case have usually done) for the vindicating and asserting their auntient rights and liberties, declare

1 Suspending power

That the pretended power of suspending of laws or the execution of laws by regall authority without consent of Parlyament is illegall.

2 Late dispensing power

That the pretended power of dispensing with laws or the execution of laws by regall authoritie as it hath been assumed and exercised of late is illegall.

3 Ecclesiastical courts illegal

That the commission for erecting the late court of commissioners for ecclesiastical causes and all other commissions and courts of like nature are illegal and pernicious.

4 Levying money

That levying money for or to the use of the Crowne by pretence of prerogative without grant of Parlyament for longer time or in other manner then the same is or shall be granted is illegal.

5 Right to petition

That it is the right of the subjects to petition the King and all commitments and prosecutions for such petitioning are illegal.

6 Standing army

That the raising or keeping a standing army within the kingdome in time of peace unlesse it be with consent of Parlyament is against law.

7 Subjects' arms

That the subjects which are protestants may have arms for their defence suitable to their conditions and as allowed by law.

8 Freedom of election

That election of members of Parlyament ought to be free.

9 Freedom of speech

That the freedome of speech and debates or proceedings in Parlyament ought not to be impeached or questioned in any court or place out of Parlyament.

10 Excessive bail

That excessive baile ought not to be required nor excessive fines imposed nor cruell and unusuall punishments inflicted.

11 Juries

That jurors ought to be duly impannelled and returned ...

As amended by the Juries Act 1825, s62; Statute Law Revision Act 1950.

ACT OF SETTLEMENT 1700

(12 & 13 Will 3 c 2)

1 The Princess Sophia, Electress and Duchess dowager of Hanover, daughter of the late Queen of Bohemia, daughter of King James the First, to inherit after the King and the Princess Anne, in default of issue of the said princess and his Majesty, respectively: and the heirs of her body, being protestants

The most excellent Princess Sophia Electress and Duchess dowager of Hanover daughter of the most excellent Princess Elizabeth late Queen of Bohemia daughter of our late sovereign lord king James the First of happy memory be and is hereby declared to be the next in succession in the protestant line to the imperiall crown and dignity of the said realms of England France and Ireland with the dominions and territories thereunto belonging after his Majesty and the Princess Ann of Denmark and in default of issue of the said Princess Ann and of his Majesty respectively and that from and after the deceases of his said Majesty our now sovereign lord and of her royall Highness the Princess Ann of Denmark and for default of issue of the said Princess Ann and of his Majesty respectively the crown and regall government of the said kingdoms of England France and Ireland and of the dominions thereunto belonging with the royall state and dignity of the said realms and all honours stiles titles regalities prerogatives powers jurisdictions and authorities to the same belonging and appertaining shall be remain and continue to the said most excellent Princess Sophia and the heirs of her body being protestants. And thereunto the said lords spirituall and temporall and commons shall and will in the name of all the people of this realm most humbly and faithfully submitt themselves their heirs and posterities and do faithfully promise that after the deceases of his Majesty and her royall Highness and the failure of the heirs of their respective bodies to stand to maintain and defend the said Princess Sophia and the heirs of her body being protestants according to the limitation and succession of the crown in this Act specified and contained to the utmost of their powers with their lives and estates against all persons whatsoever that shall attempt any thing to the contrary.

2 The persons inheritable by this Act, holding communion with the church of Rome, incapacitated as by the former Act, to take the oath at their coronation, according to Stat 1 W & M c 6

Provided always and it is hereby enacted that all and every person and persons who shall or may take or inherit the said crown by vertue of the limitation of this present

Act and is are or shall be reconciled to or shall hold communion with the see or church of Rome or shall profess the popish religion or shall marry a papist shall be subject to such incapacities as in such case or cases are by the said recited Act provided enacted and established. And that every King and Queen of this realm who shall come to and succeed in the imperiall crown of this kingdom by vertue of this Act shall have the coronation oath administered to him her or them at their respective coronations according to the Act of Parliament made in the first year of the reign of his Majesty and the said late Queen Mary intituled An Act for establishing the coronation oath and shall make subscribe and repeat the declaration in the Act first above recited mentioned or referred to in the manner and form thereby prescribed.

3 Further provisions for securing the religion, laws, and liberties of these realms

And whereas it is requisite and necessary that some further provision be made for securing our religion laws and liberties from and after the death of his Majesty and the Princess Ann of Denmark and in default of issue of the body of the said princess and of his Majesty respectively. Be it enacted by the Kings most excellent Majesty by and with the advice and consent of the lords spirituall and temporall and commons in Parliament assembled and by the authority of the same.

That whosoever shall hereafter come to the possession of this crown shall joyn in communion with the Church of England as by law established.

That in case the crown and imperiall dignity of this realm shall hereafter come to any person not being a native of this kingdom of England this nation be not obliged to ingage in any warr for the defence of any dominions or territories which do not belong to the crown of England without the consent of Parliament.

That after the said limitation shall take effect as aforesaid no person born out of the kingdoms of England Scotland or Ireland or the dominions thereunto belonging (although he be made a denizen) (except such as are born of English parents) shall be capable to be of the privy council or a member of either House of Parliament or to enjoy any office or place of trust either civill or military or to have any grant of land tenements or hereditaments from the Crown to himself or to any other or others in trust for him.

That no pardon under the great seal of England be pleadable to an impeachment by the commons in Parliament.

4 The laws and statutes of the realm confirmed

And whereas the laws of England are the birthright of the people thereof and all the Kings and Queens who shall ascend the throne of this realm ought to administer the government of the same according to the said laws and all their officers and ministers ought to serve them respectively according to the same. The said lords spirituall and temporall and commons do therefore further humbly pray that all the laws and statutes of this realm for securing the established religion and the rights and liberties of the people thereof and all other laws and statutes of the same now in force may be ratified and confirmed. And the same are by his Majesty by and with the advice and consent of the said lords spirituall and temporall and commons and by authority of the same ratified and confirmed accordingly.

NB Section 42 of the Courts Act 2003 provides that nothing in section 3, above (certain persons born outside the United Kingdom), invalidates any appointment, whether made before or after the passing of that Act, of a justice of the peace, or any act done by virtue of such an appointment.

As amended by 4 & 5 Anne c 20, ss27, 28; 1 Geo 1 stat 2 c 51; Status of Aliens Act 1914, s28, Schedule 3.

PARLIAMENT ACT 1911
(1 & 2 Geo 5 c 13)

Whereas it is expedient that provision should be made for regulating the relations between the two Houses of Parliament:

And whereas it is intended to substitute for the House of Lords as it at present exists a Second Chamber constituted on a popular instead of hereditary basis, but such substitution cannot be immediately brought into operation:

And whereas provision will require hereafter to be made by Parliament in a measure effecting such substitution for limiting and defining the powers of the new Second Chamber, but it is expedient to make such provision as in this Act appears for restricting the existing powers of the House of Lords.

1 Powers of House of Lords as to Money Bills

(1) If a Money Bill, having been passed by the House of Commons, and sent up to the House of Lords at least one month before the end of the session, is not passed by the House of Lords without amendment within one month after it is so sent up to that House, the Bill shall, unless the House of Commons direct to the contrary, be presented to His Majesty and become an Act of Parliament on the Royal Assent being signified, notwithstanding that the House of Lords have not consented to the Bill.

(2) A Money Bill means a Public Bill which in the opinion of the Speaker of the House of Commons contains only provisions dealing with all or any of the following subjects, namely, the imposition, repeal, remission, alteration, or regulation of taxation; the imposition for the payment of debt or other financial purposes of charges on the Consolidated Fund, the National Loans Fund or on money provided by Parliament, or the variation or repeal of any such charges; supply; the appropriation, receipt, custody, issue or audit of accounts of public money; the raising or guarantee of any loan or the repayment thereof; or subordinate matters incidental to those subjects or any of them. In this subsection the expressions 'taxation', 'public money', and 'loan' respectively do not include any taxation, money, or loan raised by local authorities or bodies for local purposes.

(3) There shall be endorsed on every Money Bill when it is sent up to the House of Lords and when it is presented to His Majesty for assent the certificate of the Speaker of the House of Commons signed by him that it is a Money Bill. Before giving his certificate, the Speaker shall consult, if practicable, two members to be appointed from the Chairmen's Panel at the beginning of each Session by the Committee of Selection.

2 Restriction of the powers of the House of Lords as to Bills other than Money Bills

(1) If any Public Bill (other than a Money Bill or a Bill containing any provision to extend the maximum duration of Parliament beyond five years) is passed by the House of Commons in two successive sessions (whether of the same Parliament or not), and, having been sent up to the House of Lords at least one month before the end of the session, is rejected by the House of Lords in each of those sessions, that Bill shall, on its rejection for the second time by the House of Lords, unless the House of Commons direct to the contrary, be presented to His Majesty and become an Act of Parliament on the Royal Assent being signified thereto, notwithstanding that the House of Lords have not consented to the Bill: Provided that this provision shall not take effect unless one year has elapsed between the date of the second reading in the first of those sessions of the Bill in the House of Commons and the date on which it passes the House of Commons in the second of those sessions.

(2) When a Bill is presented to His Majesty for assent in pursuance of the provisions of this section, there shall be endorsed on the Bill the certificate of the Speaker of the House of Commons signed by him that the provisions of this section have been duly complied with.

(3) A Bill shall be deemed to be rejected by the House of Lords if it is not passed by the House of Lords either without amendment or with such amendments only as may be agreed to by both Houses.

(4) A Bill shall be deemed to be the same Bill as a former Bill sent up to the House of Lords in the preceding session if, when it is sent up to the House of Lords, it is identical with the former Bill or contains only such alterations as are certified by the Speaker of the House of Commons to be necessary owing to the time which has elapsed since the date of the former Bill, or to represent any amendments which have been made by the House of Lords in the former Bill in the preceding session, and any amendments which are certified by the Speaker to have been made by the House of Lords in the second session and agreed to by the House of Commons shall be inserted in the Bill as presented for Royal Assent in pursuance of this section: Provided that the House of Commons may, if they think fit, on the passage of such a Bill through the House in the second session, suggest any further amendments without inserting the amendments in the Bill, and any such suggested amendments shall be considered by the House of Lords, and, if agreed to by that House, shall be treated as amendments made by the House of Lords and agreed to by the House of Commons; but the exercise of this power by the House of Commons shall not affect the operation of this section in the event of the Bill being rejected by the House of Lords.

3 Certificate of Speaker

Any certificate of the Speaker of the House of Commons given under this Act shall be conclusive for all purposes, and shall not be questioned in any court of law.

4 Enacting words

(1) In every Bill presented to His Majesty under the preceding provisions of this Act, the words of enactment shall be as follows, that is to say:

'Be it enacted by the King's most Excellent Majesty, by and with the advice and consent of the Commons in this present Parliament assembled, in accordance with the provisions of the Parliament Acts 1911 and 1949 and by authority of the same, as follows.'

(2) Any alteration of a Bill necessary to give effect to this section shall not be deemed to be an amendment of the Bill.

5 Provisional Order Bills excluded

In this Act the expression 'Public Bill' does not include any Bill for confirming a Provisional Order.

6 Saving for existing rights and privileges of the House of Commons

Nothing in this Act shall diminish or qualify the existing rights and privileges of the House of Commons.

7 Duration of Parliament

Five years shall be substituted for seven years as the time fixed for the maximum duration of Parliament under the Septennial Act 1715.

As amended by the Parliament Act 1949, ss1, 2(2); National Loans Act 1968, s1(5).

OFFICIAL SECRETS ACT 1911

(1 & 2 Geo 5 c 28)

1 Penalties for spying

(1) If any person for any purpose prejudicial to the safety or interests of the State –

(a) approaches, inspects, passes over, or is in the neighbourhood of, or enters any prohibited place within the meaning of this Act; or

(b) makes any sketch, plan, model, or note which is calculated to be or might be or is intended to be directly or indirectly useful to an enemy; or

(c) obtains, collects, records, or publishes, or communicates to any other person any secret official code word, or pass word, or any sketch, plan, model, article, or note, or other document or information which is calculated to be or might be or is intended to be directly or indirectly useful to an enemy;

he shall be guilty of [an offence].

(2) On a prosecution under this section, it shall not be necessary to show that the accused person was guilty of any particular act tending to show a purpose prejudicial to the safety or interests of the State, and, notwithstanding that no such act is proved against him, he may be convicted if, from the circumstances of the case, or his conduct, or his known character as proved, it appears that his purpose was a purpose prejudicial to the safety or interests of the State; and if any sketch, plan, model, article, note, document, or information relating to or used in any prohibited place within the meaning of this Act, or anything in such a place or any secret official code word or pass word, is made, obtained, collected, recorded, published, or communicated by any person other than a person acting under lawful authority, it shall be deemed to have been made, obtained, collected, recorded, published or communicated for a purpose prejudicial to the safety or interests of the State unless the contrary is proved.

3 Definition of prohibited place

For the purposes of this Act, the expression 'prohibited place' means –

(a) Any work of defence, arsenal, naval or air force establishment or station, factory, dockyard, mine, minefield, camp, ship, or aircraft belonging to or occupied by or on behalf of His Majesty, or any telegraph, telephone, wireless or signal station, or office so belonging or occupied, and any place belonging to or occupied by or on behalf of His Majesty and used for the purpose of building, repairing, making or storing any munitions of war, or any sketches, plans, models, or documents relating thereto, or for the purpose of getting any metals, oil, or minerals of use in time of war; and

(b) any place not belonging to His Majesty where any munitions of war, or any sketches, models, plans or documents relating thereto, are being made, repaired, gotten, or stored under contract with, or with any person on behalf of, His Majesty, or otherwise on behalf of His Majesty; and

(c) any place belonging to or used for the purposes of His Majesty which is for the time being declared by order of a Secretary of State to be a prohibited place for the purposes of this section on the ground that information with respect thereto, or damage thereto, would be useful to an enemy; and

(d) any railway, road, way, or channel, or other means of communication by land or water (including any works or structures being part thereof or connected therewith), or any place used for gas, water, or electricity works or other works for purposes of a public character, or any place where any munitions of war, or any sketches, models, plans or documents relating thereto, are being made, repaired, or stored otherwise than on behalf of His Majesty, which is for the time being declared by order of a Secretary of State to be a prohibited place for the purposes of this section, on the ground that information with respect thereto, or the destruction or obstruction thereof, or interference therewith, would be useful to an enemy.

As amended by the Official Secrets Act 1920, ss10, 11, Schedules 1, 2.

EMERGENCY POWERS ACT 1920

(10 & 11 Geo 5 c 55)

1 Issue of proclamations of emergency

(1) If at any time it appears to His Majesty that there have occurred, or are about to occur, events of such a nature as to be calculated, by interfering with the supply and distribution of food, water, fuel, or light, or with the means of locomotion, to deprive the community, or any substantial portion of the community, of the essentials of life, His Majesty may, by proclamation (hereinafter referred to as a proclamation of emergency), declare that a state of emergency exists. No such proclamation shall be in force for more than one month, without prejudice to the issue of another proclamation at or before the end of that period.

(2) Where a proclamation of emergency has been made the occasion thereof shall forthwith be communicated to Parliament, and, if Parliament is then separated by such adjournment or prorogation as will not expire within five days, a proclamation shall be issued for the meeting of Parliament within five days, and Parliament shall accordingly meet and sit upon the day appointed by that proclamation, and shall continue to sit and act in like manner as if it had stood adjourned or prorogued to the same day.

2 Emergency regulations

(1) Where a proclamation of emergency has been made, and so long as the proclamation is in force, it shall be lawful for His Majesty in Council, by Order, to make regulations for securing the essentials of life to the community, and those regulations may confer or impose on a Secretary of State or other Government department, or any other persons in His Majesty's service or acting on His Majesty's behalf, such powers and duties as His Majesty may deem necessary for the preservation of the peace, for securing and regulating the supply and distribution of food, water, fuel, light, and other necessities, for maintaining the means of transit or locomotion, and for any other purposes essential to the public safety and the life of the community, and may make such provisions incidental to the powers aforesaid as may appear to His Majesty to be required for making the exercise of those powers effective: Provided that nothing in this Act shall be construed to authorise the making of any regulations imposing any form of compulsory military service or industrial conscription: Provided also that no such regulation shall make it an offence for any person or persons to take part in a strike, or peacefully to persuade any other person or persons to take part in a strike.

(2) Any regulations so made shall be laid before Parliament as soon as may be after they are made, and shall not continue in force after the expiration of seven days from the time when they are so laid unless a resolution is passed by both Houses providing for the continuance thereof.

(3) The regulations may provide for the trial, by courts of summary jurisdiction, of persons guilty of offences against the regulations; so, however, that the maximum penalty which may be inflicted for any offence against any such regulations shall be imprisonment with or without hard labour for a term of three months, or a fine not exceeding level 5 on the standard scale, or not exceeding a lesser amount, or both such imprisonment and fine, together with the forfeiture of any goods or money in respect of which the offence has been committed: Provided that no such regulations shall alter any existing procedure in criminal cases, or confer any right to punish by fine or imprisonment without trial.

(4) The regulations so made may be added to, altered, or revoked by resolution of both Houses of Parliament or by regulations made in like manner and subject to the like provisions as the original regulations.

(5) The expiry or revocation of any regulations so made shall not be deemed to have affected the previous operation thereof, or the validity of any action taken thereunder, or any penalty or punishment incurred in respect of any contravention or failure to comply therewith, or any proceeding or remedy in respect of any such punishment or penalty.

As amended by the Statute Law Revision Act 1963; Emergency Powers Act 1964, s1; Criminal Justice Act 1982, s41; Statute Law (Repeals) Act 1986; Statute Law (Repeals) Act 1993, s1(1), Schedule 1, Part XIV.

OFFICIAL SECRETS ACT 1920

(10 & 11 Geo 5 c 75)

1 Unauthorised use of uniforms; falsification of reports, forgery, personation, and false documents

(1) If any person for the purpose of gaining admission, or of assisting any other person to gain admission, to a prohibited place, within the meaning of the Official Secrets Act 1911 (hereinafter referred to as 'the principal Act'), or for any other purpose prejudicial to the safety or interests of the State within the meaning of the said Act –

(a) uses or wears, without lawful authority, any naval, military, air-force, police, or other official uniform, or any uniform so nearly resembling the same as to be calculated to deceive, or falsely represents himself to be a person who is or has been entitled to use or wear any such uniform; or

(b) orally, or in writing in any declaration or application, or in any document signed by him or on his behalf, knowingly makes or connives at the making of any false statement or any omission; or

(c) tampers with any passport or any naval, military, air-force, police, or official pass, permit, certificate, licence, or other document of a similar character (hereinafter in this section referred to as an official document), or has in his possession any forged, altered, or irregular official document; or

(d) personates, or falsely represents himself to be a person holding, or in the employment of a person holding office under His Majesty, or to be or not to be a person to whom an official document or secret official code word, or pass word, has been duly issued or communicated, or with intent to obtain an official document, secret official code word or pass word, whether for himself or any other person, knowingly makes any false statement; or

(e) uses, or has in his possession or under his control, without the authority of the Government Department or the authority concerned, any die, seal, or stamp of or belonging to, or used, made or provided by any Government Department, or by any diplomatic, naval, military, or air force authority appointed by or acting under the authority of His Majesty, or any die, seal or stamp so nearly resembling any such die, seal or stamp as to be calculated to deceive, or counterfeits any such die, seal or stamp, or uses, or has in his possession, or under his control, any such counterfeited die, seal or stamp;

he shall be guilty of [an offence] ...

(3) In the case of any prosecution under this section involving the proof of a purpose

prejudicial to the safety or interests of the State, subsection (2) of section one of the principal Act shall apply in like manner as it applies to prosecutions under that section.

6 Duty of giving information as to commission of offences

(1) Where a chief officer of police is satisfied that there is reasonable ground for suspecting that an offence under section 1 of the principal Act has been committed and for believing that any person is able to furnish information as to the offence or suspected offence, he may apply to a Secretary of State for permission to exercise the powers conferred by this subsection and, if such permission is granted, he may authorise a superintendent of police, or any police officer not below the rank of inspector, to require the person believed to be able to furnish information to give any information in his power relating to the offence or suspected offence, and, if so required and on tender of his reasonable expenses, to attend at such reasonable time and place as may be specified by the superintendent or other officer; and if a person required in pursuance of such an authorisation to give information, or to attend as aforesaid, fails to comply with any such requirement or knowingly gives false information, he shall be guilty of [an offence].

(2) Where a chief officer of police has reasonable grounds to believe that the case is one of great emergency and that in the interest of the State immediate action is necessary, he may exercise the powers conferred by the last foregoing subsection without applying for or being granted the permission of a Secretary of State, but if he does so shall forthwith report the circumstances to the Secretary of State.

(3) References in this section to a chief officer of police shall be construed as including references to any other officer of police expressly authorised by a chief officer of police to act on his behalf for the purposes of this section when by reason of illness, absence, or other cause he is unable to do so.

As amended by the Official Secrets Act 1939, s1; Forgery and Counterfeiting Act 1981, s30, Schedule, Pt I.

STATUTE OF WESTMINSTER 1931

(22 & 23 Geo 5 c 4)

Preamble

Whereas the delegates of His Majesty's Governments in the United Kingdom, the Dominion of Canada, the Commonwealth of Australia, the Dominion of New Zealand, the Union of South Africa, the Irish Free State and Newfoundland, at Imperial Conferences holden at Westminster in the years of our Lord nineteen hundred and twenty-six and nineteen hundred and thirty did concur in making the declarations and resolutions set forth in the Reports of the said Conferences:

And whereas it is meet and proper to set out by way of preamble to this Act that, inasmuch as the Crown is the symbol of the free association of the members of the British Commonwealth of Nations, and as they are united by a common allegiance to the Crown, it would be in accord with the established constitutional position of all the members of the Commonwealth in relation to one another that any alteration in the law touching the Succession to the Throne or the Royal Style and Titles shall hereafter require the assent as well of the Parliaments of all the Dominions as of the Parliament of the United Kingdom:

And whereas it is in accord with the established constitutional position that no law hereafter made by the Parliament of the United Kingdom shall extend to any of the said Dominions as part of the law of that Dominion otherwise than at the request and with the consent of that Dominion:

And whereas it is necessary for the ratifying, confirming and establishing of certain of the said declarations and resolutions of the said Conferences that a law be made and enacted in due form by authority of the Parliament of the United Kingdom:

And whereas the Dominion of Canada, the Commonwealth of Australia, the Dominion of New Zealand, the Union of South Africa, the Irish Free State and Newfoundland have severally requested and consented to the submission of a measure to the Parliament of the United Kingdom for making such provision with regard to the matters aforesaid as is hereafter in that Act contained:

Now, therefore, be it enacted by the King's most Excellent Majesty by and with the advice and consent of the Lords Spiritual and Temporal, and Commons, in this present Parliament assembled, and by the authority of the same, as follows –

1 Meaning of 'Dominion' in this Act

In this Act the expression 'Dominion' means any of the following Dominions, that is to say, the Dominion of Canada, the Commonwealth of Australia, the Dominion of New Zealand, the Irish Free State and Newfoundland.

2 Validity of laws made by Parliament of a Dominion

(1) The Colonial Laws Validity Act 1865, shall not apply to any law made after the commencement of this Act by the Parliament of a Dominion.

(2) No law and no provision of any law made after the commencement of this Act by the Parliament of a Dominion shall be void or inoperative on the ground that it is repugnant to the law of England, or to the provisions of any existing or future Act of Parliament of the United Kingdom, or to any order, rule or regulation made under any such Act, and the powers of the Parliament of a Dominion shall include the power to repeal or amend any such Act, order, rule or regulation in so far as the same is part of the law of the Dominion.

3 Power of Parliament of Dominion to legislate extra-territorially

It is hereby declared and enacted that the Parliament of a Dominion has full power to make laws having extra-territorial operation.

4 Parliament of United Kingdom not to legislate for Dominion except by consent

No Act of Parliament of the United Kingdom passed after the commencement of this Act shall extend, or be deemed to extend, to a Dominion as part of the law of that Dominion unless it is expressly declared in that Act that that Dominion has requested, and consented to, the enactment thereof.

NB. In so far as s4, above, applies to Canada and Australia, it was repealed by the Canada Act 1982 and Australia Act 1986 respectively. By virtue of the Ireland Act 1949, the Irish Free State (now Republic of Ireland) ceased to be part of Her Majesty's dominions.

As amended by the South Africa Act 1962, s2(3), Schedule 5.

PUBLIC ORDER ACT 1936
(1 Edw 8 & 1 Geo 6 c 6)

1 Prohibition of uniforms in connection with political objects

(1) Subject as hereinafter provided, any person who in any public place or at any public meeting wears uniform signifying his association with any political organisation or with the promotion of any political object shall be guilty of an offence: Provided that, if the chief officer of police is satisfied that the wearing of any such uniform as aforesaid on any ceremonial, anniversary, or other special occasion will not be likely to involve risk of public disorder, he may, with the consent of a Secretary of State, by order permit the wearing of such uniform on that occasion either absolutely or subject to such conditions as may be specified in the order.

(2) Where any person is charged before any court with an offence under this section, no further proceedings in respect thereof shall be taken against him without the consent of the Attorney-General except such as are authorised by section 6 of the Prosecution of Offences Act 1979 so, however, that if that person is remanded in custody he shall, after the expiration of a period of eight days from the date on which he was so remanded, be entitled to be released on bail without sureties unless within that period the Attorney-General has consented to such further proceedings as aforesaid.

2 Prohibition of quasi-military organisations

(1) If the members or adherents of any association of persons, whether incorporated or not, are –

(a) organised or trained or equipped for the purpose of enabling them to be employed in usurping the functions of the police or of the armed forces of the Crown; or

(b) organised and trained or organised and equipped either for the purpose of enabling them to be employed for the use or display of physical force in promoting any political object, or in such manner as to arouse reasonable apprehension that they are organised and either trained or equipped for that purpose;

then any person who takes part in the control or management of the association, or in so organising or training as aforesaid any members or adherents thereof, shall be guilty of an offence under this section: Provided that in any proceedings against a person charged with the offence of taking part in the control or management of such an association as aforesaid it shall be a defence to that charge to prove that he neither consented to nor connived at the organisation, training, or equipment of members or adherents of the association in contravention of the provisions of this section.

(2) No prosecution shall be instituted under this section without the consent of the Attorney-General ...

(5) If a judge of the High Court is satisfied by information on oath that there is reasonable ground for suspecting that an offence under this section has been committed, and that evidence of the commission thereof is to be found at any premises or place specified in the information, he may, on an application made by an officer of police of a rank not lower than that of inspector, grant a search warrant authorising any such officer as aforesaid named in the warrant together with any other persons named in the warrant and any other officers of police to enter the premises or place at any time within one month from the date of the warrant, if necessary by force, and to search the premises or place and every person found therein, and to seize anything found on the premises or place or on any such person which the officer has reasonable ground for suspecting to be evidence of the commission of such an offence as aforesaid: Provided that no woman shall, in pursuance of a warrant issued under this subsection, be searched except by a woman.

(6) Nothing in this section shall be construed as prohibiting the employment of a reasonable number of persons as stewards to assist in the preservation of order at any public meeting held upon private premises, or the making of arrangements for that purpose or the instruction of the persons to be so employed in their lawful duties as such stewards, or their being furnished with badges or other distinguishing signs.

As amended by the Criminal Jurisdiction Act 1975, s14(4), Schedule 5, para 1; Bail Act 1976, s12, Schedule 2, para 10; Prosecution of Offences Act 1979, s11(1), Schedule 1.

STATUTORY INSTRUMENTS ACT 1946

(9 & 10 Geo 6 c 36)

1 Definition of 'Statutory Instrument'

(1) Where by this Act or any Act passed after the commencement of this Act power to make, confirm or approve orders, rules, regulations or other subordinate legislation is conferred on His Majesty in Council or on any Minister of the Crown then, if the power is expressed –

(a) in the case of a power conferred on His Majesty, to be exercisable by Order in Council;

(b) in the case of a power conferred on a Minister of the Crown, to be exercisable by statutory instrument,

any document by which that power is exercised shall be known as a 'statutory instrument' and the provisions of this Act shall apply thereto accordingly.

(1A) The references in subsection (1) to a Minister of the Crown shall be construed as including references to the National Assembly for Wales.

(2) Where by any Act passed before the commencement of this Act power to make statutory rules within the meaning of the Rules Publication Act 1893 was conferred on any rule-making authority within the meaning of that Act, any document by which that power is exercised after the commencement of this Act shall, save as is otherwise provided by regulations made under this Act, be known as a 'statutory instrument' and the provisions of this Act shall apply thereto accordingly.

2 Numbering, printing, publication and citation

(1) Immediately after the making of any statutory instrument, it shall be sent to the King's printer of Acts of Parliament and numbered in accordance with regulations made under this Act, and except in such cases as may be provided by any Act passed after the commencement of this Act or prescribed by regulations made under this Act, copies thereof shall as soon as possible be printed and sold by or under the authority of the King's printer of Acts of Parliament.

(2) Any statutory instrument may, without prejudice to any other mode of citation, be cited by the number given to it in accordance with the provisions of this section, and the calendar year.

3 Supplementary provisions as to publication

(1) Regulations made for the purposes of this Act shall make provision for the publication by His Majesty's Stationery Office of lists showing the date upon which every statutory instrument printed and sold by or under the authority of the King's printer of Acts of Parliament was first issued by or under the authority of that office; and in any legal proceedings a copy of any list so published shall be received in evidence as a true copy, and an entry therein shall be conclusive evidence of the date on which any statutory instrument was first issued by or under the authority of His Majesty's Stationery Office.

(2) In any proceedings against any person for an offence consisting of a contravention of any such statutory instrument, it shall be a defence to prove that the instrument had not been issued by or under the authority of His Majesty's Stationery Office at the date of the alleged contravention unless it is proved that at that date reasonable steps had been taken for the purpose of bringing the purport of the instrument to the notice of the public, or of persons likely to be affected by it, or of the person charged.

(3) Save as therein otherwise expressly provided, nothing in this section shall affect any enactment or rule of law relating to the time at which any statutory instrument comes into operation.

4 Statutory instruments which are required to be laid before Parliament

(1) Where by this Act or any Act passed after the commencement of this Act any statutory instrument is required to be laid before Parliament after being made, a copy of the instrument shall be laid before each House of Parliament and, subject as hereinafter provided, shall be so laid before the instrument comes into operation: Provided that if it is essential that any such instrument should come into operation before copies thereof can be so laid as aforesaid, the instrument may be made so as to come into operation before it has been so laid; and where any statutory instrument comes into operation before it is laid before Parliament, notification shall forthwith be sent to the Lord Chancellor and to the Speaker of the House of Commons drawing attention to the fact that copies of the instrument have yet to be laid before Parliament and explaining why such copies were not so laid before the instrument came into operation.

(2) Every copy of any such statutory instrument sold by or under the authority of the King's printer of Acts of Parliament shall bear on the face thereof –

(a) a statement showing the date on which the statutory instrument came or will come into operation; and

(b) either a statement showing the date on which copies thereof were laid before Parliament or a statement that such copies are to be laid before Parliament.

5 Statutory instruments which are subject to annulment by resolution of either House of Parliament

(1) Where by this Act or any Act passed after the commencement of this Act, it is provided that any statutory instrument shall be subject to annulment in pursuance of resolution of either House of Parliament, the instrument shall be laid before Parliament after being made and the provisions of the last foregoing section shall apply thereto accordingly, and if either House, within the period of forty days beginning with the day on which a copy thereof is laid before it, resolves that an Address be presented to His Majesty praying that the instrument be annulled, no further proceedings shall be taken thereunder after the date of the resolution, and His Majesty may by Order in Council revoke the instrument, so, however, that any such resolution and revocation shall be without prejudice to the validity of anything previously done under the instrument or to the making of a new statutory instrument ...

6 Statutory instruments of which drafts are to be laid before Parliament

(1) Where by this Act or any Act passed after the commencement of this Act it is provided that a draft of any statutory instrument shall be laid before Parliament, but the Act does not prohibit the making of the instrument without the approval of Parliament, then, in the case of an Order in Council the draft shall not be submitted to His Majesty in Council, and in any other case the statutory instrument shall not be made, until after the expiration of a period of forty days beginning with the day on which a copy of the draft is laid before each House of Parliament, or, if such copies are laid on different days, with the later of the two days, and if within that period either House resolves that the draft be not submitted to His Majesty or that the statutory instrument be not made, as the case may be, no further proceedings shall be taken thereon, but without prejudice to the laying before Parliament of a new draft ...

7 Supplementary provisions as to sections 4, 5 and 6

(1) In reckoning for the purposes of either of the last two foregoing sections any period of forty days, no account shall be taken of any time during which Parliament is dissolved or prorogued or during which both Houses are adjourned for more than four days.

(2) In relation to any instrument required by any Act, whether passed before or after the commencement of this Act, to be laid before the House of Commons only, the provisions of the last three foregoing sections shall have effect as if references to that House were therein substituted for references to Parliament and for references to either House and each House thereof.

(3) The provisions of sections four and five of this Act shall not apply to any statutory instrument being an order which is subject to special Parliamentary procedure, or to any other instrument which is required to be laid before

Parliament, or before the House of Commons, for any period before it comes into operation.

8 Regulations

(1) The Minister for the Civil Service may, with the concurrence of the Lord Chancellor and the Speaker of the House of Commons, by statutory instrument make regulations for the purposes of this Act, and such regulations may, in particular –

(a) provide for the different treatment of instruments which are of the nature of a public Act, and of those which are of the nature of a local and personal or private Act;

(b) make provisions as to the numbering, printing, and publication of statutory instruments including provision for postponing the numbering of any such instrument which does not take effect until it has been approved by Parliament, or by the House of Commons, until the instrument has been so approved;

(c) provide with respect to any classes or descriptions of statutory instrument that they shall be exempt, either altogether or to such extent as may be determined by or under the regulations, from the requirement of being printed and of being sold by or under the authority of the King's printer of Acts of Parliament, or from either of those requirements;

(d) determine the classes of cases in which the exercise of a statutory power by any rule-making authority constitutes or does not constitute the making of such a statutory rule as is referred to in subsection (2) of section one of this Act, and provide for the exclusion from that subsection of any such classes;

(e) provide for the determination by a person or persons nominated by the Lord Chancellor and the Speaker of the House of Commons of any question –

(i) as to the numbering, printing, or publication of any statutory instrument or class or description of such instruments:

(ii) whether or to what extent any statutory instrument or class or description of such instruments is, under the regulations, exempt from any such requirement as is mentioned in paragraph (c) of this subsection:

(iii) whether any statutory instrument or class or description of such instruments is in the nature of a public Act or of a local and personal or private Act:

(iv) whether the exercise of any power conferred by an Act passed before the commencement of this Act is or is not the exercise of a power to make a statutory rule.

(2) Every statutory instrument made under this section shall be subject to annulment in pursuance of resolution of either House of Parliament.

As amended by the Minister for the Civil Service Order 1968, art 2(2), Schedule; Statutory Instruments (Production and Sale) Act 1996, s1(1); Government of Wales Act 1998, s125, Schedule 12, para 2.

CROWN PROCEEDINGS ACT 1947

(10 & 11 Geo 6 c 44)

PART I

SUBSTANTIVE LAW

1 Right to sue the Crown

Where any person has a claim against the Crown after the commencement of this Act, and, if this Act had not been passed, the claim might have been enforced, subject to the grant of His Majesty's fiat, by petition of right, or might have been enforced by a proceeding provided by any statutory provision repealed by this Act, then, subject to the provisions of this Act, the claim may be enforced as of right, and without the fiat of His Majesty, by proceedings taken against the Crown for that purpose in accordance with the provisions of this Act.

2 Liability of the Crown in tort

(1) Subject to the provisions of this Act, the Crown shall be subject to all those liabilities in tort to which, if it were a private person of full age and capacity, it would be subject –

(a) in respect of torts committed by its servants or agents;

(b) in respect of any breach of those duties which a person owes to his servants or agents at common law by reason of being their employer; and

(c) in respect of any breach of the duties attaching at common law to the ownership, occupation, possession or control of property:

Provided that no proceedings shall lie against the Crown by virtue of paragraph (a) of this subsection in respect of any act or omission of a servant or agent of the Crown unless the act or omission would apart from the provisions of this Act have given rise to a cause of action in tort against that servant or agent or his estate.

(2) Where the Crown is bound by a statutory duty which is binding also upon persons other than the Crown and its officers, then, subject to the provisions of this Act, the Crown shall, in respect of a failure to comply with that duty, be subject to all those liabilities in tort (if any) to which it would be so subject if it were a private person of full age and capacity.

(3) Where any functions are conferred or imposed upon an officer of the Crown as such either by any rule of the common law or by statute, and that officer commits

a tort while performing or purporting to perform those functions, the liabilities of the Crown in respect of the tort shall be such as they would have been if those functions had been conferred or imposed solely by virtue of instructions lawfully given by the Crown.

(4) Any enactment which negatives or limits the amount of the liability of any Government department, part of the Scottish Administration or officer of the Crown in respect of any tort committed by that department, part or officer shall, in the case of proceedings against the Crown under this section in respect of a tort committed by that department, part or officer, apply in relation to the Crown as it would have applied in relation to that department, part or officer if the proceedings against the Crown had been proceedings against that department, part or officer.

(5) No proceedings shall lie against the Crown by virtue of this section in respect of anything done or omitted to be done by any person while discharging or purporting to discharge any responsibilities of a judicial nature vested in him, or any responsibilities which he has in connection with the execution of judicial process.

(6) No proceedings shall lie against the Crown by virtue of this section in respect of any act, neglect or default of any officer of the Crown, unless that officer has been directly or indirectly appointed by the Crown and was at the material time paid in respect of his duties as an officer of the Crown wholly out of the Consolidated Fund of the United Kingdom, moneys provided by Parliament, the Scottish Consolidated Fund or any other Fund certified by the Treasury for the purposes of this subsection or was at the material time holding an office in respect of which the Treasury certify that the holder thereof would normally be so paid.

10 Provisions relating to the armed forces

(1) Nothing done or omitted to be done by a member of the armed forces of the Crown while on duty as such shall subject either him or the Crown to liability in tort for causing the death of another person, or for causing personal injury to another person, in so far as the death or personal injury is due to anything suffered by that other person while he is a member of the armed forces of the Crown if –

(a) at the time when that thing is suffered by that other person, he is either on duty as a member of the armed forces of the Crown or is, though not on duty as such, on any land, premises, ship, aircraft or vehicle for the time being used for the purposes of the armed forces of the Crown; and

(b) the Secretary of State certifies that his suffering that thing has been or will be treated as attributable to service for the purposes of entitlement to an award under the Royal Warrant, Order in Council or Order of His Majesty relating to the disablement or death of members of the force of which he is a member:

Provided that this subsection shall not exempt a member of the said forces from liability in tort in any case in which the court is satisfied that the act or omission was not connected with the execution of his duties as a member of those forces.

(2) No proceedings in tort shall lie against the Crown for death or personal injury due to anything suffered by a member of the armed forces of the Crown if –

(a) that thing is suffered by him in consequence of the nature or condition of any such land, premises, ship, aircraft or vehicle as aforesaid, or in consequence of the nature or condition of any equipment or supplies used for the purposes of those forces; and

(b) the Secretary of State certifies as mentioned in the preceding subsection;

nor shall any act or omission of an officer of the Crown subject him to liability in tort for death or personal injury, in so far as the death or personal injury is due to anything suffered by a member of the armed forces of the Crown being a thing as to which the conditions aforesaid are satisfied.

(3) A Secretary of State, if satisfied that it is the fact –

(a) that a person was or was not on any particular occasion on duty as a member of the armed forces of the Crown; or

(b) that at any particular time any land, premises, ship, aircraft, vehicle, equipment or supplies was or was not, or were or were not, used for the purposes of the said forces;

may issue a certificate certifying that to be the fact; and any such certificate shall, for the purposes of this section, be conclusive as to the facts which it certifies.

PART II

JURISDICTION AND PROCEDURE

21 Nature of relief

(1) In any civil proceedings by or against the Crown the court shall, subject to the provisions of this Act, have power to make all such orders as it has power to make in proceedings between subjects, and otherwise to give such appropriate relief as the case may require: Provided that –

(a) where in any proceedings against the Crown any such relief is sought as might in proceedings between subjects be granted by way of injunction or specific performance, the court shall not grant an injunction or make an order for specific performance, but may in lieu thereof make an order declaratory of the rights of the parties; and

(b) in any proceedings against the Crown for the recovery of land or other property the court shall not make an order for the recovery of the land or the delivery of the property, but may in lieu thereof make an order declaring that the plaintiff is entitled as against the Crown to the land or property or to the possession thereof.

(2) The court shall not in any civil proceedings grant any injunction or make any order against an officer of the Crown if the effect of granting the injunction or

making the order would be to give any relief against the Crown which could not have been obtained in proceedings against the Crown.

PART III

JUDGMENTS AND EXECUTION

25 Satisfaction of orders against the Crown

(1) Where in any civil proceedings by or against the Crown, or in any proceedings on the Crown side of the King's Bench Division, or in connection with any arbitration to which the Crown is a party, any order (including an order for costs) is made by any court in favour of any person against the Crown or against a Government department or against an officer of the Crown as such, the proper officer of the court shall, on an application in that behalf made by or on behalf of that person at any time after the expiration of twenty-one days from the date of the order or, in case the order provides for the payment of costs and the costs require to be taxed, at any time after the costs have been taxed, whichever is the later, issue to that person a certificate in the prescribed form containing particulars of the order: Provided that, if the court so directs, a separate certificate shall be issued with respect to the costs (if any) ordered to be paid to the applicant.

(2) A copy of any certificate issued under this section may be served by the person in whose favour the order is made upon the person for the time being named in the record as the solicitor, or as the person acting as solicitor, for the Crown or for the Government department or officer concerned.

(3) If the order provides for the payment of any money by way of damages or otherwise, or of any costs, the certificate shall state the amount so payable, and the appropriate Government department shall, subject as hereinafter provided, pay to the person entitled or to his solicitor the amount appearing by the certificate to be due to him together with the interest, if any, lawfully due thereon: Provided that the court by which any such order as aforesaid is made or any court to which an appeal against the order lies may direct that, pending an appeal or otherwise, payment of the whole of any amount so payable, or any part thereof, shall be suspended, and if the certificate has not been issued may order any such directions to be inserted therein.

(4) Save as aforesaid no execution or attachment or process in the nature thereof shall be issued out of any court for enforcing payment by the Crown of any such money or costs as aforesaid, and no person shall be individually liable under any order for the payment by the Crown, or any Government department, or any officer of the Crown as such, of any such money or costs.

PART IV

MISCELLANEOUS AND SUPPLEMENTAL

28 Discovery

(1) Subject to and in accordance with rules of court and county court rules –

(a) in any civil proceedings in the High Court or a county court to which the Crown is a party, the Crown may be required by the court to make discovery of documents and produce documents for inspection; and

(b) in any such proceedings as aforesaid, the Crown may be required by the court to answer interrogatories:

Provided that this section shall be without prejudice to any rule of law which authorises or requires the withholding of any document or the refusal to answer any question on the ground that the disclosure of the document or the answering of the question would be injurious to the public interest. Any order of the court made under the powers conferred by paragraph (b) of this subsection shall direct by what officer of the Crown the interrogatories are to be answered.

(2) Without prejudice to the proviso to the preceding subsection, any rules made for the purposes of this section shall be such as to secure that the existence of a document will not be disclosed if, in the opinion of a Minister of the Crown, it would be injurious to the public interest to disclose the existence thereof.

NB. Section 10, above, was repealed by the Crown Proceedings (Armed Forces) Act 1987, s1, save that it may be revived by order of the Secretary of State at any time.

As amended by the Defence (Transfer of Functions) Order 1964; Statute Law (Repeals) Act 1981; Statute Law (Repeals) Act 1993, s1(1), Schedule 1, Part I; Scotland Act 1998 (Consequential Modifications) (No 1) Order 1999, art 4, Schedule 2, Pt I, para 4(1), (2); Scotland Act 1998 (Consequential Modifications) (No 2) Order 1999, art 4, Schedule 2, Pt I, para 21.

LIFE PEERAGES ACT 1958

(6 & 7 Eliz 2 c 21)

1 Power to create life peerages carrying right to sit in the House of Lords

(1) Without prejudice to Her Majesty's powers as to the appointment of Lords of Appeal in Ordinary, Her Majesty shall have power by letters patent to confer on any person a peerage for life having the incidents specified in subsection (2) of this section.

(2) A peerage conferred under this section shall, during the life of the person on whom it is conferred, entitled him –

(a) to rank as a baron under such style as may be appointed by the letters patent; and

(b) subject to subsection (4) of this section, to receive writs of summons to attend the House of Lords and sit and vote therein accordingly,

and shall expire on his death.

(3) A life peerage may be conferred under this section on a woman.

(4) Nothing in this section shall enable any person to receive a writ of summons to attend the House of Lords, or to sit and vote in that House, at any time when disqualified therefor by law.

OBSCENE PUBLICATIONS ACT 1959

(7 & 8 Eliz 2 c 66)

1 Test of obscenity

(1) For the purposes of this Act an article shall be deemed to be obscene if its effect or (where the article comprises two or more distinct items) the effect of any one of its items, is, if taken as a whole, such as to tend to deprave and corrupt persons who are likely, having regard to all relevant circumstances, to read, see or hear the matter contained or embodied in it.

(2) In this Act 'article' means any description of article containing or embodying matter to be read or looked at or both, any sound record, and any film or other record of a picture or pictures.

(3) For the purposes of this Act a person publishes an article who –

(a) distributes, circulates, sells, lets on hire, gives, or lends it or who offers it for sale or for letting on hire; or

(b) in the case of an article containing or embodying matter to be looked at or a record, shows, plays or projects it, or, where the matter is data stored electronically, transmits that data.

(4) For the purposes of this Act a person also publishes an article to the extent that any matter recorded on it is included by him in a programme included in a programme service.

(5) Where the inclusion of any matter in a programme so included would, if that matter were recorded matter, constitute the publication of an obscene article for the purposes of this Act by virtue of subsection (4) above, this Act shall have effect in relation to the inclusion of that matter in that programme as if it were recorded matter.

(6) In this section 'programme' and 'programme service' have the same meaning as in the Broadcasting Act 1990.

2 Prohibition of publication of obscene matter

(1) Subject as hereinafter provided, any person who, whether for gain or not, publishes an obscene article or who has an obscene article for publication for gain (whether gain to himself or gain to another) shall be liable –

(a) on summary conviction to a fine not exceeding the prescribed sum or to imprisonment for a term not exceeding six months;

(b) on conviction on indictment to a fine or to imprisonment for a term not exceeding three years or both.

(3) A prosecution for an offence against this section shall not be commenced more than two years after the commission of the offence.

(3A) Proceedings for an offence under this section shall not be instituted except by or with the consent of the Director of Public Prosecutions in any case where the article in question is a moving picture film of a width of not less than sixteen millimetres and the relevant publication or the only other publication which followed or could reasonably have been expected to follow from the relevant publication took place or (as the case may be) was to take place in the course of a film exhibition; and in this subsection 'the relevant publication' means –

(a) in the case of any proceedings under this section for publishing an obscene article, the publication in respect of which the defendant would be charged if the proceedings were brought; and

(b) in the case of any proceedings under this section for having an obscene article for publication for gain, the publication which, if the proceedings were brought, the defendant would be alleged to have had in contemplation.

(4) A person publishing an article shall not be proceeded against for an offence at common law consisting of the publication of any matter contained or embodied in the article where it is of the essence of the offence that the matter is obscene.

(4A) Without prejudice to subsection (4) above, a person shall not be proceeded against for an offence at common law –

(a) in respect of a film exhibition or anything said or done in the course of a film exhibition, where it is of the essence of the common law offence that the exhibition or, as the case may be, what was said or done was obscene, indecent, offensive, disgusting or injurious to morality; or

(b) in respect of an agreement to give a film exhibition or to cause anything to be said or done in the course of such an exhibition where the common law offence consists of conspiring to corrupt public morals or to do any act contrary to public morals or decency.

(5) A person shall not be convicted of an offence against this section if he proves that he had not examined the article in respect of which he is charged and had no reasonable cause to suspect that it was such that his publication of it would make him liable to be convicted of an offence against this section.

(6) In any proceedings against a person under this section the question whether an article is obscene shall be determined without regard to any publication by another person unless it could reasonably have been expected that the publication by the other person would follow from publication by the person charged.

(7) In this section 'film exhibition' has the same meaning as in the Cinemas Act 1985.

3 Powers of search and seizure

(1) If a justice of the peace is satisfied by information on oath that there is reasonable ground for suspecting that, in any premises in the petty sessions area for which he acts, or on any stall or vehicle in that area, being premises or a stall or vehicle specified in the information, obscene articles are, or are from time to time, kept for publication for gain, the justice may issue a warrant under his hand empowering any constable to enter (if need be by force) and search the premises, or to search the stall or vehicle, and to seize and remove any articles found therein or thereon which the constable has reason to believe to be obscene articles and to be kept for publication for gain.

(2) A warrant under the foregoing subsection shall, if any obscene articles are seized under the warrant, also empower the seizure and removal of any documents found in the premises or, as the case may be, on the stall or vehicle which relate to a trade or business carried on at the premises or from the stall or vehicle.

(3) Subject to subsection 3A of this section any articles seized under subsection (1) of this section shall be brought before a justice of the peace acting for the same petty sessions area as the justice who issued the warrant, and the justice before whom the articles are brought may thereupon issue a summons to the occupier of the premises or, as the case may be, the user of the stall or vehicle to appear on a day specified in the summons before a magistrates' court for that petty sessions area to show cause why the articles or any of them should not be forfeited; and if the court is satisfied, as respects any of the articles, that at the time when they were seized they were obscene articles kept for publication for gain, the court shall order those articles to be forfeited: Provided that if the person summoned does not appear, the court shall not make an order unless service of the summons is proved. Provided also that this subsection does not apply in relation to any article seized under subsection (1) of this section which is returned to the occupier of the premises or, as the case may be, to the user of the stall or vehicle in or on which it was found.

(3A) Without prejudice to the duty of a court to make an order for the forfeiture of an article where section 1(4) of the Obscene Publications Act 1964 applies (orders made on conviction), in a case where by virtue of subsection (3A) of section 2 of this Act proceedings under the said section 2 for having an article for publication for gain could not be instituted except by or with the consent of the Director of Public Prosecutions, no order for the forfeiture of the article shall be made under this section unless the warrant under which the article was seized was issued on an information laid by or on behalf of the Director of Public Prosecutions.

(4) In addition to the person summoned, any other person being the owner, author or maker of any of the articles brought before the court, or any other person through whose hands they had passed before being seized, shall be entitled to appear before the court on the day specified in the summons to show cause why they should not be forfeited.

(5) Where an order is made under this section for the forfeiture of any articles, any person who appeared, or was entitled to appear, to show cause against the making of the order may appeal to the Crown Court; and no such order shall take effect

until the expiration of the period within which the notice of appeal to the Crown Court may be given against the order or, if before the expiration thereof notice of appeal is duly given or application is made for the statement of a case for the opinion of the High Court, until the final determination or abandonment of the proceedings on the appeal or case.

(6) If as respects any articles brought before it the court does not order forfeiture, the court may if it thinks fit order the person on whose information the warrant for the seizure of the articles was issued to pay such costs as the court thinks reasonable to any person who has appeared before the court to show cause why those articles should not be forfeited; and costs ordered to be paid under this subsection shall be enforceable as a civil debt.

(7) For the purposes of this section the question whether an article is obscene shall be determined on the assumption that copies of it would be published in any manner likely having regard to the circumstances in which it was found, but in no other manner ...

4 Defence of public good

(1) Subject to subsection 1A of this section a person shall not be convicted of an offence against section 2 of this Act, and an order for forfeiture shall not be made under the foregoing section, if it is proved that publication of the article in question is justified as being for the public good on the ground that it is in the interests of science, literature, art or learning, or of other objects of general concern.

(1A) Subsection (1) of this section shall not apply where the article in question is a moving picture film or soundtrack, but –

(a) a person shall not be convicted of an offence against section 2 of this Act in relation to any such film or soundtrack, and

(b) an order for forfeiture of any such film or soundtrack shall not be made under section 3 of this Act,

if it is proved that publication of the film or soundtrack is justified as being for the public good on the ground that it is in the interests of drama, opera, ballet or any other art, or of literature or learning.

(2) It is hereby declared that the opinion of experts as to the literary, artistic, scientific or other merits of an article may be admitted in any proceedings under this Act either to establish or to negative the said ground.

(3) In this section 'moving picture soundtrack' means any sound record designed for playing with a moving picture film, whether incorporated with the film or not.

As amended by the Obscene Publications Act 1964, s1(1); Courts Act 1971, s56(2), Schedule 8, para 37, Schedule 9, Part I; Criminal Law Act 1977, ss53(1), (5), (6), (7), 65(4), (5), Schedules 12, 13; Magistrates' Courts Act 1980, s32(2); Police and Criminal Evidence Act 1984, s119(2), Schedule 7, Part I; Cinemas Act 1985, s24(1), Schedule 2, para 6; Broadcasting Act 1990, ss162(1), 203(3), Schedule 21; Criminal Justice and Public Order Act 1994, s168(1), Schedule 9, para 3.

PEERAGE ACT 1963
(1963 c 48)

1 Disclaimer of certain hereditary peerages

(1) Subject to the provisions of this section, any person who, after the commencement of this Act, succeeds to a peerage in the peerage of England, Scotland, Great Britain or the United Kingdom may, by an instrument of disclaimer delivered to the Lord Chancellor within the period prescribed by this Act, disclaim that peerage for his life.

(2) Any instrument of disclaimer to be delivered under this section in respect of a peerage shall be delivered within the period of twelve months beginning with the day on which the person disclaiming succeeds to that peerage or, if he is under the age of twenty-one when he so succeeds, the period of twelve months beginning with the day on which he attains that age; and no such instrument shall be delivered in respect of a peerage by a person who is excepted from section 1 of the House of Lords Act 1999 by virtue of section 2 of that Act. …

(4) In reckoning any period prescribed by this section for the delivery of an instrument of disclaimer by any person no account shall be taken of any time during which that person is shown to the satisfaction of the Lord Chancellor to have been subject to any infirmity of body or mind rendering him incapable of exercising or determining whether to exercise his rights under this section.

(5) The provisions of Schedule 1 to this Act shall have effect with respect to the form of instruments of disclaimer under this section, and the delivery, certification and registration of such instruments.

3 Effects of disclaimer

(1) The disclaimer of a peerage by any person under this Act shall be irrevocable and shall operate, from the date on which the instrument of disclaimer is delivered –

(a) to divest that person (and, if he is married, his wife) of all right or interest to or in the peerage, and all titles, rights, offices, privileges and precedence attaching thereto; and

(b) to relieve him of all obligations and disabilities arising therefrom,

but shall not accelerate the succession to that peerage nor affect its devolution on his death.

(2) Where a peerage is disclaimed under this Act, no other hereditary peerage shall be conferred upon the person by whom it is disclaimed.

(3) The disclaimer of a peerage under this Act shall not affect any right, interest or power (whether arising before or after the disclaimer) of the person by whom the peerage is disclaimed, or of any other person, to, in or over any estates or other property limited or settled to devolve with that peerage.

(4) The reference in the foregoing subsection to estates or other property limited or settled to devolve with a peerage shall, for the purposes of the application of this Act to Scotland, be construed as including a reference to estates or other land devolving as aforesaid under an entail or special destination, or the beneficial interest in which so devolves under a trust.

4 Scottish peerages

The holder of a peerage in the peerage of Scotland shall have the same right to receive writs of summons to attend the House of Lords, and to sit and vote in that House, as the holder of a peerage in the peerage of the United Kingdom; and the enactments relating to the election of Scottish representative peers shall cease to have effect.

6 Peeresses in own right

A woman who is the holder of a hereditary peerage in the peerage of England, Scotland, Great Britain or the United Kingdom shall (whatever the terms of the letters patent or other instrument, if any, creating that peerage) have the same right to receive writs of summons to attend the House of Lords, or to sit and vote in that House, and shall be subject to the same disqualifications in respect of membership of the House of Commons and elections to that House, as a man holding that peerage.

As amended by the House of Lords Act 1999, s4, Schedule 1, para 1, Schedule 2.

OBSCENE PUBLICATIONS ACT 1964

(1964 c 74)

1 Obscene articles intended for publication for gain ...

(2) For the purpose of any proceedings for an offence against ... section 2 [of the Obscene Publications Act 1959] a person shall be deemed to have an article for publication for gain if with a view to such publication he had the article in his ownership, possession or control.

(3) In proceedings brought against a person under the said section 2 for having an obscene article for publication for gain the following provisions shall apply in place of subsections (5) and (6) of that section, that is to say –

(a) he shall not be convicted of that offence if he proves that he had not examined the article and had no reasonable cause to suspect that it was such that his having it would make him liable to be convicted of an offence against that section; and

(b) the question whether the article is obscene shall be determined by reference to such publication for gain of the article as in the circumstances it may reasonably be inferred he had in contemplation and to any further publication that could reasonably be expected to follow from it, but not to any other publication.

(4) Where articles are seized under section 3 of the Obscene Publications Act 1959 (which provides for the seizure and forfeiture of obscene articles kept for publication for gain), and a person is convicted under section 2 of that Act of having them for publication for gain, the Court on his conviction shall order the forfeiture of those articles: Provided that an order made by virtue of this subsection (including an order so made on appeal) shall not take effect until the expiration of the ordinary time within which an appeal in the matter of the proceedings in which the order was made may be instituted or, where such an appeal is duly instituted, until the appeal is finally decided or abandoned; and for this purpose –

(a) an application for a case to be stated or for leave to appeal shall be treated as the institution of an appeal; and

(b) where a decision on appeal is subject to a further appeal, the appeal shall not be deemed to be finally decided until the expiration of the ordinary time within which a further appeal may be instituted or, where a further appeal is duly instituted, until the further appeal is finally decided or abandoned.

(5) References in section 3 of the Obscene Publications Act 1959 and this section to

publication for gain shall apply to any publication with a view to gain, whether the gain is to accrue by way of consideration for the publication or in any other way.

2 Negatives, etc for production of obscene articles

(1) The Obscene Publications Act 1959 (as amended by this Act) shall apply in relation to anything which is intended to be used, either alone or as one of a set, for the reproduction or manufacture therefrom of articles containing or embodying matter to be read, looked at or listened to, as if it were an article containing or embodying that matter so far as that matter is to be derived from it or from the set.

(2) For the purposes of the Obscene Publications Act 1959 (as so amended) an article shall be deemed to be had or kept for publication if it is had or kept for the reproduction or manufacture therefrom of articles for publication; and the question whether an article so had or kept is obscene shall –

(a) for purposes of section 2 of the Act be determined in accordance with section 1(3)(b) above as if any reference there to publication of the article were a reference to publication of articles reproduced or manufactured from it; and

(b) for purposes of section 3 of the Act be determined on the assumption that articles reproduced or manufactured from it would be published in any manner likely having regard to the circumstances in which it was found, but in no other manner.

WAR DAMAGE ACT 1965

(1965 c 18)

1 Abolition of rights at common law to compensation for certain damage to or destruction of property

(1) No person shall be entitled at common law to receive from the Crown compensation in respect of damage to, or destruction of, property caused (whether before or after the passing of this Act, within or outside the United Kingdom) by Acts lawfully done by, or on the authority of, the Crown during, or in contemplation of the outbreak of, a war in which the Sovereign was, or is, engaged.

As amended by the Statute Law (Repeals) Act 1995, s1(1), Schedule 1, Pt VI.

PARLIAMENTARY COMMISSIONER ACT 1967

(1967 c 13)

1 Appointment and tenure of office

(1) For the purpose of conducting investigations in accordance with the following provisions of this Act there shall be appointed a Commissioner, to be known as the Parliamentary Commissioner for Administration.

(2) Her Majesty may by Letters Patent from time to time appoint a person to be the Commissioner, and any person so appointed shall (subject to subsections (3) and (3A) of this section) hold office during good behaviour.

(3) A person appointed to be the Commissioner may be relieved of office by Her Majesty at his own request, or may be removed from office by Her Majesty in consequence of Addresses from both Houses of Parliament, and shall in any case vacate office on completing the year of service in which he attains the age of sixty-five years.

(3A) Her majesty may declare the office of Commissioner to have been vacated if satisfied that the person appointed to be the Commissioner is incapable for medical reasons –

(a) of performing the duties of his office; and

(b) of requesting to be relieved of it.

3 Administrative provisions

(1) The Commissioner may appoint such officers as he may determine with the approval of the Treasury as to numbers and conditions of service.

(2) Any function of the Commissioner under this Act may be performed by any officer of the Commissioner authorised for that purpose by the Commissioner, by any member of the staff so authorised of the Welsh Administration Ombudsman or of the Health Service Commissioner for Wales or by any officer so authorised of the Health Service Commissioner for England. …

3A Appointment of acting Commissioner

(1) Where the office of Commissioner becomes vacant, Her Majesty may, pending the appointment of a new Commissioner, appoint a person under this section to

act as the Commissioner at any time during the period of twelve months beginning with the date on which the vacancy arose.

(2) A person appointed under this section shall hold office during Her Majesty's pleasure and, subject to that, shall hold office –

(a) until the appointment of a new Commissioner or the expiry of the period of twelve months beginning with the date on which the vacancy arose, whichever occurs first; and

(b) in other respects, in accordance with the terms and conditions of his appointment which shall be such as the Treasury may determine.

(3) A person appointed under this section shall, while he holds office, be treated for all purposes, except those of section 2 of this Act, as the Commissioner.

(4) Any salary, pension or other benefit payable by virtue of this section shall be charged on and issued out of the Consolidated Fund.

4 Departments, etc subject to investigation

(1) Subject to the provisions of this section and to the notes contained in Schedule 2 to this Act, this Act applies to the government departments, corporations and unincorporated bodies listed in that Schedule; and references in this Act to an authority to which this Act applies are references to any such corporation or body.

(2) Her Majesty may by Order in Council amend Schedule 2 to this Act by the alteration of any entry or note, the removal of any entry or note or the insertion of any additional entry or note.

(3) An Order in Council may only insert an entry if –

(a) it relates –

(i) to a government department; or

(ii) to a corporation or body whose functions are exercised on behalf of the Crown; or

(b) it relates to a corporation or body –

(i) which is established by virtue of Her Majesty's prerogative or by an Act of Parliament or an Order in Council or order made under an Act of Parliament or which is established in any other way by a Minister of the Crown in his capacity as a Minister or by a government department;

(ii) at least half of whose revenues derive directly from money provided by Parliament, a levy authorised by an enactment, a fee or charge of any other description so authorised or more than one of those sources; and

(iii) which is wholly or partly constituted by appointment made by Her Majesty or a Minister of the Crown or government department.

(3A) No entry shall be made if the result of making it would be that the Parliamentary Commissioner could investigate action which can be investigated by the Welsh Administration Ombudsman under Schedule 9 to the Government of Wales Act 1998.

(3B) No entry shall be made in respect of –

(a) the Scottish Administration of any part of it;

(b) any Scottish public authority with mixed functions or no reserved functions within the meaning of the Scotland Act 1998; or

(c) the Scottish Parliamentary Corporate Body.

(4) No entry shall be made in respect of a corporation or body whose sole activity is, or whose main activities are, included among the activities specified in subsection (5) below.

(5) The activities mentioned in subsection (4) above are –

(a) the provision of education, or the provision of training otherwise than under the Industrial Training Act 1982;

(b) the development of curricula, the conduct of examinations or the validation of educational courses;

(c) the control of entry to any profession or the regulation of the conduct of members of any profession;

(d) the investigation of complaints by members of the public regarding the actions of any person or body, or the supervision or review or such investigations or of steps taken following them.

(6) No entry shall be made in respect of a corporation or body operating in an exclusively or predominantly commercial manner or a corporation carrying on under national ownership an industry or undertaking or part of an industry or undertaking.

(7) Any statutory instrument made by virtue of this section shall be subject to annulment in pursuance of a resolution of either House of Parliament.

(8) In this Act –

(a) any reference to a government department to which this Act applies includes a reference to any of the Ministers or officers of such a department; and

(b) any reference to an authority to which this Act applies includes a reference to any members or officers of such an authority.

5 Matters subject to investigation

(1) Subject to the provisions of this section, the Commissioner may investigate any action taken by or on behalf of a government department or other authority to which this Act applies, being action taken in the exercise of administrative functions of that department or authority, in any case where –

(a) a written complaint is duly made to a member of the House of Commons by a member of the public who claims to have sustained injustice in consequence of maladministration in connection with the action so taken; and

(b) the complaint is referred to the Commissioner, with the consent of the person who made it, by a member of that House with a request to conduct an investigation thereon.

(2) Except as hereinafter provided, the Commissioner shall not conduct an investigation under this Act in respect of any of the following matters, that is to say –

(a) any action in respect of which the person aggrieved has or had a right of appeal, reference or review to or before a tribunal constituted by or under any enactment or by virtue of Her Majesty's prerogative;

(b) any action in respect of which the person aggrieved has or had a remedy by way of proceedings in any court of law:

Provided that the Commissioner may conduct an investigation notwithstanding that the person aggrieved has or had such a right or remedy if satisfied that in the particular circumstances it is not reasonable to expect him to resort or have resorted to it. ...

(3) Without prejudice to subsection (2) of this section, the Commissioner shall not conduct an investigation under this Act in respect of any such action or matter as is described in Schedule 3 to this Act.

(4) Her Majesty may by Order in Council amend the said Schedule 3 so as to exclude from the provisions of that Schedule such actions or matters as may be described in the Order; and any statutory instrument made by virtue of this subsection shall be subject to annulment in pursuance of a resolution of either House of Parliament.

(5) In determining whether to initiate, continue or discontinue an investigation under this Act, the Commissioner shall, subject to the foregoing provisions of this section, act in accordance with his own discretion; and any question whether a complaint is duly made under this Act shall be determined by the Commissioner.

(5A) For the purpose of this section, administrative functions of a government department to which this Act applies include functions exercised by the department on behalf of the Scottish Ministers by virtue of section 93 of the Scotland Act 1998.

(5B) The Commissioner shall not conduct an investigation under this Act in respect of any action concerning Scotland and not relatiing to reserved matters which is taken by or on behalf of a cross-border public authority within the meaning of the Scotland Act 1998.

(6) For the purposes of this section, administrative functions exercisable by any person appointed by the Lord Chancellor as a member of the administrative staff of any court or tribunal shall be taken to be administrative functions of the Lord Chancellor's Department or, in Northern Ireland, of the Northern Ireland Court Service.

(7) For the purposes of this section, administrative functions exercisable by any person appointed as a member of the administative staff of a relevant tribunal –

(a) by a government department or authority to which this Act applies; or

(b) with the consent (whether as to remuneration and other terms and conditions of service or otherwise) of such a department or authority,

shall be taken to be administrative functions of that department or authority.

(8) In subsection (7) of this section, 'relevant tribunal' means a tribunal listed in Schedule 4 to this Act.

(9) Her Majesty may by Order in Council amend the said Schedule 4 by the alteration or removal of any entry or the insertion of any additional entry; and any statutory instrument made by virtue of this subsection shall be subject to annulment in pursuance of a resolution of either House of Parliament. ...

6 Provisions relating to complaints

(1) A complaint under this Act may be made by any individual, or by any body of persons whether incorporated or not, not being –

(a) a local authority or other authority or body constituted for purposes of the public service or of local government or for the purposes of carrying on under national ownership any industry or undertaking or part of an industry or undertaking;

(b) any other authority or body within subsection (1A) below.

(1A) An authority or body is within this subsection if –

(a) its members are appointed by –

(i) Her Majesty;

(ii) any Minister of the Crown;

(iii) any government department;

(iv) the Scottish Ministers;

(v) the First Minister; or

(vi) the Lord Advocate, or

(b) its revenues consist wholly or mainly of –

(i) money provided by Parliament; or

(ii) sums payable out of the Scottish Consolidated Fund (directly or indirectly).

(2) Where the person by whom a complaint might have been made under the foregoing provisions of this Act has died or is for any reason unable to act for himself, the complaint may be made by his personal representative or by a member of his family or other individual suitable to represent him; but except as aforesaid a complaint shall not be entertained under this Act unless made by the person aggrieved himself.

(3) A complaint shall not be entertained under this Act unless it is made to a member of the House of Commons not later than twelve months from the day on which the person aggrieved first had notice of the matters alleged in the complaint; but the Commissioner may conduct an investigation pursuant to a complaint not

made within that period if he considers that there are special circumstances which make it proper to do so.

(4) Except as provided in subsection (5) below a complaint shall not be entertained under this Act unless the person aggrieved is resident in the United Kingdom (or, if he is dead, was so resident at the time of his death) or the complaint relates to action taken in relation to him while he was present in the United Kingdom or on an installation in a designated area within the meaning of the Continental Shelf Act 1964 or on a ship registered in the United Kingdom or an aircraft so registered, or in relation to rights or obligations which accrued or arose in the United Kingdom or on such an installation, ship or aircraft.

(5) A complaint may be entertained under this Act in circumstances not falling within subsection (4) above where –

(a) the complaint relates to action taken in any country or territory outside the United Kingdom by an officer (not being an honorary consular officer) in the exercise of a consular function on behalf of the Government of the United Kingdom; and

(b) the person aggrieved is a citizen of the United Kingdom and Colonies who, under section 2 of the Immigration Act 1971, has the right of abode in the United Kingdom.

7 Procedure in respect of investigations

(1) Where the Commissioner proposes to conduct an investigation pursuant to a complaint under this Act, he shall afford to the principal officer of the department or authority concerned, and to any person who is alleged in the complaint to have taken or authorised the action complained of, an opportunity to comment on any allegations contained in the complaint.

(2) Every such investigation shall be conducted in private, but except as aforesaid the procedure for conducting an investigation shall be such as the Commissioner considers appropriate in the circumstances of the case; and without prejudice to the generality of the foregoing provision the Commissioner may obtain information from such persons and in such manner, and make such inquiries, as he thinks fit, and may determine whether any person may be represented, by counsel or solicitor or otherwise, in the investigation.

(3) The Commissioner may, if he thinks fit, pay to the person by whom the complaint was made and to any other person who attends or furnishes information for the purposes of an investigation under this Act –

(a) sums in respect of expenses properly incurred by them;

(b) allowances by way of compensation for the loss of their time,

in accordance with such scales and subject to such conditions as may be determined by the Treasury.

(4) The conduct of an investigation under this Act shall not affect any action taken by the department or authority concerned, or any power or duty of that department

or authority to take further action with respect to any matters subject to the investigation ...

8 Evidence

(1) For the purposes of an investigation under this Act the Commissioner may require any Minister, officer or member of the department or authority concerned or any other person who in his opinion is able to furnish information or produce documents relevant to the investigation to furnish any such information or produce any such document.

(2) For the purposes of any such investigation the Commissioner shall have the same powers as the Court in respect of the attendance and examination of witnesses (including the administration of oaths or affirmations and the examination of witnesses abroad) and in respect of the production of documents.

(3) No obligation to maintain secrecy or other restriction upon the disclosure of information obtained by or furnished to persons in Her Majesty's service, whether imposed by any enactment or by any rule of law, shall apply to the disclosure of information for the purposes of an investigation under this Act; and the Crown shall not be entitled in relation to any such investigation to any such privilege in respect of the production of documents or the giving of evidence as is allowed by law in legal proceedings.

(4) No person shall be required or authorised by virtue of this Act to furnish any information or answer any question relating to proceedings of the Cabinet or of any committee of the Cabinet or to produce so much of any document as relates to such proceedings; and for the purposes of this subsection a certificate issued by the Secretary of the Cabinet with the approval of the Prime Minister and certifying that any information, question, document or part of a document so relates shall be conclusive.

(5) Subject to subsection (3) of this section, no person shall be compelled for the purposes of an investigation under this Act to give any evidence or produce any document which he could not be compelled to give or produce in civil proceedings before the Court.

9 Obstruction and contempt

(1) If any person without lawful excuse obstructs the Commissioner or any officer of the Commissioner in the performance of his functions under this Act, or is guilty of any act or omission in relation to any investigation under this Act which, if that investigation were a proceeding in the Court, would constitute contempt of court, the Commissioner may certify the offence to the Court.

(2) Where an offence is certified under this section, the Court may inquire into the matter and, after hearing any witnesses who may be produced against or on behalf of the person charged with the offence, and after hearing any statement that may be offered in defence, deal with him in any manner in which the Court could deal with him if he had committed the like offence in relation to the Court.

(3) Nothing in this section shall be construed as applying to the taking of any such action as is mentioned in subsection (4) of section 7 of this Act.

10 Reports by Commissioner

(1) In any case where the Commissioner conducts an investigation under this Act or decides not to conduct such an investigation, he shall sent to the member of the House of Commons by whom the request for investigation was made (or if he is no longer a member of that House, to such member of that House as the Commissioner thinks appropriate) a report of the results of the investigation or, as the case may be, a statement of his reasons for not conducting an investigation.

(2) In any case where the Commissioner conducts an investigation under this Act, he shall also send a report of the results of the investigation to the principal officer of the department or authority concerned and to any other person who is alleged in the relevant complaint to have taken or authorised the action complained of.

(3) If, after conducting an investigation under this Act, it appears to the Commissioner that injustice has been caused to the person aggrieved in consequence of maladministration and that the injustice has not been, or will not be, remedied, he may, if he thinks fit, lay before each House of Parliament a special report upon the case.

(4) The Commissioner shall annually lay before each House of Parliament a general report on the performance of his functions under this Act and may from time to time lay before each House of Parliament such other reports with respect to those functions as he thinks fit.

(5) For the purposes of the law of defamation, any such publication as is hereinafter mentioned shall be absolutely privileged, that is to say –

(a) the publication of any matter by the Commissioner in making a report to either House of Parliament for the purposes of this Act;

(b) the publication of any matter by a member of the House of Commons in communicating with the Commissioner or his officers for those purposes or by the Commissioner or his officers in communicating with such a member for those purposes;

(c) the publication by such a member to the person by whom a complaint was made under this Act of a report or statement sent to the member in respect of the complaint in pursuance of subsection (1) of this section;

(d) the publication by the Commissioner to such a person as is mentioned in subsection (2) of this section of a report to that person in pursuance of that subsection.

11 Provision for secrecy of information

(2) Information obtained by the Commissioner or his officers in the course of or for the purposes of an investigation under this Act shall not be disclosed except –

(a) for the purposes of the investigation and of any report to be made thereon under this Act;

(b) for the purposes of any proceedings for an offence under the Official Secrets Acts 1911 to 1989 alleged to have been committed in respect of information obtained by the Commissioner or any of his officers by virtue of this Act or for an offence of perjury alleged to have been committed in the course of an investigation under this Act or for the purposes of an inquiry with a view to the taking of such proceedings; or

(c) for the purposes of any proceedings under section 9 of this Act;

and the Commissioner and his officers shall not be called upon to give evidence in any proceedings (other than such proceedings as aforesaid) of matters coming to his or their knowledge in the course of an investigation under this Act.

(2A) Where the Commissioner also holds office as Welsh Administration Ombudsman or a Health Service Commissioner and a person initiates a complaint to him in his capacity as Welsh Administration Ombudsman or a Health Service Commissioner which relates partly to a matter with respect to which that person has previously initiated a complaint under this Act, or subsequently initiates such a complaint, information obtained by the Commissioner or his officers in the course of or for the purposes of investigating the complaint under this Act may be disclosed for the purposes of his carrying out his functions in relation to the other complaint.

(3) A Minister of the Crown may give notice in writing to the Commissioner, with respect to any document or information specified in the notice, or any class of documents or information so specified, that in the opinion of the Minister the disclosure of that document or information, or of documents or information of that class, would be prejudicial to the safety of the State or otherwise contrary to the public interest; and where such a notice is given nothing in this Act shall be construed as authorising or requiring the Commissioner or any officer of the Commissioner to communicate to any person or for any purpose any document or information specified in the notice, or any document or information of a class so specified.

(4) The references in this section to a Minister of the Crown include references to the Commissioners of Customs and Excise and the Commissioners of Inland Revenue.

(5) Information obtained from the Information Commissioner by virtue of section 76(1) of the Freedom of Information Act 2000 shall be treated for the purposes of subsection (2) of this section as obtained for the purposes of an investigation under this Act and, in relation to such information, the reference in paragraph (a) of that subsection to the investigation shall have effect as a reference to any investigation.

11A Consultations between Parliamentary Commissioner and Welsh Administration Ombudsman or Health Service Commissioners

(1) Where, at any stage in the course of conducting an investigation under this Act, the Commissioner forms the opinion that the complaint relates partly to a

matter within the jurisdiction of the Welsh Administration Ombudsman, the Scottish Public Services Ombudsman or of the Health Service Commissioner for England or Wales, he shall –

(a) unless he also holds the office concerned, consult about the complaint with him; and

(b) if he considers it necessary, inform the person initiating the complaint under this Act of the steps necessary to initiate a complaint under the Government of Wales Act 1998, or the Health Services Commissioners Act 1993, or the Scottish Public Services Ombudsman Act 2002.

(2) Where by virtue of subsection (1) above the Commissioner consults with the Welsh Administration Ombudsman, the Scottish Public Services Ombudsman or a Health Service Commissioner in relation to a complaint under this Act, he may consult him about any matter relating to the complaint, including –

(a) the conduct of any investigation into the complaint; and

(b) the form, content and publication of any report of the results of such an investigation.

(2A) Where an authority to which this Act applies is also a listed authority to which the Scottish Public Services Ombudsman Act 2002 applies, the Commissioner must co-operate with the Scottish Public Services Ombudsman to such an extent as appears appropriate when exercising any function in relation to that authority.

(3) Nothing in section 11(2) of this Act shall apply in relation to the disclosure of information by the Commissioner or any of his officers in the course of consultations held in accordance with this section.

11AA Disclosure of information by Parliamentary Commissioner to Information Commissioner

(1) The Commissioner may disclose to the Information Commissioner any information obtained by, or furnished to, the Commissioner under or for the purposes of this Act if the information appears to the Commissioner to relate to –

(a) a matter in respect of which the Information Commissioner could exercise any power conferred by –

(i) Part V of the Data Protection Act 1998 (enforcement)

(ii) section 48 of the Freedom of Information Act 2000 (practice recommendations), or

(iii) Part IV of that Act (enforcement), or

(b) the commission of an offence under –

(i) any provision of the Data Protection Act 1998 other than paragraph 12 of Schedule 9 (obstruction of execution of warrant), or

(ii) section 77 of the Freedom of Information Act 2000 (offence of altering etc records with intent to previous disclosure).

(2) Nothing in section 11(2) of this Act shall apply in relation to the disclosure of information in accordance with this section.

11B The Criminal Injuries Compensation Scheme

(1) For the purposes of this Act, administration functions exercisable by an administrator of the Criminal Injuries Compensation Scheme ('Scheme functions') shall be taken to be administrative functions of a government department to which this Act applies.

(2) For the purposes of this section, the following are administrators of the Scheme –

(a) a claims officer appointed under section 3(4)(b) of the Criminal Injuries Compensation Act 1995;

(b) a person appointed under section 5(3)(c) of that Act;

(c) the Scheme manager, as defined by section 1(4) of that Act, and any person assigned by him to exercise functions in relation to the Scheme.

(3) The principal officer in relation to any complaint made in respect of any action taken in respect of Scheme functions is –

(a) in the case of action taken by a claims officer, such person as may from time to time be designated by the Secretary of State for the purposes of this paragraph;

(b) in the case of action taken by a person appointed under section 5(3)(c) of the Act of 1995, the chairman appointed by the Secretary of State under section 5(3)(b) of that Act; or

(c) in the case of action taken by the Scheme manager or by any other person mentioned in subsection (2)(c) of this section, the Scheme manager.

(4) The conduct of an investigation under this Act in respect of any action taken in respect of Scheme functions shall not affect –

(a) any action so taken; or

(b) any power or duty of any person to take further action with respect to any matters subject to investigation.

12 Interpretation

(1) In this Act the following expressions have the meanings hereby respectively assigned to them, that is to say –

'action' includes failure to act, and other expressions connoting action shall be construed accordingly;

'the Commissioner' means the Parliamentary Commissioner for Administration;

'the Court' means, in relation to England and Wales the High Court, in relation to Scotland the Court of Session, and in relation to Northern Ireland the High Court of Northern Ireland;

'enactment' includes an enactment of the Parliament of Northern Ireland and any instrument made by virtue of an enactment;

'officer' includes employee;

'person aggrieved' means the person who claims or is alleged to have sustained such injustice as is mentioned in section 5(1)(a) of this Act;

'tribunal' includes the person constituting a tribunal consisting of one person.

(2) References in this Act to any enactment are references to that enactment as amended or extended by or under any other enactment.

(3) It is hereby declared that nothing in this Act authorises or requires the Commissioner to question the merits of a decision taken without maladministration by a government department or other authority in the exercise of a discretion vested in that department or authority.

SCHEDULE 2

DEPARTMENTS, ETC SUBJECT TO INVESTIGATION

[NB The departments, etc, here listed are merely examples of the bodies subject to investigation.]

Advisory, Conciliation and Arbitration Service ...

Appeal Officer for Community Interest Companies ...

Arts Council of England ...

British Council ...

Cabinet Office ...

Charity Commission

Children and Family Court Advisory and Support Service ...

Civil Justice Council ...

Commission for Patient and Public Involvement in Health ...

Countryside Agency ...

Customs and Excise ...

Department for Constitutional Affairs

Department for Culture, Media and Sport

Department for Education and Skills

Department for Environment, Food and Rural Affairs

Department for International Development ...

Department for Transport ...

Department of Health

Department of Trade and Industry …

Disability Rights Commission …

English Nature …

Equal Opportunities Commission …

Export Credits Guarantee Department …

Foreign and Commonwealth Office

Forestry Commission …

Gangmasters Licensing Authority …

Health and Safety Commission

Health and Safety Executive …

Home Office …

Housing Corporation

Human Fertilisation and Embryology Authority …

Immigration Services Commissioner …

Information Commissioner

Inland Revenue …

Investors in People UK …

Land Registry

Legal Services Commission …

National Endowment for Science, Technology and the Arts …

National Lottery Charities Board …

Office of Fair Trading

Office of the Deputy Prime Minister …

Ordnance Survey …

Parole Board …

Public Record Office …

Royal Mint …

Teacher Training Agency …

Treasury Solicitor …

Victoria and Albert Museum …

Wales Office …

War Pensions Committees ...

Women's National Commission ...

Youth Justice Board for England and Wales. ...

NOTES ...

A2. The reference to the Department for Constitutional Affairs includes the Lord Chancellor's Department and the Public Trustee. ...

SCHEDULE 3

MATTERS NOT SUBJECT TO INVESTIGATION

1. Action taken in matters certified by a Secretary of State or other Minister of the Crown to affect relations or dealings between the Government of the United Kingdom and any other Government or any international organisation of States or Governments.

2. Action taken, in any country or territory outside the United Kingdom, by or on behalf of any officer representing or acting under the authority of Her Majesty in respect of the United Kingdom, or any other officer of the Government of the United Kingdom other than action which is taken by an officer (not being an honorary consular officer) in the exercise of a consular function on behalf of the Government of the United Kingdom.

3. Action taken in connection with the administration of the government of any country or territory outside the United Kingdom which forms part of Her Majesty's dominions or in which Her Majesty has jurisdiction.

4. Action taken by the Secretary of State under the Extradition Act 2003.

5. Action taken by or with the authority of the Secretary of State for the purposes of investigating crime or of protecting the security of the State, including action so taken with respect to passports.

6. The commencement or conduct of civil or criminal proceedings before any court of law in the United Kingdom, of proceedings at any place under the Naval Discipline Act 1957, the Army Act 1955 or the Air Force Act 1955, or of proceedings before any international court or tribunal.

6A. Action taken by any person appointed by the Lord Chancellor as a member of the administrative staff of any court or tribunal, so far as that action is taken at the direction, or on the authority (whether express or implied), of any person acting in a judicial capacity or in his capacity as a member of the tribunal.

6B. – (1) Action taken by any member of the administrative staff of a relevant tribunal, so far as that action is taken at the direction, or on the authority (whether express or implied), of any person acting in his capacity as a member of the tribunal.

(2) In this paragraph, 'relevant tribunal' has the meaning given by section 5(8) of this Act.

6C. Action taken by any person appointed under section 5(3)(c) of the Criminal Injuries Compensation Act 1995, so far as that action is taken at the direction, or on the authority (whether express or implied), of any person acting in his capacity as an adjudicator appointed under section 5 of that Act to determine appeals.

7. Any exercise of the prerogative of mercy or of the power of a Secretary of State to make a reference in respect of any person to the High Court of Justiciary or the Courts-Martial Appeal Court.

8. – (1) Action taken on behalf of the Minister of Health or the Secretary of State by a Strategic Health Authority, a Health Authority, a Primary Care Trust, a Special Health Authority except the Rampton Hospital Review Board, the Rampton Hospital Board, the Broadmoor Hospital Board or the Moss Side and Park Lane Hospitals Board, a Health Board or the Common Services Agency for the Scottish Health Service, by the Dental Practice Board or the Scottish Dental Practice Board or by the Public Health Laboratory Service Board.

(2) For the purposes of this paragraph, action taken by a Strategic Health Authority, Health Authority, Special Health Authority or Primary Care Trust in the exercise of functions of the Secretary of State shall be regarded as action taken on his behalf.

9. Action taken in matters relating to contractual or other commercial transactions, whether within the United Kingdom or elsewhere, being transactions of a government department or authority to which this Act applies or of any such authority or body as is mentioned in paragraph (a) or (b) of subsection (1) of section 6 of this Act and not being transactions for or relating to –

(a) the acquisition of land compulsorily or in circumstances in which it could be acquired compulsorily;

(b) the disposal as surplus of land acquired compulsorily or in such circumstances as aforesaid.

10. – (1) Action taken in respect of appointments or removals, pay, discipline, superannuation or other personnel matters, in relation to –

(a) service in any of the armed forces of the Crown, including reserve and auxiliary and cadet forces;

(b) service in any office or employment under the Crown or under any authority to which this Act applies; or

(c) service in any office or employment, or under any contract for services, in respect of which power to take action, or to determine or approve the action to be taken, in such matters is vested in Her Majesty, any Minister of the Crown or any such authority as aforesaid.

(2) Sub-paragraph (1)(c) above shall not apply to any action (not otherwise excluded from investigation by this Schedule) which is taken by the Secretary of State in connection with –

(a) the provision of information relating to the terms and conditions of any employment covered by an agreement entered into by him under section 12(1) of the Overseas Development and Cooperation Act 1980 or pursuant to the exercise of his powers under Part I of the International Development Act 2002, or

(b) the provision of any allowance, grant or supplement or any benefit (other than those relating to superannuation) arising from the designation of any person in accordance with such an agreement.

11. The grant of honours, awards or privileges within the gift of the Crown, including the grant of Royal Charters.

SCHEDULE 4

RELEVANT TRIBUNALS FOR PURPOSES OF SECTION 5(7)

[NB The tribunals, etc, here listed are merely examples of the bodies which are relevant tribunals for these purposes.]

Appeal Tribunals constituted under Chapter I of Part I of the Social Security Act 1998. …

Copyright Tribunal constituted under section 145 of the Copyright Designs and Patents Act 1988. …

Financial Services and Markets Tribunal constituted under section 132 of the Financial Services and Markets Act 2000 …

Information Tribunal constituted under section 6 of the Data Protection Act 1998. …

Persons hearing estate agents' appeals appointed under regulation 19 of the Estate Agents (Appeals) Regulations 1981. …

As amended by the Civil Evidence Act 1968, s17(1)(b); Parliamentary Commissioner (Consular Complaints) Act 1981, s1; Parliamentary and Health Service Commissioners Act 1987, ss1(1), (2), (3)(c), 2(1), 4(1), (2), 6(1); Official Secrets Act 1989, s16(4), Schedules 1, para 1(a), 2; Courts and Legal Services Act 1990, ss10(2), 110(1); Trade Union Reform and Employment Rights Act 1993, s49(2), Schedule 8, para 2; Health Service Commissioners Act 1993, s20(1), Schedule 2, paras 1, 2; Welsh Language Act 1993, s4(2), Schedule 1, para 5; Trade Union Reform and Employment Rights Act 1993, s49(2), Schedule 8, para 2; National Lottery Act 1993, s3(2), Schedule 2, para 7; Parliamentary Commissioner Act 1994, s1; Criminal Injuries Compensation Act 1995, s10(1), (2); Government of Wales Act 1998, s125, Schedule 12, paras 4–8; Scotland Act 1999 (Consequential Modifications) (No 2) Order 1999, art 4, Schedule 2, Pt I, para 39; Freedom of Information Act 2000, s76(2), Schedule 7, paras 1, 2; Scottish Public Services Ombudsman Act 2002 (Consequential Provisions and Modifications) Order 2004, art 5(1)–(3). Detailed amendments were made to Schedules 2–4, above, by relevant Acts and orders.

CRIMINAL LAW ACT 1967

(1967 c 58)

3 Use of force in making arrest, etc

(1) A person may use such force as is reasonable in the circumstances in the prevention of crime, or in effecting or assisting in the lawful arrest of offenders or suspected offenders or of persons unlawfully at large.

(2) Subsection (1) above shall replace the rules of the common law on the question when force used for a purpose mentioned in the subsection is justified by that purpose.

IMMIGRATION ACT 1971

(1971 c 77)

1 General principles

(1) All those who are in this Act expressed to have the right of abode in the United Kingdom shall be free to live in, and to come and go into and from, the United Kingdom without let or hindrance except such as may be required under and in accordance with this Act to enable their right to be established or as may be otherwise lawfully imposed on any person.

(2) Those not having the right may live, work and settle in the United Kingdom by permission and subject to such regulation and control of their entry into, stay in and departure from the United Kingdom as is imposed by this Act; and indefinite leave to enter or remain in the United Kingdom shall by virtue of this provision, be treated as having been given under this Act to those in the United Kingdom at its coming into force, if they are then settled there (and not exempt under this Act from the provisions relating to leave to enter or remain) ...

2 Statement of right of abode in the United Kingdom

(1) A person is under this Act to have the right of abode in the United Kingdom if –

(a) he is a British citizen; or

(b) he is a Commonwealth citizen who –

(i) immediately before the commencement of the British Nationality Act 1981 was a Commonwealth citizen having the right of abode in the United Kingdom by virtue of section 2(1)(d) or section 2(2) of this Act as then in force; and

(ii) has not ceased to be a Commonwealth citizen in the meanwhile.

(2) In relation to Commonwealth citizens who have the right of abode in the United Kingdom by virtue of subsection (1)(b) above, this Act, except this section and section 5(2), shall apply as if they were British citizens; and in this Act (except as aforesaid) 'British citizen' shall be construed accordingly.

3 General provisions for regulation and control

(1) Except as otherwise provided by or under this Act, where a person is not a British citizen –

(a) he shall not enter the United Kingdom unless given leave to do so in accordance with the provisions of, or made under, this Act;

(b) he may be given leave to enter the United Kingdom (or, when already there, leave to remain in the United Kingdom) either for a limited or for an indefinite period;

(c) if he is given limited leave to enter or remain in the United Kingdom, it may be given subject to all or any of the following conditions, namely –

(i) a condition restricting his employment or occupation in the United Kingdom;

(ii) a condition requiring him to maintain and accommodate himself, and any dependents of his, without recourse to public funds; and

(iii) a condition requiring him to register with the police.

(3) In the case of a limited leave to enter or remain in the United Kingdom –

(a) a person's leave may be varied, whether by restricting, enlarging or removing the limit on its duration, or by adding, varying or revoking conditions, but if the limit on its duration is removed, any conditions attached to the leave shall cease to apply; and

(b) the limitation on and any conditions attached to a person's leave whether imposed originally or on a variation shall, if not superseded, apply also to any subsequent leave he may obtain after an absence from the United Kingdom within the period limited for the duration of earlier leave ...

(5) A person who is not a British citizen shall be liable to deportation from the United Kingdom if –

(a) the Secretary of State deems his deportation to be conducive to the public good; or

(b) another person to whose family he belongs is or has been ordered to be deported.

(6) Without prejudice to the operation of subsection (5) above, a person who is not a British citizen shall also be liable to deportation from the United Kingdom if, after he has attained the age of seventeen, he is convicted of an offence for which he is punishable with imprisonment and on his conviction is recommended for deportation by a court empowered by this Act to do so ...

(8) Where any question arises under this Act whether or not a person is a British citizen, or is entitled to any exemption under this Act, it shall lie on the person asserting it to prove that he is ...

(9) A person seeking to enter the United Kingdom and claiming to have the right of abode there shall prove that he has that right by means of either –

(a) a United Kingdom passport describing him as a British citizen or as a citizen of the United Kingdom and Colonies having the right of abode in the United Kingdom; or

(b) a certificate of entitlement.

3A Further provision as to leave to enter

(1) The Secretary of State may by order make further provision with respect to the giving, refusing or varying of leave to enter the United Kingdom.

(2) An order under subsection (1) may, in particular, provide for –

(a) leave to be given or refused before the person concerned arrives in the United Kingdom;

(b) the form or manner in which leave may be given, refused or varied;

(c) the imposition of conditions;

(d) a person's leave to enter not to lapse on his leaving the common travel area.

(3) The Secretary of State may by order provide that, in such circumstances as may be prescribed –

(a) an entry visa, or

(b) such other form of entry clearance as may be prescribed,

is to have effect as leave to enter the United Kingdom. …

3B Further provision as to leave to remain

(1) The Secretary of State may by order make provision as to further provision with respect to the giving, refusing or varying of leave to remain in the United Kingdom.

(2) An order under subsection (1) may, in particular, provide for –

(a) the form or manner in which leave may be given, refused or varied;

(b) the imposition of conditions;

(c) a person's leave to remain in the United Kingdom not to lapse on his leaving the common travel area.…

3C Continuation of leave pending variation decision

(1) This section applies if –

(a) a person who has a limited leave to enter or remain in the United Kingdom applies to the Secretary of State for variation of the leave,

(b) the application for variation is made before the leave expires, and

(c) the leave expires without the application for variation having been decided.

(2) The leave is extended by virtue of this section during any period when –

(a) the application for variation is neither decided nor withdrawn,

(b) an appeal under section 82(1) of the Nationality, Asylum and Immigration Act 2002 could be brought against the decision on the application for variation (ignoring any possibility of an appeal out of time with permission), or

(c) an appeal under that section against that decision is pending (within the meaning of section 104 of that Act).

(3) Leave extended by virtue of this section shall lapse if the applicant leaves the United Kingdom.

(4) A person may not make an application for variation of his leave to enter or remain in the United Kingdom while that leave is extended by virtue of this section.

(5) But subsection (4) does not prevent the variation of the application mentioned in subsection (1)(a).

(6) In this section a reference to an application being decided is a reference to notice of the decision being given in accordance with regulations under section 105 of that Act (notice of immigration decision).

4 Administration of control

(1) The power under this Act to give or refuse leave to enter the United Kingdom shall be exercised by immigration officers, and the power to give leave to remain in the United Kingdom, or to vary any leave under section 3(3)(a) (whether as regards duration or conditions), shall be exercised by the Secretary of State; and, unless otherwise allowed by or under this Act, those powers shall be exercised by notice in writing given to the person affected ...

5 Procedure for, and further provision as to, deportation

(1) Where a person is under section 3(5) or (6) above liable to deportation, then subject to the following provisions of this Act the Secretary of State may make a deportation order against him, that is to say an order requiring him to leave and prohibiting him from entering the United Kingdom; and a deportation order against a person shall invalidate any leave to enter or remain in the United Kingdom given him before the order is made or while it is in force.

(2) A deportation order against a person may at any time be revoked by a further order of the Secretary of State, and shall cease to have effect if he becomes a British citizen.

(3) A deportation order shall not be made against a person as belonging to a family of another person if more than eight weeks have elapsed since the other person left the United Kingdom after the making of the deportation order against him; and a deportation order made against a person on that ground shall cease to have effect if he ceases to belong to the family of the other person, or if the deportation order made against the other person ceases to have effect.

(4) For purposes of deportation the following shall be those who are regarded as belonging to another person's family –

(a) where that other person is a man, his wife and his or her children under the age of eighteen; and

(b) where that other person is a woman, her husband and her or his children under the age of eighteen;

and for purposes of this subsection an adopted child, whether legally adopted or not, may be treated as the child of the adopter and, if legally adopted, shall be regarded as the child only of the adopter; an illegitimate child (subject to the foregoing rule as to adoptions) shall be regarded as the child of the mother; and 'wife' includes each of two or more wives ...

(6) Where a person is liable to deportation under section 3(5) or (6) above but, without a deportation order being made against him, leaves the United Kingdom to live permanently abroad, the Secretary of State may make payments of such amounts as he may determine to meet the person's expenses in so leaving the United Kingdom, including travelling expenses for members of his family or household.

6 Recommendation by court for deportation

(1) Where under section 3(6) above a person convicted of an offence is liable to deportation on the recommendation of a court, he may be recommended for deportation by any court having power to sentence him for the offence unless the court commits him to be sentenced or further dealt with for that offence by another court ...

(2) A court shall not recommend a person for deportation unless he has been given not less than seven days' notice in writing stating that a person is not liable to deportation if he is a British citizen, describing the persons who are British citizens and stating (so far as material) the effect of section 3(8) above and section 7 below ...

(5) Where a court recommends or purports to recommend a person for deportation, the validity of the recommendation shall not be called in question except on an appeal against the recommendation or against the conviction on which it is made; but the recommendation shall be treated as a sentence for the purpose of any enactment providing an appeal against sentence ...

(6) A deportation order shall not be made on the recommendation of a court so long as an appeal or further appeal is pending against the recommendation or against the conviction on which it was made; and for this purpose an appeal or further appeal shall be treated as pending (where one is competent but has not been brought) until the expiration of the time for bringing that appeal ...

7 Exemption from deportation for certain existing residents

(1) Notwithstanding anything in section 3(5) or (6) above but subject to the provisions of this section, a Commonwealth citizen or citizen of the Republic of Ireland who was such a citizen at the coming into force of this Act and was then ordinarily resident in the United Kingdom –

(b) shall not be liable to deportation under section 3(5) if at the time of the Secretary of State's decision he had for the last five years been ordinarily resident in the United Kingdom and Islands; and

(c) shall not on conviction of an offence be recommended for deportation under section 3(6) if at the time of the conviction he had for the last five years been ordinarily resident in the United Kingdom and Islands.

(2) A person who has at any time become ordinarily resident in the United Kingdom or in any of the Islands shall not be treated for the purposes of this section as having ceased to be so by reason only of his having remained there in breach of the immigration laws.

(3) The 'last five years' before the material time under subsection (1)(b) or (c) above is to be taken as a period amounting in total to five years exclusive of any time during which the person claiming exemption under this section was undergoing imprisonment or detention by virtue of a sentence passed for an offence on a conviction in the United Kingdom and Islands, and the period for which he was imprisoned or detained by virtue of the sentence amounted to six months or more ...

As amended by the Criminal Justice (Scotland) Act 1980, s83(3), Schedule 8; British Nationality Act 1981, s39(2), (3), (6), Schedule 4, paras 2, 3(1), 4; Criminal Justice Act 1982, ss77, 78, Schedule 15, para 16, Schedule 16; Immigration Act 1988, ss3(1), (2), (3), 10, Schedule, paras 1, 2, 3; Asylum and Immigration Appeals Act 1993, ss10, 11(1); Asylum and Immigration Act 1996, s12(1), Schedule 2, paras 1(1), (2), 2; Immigration and Asylum Act 1999, ss1, 2, 169(1), Schedule 14, paras 43, 44(1), (2), 45, 46; Nationality, Immigration and Asylum Act 2002, ss10(5)(a), 75, 118, 161, Schedule 9.

EUROPEAN COMMUNITIES ACT 1972

(1972 c 68)

1 Short title and interpretation

(1) This Act may be cited as the European Communities Act 1972.

(2) In this Act –

'the Communities' means the European Economic Community, the European Coal and Steel Community and the European Atomic Energy Community;

'the Treaties' or 'the Community Treaties' means, subject to subsection (3) below, the pre-accession treaties, that is to say, those described in Part I of Schedule 1 to this Act, taken with –

(a) the treaty relating to the accession of the United Kingdom to the European Economic Community and to the European Atomic Energy Community, signed at Brussels on the 22nd January 1972; and

(b) the decision, of the same date, of the Council of the European Communities relating to the accession of the United Kingdom to the European Coal and Steel Community; and

(c) the treaty relating to the accession of the Hellenic Republic to the European Economic Community and to the European Atomic Energy Community, signed at Athens on 28th May 1979; and

(d) the decision, of 24th May 1979, of the Council relating to the accession of the Hellenic Republic to the European Coal and Steel Community; and

(e) the decisions of the Council of 7th May 1985, 24th June 1988, and 31st October 1994 and 29th September 2000, on the Communities' system of own resources; and

(g) the treaty relating to the accession of the Kingdom of Spain and the Portuguese Republic to the European Economic Community and to the European Atomic Energy Community, signed at Lisbon and Madrid on 12th June 1985; and

(h) the decision, of 11th June 1985, of the Council relating to the accession of the Kingdom of Spain and the Portuguese Republic to the European Coal and Steel Community; and

(j) the following provisions of the Single European Act signed at Luxembourg and The Hague on 17th and 28th February 1986, namely Title II (amendment of the treaties establishing the Communities) and, so far as they relate to any of the Communities or any Community institution, the preamble and Titles I (common provisions) and IV (general and final provisions); and

(k) Titles II, III and IV of the Treaty on European Union signed at Maastricht on 7th February 1992, together with the other provisions of the Treaty so far as they relate to those Titles, and the Protocols adopted at Maastricht on that date and annexed to the Treaty establishing the European Community with the exception of the Protocol on Social Policy on page 117 of Cm 1934; and

(l) the decision, of 1st February 1993, of the Council amending the Act concerning the election of the representatives of the European Parliament by direct universal suffrage annexed to Council Decision 76/787/ECSC, EEC, Euratom of 20th September 1976; and

(m) the Agreement on the European Economic Area signed at Oporto on 2nd May 1992 together with the Protocol adjusting that Agreement signed at Brussels on 17th March 1993; and

(n) the treaty concerning the accession of the Kingdom of Norway, the Republic of Austria, the Republic of Finland and the Kingdom of Sweden to the European Union, signed at Corfu on 24th June 1994; and

(o) the following provisions of the Treaty signed at Amsterdam on 2nd October 1997 amending the Treaty on European Union, the Treaties establishing the European Communities and certain related Acts –

(i) Articles 2 and 9,

(ii) Article 12, and

(iii) the other provisions of the Treaty so far as they relate to those Articles,

and the Protocols adopted on that occasion other than the Protocol on Article J.7 of the Treaty on European Union; and

(p) the following provisions of the Treaty signed at Nice on 26th February 2001 amending the Treaty on European Union, the Treaties establishing the European Communities and certain related Acts –

(i) Articles 2 to 10, and

(ii) the other provisions of the Treaty so far as they relate to those Articles,

and the Protocols adopted on that occasion; and

(q) the treaty concerning the accession of the Czech Republic, the Republic of Estonia, the Republic of Cyprus, the Republic of Latvia, the Republic of Lithuania, the Republic of Hungary, the Republic of Malta, the Republic of Poland, the Republic of Slovenia and the Slovak Republic to the European Union, signed at Athens on 16th April 2003;

and any other treaty entered into by any of the Communities, with or without any of the Member States, or entered into, as a treaty ancillary to any of the Treaties, by the United Kingdom;

and any expression defined in Schedule 1 to this Act has the meaning there given to it.

(3) If Her Majesty by Order in Council declares that a treaty specified in the Order

is to be regarded as one of the Community Treaties as herein defined, the Order shall be conclusive that it is to be so regarded; but a treaty entered into by the United Kingdom after the 22nd January 1972, other than a pre-accession treaty to which the United Kingdom accedes on terms settled on or before that date, shall not be so regarded unless it is so specified, nor be so specified unless a draft of the Order in Council has been approved by resolution of each House of Parliament.

(4) For purposes of subsection (2) and (3) above, 'treaty' includes any international agreement, and any protocol or annex to a treaty or international agreement.

2 General implementation of treaties

(1) All such rights, powers, liabilities, obligations and restrictions from time to time created or arising by or under the Treaties, and all such remedies and procedures from time to time provided for by or under the Treaties, as in accordance with the Treaties are without further enactment to be given legal effect or used in the United Kingdom, shall be recognised and available in law, and be enforced, allowed or followed accordingly; and the expression 'enforceable Community right' and similar expressions shall be read as referring to one to which this subsection applies.

(2) Subject to Schedule 2 to this Act, at any time after its passing Her Majesty may by Order in Council, and any designated Minister or department may by regulations, make provision –

(a) for the purpose of implementing any Community obligation of the United Kingdom, or enabling any rights enjoyed or to be enjoyed by the United Kingdom under or by virtue of the Treaties to be exercised; or

(b) for the purpose of dealing with matters arising out of or related to any such obligation or rights or the coming into force, or the operation from time to time, of subsection (1) above; and in the exercise of any statutory power or duty, including any power to give directions or to legislate by means of orders, rules, regulations or other subordinate instrument, the person entrusted with the power or duty may have regard to the objects of the Communities and to any such obligations or rights as aforesaid ...

(4) The provision that may be made under subsection (2) above includes, subject to Schedule 2 to this Act, any such provision (of any such extent) as might be made by Act of Parliament, and any enactment passed or to be passed, other than one contained in this part of this Act, shall be construed and have effect subject to the foregoing provisions of this section; but, except as may be provided by any Act passed after this Act, Schedule 2 shall have effect in connection with the powers conferred by this and the following sections of this Act to make Orders in Council and regulations ...

3 Decisions on and proof of treaties and Community instruments

(1) For the purpose of all legal proceedings any question as to the meaning or effect of any of the Treaties, or as to the validity, meaning or effect of any Community

instrument, shall be treated as a question of law (and, if not referred to the European Court, be for determination as such in accordance with the principles laid down by and any relevant decision of the European Court or any court attached thereto).

(2) Judicial notice shall be taken of the Treaties, of the Official Journal of the Communities and of any decision of, or expression of opinion by, the European Court or any court attached thereto on any such question as aforesaid; and the Official Journal shall be admissible as evidence of any instrument or other act thereby communicated of any of the Communities or of any Community institution.

(3) Evidence of any instrument issued by a Community institution, including any judgment or order of the European Court or any court attached thereto, or of any document in the custody of a Community institution, or any entry in or extract from such a document, may be given by an official of that institution; and any document purporting to be such a copy shall be received in evidence without proof of the official position or handwriting of the person signing the certificate.

(4) Evidence of any Community instrument may also be given in any legal proceedings –

(a) by production of a copy purporting to be printed by the Queen's Printer;

(b) where the instrument is in the custody of a government department ... by production of a copy certified on behalf of the department to be a true copy by an officer of the department generally or specially authorised so to do;

and any document purporting to be such a copy as is mentioned in paragraph (b) above of an instrument in the custody of a department shall be received in evidence without proof of the official position or handwriting of the person signing the certificate, or of his authority to do so, or of the document being in the custody of the department ...

As amended by the Interpretation Act 1978, s25(1), Schedule 3; European Communities (Greek Accession) Act 1979, s1; European Communities (Spanish and Portuguese) Accession Act 1985, s1; European Communities (Amendment) Act 1986, ss1, 2; European Communities (Amendment) Act 1993, s1(1); European Parliamentary Elections Act 1993, s3(2); European Economic Area Act 1993, s1; European Union (Accession) Act 1994, s1; European Communities (Amendment) Act 1998, s1; European Communities (Finance) Act 2001, s1; European Communities (Amendment) Act 2002, s1(1); European Union (Accessions) Act 2003, s1(1).

HOUSE OF COMMONS DISQUALIFICATION ACT 1975

(1975 c 24)

1 Disqualification of holders of certain offices and places

(1) Subject to the provisions of this Act, a person is disqualified for membership of the House of Commons who for the time being –

(za) is a Lord Spiritual;

(a) holds any of the judicial offices specified in Part I of Schedule 1 to this Act;

(b) is employed in the civil service of the Crown, whether in an established capacity or not, and whether for the whole or part of his time;

(c) is a member of any of the regular armed forces of the Crown or the Ulster Defence Regiment.

(d) is a member of any police force maintained by a police authority;

(da) is a member of the National Criminal Intelligence Service or the National Crime Squad;

(e) is a member of the legislature of any country or territory outside the Commonwealth (other than Ireland); or

(f) holds any office described in Part II or Part III of Schedule 1.

(2) A person who for the time being holds any office described in Part IV of Schedule 1 is disqualified for membership of the House of Commons for any constituency specified in relation to that office in the second column of Part IV ...

(4) Except as provided by this Act, a person shall not be disqualified for membership of the House of Commons by reason of his holding an office or place of profit under the Crown or any other office or place; and a person shall not be disqualified for appointment to or for holding any office or place by reason of his being a member of that House.

2 Ministerial offices

(1) No more than ninety-five persons being the holders of office specified in Schedule 2 to this Act (in this section referred to as Ministerial offices) shall be entitled to sit and vote in the House of Commons at any one time.

(2) If at any time the number of members of the House of Commons who are holders of Ministerial offices exceeds the number entitled to sit and vote in that House

under subsection (1) above, none except any who were both members of that House and holders of Ministerial offices before the excess occurred shall sit or vote therein until the number has been reduced, by death, resignation or otherwise, to the number entitled to sit and vote as aforesaid.

(3) A person holding a Ministerial office is not disqualified by this Act by reason of any office held by him ex officio as the holder of that Ministerial office.

4 Stewardship of the Chiltern Hundreds, etc

For the purposes of the provisions of this Act relating to the vacation of the seat of a member of the House of Commons who becomes disqualified by this Act for membership of that House, the office of steward or bailiff of Her Majesty's three Chiltern Hundreds of Stoke, Desborough and Burnham, or of the Manor of Northstead, shall be treated as included among the office described in Part III of Schedule 1 to this Act.

6 Effect of disqualification and provisions for relief

(1) Subject to any order made by the House of Commons under this section –

(a) if any person disqualified by this Act for membership of that House, or for membership for a particular constituency, is elected as a member or that House, or as a member for that constituency, as the case may be, his election shall be void; and

(b) if any person being a member of that House becomes disqualified by this Act for membership, or for membership for the constituency for which he is sitting, his seat shall be vacated.

(2) If, in a case falling or alleged to fall within subsection (1) above, it appears to the House of Commons that the grounds of disqualification or alleged disqualification under this Act which subsisted or arose at the material time have been removed, and that it is otherwise proper so to do, that House may by order direct that any such disqualification incurred on those grounds at that time shall be disregarded for the purposes of this section ...

7 Jurisdiction of Privy Council as to disqualification

(1) Any person who claims that a person purporting to be a member of the House of Commons is disqualified by this Act, or has been so disqualified at any time since his election, may apply to Her Majesty in Council, in accordance with such rules as Her Majesty in Council may prescribe, for a declaration to that effect. ...

(4) For the purpose of determining any issue of fact arising on an application under this section the Judicial Committee may direct the issue to be tried –

(a) if the constituency for which the respondent purports to be a member is in England or Wales, in the High Court; ...

and the decision of that Court shall be final. ...

8 Relaxation of obligation to accept office

(1) No person being a member of the House of Commons, or for the time being nominated as a candidate for election to that House, shall be required to accept any office or place by virtue of which he would be disqualified by this Act for membership of that House, or for membership of that House for the constituency for which he is sitting or is a candidate.

(2) This section does not affect any obligation to serve in the armed forces of the Crown, whether imposed by an enactment or otherwise.

SCHEDULE 1

OFFICES DISQUALIFYING FOR MEMBERSHIP

PART I

JUDICIAL OFFICES

Judge of the High Court of Justice or Court of Appeal

Judge of the Court of Session, or Temporary Judge appointed under the Law Reform (Miscellaneous Provisions) (Scotland) Act 1990

Judge of the High Court of Justice or Court of Appeal in Northern Ireland

Judge of the Courts-Martial Appeal Court

Chairman of the Scottish Land Court

Circuit Judge

Sheriff Principal or Sheriff (other than Honorary Sheriff) appointed under the Sheriff Courts (Scotland) Act 1907, or Temporary Sheriff Principal or Temporary Sheriff appointed under the Sheriff Courts (Scotland) Act 1971

County Court Judge or deputy County Court Judge in Northern Ireland

District Judge (Magistrates' Courts) (but not Deputy District Judge (Magistrates' Courts))

Stipendiary Magistrate in Scotland

Resident Magistrate or Deputy Resident Magistrate appointed under the Magistrates' Courts Act (Northern Ireland) 1964

Chief of other Child Support Commissioner (excluding a person appointed under paragraph 4 of Schedule 4 to the Child Support Act 1991) ...

Chief or other Social Security Commissioner (not including a deputy Commissioner) ...

Commissioner for the special purposes of the Income Tax Acts appointed under section 4 of the Taxes Management Act 1970

Member of the Immigration Services Tribunal

Adjudicator to Her Majesty's Land Registry

PART II

[Lists bodies of which all members are disqualified, eg the Authorised Conveyancing Practitioners Board, Council for the Regulation of Health Care Professionals, Gaming Board for Great Britain, Gangmasters Licensing Authority and the Youth Justice Board for England and Wales.]

PART III

[Lists other disqualifying offices, eg Appeal Officer for Community Interest Companies, Chairman of the Board of Governors of the Commonwealth Institute, District Judge appointed under section 6 of the County Courts Act 1984, Pensions Ombudsman and Welsh Administration Ombudsman.]

PART IV

[Lists offices disqualifying for particular constituencies, eg Governor of the Isle of Wight (Isle of Wight) and the High Sheriff of a county in England and Wales (any constituency comprising the whole or part of the area for which he is appointed).]

SCHEDULE 2

MINISTERIAL OFFICES

Prime Minister and First Lord of the Treasury

Lord President of the Council

Lord Privy Seal

Chancellor of the Duchy of Lancaster

Paymaster General

President of the Board of Trade

Secretary of State

Chancellor of the Exchequer

Minister of State

Chief Secretary to the Treasury

Minister in charge of a public department of Her Majesty's Government in the United Kingdom (if not within the other provisions of this Schedule)

Attorney General

Advocate General for Scotland

Solicitor General

Parliamentary Secretary to the Treasury

Financial Secretary to the Treasury

Parliamentary Secretary in a Government department other than the Treasury, or not in a department

Junior Lord of the Treasury

Treasurer of Her Majesty's Household

Comptroller of Her Majesty's Household

Vice-Chamberlain of Her Majesty's Household

Assistant Government Whip

As amended by the Child Support Act 1991, s58(13), Schedule 5, para 3(1), (2); Social Security (Consequential Provisions) Act 1992, s4, Schedule 2, para 16; Police Act 1997, s134(1), Schedule 9, para 29(2); House of Commons Disqualification Order 1997, art 2, Schedule, para 1; Justices of the Peace Act 1997, s73(2), Schedule 5, para 17; Scotland Act 1998, ss48(6), 87(1), 125(2), Schedule 9; Access to Justice Act 1999, s78(2), Schedule 11, para 24; Immigration and Asylum Act 1999, s87(5), Schedule 7, para 12; Disqualifications Act 2000, s1; House of Commons (Removal of Clergy Disqualification) Act 2001, s1, Schedule 1, para 1; Land Registration Act 2002, s107(3), Schedule 9, para 9. Detailed amendments were made to Schedule 1, Parts II, III and IV, above, by relevant Acts and orders.

MINISTERS OF THE CROWN ACT 1975
(1975 c 26)

1 Power by Order in Council to transfer functions of Ministers

(1) Her Majesty may by Order in Council –

(a) provide for the transfer to any Minister of the Crown of any functions previously exercisable by another Minister of the Crown;

(b) provide for the dissolution of the government department in the charge of any Minister of the Crown and the transfer to or distribution among such other Minister or Ministers of the Crown as may be specified in the Order of any functions previously exercisable by the Minister in charge of that department;

(c) direct that functions of any Minister of the Crown shall be exercisable concurrently with another Minister of the Crown, or shall cease to be so exercisable.

(2) An Order in Council under this section may contain such incidental, consequential and supplemental provisions as may be necessary or expedient for the purpose of giving full effect to the Order, including provisions –

(a) for the transfer of any property, rights and liabilities held, enjoyed or incurred by any Minister of the Crown in connection with any functions transferred or distributed;

(b) for the carrying on and completion by or under the authority of the Minister to whom any functions are transferred of anything commenced by or under the authority of a minister of the Crown before the date when the Order takes effect;

(c) for such adaptations of the enactments relating to any functions transferred as may be necessary to enable them to be exercised by the Minister to whom they are transferred and his officers;

(d) for making in the enactments regulating the number of offices in respect of which salaries may be paid or in section 2 of, and Schedule 2 to, the House of Commons Disqualification Act 1975 (which regulate the number of office holders who may be elected, and sit and vote, as members of the House of Commons), such modifications as may be expedient by reason of any transfer of functions or dissolutions of a Department effected by the Order;

(e) for the substitution of the Minister to whom functions are transferred for any other Minister of the Crown in any instrument, contract, or legal proceedings made or commenced before the date when the Order takes effect.

(3) No modifications shall be made by virtue of paragraph (d) of subsection (2) above, in any of the enactments mentioned in that paragraph, so as to increase the amount of any salary which may be paid, or the aggregate number of persons to whom salaries may be paid, under those enactments or the aggregate number of persons capable thereunder of sitting and voting as Members of the House of Commons.

(4) Where by any Order made under this section provision is made for the transfer of functions in respect of which any Minister may sue or be sued by virtue of any enactment, the Order shall make any provisions which may be required for enabling the Minister to whom those functions are transferred to sue or be sued in like manner.

(5) A certificate issued by a Minister of the Crown that any property vested in any other Minister immediately before an Order under this section takes effect has been transferred by virtue of the Order to the Minister issuing the certificate shall be conclusive evidence of the transfer.

2 Changes in departments of office of Secretary of State, or in their functions

(1) Her Majesty may in connection with any change in the departments of the office of Secretary of State, or any change in the functions of a Secretary of State, by Order in Council make such incidental, consequential and supplemental provisions as may be necessary or expedient in connection with the change, including provisions –

(a) for making a Secretary of State a corporation sole,

(b) for the transfer of any property, rights or liabilities to or from a Secretary of State,

(c) for any adaptations of enactments relating to a Secretary of State, or to the department of a Secretary of State,

(d) for the substitution of one Secretary of State, or department of a Secretary of State, for another in any instrument, contract or legal proceedings made or commenced before the date when the Order takes effect.

(2) A certificate issued by a Minister of the Crown that any property vested in any other Minister immediately before an Order under this section takes effect has been transferred by virtue of the Order to the Minister issuing the certificate shall be conclusive evidence of the transfer.

(3) This section applies only to changes after 27th June 1974, and to the creation (in that year) of the Departments of Energy, Industry, Trade, and Prices and Consumer Protection.

3 Transfer of property etc by or to Secretary of State

(1) This section applies where any enactment (including an order under this Act) provides that a named Secretary of State and his successors shall be a corporation

sole, and applies whether or not the office of corporation sole is for the time being vacant.

(2) Anything done by or in relation to any other Secretary of State for the named Secretary of State as a corporation sole shall have effect as if done by or in relation to the named Secretary of State.

(3) Without prejudice to the preceding provisions of this section, any deed, contract or other instrument to be executed by or on behalf of the named Secretary of State as a corporation sole shall be valid if under the corporate seal of that Secretary of State authenticated by the signature of any other Secretary of State, or of a Secretary to any department of a Secretary of State, or of a person authorised by any Secretary of State to act in that behalf.

4 Change of title of Ministers

If Her Majesty is pleased by Order in Council to direct that any change shall be made in the style and title of a Minister of the Crown, the Order may contain provisions substituting the new style and title –

(a) in the enactments (including those mentioned in section 1(2)(d) above) relating to the Minister;

(b) in any instrument, contract, or legal proceedings made or commenced before the date when the Order takes effect.

REPRESENTATION OF THE PEOPLE ACT 1981

(1981 c 34)

1 Disqualification of certain offenders for membership of the House of Commons

A person found guilty of one or more offences (whether before or after the passing of this Act and whether in the United Kingdom or elsewhere), and sentenced or ordered to be imprisoned or detained indefinitely or for more than one year, shall be disqualified for membership of the House of Commons while detained anywhere in the British Islands or the Republic of Ireland in pursuance of the sentence or order or while unlawfully at large at a time when he would otherwise be so detained.

2 Effects of disqualification

(1) If a person disqualified by this Act for membership of the House of Commons is elected to that House his election shall be void; and if such a person is nominated for election as a member of that House his nomination shall be void.

(2) If a member of the House of Commons becomes disqualified by this Act for membership of that House his seat shall be vacated.

CONTEMPT OF COURT ACT 1981

(1981 c 49)

1 The strict liability rule

In this Act 'the strict liability rule' means the rule of law whereby conduct may be treated as a contempt of court as tending to interfere with the course of justice in particular legal proceedings regardless of intent to do so.

2 Limitation of scope of strict liability

(1) The strict liability rule applies only in relation to publications, and for this purpose 'publication' includes any speech, writing, programme included in a service or other communication in whatever form, which is addressed to the public at large or any section of the public.

(2) The strict liability rule applies only to a publication which creates a substantial risk that the course of justice in the proceedings in question will be seriously impeded or prejudiced.

(3) The strict liability rule applies to a publication only if the proceedings in question are active within the meaning of this section at the time of the publication.

(4) Schedule 1 applies for determining the times at which proceedings are to be treated as active within the meaning of this section.

(5) In this section 'programme service' has the same meaning as in the Broadcasting Act 1990.

3 Defence of innocent publication or distribution

(1) A person is not guilty of contempt of court under the strict liability rule as the publisher of any matter to which that rule applies if at the time of publication (having taken all reasonable care) he does not know and has no reason to suspect that relevant proceedings are active.

(2) A person is not guilty of contempt of court under the strict liability rule as the distributor of a publication containing any such matter if at the time of distribution (having taken all reasonable care) he does not know that it contains such matter and has no reason to suspect that it is likely to do so.

(3) The burden of proof of any fact tending to establish a defence afforded by this section to any person lies upon that person.

4 Contemporary reports of proceedings

(1) Subject to this section a person is not guilty of contempt of court under the strict liability rule in respect of a fair and accurate report of legal proceedings held in public, published contemporaneously and in good faith.

(2) In any such proceedings the court may, where it appears to be necessary for avoiding a substantial risk of prejudice to the administration of justice in those proceedings, or in any other proceedings pending or imminent, order that the publication of any report of the proceedings, or any part of the proceedings, be postponed for such period as the court thinks necessary for that purpose.

(2A) Where in proceedings for any offence whihc is an administration of justice offence for the purposes of section 54 of the Criminal Procedure and Investigations Act 1996 (acquittal tainted by an administration of justice offence) it appears to the court that there is a possibility that (by virtue of that section) proceedings may be taken against a person for an offence of which he has been acquitted, subsection (2) of this section shall apply as if those proceedings were pending or imminent.

(3) For the purposes of subsection (1) of this section a report of proceedings shall be treated as published contemporaneously –

(a) in the case of a report of which publication is postponed pursuant to an order under subsection (2) of this section, if published as soon as practicable after that order expires;

(b) in the case of a report of an application for dismissal under section 6 of the Magistrates' Courts Act 1980 of which publication is permitted by virtue only of subsection (5) or (7) of section 8A of that Act, if published as soon as practicable after publication is so permitted.

5 Discussion of public affairs

A publication made as or as part of a discussion in good faith of public affairs or other matters of general public interest is not to be treated as a contempt of court under the strict liability rule if the risk of impediment or prejudice to particular legal proceedings is merely incidental to the discussion.

6 Savings

Nothing in the foregoing provisions of this Act –

(a) prejudices any defence available at common law to a charge of contempt of court under the strict liability rule;

(b) implies that any publication is punishable as contempt of court under that rule which would not be so punishable apart from those provisions;

(c) restricts liability for contempt of court in respect of conduct intended to impede or prejudice the administration of justice.

7 Consent required for institution of proceedings

Proceedings for a contempt of court under the strict liability rule (other than Scottish proceedings) shall not be instituted except by or with the consent of the Attorney-General or on the motion of a court having jurisdiction to deal with it.

8 Confidentiality of jury's deliberations

(1) Subject to subsection (2) below, it is a contempt of court to obtain, disclose or solicit any particulars of statements made, opinions expressed, arguments advanced or votes cast by members of a jury in the course of their deliberations in any legal proceedings.

(2) This section does not apply to any disclosure of any particulars –

(a) in the proceedings in question for the purpose of enabling the jury to arrive at their verdict, or in connection with the delivery of that verdict, or

(b) in evidence in any subsequent proceedings for an offence alleged to have been committed in relation to the jury in the first mentioned proceedings,

or to the publication of any particulars so disclosed.

(3) Proceedings for a contempt of court under this section (other than Scottish proceedings) shall not be instituted except by or with the consent of the Attorney-General or on the motion of a court having jurisdiction to deal with it.

10 Sources of information

No court may require a person to disclose, nor is any person guilty of contempt of court for refusing to disclose, the source of information contained in a publication for which he is responsible, unless it be established to the satisfaction of the court that disclosure is necessary in the interests of justice or national security or for the prevention of disorder or crime.

11 Publication of matters exempted from disclosure in court

In any case where a court (having power to do so) allows a name or other matter to be withheld from the public in proceedings before the court, the court may give such directions prohibiting the publication of that name or matter in connection with the proceedings as appear to the court to be necessary for the purpose for which it was so withheld.

19 Interpretation

In this Act –

'court' includes any tribunal or body exercising the judicial power of the State, and 'legal proceedings' shall be construed accordingly ...

SCHEDULE 1

TIMES WHEN PROCEEDINGS ARE ACTIVE FOR PURPOSES OF SECTION 2

Preliminary

1. In this Schedule 'criminal proceedings' means proceedings against a person in respect of an offence, not being appellate proceedings or proceedings commenced by motion for committal or attachment in England and Wales or Northern Ireland; and 'appellate proceedings' means proceedings on appeal from or for the review of the decision of a court in any proceedings.

2. Criminal, appellate and other proceedings are active within the meaning of section 2 at the times respectively prescribed by the following paragraphs of this Schedule; and in relation to proceedings in which more than one of the steps described in any of those paragraphs is taken, the reference in that paragraph is a reference to the first of those steps.

Criminal proceedings

3. Subject to the following provisions of this Schedule, criminal proceedings are active from the relevant initial step specified in paragraph 4 or 4A until concluded as described in paragraph 5.

4. The initial steps of criminal proceedings are:

(a) arrest without warrant;

(b) the issue, or in Scotland the grant, of a warrant for arrest;

(c) the issue of a summons to appear, or in Scotland the grant of a warrant to cite;

(d) the service of an indictment or other document specifying the charge;

(e) except in Scotland, oral charge.

4A. Where as a result of an order under section 54 of the Criminal Procedure and Investigations Act 1996 (acquittal tainted by an administration of justice offence) proceedings are brought against a person for an offence of which he has previously been acquitted, the initial step of proceedings is a certification under subsection (2) of that section; and paragraph 4 has effect subject to this.

5. Criminal proceedings are concluded –

(a) by acquittal or, as the case may be, by sentence;

(b) by any other verdict, finding, order or decision which puts an end to the proceedings;

(c) by discontinuance or by operation of law.

6. The reference in paragraph 5(a) to sentence includes any order or decision consequent on conviction or finding of guilt which disposes of the case, either

absolutely or subject to future events, and a deferment of sentence under section 1 of the Powers of Criminal Courts (Sentencing) Act 2000, section 219 or 432 of the Criminal Procedure (Scotland) Act 1975 or Article 14 of the Treatment of Offenders (Northern Ireland) Order 1976.

7. Proceedings are discontinued within the meaning of paragraph 5(c) –

(a) in England and Wales or Northern Ireland, if the charge or summons is withdrawn or a nolle prosequi entered;

(aa) in England and Wales, if they are discontinued by virtue of section 23 of the Prosecution of Offences Act 1985 ...

(c) in the case of proceedings in England and Wales or Northern Ireland commenced by arrest without warrant, if the person arrested is released, otherwise than on bail, without having been charged.

8. Criminal proceedings before a court-martial or standing civilian court are not concluded until the completion of any review of finding or sentence.

9. Criminal proceedings in England and Wales or Northern Ireland cease to be active if an order is made for the charge to lie on the file, but become active again if leave is later given for the proceedings to continue.

9A. Where proceedings in England and Wales have been discontinued by virtue of section 23 of the Prosecution of Offences Act 1985, but notice is given by the accused under subsection (7) of that section to the effect that he wants the proceedings to continue, they become active again with the giving of that notice.

10. Without prejudice to paragraph 5(b) above, criminal proceedings against a person cease to be active –

(a) if the accused is found to be under a disability such as to render him unfit to be tried or unfit to plead ...; or

(b) if a hospital order is made in his case ...

but become active again if they are later resumed.

11. Criminal proceedings against a person which become active on the issue or the grant of a warrant for his arrest cease to be active at the end of the period of twelve months beginning with the date of the warrant unless he has been arrested within that period, but become active again if he is subsequently arrested.

Other proceedings at first instance

12. Proceedings other than criminal proceedings and appellate proceedings are active from the time when arrangements for the hearing are made or, if no such arrangements are previously made, from the time the hearing begins, until the proceedings are disposed of or discontinued or withdrawn; and for the purposes of this paragraph any motion or application made in or for the purposes of any proceedings, and any pre-trial review in the county curt, is to be treated as a distinct proceeding.

13. In England and Wales or Northern Ireland arrangements for the hearing of proceedings to which paragraph 12 applies are made within the meaning of that paragraph –

(a) in the case of proceedings in the High Court for which provision is made by rules of court for setting down for trial, when the case is set down;

(b) in the case of any proceedings, when a date for the trial or hearing is fixed ...

Appellate proceedings

15. Appellate proceedings are active from the time when they are commenced –

(a) by application for leave to appeal or apply for review, or by notice of such an application;

(b) by notice of appeal or of application for review;

(c) by other originating process,

until disposed of or abandoned, discontinued or withdrawn.

16. Where, in appellate proceedings relating to criminal proceedings, the court –

(a) remits the case to the court below; or

(b) orders a new trial or a venire de novo ...

any further or new proceedings which result shall be treated as active from the conclusion of the appellate proceedings.

As amended by the Prosecution of Offences Act 1985, s31(5), Schedule 1, Part I, paras 4, 5; Broadcasting Act 1990, s203(1), Schedule 20, para 31(1); Criminal Justice and Public Order Act 1994, Schedule 4, para 50; Criminal Procedure and Investigations Act 1996, s57(2)–(4); Defamation Act 1996, s16, Schedule 2; Powers of Criminal Courts (Sentencing) Act 2000, s165(1), Schedule 9, para 86; Statute Law (Repeals) Act 2004, s1(1), Schedule 1, Pt 1, Group 4.

SUPREME COURT ACT 1981

(1981 c 54)

30 Injunctions to restrain persons from acting in offices in which they are not entitled to act

(1) Where a person not entitled to do so acts in an office to which this section applies, the High Court may –

(a) grant an injunction restraining him from so acting; and
(b) if the case so requires, declare the office to be vacant.

(2) This section applies to any substantive office of a public nature and permanent character which is held under the Crown or which has been created by any statutory provision or royal charter.

31 Application for judicial review

(1) An application to the High Court for one or more of the following forms of relief, namely –

(a) a mandatory, prohibiting or quashing order;
(b) a declaration or injunction under subsection (2); or
(c) an injunction under section 30 restraining a person not entitled to do so from acting in an office to which that section applies,

shall be made in accordance with rules of court by a procedure to be known as an application for judicial review.

(2) A declaration may be made or an injunction granted under this subsection in any case where an application for judicial review, seeking that relief, has been made and the High Court considers that, having regard to –

(a) the nature of the matters in respect of which relief may be granted by mandatory, prohibiting or quashing orders;
(b) the nature of the persons and bodies against whom relief may be granted by such orders; and
(c) all the circumstances of the case,

it would be just and convenient for the declaration to be made or the injunction to be granted, as the case may be.

(3) No application for judicial review shall be made unless the leave of the High

Court has been obtained in accordance with rules of court; and the court shall not grant leave to make such an application unless it considers that the applicant has a sufficient interest in the matter to which the application relates.

(4) On an application for judicial review the High Court may award to the applicant damages, rstitution or the recovery of a sum due if –

(a) the application includes a claim for such an award arising from any matter to which the application relates; and

(b) the court is satisfied that such an award would have been made if the claim had been made in an action begun by the applicant at the time of making the application.

(5) If, on an application for judicial review seeking a quashing order, the High Court quashes the decision to which the application relates, the High Court may remit the matter to the court, tribunal or authority concerned, with a direction to reconsider it and reach a decision in accordance with the findings of the High Court.

(6) Where the High Court considers that there has been undue delay in making an application for judicial review, the court may refuse to grant –

(a) leave for the making of the application; or

(b) any relief sought on the application,

if it considers that the granting of the relief sought would be likely to cause substantial hardship to, or substantially prejudice the rights of, any person or would be detrimental to good administration.

(7) Subsection (6) is without prejudice to any enactment or rule of court which has the effect of limiting the time within which an application for judicial review may be made.

As amended by the Civil Procedure (Modification of Supreme Court Act 1981) Order 2004, arts 2, 4.

REPRESENTATION OF THE PEOPLE ACT 1983

(1983 c 2)

1 Parliamentary electors

(1) A person is entitled to vote as an elector at a parliamentary election in any constituency if on the date of the poll he –

(a) is registered in the register of parliamentary electors for that constituency;

(b) is not subject to any legal incapacity to vote (age apart);

(c) is either a Commonwealth citizen or a citizen of the Republic of Ireland; and

(d) is of voting age (that is, 18 years or over).

(2) A person is not entitled to vote as an elector –

(a) more than once in the same constituency at any parliamentary election; or

(b) in more than one constituency at a general election.

2 Local government electors

(1) A person is entitled to vote as an elector at a local government election in any electoral area if on the date of the poll he –

(a) is registered in the register of local government electors for that area;

(b) is not subject to any legal incapacity to vote (age apart);

(c) is a Commonwealth citizen, a citizen of the Republic of Ireland or a relevant citizen of the Union; and

(d) is of voting age (that is, 18 years or over).

(2) A person is not entitled to vote as an elector –

(a) more than once in the same electoral area at any local government election; or

(b) in more than one electoral area at an ordinary election for a local government area which is not a single electoral area.

3 Disfranchisement of offenders in prison, etc

(1) A convicted person during the time that he is detained in a penal institution in

pursuance of his sentence or unlawfully at large when he would otherwise be so detained is legally incapable of voting at any parliamentary or local government election. ...

3A Disfranchisement of offenders detained in mental hospitals

(1) A person to whom this section applies is, durng the time that he is –

(a) detained at any place in pursuance of the order or direction by virtue of which this section applies to him, or

(b) unlawfully at large when he would otherwise be so detained,

legally capable of voting at any parliamentary or local government election. ...

4 Entitlement to be registered as parliamentary or local government elector

(1) A person is entitled to be registered in the register of parliamentary electors for any constituency or part of a constituency if on the relevant date he –

(a) is resident in the constituency or that part of it;

(b) is not subject to any legal incapacity to vote (age apart);

(c) is either a qualifying Commonwealth citizen or a citizen of the Republic of Ireland; and

(d) is of voting age. ...

(3) A person is entitled to be registered in the register of local government electors for any electoral area if on the relevant date he –

(a) is resident in that area;

(b) is not subject to any legal incapacity to vote (age apart);

(c) is a qualifying Commonwealth citizen, a citizen of the Republic of Ireland or a relevant citizen of the Union; and

(d) is of voting age.

(4) The preceding provisions have effect –

(a) subject to –

(i) any enactment imposing a disqualification for registration as a parliamentary, or (as the case may be) local government, elector; and

(ii) compliance with any prescribed requirements; and

(b) (as respects registration as a parliamentary elector) without prejudice to section 2(1) of the Representation of the People Act 1985 (registration of British citizens overseas).

(5) A person otherwise qualified is (despite subsection (1)(d) or (3)(d), as the case may be) entitled to be registered in a register of parliamentary electors or local government electors if he will attain voting age before the end of the period of 12 months beginning with the 1st December next following the relevant date, but –

(a) his entry in the register shall give the date on which he will attain that age; and

(b) until the date given in the entry he shall not by virtue of the entry be treated as an elector for any purposes other than those of an election the date of the poll for which is the date so given or any later date.

(6) In this section –

'qualifying Commonwealth citizen' means a Commonwealth citizen who either –

(a) is not a person who requires leave under the Immigration Act 1971 to enter or remain in the United Kingdom, or

(b) is such a person but for the time being has (or is, by virtue of any enactment, to be treated as having) any description of such leave;

'the relevant date', in relation to a person, means –

(a) the date on which an application for registration is made (or, by virtue of section 10A(2) below, is treated as having been made) by him;

(b) in the case of a person applying for registration in pursuance of a declaration of local connection or a service declaration, the date on which the declaration was made.

5 Residence: general

(1) This section applies where the question whether a person is resident at a particular address on the relevant date for the purposes of section 4 above falls to be determined for the purposes of that section.

(2) Regard shall be had, in particular, to the purpose and other circumstances, as well as to the fact, of his presence at, or absence from, the address on that date. For example, where at a particular time a person is staying at any place otherwise than on a permanent basis, he may in all the circumstances be taken to be at that time –

(a) resident there if he has no home elsewhere, or

(b) not resident there if he does have a home elsewhere.

(3) For the purpose of determining whether a person is resident in a dwelling on the relevant date for the purposes of section 4 above, his residence in the dwelling shall not be taken to have been interrupted by reason of his absence in the performance of any duty arising from or incidental to any office, service or employment held or undertaken by him if –

(a) he intends to resume actual residence within six months of giving up such residence, and will not be prevented from doing so by the performance of that duty; or

(b) the dwelling serves as a permanent place of residence (whether for himself or for himself and other persons) and he would be in actual residence there but for his absence in the performance of that duty.

(4) For the purposes of subsection (3) above any temporary period of unemployment shall be disregarded.

(5) Subsection (3) above shall apply in relation to a person's absence by reason of his attendance on a course provided by an educational institution as it applies in relation to a person's absence in the performance of any duty such as is mentioned in that subsection.

(6) Subject to sections 7 [patients in mental hospitals who are not detained offenders or on remand] and 7A [persons remanded in custody, etc] below, a person who is detained at any place in legal custody shall not, by reason of his presence there, be treated for the purposes of section 4 above as resident there.

67 Appointment of election agent

(1) Not later than the latest time for the delivery of notices of withdrawals for an election, a person shall be named by or on behalf of each candidate as the candidate's election agent, and the name and address of the candidate's election agent shall be declared in writing by the candidate or some other person on his behalf to the appropriate officer not later than that time. …

(2) A candidate may name himself as election agent, and upon doing so shall, so far as circumstances admit, be subject to the provisions of this Act both as a candidate and as an election agent, and, except where the context otherwise requires, any reference in this Act to an election agent shall be construed to refer to the candidate acting in his capacity of election agent. …

(3) … one election agent only shall be appointed for each candidate, but the appointment, whether the election agent appointed be the candidate himself or not, may be revoked …

73 Payment of expenses through election agent

(1) Subject to subsection (5) below, no payment (of whatever nature) shall be made by –

(a) a candidate at an election, or

(b) any other person,

in respect of election expenses incurred by or on behalf of the candidate unless it is made by or through the candidate's election agent.

(2) Every payment made by an election agent in respect of any election expenses shall, except where less than £20, be vouched for by a bill stating the particulars and by a receipt.

(3) The references in the foregoing provisions of this section to an election agent shall, in relation to a parliamentary … election where sub-agents are allowed, be taken as references to the election agent acting by himself or a sub-agent.

(5) This section does not apply to:

(a) any expenses which are, in accordance with section 74(1) or (1B), 78(5) or 79(2) below, paid by the candidate;

(b) any expenses which are paid in accordance with section 74(3) below by a person authorised as mentioned in that provision;

(c) any expenses included in a declaration made by the election agent under section 74A below; or

(d) any expenses which are to be regarded as incurred by or on behalf of the candidate by virtue of section 90A(5)(b) below.

(6) A person who makes any payment (of whatever nature) in contravention of subsection (1) above shall be guilty of an illegal practice.

75 Prohibition of expenses not authorised by election agent

(1) No expenses shall, with a view to promoting or procuring the election of a candidate ... at an election, be incurred by any person other than the candidate, his election agent and persons authorised in writing by the election agent on account –

(a) of holding public meetings or organising any public display; or

(b) of issuing advertisements, circulars or publications; or

(c) of otherwise presenting to the electors the candidate or his views or the extent or nature of his backing or disparaging another candidate, ...

but paragraph (c) ... of this subsection shall not –

(i) restrict the publication of any matter relating to the election in a newspaper or other periodical or in a broadcast made by the British Broadcasting Corporation or by Sianel Pedwar Cymru or in a programme included in any service licensed under Part I or III of the Broadcasting Act 1990 or Part I or II of the Broadcasting Act 1996; or

(ii) apply to any expenses incurred by any person which do not exceed in the aggregate the permitted sum (and are not incurred by that person as part of a concerted plan of action), or to expenses incurred by any person in travelling or in living away from home or similar personal expenses.

(1ZA) For the purposes of subsection (1)(ii) above, 'the permitted sum' means –

(a) in respect of a candidate at a parliamentary election, £500;

(b) in respect of a candidate at a local government election, £50 together with an additional 0.5p for every entry in the register of local government electors for the electoral area in question as it has effect on the last day for publication of notice of the election;

and expenses shall be regarded as incurred by a person 'as part of a concerted plan of action' if they are incurred by that person in pursuance of any plan or other arrangement whereby that person and one or more other persons are to incur, with a view to promoting or procuring the election of the same candidate, expenses which (disregarding subsection (1)(ii)) fall within subsection (1) above. ...

As amended by the Representation of the People Act 1985, ss14(1), (3), 24, Schedule 4, para 1; Broadcasting Act 1990, s203(1), (4), Schedule 20, para 35(1), (2), Schedule 21, para 5; Broadcasting Act 1996, s148(1), Schedule 10, Pt III, para 28; Representation of the People Act 2000, ss1(1), (2), 3; Political Parties, Elections and Referendums Act 2000, ss131, 138(1), 158(2), Schedule 18, paras 1, 3(1), (2), (4)–(6), Schedule 22.

POLICE AND CRIMINAL EVIDENCE ACT 1984

(1984 c 60)

PART I

POWERS TO STOP AND SEARCH

1 Power of constable to stop and search persons, vehicles, etc

(1) A constable may exercise any power conferred by this section –

(a) in any place to which at the time when he proposes to exercise the power the public or any section of the public has access, on payment or otherwise, as of right or by virtue of express or implied permission; or

(b) in any other place to which people have ready access at the time when he proposes to exercise the power but which is not a dwelling.

(2) Subject to subsections (3) to (5) below, a constable –

(a) may search –

(i) any person or vehicle;

(ii) anything which is in or on a vehicle,

for stolen or prohibited articles or any article to which subsection (8A) below applies; and

(b) may detain a person or vehicle for the purpose of such a search.

(3) This section does not give a constable power to search a person or vehicle or anything in or on a vehicle unless he has reasonable grounds for suspecting that he will find stolen or prohibited articles or any article to which subsection (8A) below applies.

(4) If a person is in a garden or yard occupied with and used for the purposes of a dwelling or on other land so occupied and used, a constable may not search him in the exercise of the power conferred by this section unless the constable has reasonable grounds for believing –

(a) that he does not reside in the dwelling; and

(b) that he is not in the place in question with the express or implied permission of a person who resides in the dwelling.

(5) If a vehicle is in a garden or yard occupied with and used for the purposes of a dwelling or on other land so occupied and used, a constable may not search the vehicle or anything in or on it in the exercise of the power conferred by this section unless he has reasonable grounds for believing –

(a) that the person in charge of the vehicle does not reside in the dwelling; and

(b) that the vehicle is not in the place in question with the express or implied permission of a person who resides in the dwelling.

(6) If in the course of such a search a constable discovers an article which he has reasonable grounds for suspecting to be a stolen or prohibited article or an article to which subsection (8A) below applies, he may seize it.

(7) An article is prohibited for the purposes of this Part of this Act if it is –

(a) an offensive weapon; or

(b) an article –

(i) made or adapted for use in the course of or in connection with an offence to which this sub-paragraph applies; or

(ii) intended by the person having it with him for such use by him or by some other person.

(8) The offences to which subsection (7)(b)(i) above applies are –

(a) burglary;

(b) theft;

(c) offences under section 12 of the Theft Act 1968 (taking motor vehicle or other conveyance without authority);

(d) offences under section 15 of that Act (obtaining property by deception); and

(e) offences under section 1 of the Criminal Damage Act 1971 (destroying or damaging property).

(8A) This subsection applies to any article in relation to which a person has committed, or is committing or is going to commit an offence under section 139 of the Criminal Justice Act 1988.

(9) In this Part of this Act 'offensive weapon' means any article –

(a) made or adapted for use for causing injury to persons; or

(b) intended by the person having it with him for such use by him or by some other person.

2 Provisions relating to search under section 1 and other powers

(1) A constable who detains a person or vehicle in the exercise –

(a) of the power conferred by section 1 above; or

(b) of any other power –

(i) to search a person without first arresting him; or

(ii) to search a vehicle without making an arrest,

need not conduct a search if it appears to him subsequently –

(i) that no search is required; or

(ii) that a search is impracticable.

(2) If a constable contemplates a search, other than a search of an unattended vehicle, in the exercise –

(a) of the power conferred by section 1 above; or

(b) of any other power, except the power conferred by section 6 below and the power conferred by section 27(2) of the Aviation Security Act 1982 –

(i) to search a person without first arresting him; or

(ii) to search a vehicle without making an arrest,

it shall be his duty, subject to subsection (4) below, to take reasonable steps before he commences the search to bring to the attention of the appropriate person –

(i) if the constable is not in uniform, documentary evidence that he is a constable; and

(ii) whether he is in uniform or not, the matters specified in subsection (3) below;

and the constable shall not commence the search until he has performed that duty.

(3) The matters referred to in subsection (2)(ii) above are –

(a) the constable's name and the name of the police station to which he is attached;

(b) the object of the proposed search;

(c) the constable's grounds for proposing to make it; and

(d) the effect of section 3(7) or (8) below, as may be appropriate.

(4) A constable need not bring the effect of section 3(7) or (8) below to the attention of the appropriate person if it appears to the constable that it will not be practicable to make the record in section 3(1) below.

(5) In this section 'the appropriate person' means –

(a) if the constable proposes to search a person, that person; and

(b) if he proposes to search a vehicle, or anything in or on a vehicle, the person in charge of the vehicle.

(6) On completing a search of an unattended vehicle or anything in or on such a vehicle in the exercise of any such power as is mentioned in subsection (2) above a constable shall leave a notice –

(a) stating that he has searched it;

(b) giving the name of the police station to which he is attached;

(c) stating that an application for compensation for any damage caused by the search may be made to that police station; and

(d) stating the effect of section 3(8) below.

(7) The constable shall leave the notice inside the vehicle unless it is not reasonably practicable to do so without damaging the vehicle.

(8) The time for which a person or vehicle may be detained for the purposes of such a search is such time as is reasonably required to permit a search to be carried out either at the place where the person or vehicle was first detained or nearby.

(9) Neither the power conferred by section 1 above nor any other power to detain and search a person without first arresting him or to detain and search a vehicle without making an arrest is to be construed –

(a) as authorising a constable to require a person to remove any of his clothing in public other than an outer coat, jacket or gloves; or

(b) as authorising a constable not in uniform to stop a vehicle.

(10) This section and section 1 above apply to vessels, aircraft and hovercraft as they apply to vehicles.

3 Duty to make records concerning searches

(1) Where a constable has carried out a search in the exercise of any such power as is mentioned in section 2(1) above, other than a search –

(a) under section 6 below; or

(b) under section 27(2) of the Aviation Security Act 1982,

he shall make a record of it in writing unless it is not practicable to do so.

(2) If –

(a) a constable is required by subsection (1) above to make a record of a search; but

(b) it is not practicable to make the record on the spot,

he shall make it as soon as practicable after the completion of the search.

(3) The record of a search of a person shall include a note of his name, if the constable knows it, but a constable may not detain a person to find out his name.

(4) If a constable does not know the name of a person whom he has searched, the record of the search shall include a note otherwise describing that person.

(5) The record of a search of a vehicle shall include a note describing the vehicle.

(6) The record of a search of a person or a vehicle –

(a) shall state –

(i) the object of the search;

(ii) the grounds for making it;

(iii) the date and time when it was made;

(iv) the place where it was made;

(v) whether anything, and if so what, was found;

(vi) whether any, and if so what, injury to a person or damage to property appears to the constable to have resulted from the search; and

(b) shall identify the constable making it.

(7) If a constable who conducted a search of a person made a record of it, the person who was searched shall be entitled to a copy of the record if he asks for one before the end of the period specified in subsection (9) below.

(8) If –

(a) the owner of a vehicle which has been searched or the person who was in charge of the vehicle at the time when it was searched asks for a copy of the record of the search before the end of the period specified in sub-section (9) below; and

(b) the constable who conducted the search made a record of it,

the person who made the request shall be entitled to a copy.

(9) The period mentioned in subsections (7) and (8) above is the period of 12 months beginning with the date on which the search was made.

(10) The requirements imposed by this section with regard to records of searches of vehicles shall apply also to records of searches of vessels, aircraft and hovercraft.

4 Road checks

(1) This section shall have effect in relation to the conduct of road checks by police officers for the purpose of ascertaining whether a vehicle is carrying –

(a) a person who has committed an offence other than a road traffic offence or a vehicle excise offence;

(b) a person who is a witness to such an offence;

(c) a person intending to commit such an offence; or

(d) a person who is unlawfully at large.

(2) For the purposes of this section a road check consists of the exercise in a locality of the power conferred by section 163 of the Road Traffic Act 1988 in such a way as to stop during the period for which its exercise in that way in that locality continues all vehicles or vehicles selected by any criterion.

(3) Subject to subsection (5) below, there may only be such a road check if a police officer of the rank of superintendent or above authorises it in writing.

(4) An officer may only authorise a road check under subsection (3) above –

(a) for the purpose specified in subsection (1)(a) above, if he has reasonable grounds –

(i) for believing that the offence is a serious arrestable offence; and

(ii) for suspecting that the person is, or is about to be, in the locality in which vehicles would be stopped if the road check were authorised;

(b) for the purpose specified in subsection (1)(b) above, if he has reasonable grounds for believing that the offence is a serious arrestable offence;

(c) for the purpose specified in subsection (1)(c) above, if he has reasonable grounds –

(i) for believing that the offence would be a serious arrestable offence; and

(ii) for suspecting that the person is, or is about to be, in the locality in which vehicles would be stopped if the road check were authorised;

(d) for the purpose specified in subsection (1)(d) above, if he has reasonable grounds for suspecting that the person is, or is about to be, in that locality.

(5) An officer below the rank of superintendent may authorise such a road check if it appears to him that it is required as a matter of urgency for one of the purposes specified in subsection (1) above.

(6) If an authorisation is given under subsection (5) above, it shall be the duty of the officer who gives it –

(a) to make a written record of the time at which he gives it; and

(b) to cause an officer of the rank of superintendent or above to be informed that it has been given.

(7) The duties imposed by subsection (6) above shall be performed as soon as it is practicable to do so.

(8) An officer to whom a report is made under subsection (6) above may, in writing, authorise the road check to continue.

(9) If such an officer considers that the road check should not continue, he shall record in writing –

(a) the fact that it took place; and

(b) the purpose for which it took place.

(10) An officer giving an authorisation under this section shall specify the locality in which vehicles are to be stopped.

(11) An officer giving an authorisation under this section, other than an authorisation under subsection (5) above –

(a) shall specify a period, not exceeding seven days, during which the road check may continue; and

(b) may direct that the road check –

(i) shall be continuous; or

(ii) shall be conducted at specified times,

during that period.

(12) If it appears to an officer of the rank of superintendent or above that a road check ought to continue beyond the period for which it has been authorised he may, from time to time, in writing specify a further period, not exceeding seven days, during which it may continue.

(13) Every written authorisation shall specify –

(a) the name of the officer giving it;

(b) the purpose of the road check; and

(c) the locality in which vehicles are to be stopped.

(14) The duties to specify the purposes of a road check imposed by subsections (9) and (13) above include duties to specify any relevant serious arrestable offence.

(15) Where a vehicle is stopped in a road check, the person in charge of the vehicle at the time when it is stopped shall be entitled to obtain a written statement of the purpose of the road check if he applies for such a statement not later than the end of the period of 12 months from the day on which the vehicle was stopped.

(16) Nothing in this section affects the exercise by police officers of any power to stop vehicles for purposes other than those specified in subsection (1) above.

6 Statutory undertakers, etc

(1) A constable employed by statutory undertakers may stop, detain and search any vehicle before it leaves a goods area included in the premises of the statutory undertakers.

(1A) Without prejudice to any powers under subsection (1) above, a constable employed by the British Transport Police Authority may stop, detain and search any vehicle before it leaves a goods area which is included in the premises of any successor of the British Railways Board and is used wholly or mainly for the purposes of a relevant undertaking.

(2) In this section 'goods area' means any area used wholly or mainly for the storage or handling of goods; and 'successor of the British Railways Board' and 'relevant undertaking' have the same meaning as in the Railways Act 1993 (Consequential Modifications) Order 1999.

(3) For the purposes of section 6 of the Public Stores Act 1875, any person appointed under the Special Constables Act 1923 to be a special constable within any premises which are in the possession or under the control of British Nuclear Fuels Limited shall be deemed to be a constable deputed by a public department and any goods and chattels belonging to or in the possession of British Nuclear Fuels Limited shall be deemed to be Her Majesty's Stores ...

7 Part I – supplementary ...

(3) In this Part of this Act 'statutory undertakers' means persons authorised by any enactment to carry on any railway, light railway, road transport, water transport, canal, inland navigation, dock or harbour undertaking.

PART II

POWERS OF ENTRY, SEARCH AND SEIZURE

8 Power of justice of the peace to authorise entry and search of premises

(1) If on an application made by a constable a justice of the peace is satisfied that there are reasonable grounds for believing –

(a) that a serious arrestable offence has been committed; and

(b) that there is material on premises specified in the application which is likely to be of substantial value (whether by itself or together with other material) to the investigation of the offence; and

(c) that the material is likely to be relevant evidence; and

(d) that it does not consist of or include items subject to legal privilege, excluded material or special procedure material; and

(e) that any of the conditions specified in subsection (3) below applies,

he may issue a warrant authorising a constable to enter and search the premises.

(2) A constable may seize and retain anything for which a search has been authorised under subsection (1) above.

(3) The conditions mentioned in subsection (1)(e) above are –

(a) that it is not practicable to communicate with any person entitled to grant entry to the premises;

(b) that it is practicable to communicate with a person entitled to grant entry to the premises but it is not practicable to communicate with any person entitled to grant access to the evidence;

(c) that entry to the premises will not be granted unless a warrant is produced;

(d) that the purpose of a search may be frustrated or seriously prejudiced unless a constable arriving at the premises can secure immediate entry to them.

(4) In this Act 'relevant evidence', in relation to an offence, means anything that would be admissible in evidence at a trial for the offence.

(5) The power to issue a warrant conferred by this section is in addition to any such power otherwise conferred.

(6) This section applies in relation to a relevant offence (as defined in section 28D(4) of the Immigration Act 1971) as it applies in relation to a serious arrestable offence.

9 Special provisions as to access

(1) A constable may obtain access to excluded material or special procedure material for the purposes of a criminal investigation by making an application under Schedule 1 below and in accordance with that Schedule.

(2) Any Act (including a local Act) passed before this Act under which a search of

premises for the purposes of a criminal investigation could be authorised by the issue of a warrant to a constable shall cease to have effect so far as it relates to the authorisation of searches –

(a) for items subject to legal privilege; or

(b) for excluded material; or

(c) for special procedure material consisting of documents or records other than documents. ...

10 Meaning of 'items subject to legal privilege'

(1) Subject to subsection (2) below, in this Act 'items subject to legal privilege' means –

(a) communications between a professional legal adviser and his client or any person representing his client made in connection with the giving of legal advice to the client;

(b) communications between a professional legal adviser and his client or any person representing his client or between such an adviser or his client or any such representative and any other person made in connection with or in contemplation of legal proceedings and for the purposes of such proceedings; and

(c) items enclosed with or referred to in such communications and made –

(i) in connection with the giving of legal advice; or

(ii) in connection with or in contemplation of legal proceedings and for the purposes of such proceedings,

when they are in the possession of a person who is entitled to possession of them.

(2) Items held with the intention of furthering a criminal purpose are not items subject to legal privilege.

11 Meaning of 'excluded material'

(1) Subject to the following provisions of this section, in this Act 'excluded material' means –

(a) personal records which a person has acquired or created in the course of any trade, business, profession or other occupation or for the purposes of any paid or unpaid office and which he holds in confidence;

(b) human tissue or tissue fluid which has been taken for the purposes of diagnosis or medical treatment and which a person holds in confidence;

(c) journalistic material which a person holds in confidence and which consists –

(i) of documents; or

(ii) of records other than documents.

(2) A person holds material other than journalistic material in confidence for the purposes of this section if he holds it subject –

(a) to an express or implied undertaking to hold it in confidence; or

(b) to a restriction on disclosure or an obligation of secrecy contained in any enactment, including an enactment contained in an Act passed after this Act.

(3) A person holds journalistic material in confidence for the purposes of this section if –

(a) he holds it subject to such an undertaking, restriction or obligation; and

(b) it has been continuously held (by one or more persons) subject to such an undertaking, restriction or obligation since it was first acquired or created for the purposes of journalism.

12 Meaning of 'personal records'

In this Part of this Act 'personal records' means documentary and other records concerning an individual (whether living or dead) who can be identified from them and relating –

(a) to his physical or mental health;

(b) to spiritual counselling or assistance given or to be given to him; or

(c) to counselling or assistance given or to be given to him, for the purposes of his personal welfare, by any voluntary organisations or by any individual who –

(i) by reason of his office or occupation has responsibilities for his personal welfare; or

(ii) by reason of an order of a court has responsibilities for his supervision.

13 Meaning of 'journalistic material'

(1) Subject to subsection (2) below, in this Act 'journalistic material' means material acquired or created for the purposes of journalism.

(2) Material is only journalistic material for the purposes of this Act if it is in the possession of a person who acquired or created it for the purposes of journalism.

(3) A person who receives material from someone who intends that the recipient shall use it for the purposes of journalism is to be taken to have acquired it for those purposes.

14 Meaning of 'special procedure material'

(1) In this Act 'special procedure material' means –

(a) material to which subsection (2) below applies; and

(b) journalistic material, other than excluded material.

(2) Subject to the following provisions of this section, this subsection applies to material, other than items subject to legal privilege and excluded material, in the possession of a person who –

(a) acquired or created it in the course of any trade, business, profession or other occupation or for the purpose of any paid or unpaid office; and

(b) holds it subject –

(i) to an express or implied undertaking to hold it in confidence; or

(ii) to a restriction or obligation such as is mentioned in section 11(2)(b) above.

(3) Where material is acquired –

(a) by an employee from his employer and in the course of his employment; or

(b) by a company from an associated company,

it is only special procedure material if it was special procedure material immediately before the acquisition.

(4) Where material is created by an employee in the course of his employment, it is only special procedure material if it would have been special procedure material had his employer created it.

(5) Where material is created by a company on behalf of an associated company, it is only special procedure material if it would have been special procedure material had the associated company created it.

(6) A company is to be treated as another's associated company for the purposes of this section if it would be so treated under section 302 of the Income and Corporation Taxes Act 1970.

15 Search warrants – safeguards

(1) This section and section 16 below have effect in relation to the issue to constables under any enactment, including an enactment contained in an Act passed after this Act, of warrants to enter and search premises; and an entry on or search of premises under a warrant is unlawful unless it complies with this section and section 16 below.

(2) Where a constable applies for any such warrant, it shall be his duty –

(a) to state –

(i) the ground on which he makes the application; and

(ii) the enactment under which the warrant would be issued;

(b) to specify the premises which it is desired to enter and search; and

(c) to identify, so far as is practicable, the articles or persons to be sought.

(3) An application for such a warrant shall be made ex parte and supported by an information in writing.

(4) The constable shall answer on oath any question that the justice of the peace or judge hearing the application asks him.

(5) A warrant shall authorise an entry on one occasion only.

(6) A warrant –

(a) shall specify –

(i) the name of the person who applies for it;

(ii) the date on which it is issued;

(iii) the enactment under which it is issued; and

(iv) the premises to be searched; and

(b) shall identify, so far as is practicable, the articles or persons to be sought.

(7) Two copies shall be made of a warrant.

(8) The copies shall be clearly certified as copies.

16 Execution of warrants

(1) A warrant to enter and search premises may be executed by any constable.

(2) Such a warrant may authorise persons to accompany any constable who is executing it.

(2A) A person so authorised has the same powers as the constable whom he accompanies in respect of –

(a) the execution of the warrant, and

(b) the seizure of anything to which the warrant relates.

(2B) But he may exercise those powers only in the company, and under the supervision, of a constable.

(3) Entry and search under a warrant must be within one month from the date of its issue.

(4) Entry and search under a warrant must be at a reasonable hour unless it appears to the constable executing it that the purpose of a search may be frustrated on an entry at a reasonable hour.

(5) Where the occupier of premises which are to be entered and searched is present at the time when a constable seeks to execute a warrant to enter and search them, the constable –

(a) shall identify himself to the occupier and, if not in uniform, shall produce to him documentary evidence that he is a constable;

(b) shall produce the warrant to him; and

(c) shall supply him with a copy of it.

(6) Where –

(a) the occupier of such premises is not present at the time when a constable seeks to execute such a warrant; but

(b) some other person who appears to the constable to be in charge of the premises is present,

subsection (5) above shall have effect as if any reference to the occupier were a reference to that other person.

(7) If there is no person present who appears to the constable to be in charge of the premises, he shall leave a copy of the warrant in a prominent place on the premises.

(8) A search under a warrant may only be a search to the extent required for the purpose for which the warrant was issued.

(9) A constable executing a warrant shall make an endorsement on it stating –

(a) whether the articles or persons sought were found; and

(b) whether any articles were seized, other than articles which were sought.

(10) A warrant which –

(a) has been executed; or

(b) has not been executed within the time authorised for its execution,

shall be returned –

(i) if it was issued by a justice of the peace, to the chief executive to the justices for the petty sessions area for which he acts; and

(ii) if it was issued by a judge, to the appropriate officer of the court from which he issued it.

(11) A warrant which is returned under subsection (10) above shall be retained for 12 months from its return –

(a) by the chief executive to the justices, if it was returned under paragraph (i) of that subsection; and

(b) by the appropriate officer, if it was returned under paragraph (ii).

(12) If during the period for which a warrant is to be retained the occupier of the premises to which it relates asks to inspect it, he shall be allowed to do so.

17 Entry for purpose of arrest, etc

(1) Subject to the following provisions of this section, and without prejudice to any other enactment, a constable may enter and search any premises for the purpose –

(a) of executing –

(i) a warrant of arrest issued in connection with or arising out of criminal proceedings; or

(ii) a warrant of commitment issued under section 76 of the Magistrates' Courts Act 1980;

(b) of arresting a person for an arrestable offence;

(c) of arresting a person for an offence under –

(i) section 1 (prohibition of uniforms in connection with political objects) of the Public Order Act 1936;

(ii) any enactment contained in sections 6 to 8 or 10 of the Criminal Law Act 1977 (offences relating to entering and remaining on property);

(iii) section 4 of the Public Order Act 1986 (fear or provocation of violence);

(iiia) section 163 of the Road Traffic Act 1988 (c 52) (failure to stop when required to do so by a constable in uniform);

(iv) section 76 of the Criminal Justice and Public Order Act 1994 (failure to comply with interim possession order);

(ca) of arresting, in pursuance of section 32(1A) of the Children and Young Persons Act 1969, any child or young person who has been remanded or committed to local authority accommodation under section 23(1) of that Act;

(cb) of recapturing any person who is, or is deemed for any purpose to be, unlawfully at large while liable to be detained –

(i) in a prison, remand centre, young offender institution or secure training centre, or

(ii) in pursuance of section 92 of the Powers of Criminal Courts (Sentencing) Act 2000 (dealing with children and young persons guilty of grave crimes), in any other place;

(d) of recapturing any person whatever who is unlawfully at large and whom he is pursuing; or

(e) of saving life or limb or preventing serious damage to property.

(2) Except for the purpose specified in paragraph (e) of subsection (1) above, the powers of entry and search conferred by this section –

(a) are only exercisable if the constable has reasonable grounds for believing that the person whom he is seeking is on the premises; and

(b) are limited, in relation to premises consisting of two or more separate dwellings, to powers to enter and search –

(i) any parts of the premises which the occupiers of any dwelling comprised in the premises use in common with the occupiers of any other such dwelling; and

(ii) any such dwelling in which the constable has reasonable grounds for believing that the person whom he is seeking may be.

(3) The powers of entry and search conferred by this section are only exercisable for the purposes specified in subsection (1)(c)(ii) or (iv) above by a constable in uniform.

(4) The power of search conferred by this section is only a power to search to the extent that is reasonably required for the purpose for which the power of entry is exercised.

(5) Subject to subsection (6) below, all the rules of common law under which a constable has power to enter premises without a warrant are hereby abolished.

(6) Nothing in subsection (5) above affects any power of entry to deal with or prevent a breach of the peace.

18 Entry and search after arrest

(1) Subject to the following provisions of this section, a constable may enter and search any premises occupied or controlled by a person who is under arrest for an arrestable offence, if he has reasonable grounds for suspecting that there is on the premises evidence, other than items subject to legal privilege, that relates –

(a) to that offence; or

(b) to some other arrestable offence which is connected with or similar to that offence.

(2) A constable may seize and retain anything for which he may search under subsection (1) above.

(3) The power to search conferred by subsection (1) above is only a power to search to the extent that is reasonably required for the purpose of discovering such evidence.

(4) Subject to subsection (5) below, the powers conferred by this section may not be exercised unless an officer of the rank of inspector or above has authorised them in writing.

(5) A constable may conduct a search under subsection (1) –

(a) before the person is taken to a police station or released on bail under section 30A, and

(b) without obtaining an authorisation under subsection (4),

if the condition in subsection (5A) is satisfied.

(5A) The condition is that the presence of the person at a place (other than a police station) is necessary for the effective investigation of the offence.

(6) If a constable conducts a search by virtue of subsection (5) above, he shall inform an officer of the rank of inspector or above that he has made the search as soon as practicable after he has made it.

(7) An officer who –

(a) authorises a search; or

(b) is informed of a search under subsection (6) above, shall make a record in writing –

(i) of the grounds for the search; and

(ii) of the nature of the evidence that was sought.

(8) If the person who was in occupation or control of the premises at the time of the search is in police detention at the time the record is to be made, the officer shall make the record as part of his custody record.

19 General power of seizure, etc

(1) The powers conferred by subsections (2), (3) and (4) below are exercisable by a constable who is lawfully on any premises.

(2) The constable may seize anything which is on the premises if he has reasonable grounds for believing –

(a) that it has been obtained in consequence of the commission of an offence; and

(b) that it is necessary to seize it in order to prevent it being concealed, lost, damaged, altered or destroyed.

(3) The constable may seize anything which is on the premises if he has reasonable grounds for believing –

(a) that it is evidence in relation to an offence which he is investigating or any other offence; and

(b) that it is necessary to seize it in order to prevent the evidence being concealed, lost, altered or destroyed.

(4) The constable may require any information which is stored in any electronic form and is accessible from the premises to be produced in a form in which it can be taken away and in which it is visible and legible or from which it can readily be produced in a visible and legible form if he has reasonable grounds for believing –

(a) that –

(i) it is evidence in relation to an offence which he is investigating or any other offence; or

(ii) it has been obtained in consequence of the commission of an offence; and

(b) that it is necessary to do so in order to prevent it being concealed, lost, tampered with or destroyed.

(5) The powers conferred by this section are in addition to any power otherwise conferred.

(6) No power of seizure conferred on a constable under any enactment (including an enactment contained in an Act passed after this Act) is to be taken to authorise the seizure of an item which the constable exercising the power has reasonable grounds for believing to be subject to legal privilege.

20 Extension of powers of seizure to computerised information

(1) Every power of seizure which is conferred by an enactment to which this section applies on a constable who has entered premises in the exercise of a power conferred by an enactment shall be construed as including a power to require any information stored in any electronic form and accessible from the premises to be produced in a form in which it can be taken away and in which it is visible and legible or from which it can readily be produced in a visble and legible form.

(2) This section applies –

(a) to any enactment contained in an Act passed before this Act;

(b) to sections 8 and 18 above;

(c) to paragraph 13 of Schedule 1 to this Act; and

(d) to any enactment contained in an Act passed after this Act.

21 Access and copying

(1) A constable who seizes anything in the exercise of a power conferred by any enactment, including an enactment contained in an Act passed after this Act, shall, if so requested by a person showing himself –

(a) to be the occupier of premises on which it was seized; or

(b) to have had custody or control of it immediately before the seizure,

provide that person with a record of what he seized.

(2) The officer shall provide the record within a reasonable time from the making of the request for it.

(3) Subject to subsection (8) below, if a request for permission to be granted access to anything which –

(a) has been seized by a constable; and

(b) is retained by the police for the purpose of investigating an offence,

is made to the officer in charge of the investigation by a person who had custody or control of the thing immediately before it was so seized or by someone acting on behalf of such a person, the officer shall allow the person who made the request access to it under the supervision of a constable.

(4) Subject to subsection (8) below, if a request for a photograph or copy of any such thing is made to the officer in charge of the investigation by a person who had custody or control of the thing immediately before it was so seized, or by someone acting on behalf of such a person, the officer shall –

(a) allow the person who made the request access to it under the supervision of a constable for the purpose of photographing or copying it; or

(b) photograph or copy it, or cause it to be photographed or copied.

(5) A constable may also photograph or copy, or have photographed or copied, anything which he has power to seize, without a request being made under subsection (4) above.

(6) Where anything is photographed or copied under subsection (4)(b) above, the photograph or copy shall be supplied to the person who made the request.

(7) The photograph or copy shall be so supplied within a reasonable time from the making of the request.

(8) There is no duty under this section to grant access to, or to supply a photograph or copy of, anything if the officer in charge of the investigation for the purposes of which it was seized has reasonable grounds for believing that to do so would prejudice –

(a) that investigation;

(b) the investigation of an offence other than the offence for the purposes of investigating which the thing was seized; or

(c) any criminal proceedings which may be brought as a result of –

(i) the investigation of which he is in charge; or

(ii) any such investigation as is mentioned in paragraph (b) above.

(9) The references to a constable in subsections (1), (2), (3)(a) and (5) include a person authorised under section 16(2) to accompany a constable executing a warrant.

22 Retention

(1) Subject to subsection (4) below, anything which has been seized by a constable or taken away by a constable following a requirement made by virtue of section 19 or 20 above may be retained so long as is necessary in all the circumstances.

(2) Without prejudice to the generality of subsection (1) above –

(a) anything seized for the purposes of a criminal investigation may be retained, except as provided by subsection (4) below –

(i) for use as evidence at a trial for an offence; or

(ii) for forensic examination or for investigation in connection with an offence; and

(b) anything may be retained in order to establish its lawful owner, where there are reasonable grounds for believing that it has been obtained in consequence of the commission of an offence.

(3) Nothing seized on the ground that it may be used –

(a) to cause physical injury to any person;

(b) to damage property;

(c) to interfere with evidence; or

(d) to assist in escape from police detention or lawful custody,

may be retained when the person from whom it was seized is no longer in police detention or the custody of a court or is in the custody of a court but has been released on bail.

(4) Nothing may be retained for either of the purposes mentioned in subsection (2)(a) above if a photograph or copy would be sufficient for that purpose.

(5) Nothing in this section affects any power of a court to make an order under section 1 of the Police (Property) Act 1897.

(6) This section also applies to anything retained by the police under section 28H(5) of the Immigration Act 1971.

(7) The reference in subsection (1) to anything seized by a constable includes anything seized by a person authorised under section 16(2) to accompany a constable executing a warrant.

23 Meaning of 'premises', etc

In this Act –

'premises' includes any place and, in particular, includes –

(a) any vehicle, vessel, aircraft or hovercraft;

(b) any offshore installation; and

(c) any tent or movable structure; and

'offshore installation' has the meaning given to it by section 1 of the Mineral Workings (Offshore Installations) Act 1971.

PART III

ARREST

24 Arrest without warrant for arrestable offences

(1) The powers of summary arrest conferred by the following subsections shall apply –

(a) to offences for which the sentence is fixed by law;

(b) to offences for which a person of 21 years of age or over (not previously convicted) may be sentenced to imprisonment for a term of five years (or might be so sentenced but for the restrictions imposed by section 33 of the Magistrates' Courts Act 1980); and

(c) to the offences listed in Schedule 1A;

and in this Act 'arrestable offence' means any such offence.

(2) Schedule 1A (which lists the offences referred to in subsection 1(c)) shall have effect.

(3) Without prejudice to section 2 of the Criminal Attempts Act 1981, the powers of summary arrest conferred by the following subsections shall also apply to the offences of –

(a) conspiring to commit any of the offences listed in Schedule 1A;

(b) attempting to commit any such offence other than one which is a summary offence;

(c) inciting, aiding, abetting, counselling or procuring the commission of any such offence;

and such offences are also arrestable offences for the purposes of this Act.

(4) Any person may arrest without a warrant –

(a) anyone who is in the act of committing an arrestable offence;

(b) anyone whom he has reasonable grounds for suspecting to be committing such an offence.

(5) Where an arrestable offence has been committed, any person may arrest without a warrant –

(a) anyone who is guilty of the offence;

(b) anyone whom he has reasonable grounds for suspecting to be guilty of it.

(6) Where a constable has reasonable grounds for suspecting that an arrestable offence has been committed, he may arrest without a warrant anyone whom he has reasonable grounds for suspecting to be guilty of the offence.

(7) A constable may arrest without a warrant –

(a) anyone who is about to commit an arrestable offence;

(b) anyone whom he has reasonable grounds for suspecting to be about to commit an arrestable offence.

25 General arrest conditions

(1) Where a constable has reasonable grounds for suspecting that any offence which is not an arrestable offence has been committed or attempted, or is being committed or attempted, he may arrest the relevant person if it appears to him that service of a summons is impracticable or inappropriate because any of the general arrest conditions is satisfied.

(2) In this section 'the relevant person' means any person whom the constable has reasonable grounds to suspect of having committed or having attempted to commit the offence or of being in the course of committing or attempting to commit it.

(3) The general arrest conditions are –

(a) that the name of the relevant person is unknown to, and cannot be readily ascertained by, the constable;

(b) that the constable has reasonable grounds for doubting whether a name furnished by the relevant person as his name is his real name;

(c) that –

(i) the relevant person has failed to furnish a satisfactory address for service; or

(ii) the constable has reasonable grounds for doubting whether an address furnished by the relevant person is a satisfactory address for service;

(d) that the constable has reasonable grounds for believing that arrest is necessary to prevent the relevant person –

(i) causing physical injury to himself or any other person;

(ii) suffering physical injury;

(iii) causing loss of or damage to property;

(iv) committing an offence against public decency; or

(v) causing an unlawful obstruction of the highway;

(e) that the constable has reasonable grounds for believing that arrest is necessary to protect a child or other vulnerable person from the relevant person.

(4) For the purposes of subsection (3) above an address is a satisfactory address for service if it appears to the constable –

(a) that the relevant person will be at it for a sufficiently long period for it to be possible to serve him with a summons; or

(b) that some other person specified by the relevant person will accept service of a summons for the relevant person at it.

(5) Nothing in subsection (3)(d) above authorises the arrest of a person under sub-paragraph (iv) of that paragraph except where members of the public going about their normal business cannot reasonably be expected to avoid the person to be arrested.

(6) This section shall not prejudice any power of arrest conferred apart from this section.

26 Repeal of statutory powers of arrest without warrant or order

(1) Subject to subsection (2) below, so much of any Act (including a local Act) passed before this Act as enables a constable –

(a) to arrest a person for an offence without a warrant; or

(b) to arrest a person otherwise than for an offence without a warrant or an order of a court,

shall cease to have effect.

(2) Nothing in subsection (1) above affects the enactments specified in Schedule 2 to this Act.

27 Fingerprinting of certain offenders

(1) If a person –

(a) has been convicted of a recordable offence;

(b) has not at any time been in police detention for the offence; and

(c) has not had his fingerprints taken –

(i) in the course of the investigation of the offence by the police; or

(ii) since the conviction,

any constable may at any time not later than one month after the date of the conviction require him to attend a police station in order that his fingerprints may be taken.

(1A) Where a person convicted of a recordable offence has already had his fingerprints taken as mentioned in paragraph (c) of subsection (1) above, that fact (together with any time when he has been in police detention for the offence) shall be disregarded for the purposes of that subsection if –

(a) the fingerprints taken on the previous occasion do not constitute a complete set of his fingerprints; or

(b) some or all of the fingerprints taken on the previous occasion are not of sufficient quality to allow satisfactory analysis, comparison or matching.

(1B) Subsections (1) and (1A) above apply –

(a) where a person has been given a caution in respect of a recordable offence which, at the time of the caution, he has admitted, or

(b) where a person has been warned or reprimanded under section 65 of the Crime and Disorder Act 1998 (c 37) for a recordable offence,

as they apply where a person has been convicted of an offence, and references to this section to a conviction shall be construed accordingly.

(2) A requirement under subsection (1) above –

(a) shall give the person a period of at least seven days within which he must so attend; and

(b) may direct him to so attend at a specified time of day or between specified times of day.

(3) Any constable may arrest without warrant a person who has failed to comply with a requirement under subsection (1) above.

(4) The Secretary of State may by regulations make provision for recording in national police records convictions for such offences as are specified in the regulations.

(5) Regulations under this section shall be made by statutory instrument and shall be subject to annulment in pursuance of a resolution of either House of Parliament.

28 Information to be given on arrest

(1) Subject to subsection (5) below, where a person is arrested, otherwise than by being informed that he is under arrest, the arrest is not lawful unless the person arrested is informed that he is under arrest as soon as is practicable after his arrest.

(2) Where a person is arrested by a constable, subsection (1) above applies regardless of whether the fact of the arrest is obvious.

(3) Subject to subsection (5) below, no arrest is lawful unless the person arrested is informed of the ground for the arrest at the time of, or as soon as is practicable after, the arrest.

(4) Where a person is arrested by a constable, subsection (3) above applies regardless of whether the ground for the arrest is obvious.

(5) Nothing in this section is to be taken to require a person to be informed –

(a) that he is under arrest; or

(b) of the ground for the arrest,

if it was not reasonably practicable for him to be so informed by reason of his having escaped from arrest before the information could be given.

29 Voluntary attendance at police station, etc

Where for the purpose of assisting with an investigation a person attends voluntarily at a police station or at any other place where a constable is present or accompanies a constable to a police station or any such other place without having been arrested –

(a) he shall be entitled to leave at will unless he is placed under arrest;

(b) he shall be informed at once that he is under arrest if a decision is taken by a constable to prevent him from leaving at will.

30 Arrest elsewhere than at police station

(1) Subsection (1A) applies where a person is, at any place other than a police station –

(a) arrested by a constable for an offence, or

(b) taken into custody by a constable after being arrested for an offence by a person other than a constable.

(1A) The person must be taken by a constable to a police station as soon as practicable after the arrest.

(1B) Subsection (1A) has effect subject to section 30A (release on bail) and subsection (7) (release without bail).

(2) Subject to subsections (3) and (5) below, the police station to which an arrested person is taken under subsection (1A) above shall be a designated police station.

(3) A constable to whom this subsection applies may take an arrested person to any police station unless it appears to the constable that it may be necessary to keep the arrested person in police detention for more than six hours.

(4) Subsection (3) above applies –

(a) to a constable who is working in a locality covered by a police station which is not a designated police station; and

(b) to a constable belonging to a body of constables maintained by an authority other than a police authority.

(5) Any constable may take an arrested person to any police station if –

(a) either of the following conditions is satisfied –

(i) the constable has arrested him without the assistance of any other constable and no other constable is available to assist him;

(ii) the constable has taken him into custody from a person other than a constable without the assistance of any other constable and no other constable is available to assist him; and

(b) it appears to the constable that he will be unable to take the arrested person to a designated police station without the arrested person injuring himself, the constable or some other person.

(6) If the first police station to which an arrested person is taken after his arrest is not a designated police station, he shall be taken to a designated police station not more than six hours after his arrival at the first police station unless he is released previously.

(7) A person arrested by a constable at any place other than a police station must be released without bail if the condition in subsection (7A) is satisfied.

(7A) The condition is that, at any time before the person arrested reaches a police station, a constable is satisfied that there are no grounds for keeping him under arrest or releasing him on bail under section 30A.

(8) A constable who releases a person under subsection (7) above shall record the fact that he has done so.

(9) The constable shall make the record as soon as is practicable after the release.

(10) Nothing in subsection (1A) or in section 30A prevents a constable delaying taking a person to a police station or releasing him on bail if the condition in subsection (10A) is satisfied.

(10A) The condition is that the presence of the person at a place (other than a police station) is necessary in order to carry out such investigations as it is reasonable to carry out immediately.

(11) Where there is such a delay the reasons for the delay must be recorded when the person first arrives at the police station or (as the case may be) is released on bail.

(12) Nothing in subsection (1A) above or section 30A shall be taken to affect –

(a) paragraphs 16(3) or 18(1) of Schedule 2 to the Immigration Act 1971;
(b) section 34(1) of the Criminal Justice Act 1972; or
(c) any provision of the Terrorism Act 2000.

(13) Nothing in subsection (10) above shall be taken to affect paragraph 18(3) of Schedule 2 to the Immigration Act 1971.

30A Bail elsewhere than at police station

(1) A constable may release on bail a person who is arrested or taken into custody in the circumstances mentioned in section 30(1).

(2) A person may be released on bail under subsection (1) at any time before he arrives at a police station.

(3) A person released on bail under subsection (1) must be required to attend a police station.

(4) No other requirement may be imposed on the person as a condition of bail.

(5) The police station which the person is required to attend may be any police station.

30B Bail under section 30A: notices

(1) Where a constable grants bail to a person under section 30A, he must give that person a notice in writing before he is released.

(2) The notice must state –

(a) the offence for which he was arrested, and

(b) the ground on which he was arrested.

(3) The notice must inform him that he is required to attend a police station.

(4) It may also specify the police station which he is required to attend and the time when he is required to attend.

(5) If the notice does not include the information mentioned in subsection (4), the person must subsequently be given a further notice in writing which contains that information.

(6) The person may be required to attend a different police station from that specified in the notice under subsection (1) or (5) or to attend at a different time.

(7) He must be given notice in writing of any such change as is mentioned in subsection (6) but more than one such notice may be given to him.

30C Bail under section 30A: supplemental

(1) A person who has been required to attend a police station is not required to do so if he is given notice in writing that his attendance is no longer required.

(2) If a person is required to attend a police station which is not a designated police station he must be –

(a) released, or

(b) taken to a designated police station,

not more than six hours after his arrival.

(3) Nothing in the Bail Act 1976 applies in relation to bail under section 30A.

(4) Nothing in section 30A or 30B or in this section prevents the re-arrest without a warrant of a person released on bail under section 30A if new evidence justifying a further arrest has come to light since his release.

30D Failure to answer to bail under section 30A

(1) A constable may arrest without a warrant a person who –

(a) has been released on bail under section 30A subject to a requirement to attend a specified police station, but

(b) fails to attend the police station at the specified time.

(2) A person arrested under subsection (1) must be taken to a police station (which may be the specified police station or any other police station) as soon as practicable after the arrest.

(3) In subsection (1), 'specified' means specified in a notice under subsection (1) or (5) of section 30B or, if notice of change has been given under subsection (7) of that section, in that notice.

(4) For the purposes of –

(a) section 30 (subject to the obligation in subsection (2)), and

(b) section 31,

an arrest under this section is to be treated as an arrest for an offence.

31 Arrest for further offence

Where –

(a) a person –

(i) has been arrested for an offence; and

(ii) is at a police station in consequence of that arrest; and

(b) it appears to a constable that, if he were released from that arrest, he would be liable to arrest for some other offence,

he shall be arrested for that other offence.

32 Search upon arrest

(1) A constable may search an arrested person, in any case where the person to be searched has been arrested at a place other than a police station, if the constable has reasonable grounds for believing that the arrested person may present a danger to himself or others.

(2) Subject to subsections (3) to (5) below, a constable shall also have power in any such case –

(a) to search the arrested person for anything –

(i) which he might use to assist him to escape from lawful custody; or

(ii) which might be evidence relating to an offence; and

(b) to enter and search any premises in which he was when arrested or immediately before he was arrested for evidence relating to the offence for which he has been arrested.

(3) The power to search conferred by subsection (2) above is only a power to search to the extent that is reasonably required for the purpose of discovering any such thing or any such evidence.

(4) The powers conferred by this section to search a person are not to be construed as authorising a constable to require a person to remove any of his clothing in

public other than an outer coat, jacket or gloves but they do authorise a search of a person's mouth.

(5) A constable may not search a person in the exercise of the power conferred by subsection (2)(a) above unless he has reasonable grounds for believing that the person to be searched may have concealed on him anything for which a search is permitted under that paragraph.

(6) A constable may not search premises in the exercise of the power conferred by subsection (2)(b) above unless he has reasonable grounds for believing that there is evidence for which a search is permitted under that paragraph on the premises.

(7) In so far as the power of search conferred by subsection (2)(b) above relates to premises consisting of two or more separate dwellings, it is limited to a power to search –

(a) any dwelling in which the arrest took place or in which the person arrested was immediately before his arrest; and

(b) any parts of the premises which the occupier of any such dwelling uses in common with the occupiers of any other dwellings comprised in the premises.

(8) A constable searching a person in the exercise of the power conferred by subsection (1) above may seize and retain anything he finds, if he has reasonable grounds for believing that the person searched might use it to cause physical injury to himself or to any other person.

(9) A constable searching a person in the exercise of the power conferred by subsection (2)(a) above may seize and retain anything he finds, other than an item subject to legal privilege, if he has reasonable grounds for believing –

(a) that he might use it to assist him to escape from lawful custody; or

(b) that it is evidence of an offence or has been obtained in consequence of the commission of an offence.

(10) Nothing in this section shall be taken to affect the power conferred by section 43 of the Terrorism Act 2000.

PART IV

DETENTION

34 Limitations on police detention

(1) A person arrested for an offence shall not be kept in police detention except in accordance with the provisions of this Part of this Act.

(2) Subject to subsection (3) below, if at any time a custody officer –

(a) becomes aware, in relation to any person in police detention, that the grounds for the detention of that person have ceased to apply; and

(b) is not aware of any other grounds on which the continued detention of that person could be justified under the provisions of this Part of this Act, it shall be the duty of the custody officer, subject to subsection (4) below, to order his immediate release from custody.

(3) No person in police detention shall be released except on the authority of a custody officer at the police station where his detention was authorised or, if it was authorised at more than one station, a custody officer at the station where it was last authorised.

(4) A person who appears to the custody officer to have been unlawfully at large when he was arrested is not to be released under subsection (2) above.

(5) A person whose release is ordered under subsection (2) above shall be released without bail unless it appears to the custody officer –

(a) that there is need for further investigation of any matter in connection with which he was detained at any time during the period of his detention; or

(b) that, in respect of any such matter, proceedings may be taken against him or he may be reprimanded or warned under section 65 of the Crime and Disorder Act 1998;

and, if it so appears, he shall be released on bail.

(6) For the purposes of this Part of this Act a person arrested under section 6(5) of the Road Traffic Act 1988 or section 30(2) of the Transport and Works Act 1992 (c 42) is arrested for an offence.

(7) For the purposes of this Part a person who –

(a) attends a police station to answer to bail granted under section 30A,

(b) returns to a police station to answer to bail granted under this Part, or

(c) is arrested under section 30D or 46A,

is to be treated as arrested with an offence and that offence is the offence in connection with which he was granted bail.

35 Designated police stations

(1) The chief officer of police for each police area shall designate the police stations in his area which, subject to sections 30(3) and (5), 30A(5) and 30D(2), are to be the stations in that area to be used for the purpose of detaining arrested persons.

(2) A chief officer's duty under subsection (1) above is to designate police stations appearing to him to provide enough accommodation for that purpose. ...

(3) Without prejudice to section 12 of the Interpretation Act 1978 (continuity of duties) a chief officer –

(a) may designate a station which was not previously designated; and

(b) may direct that a designation of a station previously made shall cease to operate.

(4) In this Act 'designated police station' means a police station for the time being designated under this section.

36 Custody officers at police stations

(1) One or more custody officers shall be appointed for each designated police station.

(2) A custody officer for a police station designated under section 35(1) above shall be appointed –

(a) by the chief officer of police for the area in which the designated police station is situated; or

(b) by such other police officer as the chief officer of police for that area may direct. ...

(3) No officer may be appointed a custody officer unless he is of at least the rank of sergeant.

(4) An officer of any rank may perform the functions of a custody officer at a designated police station if a custody officer is not readily available to perform them.

(5) Subject to the following provisions of this section and to section 39(2) below, none of the functions of a custody officer in relation to a person shall be performed by an officer who at the time when the function falls to be performed is involved in the investigation of an offence for which that person is in police detention at that time.

(6) Nothing in subsection (5) above is to be taken to prevent a custody officer –

(a) performing any function assigned to custody officers –

(i) by this Act; or

(ii) by a code of practice issued under this Act;

(b) carrying out the duty imposed on custody officers by section 39 below;

(c) doing anything in connection with the identification of a suspect; or

(d) doing anything under sections 7 and 8 of the Road Traffic Act 1988.

(7) Where an arrested person is taken to a police station which is not a designated police station, the functions in relation to him which at a designated police station would be the functions of a custody officer shall be performed –

(a) by an officer who is not involved in the investigation of an offence for which he is in police detention, if such an officer is readily available; and

(b) if no such officer is readily available, by the officer who took him to the station or any other officer.

(7A) Subject to subsection (7B), subsection (7) applies where a person attends a police station which is not a designated station to answer to bail granted under section 30A as it applies where a person is taken to such a station.

(7B) Where subsection (7) applies because of subsection (7A), the reference in subsection (7)(b) to the officer who took him to the station is to be read as a reference to the officer who granted him bail.

(8) References to a custody officer in the following provisions of this Act include

references to an officer other than a custody officer who is performing the functions of a custody officer by virtue of subsection (4) or (7) above.

(9) Where by virtue of subsection (7) above an officer of a force maintained by a police authority who took an arrested person to a police station is to perform the functions of a custody officer in relation to him, the officer shall inform an officer who –

(a) is attached to a designated police station; and

(b) is of at least the rank of inspector,

that he is to do so.

(10) The duty imposed by subsection (9) above shall be performed as soon as it is practicable to perform it.

37 Duties of custody officer before charge

(1) Where –

(a) a person is arrested for an offence –

(i) without a warrant; or

(ii) under a warrant not endorsed for bail,

the custody officer at each police station where he is detained after his arrest shall determine whether he has before him sufficient evidence to charge that person with the offence for which he was arrested and may detain him at the police station for such period as is necessary to enable him to do so.

(2) If the custody officer determines that he does not have such evidence before him, the person arrested shall be released either on bail or without bail, unless the custody officer has reasonable grounds for believing that his detention without being charged is necessary to secure or preserve evidence relating to an offence for which he is under arrest or to obtain such evidence by questioning him.

(3) If the custody officer has reasonable grounds for so believing, he may authorise the person arrested to be kept in police detention.

(4) Where a custody officer authorises a person who has not been charged to be kept in police detention, he shall, as soon as is practicable, make a written record of the grounds for the detention.

(5) Subject to subsection (6) below, the written record shall be made in the presence of the person arrested who shall at that time be informed by the custody officer of the grounds for his detention.

(6) Subsection (5) above shall not apply where the person arrested is, at the time when the written record is made –

(a) incapable of understanding what is said to him;

(b) violent or likely to become violent; or

(c) in urgent need of medical attention.

(7) Subject to section 41(7) below, if the custody officer determines that he has before him sufficient evidence to charge the person arrested with the offence for which he was arrested, the person arrested –

(a) shall be released without charge and on bail for the purpose of enabling the Director of Public Prosecutions to make a decision under section 37B below,

(b) shall be released without charge and on bail but not for that purpose,

(c) shall be released without charge and without bail, or

(d) shall be charged.

(7A) The decision as to how a person is to be dealt with under subsection (7) above shall be that of the custody officer.

(7B) Where a person is released under subsection (7)(a) above, it shall be the duty of the custody officer to inform him that he is being released to enable the Director of Public Prosecutions to make a decision under section 37B below.

(8) Where –

(a) a person is released under subsection (7)(b) or (c) above; and

(b) at the time of his release a decision whether he should be prosecuted for the offence for which he was arrested has not been taken,

it shall be the duty of the custody officer so to inform him.

(9) If the person arrested is not in a fit state to be dealt with under subsection (7) above, he may be kept in police detention until he is.

(10) The duty imposed on the custody officer under subsection (1) above shall be carried out by him as soon as practicable after the person arrested arrives at the police station or, in the case of a person arrested at the police station, as soon as practicable after the arrest.

(15) In this Part of this Act –

'arrested juvenile' means a person arrested with or without a warrant who appears to be under the age of 17;

'endorsed for bail' means endorsed with a direction for bail in accordance with section 117(2) of the Magistrates' Courts Act 1980.

37A Guidance

(1) The Director of Public Prosecutions may issue guidance –

(a) for the purpose of enabling custody officers to decide how persons should be dealt with under section 37(7) above or 37C(2) below, and

(b) as to the information to be sent to the Director of Public Prosecutions under section 37B(1) below.

(2) The Director of Public Prosecutions may from time to time revise guidance issued under this section.

(3) Custody officers are to have regard to guidance under this section in deciding how persons should be dealt with under section 37(7) above or 37C(2) below. ...

37B Consultation with the Director of Public Prosecutions

(1) Where a person is released on bail under section 37(7)(a) above, an officer involved in the investigation of the offence shall, as soon as is practicable, send to the Director of Public Prosecutions such information as may be specified in guidance under section 37A above.

(2) The Director of Public Prosecutions shall decide whether there is sufficient evidence to charge the person with an offence.

(3) If he decides that there is sufficient evidence to charge the person with an offence, he shall decide –

(a) whether or not the person should be charged and, if so, the offence with which he should be charged, and

(b) whether or not the person should be given a caution and, if so, the offence in respect of which he should be given a caution.

(4) The Director of Public Prosecutions shall give written notice of his decision to an officer involved in the investigation of the offence.

(5) If his decision is –

(a) that there is not sufficient evidence to charge the person with an offence, or

(b) that there is sufficient evidence to charge the person with an offence but that the person should not be charged with an offence or given a caution in respect of an offence,

a custody officer shall give the person notice in writing that he is not to be prosecuted.

(6) If the decision of the Director of Public Prosecutions is that the person should be charged with an offence, or given a caution in respect of an offence, the person shall be charged or cautioned accordingly.

(7) But if his decision is that the person should be given a caution in respect of the offence and it proves not to be possible to give the person such a caution, he shall instead be charged with the offence.

(8) For the purposes of this section, a person is to be charged with an offence either –

(a) when he is in police detention after returning to a police station to answer bail or is otherwise in police detention at a police station, or

(b) in accordance with section 29 of the Criminal Justice Act 2003.

(9) In this section 'caution' includes –

(a) a conditional caution within the meaning of Part 3 of the Criminal Justice Act 2003, and

(b) a warning or reprimand under section 65 of the Crime and Disorder Act 1998.

37C Breach of bail following release under section 37(7)(a)

(1) This section applies where –

(a) a person released on bail under section 37(7)(a) above or subsection (2)(b) below is arrested under section 46A below in respect of that bail, and

(b) at the time of his detention following that arrest at the police station mentioned in section 46A(2) below, notice under section 37B(4) above has not been given.

(2) The person arrested –

(a) shall be charged, or

(b) shall be released without charge, either on bail or without bail.

(3) The decision as to how a person is to be dealt with under subsection (2) above shall be that of a custody officer.

(4) A person released on bail under subsection (2)(b) above shall be released on bail subject to the same conditions (if any) which applied immediately before his arrest.

37D Release under section 37(7)(a): further provision

(1) Where a person is released on bail under section 37(7)(a) or section 37C(2)(b) above, a custody officer may subsequently appoint a different time, or an additional time, at which the person is to attend at the police station to answer bail.

(2) The custody officer shall give the person notice in writing of the exercise of the power under subsection (1).

(3) The exercise of the power under subsection (1) shall not affect the conditions (if any) to which bail is subject.

(4) Where a person released on bail under section 37(7)(a) or 37C(2)(b) above returns to a police station to answer bail or is otherwise in police detention at a police station, he may be kept in police detention to enable him to be dealt with in accordance with section 37B or 37C above or to enable the power under subsection (1) above to be exercised.

(5) If the person is not in a fit state to enable him to be so dealt with or to enable that power to be exercised, he may be kept in police detention until he is.

(6) Where a person is kept in police detention by virtue of subsection (4) or (5) above, section 37(1) to (3) and (7) above (and section 40(8) below so far as it relates to section 37(1) to (3)) shall not apply to the offence in connection with which he was released on bail under section 37(7)(a) or 37C(2)(b) above.

38 Duties of custody officer after charge

(1) Where a person arrested for an offence otherwise than under a warrant endorsed for bail is charged with an offence, the custody officer shall, subject to section 25 of the Criminal Justice and Public Order Act 1994, order his release from police detention, either on bail or without bail, unless –

(a) if the person arrested is not an arrested juvenile –

(i) his name or address cannot be ascertained or the custody officer has reasonable grounds for doubting whether a name or address furnished by him as his name or address is his real name or address;

(ii) the custody officer has reasonable grounds for believing that the person arrested will fail to appear in court to answer to bail;

(iii) in the case of a person arrested for an imprisonable offence, the custody officer has reasonable grounds for believing that the detention of the person arrested is necessary to prevent him from committing an offence;

(iiia) except in a case where (by virtue of subsection (9) of section 63B below) that section does not apply, the custody officer has reasonable grounds for believing that the detention of the person is necessary to enable a sample to be taken from him under that section;

(iv) in the case of a person arrested for an offence which is not an imprisonable offence, the custody officer has reasonable grounds for believing that the detention of the person arrested is necessary to prevent him from causing physical injury to any other person or from causing loss of or damage to property;

(v) the custody officer has reasonable grounds for believing that the detention of the person arrested is necessary to prevent him from interfering with the administration of justice or with the investigation of offences or of a particular offence; or

(vi) the custody officer has reasonable grounds for believing that the detention of the person arrested is necessary for his own protection;

(b) if he is an arrested juvenile –

(i) any of the requirements of paragraph (a) above is satisfied (but, in the case of paragraph (a)(iiia) above, only if the arrested juvenile has attained the minimum age); or

(ii) the custody officer has reasonable grounds for believing that he ought to be detained in his own interests.

(2) If the release of a person arrested is not required by subsection (1) above, the custody officer may authorise him to be kept in police detention but may not authorise a person to be kept in police detention by virtue of subsection (1)(a)(iiia) after the end of the period of six hours beginning when he was charged with the offence.

(2A) The custody officer, in taking the decisions required by subsection 1(a) and (b) above (except (a)(i) and (vi) and (b)(ii)), shall have regard to the same considerations as those which a court is required to have regard to in taking the corresponding decisions under paragraph 2(1) of Part I of Schedule 1 to the Bail Act 1976 (disregarding paragraph 2(2) of that Part).

(3) Where a custody officer authorises a person who has been charged to be kept in police detention, he shall, as soon as practicable, make a written record of the grounds for the detention.

(4) Subject to subsection (5) below, the written record shall be made in the presence of the person charged who shall at that time be informed by the custody officer of the grounds for his detention.

(5) Subsection (4) above shall not apply where the person charged is, at the time when the written record is made –

(a) incapable of understanding what is said to him;

(b) violent or likely to become violent; or

(c) in urgent need of medical attention.

(6) Where a custody officer authorises an arrested juvenile to be kept in police detention under subsection (1) above, the custody officer shall, unless he certifies –

(a) that, by reason of such circumstances as are specified in the certificate, it is impracticable for him to do so; or

(b) in the case of an arrested juvenile who has attained the age of 12 years, that no secure accommodation is available and that keeping him in other local authority accommodation would not be adequate to protect the public from serious harm from him,

secure that the arrested juvenile is moved to local authority accommodation.

(6A) In this section –

'local authority accommodation' means accommodation provided by or on behalf of a local authority (within the meaning of the Children Act 1989);

'minimum age' means the age specified in section 63B(3) below;

'secure accommodation' means accommodation provided for the purposes of restricting liberty;

'sexual offence' and 'violent offence' have the same meanings as in the Powers of Criminal Courts (Sentencing) Act 2000;

and any reference, in relation to an arrested juvenile charged with a violent or sexual offence, to protecting the public from serious harm from him shall be construed as a reference to protecting members of the public from death or serious personal injury, whether physical or psychological, occasioned by further such offences committed by him.

(6B) Where an arrested juvenile is moved to local authority accommodation under subsection (6) above, it shall be lawful for any person acting on behalf of the authority to detain him.

(7) A certificate made under subsection (6) above in respect of an arrested juvenile shall be produced to the court before which he is first brought thereafter.

(7A) In this section 'imprisonable offence' has the same meaning as in Schedule 1 to the Bail Act 1976.

(8) In this Part of this Act 'local authority' has the same meaning as in the Children Act 1989.

39 Responsibilities in relation to persons detained

(1) Subject to subsections (2) and (4) below, it shall be the duty of the custody officer at a police station to ensure –

(a) that all persons in police detention at that station are treated in accordance with this Act and any code of practice issued under it and relating to the treatment of persons in police detention; and

(b) that all matters relating to such persons which are required by this Act or by such codes of practice to be recorded are recorded in the custody records relating to such persons.

(2) If the custody officer, in accordance with any code of practice issued under this Act, transfers or permits the transfer of a person in police detention –

(a) to the custody of a police officer investigating an offence for which that person is in police detention; or

(b) to the custody of an officer who has charge of that person outside the police station,

the custody officer shall cease in relation to that person to be subject to the duty imposed on him by subsection (1)(a) above; and it shall be the duty of the officer to whom the transfer is made to ensure that he is treated in accordance with the provisions of this Act and of any such codes of practice as are mentioned in subsection (1) above.

(3) If the person detained in subsequently returned to the custody of the custody officer, it shall be the duty of the officer investigating the offence to report to the custody officer as to the manner in which this section and the codes of practice have been complied with while that person was in his custody.

(4) If an arrested juvenile is moved to local authority accommodation in pursuance of arrangements made under section 38(6) above, the custody officer shall cease in relation to that person to be subject to the duty imposed on him by subsection (1) above. ...

40 Review of police detention

(1) Reviews of the detention of each person in police detention in connection with the investigation of an offence shall be carried out periodically in accordance with the following provisions of this section –

(a) in the case of a person who has been arrested and charged, by the custody officer; and

(b) in the case of a person who has been arrested but not charged, by an officer of at least the rank of inspector who has not been directly involved in the investigation.

(2) The officer to whom it falls to carry out a review is referred to in this section as a 'review officer'.

(3) Subject to subsection (4) below –

(a) the first review shall be not later than six hours after the detention was first authorised;

(b) the second review shall be not later than nine hours after the first;

(c) subsequent reviews shall be at intervals of not more than nine hours.

(4) A review may be postponed –

(a) if, having regard to all the circumstances prevailing at the latest time for it specified in subsection (3) above, it is not practicable to carry out the review at that time;

(b) without prejudice to the generality of paragraph (a) above –

(i) if at that time the person in detention is being questioned by a police officer and the review officer is satisfied that an interruption of the questioning for the purpose of carrying out the review would prejudice the investigation in connection with which he is being questioned; or

(ii) if at that time no review officer is readily available.

(5) If a review is postponed under subsection (4) above it shall be carried out as soon as practicable after the latest time specified for it in subsection (3) above.

(6) If a review is carried out after postponement under subsection (4) above, the fact that it was so carried out shall not affect any requirements of this section as to the time at which any subsequent review is to be carried out.

(7) The review officer shall record the reasons for any postponement of a review in the custody record.

(8) Subject to subsection (9) below, where the person whose detention is under review has not been charged before the time of the review, section 37(1) to (6) above shall have effect in relation to him, but with the modifications specified in subsection (8A).

(8A) The modifications are –

(a) the substitution of references to the person whose detention is under review for references to the person arrested;

(b) the substitution of references to the review officer for references to the custody officer; and

(c) in subsection (6), the insertion of the following paragraph after paragraph (a) –

'(aa) asleep;'.

(9) Where a person has been kept in police detention by virtue of section 37(9) or

37D(5) above, section 37(1) to (6) shall not have effect in relation to him but it shall be the duty of the review officer to determine whether he is yet in a fit state.

(10) Where the person whose detention is under review has been charged before the time of the review, section 38(1) to (6B) above shall have effect in relation to him, but with the modifications specified in subsection (10A).

(10A) The modifications are –

(a) the substitution of a reference to the person whose detention is under review for any reference to the person arrested or to the person charged; and

(b) in subsection (5), the insertion of the following paragraph after paragraph (a) –

'(aa) asleep;'.

(11) Where –

(a) an officer of higher rank than the review officer gives directions relating to a person in police detention; and

(b) the directions are at variance –

(i) with any decision made or action taken by the review officer in the performance of a duty imposed on him under this Part of this Act; or

(ii) with any decision or action which would but for the directions have been made or taken by him in the performance of such a duty,

the review officer shall refer the matter at once to an officer of the rank of superintendent or above who is responsible for the police station for which the review officer is acting as review officer in connection with the detention.

(12) Before determining whether to authorise a person's continued detention the review officer shall give –

(a) that person (unless he is asleep); or

(b) any solicitor representing him who is available at the time of the review,

an opportunity to make representations to him about the detention.

(13) Subject to subsection (14) below, the person whose detention is under review or his solicitor may make representations under subsection (12) above either orally or in writing.

(14) The review officer may refuse to hear oral representations from the person whose detention is under review if he considers that he is unfit to make such representations by reason of his condition or behaviour.

40A Use of telephone for review under s40

(1) A review under section 40(1)(b) may be carried out by means of a discussion, conducted by telephone, with one or more persons at the police station where the arrested person is held.

(2) But subsection (1) does not apply if –

(a) the review is of a kind authorised by regulations under section 45A to be carried out using video-conferencing facilities; and

(b) it is reasonably practicable to carry it out in accordance with those regulations.

(3) Where any review is carried out under this section by an officer who is not present at the station where the arrested person is held –

(a) any obligation of that officer to make a record in connection with the carrying out of the review shall have effect as an obligation to cause another officer to make the record;

(b) any requirement for the record to be made in the presence of the arrested person shall apply to the making of that record by that other officer; and

(c) the requirements under section 40(12) and (13) above for –

(i) the arrested person, or

(ii) a solicitor representing him,

to be given any opportunity to make representations (whether in writing or orally) to that officer shall have effect as a requirement for that person, or such a solicitor, to be given an opportunity to make representations in a manner authorised by subsection (4) below.

(4) Representations are made in a manner authorised by this subsection –

(a) in a case where facilities exist for the immediate transmission of written representations to the officer carrying out the review, if they are made either –

(i) orally by telephone to that officer; or

(ii) in writing to that officer by means of those facilities;

and

(b) in any other case, if they are made orally by telephone to that officer.

(5) In this section 'video-conferencing facilities' has the same meaning as in section 45A below.

41 Limits on period of detention without charge

(1) Subject to the following provisions of this section and to sections 42 and 43 below, a person shall not be kept in police detention for more than 24 hours without being charged.

(2) The time from which the period of detention of a person is to be calculated (in this Act referred to as 'the relevant time') –

(a) in the case of a person to whom this paragraph applies, shall be –

(i) the time at which that person arrives at the relevant police station; or

(ii) the time 24 hours after the time of that person's arrest,

whichever is the earlier;

(b) in the case of a person arrested outside England and Wales, shall be –

(i) the time at which that person arrives at the first police station to which he is taken in the police area in England or Wales in which the offence for which he was arrested is being investigated; or

(ii) the time 24 hours after the time of that person's entry into England and Wales,

whichever is the earlier;

(c) in the case of a person who –

(i) attends voluntarily at a police station; or

(ii) accompanies a constable to a police station without having been arrested,

and is arrested at the police station, the time of his arrest;

(ca) in the case of a person who attends a police station to answer to bail granted under section 30A, the time when he arrives at the police station;

(d) in any other case, except where subsection (5) below applies, shall be the time at which the person arrested arrives at the first police station to which he is taken after his arrest.

(3) Subsection (2)(a) above applies to a person if –

(a) his arrest is sought in one police area in England and Wales;

(b) he is arrested in another police area; and

(c) he is not questioned in the area in which he is arrested in order to obtain evidence in relation to an offence for which he is arrested;

and in sub-paragraph (i) of that paragraph 'the relevant police station' means the first police station to which he is taken in the police area in which his arrest was sought.

(4) Subsection (2) above shall have effect in relation to a person arrested under section 31 above as if every reference in it to his arrest or his being arrested were a reference to his arrest or his being arrested for the offence for which he was originally arrested.

(5) If –

(a) a person is in police detention in a police area in England and Wales ('the first area'); and

(b) his arrest for an offence is sought in some other police area in England and Wales ('the second area'); and

(c) he is taken to the second area for the purposes of investigating that offence, without being questioned in the first area in order to obtain evidence in relation to it,

the relevant time shall be –

(i) the time 24 hours after he leaves the place where he is detained in the first area; or

(ii) the time at which he arrives at the first police station to which he is taken in the second area,

whichever is the earlier.

(6) When a person who is in police detention is removed to hospital because he is in need of medical treatment, any time during which he is being questioned in hospital or on the way there or back by a police officer for the purpose of obtaining evidence relating to an offence shall be included in any period which falls to be calculated for the purposes of this Part of this Act, but any other time while he is in hospital or on his way there or back shall not be so included.

(7) Subject to subsection (8) below, a person who at the expiry of 24 hours after the relevant time is in police detention and has not been charged shall be released at that time either on bail or without bail.

(8) Subsection (7) above does not apply to a person whose detention for more than 24 hours after the relevant time has been authorised or is otherwise permitted in accordance with section 42 or 43 below.

(9) A person released under subsection (7) above shall not be re-arrested without a warrant for the offence for which he was previously arrested unless new evidence justifying a further arrest has come to light since his release; but this subsection does not prevent an arrest under section 46A below.

42 Authorisation of continued detention

(1) Where a police officer of the rank of superintendent or above who is responsible for the police station at which a person is detained has reasonable grounds for believing that –

(a) the detention of that person without charge is necessary to secure or preserve evidence relating to an offence for which he is under arrest or to obtain such evidence by questioning him;

(b) an offence for which he is under arrest is an arrestable offence; and

(c) the investigation is being conducted diligently and expeditiously,

he may authorise the keeping of that person in police detention for a period expiring at or before 36 hours after the relevant time.

(2) Where an officer such as is mentioned in subsection (1) above has authorised the keeping of a person in police detention for a period expiring less than 36 hours after the relevant time, such an officer may authorise the keeping of that person in police detention for a further period expiring not more than 36 hours after that time if the conditions specified in subsection (1) above are still satisfied when he gives the authorisation.

(3) If it is proposed to transfer a person in police detention to another police area, the officer determining whether or not to authorise keeping him in detention under subsection (1) above shall have regard to the distance and the time the journey would take.

(4) No authorisation under subsection (1) above shall be given in respect of any person –

(a) more than 24 hours after the relevant time; or

(b) before the second review of his detention under section 40 above has been carried out.

(5) Where an officer authorises the keeping of a person in police detention under subsection (1) above, it shall be his duty –

(a) to inform that person of the grounds for his continued detention; and

(b) to record the grounds in that person's custody record.

(6) Before determining whether to authorise the keeping of a person in detention under subsection (1) or (2) above, an officer shall give –

(a) that person; or

(b) any solicitor representing him who is available at the time when it falls to the officer to determine whether to give the authorisation,

an opportunity to make representations to him about the detention.

(7) Subject to subsection (8) below, the person in detention or his solicitor may make representations under subsection (6) above either orally or in writing.

(8) The officer to whom it falls to determine whether to give the authorisation may refuse to hear oral representations from the person in detention if he considers that he is unfit to make such representations by reason of his condition or behaviour.

(9) Where –

(a) an officer authorises the keeping of a person in detention under subsection (1) above; and

(b) at the time of the authorisation he has not yet exercised a right conferred on him by section 56 or 58 below,

the officer –

(i) shall inform him of that right;

(ii) shall decide whether he should be permitted to exercise it;

(iii) shall record the decision in his custody record; and

(iv) if the decision is to refuse to permit the exercise of the right, shall also record the grounds for the decision in that record.

(10) Where an officer has authorised the keeping of a person who has not been charged in detention under subsection (1) or (2) above, he shall be released from detention, either on bail or without bail, not later than 36 hours after the relevant time, unless –

(a) he has been charged with an offence; or

(b) his continued detention is authorised or otherwise permitted in accordance with section 43 below.

(11) A person released under subsection (10) above shall not be re-arrested without a warrant for the offence for which he was previously arrested unless new evidence justifying a further arrest has come to light since his release; but this subsection does not prevent an arrest under section 46A below.

43 Warrants of further detention

(1) Where, on an application on oath made by a constable and supported by an information, a magistrates' court is satisfied that there are reasonable grounds for believing that the further detention of the person to whom the application relates is justified, it may issue a warrant of further detention authorising the keeping of that person in police detention.

(2) A court may not hear an application for a warrant of further detention unless the person to whom the application relates –

(a) has been furnished with a copy of the information; and

(b) has been brought before the court for the hearing.

(3) The person to whom the application relates shall be entitled to be legally represented at the hearing and, if he is not so represented but wishes to be so represented –

(a) the court shall adjourn the hearing to enable him to obtain representation; and

(b) he may be kept in police detention during the adjournment.

(4) A person's further detention is only justified for the purposes of this section or section 44 below if –

(a) his detention without charge is necessary to secure or preserve evidence relating to an offence for which he is under arrest or to obtain such evidence by questioning him;

(b) an offence for which he is under arrest is a serious arrestable offence; and

(c) the investigation is being conducted diligently and expeditiously.

(5) Subject to subsection (7) below, an application for a warrant of further detention may be made –

(a) at any time before the expiry of 36 hours after the relevant time; or

(b) in a case where –

(i) it is not practicable for the magistrates' court to which the application will be made to sit at the expiry of 36 hours after the relevant time; but

(ii) the court will sit during the six hours following the end of that period,

at any time before the expiry of the said six hours.

(6) In a case to which subsection (5)(b) above applies –

(a) the person to whom the application relates may be kept in police detention until the application is heard; and

(b) the custody officer shall make a note in that person's custody record –

(i) of the fact that he was kept in police detention for more than 36 hours after the relevant time; and

(ii) of the reason why he was so kept.

(7) If –

(a) an application for a warrant of further detention is made after the expiry of 36 hours after the relevant time; and

(b) it appears to the magistrates' court that it would have been reasonable for the police to make it before the expiry of that period,

the court shall dismiss the application.

(8) Where on an application such as is mentioned in subsection (1) above a magistrates' court is not satisfied that there are reasonable grounds for believing that the further detention of the person to whom the application relates is justified, it shall be its duty –

(a) to refuse the application; or

(b) to adjourn the hearing of it until a time not later than 36 hours after the relevant time.

(9) The person to whom the application relates may be kept in police detention during the adjournment.

(10) A warrant of further detention shall –

(a) state the time at which it is issued;

(b) authorise the keeping in police detention of the person to whom it relates for the period stated in it.

(11) Subject to subsection (12) below, the period stated in a warrant of further detention shall be such period as the magistrates' court thinks fit, having regard to the evidence before it.

(12) The period shall not be longer than 36 hours.

(13) If it is proposed to transfer a person in police detention to a police area other than that in which he is detained when the application for a warrant of further detention is made, the court hearing the application shall have regard to the distance and the time the journey would take.

(14) Any information submitted in support of an application under this section shall state –

(a) the nature of the offence for which the person to whom the application relates has been arrested;

(b) the general nature of the evidence on which that person was arrested;

(c) what inquiries relating to the offence have been made by the police and what further inquiries are proposed by them;

(d) the reasons for believing the continued detention of that person to be necessary for the purposes of such further inquiries.

(15) Where an application under this section is refused, the person to whom the application relates shall forthwith be charged or, subject to subsection (16) below, released, either on bail or without bail.

(16) A person need not be released under subsection (15) above –

(a) before the expiry of 24 hours after the relevant time; or

(b) before the expiry of any longer period for which his continued detention is or has been authorised under section 42 above.

(17) Where an application under this section is refused, no further application shall be made under this section in respect of the person to whom the refusal relates, unless supported by evidence which has come to light since the refusal.

(18) Where a warrant of further detention is issued, the person to whom it relates shall be released from police detention, either on bail or without bail, upon or before the expiry of the warrant unless he is charged.

(19) A person released under subsection (18) above shall not be re-arrested without a warrant for the offence for which he was previously arrested unless new evidence justifying a further arrest has come to light since his release; but this subsection does not prevent an arrest under section 46A below.

44 Extension of warrants of further detention

(1) On an application on oath made by a constable and supported by an information a magistrates' court may extend a warrant of further detention issued under section 43 above if it is satisfied that there are reasonable grounds for believing that the further detention of the person to whom the application relates is justified.

(2) Subject to subsection (3) below, the period for which a warrant of further detention may be extended shall be such period as the court thinks fit, having regard to the evidence before it.

(3) The period shall not –

(a) be longer than 36 hours; or

(b) end later than 96 hours after the relevant time.

(4) Where a warrant of further detention has been extended under subsection (1) above, or further extended under this subsection, for a period ending before 96 hours after the relevant time, on an application such as is mentioned in that subsection a magistrates' court may further extend the warrant if it is satisfied as there mentioned; and subsections (2) and (3) above apply to such further extensions as they apply to extensions under subsection (1) above.

(5) A warrant of further detention shall, if extended or further extended under this section, be endorsed with a note of the period of the extension.

(6) Subsections (2), (3) and (14) of section 43 above shall apply to an application made under this section as they apply to an application made under that section.

(7) Where an application under this section is refused, the person to whom the application relates shall forthwith be charged or, subject to subsection (8) below, released, either on bail or without bail.

(8) A person need not be released under subsection (7) above before the expiry of any period for which a warrant of further detention issued in relation to him has been extended or further extended on an earlier application made under this section.

45 Detention before charge – supplementary

(1) In sections 43 and 44 of this Act 'magistrates' court' means a court consisting of two or more justices of the peace sitting otherwise than in open court.

(2) Any reference in this Part of this Act to a period of time or a time of day is to be treated as approximate only.

45A Use of video-conferencing facilities for decisions about detention

(1) Subject to the following provisions of this section, the Secretary of State may by regulations provide that, in the case of an arrested person who is held in a police station, some or all of the functions mentioned in subsection (2) may be performed (notwithstanding anything in the preceding provisions of this Part) by an officer who –

(a) is not present in that police station; but

(b) has access to the use of video-conferencing facilities that enable him to communicate with persons in that station.

(2) Those functions are –

(a) the functions in relation to an arrested person taken to, or answering to bail at, a police station that is not a designated police station which, in the case of an arrested person taken to a station that is a designated police station, are functions of a custody officer under section 37, 38 or 40 above; and

(b) the function of carrying out a review under section 40(1)(b) above (review, by an officer of at least the rank of inspector, of the detention of person arrested but not charged).

(3) Regulations under this section shall specify the use to be made in the performance of the functions mentioned in subsection (2) above of the facilities mentioned in subsection (1) above.

(4) Regulations under this section shall not authorise the performance of any of the functions mentioned in subsection (2)(a) above by such an officer as is mentioned in subsection (1) above unless he is a custody officer for a designated police station.

(5) Where any functions mentioned in subsection (2) above are performed in a manner authorised by regulations under this section –

(a) any obligation of the officer performing those functions to make a record in connection with the performance of those functions shall have effect as an obligation to cause another officer to make the record; and

(b) any requirement for the record to be made in the presence of the arrested person shall apply to the making of that record by that other officer.

(6) Where the functions mentioned in subsection (2)(b) are performed in a manner authorised by regulations under this section, the requirements under section 40(12) and (13) above for –

(a) the arrested person, or

(b) a solicitor representing him,

to be given any opportunity to make representations (whether in writing or orally) to the person performing those functions shall have effect as a requirement for that person, or such a solicitor, to be given an opportunity to make representations in a manner authorised by subsection (7) below.

(7) Representations are made in a manner authorised by this subsection –

(a) in a case where facilities exist for the immediate transmission of written representations to the officer performing the functions, if they are made either –

(i) orally to that officer by means of the video-conferencing facilities used by him for performing those functions; or

(ii) in writing to that officer by means of the facilities available for the immediate transmission of the representations;

and

(b) in any other case if they are made orally to that officer by means of the video-conferencing facilities used by him for performing the functions.

(8) Regulations under this section may make different provision for different cases and may be made so as to have effect in relation only to the police stations specified or described in the regulations.

(9) Regulations under this section shall be made by statutory instrument and shall be subject to annulment in pursuance of a resolution of either House of Parliament.

(10) Any reference in this section to video-conferencing facilities, in relation to any functions, is a reference to any facilities (whether a live television link or other facilities) by means of which the functions may be performed with the officer performing them, the person in relation to whom they are performed and any legal representative of that person all able to both see and to hear each other.

46 Detention after charge

(1) Where a person –

(a) is charged with an offence; and

(b) after being charged –

(i) is kept in police detention; or

(ii) is detained by a local authority in pursuance of arrangements made under section 38(6) above,

he shall be brought before a magistrates' court in accordance with the provisions of this section.

(2) If he is to be brought before a magistrates' court for the petty sessions area in which the police station at which he was charged is situated, he shall be brought before such a court as soon as is practicable and in any event not later than the first sitting after he is charged with the offence.

(3) If no magistrates' court for that area is due to sit either on the day on which he is charged or on the next day, the custody officer for the police station at which he was charged shall inform the justices' chief executive for the area that there is a person in the area to whom subsection (2) above applies.

(4) If the person charged is to be brought before a magistrates' court for a petty sessions area other than that in which the police station at which he was charged is situated, he shall be removed to that area as soon as is practicable and brought before such a court as soon as is practicable after his arrival in the area and in any event not later than the first sitting of a magistrates' court for that area after his arrival in the area.

(5) If no magistrates' court for that area is due to sit either on the day on which he arrives in the area or on the next day –

(a) he shall be taken to a police station in the area; and

(b) the custody officer at that station shall inform the justices' chief executive for the area that there is a person in the area to whom subsection (4) applies.

(6) Subject to subsection (8) below, where the justices' chief executive for a petty sessions area has been informed –

(a) under subsection (3) above that there is a person in the area to whom subsection (2) above applies; or

(b) under subsection (5) above that there is a person in the area to whom subsection (4) above applies,

the justices' chief executive shall arrange for a magistrates' court to sit not later than the day next following the relevant day.

(7) In this section 'the relevant day' –

(a) in relation to a person who is to be brought before a magistrates' court for the petty sessions area in which the police station at which he was charged is situated, means the day on which he was charged; and

(b) in relation to a person who is to be brought before a magistrates' court for any other petty sessions area, means the day on which he arrives in the area.

(8) Where the day next following the relevant day is Christmas Day, Good Friday or a Sunday, the duty of the justices' chief executive under subsection (6) above is a

duty to arrange for a magistrates' court to sit not later than the first day after the relevant day which is not one of those days.

(9) Nothing in this section requires a person who is in hospital to be brought before a court if he is not well enough.

46A Power of arrest for failure to answer to police bail

(1) A constable may arrest without a warrant any person who, having been released on bail under this Part of this Act subject to a duty to attend at a police station, fails to attend at that police station at the time appointed for him to do so.

(1A) A person who has been released on bail under section 37(7)(a) or 37C(2)(b) above may be arrested without warrant by a constable if the constable has reasonable grounds for suspecting that the person has broken any of the conditions of bail.

(2) A person who is arrested under this section shall be taken to the police station appointed as the place at which he is to surrender to custody as soon as practicable after the arrest.

(3) For the purposes of –

(a) section 30 above (subject to the obligation in subsection (2) above), and

(b) section 31 above,

an arrest under this section shall be treated as an arrest for an offence.

47 Bail after arrest

(1) Subject to the following provisions of this section, a release on bail of a person under this Part of this Act shall be a release on bail granted in accordance with sections 3, 3A, 5 and 5A of the Bail Act 1976 as they apply to bail granted by a constable.

(1A) The normal powers to impose conditions of bail shall be available to him where a custody officer releases a person on bail under section 37(7)(a) above or section 38(1) above (including that subsection as applied by section 40(10) above) but not in any other cases.

In this subsection, 'the normal powers to impose conditions of bail' has the meaning given in section 3(6) of the Bail Act 1976.

(1B) No application may be made under section 5B of the Bail Act 1976 if a person is released on bail under section 37(7)(a) or 37C(2)(b) above.

(1C) Subsections (1D) to (1F) below apply where a person released on bail under section 37(7)(a) or 37C(2)(b) above is on bail subject to conditions.

(1D) The person shall not be entitled to make an application under section 43B of the Magistrates' Courts Act 1980.

(1E) A magistrates' court may, on an application by or on behalf of the person, vary the conditions of bail; and in this subsection 'vary' has the same meaning as in the Bail Act 1976.

(1F) Where a magistrates' court varies the conditions of bail under subsection (1E) above, that bail shall not lapse but shall continue subject to the conditions as so varied.

(2) Nothing in the Bail Act 1976 shall prevent the re-arrest without warrant of a person released on bail subject to a duty to attend at a police station if new evidence justifying a further arrest has come to light since his release.

(3) Subject to subsections (3A) and (4) below, in this Part of this Act references to 'bail' are references to bail subject to a duty –

(a) to appear before a magistrates' court at such time and such place; or

(b) to attend at such police station at such time,

as the custody officer may appoint.

(3A) Where a custody officer grants bail to a person subject to a duty to appear before a magistrates' court, he shall appoint for the appearance –

(a) a date which is not later than the first sitting of the court after the person is charged with the offence; or

(b) where he is informed by the justices' chief executive for the relevant petty sessions area that the appearance cannot be accommodated until a later date, that later date.

(4) Where a custody officer has granted bail to a person subject to a duty to appear at a police station, the custody officer may give notice in writing to that person that his attendance at the police station is not required.

(6) Where a person who has been granted bail under this Part and either has attended at the police station in accordance with the grant of bail or has been arrested under section 46A above is detained at a police station, any time during which he was in police detention prior to being granted bail shall be included as part of any period which falls to be calculated under this Part of this Act.

(7) Where a person who was released on bail under this Part subject to a duty to attend at a police station is re-arrested, the provisions of this Part of this Act shall apply to him as they apply to a person arrested for the first time, but this subsection does not apply to a person who is arrested under section 46A above or has attended a police station in accordance with the grant of bail (and who accordingly is deemed by section 34(7) above to have been arrested for an offence). …

47A Early administrative hearings conducted by justices' clerks

Where a person has been charged with an offence at a police station, any requirement imposed under this Part for the person to appear or be brought before a magistrates' court shall be taken to be satisfied if the person appears or is brought before the clerk to the justices for a petty sessions area in order for the clerk to conduct a hearing under section 50 of the Crime and Disorder Act 1998 (early administrative hearings).

51 Savings

Nothing in this Part of this Act shall affect –

(a) the powers conferred on immigration officers by section 4 of and Schedule 2 to the Immigration Act 1971 (administrative provisions as to control on entry, etc);

(b) the powers conferred by virtue of section 41 of, or Schedule 7 to, the Terrorism Act 2000 (powers of arrest and detention);

(c) any duty of a police officer under –

(i) sections 129, 190 or 202 of the Army Act 1955 (duties of governors of prisons and others to receive prisoners, deserters, absentees and persons under escort);

(ii) sections 129, 190 or 202 of the Air Force Act 1955 (duties of governors of prisons and others to receive prisoners, deserters, absentees and persons under escort);

(iii) section 107 of the Naval Discipline Act 1957 (duties of governors of civil prisons, etc); or

(iv) paragraph 5 of Schedule 5 to the Reserve Forces Act 1980 (duties of governors of civil prisons); or

(d) any right of a person in police detention to apply for a writ of habeas corpus or other prerogative remedy.

PART V

QUESTIONING AND TREATMENT OF PERSONS BY POLICE

53 Abolition of certain powers of constables to search persons

(1) Subject to subsection (2) below, there shall cease to have effect any Act (including a local Act) passed before this Act in so far as it authorises –

(a) any search by a constable of a person in police detention at a police station; or

(b) an intimate search of a person by a constable;

and any rule of common law which authorises a search such as is mentioned in paragraph (a) or (b) above is abolished.

54 Searches of detained persons

(1) The custody officer at a police station shall ascertain everything which a person has with him when he is –

(a) brought to the station after being arrested elsewhere or after being committed to custody by an order or sentence of a court; or

(b) arrested at the station or detained there, as a person falling within section 34(7), under section 37 above.

(2) The custody officer may record or cause to be recorded all or any of the things which he ascertains under subsection (1).

(2A) In the case of an arrested person, any such record may be made as part of his custody record.

(3) Subject to subsection (4) below, a custody officer may seize and retain any such thing or cause any such thing to be seized and retained.

(4) Clothes and personal effects may only be seized if the custody officer –

(a) believes that the person from whom they are seized may use them –

(i) to cause physical injury to himself or any other person;

(ii) to damage property;

(iii) to interfere with evidence; or

(iv) to assist him to escape; or

(b) has reasonable grounds for believing that they may be evidence relating to an offence.

(5) Where anything is seized, the person from whom it is seized shall be told the reason for the seizure unless he is –

(a) violent or likely to become violent; or

(b) incapable of understanding what is said to him.

(6) Subject to subsection (7) below, a person may be searched if the custody officer considers it necessary to enable him to carry out his duty under subsection (1) above and to the extent that the custody officer considers necessary for that purpose.

(6A) A person who is in custody at a police station or is in police detention otherwise than at a police station may at any time be searched in order to ascertain whether he has with him anything which he could use for the purposes specified in subsection (4)(a) above.

(6B) Subject to subsection (6C) below, a constable may seize and retain, or cause to be seized and retained, anything found on such a search.

(6C) A constable may only seize clothes and personal effects in the circumstances specified in subsection (4) above.

(7) An intimate search may not be conducted under this section.

(8) A search under this section shall be carried out by a constable.

(9) The constable carrying out a search shall be of the same sex as the person searched.

54A Searches and examination to ascertain identity

(1) If an officer of at least the rank of inspector authorises it, a person who is detained in a police station may be searched or examined, or both –

(a) for the purpose of ascertaining whether he has any mark that would tend to identify him as a person involved in the commission of an offence; or

(b) for the purpose of facilitating the ascertainment of his identity.

(2) An officer may only give an authorisation under subsection (1) for the purpose mentioned in paragraph (a) of that subsection if –

(a) the appropriate consent to a search or examination that would reveal whether the mark in question exists has been withheld; or

(b) it is not practicable to obtain such consent.

(3) An officer may only give an authorisation under subsection (1) in a case in which subsection (2) does not apply if –

(a) the person in question has refused to identify himself; or

(b) the officer has reasonable grounds for suspecting that that person is not who he claims to be.

(4) An officer may give an authorisation under subsection (1) orally or in writing but, if he gives it orally, he shall confirm it in writing as soon as is practicable.

(5) Any identifying mark found on a search or examination under this section may be photographed –

(a) with the appropriate consent; or

(b) if the appropriate consent is withheld or it is not practicable to obtain it, without it.

(6) Where a search or examination may be carried out under this section, or a photograph may be taken under this section, the only persons entitled to carry out the search or examination, or to take the photograph, are constables.

(7) A person may not under this section carry out a search or examination of a person of the opposite sex or take a photograph of any part of the body of a person of the opposite sex.

(8) An intimate search may not be carried out under this section.

(9) A photograph taken under this section –

(a) may be used by, or disclosed to, any person for any purpose related to the prevention or detection of crime, the investigation of an offence or the conduct of a prosecution; and

(b) after being so used or disclosed, may be retained but may not be used or disclosed except for a purpose so related.

(10) In subsection –

(a) the reference to crime includes a reference to any conduct which –

(i) constitutes one or more criminal offences (whether under the law of a part of the United Kingdom or of a country or territory outside the United Kingdom); or

(ii) is, or corresponds to, any conduct which, if it all took place in any one part of the United Kingdom, would constitute one or more criminal offences;

and

(b) the references to an investigation and to a prosecution include references, respectively, to any investigation outside the United Kingdom of any crime or suspected crime and to a prosecution brought in respect of any crime in a country or territory outside the United Kingdom.

(11) In this section –

(a) references to ascertaining a person's identity include references to showing that he is not a particular person; and

(b) references to taking a photograph include references to using any process by means of which a visual image may be produced, and references to photographing a person shall be construed accordingly.

(12) In this section 'mark' includes features and injuries; and a mark is an identifying mark for the purposes of this section if its existence in any person's case facilitates the ascertainment of his identity or his identification as a person involved in the commission of an offence.

(13) Nothing in this section applies to a person arrested under an extradition arrest power.

55 Intimate searches

(1) Subject to the following provisions of this section, if an officer of at least the rank of inspector has reasonable grounds for believing –

(a) that a person who has been arrested and is in police detention may have concealed on him anything which –

(i) he could use to cause physical injury to himself or others; and

(ii) he might so use while he is in police detention or in the custody of a court; or

(b) that such a person –

(i) may have a Class A drug concealed on him; and

(ii) was in possession of it with the appropriate criminal intent before his arrest,

he may authorise an intimate search of that person.

(2) An officer may not authorise an intimate search of a person for anything unless he has reasonable grounds for believing that it cannot be found without his being intimately searched.

(3) An officer may give an authorisation under subsection (1) above orally or in writing but, if he gives it orally, he shall confirm it in writing as soon as is practicable.

(4) An intimate search which is only a drug offence search shall be by way of examination by a suitably qualified person.

(5) Except as provided by subsection (4) above, an intimate search shall be by way of examination by a suitably qualified person unless an officer of at least the rank of inspector considers that this is not practicable.

(6) An intimate search which is not carried out as mentioned in subsection (5) above shall be carried out by a constable.

(7) A constable may not carry out an intimate search of a person of the opposite sex.

(8) No intimate search may be carried out except –

(a) at a police station;

(b) at a hospital;

(c) at a registered medical practitioner's surgery; or

(d) at some other place used for medical purposes.

(9) An intimate search which is only a drug offence search may not be carried out at a police station.

(10) If an intimate search of a person is carried out, the custody record relating to him shall state –

(a) which parts of his body were searched; and

(b) why they were searched.

(11) The information required to be recorded by subsection (10) above shall be recorded as soon as practicable after the completion of the search.

(12) The custody officer at a police station may seize and retain anything which is found on an intimate search of a person, or cause any such thing to be seized and retained –

(a) if he believes that the person from whom it is seized may use it –

(i) to cause physical injury to himself or any other person;

(ii) to damage property;

(iii) to interfere with evidence; or

(iv) to assist him to escape; or

(b) if he has reasonable grounds for believing that it may be evidence relating to an offence.

(13) Where anything is seized under this section, the person from whom it is seized shall be told the reason for the seizure unless he is –

(a) violent or likely to become violent; or

(b) incapable of understanding what is said to him ...

(17) In this section –

'the appropriate criminal intent' means an intent to commit an offence under –

(a) section 5(3) of the Misuse of Drugs Act 1971 (possession of controlled drug with intent to supply to another); or

(b) section 68(2) of the Customs and Excise Management Act 1979 (exportation etc with intent to evade a prohibition of restriction);

'Class A drug' has the meaning assigned to it by section 2(1)(b) of the Misuse of Drugs Act 1971;

'drug offence search' means an intimate search for a Class A drug which an officer has authorised by virtue of subsection (1)(b) above; and

'suitably qualified person' means –

(a) a registered medical practitioner; or

(b) a registered nurse.

56 Right to have someone informed when arrested

(1) Where a person has been arrested and is being held in custody in a police station or other premises, he shall be entitled, if he so requests, to have one friend or relative or other person who is known to him or who is likely to take an interest in his welfare told, as soon as is practicable except to the extent that delay is permitted by this section, that he has been arrested and is being detained there.

(2) Delay is only permitted –

(a) in the case of a person who is in police detention for a serious arrestable offence; and

(b) if an officer of at least the rank of inspector authorises it.

(3) In any case the person in custody must be permitted to exercise the right conferred by subsection (1) above within 36 hours from the relevant time, as defined in section 41(2) above.

(4) An officer may give an authorisation under subsection (2) above orally or in writing but, if he gives it orally, he shall confirm it in writing as soon as is practicable.

(5) Subject to subsection (5A) below, an officer may only authorise delay where he has reasonable grounds for believing that telling the named person of the arrest –

(a) will lead to interference with or harm to evidence connected with a serious arrestable offence or interference with or physical injury to other persons; or

(b) will lead to the alerting of other persons suspected of having committed such an offence but not yet arrested for it; or

(c) will hinder the recovery of any property obtained as a result of such an offence.

(5A) An officer may also authorise delay where he has reasonable grounds for believing that –

(a) the person detained for the serious arrestable offence has benefited from his criminal conduct, and

(b) the recovery of the value of the property constituting the benefit will be hindered by telling the named person of the arrest.

(5B) For the purposes of subsection (5A) above the question whether a person has benefited from his criminal conduct is to be deciced with Part 2 of the Proceeds of Crime Act 2002

(6) If a delay is authorised –

(a) the detained person shall be told the reason for it; and

(b) the reason shall be noted on his custody record.

(7) The duties imposed by subsection (6) above shall be performed as soon as is practicable.

(8) The rights conferred by this section on a person detained at a police station or other premises are exercisable whenever he is transferred from one place to another; and this section applies to each subsequent occasion on which they are exercisable as it applies to the first such occasion.

(9) There may be no further delay in permitting the exercise of the right conferred by subsection (1) above once the reason for authorising delay ceases to subsist.

(10) Nothing in this section applies to a person arrested or detained under the terrorism provisions.

58 Access to legal advice

(1) A person arrested and held in custody in a police station or other premises shall be entitled, if he so requests, to consult a solicitor privately at any time.

(2) Subject to subsection (3) below, a request under subsection (1) above and the time at which it was made shall be recorded in the custody record.

(3) Such a request need not be recorded in the custody record of a person who makes it at a time while he is at a court after being charged with an offence.

(4) If a person makes such a request, he must be permitted to consult a solicitor as soon as is practicable except to the extent that delay is permitted by this section.

(5) In any case he must be permitted to consult a solicitor within 36 hours from the relevant time, as defined in section 41(2) above.

(6) Delay in compliance with a request is only permitted –

(a) in the case of a person who is in police detention for a serious arrestable offence; and

(b) if an officer of at least the rank of superintendent authorises it.

(7) An officer may give an authorisation under subsection (6) above orally or in

writing but, if he gives it orally, he shall confirm it in writing as soon as is practicable.

(8) Subject to subsection (8A) below, an officer may only authorise delay where he has reasonable grounds for believing that the exercise of the right conferred by subsection (1) above at the time when the person detained desires to exercise it –

(a) will lead to interference with or harm to evidence connected with a serious arrestable offence or interference with or physical injury to other persons; or

(b) will lead to the alerting of other persons suspected of having committed such an offence but not yet arrested for it; or

(c) will hinder the recovery of any property obtained as a result of such an offence.

(8A) An officer may also authorise delay where he has reasonable grounds for believing that –

(a) the person detained for the serious arrestable offence has benefited from his criminal conduct, and

(b) the recovery of the value of the property constituting the benefit will be hindered by the exercise of the right conferred by subsection (1) above.

(8B) For the purposes of subsection (8A) above the question whether a person has benefited from his criminal conduct is to be decided in accordance with Part 2 of the Proceeds of Crime Act 2002.

(9) If delay is authorised –

(a) the detained person shall be told the reason for it; and

(b) the reason shall be noted on his custody record.

(10) The duties imposed by subsection (9) above shall be performed as soon as is practicable.

(11) There may be no further delay in permitting the exercise of the right conferred by subsection (1) above once the reason for authorising delay ceases to subsist.

(12) Nothing in this section applies to a person arrested or detained under the terrorism provisions.

61 Fingerprinting

(1) Except as provided by this section no person's fingerprints may be taken without the appropriate consent.

(2) Consent to the taking of a person's fingerprints must be in writing if it is given at a time when he is at a police station.

(3) The fingerprints of a person detained at a police station may be taken without the appropriate consent if –

(a) he is detained in consequence of his arrest for a recordable offence; and

(b) he has not had his fingerprints taken in the course of the investigation of the offence by the police.

(3A) Where a person mentioned in paragraph (a) of subsection (3) or (4) has already had his fingerprints taken in the course of the investigation of the offence by the police, that fact shall be disregarded for the purposes of that subsection if –

(a) the fingerprints taken on the previous occasion do not constitute a complete set of his fingerprints; or

(b) some or all of the fingerprints taken on the previous occasion are not of sufficient quality to allow satisfactory analysis, comparison or matching (whether in the case in question or generally).

(4) The fingerprints of a person detained at a police station may be taken without the appropriate consent if –

(a) he has been charged with a recordable offence or informed that he will be reported for such an offence; and

(b) he has not had his fingerprints taken in the course of the investigation of the offence by the police.

(4A) The fingerprints of a person who has answered to bail at a court or police station may be taken without the appropriate consent at the court or station if –

(a) the court, or

(b) an officer of at least the rank of inspector,

authorises them to be taken.

(4B) A court of officer may only give an authorisation under subsection (4A) if –

(a) the person who has answered to bail has answered to it for a person whose fingerprints were taken on a previous occasion and there are reasonable grounds for believing that he is not the same person; or

(b) the person who has answered to bail claims to be a different person from a person whose fingerprints were taken on a previous occasion.

(5) An officer may give an authorisation under subsection (4A) above orally or in writing but, if he gives it orally, he shall confirm it in writing as soon as is practicable.

(6) Any person's fingerprints may be taken without the appropriate consent if –

(a) he has been convicted of a recordable offence;

(b) he has been given a caution in respect of a recordable offence which, at the time of the caution, he has admitted; or

(c) he has been warned or reprimanded under section 65 of the Crime and Disorder Act 1998 (c 37) for a recordable offence.

(7) In a case where by virtue of subsection (3), (4) or (6) above a person's fingerprints are taken without the appropriate consent –

(a) he shall be told the reason before his fingerprints are taken; and

(b) the reason shall be recorded as soon as is practicable after the fingerprints are taken.

(7A) If a person's fingerprints are taken at a police station, whether with or without the appropriate consent –

(a) before the fingerprints are taken, an officer shall inform him that they may be the subject of a speculative search; and

(b) the fact that the person has been informed of this possibility shall be recorded as soon as is practicable after the fingerprints have been taken.

(8) If he is detained at a police station when the fingerprints are taken, the reason for taking them and, in the case falling within subsection (7A) above, the fact referred to in paragraph (b) of that subsection shall be recorded on his custody record.

(8A) Where a person's fingerprints are taken electronically, they must be taken only in such a manner, and using such devices, as the Secretary of State has approved for the purposes of electronic fingerprinting.

(8B) The power to take the fingerprints of a person detained at a police station without the appopriate consent shall be exercisable by any constable.

(9) Nothing in this section –

(a) affects any power conferred by paragraph 18(2) of Schedule 2 to the Immigration Act 1971, section 141 of the Immigration and Asylum Act 1999 or regulations made under section 144 of that Act; or

(b) applies to a person arrested or detained under the terrorism provisions.

(10) Nothing in this section applies to a person arrested under an extradition arrest power.

62 Intimate samples

(1) Subject to section 63B below an intimate sample may be taken from a person in police detention only –

(a) if a police officer of at least the rank of inspector authorises it to be taken; and

(b) if the appropriate consent is given.

(1A) An intimate sample may be taken from a person who is not in police detention but from whom, in the course of the investigation of an offence, two or more non-intimate samples suitable for the means of analysis have been taken which have proved insufficient –

(a) if a police officer of at least the rank of inspector authorises it to be taken; and

(b) if the appropriate consent is given.

(2) An officer may only give an authorisation under subsection (1) or (1A) above if he has reasonable grounds –

(a) for suspecting the involvement of the person from whom the sample is to be taken in a recordable offence; and

(b) for believing that the sample will tend to confirm or disprove his involvement.

(3) An officer may give an authorisation under subsection (1) or (1A) above orally or in writing but, if he gives it orally, he shall confirm it in writing as soon as is practicable.

(4) The appropriate consent must be given in writing.

(5) Where –

(a) an authorisation has been given; and

(b) it is proposed that an intimate sample shall be taken in pursuance of the authorisation,

an officer shall inform the person from whom the sample is to be taken –

(i) of the giving of the authorisation; and

(ii) of the grounds for giving it.

(6) The duty imposed by subsection (5)(ii) above includes a duty to state the nature of the offence in which it is suspected that the person from whom the sample is to be taken has been involved.

(7) If an intimate sample is taken from a person –

(a) the authorisation by virtue of which it was taken;

(b) the grounds for giving the authorisation; and

(c) the fact that the appropriate consent was given,

shall be recorded as soon as is practicable after the sample is taken.

(7A) If an intimate sample is taken from a person at a police station –

(a) before the sample is taken, an officer shall inform him that it may be the subject of a speculative search; and

(b) the fact that the person has been informed of this possibility shall be recorded as soon as practicable after the sample has been taken.

(8) If an intimate sample is taken from a person detained at a police station, the matters required to be recorded by subsection (7) or (7A) above shall be recorded in his custody record.

(9) In the case of an intimate sample which is a dental impression, the sample may be taken from a person only by a registered dentist.

(9A) In the case of any other form of intimate sample, except in the case of a sample of urine, the sample may be taken from a person only by –

(a) a registered medical practitioner; or

(b) a registered health care professional.

(10) Where the appropriate consent to the taking of an intimate sample from a

person was refused without good cause, in any proceedings against that person for an offence –

(a) the court, in determining –

(i) whether to grant an application for dismissal made by that person under section 6 of the Magistrates' Courts Act 1980 (application for dismissal of charge in course of proceedings with a view to transfer for trial); or

(ii) whether there is a case to answer; and

(aa) a judge, in deciding whether to grant an application made by the accused under –

(i) section 6 of the Criminal Justice Act 1987 (application for dismissal of charge of serious fraud in respect of which notice of transfer has been given under section 4 of that Act);

or

(ii) paragraph 5 of Schedule 6 to the Criminal Justice Act 1991 (application for dismissal of charge of violent or sexual offence involving child in respect of which notice of transfer has been given under section 53 of that Act); and

(b) the court or jury, in determining whether that person is guilty of the offence charged,

may draw such inferences from the refusal as appear proper.

(11) Nothing in this section applies to the taking of a specimen for the purposes of any of the provisions of sections 4 to 11 of the Road Traffic Act 1988 or of sections 26 to 38 of the Transport and Works Act 1992.

(12) Nothing in this section applies to a person arrested or detained under the terrorism provisions; and subsection (1A) shall not apply where the non-intimate samples mentioned in that subsection were taken under paragraph 10 of Schedule 8 to the Terrorism Act 2000.

63 Other samples

(1) Except as provided by this section, a non-intimate sample may not be taken from a person without the appropriate consent.

(2) Consent to the taking of a non-intimate sample must be given in writing.

(2A) A non-intimate sample may be taken from a person without the appropriate consent if two conditions are satisfied.

(2B) The first is that the person is in police detention in consequence of his arrest for a recordable offence.

(2C) The second is that –

(a) he has not had a non-intimate sample of the same type and from the same part of the body taken in the course of the investigation of the offence by the police, or

(b) he has had such a sample taken but it proved insufficient.

(3) A non-intimate sample may be taken from a person without the appropriate consent if –

(a) he is being held in custody by the police on the authority of a court; and

(b) an officer of at least the rank of inspector authorises it to be taken without the appropriate consent.

(3A) A non-intimate sample may be taken from a person (whether or not he is in police detention or held in custody by the police on the authority of a court) without the appropriate consent if –

(a) he has been charged with a recordable offence or informed that he will be reported for such an offence; and

(b) either he has not had a non-intimate sample taken from him in the course of the investigation of the offence by the police or he has had a non-intimate sample taken from him but either it was not suitable for the same means of analysis or, though so suitable, the sample proved insufficient.

(3B) A non-intimate sample may be taken from a person without the appropriate consent if he has been convicted of a recordable offence.

(3C) A non-intimate sample may also be taken from a person without the appropriate consent if he is a person to whom section 2 of the Criminal Evidence (Amendment) Act 1997 applies (persons detained following acquittal on grounds of insanity or finding of unfitness to plead).

(4) An officer may only give an authorisation under subsection (3) above if he has reasonable grounds –

(a) for suspecting the involvement of the person from whom the sample is to be taken in a recordable offence; and

(b) for believing that the sample will tend to confirm or disprove his involvement.

(5) An officer may give an authorisation under subsection (3) above orally or in writing but, if he gives it orally, he shall confirm it in writing as soon as is practicable.

(5A) An officer shall not give an authorisation under subsection (3) above for the taking from any person of a non-intimate sample consisting of a skin impression if –

(a) a skin impression of the same part of the body has already been taken from that person in the course of the investigation of the offence; and

(b) the impression previously taken is not one that has proved insufficient.

(6) Where –

(a) an authorisation has been given; and

(b) it is proposed that a non-intimate sample shall be taken in pursuance of the authorisation, an officer shall inform the person from whom the sample is to be taken –

(i) of the giving of the authorisation; and

(ii) of the grounds for giving it.

(7) The duty imposed by subsection (6)(ii) above includes a duty to state the nature of the offence in which it is suspected that the person from whom the sample is to be taken has been involved.

(8) If a non-intimate sample is taken from a person by virtue of subsection (3) above –

(a) the authorisation by virtue of which it was taken; and

(b) the grounds for giving the authorisation,

shall be recorded as soon as is practicable after the sample is taken.

(8A) In a case where by virtue of subsection (2A), (3A), (3B) or (3C) above a sample is taken from a person without the appropriate consent –

(a) he shall be told the reason before the sample is taken; and

(b) the reason shall be recorded as soon as practicable after the sample is taken.

(8B) If a non-intimate sample is taken from a person at a police station, whether with or without the appropriate consent –

(a) before the sample is taken, an officer shall inform him that it may be the subject of a speculative search; and

(b) the fact that the person has been informed of this possibility shall be recorded as soon as practicable after the sample has been taken.

(9) If a non-intimate sample is taken from a person detained at a police station, the matters required to be recorded by subsection (8) or (8A) or (8B) above shall be recorded in his custody record.

(9A) Subsection (3B) above shall not apply to any person convicted before 10th April 1995 unless he is a person to whom section 1 of the Criminal Evidence (Amendment) Act 1997 applies (persons imprisoned or detained by virtue of pre-existing conviction for sexual offence etc).

(9ZA) The power to take a non-intimate sample from a person without the appropriate consent shall be exercisable by any constable.

(10) Nothing in this section applies to a person arrested or detained under the terrorism provisions.

(11) Nothing in this section applies to a person arrested under an extradition arrest power.

63A Fingerprints and samples: supplementary provisions

(1) Where a person has been arrested on suspicion of being involved in a recordable offence or has been charged with such an offence or has been informed that he will be reported for such an offence, fingerprints or samples or the information derived

from samples taken under any power conferred by this Part of this Act from the person may be checked against –

(a) other fingerprints or samples to which the person seeking to check has access and which are held by or on behalf of any one or more relevant law-enforcement authorities or which are held in connection with or as a result of an investigation of an offence;

(b) information derived from other samples if the information is contained in records to which the person seeking to check has access and which are held as mentioned in paragraph (a) above.

(1A) In subsection (1) above 'relevant law-enforcement authority' means –

(a) a police force;

(b) the National Criminal Intelligence Service;

(c) the National Crime Squad;

(d) a public authority (not falling within paragraphs (a) to (c)) with functions in any part of the British Islands which consist of or include the investigation of crimes or the charging of offenders; ...

(1B) The reference in subsection (1A) above to a police force is a reference to any of the following –

(a) any police force maintained under section 2 of the Police Act 1996 (c 16) (police forces in England and Wales outside London);

(b) the metropolitan police force;

(c) the City of London police force; ...

(1C) Where –

(a) fingerprints or samples have been taken from any person in connection with the investigation of an offence but otherwise than in circumstances to which subsection (1) above applies, and

(b) that person has given his consent in writing to the use in a speculative search of the fingerprints or of the samples and of information derived from them,

the fingerprints or, as the case may be, those samples and that information may be checked against any of the fingerprints, samples or information mentioned in paragraph (a) or (b) of that subsection.

(1D) A consent given for the purposes of subsection (1C) above shall not be capable of being withdrawn.

(3) Where any power to take a sample is exercisable in relation to a person the sample may be taken in a prison or other institution to which the Prison Act 1952 applies.

(3A) Where –

(a) the power to take a non-intimate sample under section 63(3B) above is exercisable in relation to any person who is detained under Part III of the Mental Health Act 1983 in pursuance of –

(i) a hospital order or interim hospital order made following his conviction for the recordable offence in question, or

(ii) a transfer direction given at a time when he was detained in pursuance of any sentence or order imposed following that conviction, or

(b) the power to take a non-intimate sample under section 63(3C) above is exercisable in relation to any person,

the sample may be taken in the hospital in which he is detained under that Part of that Act. Expressions used in this subsection and in the Mental Health Act 1983 have the same meaning as in that Act.

(3B) Where the power to take a non-intimate sample under section 63(3B) above is exercisable in relation to a person detained in pursuance of directions of the Secretary of State under section 92 of the Powers of Criminal Courts (Sentencing) Act 2000 the sample may be taken at the place where he is so detained.

(4) Any constable may, within the allowed period, require a person who is neither in police detention nor held in custody by the police on the authority of a court to attend a police station in order to have a sample taken where –

(a) the person has been charged with a recordable offence or informed that he will be reported for such an offence and either he has not had a sample taken from him in the course of the investigation of the offence by the police or he has had a sample so taken from him but either it was not suitable for the same means of analysis or, though so suitable, the sample proved insufficient; or

(b) the person has been convicted of a recordable offence and either he has not had a sample taken from him since the conviction or he has had a sample taken from him (before or after his conviction) but either it was not suitable for the same means of analysis or, though so suitable, the sample proved insufficient.

(5) The period allowed for requiring a person to attend a police station for the purpose specified in subsection (4) above is –

(a) in the case of a person falling within paragraph (a), one month beginning with the date of the charge or of his being informed as mentioned in that paragraph or one month beginning with the date on which the appropriate officer is informed of the fact that the sample is not suitable for the same means of analysis or has proved insufficient, as the case may be;

(b) in the case of a person falling within paragraph (b), one month beginning with the date of the conviction or one month beginning with the date on which the appropriate officer is informed of the fact that the sample is not suitable for the same means of analysis or has proved insufficient, as the case may be.

(6) A requirement under subsection (4) above –

(a) shall give the person at least 7 days within which he must so attend; and

(b) may direct him to attend at a specified time of day or between specified times of day.

(7) Any constable may arrest without a warrant a person who has failed to comply with a requirement under subsection (4) above.

(8) In this section 'the appropriate officer' is –

(a) in the case of a person falling within subsection (4)(a), the officer investigating the offence with which that person has been charged or as to which he was informed that he would be reported;

(b) in the case of a person falling within subsection (4)(b), the officer in charge of the police station from which the investigation of the offence of which he was convicted was conducted.

63B Testing for presence of Class A drugs

(1) A sample of urine or a non-intimate sample may be taken from a person in police detention for the purpose of ascertaining whether he has any specified Class A drug in his body if the following conditions are met.

(2) The first condition is –

(a) that the person concerned has been charged with a trigger offence; or

(b) that the person concerned has been charged with an offence and a police officer of at least the rank of inspector, who has reasonable grounds for suspecting that the misuse by that person of any specified Class A drug caused or contributed to the offence, has authorised the sample to be taken.

(3) The second condition is that the person concerned has attained the age of 14.

(4) The third condition is that a police officer has requested the person concerned to give the sample.

(5) Before requesting the person concerned to give a sample, an officer must –

(a) warn him that if, when so requested, he fails without good cause to do so he may be liable to prosecution, and

(b) in a case within subsection (2)(b) above, inform him of the giving of the authorisation and of the grounds in question.

(5A) In the case of a person who has not attained the age of 17 –

(a) the making of the request under subsection (4) above;

(b) the giving of a warning and (where applicable) the information under subsection (5) above; and

(c) the taking of the sample.

may not take place except in the presence of an appropriate adult.

(6) A sample may be taken under this section only by a person prescribed by regulations made by the Secretary of State by statutory instrument.

No regulations shall be made under this subsection unless a draft has been laid before, and approved by resolution of, each House of Parliament.

(6A) The Secretary of State may by order made by statutory instrument amend subsection (3) above by substituting for the age for the time being specified a different age specified in the order.

(6B) A statutory instrument containing an order under subsection (6A) above shall not be made unless a draft of the instrument has been laid before, and approved by a resolution of, each House of Parliament.

(7) Information obtained from a sample taken under this section may be disclosed –

(a) for the purpose of informing any decision about granting bail in criminal proceedings (within the meaning of the Bail Act 1976) to the person concerned;

(b) where the person concerned is in police detention or is remanded in or committed to custody by an order of a court or has been granted such bail, for the purpose of informing any decision about his supervision;

(c) where the person concerned is convicted of an offence, for the purpose of informing any decision about the appropriate sentence to be passed by a court and any decision about his supervision or release;

(d) for the purpose of ensuring that appropriate advice and treatment is made available to the person concerned.

(8) A person who fails without good cause to give any sample which may be taken from him under this section shall be guilty of an offence.

(9) In relation to a person who has not attained the age of 18, this section applies only where –

(a) the relevant chief officer has been notified by the Secretary of State that arrangements for the taking of samples under this section from persons who have not attained the age of 18 have been made for the police area as a whole, or for the particular police station, in which the person is in police detention; and

(b) the notice has not been withdrawn.

(10) In this section –

'appropriate adult', in relation to a person who has not attained the age of 17, means –

(a) his parent or guardian or, if he is in the care of a local authority or voluntary organisation,a person representing that authority or organisation; or

(b) a social worker of a local authority social services department; or

(c) if no person falling within paragraph (a) or (b) is available, any responsible person aged 18 or over who is not a police officer or a person employed by the police;

'relevant chief officer' means –

(a) in relation to a police area, the chief officer of police of the police force for that police area; or

(b) in relation to a police station, the chief officer of police of the police force for the police area in which the police station is situated.

63C Testing for presence of Class A drugs: supplementary

(1) A person guilty of an offence under section 63B above shall be liable on summary conviction to imprisonment for a term not exceeding three months, or to a fine not exceeding level 4 on the standard scale, or to both.

(2) A police officer may give an authorisation under section 63B above orally or in writing but, if he gives it orally, he shall confirm it in writing as soon as is practicable.

(3) If a sample is taken under section 63B above by virtue of an authorisation, the authorisation and the grounds for the suspicion shall be recorded as soon as is practicable after the sample is taken.

(4) If the sample is taken from a person detained at a police station, the matters required to be recorded by subsection (3) above shall be recorded in his custody record.

(5) Subsections (11) and (12) of section 62 above apply for the purposes of section 63B above as they do for the purposes of that section; and section 63B above does not prejudice the generality of sections 62 and 63 above.

(6) In section 63B above –

'Class A drug' and 'misuse' have the same meanings as in the Misuse of Drugs Act 1971;

'specified' (in relation to a Class A drug) and 'trigger offence' have the same meanings as in Part III of the Criminal Justice and Court Services Act 2000.

64 Destruction of fingerprints and samples

(1A) Where –

(a) fingerprints or samples are taken from a person in connection with the investigation of an offence, and

(b) subsection (3) below does not require them to be destroyed,

the fingerprints or samples may be retained after they have fulfilled the purposes for which they were taken but shall not be used by any person except for purposes related to the prevention or detection of crime, the investigation of an offence or the conduct of a prosecution.

(1B) In subsection (1A) above –

(a) the reference to using a fingerprint includes a reference to allowing any check to be made against it under section 63A(1) or (1C) above and to disclosing it to any person;

(b) the reference to using a sample includes a reference to allowing any check to be made under section 63A(1) or (1C) above against it or against information derived from it and to disclosing it or any such information to any person;

(c) the reference to crime includes a reference to any conduct which –

(i) constitutes one or more criminal offences (whether under the law of a part of the United Kingdom or of a country or territory outside the United Kingdom); or

(ii) is, or corresponds to, any conduct which, if it all took place in any one part of the United Kingdom, would constitute one or more criminal offences; and

(d) the references to an investigation and to a prosecution include references, respectively, to any investigation outside the United Kingdom of any crime or suspected crime and to a prosecution brought in respect of any crime in a country or territory outside the United Kingdom.

(3) If –

(a) fingerprints or samples are taken from a person in connection with the investigation of an offence; and

(b) that person is not suspected of having committed the offence,

they must, except as provided in the following provisions of this section, be destroyed as soon as they have fulfilled the purpose for which they were taken.

(3AA) Samples and fingerprints are not required to be destroyed under subsection (3) above if –

(a) they were taken for the purposes of the investigation of an offence of which a person has been convicted; and

(b) a sample or, as the case may be, fingerprint was also taken from the convicted person for the purposes of that investigation.

(3AB) Subject to subsection (3AC) below, where a person is entitled under subsection (3) above to the destruction of any fingerprint or sample taken from him (or would be but for subsection (3AA) above), neither the fingerprint nor the sample, nor any information derived from the sample, shall be used –

(a) in evidence against the person who is or would be entitled to the destruction of that fingerprint or sample; or

(b) for the purposes of the investigation of any offence;

and subsection (1B) above applies for the purposes of this subsection as it applies for the purposes of subsection (1A) above.

(3AC) Where a person from whom a fingerprint or sample has been taken consents in writing to its retention –

(a) that sample need not be destroyed under subsection (3) above;

(b) subsection (3AB) above shall not restrict the use that may be made of the fingerprint or sample or, in the case of a sample, of any information derived from it; and

(c) that consent shall be treated as comprising a consent for the purposes of section 63A(1C) above;

and a consent given for the purpose of this subsection shall not be capable of being withdrawn.

(3AD) For the purposes of subsection (3AC) above it shall be immaterial whether the consent is given at, before or after the time when the entitlement to the destruction of the fingerprint or sample arises.

(5) If fingerprints are destroyed –

(a) any copies of the fingerprints shall also be destroyed; and

(b) any chief officer of police controlling access to computer data relating to the fingerprints shall make access to the data impossible, as soon as it is practicable to do so.

(6) A person who asks to be allowed to witness the destruction of his fingerprints or copies of them shall have a right to witness it.

(6A) If –

(a) subsection (5)(b) above falls to be complied with; and

(b) the person to whose fingerprints the data relate asks for a certificate that it has been complied with,

such a certificate shall be issued to him, not later than the end of the period of three months beginning with the day on which he asks for it, by the responsible chief officer of police or a person authorised by him or on his behalf for the purposes of this section.

(6B) In this section –

'the responsible chief officer of police' means the chief officer of police in whose police area the computer data were put on to the computer.

(7) Nothing in this section –

(a) affects any power conferred by paragraph 18(2) of Schedule 2 to the Immigration Act 1971 or section 20 of the Immigration and Asylum Act 1999 (c 33) (disclosure of police information to the Secretary of State for use for immigration purposes); or

(b) applies to a person arrested or detained under the terrorism provisions.

64A Photographing of suspects, etc

(1) A person who is detained at a police station may be photographed –

(a) with the appropriate consent; or

(b) if the appropriate consent is withheld or it is not practicable to obtain it, without it.

(2) A person proposing to take a photograph of any person under this section –

(a) may, for the purpose of doing so, require the removal of any item or substance worn on or over the whole or any part of the head or face of the person to be photographed; and

(b) if the requirement is not complied with, may remove the item or substance himself.

(3) Where a photograph may be taken under this section, the only persons entitled to take the photograph are constables.

(4) A photograph taken under this section –

(a) may be used by, or disclosed to, any person for any purpose related to the prevention or detection of crime, the investigation of an offence or the conduct of a prosecution; and

(b) after being so used or disclosed, may be retained but may not be used or disclosed except for a purpose so related.

(5) In subsection (4) –

(a) the reference to crime includes a reference to any conduct which –

(i) constitutes one or more criminal offences (whether under the law of a part of the United Kingdom or of a country or territory outside the United Kingdom); or

(ii) is, or corresponds to, any conduct which, if it all took place in any one part of the United Kingdom, would constitute one or more criminal offences; and

(b) the references to an investigation and to a prosecution include references, respectively, to any investigation outside the United Kingdom of any crime or suspected crime and to a prosecution brought in respect of any crime in a country or territory outside the United Kingdom.

(6) References in this section to taking a photograph include references to using any process by means of which a visual image may be produced; and references to photographing a person shall be construed accordingly.

(7) Nothing in this section applies to a person arrested under an extradition arrest power.

65 Part V – supplementary

(1) In this Part of this Act –

'analysis', in relation to a skin impression, includes comparison and matching;
'appropriate consent' means –

(a) in relation to a person who has attained the age of 17 years, the consent of that person;

(b) in relation to a person who has not attained that age but has attained the age of 14 years, the consent of that person and his parent or guardian; and

(c) in relation to a person who has not attained the age of 14 years, the consent of his parent or guardian;

'extradition arrest power' means any of the following –

(a) a Part 1 warrant (within the meaning given by the Extradition Act 2003) in respect of which a certificate under section 2 of that Act has been issued;

(b) section 5 of that Act;

(c) a warrant issued under section 71 of that Act;

(d) a provisional warrant (within the meaning given by that Act).

'fingerprints', in relation to any person, means a record (in any form and produced by any method) of the skin pattern and other physical characteristics or features of –

(a) any of that person's fingers; or

(b) either of his palms;

'intimate sample' means

(a) a sample of blood, semen or any other tissue fluid, urine or pubic hair;

(b) a dental impression;

(c) a swab taken from a person's body orifice other than the mouth;

'intimate search' means a search which consists of the physical examination of a person's body orifices other than the mouth;

'non-intimate sample' means –

(a) a sample of hair other than pubic hair;

(b) a sample taken from a nail or from under a bail;

(c) a swab taken from any part of a person's body including the mouth but not any other body orifice;

(d) saliva;

(e) a skin impression;

'registered dentist' has the same meaning as in the Dentists Act 1984;

'registered health care professional' means a person (other than a medical practitioner) who is –

(a) a registered nurse; or

(b) a registered member of a health care profession which is designated for the purposes of this paragraph by an order made by the Secretary of State;

'skin impression', in relation to any person, means any record (other than a fingerprint) which is a record (in any form and produced by any method) of the skin pattern and other physical characteristics or features of the whole or any part of his foot or of any other part of his body;

'speculative search', in relation to a person's fingerprints or samples, means such a check against other fingerprints or samples or against information derived from other samples as is referred to in section 63A(1) above;

'sufficient' and 'insufficient', in relation to a sample, means (subject to subsection (2) below) sufficient or insufficient (in point of quantity or quality) for the purpose of enabling information to be produced by the means of analysis used or to be used in relation to the sample.

'the terrorism provisions' means section 41 of the Terrorism Act 2000 and any provision of Schedule 7 to that Act conferring a power of detention; and

'terrorism' has the meaning assigned to it by section 1 of that Act.

(1A) A health care profession is any profession mentioned in section 60(2) of the Health Act 1999 (c 8) other than the profession of practising medicine and the profession of nursing.

(1B) An order under subsection (1) shall be made by statutory instrument and shall be subject to annulment in pursuance of a resolution of either House of Parliament.

(2) References in this Part of this Act to a sample's proving insufficient include references to where, as a consequence of –

(a) the loss, destruction or contamination of the whole or any part of the sample,

(b) any damage to the whole or a part of the sample, or

(c) the use of the whole or a part of the sample for an analysis which produced no results or which produced results some or all of which must be regarded, in the circumstances, as unreliable.

the sample has become unavailable or insufficient for the purpose of enabling information, or information of a particular description, to be obtained by means of analysis of the sample.

PART VI

CODES OF PRACTICE – GENERAL

66 Codes of practice

(1) The Secretary of State shall issue codes of practice in connection with –

(a) the exercise by police officers of statutory powers –

(i) to search a person without first arresting him; or

(ii) to search a vehicle without making an arrest;

(b) the detention, treatment, questioning and identification of persons by police officers;

(c) searches of premises by police officers; and

(d) the seizure of property found by police officers on persons or premises.

(2) Codes shall (in particular) include provision in connection with the exercise by police officers of powers under section 63B above.

67 Codes of practice – supplementary

(1) In this section, 'code' means a code of practice under section 60, 60A or 66.

(2) The Secretary of State may at any time revise the whole or any part of a code.

(3) A code may be made, or revised, so as to –

(a) apply only in relation to one or more specified areas,

(b) have effect only for a specified period,

(c) apply only in relation to specified offences or descriptions of offender.

(4) Before issuing a code, or any revision of a code, the Secretary of State must consult –

(a) persons whom he considers to represent the interests of police authorities,

(b) persons whom he considers to represent the interests of chief officers of police,

(c) the General Council of the Bar,

(d) the Law Society of England and Wales,

(e) the Institute of Legal Executives, and

(f) such other persons as he thinks fit.

(5) A code, or a revision of a code, does not come into operation until the Secretary of State by order so provides.

(6) The power conferred by subsection (5) is exercisable by statutory instrument.

(7) An order bringing a code into operation may not be made unless a draft of the order has been laid before Parliament and approved by a resolution of each House.

(7A) An order bringing a revision of a code into operation must be laid before Parliament if the order has been made without a draft having been so laid and approved by a resolution of each House.

(7B) When an order or draft of an order is laid, the code or revision of a code to which it relates must also be laid.

(7C) No order or draft of an order may be laid until the consultation required by subsection (4) has taken place.

(7D) An order bringing a code, or a revision of a code, into operation may include transitional or saving provisions.

(9) Persons other than police officers who are charged with the duty of investigating offences or charging offenders shall in the discharge of that duty have regard to any relevant provision of such a code.

(9A) Persons on whom powers are conferred by –

(a) any designation under section 38 or 39 of the Police Reform Act 2002 (c 30) (police powers for police authority employees), or

(b) any accreditation under section 41 of that Act (accreditation under community safety accreditation schemes),

shall have regard to any relevant provisions of a code of practice to which this section applies in the exercise or performance of the powers and duties conferred or imposed on them by that designation or accreditation.

(10) A failure on the part –

(a) of a police officer to comply with any provision of such a code;

(b) of any person other than a police officer who is charged with the duty of investigating offences or charging offenders to have regard to any relevant provision of such a code in the discharge of that duty, or

(c) of a person designated under section 38 or 39 or accredited under section 41 of the Police Reform Act 2002 (c 30) to have regard to any relevant provision of such a code in the exercise or performance of the powers and duties conferred or imposed on him by that designation or accreditation.

shall not of itself render him liable to any criminal or civil proceedings.

(11) In all criminal and civil proceedings any such code shall be admissible in evidence; and if any provision of such a code appears to the court or tribunal conducting the proceedings to be relevant to any question arising in the proceedings it shall be taken into account in determining that question.

(12) In this section 'criminal proceedings' includes –

(a) proceedings in the United Kingdom or elsewhere before a court-martial constituted under the Army Act 1955, the Air Force Act 1955 or the Naval Discipline Act 1957;

(b) proceedings before the Courts-Martial Appeal Court; and

(c) proceedings before a Standing Civilian Court.

PART VIII

EVIDENCE IN CRIMINAL PROCEEDINGS – GENERAL

76 Confessions

(1) In any proceedings a confession made by an accused person may be given in evidence against him in so far as it is relevant to any matter in issue in the proceedings and is not excluded by the court in pursuance of this section.

(2) If, in any proceedings where the prosecution proposes to give in evidence a confession made by an accused person, it is represented to the court that the confession was or may have been obtained –

(a) by oppression of the person who made it; or

(b) in consequence of anything said or done which was likely, in the circumstances existing at the time, to render unreliable any confession which might be made by him in consequence thereof,

the court shall not allow the confession to be given in evidence against him except in so far as the prosecution proves to the court beyond reasonable doubt that the confession (notwithstanding that it may be true) was not obtained as aforesaid.

(3) In any proceedings where the prosecution proposes to give in evidence a confession made by an accused person, the court may of its own motion require the prosecution, as a condition of allowing it to do so, to prove that the confession was not obtained as mentioned in subsection (2) above.

(4) The fact that a confession is wholly or partly excluded in pursuance of this section shall not affect the admissibility in evidence –

(a) of any facts discovered as a result of the confession; or

(b) where the confession is relevant as showing that the accused speaks, writes or expresses himself in a particular way, of so much of the confession as is necessary to show that he does so.

(5) Evidence that a fact to which this subsection applies was discovered as a result of a statement made by an accused person shall not be admissible unless evidence of how it was discovered is given by him or on his behalf.

(6) Subsection (5) above applies –

(a) to any fact discovered as a result of a confession which is wholly excluded in pursuance of this section; and

(b) to any fact discovered as a result of a confession which is partly so excluded, if the fact is discovered as a result of the excluded part of the confession.

(7) Nothing in Part VII of this Act shall prejudice the admissibility of a confession made by an accused person.

(8) In this section 'oppression' includes torture, inhuman or degrading treatment, and the use or threat of violence (whether or not amounting to torture).

(9) Where the proceedings mentioned in subsection (1) above are proceedings before a magistrates' court inquiring into an offence as examining justices this section shall have effect with the omission of

(a) in subsection (1) the words 'and is not excluded by the court in pursuance of this section', and

(b) subsections (2) to (6) and (8).

77 Confessions by mentally handicapped persons

(1) Without prejudice to the general duty of the court at a trial on indictment to direct the jury on any matter on which it appears to the court appropriate to do so, where at such a trial –

(a) the case against the accused depends wholly or substantially on a confession by him; and

(b) the court is satisfied –

(i) that he is mentally handicapped; and

(ii) that the confession was not made in the presence of an independent person,

the court shall warn the jury that there is special need for caution before convicting the accused in reliance on the confession, and shall explain that the need arises because of the circumstances mentioned in paragraphs (a) and (b) above.

(2) In any case where at the summary trial of a person for an offence it appears to the court that a warning under subsection (1) above would be required if the trial were on indictment, the court shall treat the case as one in which there is a special need for caution before convicting the accused on his confession.

(3) In this section –

'independent person' does not include a police officer or a person employed for, or engaged on, police purposes;

'mentally handicapped', in relation to a person, means that he is in a state of arrested or incomplete development of mind which includes significant impairment of intelligence and social functioning; and

'police purposes' has the meaning assigned to it by section 101(2) of the Police Act 1996.

78 Exclusion of unfair evidence

(1) In any proceedings the court may refuse to allow evidence on which the prosecution proposes to rely to be given if it appears to the court that, having regard to all the circumstances, including the circumstances in which the evidence was obtained, the admission of the evidence would have such an adverse effect on the fairness of the proceedings that the court ought not to admit it.

(2) Nothing in this section shall prejudice any rule of law requiring a court to exclude evidence.

(3) This section shall not apply in the case of proceedings before a magistrates' court inquiring into an offence as examining justices.

82 Part VIII – interpretation

(1) In this Part of this Act –

'confession' includes any statement wholly or partly adverse to the person who made it, whether made to a person in authority or not and whether made in words or otherwise;

'court-martial' means a court-martial constituted under the Army Act 1955, the Air Force Act 1955 or the Naval Discipline Act 1957;

'proceedings' means criminal proceedings, including –

(a) proceedings in the United Kingdom or elsewhere before a court-martial constituted under the Army Act 1955, the Air Force Act 1955 or the Naval Discipline Act 1957;

(b) proceedings in the United Kingdom or elsewhere before the Courts-Martial Appeal Court –

(i) on an appeal from a court-martial so constituted; or

(ii) on a reference under section 34 of the Courts-Martial (Appeals) Act 1968; and

(b) proceedings before a Standing Civilian Court; and

'Service court' means a court-martial or a Standing Civilian Court.

(2) In this Part of this Act references to conviction before a Service court are references to a finding of guilty which is, or falls to be treated as, the finding of the court; and 'convicted' shall be construed accordingly.

(3) Nothing in this Part of this Act shall prejudice any power of a court to exclude evidence (whether by preventing questions from being put or otherwise) at its discretion.

PART XI

MISCELLANEOUS AND SUPPLEMENTARY

116 Meaning of 'serious arrestable offence'

(1) This section has effect for determining whether an offence is a serious arrestable offence for the purposes of this Act.

(2) The following arrestable offences are always serious –

(a) an offence (whether at common law or under any enactment) specified in Part I of Schedule 5 to this Act;

(b) an offence under an enactment specified in Part II of that Schedule;

(c) any offence which is specified in paragraph 1 of Schedule 2 to the Proceeds of Crime Act 2002 (drug trafficking offences);

(d) any offence under section 327, 328 or 329 of that Act (certain money laundering offences).

(3) Subject to subsection (4) below, any other arrestable offence is serious only if its commission –

(a) has led to any of the consequences specified in subsection (6) below; or

(b) is intended or is likely to lead to any of those consequences.

(4) An arrestable offence which consists of making a threat is serious if carrying out the threat would be likely to lead to any of the consequences specified in subsection (6) below.

(6) The consequences mentioned in subsections (3) and (4) above are –

(a) serious harm to the security of the State or to public order;

(b) serious interference with the administration of justice or with the investigation of offences or of a particular offence;

(c) the death of any person;

(d) serious injury to any person;

(e) substantial financial gain to any person; and

(f) serious financial loss to any person.

(7) Loss is serious for the purposes of this section if, having regard to all the circumstances, it is serious for the person who suffers it.

(8) In this section 'injury' includes any disease and any impairment of a person's physical or mental condition.

117 Power of constable to use reasonable force

Where any provision of this Act –

(a) confers a power on a constable; and

(b) does not provide that the power may only be exercised with the consent of some person, other than a police officer,

the officer may use reasonable force, if necessary, in the exercise of the power.

118 General interpretation

(1) In this Act –

'arrestable offence' has the meaning assigned to it by section 24 above; …

'designated police station' has the meaning assigned to it by section 35 above;

'document' means anything in which information of any description is recorded;

'item subject to legal privilege' has the meaning assigned to it by section 10 above;

'parent or guardian' means –

(a) in the case of a child or young person in the care of a local authority, that authority;

'premises' has the meaning assigned to it by section 23 above;

'recordable offence' means any offence to which regulations under section 27 above apply;

'vessel' includes any ship, boat, raft or other apparatus constructed or adapted for floating on water.

(2) Subject to subsection (2A) a person is in police detention for the purposes of this Act if –

(a) he has been taken to a police station after being arrested for an offence or after being arrested under section 41 of the Terrorism Act 2000; or

(b) he is arrested at a police station after attending voluntarily at the station or accompanying a constable to it,

and is detained there or is detained elsewhere in the charge of a constable, except that a person who is at a court after being charged is not in police detention for those purposes.

(2A) Where a person is in another's lawful custody by virtue of paragraph 22, 34(1) or 35(3) of Schedule 4 to the Police Reform Act 2002, he shall be treated as in police detention.

SCHEDULE 1

SPECIAL PROCEDURE

1. If on an application made by a constable a circuit judge is satisfied that one or other of the sets of access conditions is fulfilled, he may make an order under paragraph 4 below.

2. The first set of access conditions is fulfilled if –

(a) there are reasonable grounds for believing –

(i) that a serious arrestable offence has been committed;
(ii) that there is material which consists of special procedure material or includes special procedure material and does not also include excluded material on premises specified in the application;
(iii) that the material is likely to be of substantial value (whether by itself or together with other material) to the investigation in connection with which the application is made; and
(iv) that the material is likely to be relevant evidence;

(b) other methods of obtaining the material –

(i) have been tried without success; or
(ii) have not been tried because it appeared that they were bound to fail; and

(c) it is in the public interest, having regard –

(i) to the benefit likely to accrue to the investigation if the material is obtained; and
(ii) to the circumstances under which the person in possession of the material holds it,

that the material should be produced or that access to it should be given.

3. The second set of access conditions is fulfilled if –

(a) there are reasonable grounds for believing that there is material which consists of or includes excluded material or special procedure material on premises specified in the application;
(b) but for section 9(2) above a search of the premises for that material could

have been authorised by the issue of a warrant to a constable under an enactment other than this Schedule; and

(c) the issue of such a warrant would have been appropriate.

4. An order under this paragraph is an order that the person who appears to the circuit judge to be in possession of the material to which the application relates shall –

(a) produce it to a constable for him to take away; or

(b) give a constable access to it,

not later than the end of the period of seven days from the date of the order or the end of such longer period as the order may specify.

5. Where the material consists of information stored in any electronic form –

(a) an order under paragraph 4(a) above shall have effect as an order to produce the material in a form in which it can be taken away and in which it is visible and legible or from which it can readily be produced in a visible and legible form; and

(b) an order under paragraph 4(b) above shall have effect as an order to give a constable access to the material in a form in which it is visible and legible or from which it can readily be produced in a visible or legible form.

6. For the purposes of sections 21 and 22 above material produced in pursuance of an order under paragraph 4(a) above shall be treated as if it were material seized by a constable ...

11. Where notice of an application for an order under paragraph 4 above has been served on a person, he shall not conceal, destroy, alter or dispose of the material to which the application relates except –

(a) with the leave of a judge; or

(b) with the written permission of a constable,

until –

(i) the application is dismissed or abandoned; or

(ii) he has complied with an order under paragraph 4 above made on the application.

12. If on an application made by a constable a circuit judge –

(a) is satisfied –

(i) that either set of access conditions is fulfilled; and

(ii) that any of the further conditions set out in paragraph 14 below is also fulfilled; or

(b) is satisfied –

(i) that the second set of access conditions is fulfilled; and

(ii) that an order under paragraph 4 above relating to the material has not been complied with, he may issue a warrant authorising a constable to enter and search the premises.

13. A constable may seize and retain anything for which a search has been authorised under paragraph 12 above.

14. The further conditions mentioned in paragraph 12(a)(ii) above are –

(a) that it is not practicable to communicate with any person entitled to grant entry to the premises to which the application relates;

(b) that it is practicable to communicate with a person entitled to grant entry to the premises but it is not practicable to communicate with any person entitled to grant access to the material;

(c) that the material contains information which –

(i) is subject to a restriction or obligation such as is mentioned in section 11(2)(b) above; and

(ii) is likely to be disclosed in breach of it if a warrant is not issued;

(d) that service of notice of an application for an order under paragraph 4 above may seriously prejudice the investigation.

15. – (1) If a person fails to comply with an order under paragraph 4 above, a circuit judge may deal with him as if he had committed a contempt of the Crown Court.

(2) Any enactment relating to contempt of the Crown Court shall have effect in relation to such a failure as if it were such a contempt.

16. The costs of any application under this Schedule and of anything done or to be done in pursuance of an order made under it shall be in the discretion of the judge.

SCHEDULE 1A

SPECIFIC OFFENCES WHICH ARE ARRESTABLE OFFENCES

Customs and Excise Acts

1. An offence for which a person may be arrested under the customs and excise Acts (within the meaning of the Customs and Excise Management Act 1979 (c 2)).

Official Secrets Act 1920

2. An offence under the Official Secrets Act 1920 (c 75) which is not an arrestable offence by virtue of the term of imprisonment for which a person may be sentenced in respect of them.

Wireless Telegraphy Act 1949

2A. An offence mentioned in section 14(1) of the Wireless Telegraphy Act 1949 (offences under that Act which are triable either way).

Criminal Justice Act 1925

2ZA. An offence under section 36 of the Criminal Justice Act 1925 (untrue statement for procuring a passport).

Prevention of Crime Act 1953

3. An offence under section 1(1) of the Prevention of Crime Act 1953 (c 14) (prohibition of carrying offensive weapons without lawful authority or excuse).

Obscene Publications Act 1959

5. An offence under section 2 of the Obscene Publications Act 1959 (c 66) (publication of obscene matter).

Firearms Act 1968

5A. An offence under section 19 of the Firearms Act 1968 (carrying firearm or imitation firearm in public place) in respect of an air weapon or imitation firearm.

Theft Act 1968

6. An offence under –

(a) section 12(1) of the Theft Act 1968 (c 60) (taking motor vehicle or other conveyance without authority etc); or

(b) section 25(1) of that Act (going equipped for stealing etc).

Misuse of Drugs Act 1971

6A. An offence under section 5(2) of the Misuse of Drugs Act 1971 (having possession of a controlled drug) in respect of cannabis or cannabis resin (within the meaning of that Act).

Theft Act 1978

7. An offence under section 3 of the Theft Act 1978 (c 31) (making off without payment).

Protection of Children Act 1978

8. An offence under section 1 of the Protection of Children Act 1978 (c 37) (indecent photographs and pseudo-photographs of children).

Wildlife and Countryside Act 1981

9. An offence under section 1(1) or (2) or 6 of the Wildlife and Countryside Act 1981 (c 69) (taking, possessing, selling etc of wild birds) in respect of a bird included in Schedule 1 to that Act or any part of, or anything derived from, such a bird.

10. An offence under –

(a) section 1(5) of the Wildlife and Countryside Act 1981 (disturbance of wild birds);
(b) section 9 or 13(1)(a) or (2) of that Act (taking, possessing, selling etc of wild animals or plants); or
(c) section 14 of that Act (introduction of new species etc).

Civil Aviation Act 1982

11. An offence under section 39(1) of the Civil Aviation Act 1982 (c 16) (trespass on aerodrome).

11A. An offence of contravening a provision of an Order in Council under section 60 of that Act (air navigation order) where the offence relates to –

(a) a provision which prohibits specified behaviour by a person in an aircraft towards or in relation to a member of the crew, or
(b) a provision wich prohibits a person from being drunk in an aircraft, in so far as it applies to passengers.

Aviation Security Act 1982

12. An offence under section 21C(1) or 21D(1) of the Aviation Security Act 1982 (c 36) (unauthorised presence in a restricted zone or on an aircraft).

Sexual Offences Act 1985

13. An offence under section 1 of the Sexual Offences Act 1985 (c 44) (kerb-crawling).

Public Order Act 1986

14. An offence under section 19 of the Public Order Act 1986 (c 64) (publishing etc material likely to stir up racial or religious hatred).

Criminal Justice Act 1988

15. An offence under –

(a) section 139(1) of the Criminal Justice Act 1988 (c 33) (offence of having article with a blade or point in public place); or

(b) section 139A(1) or (2) of that Act (offence of having article with a blade or point or offensive weapon on school premises).

Road Traffic Act 1988

16. An offence under section 103(1)(b) of the Road Traffic Act 1988 (c 52) (driving while disqualified).

17. An offence under subsection (4) of section 170 of the Road Traffic Act 1988 (failure to stop and report an accident) in respect of an accident to which that section applies by virtue of subsection (1)(a) of that section (accidents causing personal injury).

17A. An offence under section 174 of the Road Traffic Act 1988 (false statements and withholding material information).

Official Secrets Act 1989

18. An offence under any provision of the Official Secrets Act 1989 (c 6) other than subsection (1), (4) or (5) of section 8 of that Act.

Football Spectators Act 1989

19. An offence under section 14J or 21C of the Football Spectators Act 1989 (c 37) (failing to comply with requirements imposed by or under a banning order or a notice under section 21B).

Football (Offences) Act 1991

20. An offence under any provision of the Football (Offences) Act 1991 (c 19).

Criminal Justice and Public Order Act 1994

21. An offence under –

(a) section 60AA(7) of the Criminal Justice and Public Order Act 1994 (c 33) (failing to comply with requirement to remove disguise);

(b) section 166 of that Act (sale of tickets by unauthorised persons); or

(c) section 167 of that Act (touting for car hire services).

Police Act 1996

22. An offence under section 89(1) of the Police Act 1996 (c 16) (assaulting a police officer in the execution of his duty or a person assisting such an officer).

Protection from Harassment Act 1997

23. An offence under section 2 of the Protection from Harassment Act 1997 (c 40) (harassment).

Crime and Disorder Act 1998

24. An offence falling within section 32(1)(a) of the Crime and Disorder Act 1998 (c 37) (racially or religiously aggravated harassment).

Criminal Justice and Police Act 2001

25. An offence under –

(a) section 12(4) of the Criminal Justice and Police Act 2001 (c 16) (failure to comply with requirements imposed by constable in relation to consumption of alcohol in public place); or

(b) section 46 of that Act (placing of advertisements in relation to prostitution).

Sexual Offences Act 2003

26. An offence under –

(a) section 66 of the Sexual Offences Act 2003 (exposure);

(b) section 67 of that Act (voyeurism);

(c) section 69 of that Act (intercourse with an animal);

(d) section 70 of that Act (sexual penetration of a corpse); or

(e) section 71 of that Act (sexual activity in public lavatory).

SCHEDULE 2

PRESERVED POWERS OF ARREST

Section 17(2) of the Military Lands Act 1892.

Section 12(1) of the Protection of Animals Act 1911.

Section 2 of the Emergency Powers Act 1920.

Section 7(3) of the Public Order Act 1936.

Section 49 of the Prison Act 1952.

Section 13 of the Visiting Forces Act 1952.

Sections 186 and 190B of the Army Act 1955.

Section 186 and 190B of the Air Force Act 1955.

Sections 104 and 105 of the Naval Discipline Act 1957.

Section 1(3) of the Street Offences Act 1959.

Section 32 of the Children and Young Persons Act 1969.

Section 24(2) of the Immigration Act 1971 and paragraphs 17, 24 and 33 of Schedule 2 and paragraph 7 of Schedule 3 to that Act.

Section 7 of the Bail Act 1976.

Sections 6(6), 7(11), 8(4), 9(7) and 10(5) of the Criminal Law Act 1977.

Sections 60(5) and 61(1) of the Animal Health Act 1981.

Rule 36 in Schedule 1 to the Representation of the People Act 1983.

Sections 18, 35(10), 36(8), 38(7), 136(1) and 138 of the Mental Health Act 1983.

Section 5(5) of the Repatriation of Prisoners Act 1984.

SCHEDULE 5

SERIOUS ARRESTABLE OFFENCES

PART I

OFFENCES MENTIONED IN SECTION 116(2)(a)

1. Treason.

2. Murder.

3. Manslaughter.

5. Kidnapping.

9. An offence under section 170 of the Customs and Excise Management Act 1979 (c 2) of being knowingly concerned, in relation to any goods, in any fraudulent evasion or attempt at evasion of a prohibition in force with respect to the goods under section 42 of the Customs Consolidation Act 1876 (c 36) (prohibition on importing indecent or obscene articles).

PART II

OFFENCES MENTIONED IN SECTION 116(2)(b)

Explosive Substances Act 1883 (c 3)

Section 2 (causing explosion likely to endanger life or property).

Firearms Act 1968 (c 27)

Section 16 (possession of firearms with intent to injure).

Section 17 (1) (use of firearms and imitation firearms to resist arrest).

Section 18 (carrying firearms with criminal intent).

Taking of Hostages Act 1982 (c 28)

Section 1 (hostage-taking).

Aviation Security Act 1982 (c 36)

Section 1 (hi-jacking).

Road Traffic Act 1988 (c 52)

Section 1 (causing death by dangerous driving).

Section 3A (causing death by careless driving when under the influence of drink or drugs).

Criminal Justice Act 1988 (c 33)

Section 134 (torture).

Aviation and Maritime Security Act 1990 (c 31)

Section 1 (endangering safety at aerodromes).

Section 9 (hijacking of ships).

Section 10 (seizing or execising control of fixed platforms).

Channel Tunnel (Security) Order 1994 (No 570)

Article 4 (hijacking of Channel Tunnel trains).

Article 5 (seizing or exercising control of the tunnel system).

Protection of Children Act 1978 (c 37)

Section 1 (indecent photographs and pseudo-photographs of children).

Obscene Publications Act 1959 (c 66)

Section 2 (publication of obscene matter).

Sexual Offences Act 2003

Section 1 (rape).

Section 2 (assault by penetration).

Section 4 (causing a person to engage in sexual activity without consent), where the activity caused involved penetration within subsection (4)(a) to (d) of that section.

Section 5 (rape of a child under 13).

Section 6 (assault of a child under 13 by penetration).

Section 8 (causing or inciting a child under 13 to engage in sexual activity), where an activity involving penetration within subsection (3)(a) to (d) of that section was caused.

Section 30 (sexual activity with a person with a mental disorder impeding choice), where the touching involved penetration within subsection (3)(a) to (d) of that section.

Section 31 (causing or inciting a person, with a mental disorder impeding choice, to engage in sexual activity), where an activity involving penetration within subsection (3)(a) to (d) of that section was caused.

NB At 1 August 2003, the insertion of section 38(1)(a)(iiia) and the relevant addition to subsection (2) of that section, and the insertion of sections 63B, 63C and 66(2), were in force in certain police areas only.

As amended by the Representation of the People Act 1985, s25(1); Public Order Act 1986, s40(2), (3), Schedule 2, para 7, Schedule 3; Drug Trafficking Offences Act 1986, ss32(1), (3), 36; Criminal Justice Act 1988, ss99(1), (2), 140(1), 147, 148, 170, Schedule 15, paras 99, 100, 102, Schedule 16; Road Traffic (Consequential Provisions) Act 1988, ss3, 4, Schedules 1, Pt I, 3, para 27(1), (3), (4), (5); Children Act 1989, s108(5), (7), Schedule 13, paras 53, 54, 55, Schedule 15; Prevention of Terrorism (Temporary Provisions) Act 1989, s25(1), Schedule 8, para 6(1), (2), (3), (4), (5), (6), (7), (8); Aviation and Maritime Security Act 1990, s53(1), Schedule 3, para 8; Criminal Justice Act 1991, s59; Road Traffic Act 1991, s48, Schedule 4, para 39; Police and Magistrates' Courts Act 1994, s37(a), Schedule 5, paras 24–26; Criminal Justice and Public Order Act 1994, ss24, 27(1), 28(2), (3), (4)(c)–(e), 29(2), (3), (4)(a) and (b), 54(2)–(5), 55(2), (3), (5), (6), 56, 57(2), (3), 58(2)–(4), 59(1)–(2), 85(1)–(3), 155, 166(4), 167(7), Schedule 4, para 58, Schedule 9, para 24, Schedule 10, paras 4(a), 53–59, 62(4)(a) and (b); Drug Trafficking Act 1994, ss65(1), 67(1), Schedule 1, paras 8, 9, Schedule 3; Channel Tunnel (Security) Order 1994, art 38, Schedule 3, para 4; Prisoners (Return to Custody) Act 1995, s2(1); Civil Evidence Act 1995, s15(1), Schedule 1, para 9(1), (3); Criminal Procedure and Investigations Act 1996, ss47, 64, Schedule 1, Pt II, paras 25, 26; Police Act 1996, s103(1), (3), Schedule 7, Pt II, paras 37, 38, Schedule 9, Pts I, II; Armed Forces Act 1996, ss5, 35, Schedule 1, Pt IV, paras 104, 105, 107, Schedule 6, para 14, Schedule 7, Pt I; Criminal Evidence (Amendment) Act 1997, ss1(2), 2(2), 3, 4; Crime and Disorder Act 1998, ss46, 119, Schedule 8, paras 61, 62, Schedule 9, para 9; Football (Offences and Disorder) Act 1999, s1(2)(f); Access to Justice Act 1999, s90(1), Schedule 13, paras 125, 126; Immigration and Asylum Act 1999, s169(1), Schedule 14, para 80(2)–(4); Railways Act 1993 (Consequential Modifications) (No 2) Order 1999, art 5; Powers of Criminal Courts (Sentencing) Act 2000, s165(1), Schedule 9, paras 95–97; Criminal Justice and Court Services Act 2000, ss56(2), 57(1)–(4), 74, Schedule 7, Pt II, paras 76, 78; Terrorism Act 2000, s125(1), Schedule 15, paras 5(1)–(9), 10–12, Schedule 16, Pt I; Criminal Justice and Police Act 2001, ss70, 72–74,

77–79, 80(1), (3), (5), (6), 81, 82, Schedule 2, Pt 2, para 13(1), (2)(a), 14, Schedule 7, Pt 2(1); Anti-terrorism, Crime and Security Act 2001, ss90(1), (2), 92, 101, Schedule 7, para 13(1), (2); Armed Forces Act 2001, s38, Schedule 7, Pt 1; Access to Justice Act 1999 (Transfer of Justices' Clerks' Functions) Order 2001, art 4; Police Reform Act 2002, ss48(1)–(6), 49(2), 52, 53(1), (2), 54(1)–(3), 107(1), Schedule 6, Schedule 7, para 9(1)–(9), Schedule 8; Proceeds of Crime Act 2002, s456, Schedule 11, para 14(1)–(4), Schedule 12; Criminal Justice Act 2003, ss1–10, 11(1), 12, 28, 331, 332, Schedule 1, paras 1–10, Schedule 2, paras 1–6, Schedule 36, Pt 1, para 5, Schedule 37, Pt 1; Extradition Act 2003, s169; Communications Act 2003, s181(1); Sexual Offences Act 2003, ss139, 140, Schedule 6, para 28(1), (3), (4), Schedule 7; Anti-social Behaviour Act 2003, s37(3); Aviation (Offences) Act 2003 s1(1); British Transport Police (Transitional and Consequential Provisions) Order 2004, art 12 (1), (e).

PARLIAMENTARY CONSTITUENCIES ACT 1986

(1986 c 56)

1 Parliamentary constituencies

(1) There shall for the purpose of parliamentary elections be the county and borough constituencies (or in Scotland the county and burgh constituencies), each returning a single member, which are described in Orders in Council made under this Act.

(2) In this Act and, except where the context otherwise requires, in any Act passed after the Representation of the People Act 1948, 'constituency' means an area having separate representation in the House of Commons.

2 The Boundary Commissions

(1) For the purpose of the continuous review of the distribution of seats at parliamentary elections, there shall continue to be four permanent Boundary Commissions, namely a Boundary Commission for England, a Boundary Commission for Scotland, a Boundary Commission for Wales and a Boundary Commission for Northern Ireland.

(2) Schedule 1 to this Act shall have effect with respect to the constitution of, and other matters relating to, the Boundary Commissions.

3 Reports of the Commissions

(1) Each Boundary Commission shall keep under review the representation in the House of Commons of the part of the United Kingdom with which they are concerned and shall, in accordance with subsection (2) below, submit to the Secretary of State reports with respect to the whole of that part of the United Kingdom, either –

(a) showing the constituencies into which they recommend that it should be divided in order to give effect to the rules set out in paragraphs 1 to 6 of Schedule 2 to this Act (read with paragraph 7 of that Schedule), or

(b) stating that, in the opinion of the Commission, no alteration is required to be made in respect of that part of the United Kingdom in order to give effect to the said rules (read with paragraph 7).

(2) Reports under subsection (1) above shall be submitted by a Boundary Commission not less than eight or more than twelve years from the date of the submission of their last report under that subsection.

(2A) A failure by a Boundary Commission to submit a report within the time limit which is appropriate to that report shall not be regarded as invalidating the report for the purposes of any enactment.

(3) Any Boundary Commission may also from time to time submit to the Secretary of State reports with respect to the area comprised in any particular constituency or constituencies in the part of the United Kingdom with which they are concerned, showing the constituencies into which they recommend that that area should be divided in order to give effect to the rules set out in paragraphs 1 to 6 of Schedule 2 to this Act (read with paragraph 7 of that Schedule).

(4) A report of a Boundary Commission under this Act showing the constituencies into which they recommend that any area should be divided shall state, as respects each constituency, the name by which they recommend that it should be known, and whether they recommend that it should be a county constituency or a borough constituency (or in Scotland a county constituency or a burgh constituency).

(5) As soon as may be after a Boundary Commission have submitted a report to the Secretary of State under this Act, he shall lay the report before Parliament together, except in a case where the report states that no alteration is required to be made in respect of the part of the United Kingdom with which the Commission are concerned, with the draft of an Order in Council for giving effect, whether with or without modifications, to the recommendations contained in the report.

(6) Schedule 2 to this Act which contains the rules referred to above and related provisions shall have effect. ...

4 Orders in Council

(1) The draft of any Order in Council laid before Parliament by the Secretary of State under this Act for giving effect, whether with or without modifications, to the recommendations contained in the report of a Boundary Commission may make provisions for any matters which appear to him to be incidental to, or consequential on, the recommendations.

(2) Where any such draft gives effect to any such recommendations with modifications, the Secretary of State shall lay before Parliament together with the draft a statement of the reasons for the modifications.

(3) If any such draft is approved by resolution of each House of Parliament, the Secretary of State shall submit it to Her Majesty in Council.

(4) If a motion for the approval of any such draft is rejected by either House of Parliament or withdrawn by leave of the House, the Secretary of State may amend the draft and lay the amended draft before Parliament, and if the draft as so amended is approved by resolution of each House of Parliament, the Secretary of State shall submit it to Her Majesty in Council.

(5) Where the draft of an Order in Council is submitted to Her Majesty in Council under this Act, Her Majesty in Council may make an Order in terms of the draft which (subject to subsection (6) below) shall come into force on such date as may

be specified in the Order and shall have effect notwithstanding anything in any enactment.

(6) The coming into force of any such Order shall not affect any parliamentary election until a proclamation is issued by Her Majesty summoning a new Parliament, or affect the constitution of the House of Commons until the dissolution of the Parliament then in being.

(7) The validity of any Order in Council purporting to be made under this Act and reciting that a draft of the Order has been approved by resolution of each House of Parliament shall not be called in question in any legal proceedings whatsoever.

SCHEDULE 1

THE BOUNDARY COMMISSIONS

1. The Speaker of the House of Commons shall be the chairman of each of the Commissions.

2. Each of the four Commissions shall consist of the chairman, a deputy chairman and other members appointed by the Secretary of State ...

NB In relation to reports under s3(1) above, the first such report due to be made after the passing of the Boundary Commissions Act 1992 had to be submitted not later than 31 December 1994: ibid, s2(2).

When the relevant provisions of s16 of, and Schedule 3 to, the Political Parties, Elections and Referendums Act 2000 are brought into force:

(a) the functions of each of the Boundary Commissions under s3(1) and (3), above, will be transferred to the Electoral Commission; and

(b) functions with respect to –

(i) the carrying out of reviews under this Act with respect to a particular part of the United Kingdom, and

(ii) the submission to the Electoral Commission of proposed recommendations following any such review,

will be conferred on the Boundary Committee established for that part of the United Kingdom under s14 of the Act of 2000.

As amended by the Boundary Commissions Act 1992, s2(1), (3), (4).

PUBLIC ORDER ACT 1986
(1986 c 64)

1 Riot

(1) Where 12 or more persons who are present together use or threaten unlawful violence for a common purpose and the conduct of them (taken together) is such as would cause a person of reasonable firmness present at the scene to fear for his personal safety, each of the persons using unlawful violence for the common purpose is guilty of riot.

(2) It is immaterial whether or not the 12 or more use or threaten unlawful violence simultaneously.

(3) The common purpose may be inferred from conduct.

(4) No person of reasonable firmness need actually be, or be likely to be, present at the scene.

(5) Riot may be committed in private as well as in public places.

(6) A person guilty of riot is liable on conviction on indictment to imprisonment for a term not exceeding ten years or a fine or both.

2 Violent disorder

(1) Where three or more persons who are present together use or threaten unlawful violence and the conduct of them (taken together) is such as would cause a person of reasonable firmness present at the scene to fear for his personal safety, each of the persons using or threatening unlawful violence is guilty of violent disorder.

(2) It is immaterial whether or not the three or more use or threaten unlawful violence simultaneously.

(3) No person of reasonable firmness need actually be, or be likely to be, present at the scene.

(4) Violent disorder may be committed in private as well as in public places.

(5) A person guilty of violent disorder is liable on conviction on indictment to imprisonment for a term not exceeding five years or a fine or both, or on summary conviction to imprisonment for a term not exceeding six months or a fine not exceeding the statutory maximum or both.

3 Affray

(1) A person is guilty of affray if he uses or threatens unlawful violence towards another and his conduct is such as would cause a person of reasonable firmness present at the scene to fear for his personal safety.

(2) Where two or more persons use or threaten the unlawful violence, it is the conduct of them taken together that must be considered for the purposes of subsection (1).

(3) For the purposes of this section a threat cannot be made by the use of words alone.

(4) No person of reasonable firmness need actually be, or be likely to be, present at the scene.

(5) Affray may be committed in private as well as in public places.

(6) A constable may arrest without warrant anyone he reasonably suspects is committing affray.

(7) A person guilty of affray is liable on conviction on indictment to imprisonment for a term not exceeding three years or a fine or both, or on summary conviction to imprisonment for a term not exceeding six months or a fine not exceeding the statutory maximum or both.

4 Fear or provocation of violence

(1) A person is guilty of an offence if he –

(a) uses towards another person threatening, abusive or insulting words or behaviour, or

(b) distributes or displays to another person any writing, sign or other visible representation which is threatening, abusive or insulting,

with intent to cause that person to believe that immediate unlawful violence will be used against him or another by any person, or to provoke the immediate use of unlawful violence by that person or another, or whereby that person is likely to believe that such violence will be used or it is likely that such violence will be provoked.

(2) An offence under this section may be committed in a public or a private place, except that no offence is committed where the words or behaviour are used, or the writing, sign or other visible representation is distributed or displayed, by a person inside a dwelling and the other person is also inside that or another dwelling.

(3) A constable may arrest without warrant anyone he reasonably suspects is committing an offence under this section.

(4) A person guilty of an offence under this section is liable on summary conviction to imprisonment for a term not exceeding six months or a fine not exceeding level 5 on the standard scale or both.

4A Intentional harassment, alarm or distress

(1) A person is guilty of an offence if, with intent to cause a person harassment, alarm or distress, he –

(a) uses threatening, abusive or insulting words or behaviour, or disorderly behaviour, or

(b) displays any writing, sign or other visible representation which is threatening, abusive or insulting,

thereby causing that or another person harassment, alarm or distress.

(2) An offence under this section may be committed in a public or a private place, except that no offence is committed where the words or behaviour are used, or the writing, sign or other visible representation is displayed, by a person inside a dwelling and the person who is harassed, alarmed or distressed is also inside that or another dwelling.

(3) It is a defence for the accused to prove –

(a) that he was inside a dwelling and had no reason to believe that the words or behaviour used, or the writing, sign or other visible representation displayed, would be heard or seen by a person outside that or any other dwelling, or

(b) that his conduct was reasonable.

(4) A constable may arrest without warrant anyone he reasonably suspects is committing an offence under this section.

(5) A person guilty of an offence under this section is liable on summary conviction to imprisonment for a term not exceeding 6 months or a fine not exceeding level 5 on the standard scale or both.

5 Harassment, alarm or distress

(1) A person is guilty of an offence if he –

(a) uses threatening, abusive or insulting words or behaviour, or disorderly behaviour, or

(b) displays any writing, sign or other visible representation which is threatening, abusive or insulting,

within the hearing or sight of a person likely to be caused harassment, alarm or distress thereby.

(2) An offence under this section may be committed in a public or a private place, except that no offence is committed where the words or behaviour are used, or the writing, sign or other visible representation is displayed, by a person inside a dwelling and the other person is also inside that or another dwelling.

(3) It is a defence for the accused to prove –

(a) that he had no reason to believe that there was any person within hearing or sight who was likely to be caused harassment, alarm or distress, or

(b) that he was inside a dwelling and had no reason to believe that the words or behaviour used, or the writing, sign or other visible representation displayed, would be heard or seen by a person outside that or any other dwelling, or

(c) that his conduct was reasonable.

(4) A constable may arrest a person without warrant if –

(a) he engages in offensive conduct which a constable warns him to stop, and

(b) he engages in further offensive conduct immediately or shortly after the warning.

(5) In subsection (4) 'offensive conduct' means conduct the constable reasonably suspects to constitute an offence under this section, and the conduct mentioned in paragraph (a) and the further conduct need not be of the same nature.

(6) A person guilty of an offence under this section is liable on summary conviction to a fine not exceeding level 3 on the standard scale.

6 Mental element: miscellaneous

(1) A person is guilty of riot only if he intends to use violence or is aware that his conduct may be violent.

(2) A person is guilty of violent disorder or affray only if he intends to use or threaten violence or is aware that his conduct may be violent or threaten violence.

(3) A person is guilty of an offence under section 4 only if he intends his words or behaviour, or the writing, sign or other visible representation, to be threatening, abusive or insulting, or is aware that it may be threatening, abusive or insulting.

(4) A person is guilty of an offence under section 5 only if he intends his words or behaviour, or the writing, sign or other visible representation, to be threatening, abusive or insulting, or is aware that it may be threatening, abusive or insulting or (as the case may be) he intends his behaviour to be or is aware that it may be disorderly.

(5) For the purposes of this section a person whose awareness is impaired by intoxication shall be taken to be aware of that of which he would be aware if not intoxicated, unless he shows either that his intoxication was not self-induced or that it was caused solely by the taking or administration of a substance in the course of medical treatment.

(6) In subsection (5) 'intoxication' means any intoxication, whether caused by drink, drugs or other means, or by a combination of means.

(7) Subsections (1) and (2) do not affect the determination for the purposes of riot or violent disorder of the number of persons who use or threaten violence.

7 Procedure: miscellaneous

(1) No prosecution for an offence of riot or incitement to riot may be instituted except by or with the consent of the Director of Public Prosecutions.

(2) For the purposes of the rules against charging more than one offence in the same count or information, each of sections 1 to 5 creates one offence.

(3) If on the trial on indictment of a person charged with violent disorder or affray the jury find him not guilty of the offence charged, they may (without prejudice to section 6(3) of the Criminal Law Act 1967) find him guilty of an offence under section 4.

(4) The Crown Court has the same powers and duties in relation to a person who is by virtue of subsection (3) convicted before it of an offence under section 4 as a magistrates' court would have on convicting him of the offence.

8 Interpretation

In this Part –

'dwelling' means any structure or part of a structure occupied as a person's home or as other living accommodation (whether the occupation is separate or shared with others) but does not include any part not so occupied, and for this purpose 'structure' includes a tent, caravan, vehicle, vessel or other temporary or movable structure;

'violence' means any violent conduct, so that –

(a) except in the context of affray, it includes violent conduct towards property as well as violent conduct towards persons, and

(b) it is not restricted to conduct causing or intended to cause injury or damage but includes any other violent conduct (for example, throwing at or towards a person a missile of a kind capable of causing injury which does not hit or falls short).

9 Offences abolished

(1) The common law offences of riot, rout, unlawful assembly and affray are abolished ...

11 Advance notice of public processions

(1) Written notice shall be given in accordance with this section of any proposal to hold a public procession intended –

(a) to demonstrate support for or opposition to the views or actions of any person or body of persons,

(b) to publicise a cause or campaign, or

(c) to mark or commemorate an event,

unless it is not reasonably practicable to give any advance notice of the procession.

(2) Subsection (1) does not apply where the procession is one commonly or customarily held in the police area (or areas) in which it is proposed to be held or

is a funeral procession organised by a funeral director acting in the normal course of his business.

(3) The notice must specify the date when it is intended to hold the procession, the time when it is intended to start it, its proposed route, and the name and address of the person (or of one of the persons) proposing to organise it.

(4) Notice must be delivered to a police station –

(a) in the police area in which it is proposed the procession will start, or

(b) where it is proposed the procession will start in Scotland and cross into England, in the first police area in England on the proposed route.

(5) If delivered not less than six clear days before the date when the procession is intended to be held, the notice may be delivered by post under the recorded delivery service; but section 7 of the Interpretation Act 1978 (under which a document sent by post is deemed to have been served when posted and to have been delivered in the ordinary course of post) does not apply.

(6) If not delivered in accordance with subsection (5), the notice must be delivered by hand not less than six clear days before the date when the procession is intended to be held or, if that is not reasonably practicable, as soon as delivery is reasonably practicable.

(7) Where a public procession is held, each of the persons organising it is guilty of an offence if –

(a) the requirements of this section as to notice have not been satisfied, or

(b) the date when it is held, the time when it starts, or its route, differs from the date, time or route specified in the notice.

(8) It is a defence for the accused to prove that he did not know of, and neither suspected nor had reason to suspect, the failure to satisfy the requirements or (as the case may be) the difference of date, time or route.

(9) To the extent that an alleged offence turns on a difference of date, time or route, it is a defence for the accused to prove that the difference arose from circumstances beyond his control or from something done with the agreement of a police officer or by his direction.

(10) A person guilty of an offence under subsection (7) is liable on summary conviction to a fine not exceeding level 3 on the standard scale.

12 Imposing conditions on public processions

(1) If the senior police officer, having regard to the time or place at which and the circumstances in which any public procession is being held or is intended to be held and to its route or proposed route, reasonably believes that –

(a) it may result in serious public disorder, serious damage to property or serious disruption to the life of the community, or

(b) the purpose of the persons organising it is the intimidation of others with a view to compelling them not to do an act they have a right to do, or to do an act they have a right not to do,

he may give directions imposing on the persons organising or taking part in the procession such conditions as appear to him necessary to prevent such disorder, damage, disruption or intimidation, including conditions as to the route of the procession or prohibiting it from entering any public place specified in the directions.

(2) In subsection (1) 'the senior police officer' means –

(a) in relation to a procession being held, or to a procession intended to be held in a case where persons are assembling with a view to taking part in it, the most senior in rank of the police officers present at the scene, and

(b) in relation to a procession intended to be held in a case where paragraph (a) does not apply, the chief officer of police.

(3) A direction given by a chief officer of police by virtue of subsection (2)(b) shall be given in writing.

(4) A person who organises a public procession and knowingly fails to comply with a condition imposed under this section is guilty of an offence, but it is a defence for him to prove that the failure arose from circumstances beyond his control.

(5) A person who takes part in a public procession and knowingly fails to comply with a condition imposed under this section is guilty of an offence, but it is a defence for him to prove that the failure arose from circumstances beyond his control.

(6) A person who incites another to commit an offence under subsection (5) is guilty of an offence.

(7) A constable in uniform may arrest without warrant anyone he reasonably suspects is committing an offence under subsection (4), (5) or (6).

(8) A person guilty of an offence under subsection (4) is liable on summary conviction to imprisonment for a term not exceeding three months or a fine not exceeding level 4 on the standard scale or both.

(9) A person guilty of an offence under subsection (5) is liable on summary conviction to a fine not exceeding level 3 on the standard scale.

(10) A person guilty of an offence under subsection (6) is liable on summary conviction to imprisonment for a term not exceeding three months or a fine not exceeding level 4 on the standard scale or both, notwithstanding section 45(3) of the Magistrates' Courts Act 1980 (inciter liable to same penalty as incited) ...

13 Prohibiting public processions

(1) If at any time the chief officer of police reasonably believes that, because of particular circumstances existing in any district or part of a district, the powers under section 12 will not be sufficient to prevent the holding of public processions in that district or part from resulting in serious public disorder, he shall apply to the council of the district for an order prohibiting for such period not exceeding three

months as may be specified in the application the holding of all public processions (or of any class of public procession so specified) in the district or part concerned.

(2) On receiving such an application, a council may with the consent of the Secretary of State make an order either in the terms of the application or with such modifications as may be approved by the Secretary of State.

(3) Subsection (1) does not apply in the City of London or the metropolitan police district.

(4) If at any time the Commissioner of Police for the City of London or the Commissioner of Police of the Metropolis reasonably believes that, because of particular circumstances existing in his police area or part of it, the powers under section 12 will not be sufficient to prevent the holding of public processions in that area or part from resulting in serious public disorder, he may with the consent of the Secretary of State make an order prohibiting for such period not exceeding three months as may be specified in the order the holding of all public processions (or of any class of public procession so specified) in the area or part concerned.

(5) An order made under this section may be revoked or varied by a subsequent order made in the same way, that is, in accordance with subsections (1) and (2) or subsection (4), as the case may be.

(6) Any order under this section shall, if not made in writing, be recorded in writing as soon as practicable after being made.

(7) A person who organises a public procession the holding of which he knows is prohibited by virtue of an order under this section is guilty of an offence.

(8) A person who takes part in a public procession the holding of which he knows is prohibited by virtue of an order under this section is guilty of an offence.

(9) A person who incites another to commit an offence under subsection (8) is guilty of an offence.

(10) A constable in uniform may arrest without warrant anyone he reasonably suspects is committing an offence under subsection (7), (8) or (9).

(11) A person guilty of an offence under subsection (7) is liable on summary conviction to imprisonment for a term not exceeding three months or a fine not exceeding level 4 on the standard scale or both.

(12) A person guilty of an offence under subsection (8) is liable on summary conviction to a fine not exceeding level 3 on the standard scale.

(13) A person guilty of an offence under subsection (9) is liable on summary conviction to imprisonment for a term not exceeding three months or a fine not exceeding level 4 on the standard scale or both, notwithstanding section 45(3) of the Magistrates' Courts Act 1980.

14 Imposing conditions on public assemblies

(1) If the senior police officer, having regard to the time or place at which and the

circumstances in which any public assembly is being held or is intended to be held, reasonably believes that –

(a) it may result in serious public disorder, serious damage to property or serious disruption to the life of the community, or

(b) the purpose of the persons organising it is the intimidation of others with a view to compelling them not to do an act they have a right to do, or to do an act they have a right not to do,

he may give directions imposing on the persons organising or taking part in the assembly such conditions as to the place at which the assembly may be (or continue to be) held, its maximum duration, or the maximum number of persons who may constitute it, as appear to him necessary to prevent such disorder, damage, disruption or intimidation.

(2) In subsection (1) 'the senior police officer' means –

(a) in relation to an assembly being held, the most senior in rank of the police officers present at the scene, and

(b) in relation to an assembly intended to be held, the chief officer of police.

(3) A direction given by a chief officer of police by virtue of subsection (2)(b) shall be given in writing.

(4) A person who organises a public assembly and knowingly fails to comply with a condition imposed under this section is guilty of an offence, but it is a defence for him to prove that the failure arose from circumstances beyond his control.

(5) A person who takes part in a public assembly and knowingly fails to comply with a condition imposed under this section is guilty of an offence, but it is a defence for him to prove that the failure arose from circumstances beyond his control.

(6) A person who incites another to commit an offence under subsection (5) is guilty of an offence.

(7) A constable in uniform may arrest without warrant anyone he reasonably suspects is committing an offence under subsection (4), (5) or (6).

(8) A person guilty of an offence under subsection (4) is liable on summary conviction to imprisonment for a term not exceeding three months or a fine not exceeding level 4 on the standard scale or both.

(9) A person guilty of an offence under subsection (5) is liable on summary conviction to a fine not exceeding level 3 on the standard scale.

(10) A person guilty of an offence under subsection (6) is liable on summary conviction to imprisonment for a term not exceeding three months or a fine not exceeding level 4 on the standard scale or both, notwithstanding section 45(3) of the Magistrates' Courts Act 1980.

14A Prohibiting trespassory assemblies

(1) If at any time the chief officer of police reasonably believes that an assembly is

intended to be held in any district at a place on land to which the public has no right of access or only a limited right of access and that the assembly –

(a) is likely to be held without the permission of the occupier of the land or to conduct itself in such a way as to exceed the limits of any permission of his or the limits of the public's right of access, and

(b) may result –

(i) in serious disruption to the life of the community, or

(ii) where the land, or a building or monument on it, is of historical, architectural, archaeological or scientific importance, in significant damage to the land, building or monument,

he may apply to the council of the district for an order prohibiting for a specified period the holding of all trespassory assemblies in the district or a part of it, as specified.

(2) On receiving such an application, a council may –

(a) in England and Wales, with the consent of the Secretary of State make an order either in the terms of the application or with such modifications as may be approved by the Secretary of State;

(3) Subsection (1) does not apply in the City of London or the metropolitan police district.

(4) If at any time the Commissioner of Police for the City of London or the Commissioner of Police of the Metropolis reasonably believes that an assembly is intended to be held at a place on land to which the public has no right of access or only a limited right of access in his police area and that the assembly –

(a) is likely to be held without the permission of the occupier of the land or to conduct itself in such a way as to exceed the limits of any permission of his or the limits of the public's right of access, and

(b) may result –

(i) in serious disruption to the life of the community, or

(ii) where the land, or a building or monument on it, is of historical, architectural, archaeological or scientific importance, in significant damage to the land, building or monument,

he may with the consent of the Secretary of State make an order prohibiting for a specified period the holding of all trespassory assemblies in the area or a part of it, as specified.

(5) An order prohibiting the holding of trespassory assemblies operates to prohibit any assembly which –

(a) is held on land to which the public has no right of access or only a limited right of access, and

(b) takes place in the prohibited circumstances, that is to say, without the permission of the occupier of the land or so as to exceed the limits of any permission of his or the limits of the public's right of access.

(6) No order under this section shall prohibit the holding of assemblies for a period exceeding 4 days or in an area exceeding an area represented by a circle with a radius of 5 miles from a specified centre.

(7) An order made under this section may be revoked or varied by a subsequent order made in the same way, that is, in accordance with subsection (1) and (2) or subsection (4), as the case may be.

(8) Any order under this section shall, if not made in writing, be recorded in writing as soon as practicable after being made.

(9) In this section and sections 14B and 14C –

'assembly' means an assembly of 20 or more persons;

'land' means land in the open air;

'limited', in relation to a right of access by the public to land, means that their use of it is restricted to use for a particular purpose (as in the case of a highway or road) or is subject to other restrictions;

'occupier' means –

(a) in England and Wales, the person entitled to possession of the land by virtue of an estate or interest held by him;

and in subsections (1) and (4) includes the person reasonably believed by the authority applying for or making the order to be the occupier;

'public' includes a section of the public; and

'specified' means specified in an order under this section. ...

(11) In relation to Wales, the references in subsection (1) above to a district and to the council of the district shall be construed, as respects applications on and after 1st April 1996, as references to a county or county borough and to the council for that county or county borough.

14B Offences in connection with trespassory assemblies and arrest therefor

(1) A person who organises an assembly the holding of which he knows is prohibited by an order under section 14A is guilty of an offence.

(2) A person who takes part in an assembly which he knows is prohibited by an order under section 14A is guilty of an offence.

(3) In England and Wales, a person who incites another to commit an offence under subsection (2) is guilty of an offence.

(4) A constable in uniform may arrest without a warrant anyone he reasonably suspects to be committing an offence under this section.

(5) A person guilty of an offence under subsection (1) is liable on summary conviction to imprisonment for a term not exceeding 3 months or a fine not exceeding level 4 on the standard scale or both.

(6) A person guilty of an offence under subsection (2) is liable of summary conviction to a fine not exceeding level 3 on the standard scale.

(7) A person guilty of an offence under subsection (3) is liable on summary conviction to imprisonment for a term not exceeding 3 months or a fine not exceeding level 4 on the standard scale or both, notwithstanding section 45(3) of the Magistrates' Courts Act 1980. ...

14C Stopping persons from proceeding to trespassory assemblies

(1) If a constable in uniform reasonably believes that a person is on his way to an assembly within the area to which an order under section 14A applies which the constable reasonably believes is likely to be an assembly which is prohibited by that order, he may, subject to subsection (2) below –

(a) stop that person, and

(b) direct him not to proceed in the direction of the assembly.

(2) The power conferred by subsection (1) may only be exercised within the area to which the order applies.

(3) A person who fails to comply with a direction under subsection (1) which he knows has been given to him is guilty of an offence.

(4) A constable in uniform may arrest without a warrant anyone he reasonably suspects to be committing an offence under this section.

(5) A person guilty of an offence under subsection (3) is liable on summary conviction to a fine not exceeding level 3 on the standard scale.

16 Interpretation

In this Part –

'the City of London' means the City as defined for the purposes of the Acts relating to the City of London police;

'the metropolitan police district' means that district as defined in section 76 of the London Government Act 1963;

'public assembly' means an assembly of 2 or more persons in a public place which is wholly or partly open to the air;

'public place' means –

(a) any highway, and

(b) any place to which at the material time the public or any section of the public has access, on payment or otherwise, as of rights or by virtue of express or implied permission;

'public procession' means a procession in a public place.

As amended by the Criminal Justice and Public Order Act 1994, ss70–71, 154; Public Order (Amendment) Act 1996, s1; Anti-social Behaviour Act 2003, s57.

CROWN PROCEEDINGS (ARMED FORCES) ACT 1987

(1987 c 25)

1 Repeal of section 10 of the Crown Proceedings Act 1947

Subject to section 2 below, section 10 of the Crown Proceedings Act 1947 (exclusions from liability in tort cases involving the armed forces) shall cease to have effect except in relation to anything suffered by a person in consequence of an act or omission committed before the date on which this Act is passed.

2 Revival of section 10

(1) Subject to the following provisions of this section, the Secretary of State may, at any time after the coming into force of section 1 above, by order –

(a) revive the effect of section 10 of the Crown Proceedings Act 1947 either for all purposes or for such purposes as may be described in the order; or

(b) where that section has effect for the time being in pursuance of an order made by virtue of paragraph (a) above, provide for that section to cease to have effect either for all of the purposes for which it so has effect or for such of them as may be described.

(2) The Secretary of State shall not make an order reviving the effect of the said section 10 for any purposes unless it appears to him necessary or expedient to do so –

(a) by reason of any imminent national danger or of any great emergency that has arisen; or

(b) for the purposes of any warlike operations in any part of the world outside the United Kingdom or of any other operations which are or are to be carried out in connection with the warlike activity of any persons in any such part of the world.

(3) Subject to subsection (4) below, an order under this section describing purposes for which the effect of the said section 10 is to be revived, or for which that section is to cease to have effect, may describe those purposes by reference to any matter whatever and may make different provisions for different cases, circumstances or persons.

(4) Nothing in any order under this section shall revive the effect of the said section

10, or provide for that section to cease to have effect, in relation to anything suffered by a person in consequence of an act or omission committed before the date on which the order comes into force.

(5) The power to make an order under this section shall be exercisable by statutory instrument subject to annulment in pursuance of a resolution of either House of Parliament.

NB. This Act came into effect on 15 May 1987.

IMMIGRATION ACT 1988
(1988 c 14)

2 Restriction on exercise of right of abode in cases of polygamy

(1) This section applies to any woman who –

(a) has the right of abode in the United Kingdom under section 2(1)(b) of the principal Act [ie the Immigration Act 1971] as, or as having been, the wife of a man ('the husband') –

(i) to whom she is or was polygamously married; and

(ii) who is or was such a citizen of the United Kingdom and Colonies, Commonwealth citizen or British subject as is mentioned in section 2(2)(a) or (b) of that Act as in force immediately before the commencement of the British Nationality Act 1981; and

(b) has not before the coming into force of this section and since her marriage to the husband been in the United Kingdom.

(2) A woman to whom this section applies shall not be entitled to enter the United Kingdom in the exercise of the right of abode mentioned in subsection (1)(a) above or to be granted a certificate of entitlement in respect of that right if there is another woman living (whether or not one to whom this section applies) who is the wife or widow of the husband and who –

(a) is, or at any time since her marriage to the husband has been, in the United Kingdom; or

(b) has been granted a certificate of entitlement in respect of the right of abode mentioned in subsection (1)(a) above or an entry clearance to enter the United Kingdom as the wife of the husband.

(3) So long as a woman is precluded by subsection (2) above from entering the United Kingdom in the exercise of her right of abode or being granted a certificate of entitlement in respect of that right the principal Act shall apply to her as it applies to a person not having a right of abode.

(4) Subsection (2) above shall not preclude a woman from re-entering the United Kingdom if since her marriage to the husband she has at any time previously been in the United Kingdom and there was at that time no such other woman living as is mentioned in that subsection.

(5) Where a woman claims that this section does not apply to her because she has

been in the United Kingdom before the coming into force of this section and since her marriage to the husband it shall be for her to prove that fact.

(6) For the purposes of this section a marriage may be polygamous although at its inception neither party has any spouse additional to the other.

(7) For the purposes of subsections (1)(b), (2)(a), (4) and (5) above there shall be disregarded presence in the United Kingdom as a visitor or an illegal entrant and presence in circumstances in which a person is deemed by section 11(1) of the principal Act not to have entered the United Kingdom.

(8) In subsection (2)(b) above the reference to a certificate of entitlement includes a reference to a certificate treated as such a certificate by virtue of section 39(8) of the British Nationality Act 1981.

(9) No application by a woman for a certificate of entitlement in respect of such a right of abode as is mentioned in subsection (1)(a) above or for an entry clearance shall be granted if another application for such a certificate or clearance is pending and that application is made by a woman as the wife or widow of the same husband.

(10) For the purposes of subsection (9) above an application shall be regarded as pending so long as it and any appeal proceedings relating to it have not been finally determined.

7 Persons exercising Community rights and nationals of Member States

(1) A person shall not under the principal Act require leave to enter or remain in the United Kingdom in any case in which he is entitled to do so by virtue of an enforceable Community right or of any provision made under section 2(2) of the European Communities Act 1972.

(2) The Secretary of State may by order made by statutory instrument give leave to enter the United Kingdom for a limited period to any class of persons who are nationals of Member States but who are not entitled to enter the United Kingdom as mentioned in subsection (1) above; and any such order may give leave subject to such conditions as may be imposed by the order.

(3) References in the principal Act to limited leave shall include references to leave given by an order under subsection (2) above and a person having leave by virtue of such an order shall be treated as having been given that leave by a notice given to him by an immigration officer within the period specified in paragraph 6(1) of Schedule 2 to that Act.

OFFICIAL SECRETS ACT 1989

(1989 c 6)

1 Security and intelligence

(1) A person who is or has been –

(a) a member of the security and intelligence services; or

(b) a person notified that he is subject to the provisions of this subsection,

is guilty of an offence if without lawful authority he discloses any information, document or other article relating to security or intelligence which is or has been in his possession by virtue of his position as a member of any of those services or in the course of his work while the notification is or was in force.

(2) The reference in subsection (1) above to disclosing information relating to security or intelligence includes a reference to making any statement which purports to be a disclosure of such information or is intended to be taken by those to whom it is addressed as being such a disclosure.

(3) A person who is or has been a Crown servant or government contractor is guilty of an offence if without lawful authority he makes a damaging disclosure of any information, document or other article relating to security or intelligence which is or has been in his possession by virtue of his position as such but otherwise than as mentioned in subsection (1) above.

(4) For the purposes of subsection (3) above a disclosure is damaging if –

(a) it causes damage to the work of, or of any part of, the security and intelligence services; or

(b) it is of information or a document or other article which is such that its unauthorised disclosure would be likely to cause such damage or which falls within a class or description of information or articles the unauthorised disclosure of which would be likely to have that effect.

(5) It is a defence for a person charged with an offence under this section to prove that at the time of the alleged offence he did not know, and has no reasonable cause to believe, that the information, document or article in question related to security or intelligence or, in the case of an offence under subsection (3), that the disclosure would be damaging within the meaning of that subsection.

(6) Notification that a person is subject to subsection (1) above shall be effected by a notice in writing served on him by a Minister of the Crown; and such a notice may be served if, in the Minister's opinion, the work undertaken by the person in

question is or includes work connected with the security and intelligence services and its nature is such that the interests of national security require that he should be subject to the provisions of that subsection.

(7) Subject to subsection (8) below, a notification for the purposes of subsection (1) above shall be in force for the period of five years beginning with the day on which it is served but may be renewed by further notices under subsection (6) above for periods of five years at a time.

(8) A notification for the purposes of subsection (1) above may at any time be revoked by a further notice in writing served by the Minister on the person concerned; and the Minister shall serve such a further notice as soon as, in his opinion, the work undertaken by that person ceases to be such as is mentioned in subsection (6) above.

(9) In this section 'security or intelligence' means the work of, or in support of, the security and intelligence services or any part of them, and references to information relating to security or intelligence include references to information held or transmitted by those services or by persons in support of, or of any part of, them.

2 Defence

(1) A person who is or has been a Crown servant or government contractor is guilty of an offence if without lawful authority he makes a damaging disclosure of any information, document or other article relating to defence which is or has been in his possession by virtue of his position as such.

(2) For the purposes of subsection (1) above a disclosure is damaging if –

(a) it damages the capability of, or of any part of, the armed forces of the Crown to carry out their tasks or leads to loss of life or injury to members of those forces or serious damage to the equipment or installation of those forces; or

(b) otherwise than as mentioned in paragraph (a) above, it endangers the interests of the United Kingdom abroad, seriously obstructs the promotion or protection by the United Kingdom of those interests or endangers the safety of British citizens abroad; or

(c) it is of information or of a document or article which is such that its unauthorised disclosure would be likely to have any of those effects.

(3) It is a defence for a person charged with an offence under this section to prove that at the time of the alleged offence he did not know, and had no reasonable cause to believe, that the information, document or article in question related to defence or that its disclosure would be damaging within the meaning of subsection (1) above.

(4) In this section 'defence' means –

(a) the size, shape, organisation, logistics, order of battle, deployment, operations, state of readiness and training of the armed forces of the Crown;

(b) the weapons, stores or other equipment of those forces and the invention, development, production and operation of such equipment and research relating to it;

(c) defence policy and strategy and military planning and intelligence;

(d) plans and measures for the maintenance of essential supplies and services that are or would be needed in time of war.

3 International relations

(1) A person who is or has been a Crown servant or government contractor is guilty of an offence if without lawful authority he makes a damaging disclosure of –

(a) any information, document or other article relating to international relations; or

(b) any confidential information, document or other article which was obtained from a State other than the United Kingdom or an international organisation,

being information or a document or article which is or has been in his possession by virtue of his position as a Crown servant or government contractor.

(2) For the purposes of subsection (1) above a disclosure is damaging if –

(a) it endangers the interests of the United Kingdom abroad, seriously obstructs the promotion or protection by the United Kingdom of those interests or endangers the safety of British citizens abroad; or

(b) it is of information or of a document or article which is such that its unauthorised disclosure would be likely to have any of those effects.

(3) In the case of information or a document or article within subsection (1)(b) above –

(a) the fact that it is confidential, or

(b) its nature or contents,

may be sufficient to establish for the purposes of subsection (2)(b) above that the information, document or article is such that its unauthorised disclosure would be likely to have any of the effects there mentioned.

(4) It is a defence for a person charged with an offence under this section to prove that at the time of the alleged offence he did not know, and had no reasonable cause to believe, that the information, document or article in question was such as is mentioned in subsection (1) above or that its disclosure would be damaging within the meaning of that subsection.

(5) In this section 'international relations' means the relations between States, between international organisations or between one or more States and one or more such organisations and includes any matter relating to a State other than the United Kingdom or to an international organisation which is capable of affecting the relations of the United Kingdom with another State or with an international organisation.

(6) For the purposes of this section any information, document or article obtained from a State or organisation is confidential at any time while the terms on which

it was obtained require it to be held in confidence or while the circumstances in which it was obtained make it reasonable for the State or organisation to expect that it would be so held.

4 Crime and special investigation powers

(1) A person who is or has been a Crown servant or government contractor is guilty of an offence if without lawful authority he discloses any information, document or other article to which this section applies and which is or has been in his possession by virtue of his position as such.

(2) This section applies to any information, document or other article –

(a) the disclosure of which –

(i) results in the commission of an offence; or

(ii) facilitates an escape from legal custody or the doing of any other act prejudicial to the safekeeping of persons in legal custody; or

(iii) impedes the prevention or detection of offences or the apprehension or prosecution of suspected offenders; or

(b) which is such that its unauthorised disclosure would be likely to have any of those effects.

(3) This section also applies to –

(a) any information obtained by reason of the interception of any communication in obedience to a warrant issued under section 2 of the Interception of Communications Act 1985 or under the authority of an interception warrant under section 5 of the Regulation of Investigatory Powers Act 2000, any information relating to the obtaining of information by reason of any such interception and any document or other article which is or has been used or held for use in, or has been obtained by reason of, any such interception; and

(b) any information obtained by reason of action authorised by a warrant issued under section 3 of the Security Service Act 1989 or under section 5 of the Intelligence Services Act 1994 or by an authorisation given under section 7 of that Act, any information relating to the obtaining of information by reason of any such action and any document or other article which is or has been used or held for use in, or has been obtained by reason of, any such action.

(4) It is a defence for a person charged with an offence under this section in respect of a disclosure falling within subsection (2)(a) above to prove that at the time of the alleged offence he did not know, and had no reasonable cause to believe, that the disclosure would have any of the effects there mentioned.

(5) It is a defence for a person charged with an offence under this section in respect of any other disclosure to prove that at the time of the alleged offence he did not know, and had no reasonable cause to believe, that the information, document or article in question was information or a document or article to which this section applies.

(6) In this section 'legal custody' includes detention in pursuance of any enactment or any instrument made under an enactment.

5 Information resulting from unauthorised disclosures or entrusted in confidence

(1) Subsection (2) below applies where –

(a) any information, document or other article protected against disclosure by the foregoing provisions of this Act has come into a person's possession as a result of having been –

(i) disclosed (whether to him or another) by a Crown servant or government contractor without lawful authority; or

(ii) entrusted to him by a Crown servant or government contractor on terms requiring it to be held in confidence or in circumstances in which the Crown servant or government contractor could reasonably expect that it would be so held; or

(iii) disclosed (whether to him or another) without lawful authority by a person to whom it was entrusted as mentioned in sub-paragraph (ii) above; and

(b) the disclosure without lawful authority of the information, document or article by the person into whose possession it has come is not an offence under any of those provisions.

(2) Subject to subsections (3) and (4) below, the person into whose possession the information, document or article has come is guilty of an offence if he discloses it without lawful authority knowing, or having reasonable cause to believe, that it is protected against disclosure by the foregoing provisions of this Act and that it has come into his possession as mentioned in subsection (1) above.

(3) In the case of information or a document or article protected against disclosure by sections 1 to 3 above, a person does not commit an offence under subsection (2) above unless –

(a) the disclosure by him is damaging; or

(b) he makes it knowing, or having reasonable cause to believe, that it would be damaging;

and the question whether a disclosure is damaging shall be determined for the purposes of this subsection as it would be in relation to a disclosure of that information, document or article by a Crown servant in contravention of section 1(3), 2(1) or 3(1) above.

(4) A person does not commit an offence under subsection (2) above in respect of information or a document or other article which has come into his possession as a result of having been disclosed –

(a) as mentioned in subsection (1)(a)(i) above by a government contractor; or

(b) as mentioned in subsection (1)(a)(iii) above,

unless that disclosure was by a British citizen or took place in the United Kingdom, in any of the Channel Islands or in the Isle of Man or a colony.

(5) For the purposes of this section information or a document or article is protected against disclosure by the foregoing provisions of this Act if –

(a) it relates to security or intelligence, defence or international relations within the meaning of section 1, 2 or 3 above or is such as is mentioned in section 3(1)(b) above; or

(b) it is information or a document or article to which section 4 above applies;

and information or a document or article is protected against disclosure by sections 1 to 3 above if it falls within paragraph (a) above.

(6) A person is guilty of an offence if without lawful authority he discloses any information, document or other article which he knows, or has reasonable cause to believe, to have come into his possession as a result of a contravention of section 1 of the Official Secrets Act 1911.

6 Information entrusted in confidence to other States or international organisations

(1) This section applies where –

(a) any information, document or other article which –

(i) relates to security or intelligence, defence or international relations; and

(ii) has been communicated in confidence by or on behalf of the United Kingdom to another State or to an international organisation,

has come into a person's possession as a result of having been disclosed (whether to him or another) without the authority of that State or organisation or, in the case of an organisation, of a member of it; and

(b) the disclosure without lawful authority of the information, document or article by the person into whose possession it has come is not an offence under any of the foregoing provisions of this Act.

(2) Subject to subsection (3) below, the person into whose possession the information, document or article has come is guilty of an offence if he makes a damaging disclosure of it knowing, or having reasonable cause to believe, that it is such as is mentioned in subsection (1) above, that it has come into his possession as there mentioned and that its disclosure would be damaging.

(3) A person does not commit an offence under subsection (2) above if the information, document or article is disclosed by him with lawful authority or has previously been made available to the public with the authority of the State or organisation concerned or, in the case of an organisation, of a member of it.

(4) For the purposes of this section 'security or intelligence', 'defence' and 'international relations' have the same meaning as in sections 1, 2 and 3 above and the question whether a disclosure is damaging shall be determined as it would

be in relation to a disclosure of the information, document or article in question by a Crown servant in contravention of section 1(3), 2(1) and 3(1) above.

(5) For the purposes of this section information or a document or article is communicated in confidence if it is communicated on terms requiring it to be held in confidence or in circumstances in which the person communicating it could reasonably expect that it would be so held.

7 Authorised disclosures

(1) For the purposes of this Act a disclosure by –

(a) a Crown servant; or

(b) a person, not being a Crown servant or government contractor, in whose case a notification for the purposes of section 1(1) above is in force,

is made with lawful authority if, and only if, it is made in accordance with his official duty.

(2) For the purposes of this Act a disclosure by a government contractor is made with lawful authority if, and only if, it is made –

(a) in accordance with an official authorisation; or

(b) for the purposes of the functions by virtue of which he is a government contractor and without contravening an official restriction.

(3) For the purposes of this Act a disclosure made by any other person is made with lawful authority if, and only if, it is made –

(a) to a Crown servant for the purposes of his functions as such; or

(b) in accordance with an official authorisation.

(4) It is a defence for a person charged with an offence under any of the foregoing provisions of this Act to prove that at the time of the alleged offence he believed that he had lawful authority to make the disclosure in question and had no reasonable cause to believe otherwise.

(5) In this section 'official authorisation' and 'official restriction' mean, subject to subsection (6) below, an authorisation or restriction duly given or imposed by a Crown servant or government contractor or by or on behalf of a prescribed body or a body of a prescribed class.

(6) In relation to subsection 5 above 'official authorisation' includes an authorisation duly given by or on behalf of the State or organisation concerned or, in the case of an organisation, a member of it.

8 Safeguarding of information

(1) Where a Crown servant or government contractor, by virtue of his position as such, has in his possession or under his control any document or other article which it would be an offence under any of the foregoing provisions of this Act for him to disclose without lawful authority he is guilty of an offence if –

(a) being a Crown servant, he retains the document or article contrary to his official duty; or

(b) being a government contractor, he fails to comply with an official direction for the return or disposal of the document or article,

or if he fails to take such care to prevent the unauthorised disclosure of the document or article as a person in his position may reasonably be expected to take.

(2) It is a defence for a Crown servant charged with an offence under subsection (1)(a) above to prove that at the time of the alleged offence he believed that he was acting in accordance with his official duty and had no reasonable cause to believe otherwise.

(3) In subsections (1) and (2) above references to a Crown servant include any person, not being a Crown servant or government contractor, in whose case a notification for the purposes of section 1(1) above is in force.

(4) Where a person has in his possession or under his control any document or other article which it would be an offence under section 5 above for him to disclose without lawful authority, he is guilty of an offence if –

(a) he fails to comply with an official direction for its return or disposal; or

(b) where he obtained it from a Crown servant or government contractor on terms requiring it to be held in confidence or in circumstances in which that servant or contractor could reasonably expect that it would be so held, he fails to take such care to prevent its unauthorised disclosure as a person in his position may reasonably be expected to take.

(5) Where a person has in his possession or under his control any document or other article which it would be an offence under section 6 above for him to disclose without lawful authority, he is guilty of an offence if he fails to comply with an official direction for its return or disposal.

(6) A person is guilty of an offence if he discloses any official information, document or other article which can be used for the purpose of obtaining access to any information, document or other article protected against disclosure by the foregoing provisions of this Act and the circumstances in which it is disclosed are such that it would be reasonable to expect that it might be used for that purpose without authority.

(7) For the purposes of subsection (6) above a person discloses information or a document or article which is official if –

(a) he had or has had it in his possession by virtue of his position as a Crown servant or government contractor; or

(b) he knows or has reasonable cause to believe that a Crown servant or government contractor has or has had it in his possession by virtue of his position as such.

(8) Subsection (5) of section 5 above applies for the purposes of subsection (6) above as it applies for the purposes of that section.

(9) In this section 'official direction' means a direction duly given by a Crown servant or government contractor or by or on behalf of a prescribed body or a body of a prescribed class.

9 Prosecutions

(1) Subject to subsection (2) below, no prosecution for an offence under this Act shall be instituted in England and Wales ... except by or with the consent of the Attorney General ....

(2) Subsection (1) above does not apply to an offence in respect of any such information, document or article as is mentioned in section 4(2) above but no prosecution for such an offence shall be instituted in England and Wales ... except by or with the consent of the Director of Public Prosecutions ... .

12 'Crown servant' and 'government contractor'

(1) In this Act 'Crown servant' means –

(a) a Minister of the Crown;

(aa) a member of the Scottish Executive or a junior Scottish Minister;

(c) any person employed in the civil service of the Crown, including Her Majesty's Diplomatic Service, Her Majesty's Overseas Civil Service, the civil service of Northern Ireland and the Northern Ireland Court Service;

(d) any member of the naval, military or air forces of the Crown including any person employed by an association established for the purposes of Part XI of the Reserve Forces Act 1996;

(e) any constable and any other person employed or appointed in or for the purposes of any police force (including the Police Service of Northern Ireland and the Police Service of Northern Ireland Reserve) or of the National Criminal Intelligence Service or the National Crime Squad;

(f) any person who is a member or employee of a prescribed body or a body of a prescribed class and either is prescribed for the purposes of this paragraph or belongs to a prescribed class of members or employees of any such body;

(g) any person who is the holder of a prescribed office or who is an employee of such a holder and either is prescribed for the purposes of this paragraph or belongs to a prescribed class of such employees.

(2) In this Act 'government contractor' means, subject to subsection (3) below, any person who is not a Crown servant but who provides, or is employed in the provision of, goods or services –

(a) for the purposes of any Minister or person mentioned in paragraph (a) or (b) of subsection (1) above, of any office-holder in the Scottish Administration, of any of the services, forces or bodies mentioned in that subsection or of the holder of any office prescribed under that subsection;

(aa) for the purposes of the National Assembly for Wales; or

(b) under an agreement or arrangement certified by the Secretary of State as being one to which the government of a State other than the United Kingdom or an international organisation is a party or which is subordinate to, or made for the purposes of implementing, any such agreement or arrangement.

(3) Where an employee or class of employees of any body, or of any holder of an office, is prescribed by an order made for the purposes of subsection (1) above –

(a) any employee of that body, or of the holder of that office, who is not prescribed or is not within the prescribed class; and

(b) any person who does not provide, or is not employed in the provision of, goods or services for the purposes of the performance of those functions of the body or the holder of the office in connection with which the employee or prescribed class of employees is engaged,

shall not be a government contractor for the purposes of this Act.

(4) In this section 'office-holder in the Scottish Administration' has the same meaning as in section 126(7)(a) of the Scotland Act 1998.

(5) This Act shall apply to the following as it applies to persons falling within the definition of Crown servant –

(a) the First Minister and deputy First Minister in Northern Ireland; and

(b) Northern Ireland Ministers and junior Ministers.

13 Other interpretation provisions

(1) In this Act –

'disclose' and 'disclosure', in relation to a document or other article, include parting with possession of it;

'international organisation' means, subject to subsections (2) and (3) below, an organisation of which only States are members and includes a reference to any organ of such an organisation;

'prescribed' means prescribed by an order made by the Secretary of State;

'State' includes the government of a State and any organ of its government and references to a State other than the United Kingdom include references to any territory outside the United Kingdom.

(2) In section 12(2)(b) above the reference to an international organisation includes a reference to any such organisation whether or not one of which only States are members and includes a commercial organisation.

(3) In determining for the purposes of subsection (1) above whether only States are members of an organisation, any member which is itself an organisation of which only States are members, or which is an organ of such an organisation, shall be treated as a State.

15 Acts done abroad and extent

(1) Any Act –

(a) done by a British citizen or Crown servant; or

(b) done by any person in any of the Channel Islands or the Isle of Man or any colony,

shall, if it would be an offence by that person under any provision of this Act other than section 8(1), (4) or (5) when done by him in the United Kingdom, be an offence under that provision.

(2) This Act extends to Northern Ireland.

(3) Her Majesty may by Order in Council provide that any provision of this Act shall extend, with such exceptions, adaptations and modifications as may be specified in the Order, to any of the Channel Islands or the Isle of Man or any colony.

As amended by the Intelligence Services Act 1994, s11(2), Schedule 4, para 4; Reserve Forces Act 1996, s131(1), Schedule 10, para 22; Police Act 1997, s134(1), Schedule 9, para 62; Scotland Act 1998, s125(1), Schedule 8, para 26; Government of Wales Act 1998, s125, Schedule 12, para 30; Police (Northern Ireland) Act 1998, s74(1), Schedule 4, para 17; Northern Ireland Act 1998, ss99, 100(2), Schedule 13, para 9, Schedule 15; Regulation of Investigatory Powers Act 2000, s82, Schedule 4, para 5; Police (Northern Ireland) Act 2000, s78(1), Schedule 6, para 9.

TRIBUNALS AND INQUIRIES ACT 1992
(1992 c 53)

1 The Council on Tribunals

(1) There shall continue to be a council entitled the Council on Tribunals (in this Act referred to as 'the Council') –

(a) to keep under review the constitution and working of the tribunals specified in Schedule 1 (being the tribunals constituted under or for the purposes of the statutory provisions specified in that Schedule) and, from time to time, to report on their constitution and working;

(b) to consider and report on such particular matters as may be referred to the Council under this Act with respect to tribunals other than the ordinary courts of law, whether or not specified in Schedule 1, or any such tribunal; and

(c) to consider and report on such matters as may be referred to the Council under this Act, or as the Council may determine to be of special importance, with respect to administrative procedures involving, or which may involve, the holding by or on behalf of a Minister of a statutory inquiry, or any such procedure.

(2) Nothing in this section authorises or requires the Council to deal with any matter with respect to which the Parliament of Northern Ireland had power to make laws.

2 Composition of the Council and the Scottish Committee

(1) Subject to subsection (3), the Council shall consist of not more than fifteen nor less than ten members appointed by the Lord Chancellor and the Scottish Ministers, and one of the members shall be so appointed to be chairman of the Council.

(2) There shall be a Scottish Committee of the Council (in this Act referred to as 'the Scottish Committee') which, subject to subsection (3), shall consist of –

(a) either two or three members of the council designated by the Scottish Ministers, and

(b) either three or four persons, not being members of the Council, appointed by the Scottish Ministers;

and the Scottish Ministers shall appoint one of the members of the Scottish Committee (being a member of the Council) to be chairman of the Scottish Committee.

(3) In addition to the persons appointed or designated under subsection (1) or (2), the Parliamentary Commissioner for Administration and the Scottish Public Services Ombudsman shall by virtue of their offices be members of the Council and of the Scottish Committee.

(4) In appointing members of the Council regard shall be had to the need for representation of the interests of persons in Wales.

4 Reports of, and references to, Council and Scottish Committee

(1) Subject to the provisions of this section, any report by, or reference to, the Council shall be made to or, as the case may be, by, the Lord Chancellor and the Scottish Ministers ...

(7) The Council shall make an annual report to the Lord Chancellor and the Scottish Ministers on their proceedings and those of the Scottish Committee, and –

(a) the Lord Chancellor shall lay the report before Parliament, and

(b) the Scottish Ministers shall lay the report before the Scottish Parliament,

with such comments (if any) as he or they think fit.

5 Recommendations of Council as to appointment of members of tribunals

(1) Subject to section 6 but without prejudice to the generality of section 1(1)(a), the Council may make to the appropriate Minister general recommendations as to the making of appointments to membership of any tribunals mentioned in Schedule 1 or of panels constituted for the purposes of any such tribunals; and (without prejudice to any statutory provisions having effect with respect to such appointments) the appropriate Minister shall have regard to recommendations under this section.

(2) In this section 'the appropriate Minister', in relation to appointments of any description, means the Minister making the appointments or, if they are not made by a Minister, the Minister in charge of the government department concerned with the tribunals in question ...

6 Appointment of chairmen of certain tribunals

(1) The chairman, or any person appointed to act as chairman, of any of the tribunals to which this subsection applies shall (without prejudice to any statutory provisions as to qualifications) be selected by the appropriate authority from a panel of persons appointed by the Lord Chancellor.

(2) Members of panels constituted under this section shall hold and vacate office under the terms of the instruments under which they are appointed, but may resign office by notice in writing to the Lord Chancellor; and any such member who ceases to hold office shall be eligible for re-appointment.

(3) Subsection (1) applies to any tribunal specified in paragraph 7(b) or 38(a) of Schedule 1.

(5) The person or persons constituting any tribunal specified in paragraph 31 of Schedule 1 shall be appointed by the Lord Chancellor, and where such a tribunal consists of more than one person the Lord Chancellor shall designate which of them is to be the chairman.

(6) In this section, 'the appropriate authority' means the Minister who apart from this Act would be empowered to appoint or select the chairman, person to act as chairman, members or members of the tribunal in question.

(7) A panel may be constituted under this section for the purposes either of a single tribunal or of two or more tribunals, whether or not of the same description ...

(9) In relation to any of the tribunals referred to in this section which sits in Northern Ireland, this section shall have effect with the substitution for any reference to the Lord Chancellor of a reference to the Lord Chief Justice of Northern Ireland.

7 Concurrence required for removal of members of certain tribunals

(1) Subject to subsection (2), the power of a Minister, other than the Lord Chancellor, to terminate a person's membership of any tribunal specified in Schedule 1, or of a panel constituted for the purposes of any such tribunal, shall be exercisable only with the consent of –

(a) the Lord Chancellor, the Lord President of the Court of Session and the Lord Chief Justice of Northern Ireland, if the tribunal sits in all parts of the United Kingdom;

(b) the Lord Chancellor and the Lord President of the Court of Session, if the tribunal sits in all parts of Great Britain;

(c) the Lord Chancellor and the Lord Chief Justice of Northern Ireland if the tribunal sits both in England and Wales and in Northern Ireland;

(d) the Lord Chancellor, if the tribunal does not sit outside England and Wales;

...

(f) the Lord Chief Justice of Northern Ireland, if the tribunal sits only in Northern Ireland.

(2) This section does not apply to any tribunal specified in paragraph 3, 12, 14, 15(f), 17, 18, 26, 33(a), 33AA, 34, 35(e), (g) or (h), 36(a), 36A(a) or (b), 39(b), 40, 48 or 56(a) or 57A of Schedule 1.

8 Procedural rules for tribunals

(1) The power of a Minister, the Lord President of the Court of Session, the Commissioners of Inland Revenue or the Foreign Compensation Commission to make, approve, confirm or concur in procedural rules for any tribunal specified in Schedule 1 shall be exercisable only after consultation with the Council.

(3) The Council shall consult the Scottish Committee in relation to the exercise of their functions under this section with respect to any tribunal specified in Part 2 of Schedule 1.

(4) In this section 'procedural rules' includes any statutory provision relating to the procedure of the tribunal in question.

9 Procedure in connection with statutory inquiries

(1) The Lord Chancellor, after consultation with the Council, may make rules regulating the procedure to be followed in connection with statutory inquiries held by or on behalf of Ministers; and different provision may be made by any such rules in relation to different classes of such inquiries.

(2) Any rules made by the Lord Chancellor under this section shall have effect, in relation to any statutory inquiry, subject to the provisions of the enactment under which the inquiry is held, and of any rules or regulations made under that enactment.

(3) Subject to subsection (2), rules made under this section may regulate procedure in connection with matters preparatory to such statutory inquiries as are mentioned in subsection (1), and in connection with matters subsequent to such inquiries, as well as in connection with the conduct of proceedings at such inquiries ...

10 Reasons to be given for decisions of tribunals and Ministers

(1) Subject to the provisions of this section and of section 14, where –

(a) any tribunal specified in Schedule 1 gives any decision, or

(b) any Minister notifies any decision taken by him –

(i) after a statutory inquiry has been held by him or on his behalf, or

(ii) in a case in which a person concerned could (whether by objecting or otherwise) have required a statutory inquiry to be so held,

it shall be the duty of the tribunal or Minister to furnish a statement, either written or oral, of the reasons for the decision if requested, on or before the giving or notification of the decision, to state the reasons.

(2) The statement referred to in subsection (1) may be refused, or the specification of the reasons restricted, on grounds of national security.

(3) A tribunal or Minister may refuse to furnish a statement under subsection (1) to a person not primarily concerned with the decision if of the opinion that to furnish it would be contrary to the interests of any person primarily concerned.

(4) Subsection (1) does not apply to any decision taken by a Minister after the holding by him or on his behalf of an inquiry or hearing which is a statutory inquiry by virtue only of an order made under section 16(2) unless the order contains a direction that this section is to apply in relation to any inquiry or hearing to which the order applies.

(5) Subsection (1) does not apply –

(a) to decisions in respect of which any statutory provision has effect, apart from this section, as to the giving of reasons,

(ba) to decisions of the Pensions Compensation Board referred to in paragraph 35(h) of Schedule 1,

(b) to decisions of a Minister in connection with the preparation, making, approval, confirmation, or concurrence in regulations, rules or bye-laws, or orders or schemes of a legislative and not executive character.

(6) Any statement of the reasons for a decision referred to in paragraph (a) or (b) of subsection (1), whether given in pursuance of that subsection or of any other statutory provision, shall be taken to form part of the decision and accordingly to be incorporated in the record.

(7) If, after consultation with the Council, it appears to the Lord Chancellor and the Secretary of State that it is expedient that –

(a) decisions of any particular tribunal or any description of such decisions, or

(b) any description of decisions of a Minister,

should be excluded from the operation of subsection (1) on the ground that the subject-matter of such decisions, or the circumstances in which they are made, make the giving of reasons unnecessary or impracticable, the Lord Chancellor and the Secretary of State may by order direct that subsection (1) shall not apply to such decisions.

(8) Where an order relating to any decisions has been made under subsection (7), the Lord Chancellor and the Secretary of State may, by a subsequent order made after consultation with the Council, revoke or vary the earlier order so that subsection (1) applies to any of those decisions.

11 Appeals from certain tribunals

(1) Subject to subsection (2), if any party to proceedings before any tribunal specified in paragraph 8, 15(a) or (d), 16, 24, 26, 31, 33(b), 37, 40A, 40B, 44 or 45 of Schedule 1 is dissatisfied in point of law with a decision of the tribunal he may, according as rules of court may provide, either appeal from the tribunal to the High Court or require the tribunal to state and sign a case for the opinion of the High Court.

(2) This section shall not apply in relation to proceedings before employment tribunals which arise under or by virtue of any of the enactments mentioned in section 21(1) of the Employment Tribunals Act 1996.

(3) Rules of court made with respect to all or any of the tribunals referred to in subsection (1) may provide for authorising or requiring a tribunal, in the course of proceedings before it, to state, in the form of a special case for the decision of the High Court, any question of law arising in the proceedings; and a decision of the High Court on a case stated by virtue of this subsection shall be deemed to be a judgment of the Court within the meaning of section 16 of the Supreme Court Act

1981 (jurisdiction of Court of Appeal to hear and determine appeals from judgments of the High Court).

(4) In relation to proceedings in the High Court or the Court of Appeal brought by virtue of this section, the power to make rules of court shall include power to make rules prescribing the powers of the High Court or the Court of Appeal with respect to –

(a) the giving of any decision which might have been given by the tribunal;

(b) the remitting of the matter with the opinion or direction of the court for re-hearing and determination by the tribunal;

(c) the giving of directions to the tribunal;

and different provisions may be made for different tribunals.

(5) An appeal to the Court of Appeal shall not be brought by virtue of this section except with the leave of the High Court or the Court of Appeal.

(6) Subsection (1) shall apply to a decision of the Secretary of State on an appeal under section 41 of the Consumer Credit Act 1974 from a determination of the Office of Fair Trading as it applies to a decision of any of the tribunals mentioned in that subsection, but with the substitution for the reference to a party to proceedings of a reference to any person who had a right to appeal to the Secretary of State (whether or not he has exercised that right); and accordingly references in subsections (1) and (4) to a tribunal shall be construed, in relation to such an appeal, as references to the Secretary of State ...

(10) In this section 'decision' includes any direction or order, and references to the giving of a decision shall be construed accordingly.

12 Supervisory functions of superior courts not excluded by Acts passed before 1st August 1958

(1) As respects England and Wales –

(a) any provision in an Act passed before 1st August 1958 that any order or determination shall not be called into question in any court, or

(b) any provision in such an Act which by similar words excludes any of the powers of the High Court,

shall not have effect so as to prevent the removal of the proceedings into the High Court by order of certiorari or to prejudice the powers of the High Court to make orders of mandamus ...

(3) Nothing in this section shall apply –

(a) to any order or determination of a court of law, or

(b) where an Act makes special provision for application to the High Court or the Court of Session within a time limited by the Act.

16 Interpretation

(1) In this Act, except where the context otherwise requires ...

'statutory inquiry' means –

(a) an inquiry or hearing held or to be held in pursuance of a duty imposed by any statutory provision, or

(b) an inquiry or hearing, or an inquiry or hearing of a class, designated for the purposes of this section by an order under subsection (2) ...

(2) The Lord Chancellor and the Secretary of State may by order designate for the purposes of this section any inquiry or hearing held or to be held in pursuance of a power conferred by any statutory provision specified or described in the order, or any class of such inquiries or hearings. ...

SCHEDULE 1

TRIBUNALS UNDER GENERAL SUPERVISION OF COUNCIL

PART I

Matters with which tribunal concerned	*Tribunal and statutory authority*
Agriculture	1 (a) The Agricultural Land Tribunals established under section 73 of the Agriculture Act 1947 (c 48)
	(b) arbitrators appointed (otherwise than by agreement) under Schedule 11 to the Agricultural Holdings Act 1986 (c 5) ...
Child support maintenance	7 (a) Appeal tribunals constituted under Chapter I of Part I of the Social Security Act 1998 (c 14);
	(b) a Child Support Commissioner appointed under section 22 of the Child Support Act 1991 (c 48) and any tribunal presided over by such a Commissioner ...
Conveyancing	10 A Conveyancing Appeals Tribunal constituted under section 39 of the Courts and Legal Services Act 1990 (c 41) ...

Criminal injuries compensation	12 The adjudicators appointed under section 5 of the Criminal Injuries Compensation Act 1995 (c 53) ...
Education	15 (a) Independent Schools Tribunals constituted under section 476 of, and Schedule 34, to the Education Act 1996 (c 56);
	(b) exclusion appeal panels constituted in accordance with regulations under section 52 of the Education Act 2002;
	(c) admission appeal panels constituted in accordance with regulations under section 94(5) or 95(3) of the School Standards and Frameword Act 1998;
	(d) a tribunal constituted in accordance with Schedule 2 to the School Inspections Act 1996 (c 57); ...
Employment	16 The employment tribunals for England and Wales established under section 1(1) of the Employment Tribunals Act 1996 (c 17).
Fair trading	17 The Office of Fair Trading in respect of its functions under the Consumer Credit Act 1974 and the Estate Agents Act 1979, and any member of the its staff authorised to exercise those functions.
Financial services and markets	18 The Financial Services Markets Tribunal ...
Immigration and asylum	22 The Asylum and Immigration Tribunal constituted under section 81 of the Nationality, Immigration and Asylum Act 2002 ...
Land	27 The Lands Tribunal constituted under section 1(1)(b) of the Lands Tribunal Act 1949 (c 42) ...
Mental health	30 The Mental Health Review Tribunals constituted or having effect as if constituted under section 65 of the Mental Health Act 1983 (c 20) ...

National Health Service	33 (a) Primary Care Trusts established under section 16A of the National Health Service Act 1977 (c 49) or Health Authorities established under section 8 of that Act in respect of their functions under the National Health Service (Service Committees and Tribunal) Regulations 1992 or any regulations amending or replacing those Regulations; (b) the Family Health Services Appeal Authority constituted under section 49S of that Act; (c) committees of Primary Care Trusts or Health Authorities established under regulation 3 of those Regulations or any provision amending or replacing that regulation. …
Rents	37 Rent assessment committees constituted in accordance with Schedule 10 to the Rent Act 1977 (c 42) …
Revenue	39 (a) The Commissioners for the general purposes of the income tax acting under section 2 of the Taxes Management Act 1970 (c 9) for any division in England and Wales; (b) the Commissioners for the special purposes of the Income Tax Acts appointed under section 4 of that Act; (c) the tribunal constituted for the purposes of Chapter I of Part XVII of the Income and Corporation Taxes Act 1988 (c 1).
Road traffic	40 (a) The traffic commissioner for any area constituted for the purposes of the Public Passenger Vehicles Act 1981 (c 14); (b) a parking adjudicator appointed under section 73(3)(a) of the Road Traffic Act 1991 (c 40);

	(c) a road user charging adjudicator appointed under regulation 3 of the Road User Charging (Enforcement and Adjudication) (London) Regulations 2001.
Sea fish (conservation)	40A The Sea Fish Licence Tribunal established under section 4AA of the Sea Fish (Conservation) Act 1967 (c 84). …
Special educational needs and disability discrimination	(a) 40B The Special Educational Needs and Disability Tribunal. …
Value added tax and duties	44 Value added tax and duties tribunals for England and Wales and for Northern Ireland, constituted in accordance with Schedule 12 to the Value Added Tax Act 1994. …

As amended by the Sea Fish (Conservation) Act 1992, s9; Friendly Societies Act 1992, s120(1), Schedule 21, paras 12, 13; Tribunals and Inquiries (Friendly Societies) Order 1993, art 2(b), (c); National Lottery, etc Act 1993, s3(2), Schedule 2, para 8(1); Education Act 1993, s181(2); Police and Magistrates' Courts Act 1994, Schedule 5, para 39(a), (b); Value Added Tax Act 1994, s100(1), Schedule 14, para 12; Health Authorities Act 1995, ss2(1), 8, Schedule 1, Pt III, para 123, Criminal Injuries Compensation Act 1995, s5(8); Pensions Act 1995, ss122, 151, 177, Schedule 3, para 21(a), (b), Schedule 5, para 16(1)–(3), Schedule 7, Pts II, III; School Inspections Act 1996, s47(1), Schedule 6, para 5; Employment Rights Act 1996, s240, Schedule 1, para 57; Industrial Tribunals Act 1996, s43, Schedule 1, para 9(1), (2); Education Act 1996, s582(1), Schedule 37, Pt I, para 118(1), (3); Police Act 1997, s134(1), Schedule 9, para 69; Employment Rights (Dispute Resolution) Act 1998, s1(1); Social Security Act 1998, s86, Schedule 7, paras 118(1), 119, 121(1), Schedule 8; School Standards and Framework Act 1998, ss25(4), Schedule 5, para 10(1); National Lottery Act 1998, ss1(5), 26, Schedule 1, Pt III, para 12(1), (2), Schedule 5, Pt I; Immigration and Asylum Act 1999, s169(1), Schedule 14, para 96; Scotland Act 1998 (Cross-Border Public Authorities) (Adaptation of Functions etc) Order 1999, arts 3, 4, Schedule 9, Pt I, Pt II, para 2; Scotland Act 1998 (Transfer of Functions to the Scottish Ministers etc) Order 1999, arts 6(1), (7), Schedule 5, para 11; Transfer of Functions (Lord Advocate and Secretary of State) Order 1999, art 2(1), Schedule; Financial Services and Markets Act 2000, s432(1), Schedule 20, para 6; Special Educational Needs and Disability Act 2001, s42(1), Schedule 8, Pt 2, paras 19–22, Schedule 9; Health and Social Care Act 2001, s67(1), Schedule 5, Pt I, para 10; Financial Services and Markets Act 2000 (Consequential Amendments and Repeals) Order 2001, arts 334–336, 338; Enterprise Act 2001, s276, Schedule 25, para 27(1), (2), (4)(b); Education Act 2002, ss195, 215, Schedule 18, para 15(a), Schedule 21, para 22; Nationality, Immigration and Asylum Act 2002, s114, Schedule 7, para 17; National Health Service Reform and Health Care Professions Act 2002 (Supplementary, Consequential, etc, Provisions) Regulations 2002, reg 4, Schedule 1, para 19; Tribunals and Inquiries (Road User Charging Adjudicators) (London) Order 2003, art 2; Scottish Public Services Ombudsman Act 2002 (Consequential Amendments and Modification) Order 2004, art 14; Asylum and Immigration (Treatment of Claimants, etc) Act 2004, s26, Schedule 2, para 7.

ASYLUM AND IMMIGRATION APPEALS ACT 1993

(1993 c 23)

1 Interpretation

In this Act –

'the 1971 Act' means the Immigration Act 1971; ...

'the Convention' means the Convention relating to the Status of Refugees done at Geneva on 28th July 1951 and the Protocol to that Convention.

2 Primacy of Convention

Nothing in the immigration rules (within the meaning of the 1971 Act) shall lay down any practice which would be contrary to the Convention.

CRIMINAL JUSTICE AND PUBLIC ORDER ACT 1994

(1994 c 23)

PART III

COURTS OF JUSTICE: EVIDENCE, PROCEDURE, ETC

34 Effect of accused's failure to mention facts when questioned or charged

(1) Where, in any proceedings against a person for an offence, evidence is given that the accused –

(a) at any time before he was charged with the offence, on being questioned under caution by a constable trying to discover whether or by whom the offence had been committed, failed to mention any fact relied on in his defence in those proceedings; or

(b) on being charged with the offence or officially informed that he might be prosecuted for it, failed to mention any such fact,

being a fact which in the circumstances existing at the time the accused could reasonably have been expected to mention when so questioned, charged or informed, as the case may be, subsection (2) below applies.

(2) Where this subsection applies –

(a) a magistrates' court inquiring into the offence as examing justices;

(b) a judge, in deciding whether to grant an application made by the accused under –

(i) section 6 of the Criminal Justice Act 1987 (application for dismissal of charge of serious fraud in respect of which notice of transfer has been given under section 4 of that Act); or

(ii) paragraph 5 of Schedule 6 to the Criminal Justice Act 1991 (application for dismissal of charge of violent or sexual offence involving child in respect of which notice of transfer has been given under section 53 of that Act);

(c) the court, in determining whether there is a case to answer; and

(d) the court or jury, in determining whether the accused is guilty of the offence charged, may draw such inferences from the failure as appear proper.

(2A) Where the accused was at an authorised place of detention at the time of the failure, subsections (1) and (2) above do not apply if he had not been allowed an opportunity to consult a solicitor prior to being questioned, charged or informed as mentioned in subsection (1) above.

(3) Subject to any directions by the court, evidence tending to establish the failure may be given before or after evidence tending to establish the fact which the accused is alleged to have failed to mention.

(4) This section applies in relation to questioning by persons (other than constables) charged with the duty of investigating offences or charging offenders as it applies in relation to questioning by constables; and in subsection (1) above 'officially informed' means informed by a constable or any such person.

(5) This section does not –

(a) prejudice the admissibility in evidence of the silence or other reaction of the accused in the face of anything said in his presence relating to the conduct in respect of which he is charged, in so far as evidence thereof would be admissible apart from this section; or

(b) preclude the drawing of any inference from any such silence or other reaction of the accused which could properly be drawn apart from this section.

(6) This section does not apply in relation to a failure to mention a fact if the failure occurred before the commencement of this section.

35 Effect of accused's silence at trial

(1) At the trial of any person for an offence, subsections (2) and (3) below apply unless –

(a) the accused's guilt is not in issue; or

(b) it appears to the court that the physical or mental condition of the accused makes it undesirable for him to give evidence;

but subsection (2) below does not apply if, at the conclusion of the evidence for the prosecution, his legal representative informs the court that the accused will give evidence or, where he is unrepresented, the court ascertains from him that he will give evidence.

(2) Where this subsection applies, the court shall, at the conclusion of the evidence for the prosecution, satisfy itself (in the case of proceedings on indictment, in the presence of the jury) that the accused is aware that the stage has been reached at which evidence can be given for the defence and that he can, if he wishes, give evidence and that, if he chooses not to give evidence, or having been sworn, without good cause refuses to answer any question, it will be permissible for the court or jury to draw such inferences as appear proper from his failure to give evidence or his refusal, without good cause, to answer any question.

(3) Where this subsection applies, the court or jury, in determining whether the

accused is guilty of the offence charged, may draw such inferences as appear proper from the failure of the accused to give evidence or his refusal, without good cause, to answer any question.

(4) This section does not render the accused compellable to give evidence on his own behalf, and he shall accordingly not be guilty of contempt of court by reason of a failure to do so.

(5) For the purposes of this section a person who, having been sworn, refuses to answer any question shall be taken to do so without good cause unless –

(a) he is entitled to refuse to answer the question by virtue of any enactment, whenever passed or made, or on the ground of privilege; or

(b) the court in the exercise of its general discretion excuses him from answering it.

(7) This section applies –

(a) in relation to proceedings on indictment for an offence, only if the person charged with the offence is arraigned on or after the commencement of this section;

(b) in relation to proceedings in a magistrates' court, only if the time when the court begins to receive evidence in the proceedings falls after the commencement of this section.

36 Effect of accused's failure or refusal to account for objects, substances or marks

(1) Where –

(a) a person is arrested by a constable, and there is –

(i) on his person; or

(ii) in or on his clothing or footwear; or

(iii) otherwise in his possession; or

(iv) in any place in which he is at the time of his arrest,

any object, substance or mark, or there is any mark on any such object; and

(b) that or another constable investigating the case reasonably believes that the presence of the object, substance or mark may be attributable to the participation of the person arrested in the commission of an offence specified by the constable; and

(c) the constable informs the person arrested that he so believes, and requests him to account for the presence of the object, substance or mark; and

(d) the person fails or refuses to do so,

then if, in any proceedings against the person for the offence so specified, evidence of those matters is given, subsection (2) below applies.

(2) Where this subsection applies –

(a) a magistrates' court inquiring into the offence as examining justices;

(b) a judge, in deciding whether to grant an application made by the accused under –

(i) section 6 of the Criminal Justice Act 1987 (application for dismissal of charge of serious fraud in respect of which notice of transfer has been given under section 4 of that Act); or

(ii) paragraph 5 of Schedule 6 to the Criminal Justice Act 1991 (application for dismissal of charge of violent or sexual offence involving child in respect of which notice of transfer has been given under section 53 of that Act);

(c) the court, in determining whether there is a case to answer; and

(d) the court or jury, in determining whether the accused is guilty of the offence charged,

may draw such in inferences from the failure or refusal as appear proper.

(3) Subsections (1) and (2) above apply to the condition of clothing or footwear as they apply to a substance or mark thereon.

(4) Subsections (1) and (2) above do not apply unless the accused was told in ordinary language by the constable when making the request mentioned in subsection (1)(c) above what the effect of this section would be if he failed or refused to comply with the request.

(4A) Where the accused was at an authorised place of detention at the time of the failure or refusal, subsections (1) and (2) above do not apply if he had not been allowed an opportunity to consult a solicitor prior to the request being made.

(5) This section applies in relation to officers of customs and exercise as it applies in relation to constables.

(6) This section does not preclude the drawing of any inference from a failure or refusal of the accused to account for the presence of an object, substance or mark or from the condition of clothing or footwear which could properly be drawn apart from this section.

(7) This section does not apply in relation to a failure or refusal which occurred before the commencement of this section.

37 Effect of accused's failure or refusal to account for presence at a particular place

(1) Where –

(a) a person arrested by a constable was found by him at a place at or about the time the offence for which he was arrested is alleged to have been committed; and

(b) that or another constable investigating the offence reasonably believes that the presence of the person at that place and at that time may be attributable to his participation in the commission of the offence; and

(c) the constable informs the person that he so believes, and requests him to account for that presence; and

(d) the person fails or refuses to do so,

then if, in any proceedings against the person for the offence, evidence of those matters is given, subsection (2) below applies.

(2) Where this subsection applies –

(a) a magistrates' court inquiring into the offence as examining justices;

(b) a judge, in deciding whether to grant an application made by the accused under –

(i) section 6 of the Criminal Justice Act 1987 (application for dismissal of charge of serious fraud in respect of which notice of transfer has been given under section 4 of that Act); or

(ii) paragraph 5 of Schedule 6 to the Criminal Justice Act 1991 (application for dismissal of charge of violent or sexual offence involving child in respect of which notice of transfer has been given under section 53 of that Act);

(c) the court, in determining whether there is a case to answer; and

(d) the court or jury, in determining whether the accused is guilty of the offence charged,

may draw such inferences from the failure or refusal as appear proper.

(3) Subsections (1) and (2) do not apply unless the accused was told in ordinary language by the constable when making the request mentioned in subsection (1)(c) above what the effect of this section would be if he failed or refused to comply with the request.

(3A) Where the accused was at an authorised place of detention at the time of the failure or refusal, subsections (1) and (2) do not apply if he had not been allowed an opportunity to consult a solicitor prior to the request being made.

(4) This section applies in relation to officers of customs and excise as it applies in relation to constables.

(5) This section does not preclude the drawing of any inference from a failure or refusal of the accused to account for his presence at a place which could properly be drawn apart from this section.

(6) This section does not apply in relation to a failure or refusal which occurred before the commencement of this section.

38 Interpretation and savings for sections 34, 35, 36 and 37

(1) In sections 34, 35, 36 and 37 of this Act –

'legal representative' means an authorised advocate or authorised litigator, as defined by section 119(1) of the Courts and Legal Services Act 1990; and

'place' includes any building or part of a building, any vehicle, vessel, aircraft or hovercraft and any other place whatsoever.

(2) In sections 34(2), 35(3), 36(2) and 37(2), references to an offence charged include references to any other offence of which the accused could lawfully be convicted on that charge.

(2A) In each of sections 34(2A), 36(4A) and 37(3A) 'authorised place of detention' means –

(a) a police station; or
(b) any other place prescribed for the purposes of that provision by order made by the Secretary of State;

and the power to make an order under this subsection shall be exercisable by statutory instrument which shall be subject to annulment in pursuance of a resolution of either House of Parliament.

(3) A person shall not have the proceedings against him transferred to the Crown Court for trial, have a case to answer or be convicted of an offence solely on an inference drawn from such a failure or refusal as is mentioned in section 34(2), 35(3), 36(2) or 37(2).

(4) A judge shall not refuse to grant such an application as is mentioned in section 34(2)(b), 36(2)(b) and 37(2)(b) solely on an inference drawn from such a failure as is mentioned in section 34(2), 36(2) or 37(2).

(5) Nothing in sections 34, 35, 36 or 37 prejudices the operation of a provision of any enactment which provides (in whatever words) that any answer or evidence given by a person in specified circumstances shall not be admissible in evidence against him or some other person in any proceedings or class of proceedings (however described, and whether civil or criminal).

In this subsection, the reference to giving evidence is a reference to giving evidence in any manner, whether by furnishing information, making discovery, producing documents or otherwise.

(6) Nothing in section 34, 35, 36 or 37 prejudices any power of a court, in any proceedings, to exclude evidence (whether by preventing questions being put or otherwise) at its discretion.

PART IV

POLICE POWERS

60 Powers to stop and search in anticipation of violence

(1) If a police officer of or above the rank of inspector reasonably believes –

(a) that incidents involving serious violence may take place in any locality in his police area, and that it is expedient to give an authorisation under this section to prevent their occurrence, or
(b) that persons are carrying dangerous instruments or offensive weapons in any locality in his police area without good reason,

he may give an authorisation that the powers conferred by this section are to be exercisable at any place within that locality for a specified period not exceeding 24 hours.

(3) If it appears to an officer of or above the rank of superintendent that it is expedient to do so, having regard to offences which have, or are reasonably suspected to have, been committed in connection with any activity falling within the authorisation, he may direct that the authorisation shall continue in being for a further 24 hours.

(3A) If an inspector gives an authorisation under subsection (1) he must, as soon as it is practicable to do so, cause an officer of or above the rank of superintendent to be informed.

(4) This section confers on any constable in uniform power –

(a) to stop any pedestrian and search him or anything carried by him for offensive weapons or dangerous instruments;

(b) to stop any vehicle and search the vehicle, its driver and any passenger for offensive weapons or dangerous instruments.

(5) A constable may, in the exercise of the powers conferred by subsection (4) above, stop any person or vehicle and make any search he thinks fit whether or not he has any grounds for suspecting that the person or vehicle is carrying weapons or articles of that kind.

(6) If in the course of a search under this section a constable discovers a dangerous instrument or an article which he has reasonable grounds for suspecting to be an offensive weapon, he may seize it.

(7) This section applies (with the necessary modifications) to ships, aircraft and hovercraft as it applies to vehicles.

(8) A person who fails –

(a) to stop, or to stop a vehicle;

when required to do so by a constable in the exercise of his powers under this section shall be liable on summary conviction to imprisonment for a term not exceeding one month or to a fine not exceeding level 3 on the standard scale or both.

(9) Any authorisation under this section shall be in writing signed by the officer giving it and shall specify the grounds on which it is given and the locality in which and the period during which the powers conferred by this section are exercisable and a direction under subsection (3) above shall also be given in writing or, where that is not practicable, recorded in writing as soon as it is practicable to do so. ...

(10) Where a vehicle is stopped by a constable under this section, the driver shall be entitled to obtain a written statement that the vehicle was stopped under the powers conferred by this section if he applies for such a statement not later than the end of the period of twelve months from the day on which the vehicle was stopped.

(10A) A person who is searched by a constable under this section shall be entitled to obtain a written statement that he was searched under the powers conferred by this section if he applies for such a statement not later than the end of the period of twelve months from the day on which he was searched.

(11) In this section –

'dangerous instruments' means instruments which have a blade or are sharply pointed;

'offensive weapon' has the meaning given by section 1(9) of the Police and Criminal Evidence Act 1984 ...; and ...

'vehicle' includes a caravan as defined in section 29(1) of the Caravan Sites and Control of Development Act 1960.

(11A) For the purposes of this section, a person carries a dangerous instrument or an offensive weapon if he has it in his possession.

(12) The powers conferred by this section are in addition to and not in derogation of, any power otherwise conferred.

60AA Powers to require removal of disguises

(1) Where –

(a) an authorisation under section 60 is for the time being in force in relation to any locality for any period, or

(b) an authorisation under subsection (3) that the powers conferred by subsection (2) shall be exercisable at any place in a locality is in force for any period,

those powers shall be exercisable at any place in that locality at any time in that period.

(2) This subsection confers power on any constable in uniform –

(a) to require any person to remove any item which the constable reasonably believes that person is wearing wholly or mainly for the purpose of concealing his identity;

(b) to seize any item which the constable reasonably believes any person intends to wear wholly or mainly for that purpose.

(3) If a police officer of or above the rank of inspector reasonably believes –

(a) that activities may take place in any locality in his police area that are likely (if they take place) to involve the commission of offences, and

(b) that it is expedient, in order to prevent or control the activities, to give an authorisation under this subsection,

he may give an authorisation that the powers conferred by this section shall be exercisable at any place within that locality for a specified period not exceeding twenty-four hours.

(4) If it appears to an officer of or above the rank of superintendent that it is expedient to do so, having regard to offences which –

(a) have been committed in connection with the activities in respect of which the authorisation was given, or

(b) are reasonably suspected to have been so committed,

he may direct that the authorisation shall continue in force for a further twenty-four hours.

(5) If an inspector gives an authorisation under subsection , he must, as soon as it is practicable to do so, cause an officer of or above the rank of superintendent to be informed.

(6) Any authorisation under this section –

(a) shall be in writing and signed by the officer giving it; and

(b) shall specify –

(i) the grounds on which it is given;

(ii) the locality in which the powers conferred by this section are exercisable;

(iii) the period during which those powers are exercisable;

and a direction under subsection (4) shall also be given in writing or, where that is not practicable, recorded in writing as soon as it is practicable to do so.

(7) A person who fails to remove an item worn by him when required to do so by a constable in the exercise of his power under this section shall be liable, on summary conviction, to imprisonment for a term not exceeding one month or to a fine not exceeding level 3 on the standard scale or both.

(10) The powers conferred by this section are in addition to, and not in derogation of, any power otherwise conferred. ...

60A Retention and disposal of things seized under section 60 [or 60AA]

(1) Any things seized by a constable under section 60 or 60AA may be retained in accordance with regulations made by the Secretary of State under this section.

(2) The Secretary of State may make regulations regulating the retention and safe keeping, and the disposal and destruction in prescribed circumstances, of such things. ...

PART V

PUBLIC ORDER: COLLECTIVE TRESPASS OR NUISANCE ON LAND

61 Power to remove trespassers on land

(1) If the senior police officer present at the scene reasonably believes that two or more persons are trespassing on land and are present there with the common

purpose of residing there for any period, that reasonable steps have been taken by or on behalf of the occupier to ask them to leave and –

(a) that any of those persons has caused damage to the land or to property on the land or used threatening, abusive or insulting words or behaviour towards the occupier, a member of his family or an employee or agent of his, or

(b) that those persons have between them six or more vehicles on the land,

he may direct those persons, or any of them, to leave the land and to remove any vehicles or other property they have with them on the land.

(2) Where the persons in question are reasonably believed by the senior police officer to be persons who were not originally trespassers but have become trespassers on the land, the officer must reasonably believe that the other conditions specified in subsection (1) are satisfied after those persons became trespassers before he can exercise the power conferred by that subsection.

(3) A direction under subsection (1) above, if not communicated to the persons referred to in subsection (1) by the police officer giving the direction, may be communicated to them by any constable at the scene.

(4) If a person knowing that a direction under subsection (1) above has been given which applies to him –

(a) fails to leave the land as soon as reasonably practicable, or

(b) having left again enters the land as a trespasser within the period of three months beginning with the day on which the direction was given,

he commits an offence and is liable on summary conviction to imprisonment for a term not exceeding three months or a fine not exceeding level 4 on the standard scale, or both. ...

(5) A constable in uniform who reasonably suspects that a person is committing an offence under this section may arrest him without a warrant.

(6) In proceedings for an offence under this section it is a defence for the accused to show –

(a) that he was not trespassing on the land, or

(b) that he had a reasonable excuse for failing to leave the land as soon as reasonably practicable or, as the case may be, for again entering the land as a trespasser.

(7) In its application in England and Wales to common land this section has effect as if in the preceding subsections of it –

(a) references to trespassing or trespassers were references to acts and persons doing acts which constitute either a trespass as against the occupier or an infringement of the commoners' rights; and

(b) references to 'the occupier' included the commoners or any of them or, in the case of common land to which the public has access, the local authority as well as any commoner.

(8) Subsection (7) above does not –

(a) require action by more than one occupier; or

(b) constitute persons trespassers as against any commoner or the local authority if they are permitted to be there by the other occupier.

(9) In this section –

'common land' means common land as defined in section 22 of the Commons Registration Act 1965;

'commoner' means a person with rights of common as defined in section 22 of the Commons Registration Act 1965;

'land' does not include –

(a) buildings other than –

(i) agricultural buildings within the meaning of, in England and Wales, paragraphs 3 to 8 of Schedule 5 to the Local Government Finance Act 1988 ..., or

(ii) scheduled monuments within the meaning of the Ancient Monuments and Archaeological Areas Act 1979;

(b) land forming part of –

(i) a highway unless it falls within the classifications in section 54 of the Wildlife and Countryside Act 1981 (footpath, bridleway or byway open to all traffic or road used as a public path) or is a cycle track under the Highways Act 1980 or the Cycle Tracks Act 1984; ...

'the local authority', in relation to common land, means any local authority which has powers in relation to the land under section 9 of the Commons Registration Act 1965;

'occupier' (and in subsection (8) 'the other occupier') means –

(a) in England and Wales, the person entitled to possession of the land by virtue of an estate or interest held by him; ...

'property', in relation to damage to property on land, means –

(a) in England and Wales, property within the meaning of section 10(1) of the Criminal Damage Act 1971; ...

and 'damage' includes the deposit of any substance capable of polluting the land;

'trespass' means, in the application of this section –

(a) in England and Wales, subject to the extensions effected by subsection (7) above, trespass as against the occupier of the land; and

'trespassing' and 'trespasser' shall be construed accordingly;

'vehicle' includes –

(a) any vehicle, whether or not it is in a fit state for use on roads, and includes any chassis or body, with or without wheels, appearing to have formed part of such a vehicle, and any load carried by, and anything attached to, such a vehicle; and

(b) a caravan as defined in section 29(1) of the Caravan Sites and Control of Development Act 1960;

and a person may be regarded for the purposes of this section as having a purpose of residing in a place notwithstanding that he has a home elsewhere.

62 Supplementary powers of seizure

(1) If a direction has been given under section 61 and a constable reasonably suspects that any person to whom the direction applies has, without reasonable excuse –

(a) failed to remove any vehicle on the land which appears to the constable to belong to him or to be in his possession or under his control; or

(b) entered the land as a trespasser with a vehicle within the period of three months beginning with the day on which the direction was given,

the constable may seize and remove the vehicle.

(2) In this section, 'trespasser' and 'vehicle' have the same meaning as in section 61.

62A Power to remove trespassers: alternative site available

(1) If the senior police officer present at a scene reasonably believes that the conditions in subsection (2) are satisfied in relation to a person and land, he may direct the person –

(a) to leave the land;

(b) to remove any vehicle and other property he has with him on the land.

(2) The conditions are –

(a) that the person and one or more others ('the trespassers') are trespassing on the land;

(b) that the trespassers have between them at least one vehicle on the land;

(c) that the trespassers are present on the land with the common purpose of residing there for any period;

(d) if it appears to the officer that the person has one or more caravans in his possession or under his control on the land, that there is a suitable pitch on a relevant caravan site for that caravan or each of those caravans;

(e) that the occupier of the land or a person acting on his behalf has asked the police to remove the trespassers from the land.

(3) A direction under subsection (1) may be communicated to the person to whom it applies by any constable at the scene.

(4) Subsection (5) applies if –

(a) a police officer proposes to give a direction under subsection (1) in relation to a person and land, and

(b) it appears to him that the person has one or more caravans in his possession or under his control on the land.

(5) The officer must consult every local authority within whose area the land is situated as to whether there is a suitable pitch for the caravan or each of the caravans on a relevant caravan site which is situated in the local authority's area.

(6) In this section –

'caravan' and 'caravan site' have the same meanings as in Part 1 of the Caravan Sites and Control of Development Act 1960;

'relevant caravan site' means a caravan site which is –

(a) situated in the area of a local authority within whose area the land is situated, and

(b) managed by a relevant site manager;

'relevant site manager' means –

(a) a local authority within whose area the land is situated;

(b) a registered social landlord;

'registered social landlord' means a body registered as a social landlord under Chapter 1 of Part 1 of the Housing Act 1996.

(7) The Secretary of State may by order amend the definition of 'relevant site manager' in subsection (6) by adding a person or description of a person.

(8) An order under subsection (7) must be made by statutory instrument and is subject to annulment in pursuance of a resolution of either House of Parliament.

62B Failure to comply with direction under section 62A: offences

(1) A person commits an offence if he knows that a direction under section 62A(1) has been given which applies to him and –

(a) he fails to leave the relevant land as soon as reasonably practicable, or

(b) he enters any land in the area of the relevant local authority as a trespasser before the end of the relevant period with the intention of residing there.

(2) The relevant period is the period of 3 months starting with the day on which the direction is given.

(3) A person guilty of an offence under this section is liable on summary conviction to imprisonment for a term not exceeding 3 months or a fine not exceeding level 4 on the standard scale or both.

(4) A constable in uniform who reasonably suspects that a person is committing an offence under this section may arrest him without a warrant.

(5) In proceedings for an offence under this section it is a defence for the accused to show –

(a) that he was not trespassing on the land in respect of which he is alleged to have committed the offence, or
(b) that he had a reasonable excuse –

(i) for failing to leave the relevant land as soon as reasonably practicable, or

(ii) for entering land in the area of the relevant local authority as a trespasser with the intention of residing there, or

(c) that, at the time the direction was given, he was under the age of 18 years and was residing with his parent or guardian.

62C Failure to comply with direction under section 62A: seizure

(1) This section applies if a direction has been given under section 62A(1) and a constable reasonably suspects that a person to whom the direction applies has, without reasonable excuse –

(a) failed to remove any vehicle on the relevant land which appears to the constable to belong to him or to be in his possession or under his control; or

(b) entered any land in the area of the relevant local authority as a trespasser with a vehicle before the end of the relevant period with the intention of residing there.

(2) The relevant period is the period of 3 months starting with the day on which the direction is given.

(3) The constable may seize and remove the vehicle.

62D Common land: modifications

(1) In their application to common land sections 62A to 62C have effect with these modifications.
(2) References to trespassing and trespassers have effect as if they were references to acts, and persons doing acts, which constitute –

(a) a trespass as against the occupier, or
(b) an infringement of the commoners' rights.

(3) References to the occupier –

(a) in the case of land to which the publc has access, include the local authority and any commoner;
(b) in any other case, include the commoners or any of them.

(4) Subsection (1) does not –

(a) require action by more than one occupier, or

(b) constitute persons trespassers as against any commoner or the local authority if they are permitted to be there by the other occupier.

(5) In this section 'common land', 'commoner' and 'the local authority' have the meanings given by section 61.

62E Sections 62A to 62D: interpretation

(1) Subsections (2) to (8) apply for the interpretation of sections 62A to 62D and this section.

(2) 'Land' does not include buildings other than –

(a) agricultural buildings within the meaning of paragraphs 3 to 8 of Schedule 5 to the Local Government Finance Act 1988, or

(b) scheduled monuments within the meaning of the Ancient Monuments and Archaeological Areas Act 1979.

(3) 'Local authority' means –

(a) in Greater London, a London borough or the Common Council of the City of London;

(b) in England outside Greater London, a county council, a district council or the Council of the Isles of Scilly;

(c) in Wales, a county council or a county borough council.

(4) 'Occupier', 'trespass', 'trespassing' and 'trespasser' have the meanings given by section 61 in relation to England and Wales.

(5) 'The relevant land' means the land in respect of which a direction under section 62A(1) is given.

(6) 'The relevant local authority' means –

(a) if the relevant land is situated in the area of more than one local authority (but is not in the Isles of Scilly), the district council or county borough council within whose area the relevant land is situated;

(b) if the relevant land is situated in the Isles of Scilly, the Council of the Isles of Scilly;

(c) in any other case, the local authority within whose area the relevant land is situated.

(7) 'Vehicle' has the meaning given by section 61.

(8) A person may be regarded as having a purpose of residing in a place even if he has a home elsewhere.

63 Powers to remove persons attending or preparing for a rave

(1) This section applies to a gathering on land in the open air of 20 or more persons (whether or not trespassers) at which amplified music is played during the night (with or without intermissions) and is such as, by reason of its loudness and duration and the time at which it is played, is likely to cause serious distress to the inhabitants of the locality; and for this purpose –

(a) such a gathering continues during intermissions in the music and, where the gathering extends over several days, throughout the period during which amplified music is played at night (with or without intermissions); and

(b) 'music' includes sounds wholly or predominantly characterised by the emission of a succession of repetitive beats.

(1A) This section also applies to a gathering if –

(a) it is a gathering on land of 20 or more persons who are trespassing on the land; and

(b) it would be a gathering of a kind mentioned in subsection (1) above if it took place on land in the open air.

(2) If, as respects any land, a police officer of at least the rank of superintendent reasonably believes that –

(a) two or more persons are making preparations for the holding there of a gathering to which this section applies,

(b) ten or more persons are waiting for such a gathering to begin there, or

(c) ten or more persons are attending such a gathering which is in progress,

he may give a direction that those persons and any other persons who come to prepare or wait for or to attend the gathering are to leave the land and remove any vehicles or other property which they have with them on the land.

(3) A direction under subsection (2) above, if not communicated to the persons referred to in subsection (2) by the police officer giving the direction, may be communicated to them by any constable at the scene.

(4) Persons shall be treated as having had a direction under subsection (2) above communicated to them if reasonable steps have been taken to bring it to their attention.

(5) A direction under subsection (2) above does not apply to an exempt person.

(6) If a person knowing that a direction has been given which applies to him –

(a) fails to leave the land as soon as reasonably practicable, or

(b) having left again enters the land within the period of 7 days beginning with the day on which the direction was given,

he commits an offence and is liable on summary conviction to imprisonment for a term not exceeding three months or a fine not exceeding level 4 on the standard scale, or both.

(7) In proceedings for an offence under subsection (6) above it is a defence for the accused to show that he had a reasonable excuse for failing to leave the land as soon as reasonably practicable or, as the case may be, for again entering the land.

(7A) A person commits an offence if –

(a) he knows that a direction under subsection (2) above has been given which applies to him, and

(b) he makes preparations for or attends a gathering to which this section applies within the period of 24 hours starting when the direction was given.

(7B) A person guilty of an offence under subsection (7A) above is liable on summary conviction to imprisonment for a term not exceeding three months or a fine not exceeding level 4 on the standard scale, or both.

(8) A constable in uniform who reasonably suspects that a person is committing an offence under this section may arrest him without a warrant.

(9) This section does not apply –

(a) in England and Wales, to a gathering licensed by an entertainment licence; or

(b) in Scotland, to a gathering in premises which, by virtue of section 41 of the Civic Government (Scotland) Act 1982, are licensed to be used as a place of public entertainment.

(10) In this section –

'entertainment licence' means a licence granted by a local authority under –

(a) Schedule 12 to the London Government Act 1963;

(b) section 3 of the Private Places of Entertainment (Licensing) Act 1967; or

(c) Schedule 1 to the Local Government (Miscellaneous Provisions) Act 1982;

'exempt person', in relation to land (or any gathering on land), means the occupier, any member of his family and any employee or agent of his and any person whose home is situated on the land;

'land in the open air' includes a place partly open to the air;

'local authority' means –

(a) in Greater London, a London borough council or the Common Council of the City of London;

(b) in England outside Greater London, a district council or the council of the Isles of Scilly;

(c) in Wales, a county council or county borough council; and

'occupier', 'trespasser' and 'vehicle' have the same meaning as in section 61.

64 Supplementary powers of entry and seizure

(1) If a police officer of at least the rank of superintendent reasonably believes that circumstances exist in relation to any land which would justify the giving of a direction under section 63 in relation to a gathering to which that section applies he may authorise any constable to enter the land for any of the purposes specified in subsection (2) below.

(2) Those purposes are –

(a) to ascertain whether such circumstances exist; and

(b) to exercise any power conferred on a constable by section 63 or subsection (4) below.

(3) A constable who is so authorised to enter land for any purpose may enter the land without a warrant.

(4) If a direction has been given under section 63 and a constable reasonably suspects that any person to whom the direction applies has, without reasonable excuse –

(a) failed to remove any vehicle or sound equipment on the land which appears to the constable to belong to him or to be in his possession or under his control; or

(b) entered the land as a trespasser with a vehicle or sound equipment within the period of 7 days beginning with the day on which the direction was given,

the constable may seize and remove that vehicle or sound equipment.

(5) Subsection (4) above does not authorise the seizure of any vehicle or sound equipment of an exempt person. ...

(6) In this section –

'exempt person' has the same meaning as in section 63;

'sound equipment' means equipment designed or adapted for amplifying music and any equipment suitable for use in connection with such equipment, and 'music' has the same meaning as in section 63; and

'vehicle' has the same meaning as in section 61.

65 Raves: power to stop persons from proceeding

(1) If a constable in uniform reasonably believes that a person is on his way to a gathering to which section 63 applies in relation to which a direction under section 63(2) is in force, he may, subject to subsections (2) and (3) below –

(a) stop that person, and

(b) direct him not to proceed in the direction of the gathering.

(2) The power conferred by subsection (1) above may only be exercised at a place within 5 miles of the boundary of the site of the gathering.

(3) No direction may be given under subsection (1) above to an exempt person.

(4) If a person knowing that a direction under subsection (1) above has been given to him fails to comply with that direction, he commits an offence and is liable on summary conviction to a fine not exceeding level 3 on the standard scale.

(5) A constable in uniform who reasonably suspects that a person is committing an offence under this section may arrest him without a warrant.

(6) In this section, 'exempt person' has the same meaning as in section 63.

66 Power of court to forfeit sound equipment

(1) Where a person is convicted of an offence under section 63 in relation to a gathering to which that section applies and the court is satisfied that any sound equipment which has been seized from him under section 64(4), or which was in his possession or under his control at the relevant time, has been used at the

gathering the court may make an order for forfeiture under this subsection in respect of that property.

(2) The court may make an order under subsection (1) above whether or not it also deals with the offender in respect of the offence in any other way and without regard to any restrictions on forfeiture in any enactment.

(3) In considering whether to make an order under subsection (1) above in respect of any property a court shall have regard –

(a) to the value of the property; and

(b) to the likely financial and other effects on the offender of the making of the order (taken together with any other order that the court contemplates making).

(4) An order under subsection (1) above shall operate to deprive the offender of his rights, if any, in the property to which it relates, and the property shall (if not already in their possession) be taken into the possession of the police.

(5) Except in a case to which subsection (6) below applies, where any property has been forfeited under subsection (1) above, a magistrates' court may, on application by a claimant of the property, other than the offender from whom it was forfeited under subsection (1) above, make an order for delivery of the property to the applicant if it appears to the court that he is the owner of the property.

(6) In a case where forfeiture under subsection (1) above has been by order of a Scottish court, a claimant such as is mentioned in subsection (5) above may, in such manner as may be prescribed by act of adjournal, apply to that court for an order for the return of the property in question.

(7) No application shall be made under subsection (5), or by virtue of subsection (6), above by any claimant of the property after the expiration of 6 months from the date on which an order under subsection (1) above was made in respect of the property.

(8) No such application shall succeed unless the claimant satisfies the court either that he had not consented to the offender having possession of the property or that he did not know, and had no reason to suspect, that the property was likely to be used at a gathering to which section 63 applies.

(9) An order under subsection (5), or by virtue of subsection (6), above shall not affect the right of any person to take, within the period of 6 months from the date of an order under subsection (5), or as the case may be by virtue of subsection (6), above, proceedings for the recovery of the property from the person in possession of it in pursuance of the order, but on the expiration of that period the right shall cease.

(10) The Secretary of State may make regulations for the disposal of property, and for the application of the proceeds of sale of property, forfeited under subsection (1) above where no application by a claimant of the property under subsection (5), or by virtue of subsection (6), above has been made within the period specified in subsection (7) above or no such application has succeeded.

(11) The regulations may also provide for the investment of money and for the audit of accounts.

(12) The power to make regulations under subsection (10) above shall be exercisable by statutory instrument which shall be subject to annulment in pursuance of a resolution of either House of Parliament.

(13) In this section –

'relevant time', in relation to a person –

(a) convicted in England and Wales of an offence under section 63, means the time of his arrest for the offence or of the issue of a summons in respect of it;

...

'sound equipment' has the same meaning as in section 64.

67 Retention and charges for seized property

(1) Any vehicles which have been seized and removed by a constable under section 62(1), 62C(3) or 64(4) may be retained in accordance with regulations made by the Secretary of State under subsection (3) below.

(2) Any sound equipment which has been seized and removed by a constable under section 64(4) may be retained until the conclusion of proceedings against the person from whom it was seized for an offence under section 63.

(3) The Secretary of State may make regulations –

(a) regulating the retention and safe keeping and the disposal and the destruction in prescribed circumstances of vehicles; and

(b) prescribing charges in respect of the removal, retention, disposal and destruction of vehicles.

(4) Any authority shall be entitled to recover from a person from whom a vehicle has been seized such charges as may be prescribed in respect of the removal, retention, disposal and destruction of the vehicle by the authority.

(5) Regulations under subsection (3) above may make different provisions for different classes of vehicles or for different circumstances.

(6) Any charges under subsection (4) above shall be recoverable as a simple contract debt.

(7) Any authority having custody of vehicles under regulations under subsection (3) above shall be entitled to retain custody until any charges under subsection (4) are paid.

(8) The power to make regulations under subsection (3) above shall be exercisable by statutory instrument which shall be subject to annulment in pursuance of a resolution of either House of Parliament.

(9) In this section –

'conclusion of proceedings' against a person means –

(a) his being sentenced or otherwise dealt with for the offence or his acquittal;

(b) the discontinuance of the proceedings; or

(c) the decision not to prosecute him,

whichever is the earlier;

'sound equipment' has the same meaning as in section 64; and

'vehicle' has the same meaning as in section 61.

68 Offence of aggravated trespass

(1) A person commits the offence of aggravated trespass if he trespasses on land and, in relation to any lawful activity which persons are engaging in or are about to engage in on that or adjoining land, does there anything which is intended by him to have the effect –

(a) of intimidating those persons or any of them so as to deter them or any of them from engaging in that activity,

(b) of obstructing that activity, or

(c) of disrupting that activity. ...

(2) Activity on any occasion on the part of a person or persons on land is 'lawful' for the purposes of this section if he or they may engage in the activity on the land on that occasion without committing an offence or trespassing on the land.

(3) A person guilty of an offence under this section is liable on summary conviction to imprisonment for a term not exceeding three months or a fine not exceeding level 4 on the standard scale, or both.

(4) A constable in uniform who reasonably suspects that a person is committing an offence under this section may arrest him without a warrant.

(5) In this section 'land' does not include –

(a) the highways and roads excluded from the application of section 61 by paragraph (b) of the definition of 'land' in subsection (9) of that section; ...

69 Powers to remove persons committing or participating in aggravated trespass

(1) If the senior police officer present at the scene reasonably believes –

(a) that a person is committing, has committed or intends to commit the offence of aggravated trespass on land; or

(b) that two or more persons are trespassing on land and are present there with the common purpose of intimidating persons so as to deter them from engaging in a lawful activity or of obstructing or disrupting a lawful activity,

he may direct that person or (as the case may be) those persons (or any of them) to leave the land.

(2) A direction under subsection (1) above, if not communicated to the persons

referred to in subsection (1) by the police officer giving the direction, may be communicated to them by any constable at the scene.

(3) If a person knowing that a direction under subsection (1) above has been given which applies to him –

(a) fails to leave the land as soon as practicable, or

(b) having left again enters the land as a trespasser within the period of three months beginning with the day on which the direction was given,

he commits an offence and is liable on summary conviction to imprisonment for a term not exceeding three months or a fine not exceeding level 4 on the standard scale, or both.

(4) In proceedings for an offence under subsection (3) it is a defence for the accused to show –

(a) that he was not trespassing on the land, or

(b) that he had a reasonable excuse for failing to leave the land as soon as practicable or, as the case may be, for again entering the land as a trespasser.

(5) A constable in uniform who reasonably suspects that a person is committing an offence under this section may arrest him without a warrant.

(6) In this section 'lawful activity' and 'land' have the same meaning as in section 68.

PART XII

MISCELLANEOUS AND GENERAL

166 Sale of tickets by unauthorised persons

(1) It is an offence for an unauthorised person to sell, or offer or expose for sale, a ticket for a designated football match in any public place or place to which the public has access or, in the course of a trade or business, in any other place.

(2) For this purpose –

(a) a person is 'unauthorised' unless he is authorised in writing to sell tickets for the match by the home club or by the organisers of the match;

(b) a 'ticket' means anything which purports to be a ticket; and

(c) a 'designated football match' means a football match of a description, or a particular footbal match, for the time being designated for the purposes of Part I of the Football Spectators Act 1989 or which is a regulated football match for the purposes of Part II of that Act.

(3) A person guilty of an offence under this section is liable on summary conviction to a fine not exceeding level 5 on the standard scale. ...

(5) Section 32 of the Police and Criminal Evidence Act 1984 (search of persons and premises (including vehicles) upon arrest) shall have effect, in its application in relation to an offence under this section, as if the power conferred on a constable

to enter and search any vehicle extended to any vehicle which the constable has reasonable grounds for believing was being used for any purpose connected with the offence. ...

As amended by the Criminal Procedure and Investigations Act 1996, ss44(1), (3), (4), (7), 80, Schedule 5(1); Knives Act 1997, s8(1)–(10); Crime and Disorder Act 1998, ss25, 26, 35, 120, Schedule 9, para 2, Schedule 10; Football (Offences and Disorder) Act 1999, s10; Youth Justice and Criminal Evidence Act 1999, s58(1)–(5); Football (Offences and Disorder) Act 1999, s10; Football (Disorder) Act 2000, s1(2), (3), Schedule 2, para 20, Schedule 3; Anti-terrorism, Crime and Security Act 2001, ss94(1), (2), 101, 125, Schedule 7, paras 15, 16(1), (2), Schedule 8, Pt 6; Anti-social Behaviour Act 2003, ss58–64.

POLICE ACT 1996
(1996 c 16)

PART V

MISCELLANEOUS AND GENERAL

89 Assaults on constables

(1) Any person who assaults a constable in the execution of his duty, or a person assisting a constable in the execution of his duty, shall be guilty of an offence and liable on summary conviction to imprisonment for a term not exceeding six months or to a fine not exceeding level 5 on the standard scale, or to both.

(2) Any person who resists or wilfully obstructs a constable in the execution of his duty, or a person assisting a constable in the execution of his duty, shall be guilty of an offence and liable on summary conviction to imprisonment for a term not exceeding one month or to a fine not exceeding level 3 on the standard scale, or to both.

(3) This section also applies to a constable who is a member of a police force maintained in Scotland or Northern Ireland when he is executing a warrant, or otherwise acting in England or Wales, by virtue of any enactment conferring powers on him in England and Wales.

(4) In this section references to a person assisting a constable in the execution of his duty include references to any person who is neither a constable nor in the company of a constable but who –

(a) is a member of an international joint investigation team that is led by a member of a police force or by a member of the National Criminal Intelligence Service or of the National Crime Squad; and

(b) is carrying out his functions as a member of that team.

(5) In this section 'international joint investigation team' means any investigation team formed in accordance with –

(a) any framework decision on joint investigation teams adopted under Article 34 of the Treaty on European Union;

(b) the Convention on Mutual Assistance in Criminal Matters between the Member States of the European Union, and the Protocol to that Convention, established in accordance with that Article of that Treaty; or

(c) any international agreements to which the United Kingdom is a party and which is specified for the purposes of this section in an order made by the Secretary of State.

(6) A statutory instrument containing an order under subsection (5) shall be subject to annulment in pursuance of a resolution of either House of Parliament.

As amended by the Police Reform Act 2002, s104(1).

DEFAMATION ACT 1996

(1996 c 31)

13 Evidence concerning proceedings in Parliament

(1) Where the conduct of a person in or in relation to proceedings in Parliament is in issue in defamation proceedings, he may waive for the purposes of those proceedings, so far as concerns him, the protection of any enactment or rule of law which prevents proceedings in Parliament being impeached or questioned in any court or place out of Parliament.

(2) Where a person waives that protection –

(a) any such enactment or rule of law shall not apply to prevent evidence being given, questions being asked or statements, submissions, comments or findings being made about his conduct, and

(b) none of those things shall be regarded as infringing the privilege of either House of Parliament.

(3) The waiver by one person of that protection does not affect its operation in relation to another person who has not waived it.

(4) Nothing in this section affects any enactment or rule of law so far as it protects a person (including a person who has waived the protection referred to above) from legal liability for words spoken or things done in the course of, or for the purposes of or incidental to, any proceedings in Parliament.

(5) Without prejudice to the generality of subsection (4), that subsection applies to –

(a) the giving of evidence before either House or a committee;

(b) the presentation or submission of a document to either House or a committee;

(c) the preparation of a document for the purposes of or incidental to the transacting of any such business;

(d) the formulation, making or publication of a document, including a report, by or pursuant to an order of either House or a committee; and

(e) any communication with the Parliamentary Commissioner for Standards or any person having functions in connection with the registration of members' interests.

In this subsection 'a committee' means a committee of either House or a joint committee of both Houses of Parliament.

15 Reports, etc protected by qualified privilege

(1) The publication of any report or other statement mentioned in Schedule 1 to this Act is privileged unless the publication is shown to be made with malice, subject as follows.

(2) In defamation proceedings in respect of the publication of a report or other statement mentioned in Part II of that Schedule, there is no defence under this section if the plaintiff shows that the defendant –

(a) was requested by him to publish in a suitable manner a reasonable letter or statement by way of explanation or contradiction, and

(b) refused or neglected to do so.

For this purpose 'in a suitable manner' means in the same manner as the publication complained of or in a manner that is adequate and reasonable in the circumstances.

(3) This section does not apply to the publication to the public, or a section of the public, of matter which is not of public concern and the publication of which is not for the public benefit.

(4) Nothing in this section shall be construed –

(a) as protecting the publication of matter the publication of which is prohibited by law, or

(b) as limiting or abridging any privilege subsisting apart from this section.

SCHEDULE 1

QUALIFIED PRIVILEGE

PART I

STATEMENTS HAVING QUALIFIED PRIVILEGE WITHOUT EXPLANATION OR CONTRADICTION

1. A fair and accurate report of proceedings in public of a legislature anywhere in the world.

2. A fair and accurate report of proceedings in public before a court anywhere in the world.

3. A fair and accurate report of proceedings in public of a person appointed to hold a public inquiry by a government or legislature anywhere in the world.

4. A fair and accurate report of proceedings in public anywhere in the world of an international organisation or an international conference.

5. A fair and accurate copy of or extract from any register or other document required by law to be open to public inspection.

6. A notice or advertisement published by or on the authority of a court, or of a judge or officer of a court, anywhere in the world.

7. A fair and accurate copy of or extract from matter published by or on the authority of a government or legislature anywhere in the world.

8. A fair and accurate copy of or extract from matter published anywhere in the world by an international organisation or an international conference.

PART II

STATEMENTS PRIVILEGED SUBJECT TO EXPLANATION OR CONTRADICTION

9. – (1) A fair and accurate copy of or extract from a notice or other matter issued for the information of the public by or on behalf of –

(a) a legislature in any member State or the European Parliament;

(b) the government of any member State, or any authority performing governmental functions in any member State or part of a member State, or the European Commission;

(c) an international organisation or international conference.

(2) In this paragraph 'governmental functions' includes police functions.

10. A fair and accurate copy of or extract from a document made available by a court in any member State or the European Court of Justice (or any court attached to that court), or by a judge or officer of any such court.

11. – (1) A fair and accurate report of proceedings at any public meeting or sitting in the United Kingdom of –

(a) a local authority or local authority committee;

(aa) in the case of a local authority which are operating executive arrangements, the executive of that authority or a committee of that executive;

(b) a justice or justices of the peace acting otherwise than as a court exercising judicial authority;

(c) a commission, tribunal, committee or person appointed for the purposes of any inquiry by any statutory provision, by Her Majesty or by a Minister of the Crown, a member of the Scottish Executive or a Northern Ireland Department;

(d) a person appointed by a local authority to hold a local inquiry in pursuance of any statutory provision;

(e) any other tribunal, board, committee or body constituted by or under, and exercising functions under, any statutory provision.

(1A) In the case of a local authority which are operating executive arrangements, a fair and accurate record of any decision made by any member of the executive where that record is required to be made and available for public inspection by virtue of section 22 of the Local Government Act 2000 or of any provision in regulations made under that section.

(2) In sub-paragraphs (1)(a), (1)(aa) and (1A) –

'local authority' means –

(a) in relation to England and Wales, a principal council within the meaning of the Local Government Act 1972, any body falling within any paragraph of section 100J(1) of that Act or an authority or body to which the Public Bodies (Admission to Meetings) Act 1960 applies, ... and

'local authority committee' means any committee of a local authority or of local authorities, and includes –

(a) any committee or sub-committee in relation to which sections 100A to 100D of the Local Government Act 1972 apply by virtue of section 100E of that Act (whether or not also by virtue of section 100J of that Act), ...

(2A) In sub-paragraphs (1) and (1A) –

'executive' and 'executive arrangements' have the same meaning as in Part II of the Local Government Act 2000.

(3) A fair and accurate report of any corresponding proceedings in any of the Channel Islands or the Isle of Man or in another member State.

12. – (1) A fair and accurate report of proceedings at any public meeting held in a member State.

(2) In this paragraph a 'public meeting' means a meeting bona fide and lawfully held for a lawful purpose and for the furtherance or discussion of a matter of public concern, whether admission to the meeting is general or restricted. ...

15. – (1) A fair and accurate report of, or copy of or extract from, any adjudication, report, statement or notice issued by a body, officer or other person designated for the purposes of this paragraph –

(a) for England and Wales or Northern Ireland, by order of the Lord Chancellor, ...

(2) An order under this paragraph shall be made by statutory instrument which shall be subject to annulment in pursuance of a resolution of either House of Parliament.

PART III

SUPPLEMENTARY PROVISIONS

16. – (1) In this Schedule –

'court' includes any tribunal or body exercising the judicial power of the State;

'international conference' means a conference attended by representatives of two or more governments;

'international organisation' means an organisation of which two or more governments are members, and includes any committee or other subordinate body of such an organisation; and 'legislature' includes a local legislature.

(2) References in this Schedule to a member State include any European dependent territory of a member State.

(3) In paragraphs 2 and 6 'court' includes –

(a) the European Court of Justice (or any court attached to that court) and the Court of Auditors of the European Communities,

(b) the European Court of Human Rights,

(c) any international criminal tribunal established by the Security Council of the United Nations or by an international agreement to which the United Kingdom is a party, and

(d) the International Court of Justice and any other judicial or arbitral tribunal deciding matters in dispute between States.

(4) In paragraphs 1, 3 and 7 'legislature' includes the European Parliament.

17. – (1) Provision may be made by order identifying –

(a) for the purposes of paragraph 11, the corresponding proceedings referred to in sub-paragraph (3); ...

(2) An order under this paragraph may be made –

(a) for England and Wales or Northern Ireland, by the Lord Chancellor, ...

(3) An order under this paragraph shall be made by statutory instrument which shall be subject to annulment in pursuance of a resolution of either House of Parliament.

NB For the amendment of Schedule 1, Pt II, para 11, above, in relation to Wales, see the Local Authorities (Executive and Alternative Arrangements) (Modification of Enactments and Other Provisions) Order 2002, arts 2(p), 30.

As amended by the Scotland Act 1998, s125(1), Schedule 8, para 33(1), (3); Local Authorities (Executive and Alternative Arrangements) (Modification of Enactments and Other Provisions) (England) Order 2001, art 31; Local Authorities (Executive Arrangements) (Modification of Enactments) (England) Order 2002, art 12.

ASYLUM AND IMMIGRATION ACT 1996

(1996 c 49)

8 Restrictions on employment

(1) Subject to subsection (2) below, if any person ('the employer') employs a person subject to immigration control ('the employee') who has attained the age of 16, the employer shall be guilty of an offence if –

(a) the employee has not been granted leave to enter or remain in the United Kingdom; or

(b) the employee's leave is not valid and subsisting, or is subject to a condition precluding him from taking up the employment,

and (in either case) the employee does not satisfy such conditions as may be specified in an order made by the Secretary of State.

(2) It is a defence for a person charged with an offence under this section to prove that before the employment began any relevant requirement of an order of the Secretary of State under subsection (2A) was complied with.

(2A) An order under this subsection may –

(a) require the production to an employer of a document of a specified description;

(b) require the production to an employer of one document of each of a number of specified descriptions;

(c) require an employer to take specified steps to retain, copy or record the content of a document produced to him in accordance with the order;

(d) make provision which applies generally or only in specified circumstances;

(e) make different provisions for different circumstances.

(3) The defence afforded by subsection (2) above shall not be available in any case where the employer knew that his employment of the employee would constitute an offence under this section. ...

(8) In this section –

'contract of employment' means a contract of service or apprenticeship, whether express or implied, and (if it is express) whether it is oral or in writing;

'employ' means employ under a contract of employment and 'employment' shall be construed accordingly.

(10) An offence under this section shall be treated as –

(a) a relevant offence for the purpose of sections 28B and 28D of that Act (search, entry and arrest), and

(b) an offence under Part III of that Act (criminal proceedings) for the purposes of sections 28E, 28G and 28H (search after arrest).

8A Code of practice

(1) The Secretary of State must issue a code of practice as to the measures which an employer is to be expected to take, or not to take, with a view to securing that, while avoiding the commission of an offence under section 8, he also avoids unlawful discrimination.

(2) 'Unlawful discrimination' means –

(a) discrimination in contravention of section 4(1) of the Race Relations Act 1976 ('the 1976 Act'); …

As amended by the Immigration and Asylum Act 1999, s22; Nationality, Immigration and Asylum Act 2002, s147(1), (2), (4); Asylum and Immigration (Treatment of Claimants, etc) Act 2004, s6(2).

BROADCASTING ACT 1996
(1996 c 55)

PART V

107 Preparation by OFCOM of code relating to avoidance of unjust or unfair treatment or interference with privacy

(1) It shall be the duty of OFCOM to draw up, and from time to time review, a code giving guidance as to principles to be observed, and practices to be followed, in connection with the avoidance of –

(a) unjust or unfair treatment in programmes in which this section applies, or

(b) unwarranted infringement of privacy in, or in connection with the obtaining of material included in, such programmes.

(3) OFCOM shall from time to time publish the code (as for the time being in force).

(4) Before drawing up or revising the code, OFCOM shall consult –

(a) each broadcasting body, and

(b) such other persons as appear to OFCOM to be appropriate.

(5) This section applies to –

(a) any programme broadcast by the BBC,

(b) any programme broadcast by the Welsh Authority or included in any public service of the Welsh Authority (within the meaning of Part 2 of Schedule 12 to the Communications Act 2003), and

(c) any programme included in a licensed service.

110 General functions of OFCOM in relation to complaints

(1) Subject to the provisions of this Part, it shall be the duty of OFCOM to consider and adjudicate on complaints which are made to them in accordance with sections 111 and 114 and relate –

(a) to unjust or unfair treatment in programmes to which section 107 applies, or

(b) to unwarranted infringement of privacy in, or in connection with the obtaining of material included in, such programmes.

(3) In exercising their functions under subsection (1), OFCOM shall take into account any relevant provisions of the code maintained by them under section 107.

(4) In this Part –

'a fairness complaint' means a complaint to OFCOM in respect of any of the matters referred to in subsection (1)(a) and (b).

111 Complaints of unfair treatment, etc

(1) A fairness complaint may be made by an individual or by a body of persons, whether incorporated or not, but, subject to subsection (2), shall not be entertained by OFCOM unless made by the person affected or by a person authorised by him to make the complaint for him.

(2) Where the person affected is an individual who has died, a fairness complaint may be made by his personal representative or by a member of the family of the person affected, or by some other person or body closely connected with him (whether as his employer, or as a body of which he was at his death a member, or in any other way).

(3) Where the person affected is an individual who is for any reason both unable to make a complaint himself and unable to authorise another person to do so for him, a fairness complaint may be made by a member of the family of the person affected, or by some other person or body closely connected with him (whether as his employer, or as a body of which he is a member, or in any other way).

(4) OFCOM shall not entertain, or proceed with the consideration of, a fairness complaint if it appears to them that the complaint relates to the broadcasting of the relevant programme, or to its inclusion in a licensed service, on an occasion more than five years after the death of the person affected, unless it appears to them that in the particular circumstances it is appropriate to do so.

(5) OFCOM may refuse to entertain a fairness complaint if it appears to them not to have been made within a reasonable time after the last occasion on which the relevant programme was broadcast or, as the case may be, included in a licensed service.

(6) Where, in the case of a fairness complaint, the relevant programme was broadcast or included in a licensed service after the death of the person affected, subsection (5) shall apply as if at the end there were added 'within five years (or such longer period as may be allowed by OFCOM in the particular case under subsection (4)) after the death of the person affected'.

(7) OFCOM may refuse to entertain –

(a) a fairness complaint which is a complaint of unjust or unfair treatment if the person named as the person affected was not himself the subject of the treatment complained of and it appears to OFCOM that he did not have a sufficiently direct interest in the subject-matter of that treatment to justify the making of a complaint with him as the person affected, or

(b) a complaint made under subsection (2) or (3) by a person other than the person affected or a person authorised by him, if it appears to OFCOM that the complainant's connection with the person affected is not sufficiently close to justify the making of the complaint by him.

119 Publication of OFCOM's findings

(1) Where OFCOM have considered and adjudicated upon a fairness complaint, they may direct the relevant person to publish the matters mentioned in subsection (3) in such manner, and within such period, as may be specified in the directions.

(3) Those matters are –

(a) a summary of the complaint;

(b) OFCOM's findings on the complaint or a summary of them.

(4) References in subsection (1) to the publication of any matter are references to the publication of that matter without its being accompanied by any observations made by a person other than OFCOM and relating to the complaint.

(5) The form and content of any such summary as is mentioned in subsection (3)(a) or (b) shall be such as may be approved by OFCOM.

(6) A relevant person shall comply with any directions given to him under this section.

(7) The regulatory regime for every licensed service includes the conditions that OFCOM consider appropriate for securing that the licence holder complies with every direction given to him under this section.

(7A) Section 263 of the Communications Act 2003 applies in relation to conditions included by virtue of subsection (7) in the regulatory regime for a licensed service as it applies in relation to conditions which are so included by virtue of a provision of Chapter 4 of Part 3 of that Act.

(7B) It is hereby declared that, where –

(a) OFCOM exercise their powers under this Part to adjudicate upon a fairness complaint or to give a direction under subsection (1), and

(b) it appears to them that the matters to which the complaint in question relates consist in or include a contravention of the conditions of the licence for a licensed service,

the exercise by OFCOM of their powers under this Part is not to preclude the exercise by them of their powers under any other enactment in respect of the contravention.

(7C) Where OFCOM are proposing to exercise any of their powers in respect of a contravention of a licence condition in a case in which the contravention relates to matters that have been the subject-matter of a fairness complaint –

(a) OFCOM may have regard, in the exercise of those powers, to any matters considered or steps taken by them for the purpose of adjudicating upon that complaint and to any direction given by them under this section; but

(b) steps taken for the purposes of this Part do not satisfy a requirement to give the licence holder in relation to whom those powers are to be exercised a reasonable opportunity, before they are exercised, of making representations to OFCOM.

(8) OFCOM shall publish, monthly or at such other intervals as they think fit and in such manner as they think fit, reports each containing, as regards every fairness complaint which falls within this subsection and has been dealt with by them in the period covered by the report –

(a) a summary of the complaint and the action taken by them on it,

(b) where they have adjudicated on it, a summary of –

(i) their findings,

(ii) any direction given under subsection (1), or other action taken by them, in relation to the complaint, and

(c) where a direction has been given under subsection (1) in relation to the complaint, a summary of any action taken by a broadcasting body or the holder of a licence to provide a licensed service in pursuance of the direction.

(9) A fairness complaint made to OFCOM falls within subsection (8) unless it is one which under section 111(1), (4) or (5) or 114(2) they have refused to entertain.

(10) OFCOM may, if they think fit, omit from any summary which is included in a report under subsection (8) and relates to a fairness complaint any information which could lead to the disclosure of the identity of any person connected with the complaint in question other than a relevant person.

(11) The references in subsections (3)(b) and (8)(b) to OFCOM findings on a complaint shall be construed, in relation to a fairness complaint which has been considered by them in two or more parts, as references to their findings on each part of the complaint.

(11A) In this section 'relevant person' means –

(a) in a case where the relevant programme was broadcast by a broadcasting body, that body; and

(b) in a case where the relevant programme was included in a licensed service, the licence holder providing that service.

120 Reports on action taken voluntarily in response to findings on complaints

(1) This section applies where OFCOM have given a direction under section 119(1) in relation to a fairness complaint.

(2) Where the relevant programme was included in a licensed service, the licence holder shall send to OFCOM a report of any supplementary action taken by him or

by any other person responsible for the making or provision of the relevant programme.

(3) Where the relevant programme was broadcast by a broadcasting body, that body shall send to OFCOM a report of any supplementary action taken by –

(a) the broadcasting body, or

(b) any other person appearing to that body to be responsible for the making or provision of the relevant programme.

(4) OFCOM may include, in any report under section 119(8), a summary of any report received by them under subsection (2) or (3) in relation to the complaint.

(5) In this section 'supplementary action' in relation to a complaint, means action which, although not taken in pursuance of a direction under section 119(1), is taken in consequence of the findings of OFCOM on the complaint.

As amended by the Communications Act 2003, ss327(1), (4), (5), 360(3), 406(7), Schedule 15, Pt 2, paras 132, 133, 136, Schedule 19(1).

POLICE ACT 1997

(1997 c 50)

PART III

AUTHORISATION OF ACTION IN RESPECT OF PROPERTY

91 The Commissioners

(1) The Prime Minister, after consultation with Scottish Ministers, shall appoint for the purposes of this Part –

(a) a Chief Commissioner, and

(b) such number of other Commissioners as the Prime Minister thinks fit.

(2) The persons appointed under subsection (1) shall be persons who hold or have held high judicial office within the meaning of the Appellate Jurisdiction Act 1876.

(3) Subject to subsections (4) to (7), each Commissioner shall hold and vacate office in accordance with the terms of his appointment.

(4) Each Commissioner shall be appointed for a term of three years.

(5) A person who ceases to be a Commissioner (otherwise than under subsection (7)) may be reappointed under this section.

(6) Subject to subsection (7), a Commissioner shall not be removed from office before the end of the term for which he is appointed unless –

(a) a resolution approving his removal has been passed by each House of Parliament; and

(b) a resolution approving his removal has been passed by the Scottish Parliament.

(7) A Commissioner may be removed from office by the Prime Minister if after his appointment –

(a) a bankruptcy order is made against him or his estate is sequestrated or he makes a composition or arrangement with, or grants a trust deed for, his creditors;

(b) a disqualification order under the Company Directors Disqualification Act 1986 or Part II of the Companies (Northern Ireland) Order 1989, or an order under section 429(2)(b) of the Insolvency Act 1986 (failure to pay under county court administration order), is made against him or his disqualification undertaking is accepted under section 7 or 8 of the Company Directors Disqualification Act 1986 or disqualification undertaking under the Company Directors Disqualification (Northern Ireland) Order 2002; or

(c) he is convicted in the United Kingdom, the Channel Islands or the Isle of Man of an offence and has passed on him a sentence of imprisonment (whether suspended or not).

(8) The Secretary of State shall pay to each Commissioner, other than a Commissioner carrying out functions as mentioned in subsection (8A), such allowances as the Secretary of State considers appropriate.

(8A) The Scottish Ministers shall pay to any Commissioner who carries out his functions under this Part wholly or mainly in Scotland such allowances as the Scottish Ministers consider appropriate.

(9) The Secretary of State shall, after consultation with the Chief Commissioner and subject to the approval of the Treasury as to numbers, provide the Commissioners and any Assistant Surveillance Commissioners holding office under section 63 of the Regulation of Investigatory Powers Act 2000, other than any Commissioner carrying out functions as mentioned in subsection (9A), with such staff as the Secretary of State considers necessary for the discharge of their functions.

(9A) The Scottish Ministers shall, after consultation with the Chief Commissioner, provide any Commissioner who carries out his functions under this Part wholly or mainly in Scotland with such staff as the Scottish Ministers consider necessary for the discharge of his functions.

(10) The decisions of the Chief Commissioner or, subject to sections 104 and 106, any other Commissioner (including decisions as to his jurisdiction) shall not be subject to appeal or liable to be questioned in any court.

92 Effect of authorisation under Part III

No entry on or interference with property or with wireless telegraphy shall be unlawful if it is authorised by an authorisation having effect under this Part.

93 Authorisations to interfere with property, etc

(1) Where subsection (2) applies, an authorising officer may authorise –

(a) the taking of such action, in respect of such property in the relevant area, as he may specify, or

(ab) the taking of such action falling within subsection (1A), in respect of property outside the relevant area, as he may specify, or

(b) the taking of such action in the relevant area as he may specify, in respect of wireless telegraphy.

(1A) The action falling within this subsection is action for maintaining or retrieving any equipment, apparatus or device the placing or use of which in the relevant area has been authorised under this Part or Part II of the Regulation of

Investigatory Powers Act 2000 or under any enactment contained in or made under an Act of the Scottish Parliament which makes provision equivalent to that made by Part II of that Act of 2000.

(1B) Subsection (1) applies where the authorising officer is a customs officer or an officer of the Office of Fair Trading with the omission of –

(a) the words 'in the relevant area', in each place where they occur; and

(b) paragraph (ab).

(2) This subsection applies where the authorising officer believes –

(a) that it is necessary for the action specified to be taken for the purpose of preventing or detecting serious crime, and

(b) that the taking of the action is proportionate to what the action seeks to achieve.

(2A) Subsection (2) applies where the authorising officer is the Chief Constable or the Deputy Chief Constable of the Police Service of Northern Ireland as if the reference in subsection (2)(a) to preventing or detecting serious crime included a reference to the interests of national security.

(2AA) Where the authorising officer is the chairman of the Office of Fair Trading, the only purpose falling within subsection (2)(a) is the purpose of preventing or detecting an offence under section 188 of the Enterprise Act 2002.

(2B) The matters to be taken into account in considering whether the requirements of subsection (2) are satisfied in the case of any authorisation shall include whether what it is thought necessary to achieve by the authorised action could reasonably be achieved by other means.

(3) An authorising officer shall not give an authorisation under this section except on an application made –

(a) if the authorising officer is within subsection (5)(a) to (ea) or (ee), by a member of his police force,

(aa) if the authorising officer is within subsection (5)(eb) to (ed), by a member, as the case may be, of the Royal Navy Regulating Branch, the Royal Military Police or the Royal Air Force Police,

(b) if the authorising officer is within subsection (5)(f), by a member of the National Criminal Intelligence Service,

(c) if the authorising officer is within subsection (5)(g), by a member of the National Crime Squad, or

(d) if the authorising officer is within subsection (5)(h), by a customs officer, or

(e) if the authorising officer is within subsection (5)(i), by an officer of the Office of Fair Trading.

(4) For the purposes of subsection (2), conduct which constitutes one or more offences shall be regarded as serious crime if, and only if, –

(a) it involves the use of violence, results in substantial financial gain or is conduct by a large number of persons in pursuit of a common purpose, or

(b) the offence or one of the offences is an offence for which a person who has attained the age of twenty-one and has no previous convictions could reasonably be expected to be sentenced to imprisonment for a term of three years or more,

and, where the authorising officer is within subsection (5)(h), it relates to an assigned matter within the meaning of section 1(1) of the Customs and Excise Management Act 1979.

(5) In this section 'authorising officer' means –

(a) the chief constable of a police force maintained under section 2 of the Police Act 1996 (maintenance of police forces for areas in England and Wales except London);

(b) the Commissioner, or an Assistant Commissioner, of Police of the Metropolis;

(c) the Commissioner of Police for the City of London; ...

(f) the Director General of the National Criminal Intelligence Service;

(g) the Director General of the National Crime Squad, or any person holding the rank of assistant chief constable in that Squad who is designated for the purposes of this paragraph by that Director General; or

(h) any customs officer designated by the Commissioners of Customs and Excise for the purposes of this paragraph; or

(i) the chairman of the Office of Fair Trading.

(6) In this section 'relevant area' –

(a) in relation to a person within paragraph (a), (b) or (c) of subsection (5), means the area in England and Wales for which his police force is maintained; ...

(d) in relation to the Director General of the National Criminal Intelligence Service, means the United Kingdom;

(e) in relation to the Director General of the National Crime Squad, means England and Wales;

and in each case includes the adjacent United Kingdom waters. ...

(7) The powers conferred by, or by virtue of, this section are additional to any other powers which a person has as a constable either at common law or under or by virtue of any other enactment and are not to be taken to affect any of those other powers.

95 Authorisations: form and duration, etc

(1) An authorisation shall be in writing, except that in an urgent case an authorisation (other than one given by virtue of section 94) may be given orally.

(2) An authorisation shall, unless renewed under subsection (3), cease to have effect –

(a) if given orally or by virtue of section 94, at the end of the period of 72 hours beginning with the time when it took effect;

(b) in any other case, at the end of the period of three months beginning with the day on which it took effect.

(3) If at any time before an authorisation would cease to have effect the authorising officer who gave the authorisation, or in whose absence it was given, considers it necessary for the authorisation to continue to have effect for the purpose for which it was issued, he may, in writing, renew it for a period of three months beginning with the day on which it would cease to have effect.

(4) A person shall cancel an authorisation given by him if satisfied that the authorisation is one in relation to which the requirements of paragraphs (a) and (b) of section 93(2) are no longer satisfied.

(5) An authorising officer shall cancel an authorisation given in his absence if satisfied that the authorisation is one in relation to which the requirements of paragraphs (a) and (b) of section 93(2) are no longer satisfied.

(6) If the authorising officer who gave the authorisation is within paragraph (b), (e) or (g) of section 93(5), the power conferred on that person by subsections (3) and (4) above shall also be exercisable by each of the other persons within the paragraph concerned.

(7) Nothing in this section shall prevent a designated deputy from exercising the powers conferred on an authorising officer within paragraph (a), (c), ... (f) or (g) of section 93(5) by subsections (3), (4) and (5) above.

96 Notification of authorisations, etc

(1) Where a person gives, renews or cancels an authorisation, he shall, as soon as is reasonably practicable and in accordance with arrangements made by the Chief Commissioner, give notice in writing that he has done so to a Commissioner appointed under section 91(1)(b).

(2) Subject to subsection (3), a notice under this section shall specify such matters as the Secretary of State may by order prescribe.

(3) A notice under this section of the giving or renewal of an authorisation shall specify –

(a) whether section 97 applies to the authorisation or renewal, and

(b) where that section does not apply by virtue of subsection (3) of that section, the grounds on which the case is believed to be one of urgency.

(4) Where a notice is given to a Commissioner under this section, he shall, as soon as is reasonably practicable, scrutinise the notice.

(5) An order under subsection (2) shall be made by statutory instrument.

(6) A statutory instrument which contains an order under subsection (2) shall not be made unless a draft has been laid before, and approved by a resolution of, each House of Parliament.

97 Authorisations requiring approval

(1) An authorisation to which this section applies shall not take effect until –

(a) it has been approved in accordance with this section by a Commissioner appointed under section 91(1)(b), and

(b) the person who gave the authorisation has been notified under subsection (4).

(2) Subject to subsection (3), this section applies to an authorisation if, at the time it is given, the person who gives it believes –

(a) that any of the property specified in the authorisation –

(i) is used wholly or mainly as a dwelling or as a bedroom in a hotel, or
(ii) constitutes office premises, or

(b) that the action authorised by it is likely to result in any person acquiring knowledge of –

(i) matters subject to legal privilege,
(ii) confidential personal information, or
(iii) confidential journalistic material.

(3) This section does not apply to an authorisation where the person who gives it believes that the case is one of urgency.

(4) Where a Commissioner receives a notice under section 96 which specifies that this section applies to the authorisation, he shall as soon as is reasonably practicable –

(a) decide whether to approve the authorisation or refuse approval, and

(b) give written notice of his decision to the person who gave the authorisation.

(5) A Commissioner shall approve an authorisation if, and only if, he is satisfied that there are reasonable grounds for believing the matters specified in section 93(2).

(6) Where a Commissioner refuses to approve an authorisation, he shall, as soon as is reasonably practicable, make a report of his findings to the authorising officer who gave it or in whose absence it was given.

(6A) The reference in subsection (6) to the authorising officer who gave the authorisation or in whose absence it was given shall be construed, in the case of an authorisation given by or in the absence of a person within paragraph (b), (e) or (g) of section 93(5), as a reference to the Commissioner of Police, Chief Constable or, as the case may be, Director General mentioned in the paragaph concerned.

(7) This section shall apply in relation to a renewal of an authorisation as it applies in relation to an authorisation (the references in subsection (2)(a) and (b) to the authorisation being construed as references to the authorisation renewed).

(8) In this section –

'office premises' has the meaning given in section 1(2) of the Offices, Shops and Railway Premises Act 1963;

'hotel' means premises used for the reception of guests who desire to sleep in the premises.

98 Matters subject to legal privilege

(1) Subject to subsection (5) below, in section 97 'matters subject to legal privilege' means matters to which subsection (2), (3) or (4) below applies.

(2) This subsection applies to communications between a professional legal adviser and –

(a) his client, or

(b) any person representing his client,

which are made in connection with the giving of legal advice to the client.

(3) This subsection applies to communications –

(a) between a professional legal adviser and his client or any person representing his client, or

(b) between a professional legal adviser or his client or any such representative and any other person,

which are made in connection with or in contemplation of legal proceedings and for the purposes of such proceedings.

(4) This subsection applies to items enclosed with or referred to in communications of the kind mentioned in subsection (2) or (3) and made –

(a) in connection with the giving of legal advice, or

(b) in connection with or in contemplation of legal proceedings and for the purposes of such proceedings.

(5) For the purposes of section 97 –

(a) communications and items are not matters subject to legal privilege when they are in the possession of a person who is not entitled to possession of them, and

(b) communications and items held, or oral communications made, with the intention of furthering a criminal purpose are not matters subject to legal privilege.

99 Confidential personal information

(1) In section 97 'confidential personal information' means –

(a) personal information which a person has acquired or created in the course of any trade, business, profession or other occupation or for the purposes of any paid or unpaid office, and which he holds in confidence, and

(b) communications as a result of which personal information –

(i) is acquired or created as mentioned in paragraph (a), and

(ii) is held in confidence.

(2) For the purposes of this section 'personal information' means information concerning an individual (whether living or dead) who can be identified from it and relating –

(a) to his physical or mental health, or

(b) to spiritual counselling or assistance given or to be given to him.

(3) A person holds information in confidence for the purposes of this section if he holds it subject –

(a) to an express or implied undertaking to hold it in confidence, or

(b) to a restriction on disclosure or an obligation of secrecy contained in any enactment (including an enactment contained in an Act passed after this Act).

100 Confidential journalistic material

(1) In section 97 'confidential journalistic material' means –

(a) material acquired or created for the purposes of journalism which –

(i) is in the possession of persons who acquired or created it for those purposes,

(ii) is held subject to an undertaking, restriction or obligation of the kind mentioned in section 99(3), and

(iii) has been continuously held (by one or more persons) subject to such an undertaking, restriction or obligation since it was first acquired or created for the purposes of journalism, and

(b) communications as a result of which information is acquired for the purposes of journalism and held as mentioned in paragraph (a)(ii).

(2) For the purposes of subsection (1), a person who receives material, or acquires information, from someone who intends that the recipient shall use it for the purposes of journalism is to be taken to have acquired it for those purposes.

103 Quashing of authorisations, etc

(1) Where, at any time, a Commissioner appointed under section 91(1)(b) is satisfied that, at the time an authorisation was given or renewed, there were no reasonable grounds for believing the matters specified in section 93(2), he may quash the authorisation or, as the case may be, renewal.

(2) Where, in the case of an authorisation or renewal to which section 97 does not apply, a Commissioner appointed under section 91(1)(b) is at any time satisfied that, at the time the authorisation was given or, as the case may be, renewed, –

(a) there were reasonable grounds for believing any of the matters specified in subsection (2) of section 97, and

(b) there were no reasonable grounds for believing the case to be one of urgency for the purposes of subsection (3) of that section,

he may quash the authorisation or, as the case may be, renewal.

(3) Where a Commissioner quashes an authorisation or renewal under subsection (1) or (2), he may order the destruction of any records relating to information obtained by virtue of the authorisation (or, in the case of a renewal, relating wholly or partly to information so obtained after the renewal) other than records required for pending criminal or civil proceedings.

(4) If a Commissioner appointed under section 91(1)(b) is satisfied that, at any time after an authorisation was given or, in the case of an authorisation renewed under section 95, after it was renewed, there were no reasonable grounds for believing the matters specified in section 93(2), he may cancel the authorisation.

(5) Where –

(a) an authorisation has ceased to have effect (otherwise than by virtue of subsection (1) or (2)), and

(b) a Commissioner appointed under section 91(1)(b) is satisfied that, at any time during the period of the authorisation, there were no reasonable grounds for believing the matters specified in section 93(2),

he may order the destruction of any records relating, wholly or partly, to information which was obtained by virtue of the authorisation after that time (other than records required for pending criminal or civil proceedings).

(6) Where a Commissioner exercises his powers under subsection (1), (2) or (4), he shall, if he is satisfied that there are reasonable grounds for doing so, order that the authorisation shall be effective, for such period as he shall specify, so far as it authorises the taking of action to retrieve anything left on property in accordance with the authorisation.

(7) Where a Commissioner exercises a power conferred by this section, he shall, as soon as is reasonably practicable, make a report of his findings –

(a) to the authorising officer who gave the authorisation or in whose absence it was given, and

(b) to the Chief Commissioner;

and subsection (6A) of section 97 shall apply for the purposes of this subsection as it applies for the purposes of subsection (6) of that section.

(8) Where –

(a) a decision is made under subsection (1) or (2) and an order for the destruction of records is made under subsection (3), or

(b) a decision to order the destruction of records is made under subsection (5),

the order shall not become operative until the period for appealing against the decision has expired and, where an appeal is made, a decision dismissing it has been made by the Chief Commissioner.

(9) A Commissioner may exercise any of the powers conferred by this section notwithstanding any approval given under section 97.

104 Appeals by authorising officers

(1) An authorising officer who gives an authorisation, or in whose absence it is given, may, within the prescribed period, appeal to the Chief Commissioner against –

(a) any refusal to approve the authorisation or any renewal of it under section 97;

(b) any decision to quash the authorisation, or any renewal of it, under subsection (1) of section 103;

(c) any decision to quash the authorisation, or any renewal of it, under subsection (2) of that section;

(d) any decision to cancel the authorisation under subsection (4) of that section;

(e) any decision to order the destruction of records under subsection (5) of that section;

(f) any refusal to make an order under subsection (6) of that section.

(2) In subsection (1), 'the prescribed period' means the period of seven days beginning with the day on which the refusal, decision or, as the case may be, determination appealed against is reported to the authorising officer.

(3) In determining an appeal within subsection (1)(a), the Chief Commissioner shall, if he is satisfied that there are reasonable grounds for believing the matters specified in section 93(2), allow the appeal and direct the Commissioner to approve the authorisation or renewal under that section.

(4) In determining –

(a) an appeal within subsection (1)(b),

the Chief Commissioner shall allow the appeal unless he is satisfied that, at the time the authorisation was given or, as the case may be, renewed there were no reasonable grounds for believing the matters specified in section 93(2).

(5) In determining –

(a) an appeal within subsection (1)(c),

the Chief Commissioner shall allow the appeal unless he is satisfied as mentioned in section 103(2).

(6) In determining –

(a) an appeal within subsection (1)(d) or (e),

the Chief Commissioner shall allow the appeal unless he is satisfied that at the time to which the decision relates there were no reasonable grounds for believing the matters specified in section 93(2).

(7) In determining an appeal within subsection (1)(f), the Chief Commissioner shall allow the appeal and order that the authorisation shall be effective to the

extent mentioned in section 103(6), for such period as he shall specify, if he is satisfied that there are reasonable grounds for making such an order.

(8) Where an appeal is allowed under this section, the Chief Commissioner shall –

(a) in the case of an appeal within subsection (1)(b) or (c), also quash any order made by the Commissioner to destroy records relating to information obtained by virtue of the authorisation concerned.

107 Supplementary provisions relating to Commissioners

(1) The Chief Commissioner shall keep under review the performance of functions under this Part.

(2) The Chief Commissioner shall make an annual report on the matters with which he is concerned to the Prime Minister and to the Scottish Ministers and may at any time report to him or them (as the case may require) on anything relating to any of those matters.

(3) The Prime Minister shall lay before each House of Parliament a copy of each annual report made by the Chief Commissioner under subsection (2) together with a statement as to whether any matter has been excluded from that copy in pursuance of subsection (4) below. ...

(4) The Prime Minister may exclude a matter from the copy of a report as laid before each House of Parliament, if it appears to him, after consultation with the Chief Commissioner and the Scottish Ministers, that the publication of that matter in the report would be prejudicial to any of the purposes for which authorisations may be given or granted under this Part of this Act or Part II of the Regulation of Investigatory Powers Act 2000 or under any enactment contained in or made under an Act of the Scottish Parliament which makes provision equivalent to that made by Part II of that Act of 2000 or to the discharge of –

(a) the functions of any police authority,

(b) the functions of the Service Authority for the National Criminal Intelligence Service or the Service Authority for the National Crime Squad, or

(c) the duties of the Commissioners of Customs and Excise.

(5) Any person having functions under this Part, and any person taking action in relation to which an authorisation was given, shall comply with any request of a Commissioner for documents or information required by him for the purpose of enabling him to discharge his functions.

(5A) It shall be the duty of –

(a) every person by whom, or on whose application, there has been given or granted any authorisation the function of giving or granting which is subject to review by the Chief Commissioner,

(b) every person who has engaged in conduct with the authority of such an authorisation,

(c) every person who holds or has held any office, rank or position with the same public authority as a person falling within paragraph (a),

(d) every person who holds or has held any office, rank or position with any public authority for whose benefit (within the meaning of Part II of the Regulation of Investigatory Powers Act 2000) activities which are or may be subject to any such review have been or may be carried out, and

(e) every person to whom a notice under section 49 of the Regulation of Investigatory Powers Act 2000 (notices imposing a disclosure requirement in respect of information protected by a key) has been given in relation to any information obtained by conduct to which such an authorisation relates,

to disclose or provide to the Chief Commissioner all such documents and information as he may require for the purpose of enabling him to carry out his functions.

(5B) It shall be the duty of every Commissioner to give the tribunal established under section 65 of the Regulation of Investigatory Powers Act 2000 all such assistance (including his opinion as to any issue falling to be determined by that tribunal) as that tribunal may require –

(a) in connection with the investigation of any matter by that tribunal; or

(b) otherwise for the purposes of that tribunal's consideration or determination of any matter.

(5C) In this section 'public authority' means any public authority within the meaning of section 6 of the Human Rights Act 1998 (acts of public authorities) other than a court or tribunal.

As amended by the Scotland Act 1998 (Cross-Border Public Authorities) (Adaptation of Functions, etc) Order 1999, arts 3–5, Schedule 6, Pt I, Pt II, para 2; Regulation of Investigatory Powers Act 2000, ss75(1)–(5), (6)(b), (c), 82, Schedule 4, para 8(1), (2), (6)–(8), (10), (11); Insolvency Act 2000, s8, Schedule 4, Pt II, para 22; Police (Northern Ireland) Act 2000, s78(1), Schedule 6, para 20(1), (2)(b); Enterprise Act 2002, s200(1), (2; Insolvency Act 2000 (Company Directors Disqualification Undertakings) Order 2004, art 3, Schedule, paras 9, 10.

SPECIAL IMMIGRATION APPEALS COMMISSION ACT 1997

(1997 c 68)

1 Establishment of the Commission

(1) There shall be a commission, known as the Special Immigration Appeals Commission, for the purpose of exercising the jurisdiction conferred by this Act.

(2) Schedule 1 to this Act shall have effect in relation to the Commission.

(3) The Commission shall be a superior court of record.

(4) A decision of the Commission shall be questioned in legal proceedings only in accordance with –

(a) section 7, or

(b) section 30(5)(a) of the Anti-terrorism, Crime and Security Act 2001 (derogation).

2 Jurisdiction: appeals

(1) A person may appeal to the Special Immigration Appeals Commission against a decision if –

(a) he would be able to appeal against the decision under section 82(1) or 83(2) of the Nationality, Immigration and Asylum Act 2002 but for a certificate of the Secretary of State under section 97 of that Act (national security, etc), or

(b) an appeal against the decision under section 82(1) or 83(2) of that Act lapsed under section 99 of that Act by virtue of a certificate of the Secretary of State under section 97 of that Act.

(2) The following provisions shall apply, with any necessary modifications, in relation to an appeal against an immigration decision under this section as they apply in relation to an appeal under section 82(1) of the Nationality, Immigration and Asylum Act 2002 –

(a) section 3C of the Immigration Act 1971 (c 77) (continuation of leave pending variation decision),

(b) section 78 of the Nationality, Immigration and Asylum Act 2002 (no removal while appeal pending),

(c) section 79 of that Act (deportation order: appeal),

(d) section 82(3) of that Act (variation or revocation of leave to enter or remain: appeal),
(e) section 84 of that Act (grounds of appeal),
(f) section 85 of that Act (matters to be considered),
(g) section 86 of that Act (determination of appeal),
(h) section 87 of that Act (successful appeal: direction),
(i) section 96 of that Act (earlier right of appeal),
(j) section 104 of that Act (pending appeal),
(k) section 105 of that Act (notice of immigration decision), and
(l) section 110 of that Act (grants).

(3) The following provisions shall apply, with any necessary modifications, in relation to an appeal against the rejection of a claim for asylum under this section as they apply in relation to an appeal under section 83(2) of the Nationality, Immigration and Asylum Act 2002 –

(a) section 85(4) of that Act (matters to be considered),
(b) section 86 of that Act (determination of appeal),
(c) section 87 of that Act (successful appeal: direction), and
(d) section 110 of that Act (grants).

(4) An appeal against the rejection of a claim for asylum under this section shall be treated as abandoned if the appellant leaves the United Kingdom.

(5) A person may bring or continue an appeal against an immigration decision under this section while he is in the United Kingdom only if he would be able to bring or continue the appeal while he was in the United Kingdom if it were an appeal under section 82(1) of that Act.

(6) In this section 'immigration decision' has the meaning given by section 82(2) of the Nationality, Immigration and Asylum Act 2002.

2B Deprivation of citizenship

A person may appeal to the Special Immigration Appeals Commission against a decision to make an order under section 40 of the British Nationality Act 1981 (c 61) (deprivation of citizenship) if he is not entitled to appeal under section 40A(1) of that Act because of a certificate under section 40A(2) (and section 40A(3)(a) shall have effect in relation to appeals under this section).

6 Appointment of person to represent the appellant's interests

(1) The relevant law officer may appoint a person to represent the interests of an appellant in any proceedings before the Special Immigration Appeals Commission from which the appellant and any legal representative of his are excluded.

(2) For the purposes of subsection (1) above, the relevant law officer is –

(a) in relation to proceedings before the Commission in England and Wales, the Attorney General … .

(3) A person appointed under subsection (1) above –

(a) if appointed for the purposes of proceedings in England and Wales, shall have a general qualification for the purposes of section 71 of the Courts and Legal Services Act 1990 … .

(4) A person appointed under subsection (1) above shall not be responsible to the person whose interests he is appointed to represent.

7 Appeals from the Commission

(1) Where the Special Immigration Appeals Commission has made a final determination of an appeal, any party to the appeal may bring a further appeal to the appropriate appeal court on any question of law material to that determination.

(2) An appeal under this section may be brought only with the leave of the Commission or, if such leave is refused, with the leave of the appropriate appeal court.

(3) In this section 'the appropriate appeal court' means –

(a) in relation to a determination made by the Commission in England and Wales, the Court of Appeal …

SCHEDULE 1

THE COMMISSION

1. – (1) The Special Immigration Appeals Commission shall consist of such number of members appointed by the Lord Chancellor as he may determine.

(2) A member of the Commission shall hold and vacate office in accordance with the terms of his appointment and shall, on ceasing to hold office, be eligible for re-appointment.

(3) A member of the Commission may resign his office at any time by notice in writing to the Lord Chancellor.

2. The Lord Chancellor shall appoint one of the members of the Commission to be its chairman. …

As amended by the Immigration and Asylum Act 1999, s169(1), Schedule 14, paras 118, 120–122, 124; Anti-terrorism, Crime and Security Act 2001, s35; Nationality, Immigration and Asylum Act 2002, ss4(2), 114, 161, Schedule 7, paras 20–22, 24, Schedule 9; Asylum and Immigration (Treatment of Claimants, etc) Act 2004, s26, Schedule 2, paras 10, 11.

CRIME AND DISORDER ACT 1998

(1998 c 37)

PART I

PREVENTION OF CRIME AND DISORDER

CHAPTER I

ENGLAND AND WALES

1 Anti-social behaviour orders

(1) An application for an order under this section may be made by a relevant authority if it appears to the authority that the following conditions are fulfilled with respect to any person aged 10 or over, namely –

(a) that the person has acted, since the commencement date, in an anti-social manner, that is to say, in a manner that caused or was likely to cause harassment, alarm or distress to one or more persons not of the same household as himself; and

(b) that such an order is necessary to protect relevant persons from further anti-social acts by him.

(1A) In this section and sections 1B and 1E 'relevant authority' means –

(a) the council for a local government area;

(aa) in relation to England, a county council;

(b) the chief office of police of any police force maintained for a police area;

(c) the chief constable of the British Transport Police Force;

(d) any person registered under section 1 of the Housing Act 1996 (c 52) as a social landlord who provides or manages any houses or hostel in a local government area; or

(e) a housing action trust established by order in pursuance of section 62 of the Housing Act 1988.

(1B) In this section 'relevant persons' means –

(a) in relation to a relevant authority falling within paragraph (a) of subsection (1A), persons within the local government area of that council;

(aa) in relation to a relevant authority falling within paragraph (aa) of subsection (1A), persons within the county of the county council;

(b) in relation to a relevant authority falling within paragraph (b) of that subsection, persons within the police area;

(c) in relation to a relevant authority falling within paragraph (c) of that subsection –

(i) persons who are within or likely to be within a place specified in section 31(1)(a) to (f) of the Railways and Transport Safety Act 2003 in a local government area; or

(ii) persons who are within or likely to be within such a place;

(d) in relation to a relevant authority falling within paragraph (d) or (e) of that subsection –

(i) persons who are residing in or who are otherwise on or likely to be on premises provided or managed by that authority; or

(ii) persons who are in the vicinity of or likely to be in the vicinity of such premises.

(3) Such an application shall be made by complaint to the magistrates' court whose commission area includes the local government area or police area concerned.

(4) If, on such an application, it is proved that the conditions mentioned in subsection (1) above are fulfilled, the magistrates' court may make an order under this section (an 'anti-social behaviour order') which prohibits the defendant from doing anything described in the order.

(5) For the purpose of determining whether the condition mentioned in subsection (1)(a) above is fulfilled, the court shall disregard any act of the defendant which he shows was reasonable in the circumstances.

(6) The prohibitions that may be imposed by an anti-social behaviour order are those necessary for the purpose of protecting persons (whether relevant persons or persons elsewhere in England and Wales) from further anti-social acts by the defendant.

(7) An anti-social behaviour order shall have effect for a period (not less than two years) specified in the order or until further order.

(8) Subject to subsection (9) below, the applicant or the defendant may apply by complaint to the court which made an anti-social behaviour order for it to be varied or discharged by a further order.

(9) Except with the consent of both parties, no anti-social behaviour order shall be discharged before the end of the period of two years beginning with the date of service of the order.

(10) If without reasonable excuse a person does anything which he is prohibited from doing by an anti-social behaviour order, he is guilty of an offence and liable –

(a) on summary conviction, to imprisonment for a term not exceeding six months or to a fine not exceeding the statutory maximum, or to both; or

(b) on conviction on indictment, to imprisonment for a term not exceeding five years or to a fine, or to both.

(10A) The following may bring proceedings for an offence under subsection (10) –

(a) a council which is a relevant authority;

(b) the council for the local government area in which a person in respect of whom an anti-social behaviour order has been made resides or appears to reside.

(10B) If proceedings for an offence under subsection (10) are brought in a youth court section 47(2) of the Children and Young Persons Act 1933 (c 12) has effect as if the persons entitled to be present at a sitting for the purposes of those proceedings include one person authorised to be present by a relevant authority.

(11) Where a person is convicted of an offence under subsection (10) above, it shall not be open to the court by or before which he is so convicted to make an order under subsection (1)(b) (conditional discharge) of section 12 of the Powers of Criminal Courts (Sentencing) Act 2000 in respect of the offence.

(12) In this section –

'the commencement date' means the date of the commencement of this section;

'local government area' means –

(a) in relation to England, a district or London borough, the City of London, the Isle of Wight and the Isles of Scilly;
(b) in relation to Wales, a county or county borough.

1A Power of Secretary of State to add to relevant authorities

The Secretary of State may by order provide that the chief officer of a body of constables maintained otherwise than by a police authority is, in such cases and circumstances as may be prescribed by the order, to be a relevant authority for the purposes of section 1 above.

1AA Individual support orders

(1) Where a court makes an anti-social behaviour order in respect of a defendant who is a child or young person when that order is made, it must consider whether the individual support conditions are fulfilled.

(2) If it is satisfied that those conditions are fulfilled, the court must make an order under this section ('an individual support order') which –

(a) requires the defendant to comply, for a period not exceeding six months, with such requirements as are specified in the order; and

(b) requires the defendant to comply with any directions given by the responsible officer with a view to the implementation of the requirements under paragraph (a) above.

(3) The individual support conditions are –

(a) that an individual support order would be desirable in the interests of preventing any repetition of the kind of behaviour which led to the making of the anti-social behaviour order;

(b) that the defendant is not already subject to an individual support order; and

(c) that the court has been notified by the Secretary of State that arrangements for implementing individual support orders are available in the area in which it appears to it that the defendant resides or will reside and the notice has not been withdrawn.

(4) If the court is not satisfied that the individual support conditions are fulfilled, it shall state in open court that it is not so satisfied and why it is not.

(5) The requirements that may be specified under subsection (2)(a) above are those that the court considers desirable in the interests of preventing any repetition of the kind of behaviour which led to the making of the anti-social behaviour order.

(6) Requirements included in an individual support order, or directions given under such an order by a responsible officer, may require the defendant to do all or any of the following things –

(a) to participate in activities specified in the requirements or directions at a time or times so specified;

(b) to present himself to a person or persons so specified at a place or places and at a time or times so specified;

(c) to comply with any arrangements for his education so specified.

(7) But requirements included in, or directions given under, such an order may not require the defendant to attend (whether at the same place or at different places) on more than two days in any week; and 'week' here means a period of seven days beginning with a Sunday.

(8) Requirements included in, and directions given under, an individual support order shall, as far as practicable, be such as to avoid –

(a) any conflict with the defendant's religious beliefs; and

(b) any interference with the times, if any, at which he normally works or attends school or any other educational establishment.

(9) Before making an individual support order, the court shall obtain from a social worker of a local authority social services department or a member of a youth offending team any information which it considers necessary in order –

(a) to determine whether the individual support conditions are fulfilled, or

(b) to determine what requirements should be imposed by an individual support order if made,

and shall consider that information.

(10) In this section and section 1AB below 'responsible officer', in relation to an individual support order, means one of the following who is specified in the order, namely –

(a) a social worker of a local authority social services department;

(b) a person nominated by a person appointed as chief education officer under section 532 of the Education Act 1996 (c. 56);

(c) a member of a youth offending team.

1AB Individual support orders: explanation, breach, amendment, etc

(1) Before making an individual support order, the court shall explain to the defendant in ordinary language –

(a) the effect of the order and of the requirements proposed to be included in it;

(b) the consequences which may follow (under subsection (3) below) if he fails to comply with any of those requirements; and

(c) that the court has power (under subsection (6) below) to review the order on the application either of the defendant or of the responsible officer.

(2) The power of the Secretary of State under section 174(4) of the Criminal Justice Act 2003 includes power by order to –

(a) prescribe cases in which subsection (1) above does not apply; and

(b) prescribe cases in which the explanation referred to in that subsection may be made in the absence of the defendant, or may be provided in written form.

(3) If the person in respect of whom an individual support order is made fails without reasonable excuse to comply with any requirement included in the order, he is guilty of an offence and liable on summary conviction to a fine not exceeding –

(a) if he is aged 14 or over at the date of his conviction, £1,000;

(b) if he is aged under 14 then, £250.

(4) No referral order under section 16(2) or (3) of the Powers of Criminal Courts (Sentencing) Act 2000 (referral of young offenders to youth offender panels) may be made in respect of an offence under subsection (3) above.

(5) If the anti-social behaviour order as a result of which an individual support order was made ceases to have effect, the individual support order (if it has not previously ceased to have effect) ceases to have effect when the anti-social behaviour order does.

(6) On an application made by complaint by –

(a) the person subject to an individual support order, or

(b) the responsible officer,

the court which made the individual support order may vary or discharge it by a further order.

(7) If the anti-social behaviour order as a result of which an individual support order was made is varied, the court varying the anti-social behaviour order may by a further order vary or discharge the individual support order.

1B Orders in county court proceedings

(1) This section applies to any proceedings in a county court ('the principal proceedings').

(2) If a relevant authority –

(a) is a party to the principal proceedings, and

(b) considers that a party to those proceedings is a person in relation to whom it would be reasonable for it to make an application under section 1,

it may make an application in those proceedings for an order under subsection (4).

(3) If a relevant authority –

(a) is not a party to the principal proceedings, and

(b) considers that a party to those proceedings is a person in relation to whom it would be reasonable for it to make an application under section 1,

it may make an application to be joined to those proceedings to enable it to apply for an order under subsection (4) and, if it is so joined, may apply for such an order.

(3A) Subsection (3B) applies if a relevant authority is a party to the principal proceedings and considers –

(a) that a person who is not a party to the proceedings has acted in an anti-social manner, and

(b) that the person's anti-social acts are material in relation to the principal proceedings.

(3B) The relevant authority may –

(a) make an application for the person mentioned in subsection (3A)(a) to be joined to the principal proceedings to enable an order under subsection (4) to be made in relation to that person;

(b) if that person is so joined, apply for an order under subsection (4).

(3C) But a person must not be joined to proceedings in pursuance of subsection (3B) unless his anti-social acts are material in relation to the principal proceedings.

(4) If, on an application for an order under this subsection, it is proved that the conditions mentioned in section 1(1) are fulfilled as respects that other party, the court may make an order which prohibits him from doing anything described in the order.

(5) Subject to subsection (6), the person against whom an order under this section has been made and the relevant authority on whose application that order was made may apply to the county court which made an order under this section for it to be varied or discharged by a further order.

(6) Except with the consent of the relevant authority and the person subject to the order, no order under this section shall be discharged before the end of the period of two years beginning with the date of service of the order.

(7) Subsections (5) to (7) and (10) to (12) of section 1 apply for the purposes of the

making and effect of orders made under this section as they apply for the purposes of the making and effect of anti-social behaviour orders.

1C Orders on conviction in criminal proceedings

(1) This section applies where a person (the 'offender') is convicted of a relevant offence.

(2) If the court considers –

(a) that the offender has acted, at any time since the commencement date, in an anti-social manner, that is to say in a manner that caused or was likely to cause harassment, alarm or distress to one or more persons not of the same household as himself, and

(b) that an order under this section is necessary to protect persons in any place in England and Wales from further anti-social acts by him,

it may make an order which prohibits the offender from doing anything described in the order.

(3) The court may make an order under this section –

(a) if the prosecutor asks it to do so, or

(b) if the court thinks it is appropriate to do so.

(3A) For the purpose of deciding whether to make an order under this section the court may consider evidence led by the prosecution and the defence.

(3B) It is immaterial whether evidence led in pursuance of subsection (3A) would have been admissible in the proceedings in which the offender was convicted.

(4) An order under this section shall not be made except –

(a) in addition to a sentence imposed in respect of the relevant offence; or

(b) in addition to an order discharging him conditionally.

(5) An order under this section takes effect on the day on which it is made, but the court may provide in any such order that such requirements of the order as it may specify shall, during any period when the offender is detained in legal custody, be suspended until his release from that custody.

(6) An offender subject to an order under this section may apply to the court which made it for it to be varied or discharged.

(7) In the case of an order under this section made by a magistrates' court, the reference in subsection (6) to the court by which the order was made includes a reference to any magistrates' court acting for the same petty sessions area as that court.

(8) No application may be made under subsection (6) for the discharge of an order before the end of the period of two years beginning with the day on which the order takes effect.

(9) Subsections (7), (10) and (11) of section 1 apply for the purposes of the making

and effect of orders made by virtue of this section as they apply for the purposes of the making and effect of anti-social behaviour orders.

(9A) The council for the local government area in which a person in respect of whom an anti-social behaviour order has been made resides or appears to reside may bring proceedings under section 1(10) (as applied by subsection (9) above) for breach of an order under subsection (2) above.

(9B) Subsection (9C) applies in relation to proceedings in which an order under subsection (2) is made against a child or young person who is convicted of an offence.

(9C) In so far as the proceedings relate to the making of the order –

(a) section 49 of the Children and Young Persons Act 1933 (c 12) (restrictions on reports of proceedings in which children and young person are concerned) does not apply in respect of the child or young person against whom the order is made;

(b) section 39 of that Act (power to prohibit publication of certain matter) does so apply.

(10) In this section –

'child' and 'young person' have the same meaning as in the Children and Young Persons Act 1933 (c 12);

'the commencement date' has the same meaning as in section 1 above;

'the court' in relation to an offender means –

(a) the court by or before which he is convicted of the relevant offence; or

(b) if he is committed to the Crown Court to be dealt with for that offence, the Crown Court; and

'relevant offence' means an offence committed after the coming into force of section 64 of the Police Reform Act 2002 (c 30).

1D Interim orders

(1) The applications to which this section applies are –

(a) an application for an anti-social behaviour order; and

(b) an application for an order under section 1B.

(2) If, before determining an application to which this section applies, the court considers that it is just to make an order under this section pending the determination of that application ('the main application'), it may make such an order.

(3) An order under this section is an order which prohibits the defendant from doing anything described in the order.

(4) An order under this section –

(a) shall be for a fixed period;

(b) may be varied, renewed or discharged;

(c) shall, if it has not previously ceased to have effect, cease to have effect on the determination of the main application.

(5) Subsections (6), (8) and (10) to (12) of section 1 apply for the purposes of the making and effect of orders under this section as they apply for the purposes of the making and effect of anti-social behaviour orders.

1E Consultation requirements

(1) This section applies to –

(a) applications for an anti-social behaviour order; and

(b) applications for an order under section 1B.

(2) Before making an application to which this section applies, the council for a local government area shall consult the chief officer of police of the police force maintained for the police area within which that local government area lies.

(3) Before making an application to which this section applies, a chief officer of police shall consult the council for the local government area in which the person in relation to whom the application is to be made resides or appears to reside.

(4) Before making an application to which this section applies, a relevant authority other than a council for a local government area or a chief officer of police shall consult –

(a) the council for the local government area in which the person in relation to whom the application is to be made resides or appears to reside; and

(b) the chief officer of police of the police force maintained for the police area within which that local government area lies.

(5) Subsection (4)(a) does not apply if the relevant authority is a county council for a county in which there are no districts.

4 Appeals against orders

(1) An appeal shall lie to the Crown Court against the making by a magistrates' court of an anti-social behaviour order, an individual support order, an order under section 1D above ...

5 Authorities responsible for strategies

(1) Subject to the provisions of this section, the functions conferred by section 6 below shall be exercisable in relation to each local government area by the responsible authorities, that is to say –

(a) the council for the area and, where the area is a district and the council is not a unitary authority, the council for the county which includes the district;

(b) every chief officer of police any part of whose police area lies within the area;

(c) every police authority any part of whose police area so lies;

(d) every fire and rescue authority any part of whose area so lies;

(e) if the local government area is in England, every Primary Care Trust the whole or any part of whose area so lies; and

(f) if the local government area is in Wales, every health authority the whole or any part of whose area so lies. ...

6 Formulation and implementation of strategies

(1) The responsible authorities for a local government area shall, in accordance with the provisions of section 5 above and this section, formulate and implement, for each relevant period –

(a) in the case of an area in England –

(i) a strategy for the reduction of crime and disorder in the area; and

(ii) a strategy for combattting the misuse of drugs in the area; and

(b) in the case of an area in Wales –

(i) a strategy for the reduction of crime and disorder in the area; and

(ii) a strategy for combatting substance misuse in the area.

(1A) In determining what matters to include or not to include in their strategy for combatting substance misuse, the responsible authorities for an area in Wales shall have regard to any guidance issued for the purposes of this section by the National Assemby for Wales. ...

6A Powers of the Secretary of State and National Assembly for Wales

(1) The Secretary of State may, by order, require –

(a) the responsible authorities for local government areas to formulate any section 6 strategy of theirs for the reduction of crime and disorder so as to include, in particular, provision for the reduction of –

(i) crime of a description specified in the order; or

(ii) disorder of a description so specified;

(b) the responsible authorities for local government areas in England to prepare any section 6 strategy of theirs for combatting the misuse of drugs so as to include in it a strategy for combatting, in the area in question, such other forms of substance misuse as may be specified or described in the order. ...

8 Parenting orders

(1) This section applies where, in any court proceedings –

(a) a child safety order is made in respect of a child;

(b) an anti-social behaviour order or sex offender order is made in respect of a child or young person;

(c) a child or young person is convicted of an offence; or

(d) a person is convicted of an offence under section 443 (failure to comply with school attendance order) or section 444 (failure to secure regular attendance at school of registered pupil) of the Education Act 1996.

(2) Subject to subsection (3) and section 9(1) below, if in the proceedings the court is satisfied that the relevant condition is fulfilled, it may make a parenting order in respect of a person who is a parent or guardian of the child or young person or, as the case may be, the person convicted of the offence under section 443 or 444 ('the parent').

(3) A court shall not make a parenting order unless it has been notified by the Secretary of State that arrangements for implementing such orders are available in the area in which it appears to the court that the parent resides or will reside and the notice has not been withdrawn.

(4) A parenting order is an order which requires the parent –

(a) to comply, for a period not exceeding twelve months, with such requirements as are specified in the order, and

(b) subject to subsection (5) below, to attend, for a concurrent period not exceeding three months, such counselling or guidance programme as may be specified in directions given by the responsible officer.

(5) A parenting order may, but need not, include such a requirement as is mentioned in subsection (4)(b) above in any case where a parenting order under this section or any other enactment has been made in respect of the parent on a previous occasion.

(6) The relevant condition is that the parenting order would be desirable in the interests of preventing –

(a) in a case falling within paragraph (a) or (b) of subsection (1) above, any repetition of the kind of behaviour which led to the child safety order, anti-social behaviour order or sex offender order being made;

(b) in a case falling within paragraph (c) of that subsection, the commission of any further offence by the child or young person;

(c) in a case falling within paragraph (d) of that subsection, the commission of any further offence under section 443 or 444 of the Education Act 1996.

(7) The requirements that may be specified under subsection (4)(a) above are those which the court considers desirable in the interests of preventing any such repetition or, as the case may be, the commission of any such further offence.

(7A) A counselling or guidance programme which a parent is required to attend by virtue of subsection (4)(b) above may be or include a residential course but only if the court is satisfied –

(a) that the attendance of the parent at a residential course is likely to be more effective than his attendance at a non-residential course in preventing any such repetition or, as the case may be, the commission of any such further offence, and

(b) that any interference with family life which is likely to result from the attendance of the parent at a residential course is proportionate in all the circumstances.

(8) In this section and section 9 below 'responsible officer', in relation to a parenting order, means one of the following who is specified in the order, namely –

(a) an officer of a local probation board;

(b) a social worker of a local authority social services department;

(bb) a person nominated by a person appointed as chief eduction officer under section 532 of the Education Act 1996; and

(c) a member of a youth offending team.

9 Parenting orders: supplemental

(1) Where a person under the age of 16 is convicted of an offence, the court by or before which he is so convicted –

(a) if it is satisfied that the relevant condition is fulfilled, shall make a parenting order; and

(b) if it is not so satisfied, shall state in open court that it is not and why it is not.

(1A) The requirements of subsection (1) do not apply where the court makes a referral order in respect of the offence.

(1B) If an anti-social behaviour order is made in respect of a person under the age of 16 the court which makes the order –

(a) must make a parenting order if it is satisfied that the relevant condition is fulfilled;

(b) if it is not so satisfied, must state in open court that it is not and why it is not.

(2) Before making a parenting order –

(a) in a case falling within paragraph (a) of subsection (1) of section 8 above;

(b) in a case falling within paragraph (b) or (c) of that subsection, where the person concerned is under the age of 16; or

(c) in a case falling within paragraph (d) of that subsection, where the person to whom the offence related is under that age,

a court shall obtain and consider information about the person's family circumstances and the likely effect of the order on those circumstances.

(2A) In a case where a court proposes to make both a referral order in respect of a child or young person convicted of an offence and a parenting order, before making the parenting order the court shall obtain and consider a report by an appropriate officer –

(a) indicating the requirements proposed by that officer to be included in the parenting order;

(b) indicating the reasons why he considers those requirements would be desirable in the interests of preventing the commission of any further offence by the child or young person; and

(c) if the child or young person is aged under 16, containing the information required by subsection (2) above.

(2B) In subsection (2A) above 'an appropriate officer' means –

(a) an officer of a local probation board;

(b) a social worker of a local authority social services department; or

(c) a member of a youth offending team.

(5) If while a parenting order is in force it appears to the court which made it, on the application of the responsible officer or the parent, that it is appropriate to make an order under this subsection, the court may make an order discharging the parenting order or varying it – ...

(7A) In this section 'referral order' means an order under section 16(2) or (3) of the Powers of Criminal Courts (Sentencing) Act 2000 (referral of offender to youth offender panel).

10 Appeals against parenting orders

(1) An appeal shall lie –

(a) to the High Court against the making of a parenting order by virtue of paragraph (a) of subsection (1) of section 8 above; and

(b) to the Crown Court against the making of a parenting order by virtue of paragraph (b) of that subsection. ...

(4) A person in respect of whom a parenting order is made by virtue of section 8(1)(c) above shall have the same right of appeal against the making of the order as if –

(a) the offence that led to the making of the order were an offence committed by him; and

(b) the order were a sentence passed on him for the offence.

(5) A person in respect of whom a parenting order is made by virtue of section 8(1)(d) above shall have the same right of appeal against the making of the order as if the order were a sentence passed on him for the offence that led to the making of the order. ...

11 Child safety orders

(1) Subject to subsection (2) below, if a magistrates' court, on the application of a local authority, is satisfied that one or more of the conditions specified in subsection (3) below are fulfilled with respect to a child under the age of 10, it may make an order (a 'child safety order') which –

(a) places the child, for a period (not exceeding the permitted maximum) specified in the order, under the supervision of the responsible officer; and

(b) requires the child to comply with such requirements as are so specified.

(2) A court shall not make a child safety order unless it has been notified by the Secretary of State that arrangements for implementing such orders are available in the area in which it appears that the child resides or will reside and the notice has not been withdrawn.

(3) The conditions are –

(a) that the child has committed an act which, if he had been aged 10 or over, would have constituted an offence;

(b) that a child safety order is necessary for the purpose of preventing the commission by the child of such an act as is mentioned in paragraph (a) above;

(c) that the child has contravened a ban imposed by a curfew notice; and

(d) that the child has acted in a manner that caused or was likely to cause harassment, alarm or distress to one or more persons not of the same household as himself.

(4) The maximum period permitted for the purposes of subsection (1)(a) above is three months or, where the court is satisfied that the circumstances of the case are exceptional, 12 months.

(5) The requirements that may be specified under subsection (1)(b) above are those which the court considers desirable in the interests of –

(a) securing that the child receives appropriate care, protection and support and is subject to proper control; or

(b) preventing any repetition of the kind of behaviour which led to the child safety order being made. ...

(8) In this section and section 12 below, 'responsible officer', in relation to a child safety order, means one of the following who is specified in the order, namely –

(a) a social worker of a local authority social services department; and

(b) a member of a youth offending team.

12 Child safety orders: supplemental

(1) Before making a child safety order, a magistrates' court shall obtain and consider information about the child's family circumstances and the likely effect of the order on those circumstances. ...

(4) If while a child safety order is in force in respect of a child it appears to the court which made it, on the application of the responsible officer or a parent or guardian of the child, that it is appropriate to make an order under this subsection, the court may make an order discharging the child safety order or varying it – ...

13 Appeals against child safety orders

(1) An appeal shall lie to the High Court against the making by a magistrates' court of a child safety order; ...

14 Local child curfew schemes

(1) A local authority or a chief officer of police may make a scheme (a 'local child curfew scheme') for enabling the authority or (as the case may be) the officer –

(a) subject to and in accordance with the provisions of the scheme; and

(b) if, after such consultation as is required by the scheme, the authority or (as the case may be) the officer considers it necessary to do so for the purpose of maintaining order,

to give a notice imposing, for a specified period (not exceeding 90 days), a ban to which subsection (2) below applies.

(2) This subsection applies to a ban on children of specified ages (under 16) being in a public place within a specified area –

(a) during specified hours (between 9 pm and 6 am); and

(b) otherwise than under the effective control of a parent or a responsible person aged 18 or over. ...

(6) A notice given under a local child curfew scheme (a 'curfew notice') may specify different hours in relation to children of different ages.

(7) A curfew notice shall be given –

(a) by posting the notice in some conspicuous place or places within the specified area; and

(b) in such other manner, if any, as appears to the local authority or (as the case may be) the chief officer of police to be desirable for giving publicity to the notice. ...

15 Contravention of curfew notices

(1) Subsections (2) and (3) below apply where a constable has reasonable cause to believe that a child is in contravention of a ban imposed by a curfew notice.

(2) The constable shall, as soon as practicable, inform the local authority for the area that the child has contravened the ban.

(3) The constable may remove the child to the child's place of residence unless he has reasonable cause to believe that the child would, if removed to that place, be likely to suffer significant harm. ...

16 Removal of truants to designated premises, etc

(1) This section applies where a local authority –

(a) designates premises in a police area ('designated premises') as premises to which children and young persons of compulsory school age may be removed under this section; and

(b) notifies the chief officer of police for that area of the designation. …

(3) If a constable has reasonable cause to believe that a child or young person found by him in a public place in a specified area during a specified period –

(a) is of compulsory school age; and

(b) is absent from a school without lawful authority,

the constable may remove the child or young person to designated premises, or to the school from which he is so absent. …

(4) A child's or young person's absence from a school shall be taken to be without lawful authority unless it falls within subsection (3) (leave, sickness, unavoidable cause or day set apart for religious observance) of section 444 of the Education Act 1996. …

As amended by the Youth Justice and Criminal Evidence Act 1999, s67(1), Schedule 4, paras 25, 27; Powers of Criminal Courts (Sentencing) Act 2000, s165(1), Schedule 9, paras 192–194, Schedule 11, Pt III, para 11(4); Criminal Justice and Court Services Act 2000, ss73, 74, Schedule 7, Pt I, para 4; Criminal Justice and Police Act 2001, ss48, 49(1), (2), (5); Police Reform Act 2002, ss61, 62(1), 63, 64, 65(1), (2), 66, 67(1)–(9), 68(1), (2), 97(1), (2), (7), (8), 98, 107(2), Schedule 8; Anti-social Behaviour Act 2003, ss18(1)–(3), 85(1)–(8), 86(1)–(4); Railways and Transport Safety Act 2003, s73, Schedule 5, para 4(1), (2)(j); Criminal Justice Act 2003, s322, 323(1), (2)(a), 324, 332, Schedule 34, paras 1, 2, Schedule 37, Pt 12; Sexual Offences Act 2003, ss139, 140, Schedule 6, para 38(1), (3)(a), Schedule 7; British Transport Police (Transitional and Consequential Provisions) Order 2004, art 12(5)(a), (b), (d); Fire and Rescue Services Act 2004, s53(1), Schedule 1, para 89(1), (2)(a).

GOVERNMENT OF WALES ACT 1998
(1998 c 38)

PART I
THE NATIONAL ASSEMBLY FOR WALES

1 The Assembly

(1) There shall be an Assembly for Wales to be known as the National Assembly for Wales or Cynulliad Cenedlaethol Cymru (but referred to in this Act as the Assembly).

(2) The Assembly shall be a body corporate.

(3) The exercise by the Assembly of its functions is to be regarded as done on behalf of the Crown.

2 Membership

(1) The Assembly shall consist of –

(a) one member for each Assembly constituency, and

(b) members for each Assembly electoral region.

(2) The Assembly constituencies and Assembly electoral regions, and the number of Assembly seats for each Assembly electoral region, shall be as provided for by or in accordance with Schedule 1.

(3) Members of the Assembly (referred to in this Act as Assembly members) shall be returned in accordance with the provision made by and under this Act for –

(a) the holding of ordinary elections of Assembly members, and

(b) the filling of vacancies in Assembly seats.

(4) An ordinary election involves the holding of elections for the return of the entire Assembly.

(5) The term of office of an Assembly member –

(a) begins when he is declared to be returned as an Assembly member, and

(b) continues until the end of the day before the day of the poll at the next ordinary election.

(6) But an Assembly member may at any time resign his seat by giving notice to –

(a) the presiding officer, or

(b) any person authorised by the standing orders of the Assembly to receive the notice.

(7) The validity of anything done by the Assembly is not affected by any vacancy in its membership.

3 Time of ordinary elections

(1) The poll at the first ordinary election shall be held on a day appointed by order made by the Secretary of State.

(2) The poll at each subsequent ordinary election shall be held on the first Thursday in May in the fourth calendar year following that in which the previous ordinary election was held.

(3) But the Secretary of State may by order require the poll at such an ordinary election to be held on a day which is neither –

(a) more than one month earlier, nor

(b) more than one month later,

than the first Thursday in May

(4) Where the poll at an ordinary election would be held on the same day as polls at ordinary elections of community councillors, the Secretary of State may by order provide for the polls at ordinary elections of community councillors to be postponed, for not more than three months, to a day specified in the order. ...

4 Voting at ordinary elections

(1) Each person entitled to vote at an ordinary election in an Assembly constituency shall have two votes.

(2) One (referred to in this Act as a constituency vote) is to be given for a candidate to be the Assembly member for the Assembly constituency.

(3) The other (referred to in this Act as an electoral region vote) is to be given for –

(a) a registered political party which has submitted a list of candidates to be Assembly members for the Assembly electoral region in which the Assembly constituency is included, or

(b) an individual who is a candidate to be an Assembly member for that Assembly electoral region.

(4) The Assembly member for the Assembly constituency shall be returned under the simple majority system.

(5) The Assembly members for the Assembly electoral region shall be returned under the additional member system of proportional representation in accordance with sections 5 to 7.

(6) The person who is to be returned as the Assembly member for each Assembly

constituency in the Assembly electoral region must be determined before it is determined who are to be returned as the Assembly members for that Assembly electoral region.

(7) At an ordinary election a person may not be a candidate to be the Assembly member for more than one Assembly constituency.

(8) In this Act 'registered political party' means a party registered under Part II of the Political Parties, Elections and Referendums Act 2000.

5 Party lists and individual candidates

(1) Any registered political party may submit a list of candidates to be Assembly members for the Assembly electoral region.

(2) The list is to be submitted to the regional returning officer.

(3) The list has effect in relation to –

(a) the ordinary election, and

(b) any vacancies in seats of Assembly members returned for Assembly electoral regions which occur after that election and before the next ordinary election.

(4) The list must not include more than twelve persons (but may include only one).

(5) The list must not include a person –

(a) who is included on any other list submitted for the Assembly electoral region or any list submitted for another Assembly electoral region,

(b) who is an individual candidate to be an Assembly member for the Assembly electoral region or another Assembly electoral region,

(c) who is a candidate to be the Assembly member for an Assembly constituency which is not included in the Assembly electoral region, or

(d) who is a candidate to be the Assembly member for an Assembly constituency included in the Assembly electoral region but is not a candidate of the party.

(6) A person may not be an individual candidate to be an Assembly member for the Assembly electoral region if he is –

(a) included on a list submitted by a registered political party for the Assembly electoral region or another Assembly electoral region,

(b) an individual candidate to be an Assembly member for another Assembly electoral region,

(c) a candidate to be the Assembly member for an Assembly constituency which is not included in the Assembly electoral region, or

(d) a candidate of any registered political party to be the Assembly member for an Assembly constituency included in the Assembly electoral region.

6 Calculation of electoral region figures

(1) For each registered political party by which a list of candidates has been submitted for the Assembly electoral region –

(a) there shall be added together the number of electoral region votes given for the party in the Assembly constituencies included in the Assembly electoral region, and

(b) the number arrived at under paragraph (a) shall then be divided by the aggregate of one and the number of candidates of the party returned as Assembly members for any of those Assembly constituencies.

(2) For each individual candidate to be an Assembly member for the Assembly electoral region there shall be added together the number of electoral region votes given for him in the Assembly constituencies included in the Assembly electoral region.

(3) The number arrived at –

(a) in the case of a registered political party, under subsection (1)(b), or

(b) in the case of an individual candidate, under subsection (2),

is referred to in this Act as the electoral region figure for that party or individual candidate.

7 Return of electoral region members

(1) The first seat for the Assembly electoral region shall be allocated to the party or individual candidate with the highest electoral region figure.

(2) The second and subsequent seats for the Assembly electoral region shall be allocated to the party or individual candidate with the highest electoral region figure after any recalculation required by subsection (3) has been carried out.

(3) This subsection requires a recalculation under section 6(1)(b) in relation to a party –

(a) for the first application of subsection (2), if the application of subsection (1) resulted in the allocation of a seat to the party, or

(b) for any subsequent application of subsection (2), if the previous application of that subsection did so;

and a recalculation shall be carried out after adding one to the aggregate mentioned in section 6(1)(b).

(4) An individual candidate already returned as an Assembly member shall be disregarded.

(5) Seats for the Assembly electoral region which are allocated to a party shall be filled by the persons on the party's list in the order in which they appear on the list.

(6) Once a party's list has been exhausted (by the return of persons included on it as Assembly members for Assembly constituencies or by the previous application of subsection (1) or (2)) the party shall be disregarded.

(7) If (on the application of subsection (1) or any application of subsection (2)) the

highest electoral region figure is the electoral region figure of two or more parties or individual candidates, the subsection shall apply to each of them.

(8) However, where subsection (7) would mean that more than the full number of seats for the Assembly electoral region were allocated, subsection (1) or (2) shall not apply until –

(a) a recalculation has been carried out under section 6(1)(b) after adding one to the number of votes given for each party with that electoral region figure, and

(b) one has been added to the number of votes given for each individual candidate with that electoral region figure.

(9) If, after that, the highest electoral region figure is still the electoral region figure of two or more parties or individual candidates, the regional returning officer shall decide between them by lots.

(10) For the purposes of subsection (5) and section 9 a person included on a list submitted by a registered political party who is returned as an Assembly member shall be treated as ceasing to be on the list (even if his return is void).

12 Disqualification from being Assembly member

(1) A person is disqualified from being an Assembly member if –

(a) he is disqualified from being a member of the House of Commons under paragraphs (a) to (e) of section 1(1) of the House of Commons Disqualification Act 1975 (judges, civil servants, members of the armed forces, members of police forces and members of foreign legislatures),

(b) he holds any of the offices for the time being designated by Order in Council as offices disqualifying persons from being Assembly members,

(c) he holds the office of Auditor General for Wales or the office of Welsh Administration Ombudsman, or

(d) he is disqualified from being a member of a local authority under section 17(2)(b) or 18(7) of the Audit Commission Act 1998 (members of local authorities who are responsible for incurring or authorising unlawful expenditure or whose wilful misconduct has caused a loss or deficiency).

(2) Subject to section 13(1) and (2), a person is also disqualified from being an Assembly member if he is disqualified otherwise than under the House of Commons Disqualification Act 1975 (either generally or in relation to a particular constituency) from being a member of the House of Commons or from sitting and voting in it.

(3) For the purposes of subsection (2) the references to the Republic of Ireland in section 1 of the Representation of the People Act 1981 (disqualification of offenders detained in, or unlawfully at large from detention in, the British Islands or the Republic of Ireland) shall be treated as references to any member State (other than the United Kingdom).

(4) A person who holds office as lord-lieutenant, lieutenant or high sheriff of any

area in Wales is disqualified from being an Assembly member for any Assembly constituency or Assembly electoral region wholly or partly included in that area.

...

13 Exceptions and relief from disqualification

(1) A person is not disqualified from being an Assembly member merely because –

(a) he is a peer (whether of the United Kingdom, Great Britain, England or Scotland), or

(b) he is a Lord Spiritual.

(2) A citizen of the European Union who is resident in the United Kingdom is not disqualified from being an Assembly member merely because of section 3 of the Act of Settlement (disqualification of persons born outside the United Kingdom other than Commonwealth citizens and citizens of the Republic of Ireland).

(3) Where a person was, or is alleged to have been, disqualified from being an Assembly member on a ground within section 12(1)(a), (b) or (c) or (4), the Assembly may resolve that any disqualification incurred by that person on that ground is to be disregarded if it appears to the Assembly –

(a) that that ground has been removed, and

(b) that it is proper so to resolve. ...

14 Effect of disqualification

(1) If a person who is disqualified from being an Assembly member, or from being an Assembly member for a particular Assembly constituency or Assembly electoral region, is returned as an Assembly member or as an Assembly member for that Assembly constituency or Assembly electoral region, his return shall be void and his seat vacant.

(2) If an Assembly member becomes disqualified from being an Assembly member or from being an Assembly member for the Assembly constituency or Assembly electoral region for which he is sitting, he shall cease to be an Assembly member (so that his seat is vacant).

(3) Subsections (1) and (2) have effect subject to any resolution of the Assembly under section 13(3).

(4) Subsection (2) also has effect subject to section 141 of the Mental Health Act 1983 (mental illness) and section 427 of the Insolvency Act 1986 (bankruptcy etc); and where, in consequence of either of those sections, the seat of a disqualified Assembly member is not vacant he shall not cease to be an Assembly member until his seat becomes vacant but –

(a) he shall not participate in any proceedings of the Assembly (including proceedings of a committee of the Assembly or of a sub-committee of such a committee), and

(b) any of his other rights and privileges as an Assembly member may be withdrawn by the Assembly.

(5) The validity of anything done by the Assembly is not affected by the disqualification of any person from being an Assembly member or from being an Assembly member for the Assembly constituency or Assembly electoral region for which he purports to sit.

15 Judicial proceedings as to disqualification

(1) Any person who claims that a person purporting to be an Assembly member is, or at any time since being returned as an Assembly member has been, disqualified from being –

(a) an Assembly member, or

(b) an Assembly member for the Assembly constituency or Assembly electoral region for which he purports to sit,

may apply to the High Court for a declaration to that effect.

(2) An application under subsection (1) in respect of any person may be made whether the grounds on which it is made are alleged to have subsisted at the time when he was returned or to have arisen subsequently.

(3) No declaration shall be made under this section in respect of any person –

(a) on grounds which subsisted when he was returned, if an election petition is pending or has been tried in which his disqualification on those grounds is or was in issue, or

(b) on any ground, if a resolution under section 13(3) requires that any disqualification incurred by him on that ground is to be disregarded. ...

20 Oath or affirmation of allegiance

(1) An Assembly member shall take the oath of allegiance set out in section 2 of the Promissory Oaths Act 1868 (or make the corresponding affirmation) as soon as may be after he is returned as an Assembly member (whether for the first time or subsequently).

(2) The oath shall be taken (or the affirmation made) before a person appointed by the Assembly (or, until the first appointment is made by the Assembly, before a person appointed by the Secretary of State).

(3) Until an Assembly member has taken the oath (or made the affirmation) he shall not do anything as an Assembly member (other than take part in proceedings of the Assembly at which Assembly members take the oath or make the affirmation, or any earlier proceedings for the election of the presiding officer or deputy presiding officer).

(4) If an Assembly member has not taken the oath (or made the affirmation) within –

(a) the period of two months beginning with the day on which he was declared to be returned as an Assembly member, or

(b) such longer period as the Assembly may have allowed before the end of that period of two months,

he shall at the end of that period of two months or longer period cease to be an Assembly member (so that his seat is vacant). ...

PART II

ASSEMBLY FUNCTIONS

21 Introductory

The Assembly shall have the functions which are –

(a) transferred to, or made exercisable by, the Assembly by virtue of this Act, or

(b) conferred or imposed on the Assembly by or under this Act or any other Act.

22 Transfer of Ministerial functions

(1) Her Majesty may by Order in Council –

(a) provide for the transfer to the Assembly of any function so far as exercisable by a Minister of the Crown in relation to Wales,

(b) direct that any function so far as so exercisable shall be exercisable by the Assembly concurrently with the Minister of the Crown, or

(c) direct that any function so far as exercisable by a Minister of the Crown in relation to Wales shall be exercisable by the Minister only with the agreement of, or after consultation with, the Assembly. ...

23 General transfer of property, rights and liabilities, etc

(1) There shall be transferred to and vest in the Assembly by virtue of this subsection all property, rights and liabilities to which a Minister of the Crown is entitled or subject, at the coming into force of an Order in Council under section 22, in connection with any function exercisable by the Minister which is transferred by the Order in Council.

(2) There may be continued by or in relation to the Assembly anything (including legal proceedings) which relates to –

(a) any function exercisable by a Minister of the Crown which is transferred by an Order in Council under section 22, or

(b) any property, rights or liabilities transferred by subsection (1) as the result of the transfer of any such function by such an Order in Council.

and which is in the process of being done by or in relation to the Minister immediately before the coming into force of the Order in Council.

(3) Anything which was done by a Minister of the Crown for the purpose of or in connection with –

(a) any function exercisable by the Minister which is transferred by an Order in Council under section 22, or

(b) any property, rights or liabilities transferred by subsection (1) as the result of the transfer of any such function by such an Order in Council,

and which is in effect immediately before the coming into force of the Order in Council shall have effect as if done by the Assembly.

(4) The Assembly shall be substituted for any Minister of the Crown in any instruments, contracts or legal proceedings which relate to –

(a) any function exercisable by the Minister which is transferred by an Order in Council under section 22, or

(b) any property, rights or liabilities transferred by subsection (1) as the result of the transfer of any such function by such an Order in Council,

and which are made or commenced before the coming into force of the Order in Council.

29 Implementation of Community law

(1) The power to designate a Minister of the Crown or government department under section 2(2) of the European Communities Act 1972 may be exercised to designate the Assembly.

(2) Accordingly, the Assembly may exercise the power to make regulations conferred by section 2(2) of the European Communities Act 1972 in relation to any matter, or for any purpose, if the Assembly has been designated in relation to that matter or for that purpose, but subject to such restrictions or conditions (if any) as may be specified by the Order in Council designating the Assembly. ...

30 Consultation about public appointments

(1) Her Majesty may by Order in Council make provision requiring any Minister of the Crown or other person to consult the Assembly before –

(a) appointing a person to a specified public post,

(b) recommending, consenting to or approving the appointment of a person to a specified public post,

(c) nominating a person for appointment to a specified public post, or

(d) selecting persons with a view to the appointment of one or more of them to a specified public post (whether or not by the person subject to the requirement).

(2) In subsection (1) 'a specified public post' means –

(a) a public office specified, or of a description specified, in the Order in Council, or

(b) membership, or membership of a description so specified, of a public body so specified or of a description so specified. ...

31 Consultation about government's legislative programme

(1) As soon as is reasonably practicable after the beginning of each session of Parliament, the Secretary of State for Wales shall undertake with the Assembly such consultation about the government's legislative programme for the session as appears to him to be appropriate but including attending and participating in proceedings of the Assembly relating to the programme on at least one occasion.

(2) For this purpose the government's legislative programme for a session of Parliament consists of the bills which (at the beginning of the session) are intended to be introduced into either House of Parliament during the session by a Minister of the Crown.

(3) If at any time after the beginning of a session of Parliament –

(a) it is decided that a bill should be introduced into either House of Parliament during the session by a Minister of the Crown, and

(b) no consultation about the bill has been undertaken under subsection (1),

the Secretary of State for Wales shall undertake with the Assembly such consultation about the bill as appears to him to be appropriate.

(4) This section does not require the Secretary of State for Wales to undertake consultation with the Assembly about a bill if he considers that there are considerations relating to the bill which make it inappropriate for him to do so.

32 Support of culture, etc

The Assembly may do anything it considers appropriate to support –

(a) museums, art galleries or libraries in Wales,

(b) buildings of historical or architectural interest, or other places of historical interest, in Wales,

(c) the Welsh language, or

(d) the arts, crafts, sport or other cultural or recreational activities in Wales.

33 Consideration of matters affecting Wales

The Assembly may consider, and make appropriate representations about, any matter affecting Wales.

34 Staff

(1) The Assembly may appoint such staff as it considers appropriate.

(2) Service as a member of the Assembly's staff shall be service in Her Majesty's Home Civil Service.

(3) Subsection (1) is subject to any provision made in relation to Her Majesty's Home Civil Service by or under any Order in Council. ...

35 Inquiries

(1) The Assembly may cause an inquiry to be held into any matter relevant to the exercise of any of its functions. ...

36 Polls for ascertaining views of the public

(1) The Assembly may hold a poll in an area consisting of Wales or any part (or parts) of Wales for the purpose of ascertaining the views of those polled about whether or how any of the Assembly's functions (other than those under section 33) should be exercised.

(2) The persons entitled to vote in a poll under this section are those who –

(a) would be entitled to vote as electors at a local government election in an electoral area wholly or partly included in the area in which the poll is held, and

(b) are registered in the register of local government electors at an address within the area in which the poll is held. ...

37 Private bills

(1) The Assembly may promote private bills in Parliament and may oppose any private bill in Parliament.

(2) But the Assembly shall not promote or oppose any private bill in Parliament unless a motion to authorise the Assembly to promote or oppose the bill is passed by the Assembly on a vote in which at least two-thirds of the Assembly members voting support the motion. ...

38 Legal proceedings

Where the Assembly considers it appropriate for the promotion or protection of the public interest it may institute in its own name, defend or appear in any legal proceedings relating to matters with respect to which any functions of the Assembly are exercisable.

39 Contracts

The Secretary of State may by order provide that the Local Government (Contracts) Act 1997 shall apply in relation to contracts entered into by the Assembly but subject to any appropriate modifications.

40 Supplementary powers

The Assembly may do anything (including the acquisition or disposal of any property or rights) which is calculated to facilitate, or is conducive or incidental to, the exercise of any of its functions.

44 Parliamentary procedures for subordinate legislation

(1) This section applies where a function to make subordinate legislation (including a function conferred or imposed by, or after the passing of, this Act) has been transferred to, or made exercisable by, the Assembly by an Order in Council under section 22.

(2) Subject to subsections (4) and (5), any relevant Parliamentary procedural provision relating to the function shall not have effect in relation to the exercise of the function of the Assembly.

(3) For the purposes of this Act 'relevant Parliamentary procedural provision' means provision –

(a) requiring any instrument made in the exercise of the function, or a draft of any such instrument, to be laid before Parliament or either House of Parliament,

(b) for the annulment or approval of any such instrument or draft by or in pursuance of a resolution of either House of Parliament or of both Houses,

(c) prohibiting the making of any such instrument without that approval,

(d) for any such instrument to be a provisional order (that is, an order which requires to be confirmed by Act of Parliament), or

(e) requiring any order (within the meaning of the Statutory Orders (Special Procedure) Act 1945) to be subject to special parliamentary procedure.

(4) Subsection (2) does not apply in the case of any instrument made in the exercise of the function, or a draft of any such instrument, if it –

(a) contains subordinate legislation made or to be made by a Minister of the Crown or government department (whether or not jointly with the Assembly),

(b) contains (or confirms or approves) subordinate legislation relating to an English border area, or

(c) contains (or confirms or approves) subordinate legislation relating to a cross-border body (and not relating only to the exercise of functions, or the carrying on of activities, by the body in or with respect to Wales or a part of Wales).

(5) Where a function transferred to, or made exercisable by, the Assembly by an Order in Council under section 22 is subject to a provision of the description specified in subsection (3)(e), the Order in Council may provide that –

(a) any order made by the Assembly in the exercise of the function, or

(b) any order so made in circumstances specified in the Order in Council,

is to be subject to special parliamentary procedure.

(6) In this section 'male' includes confirm or approve and related expressions (except 'made exercisable') shall be construed accordingly; but an instrument (or draft) does not fall within subsection (4)(a) just because it contains subordinate legislation made (or to be made) by the Assembly with the agreement of a Minister of the Crown or government department.

PART III

ASSEMBLY PROCEDURE

46 Regulation of procedure

(1) The procedure of the Assembly (including that of committees of the Assembly and sub-committees of such committees) shall be regulated by the standing orders of the Assembly.

(2) But subsection (1) is subject to any other provision of this Act or any other enactment which regulates, or provides for the regulation of, the procedure of the Assembly (or of committees of the Assembly or sub-committees of such committees). ...

(5) The Assembly may not delegate the function of remaking or revising the standing orders.

(6) The standing orders shall not be remade or revised unless a motion to approve the standing orders or revisions is passed by the Assembly on a vote in which at least two-thirds of the Assembly members voting support the motion.

47 Equal treatment of English and Welsh languages

(1) The Assembly shall in the conduct of its business give effect, so far as is both appropriate in the circumstances and reasonably practicable, to the principle that the English and Welsh languages should be treated on a basis of equality. ...

48 Equal opportunities in conduct of business

The Assembly shall make appropriate arrangements with a view to securing that its business is conducted with due regard to the principle that there should be equality of opportunity for all people.

52 Presiding officer and deputy

(1) The Assembly shall elect from among the Assembly members –

(a) the presiding officer, and

(b) the deputy presiding officer.

(2) The offices specified in subsection (1) shall be known by such titles as the standing orders may provide (but are referred to in this Act as the presiding officer and the deputy presiding officer).

(3) The presiding officer and the deputy presiding officer may not be Assembly members who represent the same party.

53 Assembly First Secretary and Assembly Secretaries

(1) The Assembly shall elect one of the Assembly members to be Assembly First Secretary or Prif Ysgrifennydd y Cynulliad.

(2) The Assembly First Secretary shall appoint Assembly Secretaries, or Ysgrifenyddion y Cynulliad, from among the Assembly members (and may at any time remove a person from office as an Assembly Secretary).

(3) The standing orders must specify the maximum number of Assembly Secretaries that may be appointed.

(4) The Assembly First Secretary, and each of the Assembly Secretaries, is a Crown servant for the purposes of the Official Secrets Act 1989.

54 Committees

(1) The Assembly –

(a) shall establish the committees in which it is required to establish by the following provisions of this Part, and

(b) may establish any other committees which it considers appropriate.

(2) The members of any committee established by the Assembly under subsection (1)(b) –

(a) shall be elected by the Assembly from among the Assembly members, and

(b) shall, unless the committee exists solely to provide advice, be elected so as to secure that, as far as is practicable, the balance of the parties in the Assembly is reflected in the membership of the committee.

56 Executive committee

(1) There shall be a committee of the Assembly whose members shall be –

(a) the Assembly First Secretary, who shall chair it, and

(b) the Assembly Secretaries.

(2) The committee shall be known by such title as the standing orders may provide (but is referred to in this Act as the executive committee).

(3) The Assembly First Secretary shall allocate accountability in the fields in which the Assembly has functions to members of the executive committee so that, in the case of each of those fields, accountability in the field is allocated either to one of the Assembly Secretaries or to him. …

57 Subject committees

(1) The Assembly shall establish committees with responsibilities in the fields in which the Assembly has functions.

(2) The committees established under this section shall be known by such titles as the standing orders may provide (but are referred to in this Act as subject committees). ...

58 Subordinate legislation scrutiny committee

(1) The Assembly shall establish a committee with responsibilities relating to the scrutiny of relevant Welsh subordinate legislation.

(2) For the purposes of this section 'relevant Welsh subordinate legislation' is any subordinate legislation –

(a) which is made or proposed to be made, or

(b) which, or a draft of which, is (or but for paragraph 2(4) of Schedule 7 would be) required to be confirmed or approved,

by the Assembly (whether or not jointly with a Minister of the Crown or government department). ...

59 Members of scrutiny committee, etc

(1) The subordinate legislation scrutiny committee shall have such number of members as the standing orders may provide.

(2) The members of the subordinate legislation scrutiny committee shall be elected by the Assembly from among Assembly members so as to secure that, as far as is practicable, the balance of the parties in the Assembly is reflected in the membership of the committee.

(3) Neither the Assembly First Secretary nor an Assembly Secretary may be a member of the subordinate legislation scrutiny committee.

(4) The Assembly shall elect one of the members of the subordinate legislation scrutinee committee to chair the committee but it may not be chaired by a member who represents the largest party with an executive role. ...

(7) For the purposes of this Act a party is the largest party with an executive role if –

(a) an Assembly member representing the party is a member of the executive committee, and

(b) it is represented by more Assembly members than any other party represented by an Assembly member who is a member of that committee.

62 Delegation of functions

(1) The Assembly may delegate functions of the Assembly (to such extent as the Assembly may determine) to –

(a) any committee of the Assembly, or

(b) the Assembly First Secretary.

(2) Any committee of the Assembly, apart from the Audit Committee, may delegate functions of the committee (to such extent as the committee may determine) to a sub-committee of the committee.

(3) In addition –

(a) the executive committee may delegate functions of the executive committee (to such extent as the executive committee may determine) to the Assembly First Secretary or an Assembly Secretary …

63 Exercise of functions by Assembly staff

(1) Each of the following –

(a) the Assembly,

(b) any committee of the Assembly, apart from the Audit Committee,

(c) any sub-committee of a committee of the Assembly,

(d) the Assembly First Secretary, and

(e) any Assembly Secretary,

may delegate functions of its or his (to such extent as it or he may determine) to the Assembly's staff. …

64 Standing orders to provide procedures

The standing orders must provide procedures (referred to in this Act as the subordinate legislation procedures) for –

(a) the preparation, and

(b) the making, confirmation and approval,

of orders, regulations, rules and other subordinate legislation.

65 Regulatory appraisals

(1) The subordinate legislation procedures must include provision for securing that an appraisal (referred to in this Act as a regulatory appraisal) as to the likely costs and benefits of complying with any proposed Assembly general subordinate legislation is carried out before a draft of the statutory instrument containing the subordinate legislation is laid before the Assembly.

(2) But the subordinate legislation procedures may provide that a regulatory appraisal need not be carried out in relation to any proposed Assembly general subordinate legislation if in the particular circumstances it is inappropriate or not reasonably practicable for one to be carried out. …

66 Making of Assembly general subordinate legislation

(1) Assembly general subordinate legislation shall be made by being signed by the presiding officer, the deputy officer, the Assembly First Secretary or such other person as may be authorised by the subordinate legislation procedures.

(2) Assembly general subordinate legislation may not be made until a draft of the statutory instrument containing it has been laid before, and approved by a resolution of, the Assembly.

(3) The subordinate legislation procedures must include provision for securing that Assembly general subordinate legislation may be made by being signed otherwise than by the presiding officer only in the absence of the presiding officer.

(4) The subordinate legislation procedures must include provision for securing that a draft of the statutory instrument containing any Assembly general subordinate legislation may be approved by the Assembly only if the draft is in both English and Welsh unless in the particular circumstances it is inappropriate or not reasonably practicable for the draft to be in both languages.

(5) The subordinate legislation procedures must include provision for securing that a draft of the statutory instrument containing any Assembly general subordinate legislation is not approved by the Assembly until the Assembly has considered –

(a) the report of the subordinate legislation scrutiny committee relating to the subordinate legislation, and

(b) the regulatory appraisal (if any) in relation to it.

(6) The Assembly First Secretary may not delegate his function of signing Assembly general subordinate legislation.

(7) The Assembly may not delegate the function of approving the draft of the statutory instrument containing any Assembly general subordinate legislation or the function of considering –

(a) the report of the subordinate legislation scrutiny committee relating to it, or

(b) the regulatory appraisal (if any) published in relation to it.

76 Attendance of Secretary of State for Wales

(1) The Secretary of State for Wales shall be entitled to attend and participate in any proceedings of the Assembly.

(2) Subsection (1) does not confer on the Secretary of State for Wales –

(a) any right to vote, or

(b) a right to attend or participate in the proceedings of a committee of the Assembly or any sub-committee of such a committee.

(3) The standing orders must include provision for any documents which –

(a) contain material relating to any proceedings of the Assembly itself which have taken place or are to take place, and

(b) are made available to all Assembly members,

to be made available to the Secretary of State for Wales no later than the time when they are made available to Assembly members who are not members of the executive committee.

78 Contempt of court

(1) The strict liability rule shall not apply in relation to any publication –

(a) made in, for the purposes of or for purposes incidental to proceedings of the Assembly (including proceedings of a committee of the Assembly or of a sub-committee of such a committee), or

(b) to the extent that it consists of a report of such proceedings which either is made by or under the authority of the Assembly or is fair and accurate and made in good faith.

(2) ... 'the strict liability rule' and 'publication' have the same meanings as in the Contempt of Court Act 1981.

PART V

OTHER PROVISIONS ABOUT THE ASSEMBLY

106 Community law

(1) A Community obligation of the United Kingdom is also an obligation of the Assembly if, and to the extent that, the obligation could be implemented (or enabled to be implemented) or complied with by the exercise by the Assembly of any of its functions.

(2) Subsection (1) does not apply in the case of a Community obligation of the United Kingdom if –

(a) it is an obligation to achieve a result defined by reference to a quantity (whether expressed as an amount, proportion or ratio or otherwise), and

(b) the quantity relates to the United Kingdom (or to an area including the United Kingdom or to an area consisting of a part of the United Kingdom which includes the whole or part of Wales).

(3) But if such a Community obligation could (to any extent) be implemented (or enabled to be implemented) or complied with by the exercise by the Assembly of any of its functions, a Minister of the Crown may by order provide for the achievement by the Assembly (in the exercise of its functions) of so much of the result to be achieved under the Community obligation as is specified in the order.

(4) The order may specify the time by which any part of the result to be achieved by the Assembly is to be achieved.

(5) No order shall be made by a Minister of the Crown under subsection (3) unless he has consulted the Assembly.

(6) Where an order under subsection (3) is in force in relation to a Community obligation, to the extent that the Community obligation involves achieving what is

specified in the order it is also an obligation of the Assembly (enforceable as if it were an obligation of the Assembly under subsection (1)).

(7) The Assembly has no power –

(a) to make, confirm or approve any subordinate legislation, or

(b) to do any other act,

so far as the subordinate legislation or act is incompatible with Community law or an obligation under subsection (6).

107 Human rights

(1) The Assembly has no power –

(a) to make, confirm or approve any subordinate legislation, or

(b) to do any other act,

so far as the subordinate legislation or act is incompatible with any of the Convention rights.

(2) Subsection (1) does not enable a person –

(a) to bring any proceedings in a court or tribunal, or

(b) to rely on any of the Convention rights in any such proceedings,

in respect of an act unless he would be a victim for the purposes of Article 34 of the Convention if proceedings were brought in the European Court of Human Rights in respect of that act.

(3) Subsection (2) does not apply to the Attorney General, the Assembly, the Advocate General for Scotland or the Attorney General for Northern Ireland.

(4) Subsection (1) –

(a) does not apply to an act which, by virtue of subsection (2) of section 6 of the Human Rights Act 1998, is not unlawful under subsection (1) of that section, and

(b) does not enable a court or tribunal to award in respect of an act any damages which it could not award on finding the act unlawful under that subsection.

(5) In this Act 'the Convention rights' has the same meaning as in the Human Rights Act 1998 and in subsection (2) 'the Convention' has the same meaning as in that Act.

108 International obligations

(1) If a Minister of the Crown considers that any action proposed to be taken by the Assembly would be incompatible with any international obligation, he may by order direct that the proposed action shall not be taken.

(2) If a Minister of the Crown considers that any action capable of being taken by

the Assembly is required for the purpose of giving effect to any international obligation, he may by order direct the Assembly to take the action.

(3) If a Minister of the Crown considers that any subordinate legislation made, or which could be revoked, by the Assembly is incompatible with any international obligation, he may by order revoke the legislation. ...

(6) In this section 'international obligation' means an international obligation of the United Kingdom other than –

(a) an obligation under Community law, or

(b) an obligation not to act (or fail to act) in a way which is incompatible with any of the Convention rights. ...

111 Welsh Administration Ombudsman

(1) There shall be an office of Welsh Administration Ombudsman or Ombwdsmon Gweinyddiaeth Cymru.

(2) Schedule 9 (which makes provision about the Welsh Administration Ombudsman and, in particular, enables him to investigate administrative action taken by the Assembly and certain other public bodies in Wales in response to complaints claiming maladministration) has effect.

155 Interpretation

(1) In this Act –

'Community law' means –

(a) all the rights, powers, liabilities, obligations and restrictions from time to time created or arising by or under the Community Treaties, and

(b) all the remedies and procedures from time to time provided for by or under the Community Treaties,

'delegate' includes further delegate,

'enactment' includes subordinate legislation,

'functions' includes powers and duties,

'Minister of the Crown' includes the Treasury,

'subordinate legislation' has the same meaning as in the Interpretation Act 1978, and

'Wales' includes the sea adjacent to Wales out as far as the seaward boundary of the territorial sea;

and related expressions shall be construed accordingly. ...

SCHEDULE 1

ASSEMBLY CONSTITUENCIES AND ASSEMBLY ELECTORAL REGIONS

1. The Assembly constituencies shall be the parliamentary constituencies in Wales.

2. – (1) There shall be five Assembly electoral regions.

(2) The Assembly electoral regions shall be the five European Parliamentary constituencies in Wales provided for by the European Parliamentary Constituencies (Wales) Order 1994.

(3) There shall be four Assembly seats for each Assembly electoral region. ...

SCHEDULE 9

WELSH ADMINISTRATION OMBUDSMAN

PART I

THE OMBUDSMAN

1. – (1) The Welsh Administration Ombudsman shall be appointed by Her Majesty.

(2) Subject to sub-paragraphs (3) and (4), the Welsh Administration Ombudsman shall hold office until the end of the year of service in which he attains the age of 65.

(3) Her Majesty may relieve the Welsh Administration Ombudsman of office before the end of that year of service –

(a) at his request, or

(b) on Her Majesty being satisfied that he is incapable for medical reasons of performing the duties of his office and of requesting to be relieved of it.

(4) Her Majesty may remove the Welsh Administration Ombudsman from office before the end of the year of service in which he attains the age of 65 if, on the ground of misbehaviour, the Secretary of State recommends that Her Majesty should do so; but the Secretary of State shall not so recommend without consulting the Assembly. ...

PART II

INVESTIGATION OF COMPLAINTS ...

27. – (1) Where the Welsh Administration Ombudsman, at any stage in the course of conducting an investigation, forms the opinion that the complaint relates partly to a matter which could be the subject of an investigation –

(a) by the Parliamentary Commissioner for Administration under the Parliamentary Commissioner Act 1967,

(b) by a Health Service Commissioner under the Health Service Commissioners Act 1993,

(c) by a Local Commissioner under Part III of the Local Government Act 1974, or

(d) by the Scottish Public Services Ombudsman under the Scottish Public Services Ombudsman Act 2002.

he shall consult about the complaint with the appropriate Commissioner or Scottish Public Services Ombudsman as the case may require and, if he considers it necessary, he shall inform the person who made the complaint of the steps necessary to make a complaint to that Commissioner or the Scottish Public Services Ombudsman. ...

As amended by the Registration of Political Parties Act 1998, s23, Schedule 3, para 5; Political Parties, Elections and Referendums Act 2000, s158(1), Schedule 21, para 12(1), (2); House of Commons (Removal of Clergy Disqualification) Act 2001, s1, Schedule 1, para 3; Scottish Public Services Ombudsman Act 2002 (Consequential Amendments and Modifications) Order 2004, art 20(a).

HUMAN RIGHTS ACT 1998
(1998 c 42)

1 The Convention Rights

(1) In this Act 'the Convention rights' means the rights and fundamental freedoms set out in –

(a) Articles 2 to 12 and 14 of the Convention,

(b) Articles 1 to 3 of the First Protocol, and

(c) Article 1 of the Thirteenth Protocol,

as read with Articles 16 to 18 of the Convention.

(2) Those Articles are to have effect for the purposes of this Act subject to any designated derogation or reservation (as to which see sections 14 and 15).

(3) The Articles are set out in Schedule 1.

(4) The Secretary of State may by order make such amendments to this Act as he considers appropriate to reflect the effect, in relation to the United Kingdom, of a protocol.

(5) In subsection (4) 'protocol' means a protocol to the Convention –

(a) which the United Kingdom has ratified; or

(b) which the United Kingdom has signed with a view to ratification.

(6) No amendment may be made by an order under subsection (4) so as to come into force before the protocol concerned is in force in relation to the United Kingdom.

2 Interpretation of Convention rights

(1) A court or tribunal determining a question which has arisen in connection with a Convention right must take into account any –

(a) judgment, decision, declaration or advisory opinion of the European Court of Human Rights,

(b) opinion of the Commission given in a report adopted under Article 31 of the Convention,

(c) decision of the Commission in connection with Article 26 or 27(2) of the Convention, or

(d) decision of the Committee of Ministers taken under Article 46 of the Convention,

whenever made or given, so far as, in the opinion of the court or tribunal, it is relevant to the proceedings in which that question has arisen.

(2) Evidence of any judgment, decision, declaration or opinion of which account may have to be taken under this section is to be given in proceedings before any court or tribunal in such manner as may be provided by rules.

(3) In this section 'rules' means rules of court or, in the case of proceedings before a tribunal, rules made for the purposes of this section –

(a) by the Secretary of State, in relation to any proceedings outside Scotland ...

3 Interpretation of legislation

(1) So far as it is possible to do so, primary legislation and subordinate legislation must be read and given effect in a way which is compatible with the Convention rights.

(2) This section –

(a) applies to primary legislation and subordinate legislation whenever enacted;

(b) does not affect the validity, continuing operation or enforcement of any incompatible primary legislation; and

(c) does not affect the validity, continuing operation or enforcement of any incompatible subordinate legislation if (disregarding any possibility of revocation) primary legislation prevents removal of the incompatibility.

4 Declaration of incompatibility

(1) Subsection (2) applies in any proceedings in which a court determines whether a provision of primary legislation is compatible with a Convention right.

(2) If the court is satisfied that the provision is incompatible with a Convention right, it may make a declaration of that incompatibility.

(3) Subsection (4) applies in any proceedings in which a court determines whether a provision of subordinate legislation, made in the exercise of a power conferred by primary legislation, is compatible with a Convention right.

(4) If the court is satisfied –

(a) that the provision is incompatible with a Convention right, and

(b) that (disregarding any possibility of revocation) the primary legislation concerned prevents removal of the incompatibility,

it may make a declaration of that incompatibility.

(5) In this section 'court' means –

(a) the House of Lords;

(b) the Judicial Committee of the Privy Council;

(c) the Courts-Martial Appeal Court; ...

(e) in England and Wales ... the High Court or the Court of Appeal.

(6) A declaration under this section ('a declaration of incompatibility') –

(a) does not affect the validity, continuing operation or enforcement of the provision in respect of which it is given; and

(b) is not binding on the parties to the proceedings in which it is made.

5 Right of Crown to intervene

(1) Where a court is considering whether to make a declaration of incompatibility, the Crown is entitled to notice in accordance with rules of court.

(2) In any case to which subsection (1) applies –

(a) a Minister of the Crown (or a person nominated by him), ...

is entitled, on giving notice in accordance with rules of court, to be joined as a party to the proceedings.

(3) Notice under subsection (2) may be given at any time during the proceedings.

(4) A person who has been made a party to criminal proceedings (other than in Scotland) as the result of a notice under subsection (2) may, with leave, appeal to the House of Lords against any declaration of incompatibility made in the proceedings.

(5) In subsection (4) –

'criminal proceedings' includes all proceedings before the Courts-Martial Appeal Court; and

'leave' means leave granted by the court making the declaration of incompatibility or by the House of Lords.

6 Acts of public authorities

(1) It is unlawful for a public authority to act in a way which is incompatible with a Convention right.

(2) Subsection (1) does not apply to an act if –

(a) as the result of one or more provisions of primary legislation, the authority could not have acted differently; or

(b) in the case of one or more provisions of, or made under, primary legislation which cannot be read or given effect in a way which is compatible with the Convention rights, the authority was acting so as to give effect to or enforce those provisions.

(3) In this section 'public authority' includes –

(a) a court or tribunal, and

(b) any person certain of whose functions are functions of a public nature,

but does not include either House of Parliament or a person exercising functions in connection with proceedings in Parliament.

(4) In subsection (3) 'Parliament' does not include the House of Lords in its judicial capacity.

(5) In relation to a particular act, a person is not a public authority by virtue only of subsection (3)(b) if the nature of the act is private.

(6) 'An act' includes a failure to act but does not include a failure to –

(a) introduce in, or lay before, Parliament a proposal for legislation; or

(b) make any primary legislation or remedial order.

7 Proceedings

(1) A person who claims that a public authority has acted (or proposes to act) in a way which is made unlawful by section 6(1) may –

(a) bring proceedings against the authority under this Act in the appropriate court or tribunal, or

(b) rely on the Convention right or rights concerned in any legal proceedings,

but only if he is (or would be) a victim of the unlawful act.

(2) In subsection (1)(a) 'appropriate court or tribunal' means such court or tribunal as may be determined in accordance with rules; and proceedings against an authority include a counterclaim or similar proceeding.

(3) If the proceedings are brought on an application for judicial review, the applicant is to be taken to have a sufficient interest in relation to the unlawful act only if he is, or would be, a victim of that act.

(4) If the proceedings are made by way of a petition for judicial review in Scotland, the applicant shall be taken to have title and interest to sue in relation to the unlawful act only if he is, or would be, a victim of that act.

(5) Proceedings under subsection (1)(a) must be brought before the end of –

(a) the period of one year beginning with the date on which the act complained of took place; or

(b) such longer period as the court or tribunal considers equitable having regard to all the circumstances,

but that is subject to any rule imposing a stricter time limit in relation to the procedure in question.

(6) In subsection (1)(b) 'legal proceedings' includes –

(a) proceedings brought by or at the instigation of a public authority; and

(b) an appeal against the decision of a court or tribunal.

(7) For the purposes of this section, a person is a victim of an unlawful act only if

he would be a victim for the purposes of Article 34 of the Convention if proceedings were brought in the European Court of Human Rights in respect of that act.

(8) Nothing in this Act creates a criminal offence.

(9) In this section 'rules' means –

(a) in relation to proceedings before a court or tribunal outside Scotland, rules made by the Secretary of State for the purposes of this section or rules of court, ...

and includes provision made by order under section 1 of the Courts and Legal Services Act 1990.

(10) In making rules, regard must be had to section 9.

(11) The Minister who has power to make rules in relation to a particular tribunal may, to the extent he considers it necessary to ensure that the tribunal can provide an appropriate remedy in relation to an act (or proposed act) of a public authority which is (or would be) unlawful as a result of section 6(1), by order add to –

(a) the relief or remedies which the tribunal may grant; or
(b) the grounds on which it may grant any of them.

(12) An order made under subsection (11) may contain such incidental, supplemental, consequential or transitional provision as the Minister making it considers appropriate. ...

8 Judicial remedies

(1) In relation to any act (or proposed act) of a public authority which the court finds is (or would be) unlawful, it may grant such relief or remedy, or make such order, within its powers as it considers just and appropriate.

(2) But damages may be awarded only by a court which has power to award damages, or to order the payment of compensation, in civil proceedings.

(3) No award of damages is to be made unless, taking account of all the circumstances of the case, including –

(a) any other relief or remedy granted, or order made, in relation to the act in question (by that or any other court), and

(b) the consequences of any decision (of that or any other court) in respect of that act,

the court is satisfied that the award is necessary to afford just satisfaction to the person in whose favour it is made.

(4) In determining –

(a) whether to award damages, or
(b) the amount of an award,

the court must take into account the principles applied by the European Court of

Human Rights in relation to the award of compensation under Article 41 of the Convention.

(5) A public authority against which damages are awarded is to be treated – …

(b) for the purposes of the Civil Liability (Contribution) Act 1978 as liable in respect of damage suffered by the person to whom the award is made.

(6) In this section –

'court' includes a tribunal;

'damages' means damages for an unlawful act of a public authority; and

'unlawful' means unlawful under section 6(1).

9 Judicial acts

(1) Proceedings under section 7(1)(a) in respect of a judicial act may be brought only –

(a) by exercising a right of appeal;

(b) on an application … for judicial review; or

(c) in such other forum as may be prescribed by rules.

(2) That does not affect any rule of law which prevents a court from being the subject of judicial review.

(3) In proceedings under this Act in respect of a judicial act done in good faith, damages may not be awarded otherwise than to compensate a person to the extent required by Article 5(5) of the Convention.

(4) An award of damages permitted by subsection (3) is to be made against the Crown; but no award may be made unless the appropriate person, if not a party to the proceedings, is joined.

(5) In this section –

'appropriate person' means the Minister responsible for the court concerned, or a person or government department nominated by him;

'court' includes a tribunal;

'judge' includes a member of a tribunal, a justice of the peace … and a clerk or other officer entitled to exercise the jurisdiction of a court;

'judicial act' means a judicial act of a court and includes an act done on the instructions, or on behalf, of a judge; and

'rules' has the same meaning as in section 7(9).

10 Power to take remedial action

(1) This section applies if –

(a) a provision of legislation has been declared under section 4 to be incompatible with a Convention right and, if an appeal lies –

(i) all persons who may appeal have stated in writing that they do not intend to do so;

(ii) the time for bringing an appeal has expired and no appeal has been brought within that time; or

(iii) an appeal brought within that time has been determined or abandoned; or

(b) it appears to a Minister of the Crown or Her Majesty in Council that, having regard to a finding of the European Court of Human Rights made after the coming into force of this section in proceedings against the United Kingdom, a provision of legislation is incompatible with an obligation of the United Kingdom arising from the Convention.

(2) If a Minister of the Crown considers that there are compelling reasons for proceeding under this section, he may by order make such amendments to the legislation as he considers necessary to remove the incompatibility.

(3) If, in the case of subordinate legislation, a Minister of the Crown considers –

(a) that it is necessary to amend the primary legislation under which the subordinate legislation in question was made, in order to enable the incompatibility to be removed, and

(b) that there are compelling reasons for proceeding under this section,

he may by order make such amendments to the primary legislation as he considers necessary.

(4) This section also applies where the provision in question is in subordinate legislation and has been quashed, or declared invalid, by reason of incompatibility with a Convention right and the Minister proposes to proceed under paragraph 2(b) of Schedule 2.

(5) If the legislation is an Order in Council, the power conferred by subsection (2) or (3) is exercisable by Her Majesty in Council.

(6) In this section 'legislation' does not include a Measure of the Church Assembly or of the General Synod of the Church of England.

(7) Schedule 2 makes further provision about remedial orders.

11 Safeguard for existing human rights

A person's reliance on a Convention right does not restrict –

(a) any other right or freedom conferred on him by or under any law having effect in any part of the United Kingdom; or

(b) his right to make any claim or bring any proceedings which he could make or bring apart from sections 7 to 9.

12 Freedom of expression

(1) This section applies if a court is considering whether to grant any relief which, if granted, might affect the exercise of the Convention right to freedom of expression.

(2) If the person against whom the application for relief is made ('the respondent') is neither present nor represented, no such relief is to be granted unless the court is satisfied –

(a) that the applicant has taken all practicable steps to notify the respondent; or

(b) that there are compelling reasons why the respondent should not be notified.

(3) No such relief is to be granted so as to restrain publication before trial unless the court is satisfied that the applicant is likely to establish that publication should not be allowed.

(4) The court must have particular regard to the importance of the Convention right to freedom of expression and, where the proceedings relate to material which the respondent claims, or which appears to the court, to be journalistic, literary or artistic material (or to conduct connected with such material), to –

(a) the extent to which –

(i) the material has, or is about to, become available to the public; or

(ii) it is, or would be, in the public interest for the material to be published;

(b) any relevant privacy code.

(5) In this section –

'court' includes a tribunal; and

'relief' includes any remedy or order (other than in criminal proceedings).

13 Freedom of thought, conscience and religion

(1) If a court's determination of any question arising under this Act might affect the exercise by a religious organisation (itself or its members collectively) of the Convention right to freedom of thought, conscience and religion, it must have particular regard to the importance of that right.

(2) In this section 'court' includes a tribunal.

14 Derogations

(1) In this Act 'designated derogation' means any derogation by the United Kingdom from an Article of the Convention, or of any protocol to the Convention, which is designated for the purposes of this Act in an order made by the Secretary of State.

(3) If a designated derogation is amended or replaced it ceases to be a designated derogation.

(4) But subsection (3) does not prevent the Secretary of State from exercising his power under subsection (1) to make a fresh designation order in respect of the Article concerned.

(5) The Secretary of State must by order make such amendments to Schedule 3 as he considers appropriate to reflect –

(a) any designation order; or

(b) the effect of subsection (3).

(6) A designation order may be made in anticipation of the making by the United Kingdom of a proposed derogation.

15 Reservations

(1) In this Act 'designated reservation' means –

(a) the United Kingdom's reservation to Article 2 of the First Protocol to the Convention; and

(b) any other reservation by the United Kingdom to an Article of the Convention, or of any protocol to the Convention, which is designated for the purposes of this Act in an order made by the Secretary of State.

(2) The text of the reservation referred to in subsection (1)(a) is set out in Part II of Schedule 3.

(3) If a designated reservation is withdrawn wholly or in part it ceases to be a designated reservation.

(4) But subsection (3) does not prevent the Secretary of State from exercising his power under subsection (1)(b) to make a fresh designation order in respect of the Article concerned.

(5) The Secretary of State must by order make such amendments to this Act as he considers appropriate to reflect –

(a) any designation order; or

(b) the effect of subsection (3).

16 Period for which designated derogations have effect

(1) If it has not already been withdrawn by the United Kingdom, a designated derogation ceases to have effect for the purposes of this Act at the end of the period of five years beginning with the date on which the order designating it was made.

(2) At any time before the period –

(a) fixed by subsection (1), or

(b) extended by an order under this subsection,

comes to an end, the Secretary of State may by order extend it by a further period of five years.

(3) An order under section 14(1) ceases to have effect at the end of the period for consideration, unless a resolution has been passed by each House approving the order.

(4) Subsection (3) does not affect –

(a) anything done in reliance on the order; or

(b) the power to make a fresh order under section 14(1).

(5) In subsection (3) 'period for consideration' means the period of forty days beginning with the day on which the order was made.

(6) In calculating the period for consideration, no account is to be taken of any time during which –

(a) Parliament is dissolved or prorogued; or

(b) both Houses are adjourned for more than four days.

(7) If a designated derogation is withdrawn by the United Kingdom, theSecretary of State must by order make such amendments to this Act as he considers are required to reflect that withdrawal.

17 Periodic review of designated reservations

(1) The appropriate Minister must review the designated reservation referred to in section 15(1)(a) –

(a) before the end of the period of five years beginning with the date on which section 1(2) came into force; and

(b) if that designation is still in force, before the end of the period of five years beginning with the date on which the last report relating to it was laid under subsection (3).

(2) The appropriate Minister must review each of the other designated reservations (if any) –

(a) before the end of the period of five years beginning with the date on which the order designating the reservation first came into force; and

(b) if the designation is still in force, before the end of the period of five years beginning with the date on which the last report relating to it was laid under subsection (3).

(3) The Minister conducting a review under this section must prepare a report on the result of the review and lay a copy of it before each House of Parliament.

18 Appointment to European Court of Human Rights

(1) In this section 'judicial office' means the office of –

(a) Lord Justice of Appeal, Justice of the High Court or Circuit judge, in England and Wales ...

(2) The holder of a judicial office may become a judge of the European Court of Human Rights ('the Court') without being required to relinquish his office.

(3) But he is not required to perform the duties of his judicial office while he is a judge of the Court.

(4) In respect of any period during which he is a judge of the Court –

(a) a Lord Justice of Appeal or Justice of the High Court is not to count as a judge of the relevant court for the purposes of section 2(1) or 4(1) of the Supreme Court Act 1981 (maximum number of judges) nor as a judge of the Supreme Court for the purposes of section 12(1) to (6) of that Act (salaries etc); ...

(d) a Circuit judge is not to count as such for the purposes of section 18 of the Courts Act 1971 (salaries etc); ...

(7) The Lord Chancellor or the Secretary of State may by order make such transitional provision (including, in particular, provision for a temporary increase in the maximum number of judges) as he considers appropriate in relation to any holder of a judicial office who has completed his service as a judge of the Court.

19 Statements of compatibility

(1) A Minister of the Crown in charge of a Bill in either House of Parliament must, before Second Reading of the Bill –

(a) make a statement to the effect that in his view the provisions of the Bill are compatible with the Convention rights ('a statement of compatibility'); or

(b) make a statement to the effect that although he is unable to make a statement of compatibility the government nevertheless wishes the House to proceed with the Bill.

(2) The statement must be in writing and be published in such manner as the Minister making it considers appropriate.

20 Orders, etc under this Act

(1) Any power of a Minister of the Crown to make an order under this Act is exercisable by statutory instrument.

(2) The power of the Secretary of State to make rules (other than rules of court) under section 2(3) or 7(9) is exercisable by statutory instrument.

(3) Any statutory instrument made under section 14, 15 or 16(7) must be laid before Parliament.

(4) No order may be made by the Secretary of State under section 1(4), 7(11) or 16(2) unless a draft of the order has been laid before, and approved by, each House of Parliament.

(5) Any statutory instrument made under section 18(7) or Schedule 4, or to which subsection (2) applies, shall be subject to annulment in pursuance of a resolution of either House of Parliament. ...

21 Interpretation, etc

(1) In this Act –

'amend' includes repeal and apply (with or without modifications);

'the appropriate Minister' means the Minister of the Crown having charge of the appropriate authorised government department (within the meaning of the Crown Proceedings Act 1947);

'the Commission' means the European Commission of Human Rights;

'the Convention' means the Convention for the Protection of Human Rights and Fundamental Freedoms, agreed by the Council of Europe at Rome on 4th November 1950 as it has effect for the time being in relation to the United Kingdom;

'declaration of incompatibility' means a declaration under section 4;

'Minister of the Crown' has the same meaning as in the Ministers of the Crown Act 1975; …

'primary legislation' means any –

(a) public general Act;

(b) local and personal Act;

(c) private Act;

(d) Measure of the Church Assembly;

(e) Measure of the General Synod of the Church of England;

(f) Order in Council –

(i) made in exercise of Her Majesty's Royal Prerogative; … or

(iii) amending an Act of a kind mentioned in paragraph (a), (b) or (c);

and includes an order or other instrument made under primary legislation (otherwise than by the National Assembly for Wales …) to the extent to which it operates to bring one or more provisions of that legislation into force or amends any primary legislation;

'the First Protocol' means the protocol to the Convention agreed at Paris on 20th March 1952;

'the Eleventh Protocol' means the protocol to the Convention (restructuring the control machinery established by the Convention) agreed at Strasbourg on 11th May 1994;

'the Thirteenth Protocol' means the protocol to the Convention (concerning the abolition of the death penalty in all circumstances) agreed at Vilnius on 3rd May 2002;

'remedial order' means an order under section 10;

'subordinate legislation' means any –

(a) Order in Council other than one –

(i) made in exercise of Her Majesty's Royal Prerogative; … or

(iii) amending an Act of a kind mentioned in the definition of primary legislation; …

(f) order, rules, regulations, scheme, warrant, byelaw or other instrument made under primary legislation (except to the extent to which it operates to bring one or more provisions of that legislation into force or amends any primary legislation); ... and

'tribunal' means any tribunal in which legal proceedings may be brought.

(2) The references in paragraphs (b) and (c) of section 2(1) to Articles are to Articles of the Convention as they had effect immediately before the coming into force of the Eleventh Protocol.

(3) The reference in paragraph (d) of section 2(1) to Article 46 includes a reference to Articles 32 and 54 of the Convention as they had effect immediately before the coming into force of the Eleventh Protocol.

(4) The references in section 2(1) to a report or decision of the Commission or a decision of the Committee of Ministers include references to a report or decision made as provided by paragraphs 3, 4 and 6 of Article 5 of the Eleventh Protocol (transitional provisions).

(5) Any liability under the Army Act 1955, the Air Force Act 1955 or the Naval Discipline Act 1957 to suffer death for an offence is replaced by a liability to imprisonment for life or any less punishment authorised by those Acts; and those Acts shall accordingly have effect with the necessary modifications.

22 Short title, commencement, application and extent ...

(4) Paragraph (b) of subsection (1) of section 7 applies to proceedings brought by or at the instigation of a public authority whenever the act in question took place; but otherwise that subsection does not apply to an act taking place before the coming into force of that section.

(5) This Act binds the Crown. ...

(7) Section 21(5), so far as it relates to any provision contained in the Army Act 1955, the Air Force Act 1955 or the Naval Discipline Act 1957, extends to any place to which that provision extends.

SCHEDULE 1

THE ARTICLES

PART I

THE CONVENTION

[See Appendix, below, although it should be noted that The Articles do not include Articles 13 and 15 of the Convention.]

PART II

THE FIRST PROTOCOL

Article 1

Every natural or legal person is entitled to the peaceful enjoyment of his possessions. No one shall be deprived of his possessions except in the public interest and subject to the conditions provided for by law and by the general principles of international law.

The preceding provisions shall not, however, in any way impair the right of a State to enforce such laws as it deems necessary to control the use of property in accordance with the general interest or to secure the payment of taxes or other contributions or penalties.

Article 2

No person shall be denied the right to education. In the exercise of any functions which it assumes in relation to education and to teaching, the State shall respect the right of parents to ensure such education and teaching in conformity with their own religious and philosophical convictions.

Article 3

The High Contracting Parties undertake to hold free elections at reasonable intervals by secret ballot, under conditions which will ensure the free expression of the opinion of the people in the choice of the legislature.

PART 3

ARTICLE 1 OF THE THIRTEENTH PROTOCOL

The death penalty shall be abolished. No one shall be condemned to such penalty or executed.

SCHEDULE 2

REMEDIAL ORDERS

1. – (1) A remedial order may –

(a) contain such incidental, supplemental, consequential or transitional provision as the person making it considers appropriate;

(b) be made so as to have effect from a date earlier than that on which it is made;

(c) make provision for the delegation of specific functions;

(d) make different provision for different cases.

(2) The power conferred by sub-paragraph (1)(a) includes –

(a) power to amend primary legislation (including primary legislation other than that which contains the incompatible provision); and

(b) power to amend or revoke subordinate legislation (including subordinate legislation other than that which contains the incompatible provision).

(3) A remedial order may be made so as to have the same extent as the legislation which it affects.

(4) No person is to be guilty of an offence solely as a result of the retrospective effect of a remedial order.

2. No remedial order may be made unless –

(a) a draft of the order has been approved by a resolution of each House of Parliament made after the end of the period of 60 days beginning with the day on which the draft was laid; or

(b) it is declared in the order that it appears to the person making it that, because of the urgency of the matter, it is necessary to make the order without a draft being so approved.

3. – (1) No draft may be laid under paragraph 2(a) unless –

(a) the person proposing to make the order has laid before Parliament a document which contains a draft of the proposed order and the required information; and

(b) the period of 60 days, beginning with the day on which the document required by this sub-paragraph was laid, has ended.

(2) If representations have been made during that period, the draft laid under paragraph 2(a) must be accompanied by a statement containing –

(a) a summary of the representations; and

(b) if, as a result of the representations, the proposed order has been changed, details of the changes.

4. – (1) If a remedial order ('the original order') is made without being approved in draft, the person making it must lay it before Parliament, accompanied by the required information, after it is made.

(2) If representations have been made during the period of 60 days beginning with the day on which the original order was made, the person making it must (after the end of that period) lay before Parliament a statement containing –

(a) a summary of the representations; and

(b) if, as a result of the representations, he considers it appropriate to make changes to the original order, details of the changes.

(3) If sub-paragraph (2)(b) applies, the person making the statement must –

(a) make a further remedial order replacing the original order; and

(b) lay the replacement order before Parliament.

(4) If, at the end of the period of 120 days beginning with the day on which the original order was made, a resolution has not been passed by each House approving the original or replacement order, the order ceases to have effect (but without that affecting anything previously done under either order or the power to make a fresh remedial order).

5. In this Schedule –

'representations' means representations about a remedial order (or proposed remedial order) made to the person making (or proposing to make) it and includes any relevant Parliamentary report or resolution; and

'required information' means –

(a) an explanation of the incompatibility which the order (or proposed order) seeks to remove, including particulars of the relevant declaration, finding or order; and

(b) a statement of the reasons for proceeding under section 10 and for making an order in those terms.

6. In calculating any period for the purposes of this Schedule, no account is to be taken of any time during which –

(a) Parliament is dissolved or prorogued; or

(b) both Houses are adjourned for more than four days. …

SCHEDULE 3

DEROGATION AND RESERVATION

PART I

DEROGATION

United Kingdom's derogation from Article 5(1)

The United Kingdom Permanent Representative to the Council of Europe presents his compliments to the Secretary General of the Council, and has the honour to convey the following information in order to ensure compliance with the obligations of Her Majesty's Government in the United Kingdom under Article 15(3) of the Convention for the Protection of Human Rights and Fundamental Freedoms signed at Rome on 4 November 1950.

Public emergency in the United Kingdom

The terrorist attacks in New York, Washington, D.C. and Pennsylvania on 11th September 2001 resulted in several thousand deaths, including many British victims and others from 70 different countries. In its resolutions 1368 (2001) and 1373 (2001), the United Nations Security Council recognised the attacks as a threat to international peace and security.

The threat from international terrorism is a continuing one. In its resolution 1373 (2001), the Security Council, acting under Chapter VII of the United Nations Charter, required all States to take measures to prevent the commission of terrorist attacks, including by denying safe haven to those who finance, plan, support or commit terrorist attacks.

There exists a terrorist threat to the United Kingdom from persons suspected of involvement in international terrorism. In particular, there are foreign nationals present in the United Kingdom who are suspected of being concerned in the commission, preparation or instigation of acts of international terrorism, of being members of organisations or groups which are so concerned or of having links with members of such organisations or groups, and who are a threat to the national security of the United Kingdom.

As a result, a public emergency, within the meaning of Article 15(1) of the Convention, exists in the United Kingdom.

The Anti-terrorism, Crime and Security Act 2001

As a result of the public emergency, provision is made in the Anti-terrorism, Crime and Security Act 2001, inter alia, for an extended power to arrest and detain a foreign national which will apply where it is intended to remove or deport the person from the United Kingdom but where removal or deportation is not for the time being possible, with the consequence that the detention would be unlawful under existing domestic law powers. The extended power to arrest and detain will apply where the Secretary of State issues a certificate indicating his belief that the person's presence in the United Kingdom is a risk to national security and that he suspects the person of being an international terrorist. That certificate will be subject to an appeal to the Special Immigration Appeals Commission ('SIAC'), established under the Special Immigration Appeals Commission Act 1997, which will have power to cancel it if it considers that the certificate should not have been issued. There will be an appeal on a point of law from a ruling by SIAC. In addition, the certificate will be reviewed by SIAC at regular intervals. SIAC will also be able to grant bail, where appropriate, subject to conditions. It will be open to a detainee to end his detention at any time by agreeing to leave the United Kingdom.

The extended power of arrest and detention in the Anti-terrorism, Crime and Security Act 2001 is a measure which is strictly required by the exigencies of the situation. It is a temporary provision which comes into force for an initial period of 15 months and then expires unless renewed by Parliament. Thereafter, it is subject to annual renewal by Parliament. If, at any time, in the Government's assessment, the public emergency no longer exists or the extended power is no longer strictly required by the exigencies of the situation, then the Secretary of State will, by Order, repeal the provision.

Domestic law powers of detention (other than under the Anti-terrorism, Crime and Security Act 2001)

The Government has powers under the Immigration Act 1971 ('the 1971 Act') to remove or deport persons on the ground that their presence in the United Kingdom is not conducive to the public good on national security grounds. Persons can also be arrested and detained under Schedules 2 and 3 to the 1971 Act pending their removal or deportation. The courts in the United Kingdom have ruled that this power of detention can only be exercised during the period necessary, in all the circumstances of the particular case, to effect removal and that, if it becomes clear that removal is not going to be possible within a reasonable time, detention will be unlawful (*R* v *Governor of Durham Prison, ex parte Singh* [1984] 1A11 ER 983).

Article 5(1)(f) of the Convention

It is well established that Article 5(1)(f) permits the detention of a person with a view to deportation only in circumstance where 'action is being taken with a view to deportation' (*Chahal* v *United Kingdom* (1996) 23 EHRR 413 at paragraph 112). In that case the European Court of Human Rights indicated that detention will cease to be permissible under Article 5(1)(f) if deportation proceedings are not prosecuted with due diligence and that it was necessary in such cases to determine whether the duration of the deportation proceedings was excessive (paragraph 113).

In some cases, where the intention remains to remove or deport a person on national security grounds, continued detention may not be consistent with Article 5(1)(f) as interpreted by the Court in the Chahal case. This may be the case, for example, if the person has established that removal to their own country might result in treatment contrary to Article 3 of the Convention. In such circumstances, irrespective of the gravity of the threat to national security posed by the person concerned, it is well established that Article 3 prevents removal or deportation to a place where there is a real risk that the person will suffer treatment contrary to that article. If no alternative destination is immediately available then removal or deportation may not, for the time being, be possible even though the ultimate intention remains to remove or deport the person once satisfactory arrangements can be made. In addition, it may not be possible to prosecute the person for a criminal offence given the strict rules on the admissibility of evidence in the criminal justice system of the United Kingdom and the high standard of proof required.

Derogation under Article 15 of the Convention

The Government has considered whether the exercise of the extended power to detain contained in the Anti-terrorism, Crime and Security Act 2001 may be inconsistent with the obligations under Article 5(1) of the Convention. As indicated above, there may be cases where, notwithstanding a continuing intention to remove or deport a person who is being detained, it is not possible to say that 'action is being taken with a view to deportation' within the meaning of Article 5(1)(f) as interpreted by the Court in the Chahal case. To the extent, therefore, that the exercise of the extended power may be inconsistent with the United Kingdom's obligations under Article 5(1), the Government has decided to avail itself of the right of derogation conferred by Article 15(1) of the Convention and will continue to do so until further notice.

Strasbourg, 18 December 2001.

PART II

RESERVATION

At the time of signing the present (First) Protocol, I declare that, in view of certain provisions of the Education Acts in the United Kingdom, the principle affirmed in the second sentence of Article 2 is accepted by the United Kingdom only so far as it is compatible with the provision of efficient instruction and training, and the avoidance of unreasonable public expenditure.

Dated 20 March 1952 Made by the United Kingdom Permanent Representative to the Council of Europe.

As amended by the Transfer of Functions (Miscellaneous) Order 2001, art 8, Schedule 2, para 7(a)–(d); Human Rights Act (Amendment) Order 2001, arts 2(a)–(c), 3(a)–(d), 4; Human Rights Act 1998 (Amendment No 2) Order 2001, art 2, Schedule; Secretary of State for Constitutional Affairs Order 2003, art 9, Schedule 2, para 10(1), (2); Human Rights Act 1998 (Amendment) Order 2004, art 2(1)–(3).

IMMIGRATION AND ASYLUM ACT 1999

(1999 c 33)

PART I

IMMIGRATION: GENERAL

10 Removal of certain persons unlawfully in the United Kingdom

(1) A person who is not a British citizen may be removed from the United Kingdom, in accordance with directions given by an immigration officer, if –

(a) having only a limited leave to enter or remain, he does not observe a condition attached to the leave or remains beyond the time limited by the leave;

(b) he uses deception in seeking (whether successfully or not) leave to remain; or

(ba) his indefinite leave to enter or remain has been revoked under section 76(3) of the Nationality, Immigration and Asylum Act 2002 (person ceasing to be refugee);

(c) directions have been given for the removal, under this section, of a person to whose family he belongs.

(2) Directions may not be given under subsection (1)(a) if the person concerned has made an application for leave to remain in accordance with regulations made under section 9.

(3) Directions for the removal of a person may not be given under subsection (1)(c) unless the Secretary of State has given the person written notice of the intention to remove him.

(4) A notice under subsection (3) may not be given if –

(a) the person whose removal under subsection (1)(a) or (b) is the cause of the proposed directions under subsection (1)(c) has left the United Kingdom, and

(b) more than eight weeks have elapsed since that person's departure.

(5) If a notice under subsection (3) is sent by first class post to a person's last known address, that subsection shall be taken to be satisfied at the end of the second day after the day of posting.

(5A) Directions for the removal of a person under subsection (1)(c) cease to have effect if he ceases to belong to the family of the person whose removal under subsection (1)(a) or (b) is the cause of the directions under subsection (1)(c).

(8) Directions for the removal of a person given under this section invalidate any leave to enter or remain in the United Kingdom given to him before the directions are given or while they are in force.

(9) The costs of complying with a direction given under this section (so far as reasonably incurred) must be met by the Secretary of State.

(10) A person shall not be liable to removal from the United Kingdom under this section at a time when section 7(1)(b) of the Immigration Act 1971 (Commonwealth and Irish citizens ordinarily resident in United Kingdom) would prevent a decision to deport him.

As amended by the Nationality, Immigration and Asylum Act 2002, ss73(2)–(4), 74, 75(1), (4), 76(7), 161, Schedule 9.

HOUSE OF LORDS ACT 1999

(1999 c 34)

1 Exclusion of hereditary peers

No-one shall be a member of the House of Lords by virtue of a hereditary peerage.

2 Exception from section 1

(1) Section 1 shall not apply in relation to anyone excepted from it by or in accordance with Standing Orders of the House.

(2) At any one time 90 people shall be excepted from section 1; but anyone excepted as holder of the office of Earl Marshal, or as performing the office of Lord Great Chamberlain, shall not count towards that limit.

(3) Once excepted from section 1, a person shall continue to be so throughout his life (until an Act of Parliament provides to the contrary).

(4) Standing Orders shall make provision for filling vacancies among the people excepted from section 1; and in any case where –

(a) the vacancy arises on a death occurring after the end of the first Session of the next Parliament after that in which this Act is passed, and

(b) the deceased person was excepted in consequence of an election,

that provision shall require the holding of a by-election.

(5) A person may be excepted from section 1 by or in accordance with Standing Orders made in anticipation of the enactment or commencement of this section.

(6) Any question whether a person is excepted from section 1 shall be decided by the Clerk of the Parliaments, whose certificate shall be conclusive.

3 Removal of disqualifications in relation to the House of Commons

(1) The holder of a hereditary peerage shall not be disqualified by virtue of that peerage for –

(a) voting at elections to the House of Commons, or

(b) being, or being elected as, a member of that House.

(2) Subsection (1) shall not apply in relation to anyone excepted from section 1 by virtue of section 2.

5 Commencement and transitional provision

(1) Sections 1 to 4 (including Schedules 1 and 2) shall come into force at the end of the Session of Parliament in which this Act is passed.

(2) Accordingly, any writ of summons issued for the present Parliament in right of a hereditary peerage shall not have effect after that Session unless it has been issued to a person who, at the end of the Session, is excepted from section 1 by virtue of section 2.

(3) The Secretary of State may by order make such transitional provision about the entitlement of holders of hereditary peerages to vote at elections to the House of Commons or the European Parliament as he considers appropriate. …

6 Interpretation and short title

(1) In this act 'hereditary peerage' indicates the principality of Wales and earldom of Chester. …

TERRORISM ACT 2000

(2000 c 11)

PART I

INTRODUCTORY

1 Terrorism: interpretation

(1) In this Act 'terrorism' means the use or threat of action where –

(a) the action falls within subsection (2),

(b) the use or threat is designed to influence the government or to intimidate the public or a section of the public, and

(c) the use or threat is made for the purpose of advancing a political, religious or ideological cause.

(2) Action falls within this subsection if it –

(a) involves serious violence against a person,

(b) involves serious damage to property,

(c) endangers a person's life, other than that of the person committing the action,

(d) creates a serious risk to the health or safety of the public or a section of the public, or

(e) is designed seriously to interfere with or seriously to disrupt an electronic system.

(3) The use or threat of action falling within subsection (2) which involves the use of firearms or explosives is terrorism whether or not subsection (1)(b) is satisfied.

(4) In this section –

(a) 'action' includes action outside the United Kingdom,

(b) a reference to any person or to property is a reference to any person, or to property, wherever situated,

(c) a reference to the public includes a reference to the public of a country other than the United Kingdom, and

(d) 'the government' means the government of the United Kingdom, of a Part of the United Kingdom or of a country other than the United Kingdom.

(5) In this Act a reference to action taken for the purposes of terrorism includes a reference to action taken for the benefit of a proscribed organisation.

PART II

PROSCRIBED ORGANISATIONS

Procedure

3 Proscription

(1) For the purposes of this Act an organisation is proscribed if –

(a) it is listed in Schedule 2, or

(b) it operates under the same name as an organisation listed in that Schedule.

(2) Subsection (1)(b) shall not apply in relation to an organisation listed in Schedule 2 if its entry is the subject of a note in that Schedule.

(3) The Secretary of State may by order –

(a) add an organisation to Schedule 2;

(b) remove an organisation from that Schedule;

(c) amend that Schedule in some other way.

(4) The Secretary of State may exercise his power under subsection (3)(a) in respect of an organisation only if he believes that it is concerned in terrorism.

(5) For the purposes of subsection (4) an organisation is concerned in terrorism if it –

(a) commits or participates in acts of terrorism,

(b) prepares for terrorism,

(c) promotes or encourages terrorism, or

(d) is otherwise concerned in terrorism.

4 Deproscription: application

(1) An application may be made to the Secretary of State for the exercise of his power under section 3(3)(b) to remove an organisation from Schedule 2. ...

5 Deproscription: appeal

(1) There shall be a commission, to be known as the Proscribed Organisations Appeal Commission.

(2) Where an application under section 4 has been refused, the applicant may appeal to the Commission.

(3) The Commission shall allow an appeal against a refusal to deproscribe an organisation if it considers that the decision to refuse was flawed when considered in the light of the principles applicable on an application for judicial review.

(4) Where the Commission allows an appeal under this section by or in respect of an organisation, it may make an order under this subsection.

(5) Where an order is made under subsection (4) the Secretary of State shall as soon as is reasonably practicable –

(a) lay before Parliament, in accordance with section 123(4), the draft of an order under section 3(3)(b) removing the organisation from the list in Schedule 2, or

(b) make an order removing the organisation from the list in Schedule 2 in pursuance of section 123(5).

(6) Schedule 3 (constitution of the Commission and procedure) shall have effect.

6 Further appeal

(1) A party to an appeal under section 5 which the Proscribed Organisations Appeal Commission has determined may bring a further appeal on a question of law to –

(a) the Court of Appeal, if the first appeal was heard in England and Wales, ...

(2) An appeal under subsection (1) may be brought only with the permission –

(a) of the Commission, or

(b) where the Commission refuses permission, of the court to which the appeal would be brought.

(3) An order under section 5(4) shall not require the Secretary of State to take any action until the final determination or disposal of an appeal under this section (including any appeal to the House of Lords).

9 Human Rights Act 1998

(1) This section applies where rules (within the meaning of section 7 of the Human Rights Act 1998 (jurisdiction)) provide for proceedings under section 7(1) of that Act to be brought before the Proscribed Organisations Appeal Commission.

(2) The following provisions of this Act shall apply in relation to proceedings under section 7(1) of that Act as they apply to appeals under section 5 of this Act –

(a) section 5(4) and (5),

(b) section 6,

(c) section 7, and

(d) paragraphs 4 to 7 of Schedule 3.

(3) The Commission shall decide proceedings in accordance with the principles applicable on an application for judicial review.

(4) In the application of the provisions mentioned in subsection (2) –

(a) a reference to the Commission allowing an appeal shall be taken as a reference to the Commission determining that an action of the Secretary of State is incompatible with a Convention right, and

(b) a reference to the refusal to deproscribe against which an appeal was brought shall be taken as a reference to the action of the Secretary of State which is found to be incompatible with a Convention right.

10 Immunity

(1) The following shall not be admissible as evidence in proceedings for an offence under any of sections 11 to 13, 15 to 19 and 56 –

(a) evidence of anything done in relation to an application to the Secretary of State under section 4,

(b) evidence of anything done in relation to proceedings before the Proscribed Organisations Appeal Commission under section 5 above or section 7(1) of the Human Rights Act 1998,

(c) evidence of anything done in relation to proceedings under section 6 (including that section as applied by section 9(2)), and

(d) any document submitted for the purposes of proceedings mentioned in any of paragraphs (a) to (c).

(2) But subsection (1) does not prevent evidence from being adduced on behalf of the accused.

11 Membership

(1) A person commits an offence if he belongs or professes to belong to a proscribed organisation.

(2) It is a defence for a person charged with an offence under subsection (1) to prove –

(a) that the organisation was not proscribed on the last (or only) occasion on which he became a member or began to profess to be a member, and

(b) that he has not taken part in the activities of the organisation at any time while it was proscribed.

12 Support

(1) A person commits an offence if –

(a) he invites support for a proscribed organisation, and

(b) the support is not, or is not restricted to, the provision of money or other property (within the meaning of section 15).

(2) A person commits an offence if he arranges, manages or assists in arranging or managing a meeting which he knows is –

(a) to support a proscribed organisation,

(b) to further the activities of a proscribed organisation, or

(c) to be addressed by a person who belongs or professes to belong to a proscribed organisation.

(3) A person commits an offence if he addresses a meeting and the purpose of his address is to encourage support for a proscribed organisation or to further its activities.

(4) Where a person is charged with an offence under subsection (2)(c) in respect of a private meeting it is a defence for him to prove that he had no reasonable cause to believe that the address mentioned in subsection (2)(c) would support a proscribed organisation or further its activities.

(5) In subsections (2) to (4) –

(a) 'meeting' means a meeting of three or more persons, whether or not the public are admitted, and

(b) a meeting is private if the public are not admitted. ...

13 Uniform

(1) A person in a public place commits an offence if he –

(a) wears an item of clothing, or

(b) wears, carries or displays an article,

in such a way or in such circumstances as to arouse reasonable suspicion that he is a member or supporter of a proscribed organisation. ...

PART III

TERRORIST PROPERTY

14 Terrorist property

(1) In this Act 'terrorist property' means –

(a) money or other property which is likely to be used for the purposes of terrorism (including any resources of a proscribed organisation),

(b) proceeds of the commission of acts of terrorism, and

(c) proceeds of acts carried out for the purposes of terrorism.

(2) In subsection (1) –

(a) a reference to proceeds of an act includes a reference to any property which wholly or partly, and directly or indirectly, represents the proceeds of the act (including payments or other rewards in connection with its commission), and

(b) the reference to an organisation's resources includes a reference to any money or other property which is applied or made available, or is to be applied or made available, for use by the organisation.

15 Fund-raising

(1) A person commits an offence if he –

(a) invites another to provide money or other property, and

(b) intends that it should be used, or has reasonable cause to suspect that it may be used, for the purposes of terrorism.

(2) A person commits an offence if he –

(a) receives money or other property, and

(b) intends that it should be used, or has reasonable cause to suspect that it may be used, for the purposes of terrorism.

(3) A person commits an offence if he –

(a) provides money or other property, and

(b) knows or has reasonable cause to suspect that it will or may be used for the purposes of terrorism.

(4) In this section a reference to the provision of money or other property is a reference to its being given, lent or otherwise made available, whether or not for consideration.

16 Use and possession

(1) A person commits an offence if he uses money or other property for the purposes of terrorism.

(2) A person commits an offence if he –

(a) possesses money or other property, and

(b) intends that it should be used, or has reasonable cause to suspect that it may be used, for the purposes of terrorism.

17 Funding arrangements

A person commits an offence if –

(a) he enters into or becomes concerned in an arrangement as a result of which money or other property is made available or is to be made available to another, and

(b) he knows or has reasonable cause to suspect that it will or may be used for the purposes of terrorism.

18 Money laundering

(1) A person commits an offence if he enters into or becomes concerned in an arrangement which facilitates the retention or control by or on behalf of another person of terrorist property –

(a) by concealment,

(b) by removal from the jurisdiction,

(c) by transfer to nominees, or

(d) in any other way.

(2) It is a defence for a person charged with an offence under subsection (1) to prove that he did not know and had no reasonable cause to suspect that the arrangement related to terrorist property.

19 Disclosure of information: duty

(1) This section applies where a person –

(a) believes or suspects that another person has committed an offence under any of sections 15 to 18, and

(b) bases his belief or suspicion on information which comes to his attention in the course of a trade, profession, business or employment.

(1A) But this section does not apply if the information came to the person in the course of a business in the regulated sector.

(2) The person commits an offence if he does not disclose to a constable as soon as is reasonably practicable –

(a) his belief or suspicion, and

(b) the information on which it is based.

(3) It is a defence for a person charged with an offence under subsection (2) to prove that he had a reasonable excuse for not making the disclosure.

(4) Where –

(a) a person is in employment,

(b) his employer has established a procedure for the making of disclosures of the matters specified in subsection (2), and

(c) he is charged with an offence under that subsection,

it is a defence for him to prove that he disclosed the matters specified in that subsection in accordance with the procedure.

(5) Subsection (2) does not require disclosure by a professional legal adviser of –

(a) information which he obtains in privileged circumstances, or

(b) a belief or suspicion based on information which he obtains in privileged circumstances.

(6) For the purpose of subsection (5) information is obtained by an adviser in privileged circumstances if it comes to him, otherwise than with a view to furthering a criminal purpose –

(a) from a client or a client's representative, in connection with the provision of legal advice by the adviser to the client,

(b) from a person seeking legal advice from the adviser, or from the person's representative, or

(c) from any person, for the purpose of actual or contemplated legal proceedings.

(7) For the purposes of subsection (1)(a) a person shall be treated as having committed an offence under one of sections 15 to 18 if –

(a) he has taken an action or been in possession of a thing, and

(b) he would have committed an offence under one of those sections if he had been in the United Kingdom at the time when he took the action or was in possession of the thing. ...

20 Disclosure of information: permission

(1) A person may disclose to a constable –

(a) a suspicion or belief that any money or other property is terrorist property or is derived from terrorist property;

(b) any matter on which the suspicion or belief is based.

(2) A person may make a disclosure to a constable in the circumstances mentioned in section 19(1) and (2).

(3) Subsections (1) and (2) shall have effect notwithstanding any restriction on the disclosure of information imposed by statute or otherwise.

(4) Where –

(a) a person is in employment, and

(b) his employer has established a procedure for the making of disclosures of the kinds mentioned in subsection (1) and section 19(2),

subsections (1) and (2) shall have effect in relation to that person as if any reference to disclosure to a constable included a reference to disclosure in accordance with the procedure. ...

21 Cooperation with police

(1) A person does not commit an offence under any of sections 15 to 18 if he is acting with the express consent of a constable.

(2) Subject to subsections (3) and (4), a person does not commit an offence under any of sections 15 to 18 by involvement in a transaction or arrangement relating to money or other property if he discloses to a constable –

(a) his suspicion or belief that the money or other property is terrorist property, and

(b) the information on which his suspicion or belief is based.

(3) Subsection (2) applies only where a person makes a disclosure –

(a) after he becomes concerned in the transaction concerned,

(b) on his own initiative, and

(c) as soon as is reasonably practicable.

(4) Subsection (2) does not apply to a person if –

(a) a constable forbids him to continue his involvement in the transaction or arrangement to which the disclosure relates, and

(b) he continues his involvement.

(5) It is a defence for a person charged with an offence under any of sections 15(2) and (3) and 16 to 18 to prove that –

(a) he intended to make a disclosure of the kind mentioned in subsections (2) and (3), and

(b) there is reasonable excuse for his failure to do so.

(6) Where –

(a) a person is in employment, and

(b) his employer has established a procedure for the making of disclosures of the same kind as may be made to a constable under subsection (2),

this section shall have effect in relation to that person as if any reference to disclosure to a constable included a reference to disclosure in accordance with the procedure.

(7) A reference in this section to a transaction or arrangement relating to money or other property includes a reference to use or possession.

23 Forfeiture

(1) The court by or before which a person is convicted of an offence under any of sections 15 to 18 may make a forfeiture order in accordance with the provisions of this section. ...

PART IV

TERRORIST INVESTIGATIONS

32 Terrorist investigation

In this Act 'terrorist investigation' means an investigation of –

(a) the commission, preparation or instigation of acts of terrorism,

(b) an act which appears to have been done for the purposes of terrorism,

(c) the resources of a proscribed organisation,

(d) the possibility of making an order under section 3(3), or

(e) the commission, preparation or instigation of an offence under this Act.

33 Cordoned areas

(1) An area is a cordoned area for the purposes of this Act if it is designated under this section.

(2) A designation may be made only if the person making it considers it expedient for the purposes of a terrorist investigation.

(3) If a designation is made orally, the person making it shall confirm it in writing as soon as is reasonably practicable.

(4) The person making a designation shall arrange for the demarcation of the cordoned area, so far as is reasonably practicable –

(a) by means of tape marked with the word 'police', or

(b) in such other manner as a constable considers appropriate.

34 Power to designate

(1) Subject to subsection … (2), a designation under section 33 may only be made –

(a) where the area is outside Northern Ireland and is wholly or partly within a police area, by an officer for the police area who is of at least the rank of superintendent …

(2) A constable who is not of the rank required by subsection (1) may make a designation if he considers it necessary by reason of urgency. …

35 Duration

(1) A designation under section 33 has effect, subject to subsections (2) to (5), during the period –

(a) beginning at the time when it is made, and

(b) ending with a date or at a time specified in the designation.

(2) The date or time specified under subsection (1)(b) must not occur after the end of the period of 14 days beginning with the day on which the designation is made.

(3) The period during which a designation has effect may be extended in writing from time to time by …

(a) the person who made it, or

(b) a person who could have made it (otherwise than by virtue of section 34(2)).

(4) An extension shall specify the additional period during which the designation is to have effect.

(5) A designation shall not have effect after the end of the period of 28 days beginning with the day on which it is made.

36 Police powers

(1) A constable in uniform may –

(a) order a person in a cordoned area to leave it immediately;

(b) order a person immediately to leave premises which are wholly or partly in or adjacent to a cordoned area;

(c) order the driver or person in charge of a vehicle in a cordoned area to move it from the area immediately;

(d) arrange for the removal of a vehicle from a cordoned area;

(e) arrange for the movement of a vehicle within a cordoned area;

(f) prohibit or restrict access to a cordoned area by pedestrians or vehicles.

(2) A person commits an offence if he fails to comply with an order, prohibition or restriction imposed by virtue of subsection (1).

(3) It is a defence for a person charged with an offence under subsection (2) to prove that he had a reasonable excuse for his failure. ...

38B Information about acts of terrorism

(1) This section applies where a person has information which he knows or believes might be of material assistance –

(a) in preventing the commission by another person of an act of terrorism, or

(b) in securing the apprehension, prosecution or conviction of another person, in the United Kingdom, for an offence involving the commission, preparation or instigation of an act of terrorism.

(2) The person commits an offence if he does not disclose the information as soon as reasonably practicable in accordance with subsection (3).

(3) Disclosure is in accordance with this subsection if it is made –

(a) in England and Wales, to a constable ...

(4) It is a defence for a person charged with an offence under subsection (2) to prove that he had a reasonable excuse for not making the disclosure.

(6) Proceedings for an offence under this section may be taken, and the offence may for the purposes of those proceedings be treated as having been committed, in any place where the person to be charged is or has at any time been since he first knew or believed that the information might be of material assistance as mentioned in subsection (1).

39 Disclosure of information, etc

(1) Subsection (2) applies where a person knows or has reasonable cause to suspect that a constable is conducting or proposes to conduct a terrorist investigation.

(2) The person commits an offence if he –

(a) discloses to another anything which is likely to prejudice the investigation, or

(b) interferes with material which is likely to be relevant to the investigation.

(3) Subsection (4) applies where a person knows or has reasonable cause to suspect that a disclosure has been or will be made under any of sections 19 to 21 or 38B.

(4) The person commits an offence if he –

(a) discloses to another anything which is likely to prejudice an investigation resulting from the disclosure under that section, or

(b) interferes with material which is likely to be relevant to an investigation resulting from the disclosure under that section.

(5) It is a defence for a person charged with an offence under subsection (2) or (4) to prove –

(a) that he did not know and had no reasonable cause to suspect that the disclosure or interference was likely to affect a terrorist investigation, or
(b) that he had a reasonable excuse for the disclosure or interference.

(6) Subsections (2) and (4) do not apply to a disclosure which is made by a professional legal adviser –

(a) to his client or to his client's representative in connection with the provision of legal advice by the adviser to the client and not with a view to furthering a criminal purpose, or
(b) to any person for the purpose of actual or contemplated legal proceedings and not with a view to furthering a criminal purpose. ...

(8) For the purposes of this section –

(a) a reference to conducting a terrorist investigation includes a reference to taking part in the conduct of, or assisting, a terrorist investigation, and

(b) a person interferes with material if he falsifies it, conceals it, destroys it or disposes of it, or if he causes or permits another to do any of those things.

PART V

COUNTER-TERRORIST POWERS

40 Terrorist: interpretation

(1) In this Part 'terrorist' means a person who –

(a) has committed an offence under any of sections 11, 12, 15 to 18, 54 and 56 to 63, or

(b) is or has been concerned in the commission, preparation or instigation of acts of terrorism.

(2) The reference in subsection (1)(b) to a person who has been concerned in the commission, preparation or instigation of acts of terrorism includes a reference to a person who has been, whether before or after the passing of this Act, concerned in the commission, preparation or instigation of acts of terrorism within the meaning given by section 1.

41 Arrest without warrant

(1) A constable may arrest without a warrant a person whom he reasonably suspects to be a terrorist.

(2) Where a person is arrested under this section the provisions of Schedule 8 (detention: treatment, review and extension) shall apply.

(3) Subject to subsections (4) to (7), a person detained under this section shall

(unless detained under any other power) be released not later than the end of the period of 48 hours beginning –

(a) with the time of his arrest under this section, or

(b) if he was being detained under Schedule 7 when he was arrested under this section, with the time when his examination under that Schedule began.

(4) If on a review of a person's detention under Part II of Schedule 8 the review officer does not authorise continued detention, the person shall (unless detained in accordance with subsection (5) or (6) or under any other power) be released.

(5) Where a police officer intends to make an application for a warrant under paragraph 29 of Schedule 8 extending a person's detention, the person may be detained pending the making of the application.

(6) Where an application has been made under paragraph 29 or 36 of Schedule 8 in respect of a person's detention, he may be detained pending the conclusion of proceedings on the application.

(7) Where an application under paragraph 29 or 36 of Schedule 8 is granted in respect of a person's detention, he may be detained, subject to paragraph 37 of that Schedule, during the period specified in the warrant.

(8) The refusal of an application in respect of a person's detention under paragraph 29 or 36 of Schedule 8 shall not prevent his continued detention in accordance with this section.

(9) A person who has the powers of a constable in one Part of the United Kingdom may exercise the power under subsection (1) in any Part of the United Kingdom.

42 Search of premises

(1) A justice of the peace may on the application of a constable issue a warrant in relation to specified premises if he is satisfied that there are reasonable grounds for suspecting that a person whom the constable reasonably suspects to be a person falling within section 40(1)(b) is to be found there.

(2) A warrant under this section shall authorise any constable to enter and search the specified premises for the purpose of arresting the person referred to in subsection (1) under section 41. ...

43 Search of persons

(1) A constable may stop and search a person whom he reasonably suspects to be a terrorist to discover whether he has in his possession anything which may constitute evidence that he is a terrorist.

(2) A constable may search a person arrested under section 41 to discover whether he has in his possession anything which may constitute evidence that he is a terrorist.

(3) A search of a person under this section must be carried out by someone of the same sex.

(4) A constable may seize and retain anything which he discovers in the course of a search of a person under subsection (1) or (2) and which he reasonably suspects may constitute evidence that the person is a terrorist.

(5) A person who has the powers of a constable in one Part of the United Kingdom may exercise a power under this section in any Part of the United Kingdom.

44 Authorisations

(1) An authorisation under this subsection authorises any constable in uniform to stop a vehicle in an area or at a place specified in the authorisation and to search –

(a) the vehicle;

(b) the driver of the vehicle;

(c) a passenger in the vehicle;

(d) anything in or on the vehicle or carried by the driver or a passenger.

(2) An authorisation under this subsection authorises any constable in uniform to stop a pedestrian in an area or at a place specified in the authorisation and to search –

(a) the pedestrian;

(b) anything carried by him.

(3) An authorisation under subsection (1) or (2) may be given only if the person giving it considers it expedient for the prevention of acts of terrorism.

(4) An authorisation may be given –

(a) where the specified area or place is the whole or part of a police area outside Northern Ireland other than one mentioned in paragraph (b) or (c), by a police officer for the area who is of at least the rank of assistant chief constable;

(b) where the specified area or place is the whole or part of the metropolitan police district, by a police officer for the district who is of at least the rank of commander of the metropolitan police;

(c) where the specified area or place is the whole or part of the City of London, by a police officer for the City who is of at least the rank of commander in the City of London police force; ...

(5) If an authorisation is given orally, the person giving it shall confirm it in writing as soon as is reasonably practicable.

45 Exercise of power

(1) The power conferred by an authorisation under section 44(1) or (2) –

(a) may be exercised only for the purpose of searching for articles of a kind which could be used in connection with terrorism, and

(b) may be exercised whether or not the constable has grounds for suspecting the presence of articles of that kind.

(2) A constable may seize and retain an article which he discovers in the course of a search by virtue of section 44(1) or (2) and which he reasonably suspects is intended to be used in connection with terrorism.

(3) A constable exercising the power conferred by an authorisation may not require a person to remove any clothing in public except for headgear, footwear, an outer coat, a jacket or gloves.

(4) Where a constable proposes to search a person or vehicle by virtue of section 44(1) or (2) he may detain the person or vehicle for such time as is reasonably required to permit the search to be carried out at or near the place where the person or vehicle is stopped.

(5) Where –

(a) a vehicle or pedestrian is stopped by virtue of section 44(1) or (2), and

(b) the driver of the vehicle or the pedestrian applies for a written statement that the vehicle was stopped, or that he was stopped, by virtue of section 44(1) or (2),

the written statement shall be provided.

(6) An application under subsection (5) must be made within the period of 12 months beginning with the date on which the vehicle or pedestrian was stopped.

46 Duration of authorisation

(1) An authorisation under section 44 has effect, subject to subsections (2) to (7), during the period –

(a) beginning at the time when the authorisation is given, and

(b) ending with a date or at a time specified in the authorisation.

(2) The date or time specified under subsection (1)(b) must not occur after the end of the period of 28 days beginning with the day on which the authorisation is given.

(3) The person who gives an authorisation shall inform the Secretary of State as soon as is reasonably practicable.

(4) If an authorisation is not confirmed by the Secretary of State before the end of the period of 48 hours beginning with the time when it is given –

(a) it shall cease to have effect at the end of that period, but

(b) its ceasing to have effect shall not affect the lawfulness of anything done in reliance on it before the end of that period.

(5) Where the Secretary of State confirms an authorisation he may substitute an earlier date or time for the date or time specified under subsection (1)(b).

(6) The Secretary of State may cancel an authorisation with effect from a specified time.

(7) An authorisation may be renewed in writing by the person who gave it or by a

person who could have given it; and subsections (1) to (6) shall apply as if a new authorisation were given on each occasion on which the authorisation is renewed.

47 Offences

(1) A person commits an offence if he –

(a) fails to stop a vehicle when required to do so by a constable in the exercise of the power conferred by an authorisation under section 44(1);
(b) fails to stop when required to do so by a constable in the exercise of the power conferred by an authorisation under section 44(2);
(c) wilfully obstructs a constable in the exercise of the power conferred by an authorisation under section 44(1) or (2). ...

48 Authorisations

(1) An authorisation under this section authorises any constable in uniform to prohibit or restrict the parking of vehicles on a road specified in the authorisation.

(2) An authorisation may be given only if the person giving it considers it expedient for the prevention of acts of terrorism.

(3) An authorisation may be given –

(a) where the road specified is outside Northern Ireland and is wholly or partly within a police area other than one mentioned in paragraphs (b) or (c), by a police officer for the area who is of at least the rank of assistant chief constable;
(b) where the road specified is wholly or partly in the metropolitan police district, by a police officer for the district who is of at least the rank of commander of the metropolitan police;
(c) where the road specified is wholly or partly in the City of London, by a police officer for the City who is of at least the rank of commander in the City of London police force; ...

(4) If an authorisation is given orally, the person giving it shall confirm it in writing as soon as is reasonably practicable.

49 Exercise of power

(1) The power conferred by an authorisation under section 48 shall be exercised by placing a traffic sign on the road concerned.

(2) A constable exercising the power conferred by an authorisation under section 48 may suspend a parking place. ...

50 Duration of authorisation

(1) An authorisation under section 48 has effect, subject to subsections (2) and (3), during the period specified in the authorisation.

(2) The period specified shall not exceed 28 days.

(3) An authorisation may be renewed in writing by the person who gave it or by a person who could have given it; and subsections (1) and (2) shall apply as if a new authorisation were given on each occasion on which the authorisation is renewed.

51 Offences

(1) A person commits an offence if he parks a vehicle in contravention of a prohibition or restriction imposed by virtue of section 48.

(2) A person commits an offence if –

(a) he is the driver or other person in charge of a vehicle which has been permitted to remain at rest in contravention of any prohibition or restriction imposed by virtue of section 48, and

(b) he fails to move the vehicle when ordered to do so by a constable in uniform.

(3) It is a defence for a person charged with an offence under this section to prove that he had a reasonable excuse for the act or omission in question.

(4) Possession of a current disabled person's badge shall not itself constitute a reasonable excuse for the purposes of subsection (3). ...

52 Interpretation

In sections 48 to 51 –

'disabled person's badge' means a badge issued, or having effect as if issued, under any regulations for the time being in force under section 21 of the Chronically Sick and Disabled Persons Act 1970 (in relation to England and Wales ...) ...;

'driver' means, in relation to a vehicle which has been left on any road, the person who was driving it when it was left there;

'parking' means leaving a vehicle or permitting it to remain at rest;

'traffic sign' has the meaning given in section 142(1) of the Road Traffic Regulation Act 1984 (in relation to England and Wales ...) ...

'vehicle' has the same meaning as in section 99(5) of the Road Traffic Regulation Act 1984 (in relation to England and Wales ...) ...

PART VI

MISCELLANEOUS ...

59 England and Wales

(1) A person commits an offence if –

(a) he incites another person to commit an act of terrorism wholly or partly outside the United Kingdom, and

(b) the act would, if committed in England and Wales, constitute one of the offences listed in subsection (2).

(2) Those offences are –

(a) murder,

(b) an offence under section 18 of the Offences against the Person Act 1861 (wounding with intent),

(c) an offence under section 23 or 24 of that Act (poison),

(d) an offence under section 28 or 29 of that Act (explosions), and

(e) an offence under section 1(2) of the Criminal Damage Act 1971 (endangering life by damaging property). ...

(4) For the purposes of subsection (1) it is immaterial whether or not the person incited is in the United Kingdom at the time of the incitement.

(5) Nothing in this section imposes criminal liability on any person acting on behalf of, or holding office under, the Crown.

62 Terrorist bombing: jurisdiction

(1) If –

(a) a person does anything outside the United Kingdom as an act of terrorism or for the purposes of terrorism, and

(b) his action would have constituted the commission of one of the offences listed in subsection (2) if it had been done in the United Kingdom,

he shall be guilty of the offence.

(2) The offences referred to in subsection (1)(b) are –

(a) an offence under section 2, 3 or 5 of the Explosive Substances Act 1883 (causing explosions, etc),

(b) an offence under section 1 of the Biological Weapons Act 1974 (biological weapons), and

(c) an offence under section 2 of the Chemical Weapons Act 1996 (chemical weapons).

63 Terrorist finance: jurisdiction

(1) If –

(a) a person does anything outside the United Kingdom, and

(b) his action would have constituted the commission of an offence under any of sections 15 to 18 if it had been done in the United Kingdom,

he shall be guilty of the offence.

(2) For the purposes of subsection (1)(b), section 18(1)(b) shall be read as if for 'the jurisdiction' there were substituted 'a jurisdiction'.

PART VIII

GENERAL

114 Police powers

(1) A power conferred by virtue of this Act on a constable –

(a) is additional to powers which he has at common law or by virtue of any other enactment, and

(b) shall not be taken to affect those powers.

(2) A constable may if necessary use reasonable force for the purpose of exercising a power conferred on him by virtue of this Act (apart from paragraphs 2 and 3 of Schedule 7).

(3) Where anything is seized by a constable under a power conferred by virtue of this Act, it may (unless the contrary intention appears) be retained for so long as is necessary in all the circumstances.

116 Powers to stop and search

(1) A power to search premises conferred by virtue of this Act shall be taken to include power to search a container.

(2) A power conferred by virtue of this Act to stop a person includes power to stop a vehicle (other than an aircraft which is airborne).

(3) A person commits an offence if he fails to stop a vehicle when required to do so by virtue of this section. …

117 Consent to prosecution

(1) This section applies to an offence under any provision of this Act other than an offence under –

(a) section 36,

(b) section 51,

(c) paragraph 18 of Schedule 7,

(d) paragraph 12 of Schedule 12, or

(e) Schedule 13.

(2) Proceedings for an offence to which this section applies –

(a) shall not be instituted in England and Wales without the consent of the Director of Public Prosecutions …

(3) Where it appears to the Director of Public Prosecutions … that an offence to which this section applies is committed for a purpose connected with the affairs of a country other than the United Kingdom –

(a) subsection (2) shall not apply, and

(b) proceedings for the offence shall not be instituted without the consent of the Attorney General ...

118 Defences

(1) Subsection (2) applies where in accordance with a provision mentioned in subsection (5) it is a defence for a person charged with an offence to prove a particular matter.

(2) If the person adduces evidence which is sufficient to raise an issue with respect to the matter the court or jury shall assume that the defence is satisfied unless the prosecution proves beyond reasonable doubt that it is not.

(3) Subsection (4) applies where in accordance with a provision mentioned in subsection (5) a court –

(a) may make an assumption in relation to a person charged with an offence unless a particular matter is proved, or

(b) may accept a fact as sufficient evidence unless a particular matter is proved.

(4) If evidence is adduced which is sufficient to raise an issue with respect to the matter mentioned in subsection (3)(a) or (b) the court shall treat it as proved unless the prosecution disproves it beyond reasonable doubt.

(5) The provisions in respect of which subsections (2) and (4) apply are –

(a) sections 12(4), 39(5)(a), 54, 57, 58, 77 and 103 of this Act ...

119 Crown servants, regulators, etc

(1) The Secretary of State may make regulations providing for any of sections 15 to 23 and 39 to apply to persons in the public service of the Crown.

(2) The Secretary of State may make regulations providing for section 19 not to apply to persons who are in his opinion performing or connected with the performance of regulatory, supervisory, investigative or registration functions of a public nature. ...

120 Evidence

(1) A document which purports to be –

(a) a notice or direction given or order made by the Secretary of State for the purposes of a provision of this Act, and

(b) signed by him or on his behalf,

shall be received in evidence and shall, until the contrary is proved, be deemed to have been given or made by the Secretary of State.

(2) A document bearing a certificate which –

(a) purports to be signed by or on behalf of the Secretary of State, and

(b) states that the document is a true copy of a notice or direction given or order made by the Secretary of State for the purposes of a provision of this Act,

shall be evidence ... of the document in legal proceedings.

(3) In subsections (1) and (2) a reference to an order does not include a reference to an order made by statutory instrument.

(4) The Documentary Evidence Act 1868 shall apply to an authorisation given in writing by the Secretary of State for the purposes of this Act as it applies to an order made by him.

121 Interpretation

In this Act –

'act' and 'action' include omission,

'article' includes substance and any other thing,

'customs officer' means an officer commissioned by the Commissioners of Customs and Excise under section 6(3) of the Customs and Excise Management Act 1979,

'dwelling' means a building or part of a building used as a dwelling, and a vehicle which is habitually stationary and which is used as a dwelling,

'explosive' means –

(a) an article or substance manufactured for the purpose of producing a practical effect by explosion,
(b) materials for making an article or substance within paragraph (a),
(c) anything used or intended to be used for causing or assisting in causing an explosion, and
(d) a part of anything within paragraph (a) or (c),

'firearm' includes an air gun or air pistol,

'immigration officer' means a person appointed as an immigration officer under paragraph 1 of Schedule 2 to the Immigration Act 1971,

'the Islands' means the Channel Islands and the Isle of Man,

'organisation' includes any association or combination of persons,

'premises' ... includes any place and in particular includes –

(a) a vehicle,
(b) an offshore installation within the meaning given in section 44 of the Petroleum Act 1998, and
(c) a tent or moveable structure,

'property' includes property wherever situated and whether real or personal, heritable or moveable, and things in action and other intangible or incorporeal property, 'public place' means a place to which members of the public have or are permitted to have access, whether or not for payment,

'road' has the same meaning as in the Road Traffic Act 1988 (in relation to England and Wales) … and includes part of a road, and

'vehicle', except in sections 48 to 52 and Schedule 7, includes an aircraft, hovercraft, train or vessel.

123 Orders and regulations

(1) An order or regulations made by the Secretary of State under this Act –

(a) shall be made by statutory instrument,

(b) may contain savings and transitional provisions, and

(c) may make different provision for different purposes. …

SCHEDULE 2

PROSCRIBED ORGANISATIONS

The Irish Republican Army …

The Red Hand Commando …

The Ulster Freedom Fighters

The Ulster Volunteer Force

The Irish National Liberation Army

The Irish People's Liberation Organisation

The Ulster Defence Association …

The Orange Volunteers …

Al-Qa'ida …

International Sikh Youth Federation …

Liberation Tigers of Tamil Eelam (LTTE) …

Palestinian Islamic Jihad-Shaqaqi …

Islamic Army of Aden …

Kurdistan Workers' Party (Partiya Karkeren Kurdistan) (PKK) …

Basque Homeland and Liberty (Euskadi ta Askatasuna) (ETA) …

SCHEDULE 3

THE PROSCRIBED ORGANISATIONS APPEAL COMMISSION

1. – (1) The Commission shall consist of members appointed by the Lord Chancellor.

(2) The Lord Chancellor shall appoint one of the members as chairman.

(3) A member shall hold and vacate office in accordance with the terms of his appointment.

(4) A member may resign at any time by notice in writing to the Lord Chancellor.

2. The Lord Chancellor may appoint officers and servants for the Commission.

3. The Lord Chancellor –

(a) may pay sums by way of remuneration, allowances, pensions and gratuities to or in respect of members, officers and servants,

(b) may pay compensation to a person who ceases to be a member of the Commission if the Lord Chancellor thinks it appropriate because of special circumstances, and

(c) may pay sums in respect of expenses of the Commission.

4. – (1) The Commission shall sit at such times and in such places as the Lord Chancellor may direct.

(2) The Commission may sit in two or more divisions.

(3) At each sitting of the Commission –

(a) three members shall attend,

(b) one of the members shall be a person who holds or has held high judicial office (within the meaning of the Appellate Jurisdiction Act 1876), and

(c) the chairman or another member nominated by him shall preside and report the Commission's decision. ...

As amended by the Regulation of Investigatory Powers Act 2000, s82(1), Schedule 4, para 12(1); Anti-terrorism, Crime and Security Act 2001, ss3, 117, Schedule 2, Pt 3, para 5(1), (3); Terrorism Act 2000 (Proscribed Organisations) (Amendment) Order 2001, art 2.

REGULATION OF INVESTIGATORY POWERS ACT 2000
(2000 c 23)

PART I
COMMUNICATIONS
CHAPTER I
INTERCEPTION

1 Unlawful interception

(1) It shall be an offence for a person intentionally and without lawful authority to intercept, at any place in the United Kingdom, any communication in the course of its transmission by means of –

(a) a public postal service; or
(b) a public telecommunication system.

(2) It shall be an offence for a person –

(a) intentionally and without lawful authority, and
(b) otherwise than in circumstances in which his conduct is excluded by subsection (6) from criminal liability under this subsection,

to intercept, at any place in the United Kingdom, any communication in the course of its transmission by means of a private telecommunication system.

(3) Any interception of a communication which is carried out at any place in the United Kingdom by, or with the express or implied consent of, a person having the right to control the operation or the use of a private telecommunication system shall be actionable at the suit or instance of the sender or recipient, or intended recipient, of the communication if it is without lawful authority and is either –

(a) an interception of that communication in the course of its transmission by means of that private system; or
(b) an interception of that communication in the course of its transmission, by means of a public telecommunication system, to or from apparatus comprised in that private telecommunication system.

(4) Where the United Kingdom is a party to an international agreement which –

(a) relates to the provision of mutual assistance in connection with, or in the form of, the interception of communications,

(b) requires the issue of a warrant, order or equivalent instrument in cases in which assistance is given, and

(c) is designated for the purposes of this subsection by an order made by the Secretary of State,

it shall be the duty of the Secretary of State to secure that no request for assistance in accordance with the agreement is made on behalf of a person in the United Kingdom to the competent authorities of a country or territory outside the United Kingdom except with lawful authority.

(5) Conduct has lawful authority for the purposes of this section if, and only if –

(a) it is authorised by or under section 3 or 4;

(b) it takes place in accordance with a warrant under section 5 ('an interception warrant'); or

(c) it is in exercise, in relation to any stored communication, of any statutory power that is exercised (apart from this section) for the purpose of obtaining information or of taking possession of any document or other property;

and conduct (whether or not prohibited by this section) which has lawful authority for the purposes of this section by virtue of paragraph (a) or (b) shall also be taken to be lawful for all other purposes.

(6) The circumstances in which a person makes an interception of a communication in the course of its transmission by means of a private telecommunication system are such that his conduct is excluded from criminal liability under subsection (2) if –

(a) he is a person with a right to control the operation or the use of the system; or

(b) he has the express or implied consent of such a person to make the interception.

(7) A person who is guilty of an offence under subsection (1) or (2) shall be liable –

(a) on conviction on indictment, to imprisonment for a term not exceeding two years or to a fine, or to both;

(b) on summary conviction, to a fine not exceeding the statutory maximum.

(8) No proceedings for any offence which is an offence by virtue of this section shall be instituted –

(a) in England and Wales, except by or with the consent of the Director of Public Prosecutions; …

2 Meaning and location of 'interception', etc

(1) In this Act –

'postal service' means any service which –

(a) consists in the following, or in any one or more of them, namely, the collection, sorting, conveyance, distribution and delivery (whether in the United Kingdom or elsewhere) of postal items; and

(b) is offered or provided as a service the main purpose of which, or one of the main purposes of which, is to make available, or to facilitate, a means of transmission from place to place of postal items containing communications;

'private telecommunication system' means any telecommunication system which, without itself being a public telecommunication system, is a system in relation to which the following conditions are satisfied –

(a) it is attached, directly or indirectly and whether or not for the purposes of the communication in question, to a public telecommunication system; and

(b) there is apparatus comprised in the system which is both located in the United Kingdom and used (with or without other apparatus) for making the attachment to the public telecommunication system;

'public postal service' means any postal service which is offered or provided to, or to a substantial section of, the public in any one or more parts of the United Kingdom;

'public telecommunications service' means any telecommunications service which is offered or provided to, or to a substantial section of, the public in any one or more parts of the United Kingdom;

'public telecommunication system' means any such parts of a telecommunication system by means of which any public telecommunications service is provided as are located in the United Kingdom;

'telecommunications service' means any service that consists in the provision of access to, and of facilities for making use of, any telecommunication system (whether or not one provided by the person providing the service); and

'telecommunication system' means any system (including the apparatus comprised in it) which exists (whether wholly or partly in the United Kingdom or elsewhere) for the purpose of facilitating the transmission of communications by any means involving the use of electrical or electro –magnetic energy.

(2) For the purposes of this Act, but subject to the following provisions of this section, a person intercepts a communication in the course of its transmission by means of a telecommunication system if, and only if, he –

(a) so modifies or interferes with the system, or its operation,

(b) so monitors transmissions made by means of the system, or

(c) so monitors transmissions made by wireless telegraphy to or from apparatus comprised in the system,

as to make some or all of the contents of the communication available, while being transmitted, to a person other than the sender or intended recipient of the communication.

(3) References in this Act to the interception of a communication do not include references to the interception of any communication broadcast for general reception.

(4) For the purposes of this Act the interception of a communication takes place in the United Kingdom if, and only if, the modification, interference or monitoring or, in the case of a postal item, the interception is effected by conduct within the United Kingdom and the communication is either –

(a) intercepted in the course of its transmission by means of a public postal service or public telecommunication system; or

(b) intercepted in the course of its transmission by means of a private telecommunication system in a case in which the sender or intended recipient of the communication is in the United Kingdom.

(5) References in this Act to the interception of a communication in the course of its transmission by means of a postal service or telecommunication system do not include references to –

(a) any conduct that takes place in relation only to so much of the communication as consists in any traffic data comprised in or attached to a communication (whether by the sender or otherwise) for the purposes of any postal service or telecommunication system by means of which it is being or may be transmitted; or

(b) any such conduct, in connection with conduct falling within paragraph (a), as gives a person who is neither the sender nor the intended recipient only so much access to a communication as is necessary for the purpose of identifying traffic data so comprised or attached.

(6) For the purposes of this section references to the modification of a telecommunication system include references to the attachment of any apparatus to, or other modification of or interference with –

(a) any part of the system; or

(b) any wireless telegraphy apparatus used for making transmissions to or from apparatus comprised in the system.

(7) For the purposes of this section the times while a communication is being transmitted by means of a telecommunication system shall be taken to include any time when the system by means of which the communication is being, or has been, transmitted is used for storing it in a manner that enables the intended recipient to collect it or otherwise to have access to it.

(8) For the purposes of this section the cases in which any contents of a communication are to be taken to be made available to a person while being transmitted shall include any case in which any of the contents of the communication, while being transmitted, are diverted or recorded so as to be available to a person subsequently.

(9) In this section 'traffic data', in relation to any communication, means –

(a) any data identifying, or purporting to identify, any person, apparatus or location to or from which the communication is or may be transmitted,

(b) any data identifying or selecting, or purporting to identify or select, apparatus through which, or by means of which, the communication is or may be transmitted,

(c) any data comprising signals for the actuation of apparatus used for the purposes of a telecommunication system for effecting (in whole or in part) the transmission of any communication, and

(d) any data identifying the data or other data as data comprised in or attached to a particular communication,

but that expression includes data identifying a computer file or computer program access to which is obtained, or which is run, by means of the communication to the extent only that the file or program is identified by reference to the apparatus in which it is stored.

(10) In this section –

(a) references, in relation to traffic data comprising signals for the actuation of apparatus, to a telecommunication system by means of which a communication is being or may be transmitted include references to any telecommunication system in which that apparatus is comprised; and

(b) references to traffic data being attached to a communication include references to the data and the communication being logically associated with each other;

and in this section 'data', in relation to a postal item, means anything written on the outside of the item.

(11) In this section 'postal item' means any letter, postcard or other such thing in writing as may be used by the sender for imparting information to the recipient, or any packet or parcel.

3 Lawful interception without an interception warrant

(1) Conduct by any person consisting in the interception of a communication is authorised by this section if the communication is one which, or which that person has reasonable grounds for believing, is both –

(a) a communication sent by a person who has consented to the interception; and

(b) a communication the intended recipient of which has so consented.

(2) Conduct by any person consisting in the interception of a communication is authorised by this section if –

(a) the communication is one sent by, or intended for, a person who has consented to the interception; and

(b) surveillance by means of that interception has been authorised under Part II.

(3) Conduct consisting in the interception of a communication is authorised by this section if –

(a) it is conduct by or on behalf of a person who provides a postal service or a telecommunications service; and

(b) it takes place for purposes connected with the provision or operation of that service or with the enforcement, in relation to that service, of any enactment relating to the use of postal services or telecommunications services.

(4) Conduct by any person consisting in the interception of a communication in the course of its transmission by means of wireless telegraphy is authorised by this section if it takes place –

(a) with the authority of a designated person under section 5 of the Wireless Telegraphy Act 1949 (misleading messages and interception and disclosure of wireless telegraphy messages); and

(b) for purposes connected with anything falling within subsection (5).

(5) Each of the following falls within this subsection –

(a) the issue of licences under the Wireless Telegraphy Act 1949;

(b) the prevention or detection of anything which constitutes interference with wireless telegraphy; and

(c) the enforcement of any enactment contained in that Act or of any enactment not so contained that relates to such interference.

4 Power to provide for lawful interception

(1) Conduct by any person ('the interceptor') consisting in the interception of a communication in the course of its transmission by means of a telecommunication system is authorised by this section if –

(a) the interception is carried out for the purpose of obtaining information about the communications of a person who, or who the interceptor has reasonable grounds for believing, is in a country or territory outside the United Kingdom;

(b) the interception relates to the use of a telecommunications service provided to persons in that country or territory which is either –

(i) a public telecommunications service; or

(ii) a telecommunications service that would be a public telecommunications service if the persons to whom it is offered or provided were members of the public in a part of the United Kingdom;

(c) the person who provides that service (whether the interceptor or another person) is required by the law of that country or territory to carry out, secure or facilitate the interception in question;

(d) the situation is one in relation to which such further conditions as may be prescribed by regulations made by the Secretary of State are required to be satisfied before conduct may be treated as authorised by virtue of this subsection; and

(e) the conditions so prescribed are satisfied in relation to that situation.

(2) Subject to subsection (3), the Secretary of State may by regulations authorise any such conduct described in the regulations as appears to him to constitute a legitimate practice reasonably required for the purpose, in connection with the carrying on of any business, of monitoring or keeping a record of –

(a) communications by means of which transactions are entered into in the course of that business; or

(b) other communications relating to that business or taking place in the course of its being carried on.

(3) Nothing in any regulations under subsection (2) shall authorise the interception of any communication except in the course of its transmission using apparatus or services provided by or to the person carrying on the business for use wholly or partly in connection with that business.

(4) Conduct taking place in a prison is authorised by this section if it is conduct in exercise of any power conferred by or under any rules made under section 47 of the Prison Act 1952 ...

(5) Conduct taking place in any hospital premises where high security psychiatric services are provided is authorised by this section if it is conduct in pursuance of, and in accordance with, any direction given under section 17 of the National Health Service Act 1977 (directions as to the carrying out of their functions by health bodies) to the body providing those services at those premises. ...

(7) In this section references to a business include references to any activities of a government department, of any public authority or of any person or office holder on whom functions are conferred by or under any enactment.

(8) In this section –

'government department' includes any part of the Scottish Administration, a Northern Ireland department and the National Assembly for Wales;

'high security psychiatric services' has the same meaning as in the National Health Service Act 1977;

'hospital premises' has the same meaning as in section 4(3) of that Act; ...

(9) In this section 'prison' means –

(a) any prison, young offender institution, young offenders centre or remand centre which is under the general superintendence of, or is provided by, the Secretary of State under the Prison Act 1952 ...

and includes any contracted out prison, within the meaning of Part IV of the Criminal Justice Act 1991 or section 106(4) of the Criminal Justice and Public Order Act 1994 ...

5 Interception with a warrant

(1) Subject to the following provisions of this Chapter, the Secretary of State may issue a warrant authorising or requiring the person to whom it is addressed, by any

such conduct as may be described in the warrant, to secure any one or more of the following –

(a) the interception in the course of their transmission by means of a postal service or telecommunication system of the communications described in the warrant;

(b) the making, in accordance with an international mutual assistance agreement, of a request for the provision of such assistance in connection with, or in the form of, an interception of communications as may be so described;

(c) the provision, in accordance with an international mutual assistance agreement, to the competent authorities of a country or territory outside the United Kingdom of any such assistance in connection with, or in the form of, an interception of communications as may be so described;

(d) the disclosure, in such manner as may be so described, of intercepted material obtained by any interception authorised or required by the warrant, and of related communications data.

(2) The Secretary of State shall not issue an interception warrant unless he believes –

(a) that the warrant is necessary on grounds falling within subsection (3); and

(b) that the conduct authorised by the warrant is proportionate to what is sought to be achieved by that conduct.

(3) Subject to the following provisions of this section, a warrant is necessary on grounds falling within this subsection if it is necessary –

(a) in the interests of national security;

(b) for the purpose of preventing or detecting serious crime;

(c) for the purpose of safeguarding the economic well –being of the United Kingdom; or

(d) for the purpose, in circumstances appearing to the Secretary of State to be equivalent to those in which he would issue a warrant by virtue of paragraph (b), of giving effect to the provisions of any international mutual assistance agreement.

(4) The matters to be taken into account in considering whether the requirements of subsection (2) are satisfied in the case of any warrant shall include whether the information which it is thought necessary to obtain under the warrant could reasonably be obtained by other means.

(5) A warrant shall not be considered necessary on the ground falling within subsection (3)(c) unless the information which it is thought necessary to obtain is information relating to the acts or intentions of persons outside the British Islands.

(6) The conduct authorised by an interception warrant shall be taken to include –

(a) all such conduct (including the interception of communications not identified by the warrant) as it is necessary to undertake in order to do what is expressly authorised or required by the warrant;

(b) conduct for obtaining related communications data; and

(c) conduct by any person which is conduct in pursuance of a requirement imposed by or on behalf of the person to whom the warrant is addressed to be provided with assistance with giving effect to the warrant.

6 Application for issue of an interception warrant

(1) An interception warrant shall not be issued except on an application made by or on behalf of a person specified in subsection (2).

(2) Those persons are –

(a) the Director-General of the Security Service;

(b) the Chief of the Secret Intelligence Service;

(c) the Director of GCHQ;

(d) the Director General of the National Criminal Intelligence Service;

(e) the Commissioner of Police of the Metropolis; …

(h) the Commissioners of Customs and Excise;

(i) the Chief of Defence Intelligence;

(j) a person who, for the purposes of any international mutual assistance agreement, is the competent authority of a country or territory outside the United Kingdom.

(3) An application for the issue of an interception warrant shall not be made on behalf of a person specified in subsection (2) except by a person holding office under the Crown.

7 Issue of warrants

(1) An interception warrant shall not be issued except –

(a) under the hand of the Secretary of State; or

(b) in a case falling within subsection (2), under the hand of a senior official.

(2) Those cases are –

(a) an urgent case in which the Secretary of State has himself expressly authorised the issue of the warrant in that case; and

(b) a case in which the warrant is for the purposes of a request for assistance made under an international mutual assistance agreement by the competent authorities of a country or territory outside the United Kingdom and either –

(i) it appears that the interception subject is outside the United Kingdom; or

(ii) the interception to which the warrant relates is to take place in relation only to premises outside the United Kingdom.

(3) An interception warrant –

(a) must be addressed to the person falling within section 6(2) by whom, or on whose behalf, the application for the warrant was made; and

(b) in the case of a warrant issued under the hand of a senior official, must contain, according to whatever is applicable –

(i) one of the statements set out in subsection (4); and

(ii) if it contains the statement set out in subsection (4)(b), one of the statements set out in subsection (5).

(4) The statements referred to in subsection (3)(b)(i) are –

(a) a statement that the case is an urgent case in which the Secretary of State has himself expressly authorised the issue of the warrant;

(b) a statement that the warrant is issued for the purposes of a request for assistance made under an international mutual assistance agreement by the competent authorities of a country or territory outside the United Kingdom.

(5) The statements referred to in subsection (3)(b)(ii) are –

(a) a statement that the interception subject appears to be outside the United Kingdom;

(b) a statement that the interception to which the warrant relates is to take place in relation only to premises outside the United Kingdom.

8 Contents of warrants

(1) An interception warrant must name or describe either –

(a) one person as the interception subject; or

(b) a single set of premises as the premises in relation to which the interception to which the warrant relates is to take place.

(2) The provisions of an interception warrant describing communications the interception of which is authorised or required by the warrant must comprise one or more schedules setting out the addresses, numbers, apparatus or other factors, or combination of factors, that are to be used for identifying the communications that may be or are to be intercepted.

(3) Any factor or combination of factors set out in accordance with subsection (2) must be one that identifies communications which are likely to be or to include –

(a) communications from, or intended for, the person named or described in the warrant in accordance with subsection (1); or

(b) communications originating on, or intended for transmission to, the premises so named or described.

(4) Subsections (1) and (2) shall not apply to an interception warrant if –

(a) the description of communications to which the warrant relates confines the conduct authorised or required by the warrant to conduct falling within subsection (5); and

(b) at the time of the issue of the warrant, a certificate applicable to the warrant has been issued by the Secretary of State certifying –

(i) the descriptions of intercepted material the examination of which he considers necessary; and

(ii) that he considers the examination of material of those descriptions necessary as mentioned in section 5(3)(a), (b) or (c).

(5) Conduct falls within this subsection if it consists in –

(a) the interception of external communications in the course of their transmission by means of a telecommunication system; and

(b) any conduct authorised in relation to any such interception by section 5(6).

(6) A certificate for the purposes of subsection (4) shall not be issued except under the hand of the Secretary of State.

9 Duration, cancellation and renewal of warrants

(1) An interception warrant –

(a) shall cease to have effect at the end of the relevant period; but

(b) may be renewed, at any time before the end of that period, by an instrument under the hand of the Secretary of State or, in a case falling within section 7(2)(b), under the hand of a senior official.

(2) An interception warrant shall not be renewed under subsection (1) unless the Secretary of State believes that the warrant continues to be necessary on grounds falling within section 5(3).

(3) The Secretary of State shall cancel an interception warrant if he is satisfied that the warrant is no longer necessary on grounds falling within section 5(3).

(4) The Secretary of State shall cancel an interception warrant if, at any time before the end of the relevant period, he is satisfied in a case in which –

(a) the warrant is one which was issued containing the statement set out in section 7(5)(a) or has been renewed by an instrument containing the statement set out in subsection (5)(b)(i) of this section, and

(b) the latest renewal (if any) of the warrant is not a renewal by an instrument under the hand of the Secretary of State,

that the person named or described in the warrant as the interception subject is in the United Kingdom.

(5) An instrument under the hand of a senior official that renews an interception warrant must contain –

(a) a statement that the renewal is for the purposes of a request for assistance made under an international mutual assistance agreement by the competent authorities of a country or territory outside the United Kingdom; and

(b) whichever of the following statements is applicable –

(i) a statement that the interception subject appears to be outside the United Kingdom;

(ii) a statement that the interception to which the warrant relates is to take place in relation only to premises outside the United Kingdom.

(6) In this section 'the relevant period' –

(a) in relation to an unrenewed warrant issued in a case falling within section 7(2)(a) under the hand of a senior official, means the period ending with the fifth working day following the day of the warrant's issue;

(b) in relation to a renewed warrant the latest renewal of which was by an instrument endorsed under the hand of the Secretary of State with a statement that the renewal is believed to be necessary on grounds falling within section 5(3)(a) or (c), means the period of six months beginning with the day of the warrant's renewal; and

(c) in all other cases, means the period of three months beginning with the day of the warrant's issue or, in the case of a warrant that has been renewed, of its latest renewal.

10 Modification of warrants and certificates

(1) The Secretary of State may at any time –

(a) modify the provisions of an interception warrant; or

(b) modify a section 8(4) certificate so as to include in the certified material any material the examination of which he considers to be necessary as mentioned in section 5(3)(a), (b) or (c).

(2) If at any time the Secretary of State considers that any factor set out in a schedule to an interception warrant is no longer relevant for identifying communications which, in the case of that warrant, are likely to be or to include communications falling within section 8(3)(a) or (b), it shall be his duty to modify the warrant by the deletion of that factor.

(3) If at any time the Secretary of State considers that the material certified by a section 8(4) certificate includes any material the examination of which is no longer necessary as mentioned in any of paragraphs (a) to (c) of section 5(3), he shall modify the certificate so as to exclude that material from the certified material.

(4) Subject to subsections (5) to (8), a warrant or certificate shall not be modified under this section except by an instrument under the hand of the Secretary of State or of a senior official.

(5) Unscheduled parts of an interception warrant shall not be modified under the hand of a senior official except in an urgent case in which –

(a) the Secretary of State has himself expressly authorised the modification; and

(b) a statement of that fact is endorsed on the modifying instrument.

(6) Subsection (4) shall not authorise the making under the hand of either –

(a) the person to whom the warrant is addressed, or

(b) any person holding a position subordinate to that person,

of any modification of any scheduled parts of an interception warrant.

(7) A section 8(4) certificate shall not be modified under the hand of a senior official except in an urgent case in which –

(a) the official in question holds a position in respect of which he is expressly authorised by provisions contained in the certificate to modify the certificate on the Secretary of State's behalf; or

(b) the Secretary of State has himself expressly authorised the modification and a statement of that fact is endorsed on the modifying instrument.

(8) Where modifications in accordance with this subsection are expressly authorised by provision contained in the warrant, the scheduled parts of an interception warrant may, in an urgent case, be modified by an instrument under the hand of –

(a) the person to whom the warrant is addressed; or

(b) a person holding any such position subordinate to that person as may be identified in the provisions of the warrant.

(9) Where –

(a) a warrant or certificate is modified by an instrument under the hand of a person other than the Secretary of State, and

(b) a statement for the purposes of subsection (5)(b) or (7)(b) is endorsed on the instrument, or the modification is made under subsection (8),

that modification shall cease to have effect at the end of the fifth working day following the day of the instrument's issue.

(10) For the purposes of this section –

(a) the scheduled parts of an interception warrant are any provisions of the warrant that are contained in a schedule of identifying factors comprised in the warrant for the purposes of section 8(2); and

(b) the modifications that are modifications of the scheduled parts of an interception warrant include the insertion of an additional such schedule in the warrant;

and references in this section to unscheduled parts of an interception warrant, and to their modification, shall be construed accordingly.

11 Implementation of warrants

(1) Effect may be given to an interception warrant either –

(a) by the person to whom it is addressed; or

(b) by that person acting through, or together with, such other persons as he may require (whether under subsection (2) or otherwise) to provide him with assistance with giving effect to the warrant.

(2) For the purpose of requiring any person to provide assistance in relation to an interception warrant the person to whom it is addressed may –

(a) serve a copy of the warrant on such persons as he considers may be able to provide such assistance; or

(b) make arrangements under which a copy of it is to be or may be so served.

(3) The copy of an interception warrant that is served on any person under subsection (2) may, to the extent authorised –

(a) by the person to whom the warrant is addressed, or

(b) by the arrangements made by him for the purposes of that subsection,

omit any one or more of the schedules to the warrant.

(4) Where a copy of an interception warrant has been served by or on behalf of the person to whom it is addressed on –

(a) a person who provides a postal service,

(b) a person who provides a public telecommunications service, or

(c) a person not falling within paragraph (b) who has control of the whole or any part of a telecommunication system located wholly or partly in the United Kingdom,

it shall (subject to subsection (5)) be the duty of that person to take all such steps for giving effect to the warrant as are notified to him by or on behalf of the person to whom the warrant is addressed.

(5) A person who is under a duty by virtue of subsection (4) to take steps for giving effect to a warrant shall not be required to take any steps which it is not reasonably practicable for him to take.

(6) For the purposes of subsection (5) the steps which it is reasonably practicable for a person to take in a case in which obligations have been imposed on him by or under section 12 shall include every step which it would have been reasonably practicable for him to take had he complied with all the obligations so imposed on him.

(7) A person who knowingly fails to comply with his duty under subsection (4) shall be guilty of an offence and liable –

(a) on conviction on indictment, to imprisonment for a term not exceeding two years or to a fine, or to both;

(b) on summary conviction, to imprisonment for a term not exceeding six months or to a fine not exceeding the statutory maximum, or to both.

(8) A person's duty under subsection (4) to take steps for giving effect to a warrant shall be enforceable by civil proceedings by the Secretary of State for an injunction … or for any other appropriate relief.

(9) For the purposes of this Act the provision of assistance with giving effect to an interception warrant includes any disclosure to the person to whom the warrant is addressed, or to persons acting on his behalf, of intercepted material obtained by any interception authorised or required by the warrant, and of any related communications data.

12 Maintenance of interception capability

(1) The Secretary of State may by order provide for the imposition by him on persons who –

(a) are providing public postal services or public telecommunications services, or

(b) are proposing to do so,

of such obligations as it appears to him reasonable to impose for the purpose of securing that it is and remains practicable for requirements to provide assistance in relation to interception warrants to be imposed and complied with.

(2) The Secretary of State's power to impose the obligations provided for by an order under this section shall be exercisable by the giving, in accordance with the order, of a notice requiring the person who is to be subject to the obligations to take all such steps as may be specified or described in the notice.

(3) Subject to subsection (11), the only steps that may be specified or described in a notice given to a person under subsection (2) are steps appearing to the Secretary of State to be necessary for securing that that person has the practical capability of providing any assistance which he may be required to provide in relation to relevant interception warrants.

(4) A person shall not be liable to have an obligation imposed on him in accordance with an order under this section by reason only that he provides, or is proposing to provide, to members of the public a telecommunications service the provision of which is or, as the case may be, will be no more than –

(a) the means by which he provides a service which is not a telecommunications service; or

(b) necessarily incidental to the provision by him of a service which is not a telecommunications service.

(5) Where a notice is given to any person under subsection (2) and otherwise than by virtue of subsection (6)(c), that person may, before the end of such period as may be specified in an order under this section, refer the notice to the Technical Advisory Board.

(6) Where a notice given to any person under subsection (2) is referred to the Technical Advisory Board under subsection (5) –

(a) there shall be no requirement for that person to comply, except in pursuance of a notice under paragraph (c)(ii), with any obligations imposed by the notice;

(b) the Board shall consider the technical requirements and the financial consequences, for the person making the reference, of the notice referred to them and shall report their conclusions on those matters to that person and to the Secretary of State; and

(c) the Secretary of State, after considering any report of the Board relating to the notice, may either –

(i) withdraw the notice; or

(ii) give a further notice under subsection (2) confirming its effect, with or without modifications.

(7) It shall be the duty of a person to whom a notice is given under subsection (2) to comply with the notice; and that duty shall be enforceable by civil proceedings by the Secretary of State for an injunction, or for specific performance of a statutory duty under section 45 of the Court of Session Act 1988, or for any other appropriate relief.

(8) A notice for the purposes of subsection (2) must specify such period as appears to the Secretary of State to be reasonable as the period within which the steps specified or described in the notice are to be taken.

(9) Before making an order under this section the Secretary of State shall consult with –

(a) such persons appearing to him to be likely to be subject to the obligations for which it provides,

(b) the Technical Advisory Board,

(c) such persons representing persons falling within paragraph (a), and

(d) such persons with statutory functions in relation to persons falling within that paragraph,

as he considers appropriate.

(10) The Secretary of State shall not make an order under this section unless a draft of the order has been laid before Parliament and approved by a resolution of each House.

(11) For the purposes of this section the question whether a person has the practical capability of providing assistance in relation to relevant interception warrants shall include the question whether all such arrangements have been made as the Secretary of State considers necessary –

(a) with respect to the disclosure of intercepted material;

(b) for the purpose of ensuring that security and confidentiality are maintained in relation to, and to matters connected with, the provision of any such assistance; and

(c) for the purpose of facilitating the carrying out of any functions in relation to this Chapter of the Interception of Communications Commissioner;

but before determining for the purposes of the making of any order, or the imposition of any obligation, under this section what arrangements he considers necessary for the purpose mentioned in paragraph (c) the Secretary of State shall consult that Commissioner.

(12) In this section 'relevant interception warrant' –

(a) in relation to a person providing a public postal service, means an interception warrant relating to the interception of communications in the course of their transmission by means of that service; and

(b) in relation to a person providing a public telecommunications service, means an interception warrant relating to the interception of communications in the course of their transmission by means of a telecommunication system used for the purposes of that service.

13 Technical Advisory Board

(1) There shall be a Technical Advisory Board consisting of such number of persons appointed by the Secretary of State as he may by order provide.

(2) The order providing for the membership of the Technical Advisory Board must also make provision which is calculated to ensure –

(a) that the membership of the Technical Advisory Board includes persons likely effectively to represent the interests of the persons on whom obligations may be imposed under section 12;

(b) that the membership of the Board includes persons likely effectively to represent the interests of the persons by or on whose behalf applications for interception warrants may be made;

(c) that such other persons (if any) as the Secretary of State thinks fit may be appointed to be members of the Board; and

(d) that the Board is so constituted as to produce a balance between the representation of the interests mentioned in paragraph (a) and the representation of those mentioned in paragraph (b).

(3) The Secretary of State shall not make an order under this section unless a draft of the order has been laid before Parliament and approved by a resolution of each House.

14 Grants for interception costs

(1) It shall be the duty of the Secretary of State to ensure that such arrangements are in force as are necessary for securing that a person who provides –

(a) a postal service, or

(b) a telecommunications service,

receives such contribution as is, in the circumstances of that person's case, a fair contribution towards the costs incurred, or likely to be incurred, by that person in consequence of the matters mentioned in subsection (2).

(2) Those matters are –

(a) in relation to a person providing a postal service, the issue of interception warrants relating to communications transmitted by means of that postal service;

(b) in relation to a person providing a telecommunications service, the issue of interception warrants relating to communications transmitted by means of a telecommunication system used for the purposes of that service;

(c) in relation to each description of person, the imposition on that person of obligations provided for by an order under section 12.

(3) For the purpose of complying with his duty under this section, the Secretary of State may make arrangements for payments to be made out of money provided by Parliament.

15 General safeguards

(1) Subject to subsection (6), it shall be the duty of the Secretary of State to ensure, in relation to all interception warrants, that such arrangements are in force as he considers necessary for securing –

(a) that the requirements of subsections (2) and (3) are satisfied in relation to the intercepted material and any related communications data; and

(b) in the case of warrants in relation to which there are section 8(4) certificates, that the requirements of section 16 are also satisfied.

(2) The requirements of this subsection are satisfied in relation to the intercepted material and any related communications data if each of the following –

(a) the number of persons to whom any of the material or data is disclosed or otherwise made available,

(b) the extent to which any of the material or data is disclosed or otherwise made available,

(c) the extent to which any of the material or data is copied, and

(d) the number of copies that are made,

is limited to the minimum that is necessary for the authorised purposes.

(3) The requirements of this subsection are satisfied in relation to the intercepted material and any related communications data if each copy made of any of the material or data (if not destroyed earlier) is destroyed as soon as there are no longer any grounds for retaining it as necessary for any of the authorised purposes.

(4) For the purposes of this section something is necessary for the authorised purposes if, and only if –

(a) it continues to be, or is likely to become, necessary as mentioned in section 5(3);

(b) it is necessary for facilitating the carrying out of any of the functions under this Chapter of the Secretary of State;

(c) it is necessary for facilitating the carrying out of any functions in relation to this Part of the Interception of Communications Commissioner or of the Tribunal;

(d) it is necessary to ensure that a person conducting a criminal prosecution has the information he needs to determine what is required of him by his duty to secure the fairness of the prosecution; or

(e) it is necessary for the performance of any duty imposed on any person by the Public Records Act 1958 ...

(5) The arrangements for the time being in force under this section for securing that the requirements of subsection (2) are satisfied in relation to the intercepted material or any related communications data must include such arrangements as the Secretary of State considers necessary for securing that every copy of the material or data that is made is stored, for so long as it is retained, in a secure manner.

(6) Arrangements in relation to interception warrants which are made for the purposes of subsection (1) –

(a) shall not be required to secure that the requirements of subsections (2) and (3) are satisfied in so far as they relate to any of the intercepted material or related communications data, or any copy of any such material or data, possession of which has been surrendered to any authorities of a country or territory outside the United Kingdom; but

(b) shall be required to secure, in the case of every such warrant, that possession of the intercepted material and data and of copies of the material or data is surrendered to authorities of a country or territory outside the United Kingdom only if the requirements of subsection (7) are satisfied.

(7) The requirements of this subsection are satisfied in the case of a warrant if it appears to the Secretary of State –

(a) that requirements corresponding to those of subsections (2) and (3) will apply, to such extent (if any) as the Secretary of State thinks fit, in relation to any of the intercepted material or related communications data possession of which, or of any copy of which, is surrendered to the authorities in question; and

(b) that restrictions are in force which would prevent, to such extent (if any) as the Secretary of State thinks fit, the doing of anything in, for the purposes of or in connection with any proceedings outside the United Kingdom which would result in such a disclosure as, by virtue of section 17, could not be made in the United Kingdom.

(8) In this section 'copy', in relation to intercepted material or related communications data, means any of the following (whether or not in documentary form) –

(a) any copy, extract or summary of the material or data which identifies itself as the product of an interception, and

(b) any record referring to an interception which is a record of the identities of the persons to or by whom the intercepted material was sent, or to whom the communications data relates,

and 'copied' shall be construed accordingly.

16 Extra safeguards in the case of certificated warrants

(1) For the purposes of section 15 the requirements of this section, in the case of a warrant in relation to which there is a section 8(4) certificate, are that the

intercepted material is read, looked at or listened to by the persons to whom it becomes available by virtue of the warrant to the extent only that it –

(a) has been certified as material the examination of which is necessary as mentioned in section 5(3)(a), (b) or (c); and

(b) falls within subsection (2).

(2) Subject to subsections (3) and (4), intercepted material falls within this subsection so far only as it is selected to be read, looked at or listened to otherwise than according to a factor which –

(a) is referable to an individual who is known to be for the time being in the British Islands; and

(b) has as its purpose, or one of its purposes, the identification of material contained in communications sent by him, or intended for him.

(3) Intercepted material falls within subsection (2), notwithstanding that it is selected by reference to any such factor as is mentioned in paragraph (a) and (b) of that subsection, if –

(a) it is certified by the Secretary of State for the purposes of section 8(4) that the examination of material selected according to factors referable to the individual in question is necessary as mentioned in subsection 5(3)(a), (b) or (c); and

(b) the material relates only to communications sent during a period of not more than three months specified in the certificate.

(4) Intercepted material also falls within subsection (2), notwithstanding that it is selected by reference to any such factor as is mentioned in paragraph (a) and (b) of that subsection, if –

(a) the person to whom the warrant is addressed believes, on reasonable grounds, that the circumstances are such that the material would fall within that subsection; or

(b) the conditions set out in subsection (5) below are satisfied in relation to the selection of the material.

(5) Those conditions are satisfied in relation to the selection of intercepted material if –

(a) it has appeared to the person to whom the warrant is addressed that there has been such a relevant change of circumstances as, but for subsection (4)(b), would prevent the intercepted material from falling within subsection (2);

(b) since it first so appeared, a written authorisation to read, look at or listen to the material has been given by a senior official; and

(c) the selection is made before the end of the first working day after the day on which it first so appeared to that person.

(6) References in this section to its appearing that there has been a relevant change of circumstances are references to its appearing either –

(a) that the individual in question has entered the British Islands; or

(b) that a belief by the person to whom the warrant is addressed in the individual's presence outside the British Islands was in fact mistaken.

17 Exclusion of matters from legal proceedings

(1) Subject to section 18, no evidence shall be adduced, question asked, assertion or disclosure made or other thing done in, for the purposes of or in connection with any legal proceedings which (in any manner) –

(a) discloses, in circumstances from which its origin in anything falling within subsection (2) may be inferred, any of the contents of an intercepted communication or any related communications data; or

(b) tends (apart from any such disclosure) to suggest that anything falling within subsection (2) has or may have occurred or be going to occur.

(2) The following fall within this subsection –

(a) conduct by a person falling within subsection (3) that was or would be an offence under section 1(1) or (2) of this Act or under section 1 of the Interception of Communications Act 1985;

(b) a breach by the Secretary of State of his duty under section 1(4) of this Act;

(c) the issue of an interception warrant or of a warrant under the Interception of Communications Act 1985;

(d) the making of an application by any person for an interception warrant, or for a warrant under that Act;

(e) the imposition of any requirement on any person to provide assistance with giving effect to an interception warrant.

(3) The persons referred to in subsection (2)(a) are –

(a) any person to whom a warrant under this Chapter may be addressed;

(b) any person holding office under the Crown;

(c) any member of the National Criminal Intelligence Service;

(d) any member of the National Crime Squad;

(e) any person employed by or for the purposes of a police force;

(f) any person providing a postal service or employed for the purposes of any business of providing such a service; and

(g) any person providing a public telecommunications service or employed for the purposes of any business of providing such a service.

(4) In this section 'intercepted communication' means any communication intercepted in the course of its transmission by means of a postal service or telecommunication system.

18 Exceptions to section 17

(1) Section 17(1) shall not apply in relation to –

(a) any proceedings for a relevant offence;

(b) any civil proceedings under section 11(8);

(c) any proceedings before the Tribunal;

(d) any proceedings on an appeal or review for which provision is made by an order under section 67(8);

(e) any proceedings before the Special Immigration Appeals Commission or any proceedings arising out of proceedings before that Commission; or

(f) any proceedings before the Proscribed Organisations Appeal Commission or any proceedings arising out of proceedings before that Commission.

(2) Subsection (1) shall not, by virtue of paragraph (e) or (f), authorise the disclosure of anything –

(a) in the case of any proceedings falling within paragraph (e), to –

(i) the appellant to the Special Immigration Appeals Commission; or

(ii) any person who for the purposes of any proceedings so falling (but otherwise than by virtue of an appointment under section 6 of the Special Immigration Appeals Commission Act 1997) represents that appellant;

or

(b) in the case of proceedings falling within paragraph (f), to –

(i) the applicant to the Proscribed Organisations Appeal Commission;

(ii) the organisation concerned (if different);

(iii) any person designated under paragraph 6 of Schedule 3 to the Terrorism Act 2000 to conduct proceedings so falling on behalf of that organisation; or

(iv) any person who for the purposes of any proceedings so falling (but otherwise than by virtue of an appointment under paragraph 7 of that Schedule) represents that applicant or that organisation.

(3) Section 17(1) shall not prohibit anything done in, for the purposes of, or in connection with, so much of any legal proceedings as relates to the fairness or unfairness of a dismissal on the grounds of any conduct constituting an offence under section 1(1) or (2), 11(7) or 19 of this Act, or section 1 of the Interception of Communications Act 1985.

(4) Section 17(1)(a) shall not prohibit the disclosure of any of the contents of a communication if the interception of that communication was lawful by virtue of section 1(5)(c), 3 or 4.

(5) Where any disclosure is proposed to be or has been made on the grounds that it is authorised by subsection (4), section 17(1) shall not prohibit the doing of anything in, or for the purposes of, so much of any legal proceedings as relates to the question whether that disclosure is or was so authorised.

(6) Section 17(1)(b) shall not prohibit the doing of anything that discloses any conduct of a person for which he has been convicted of an offence under section 1(1) or (2), 11(7) or 19 of this Act, or section 1 of the Interception of Communications Act 1985.

(7) Nothing in section 17(1) shall prohibit any such disclosure of any information that continues to be available for disclosure as is confined to –

(a) a disclosure to a person conducting a criminal prosecution for the purpose only of enabling that person to determine what is required of him by his duty to secure the fairness of the prosecution; or

(b) a disclosure to a relevant judge in a case in which that judge has ordered the disclosure to be made to him alone.

(8) A relevant judge shall not order a disclosure under subsection (7)(b) except where he is satisfied that the exceptional circumstances of the case make the disclosure essential in the interests of justice.

(9) Subject to subsection (10), where in any criminal proceedings –

(a) a relevant judge does order a disclosure under subsection (7)(b), and

(b) in consequence of that disclosure he is of the opinion that there are exceptional circumstances requiring him to do so,

he may direct the person conducting the prosecution to make for the purposes of the proceedings any such admission of fact as that judge thinks essential in the interests of justice.

(10) Nothing in any direction under subsection (9) shall authorise or require anything to be done in contravention of section 17(1).

(11) In this section 'a relevant judge' means –

(a) any judge of the High Court or of the Crown Court or any Circuit judge; ...

(c) in relation to a court –martial, the judge advocate appointed in relation to that court –martial under section 84B of the Army Act 1955, section 84B of the Air Force Act 1955 or section 53B of the Naval Discipline Act 1957; or

(d) any person holding any such judicial office as entitles him to exercise the jurisdiction of a judge falling within paragraph (a) or (b).

(12) In this section 'relevant offence' means –

(a) an offence under any provision of this Act;

(b) an offence under section 1 of the Interception of Communications Act 1985;

(c) an offence under section 5 of the Wireless Telegraphy Act 1949;

(d) an offence under section 83 or 84 of the Postal Services Act 2000;

(f) an offence under section 4 of the Official Secrets Act 1989 relating to any such information, document or article as is mentioned in subsection (3)(a) of that section;

(g) an offence under section 1 or 2 of the Official Secrets Act 1911 relating to any sketch, plan, model, article, note, document or information which incorporates or relates to the contents of any intercepted communication or any related communications data or tends to suggest as mentioned in section 17(1)(b) of this Act;

(h) perjury committed in the course of any proceedings mentioned in subsection (1) or (3) of this section;

(i) attempting or conspiring to commit, or aiding, abetting, counselling or procuring the commission of, an offence falling within any of the preceding paragraphs; and

(j) contempt of court committed in the course of, or in relation to, any proceedings mentioned in subsection (1) or (3) of this section.

(13) In subsection (12) 'intercepted communication' has the same meaning as in section 17.

19 Offence for unauthorised disclosures

(1) Where an interception warrant has been issued or renewed, it shall be the duty of every person falling within subsection (2) to keep secret all the matters mentioned in subsection (3).

(2) The persons falling within this subsection are –

(a) the persons specified in section 6(2);

(b) every person holding office under the Crown;

(c) every member of the National Criminal Intelligence Service;

(d) every member of the National Crime Squad;

(e) every person employed by or for the purposes of a police force;

(f) persons providing postal services or employed for the purposes of any business of providing such a service;

(g) persons providing public telecommunications services or employed for the purposes of any business of providing such a service;

(h) persons having control of the whole or any part of a telecommunication system located wholly or partly in the United Kingdom.

(3) Those matters are –

(a) the existence and contents of the warrant and of any section 8(4) certificate in relation to the warrant;

(b) the details of the issue of the warrant and of any renewal or modification of the warrant or of any such certificate;

(c) the existence and contents of any requirement to provide assistance with giving effect to the warrant;

(d) the steps taken in pursuance of the warrant or of any such requirement; and

(e) everything in the intercepted material, together with any related communications data.

(4) A person who makes a disclosure to another of anything that he is required to keep secret under this section shall be guilty of an offence and liable –

(a) on conviction on indictment, to imprisonment for a term not exceeding five years or to a fine, or to both;

(b) on summary conviction, to imprisonment for a term not exceeding six months or to a fine not exceeding the statutory maximum, or to both.

(5) In proceedings against any person for an offence under this section in respect of any disclosure, it shall be a defence for that person to show that he could not reasonably have been expected, after first becoming aware of the matter disclosed, to take steps to prevent the disclosure.

(6) In proceedings against any person for an offence under this section in respect of any disclosure, it shall be a defence for that person to show that –

(a) the disclosure was made by or to a professional legal adviser in connection with the giving, by the adviser to any client of his, of advice about the effect of provisions of this Chapter; and

(b) the person to whom or, as the case may be, by whom it was made was the client or a representative of the client.

(7) In proceedings against any person for an offence under this section in respect of any disclosure, it shall be a defence for that person to show that the disclosure was made by a legal adviser –

(a) in contemplation of, or in connection with, any legal proceedings; and

(b) for the purposes of those proceedings.

(8) Neither subsection (6) nor subsection (7) applies in the case of a disclosure made with a view to furthering any criminal purpose.

(9) In proceedings against any person for an offence under this section in respect of any disclosure, it shall be a defence for that person to show that the disclosure was confined to a disclosure made to the Interception of Communications Commissioner or authorised –

(a) by that Commissioner;

(b) by the warrant or the person to whom the warrant is or was addressed;

(c) by the terms of the requirement to provide assistance; or

(d) by section 11(9).

20 Interpretation of Chapter I

In this Chapter –

'certified', in relation to a section 8(4) certificate, means of a description certified by the certificate as a description of material the examination of which the Secretary of State considers necessary;

'external communication' means a communication sent or received outside the British Islands;

'intercepted material', in relation to an interception warrant, means the contents of any communications intercepted by an interception to which the warrant relates;

'the interception subject', in relation to an interception warrant, means the person about whose communications information is sought by the interception to which the warrant relates;

'international mutual assistance agreement' means an international agreement designated for the purposes of section 1(4);

'related communications data', in relation to a communication intercepted in the course of its transmission by means of a postal service or telecommunication system, means so much of any communications data (within the meaning of Chapter II of this Part) as –

(a) is obtained by, or in connection with, the interception; and

(b) relates to the communication or to the sender or recipient, or intended recipient, of the communication;

'section 8(4) certificate' means any certificate issued for the purposes of section 8(4).

PART II

SURVEILLANCE AND COVERT HUMAN INTELLIGENCE SOURCES

26 Conduct to which Part II applies

(1) This Part applies to the following conduct –

(a) directed surveillance;

(b) intrusive surveillance; and

(c) the conduct and use of covert human intelligence sources.

(2) Subject to subsection (6), surveillance is directed for the purposes of this Part if it is covert but not intrusive and is undertaken –

(a) for the purposes of a specific investigation or a specific operation;

(b) in such a manner as is likely to result in the obtaining of private information about a person (whether or not one specifically identified for the purposes of the investigation or operation); and

(c) otherwise than by way of an immediate response to events or circumstances the nature of which is such that it would not be reasonably practicable for an authorisation under this Part to be sought for the carrying out of the surveillance.

(3) Subject to subsections (4) to (6), surveillance is intrusive for the purposes of this Part if, and only if, it is covert surveillance that –

(a) is carried out in relation to anything taking place on any residential premises or in any private vehicle; and

(b) involves the presence of an individual on the premises or in the vehicle or is carried out by means of a surveillance device.

(4) For the purposes of this Part surveillance is not intrusive to the extent that –

(a) it is carried out by means only of a surveillance device designed or adapted principally for the purpose of providing information about the location of a vehicle; or

(b) it is surveillance consisting in any such interception of a communication as falls within section 48(4).

(5) For the purposes of this Part surveillance which –

(a) is carried out by means of a surveillance device in relation to anything taking place on any residential premises or in any private vehicle, but

(b) is carried out without that device being present on the premises or in the vehicle,

is not intrusive unless the device is such that it consistently provides information of the same quality and detail as might be expected to be obtained from a device actually present on the premises or in the vehicle.

(6) For the purposes of this Part surveillance which –

(a) is carried out by means of apparatus designed or adapted for the purpose of detecting the installation or use in any residential or other premises of a television receiver (within the meaning of Part 4 of the Communications Act 2003), and

(b) is carried out from outside those premises exclusively for that purpose,

is neither directed nor intrusive.

(7) In this Part –

(a) references to the conduct of a covert human intelligence source are references to any conduct of such a source which falls within any of paragraphs (a) to (c) of subsection (8), or is incidental to anything falling within any of those paragraphs; and

(b) references to the use of a covert human intelligence source are references to inducing, asking or assisting a person to engage in the conduct of such a source, or to obtain information by means of the conduct of such a source.

(8) For the purposes of this Part a person is a covert human intelligence source if –

(a) he establishes or maintains a personal or other relationship with a person for the covert purpose of facilitating the doing of anything falling within paragraph (b) or (c);

(b) he covertly uses such a relationship to obtain information or to provide access to any information to another person; or

(c) he covertly discloses information obtained by the use of such a relationship, or as a consequence of the existence of such a relationship.

(9) For the purposes of this section –

(a) surveillance is covert if, and only if, it is carried out in a manner that is calculated to ensure that persons who are subject to the surveillance are unaware that it is or may be taking place;

(b) a purpose is covert, in relation to the establishment or maintenance of a personal or other relationship, if and only if the relationship is conducted in a manner that is calculated to ensure that one of the parties to the relationship is unaware of the purpose; and

(c) a relationship is used covertly, and information obtained as mentioned in subsection (8)(c) is disclosed covertly, if and only if it is used or, as the case may be, disclosed in a manner that is calculated to ensure that one of the parties to the relationship is unaware of the use or disclosure in question.

(10) In this section 'private information', in relation to a person, includes any information relating to his private or family life.

(11) References in this section, in relation to a vehicle, to the presence of a surveillance device in the vehicle include references to its being located on or under the vehicle and also include references to its being attached to it.

27 Lawful surveillance, etc

(1) Conduct to which this Part applies shall be lawful for all purposes if –

(a) an authorisation under this Part confers an entitlement to engage in that conduct on the person whose conduct it is; and

(b) his conduct is in accordance with the authorisation.

(2) A person shall not be subject to any civil liability in respect of any conduct of his which –

(a) is incidental to any conduct that is lawful by virtue of subsection (1); and

(b) is not itself conduct an authorisation or warrant for which is capable of being granted under a relevant enactment and might reasonably have been expected to have been sought in the case in question.

(3) The conduct that may be authorised under this Part includes conduct outside the United Kingdom.

(4) In this section 'relevant enactment' means –

(a) an enactment contained in this Act;

(b) section 5 of the Intelligence Services Act 1994 (warrants for the intelligence services); or

(c) an enactment contained in Part III of the Police Act 1997 (powers of the police and of customs officers).

27A Authorisation of detection of television receivers

(1) Subject to the following provisions of this Part, the persons designated for the purposes of this section shall each have power to grant authorisations for the detection of television receivers, that is to say, surveillance which –

(a) is carried out by means of apparatus designed or adapted for the purpose of detecting the installation or use in any residential or other premises of a television receiver (within the meaning of section 1 of the Wireless Telegraphy Act 1949), and

(b) is carried out from outside those premises exclusively for that purpose.

(2) The persons designated for the purposes of this section are –

(a) any person holding the position of head of sales or head of marketing within the Television Licence Management Unit of the British Broadcasting Corporation, and

(b) any person holding a position within that Unit which is more senior than the positions mentioned in paragraph (a).

(3) A person shall not grant an authorisation for the detection of television receivers unless he believes –

(a) that the authorisation is necessary –

(i) for the purpose of preventing or detecting crime constituting an offence under section 1 or 1A of the Wireless Telegraphy Act 1949; or

(ii) for the purpose of assessing or collecting sums payable to the British Broadcasting Corporation under regulations made under section 2 of the Wireless Telegraphy Act 1949; and

(b) that the authorised surveillance is proportionate to what is sought to be achieved by carrying it out.

(4) The conduct that is authorised by an authorisation for the detection of television receivers is any conduct that –

(a) consists in the carrying out of the detection of television receivers, and

(b) is carried out by the persons described in the authorisation in the circumstances described in the authorisation.

28 Authorisation of directed surveillance

(1) Subject to the following provisions of this Part, the persons designated for the purposes of this section shall each have power to grant authorisations for the carrying out of directed surveillance.

(2) A person shall not grant an authorisation for the carrying out of directed surveillance unless he believes –

(a) that the authorisation is necessary on grounds falling within subsection (3); and

(b) that the authorised surveillance is proportionate to what is sought to be achieved by carrying it out.

(3) An authorisation is necessary on grounds falling within this subsection if it is necessary –

(a) in the interests of national security;

(b) for the purpose of preventing or detecting crime or of preventing disorder;

(c) in the interests of the economic well –being of the United Kingdom;

(d) in the interests of public safety;

(e) for the purpose of protecting public health;

(f) for the purpose of assessing or collecting any tax, duty, levy or other imposition, contribution or charge payable to a government department; or

(g) for any purpose (not falling within paragraphs (a) to (f)) which is specified for the purposes of this subsection by an order made by the Secretary of State.

(4) The conduct that is authorised by an authorisation for the carrying out of directed surveillance is any conduct that –

(a) consists in the carrying out of directed surveillance of any such description as is specified in the authorisation; and

(b) is carried out in the circumstances described in the authorisation and for the purposes of the investigation or operation specified or described in the authorisation.

(5) The Secretary of State shall not make an order under subsection (3)(g) unless a draft of the order has been laid before Parliament and approved by a resolution of each House.

29 Authorisation of covert human intelligence sources

(1) Subject to the following provisions of this Part, the persons designated for the purposes of this section shall each have power to grant authorisations for the conduct or the use of a covert human intelligence source.

(2) A person shall not grant an authorisation for the conduct or the use of a covert human intelligence source unless he believes –

(a) that the authorisation is necessary on grounds falling within subsection (3);

(b) that the authorised conduct or use is proportionate to what is sought to be achieved by that conduct or use; and

(c) that arrangements exist for the source's case that satisfy the requirements of subsection (5) and such other requirements as may be imposed by order made by the Secretary of State.

(3) An authorisation is necessary on grounds falling within this subsection if it is necessary –

(a) in the interests of national security;

(b) for the purpose of preventing or detecting crime or of preventing disorder;

(c) in the interests of the economic well-being of the United Kingdom;

(d) in the interests of public safety;

(e) for the purpose of protecting public health;

(f) for the purpose of assessing or collecting any tax, duty, levy or other imposition, contribution or charge payable to a government department; or

(g) for any purpose (not falling within paragraphs (a) to (f)) which is specified for the purposes of this subsection by an order made by the Secretary of State.

(4) The conduct that is authorised by an authorisation for the conduct or the use of a covert human intelligence source is any conduct that –

(a) is comprised in any such activities involving conduct of a covert human intelligence source, or the use of a covert human intelligence source, as are specified or described in the authorisation;

(b) consists in conduct by or in relation to the person who is so specified or described as the person to whose actions as a covert human intelligence source the authorisation relates; and

(c) is carried out for the purposes of, or in connection with, the investigation or operation so specified or described.

(5) For the purposes of this Part there are arrangements for the source's case that satisfy the requirements of this subsection if such arrangements are in force as are necessary for ensuring –

(a) that there will at all times be a person holding an office, rank or position with the relevant investigating authority who will have day-to-day responsibility for dealing with the source on behalf of that authority, and for the source's security and welfare;

(b) that there will at all times be another person holding an office, rank or position with the relevant investigating authority who will have general oversight of the use made of the source;

(c) that there will at all times be a person holding an office, rank or position with the relevant investigating authority who will have responsibility for maintaining a record of the use made of the source;

(d) that the records relating to the source that are maintained by the relevant investigating authority will always contain particulars of all such matters (if any) as may be specified for the purposes of this paragraph in regulations made by the Secretary of State; and

(e) that records maintained by the relevant investigating authority that disclose the identity of the source will not be available to persons except to the extent that there is a need for access to them to be made available to those persons.

(6) The Secretary of State shall not make an order under subsection (3)(g) unless a draft of the order has been laid before Parliament and approved by a resolution of each House.

(7) The Secretary of State may by order –

(a) prohibit the authorisation under this section of any such conduct or uses of covert human intelligence sources as may be described in the order; and

(b) impose requirements, in addition to those provided for by subsection (2), that must be satisfied before an authorisation is granted under this section for any such conduct or uses of covert human intelligence sources as may be so described.

(8) In this section 'relevant investigating authority', in relation to an authorisation for the conduct or the use of an individual as a covert human intelligence source, means (subject to subsection (9)) the public authority for whose benefit the activities of that individual as such a source are to take place.

(9) In the case of any authorisation for the conduct or the use of a covert human intelligence source whose activities are to be for the benefit of more than one public authority, the references in subsection (5) to the relevant investigating authority are references to one of them (whether or not the same one in the case of each reference).

30 Persons entitled to grant authorisations under ss28 and 29

(1) Subject to subsection (3), the persons designated for the purposes of sections 28 and 29 are the individuals holding such offices, ranks or positions with relevant public authorities as are prescribed for the purposes of this subsection by an order under this section.

(2) For the purposes of the grant of an authorisation that combines –

(a) an authorisation under section 28 or 29, and

(b) an authorisation by the Secretary of State for the carrying out of intrusive surveillance,

the Secretary of State himself shall be a person designated for the purposes of that section.

(3) An order under this section may impose restrictions –

(a) on the authorisations under sections 28 and 29 that may be granted by any individual holding an office, rank or position with a specified public authority; and

(b) on the circumstances in which, or the purposes for which, such authorisations may be granted by any such individual.

(4) A public authority is a relevant public authority for the purposes of this section –

(a) in relation to section 28 if it is specified in Part I or II of Schedule 1; and

(b) in relation to section 29 if it is specified in Part I of that Schedule.

(5) An order under this section may amend Schedule 1 by –

(a) adding a public authority to Part I or II of that Schedule;

(b) removing a public authority from that Schedule;

(c) moving a public authority from one Part of that Schedule to the other;

(d) making any change consequential on any change in the name of a public authority specified in that Schedule.

(6) Without prejudice to section 31, the power to make an order under this section shall be exercisable by the Secretary of State.

(7) The Secretary of State shall not make an order under subsection (5) containing any provision for –

(a) adding any public authority to Part I or II of that Schedule, or

(b) moving any public authority from Part II to Part I of that Schedule,

unless a draft of the order has been laid before Parliament and approved by a resolution of each House.

32 Authorisation of intrusive surveillance

(1) Subject to the following provisions of this Part, the Secretary of State and each of the senior authorising officers shall have power to grant authorisations for the carrying out of intrusive surveillance.

(2) Neither the Secretary of State nor any senior authorising officer shall grant an authorisation for the carrying out of intrusive surveillance unless he believes –

(a) that the authorisation is necessary on grounds falling within subsection (3); and

(b) that the authorised surveillance is proportionate to what is sought to be achieved by carrying it out.

(3) Subject to the following provisions of this section, an authorisation is necessary on grounds falling within this subsection if it is necessary –

(a) in the interests of national security;

(b) for the purpose of preventing or detecting serious crime; or

(c) in the interests of the economic well-being of the United Kingdom.

(3A) In the case of an authorisation granted by the chairman of the OFT, the authorisation is necessary on grounds falling within subsection (3) only if it is necessary for the purpose of preventing or detecting an offence under section 188 of the Enterprise Act 2002 (cartel offence).

(4) The matters to be taken into account in considering whether the requirements of subsection (2) are satisfied in the case of any authorisation shall include whether the information which it is thought necessary to obtain by the authorised conduct could reasonably be obtained by other means.

(5) The conduct that is authorised by an authorisation for the carrying out of intrusive surveillance is any conduct that –

(a) consists in the carrying out of intrusive surveillance of any such description as is specified in the authorisation;

(b) is carried out in relation to the residential premises specified or described in the authorisation or in relation to the private vehicle so specified or described; and

(c) is carried out for the purposes of, or in connection with, the investigation or operation so specified or described.

(6) For the purposes of this section the senior authorising officers are –

(a) the chief constable of every police force maintained under section 2 of the Police Act 1996 (police forces in England and Wales outside London);

(b) the Commissioner of Police of the Metropolis and every Assistant Commissioner of Police of the Metropolis;

(c) the Commissioner of Police for the City of London; ...

(f) the Chief Constable of the Ministry of Defence Police;

(g) the Provost Marshal of the Royal Navy Regulating Branch;

(h) the Provost Marshal of the Royal Military Police;

(i) the Provost Marshal of the Royal Air Force Police;

(j) the Chief Constable of the British Transport Police;

(k) the Director General of the National Criminal Intelligence Service;

(l) the Director General of the National Crime Squad and any person holding the rank of assistant chief constable in that Squad who is designated for the purposes of this paragraph by that Director General;

(m) any customs officer designated for the purposes of this paragraph by the Commissioners of Customs and Excise; and

(n) the chairman of the OFT.

33 Rules for grant of authorisations

(1) A person who is a designated person for the purposes of section 28 or 29 by reference to his office, rank or position with a police force, the National Criminal Intelligence Service or the National Crime Squad shall not grant an authorisation under that section except on an application made by a member of the same force, Service or Squad.

(2) A person who is designated for the purposes of section 28 or 29 by reference to his office, rank or position with the Commissioners of Customs and Excise shall not grant an authorisation under that section except on an application made by a customs officer.

(3) A person who is a senior authorising officer by reference to a police force, the National Criminal Intelligence Service or the National Crime Squad shall not grant an authorisation for the carrying out of intrusive surveillance except –

(a) on an application made by a member of the same force, Service or Squad; and

(b) in the case of an authorisation for the carrying out of intrusive surveillance in relation to any residential premises, where those premises are in the area of operation of that force, Service or Squad.

(4) A person who is a senior authorising officer by virtue of a designation by the Commissioners of Customs and Excise shall not grant an authorisation for the carrying out of intrusive surveillance except on an application made by a customs officer.

(4A) The chairman of the OFT shall not grant an authorisation for the carrying out of intrusive surveillance except on an application made by an officer of the OFT.

(5) A single authorisation may combine both –

(a) an authorisation granted under this Part by, or on the application of, an individual who is a member of a police force, the National Criminal Intelligence Service or the National Crime Squad, or who is a customs officer or the chairman or an officer of the OFT; and

(b) an authorisation given by, or on the application of, that individual under Part III of the Police Act 1997;

but the provisions of this Act or that Act that are applicable in the case of each of the authorisations shall apply separately in relation to the part of the combined authorisation to which they are applicable.

(6) For the purposes of this section –

(a) the area of operation of a police force maintained under section 2 of the Police Act 1996, of the metropolitan police force, of the City of London police force ... is the area for which that force is maintained;...

(c) residential premises are in the area of operation of the Ministry of Defence Police if they are premises where the members of that police force, under section 2 of the Ministry of Defence Police Act 1987, have the powers and privileges of a constable;

(d) residential premises are in the area of operation of the Royal Navy Regulating Branch, the Royal Military Police or the Royal Air Force Police if they are premises owned or occupied by, or used for residential purposes by, a person subject to service discipline;

(e) the area of operation of the British Transport Police and also of the National Criminal Intelligence Service is the United Kingdom;

(f) the area of operation of the National Crime Squad is England and Wales;

and references in this section to the United Kingdom or to any part or area of the United Kingdom include any adjacent waters within the seaward limits of the territorial waters of the United Kingdom.

(7) For the purposes of this section a person is subject to service discipline –

(a) in relation to the Royal Navy Regulating Branch, if he is subject to the Naval Discipline Act 1957 or is a civilian to whom Parts I and II of that Act for the time being apply by virtue of section 118 of that Act ;

(b) in relation to the Royal Military Police, if he is subject to military law or is a civilian to whom Part II of the Army Act 1955 for the time being applies by virtue of section 209 of that Act; and

(c) in relation to the Royal Air Force Police, if he is subject to air-force law or is a civilian to whom Part II of the Air Force Act 1955 for the time being applies by virtue of section 209 of that Act.

34 Grant of authorisations in the senior officer's absence

(1) This section applies in the case of an application for an authorisation for the carrying out of intrusive surveillance where –

(a) the application is one made by a member of a police force, of the National Criminal Intelligence Service or of the National Crime Squad or by an officer of the OFT or a customs officer; and

(b) the case is urgent.

(2) If –

(a) it is not reasonably practicable, having regard to the urgency of the case, for the application to be considered by any person who is a senior authorising officer by reference to the force, Service or Squad in question or, as the case may be, as chairman of the OFT or by virtue of a designation by the Commissioners of Customs and Excise, and

(b) it also not reasonably practicable, having regard to the urgency of the case, for the application to be considered by a person (if there is one) who is entitled, as a designated deputy of a senior authorising officer, to exercise the functions in relation to that application of such an officer,

the application may be made to and considered by any person who is entitled under subsection (4) to act for any senior authorising officer who would have been entitled to consider the application.

(3) A person who considers an application under subsection (1) shall have the same power to grant an authorisation as the person for whom he is entitled to act.

(4) For the purposes of this section –

(a) a person is entitled to act for the chief constable of a police force maintained under section 2 of the Police Act 1996 if he holds the rank of assistant chief constable in that force;

(b) a person is entitled to act for the Commissioner of Police of the Metropolis, or for an Assistant Commissioner of Police of the Metropolis, if he holds the rank of commander in the metropolitan police force;

(c) a person is entitled to act for the Commissioner of Police for the City of London if he holds the rank of commander in the City of London police force;

…

(f) a person is entitled to act for the Chief Constable of the Ministry of Defence Police if he holds the rank of deputy or assistant chief constable in that force;

(g) a person is entitled to act for the Provost Marshal of the Royal Navy Regulating Branch if he holds the position of assistant Provost Marshal in that Branch;

(h) a person is entitled to act for the Provost Marshal of the Royal Military Police or the Provost Marshal of the Royal Air Force Police if he holds the position of deputy Provost Marshal in the police force in question;

(i) a person is entitled to act for the Chief Constable of the British Transport Police if he holds the rank of deputy or assistant chief constable in that force;

(j) a person is entitled to act for the Director General of the National Criminal Intelligence Service if he is a person designated for the purposes of this paragraph by that Director General;

(k) a person is entitled to act for the Director General of the National Crime Squad if he is designated for the purposes of this paragraph by that Director General as a person entitled so to act in an urgent case;

(l) a person is entitled to act for a person who is a senior authorising officer by virtue of a designation by the Commissioners of Customs and Excise, if he is designated for the purposes of this paragraph by those Commissioners as a person entitled so to act in an urgent case;

(m) a person is entitled to act for the chairman of the OFT if he is an officer of the OFT designated by it for the purposes of this paragraph as a person entitled so to act in an urgent case.

(5) A police member of the National Criminal Intelligence Service or the National Crime Squad appointed under section 9(1)(b) or 55(1)(b) of the Police Act 1997 (police members) may not be designated under subsection (4)(j) or (k) unless he holds the rank of assistant chief constable in that Service or Squad.

(6) In this section 'designated deputy' –

(a) in relation to a chief constable, means a person holding the rank of assistant chief constable who is designated to act under section 12(4) of the Police Act 1996 ...;

(b) in relation to the Commissioner of Police for the City of London, means a person authorised to act under section 25 of the City of London Police Act 1839;

(c) in relation to the Director General of the National Criminal Intelligence Service or the Director General of the National Crime Squad, means a person designated to act under section 8 or, as the case may be, section 54 of the Police Act 1997.

35 Notification of authorisations for intrusive surveillance

(1) Where a person grants or cancels a police. customs or OFT authorisation for the carrying out of intrusive surveillance, he shall give notice that he has done so to an ordinary Surveillance Commissioner.

(2) A notice given for the purposes of subsection (1) –

(a) must be given in writing as soon as reasonably practicable after the grant or, as the case may be, cancellation of the authorisation to which it relates;

(b) must be given in accordance with any such arrangements made for the purposes of this paragraph by the Chief Surveillance Commissioner as are for the time being in force; and

(c) must specify such matters as the Secretary of State may by order prescribe.

(3) A notice under this section of the grant of an authorisation shall, as the case may be, either –

(a) state that the approval of a Surveillance Commissioner is required by section 36 before the grant of the authorisation will take effect; or

(b) state that the case is one of urgency and set out the grounds on which the case is believed to be one of urgency.

(4) Where a notice for the purposes of subsection (1) of the grant of an authorisation has been received by an ordinary Surveillance Commissioner, he shall, as soon as practicable –

(a) scrutinise the authorisation; and

(b) in a case where notice has been given in accordance with subsection (3)(a), decide whether or not to approve the authorisation.

(5) Subject to subsection (6), the Secretary of State shall not make an order under subsection (2)(c) unless a draft of the order has been laid before Parliament and approved by a resolution of each House.

(6) Subsection (5) does not apply in the case of the order made on the first occasion on which the Secretary of State exercises his power to make an order under subsection (2)(c).

(7) The order made on that occasion shall cease to have effect at the end of the period of forty days beginning with the day on which it was made unless, before the end of that period, it has been approved by a resolution of each House of Parliament.

(8) For the purposes of subsection (7) –

(a) the order's ceasing to have effect shall be without prejudice to anything previously done or to the making of a new order; and

(b) in reckoning the period of forty days no account shall be taken of any period during which Parliament is dissolved or prorogued or during which both Houses are adjourned for more than four days.

(9) Any notice that is required by any provision of this section to be given in writing may be given, instead, by being transmitted by electronic means.

(10) In this section references to a police, customs or OFT authorisation are references to an authorisation granted by –

(a) a person who is a senior authorising officer by reference to a police force, the National Criminal Intelligence Service or the National Crime Squad;

(b) a person who is a senior authorising officer by virtue of a designation by the Commissioners of Customs and Excise;

(ba) the chairman of the OFT; or

(c) a person who for the purposes of section 34 is entitled to act for a person falling within paragraph (a) or for a person falling within paragraph (b) or for a person falling within paragraph (ba).

36 Approval required for authorisations to take effect

(1) This section applies where an authorisation for the carrying out of intrusive surveillance has been granted on the application of –

(a) a member of a police force;

(b) a member of the National Criminal Intelligence Service;

(c) a member of the National Crime Squad;

(d) a customs officer; or

(e) an officer of the OFT.

(2) Subject to subsection (3), the authorisation shall not take effect until such time (if any) as –

(a) the grant of the authorisation has been approved by an ordinary Surveillance Commissioner; and

(b) written notice of the Commissioner's decision to approve the grant of the authorisation has been given, in accordance with subsection (4), to the person who granted the authorisation.

(3) Where the person who grants the authorisation –

(a) believes that the case is one of urgency, and

(b) gives notice in accordance with section 35(3)(b),

subsection (2) shall not apply to the authorisation, and the authorisation shall have effect from the time of its grant.

(4) Where subsection (2) applies to the authorisation –

(a) a Surveillance Commissioner shall give his approval under this section to the authorisation if, and only if, he is satisfied that there are reasonable grounds for believing that the requirements of section 32(2)(a) and (b) are satisfied in the case of the authorisation; and

(b) a Surveillance Commissioner who makes a decision as to whether or not the authorisation should be approved shall, as soon as reasonably practicable after making that decision, give written notice of his decision to the person who granted the authorisation.

(5) If an ordinary Surveillance Commissioner decides not to approve an authorisation to which subsection (2) applies, he shall make a report of his findings to the most senior relevant person.

(6) In this section 'the most senior relevant person' means –

(a) where the authorisation was granted by the senior authorising officer with any police force who is not someone's deputy, that senior authorising officer;

(b) where the authorisation was granted by the Director General of the National Criminal Intelligence Service or the Director General of the National Crime Squad, that Director General;

(c) where the authorisation was granted by a senior authorising officer with a police force who is someone's deputy, the senior authorising officer whose deputy granted the authorisation;

(d) where the authorisation was granted by the designated deputy of the Director General of the National Criminal Intelligence Service or a person entitled to act for him by virtue of section 34(4)(j), that Director General;

(e) where the authorisation was granted by the designated deputy of the Director General of the National Crime Squad or by a person designated by that Director General for the purposes of section 32(6)(l) or 34(4)(k), that Director General;

(f) where the authorisation was granted by a person entitled to act for a senior authorising officer under section 34(4)(a) to (i), the senior authorising officer in the force in question who is not someone's deputy;

(g) where the authorisation was granted by a customs officer, the customs officer for the time being designated for the purposes of this paragraph by a written notice given to the Chief Surveillance Commissioner by the Commissioners of Customs and Excise; and

(h) where the authorisation was granted by the chairman of the OFT or a person entitled to act for him by virtue of section 34(4)(m), that chairman.

(7) The references in subsection (6) to a person's deputy are references to the following –

(a) in relation to –

(i) a chief constable of a police force maintained under section 2 of the Police Act 1996,

(ii) the Commissioner of Police for the City of London, …

to his designated deputy;

(b) in relation to the Commissioner of Police of the Metropolis, to an Assistant Commissioner of Police of the Metropolis; …

and in this subsection and that subsection 'designated deputy' has the same meaning as in section 34.

(8) Any notice that is required by any provision of this section to be given in writing may be given, instead, by being transmitted by electronic means.

37 Quashing of police and customs authorisations, etc

(1) This section applies where an authorisation for the carrying out of intrusive surveillance has been granted on the application of –

(a) a member of a police force;

(b) a member of the National Criminal Intelligence Service;

(c) a member of the National Crime Squad;

(d) a customs officer; or

(e) an officer of the OFT.

(2) Where an ordinary Surveillance Commissioner is at any time satisfied that, at the time when the authorisation was granted or at any time when it was renewed, there were no reasonable grounds for believing that the requirements of section 32(2)(a) and (b) were satisfied, he may quash the authorisation with effect, as he thinks fit, from the time of the grant of the authorisation or from the time of any renewal of the authorisation.

(3) If an ordinary Surveillance Commissioner is satisfied at any time while the authorisation is in force that there are no longer any reasonable grounds for believing that the requirements of section 32(2)(a) and (b) are satisfied in relation to the authorisation, he may cancel the authorisation with effect from such time as appears to him to be the time from which those requirements ceased to be so satisfied.

(4) Where, in the case of any authorisation of which notice has been given in accordance with section 35(3)(b), an ordinary Surveillance Commissioner is at any time satisfied that, at the time of the grant or renewal of the authorisation to which that notice related, there were no reasonable grounds for believing that the case was one of urgency, he may quash the authorisation with effect, as he thinks fit, from the time of the grant of the authorisation or from the time of any renewal of the authorisation.

(5) Subject to subsection (7), where an ordinary Surveillance Commissioner quashes an authorisation under this section, he may order the destruction of any records relating wholly or partly to information obtained by the authorised conduct after the time from which his decision takes effect.

(6) Subject to subsection (7), where –

(a) an authorisation has ceased to have effect (otherwise than by virtue of subsection (2) or (4)), and

(b) an ordinary Surveillance Commissioner is satisfied that there was a time while the authorisation was in force when there were no reasonable grounds for believing that the requirements of section 32(2)(a) and (b) continued to be satisfied in relation to the authorisation,

he may order the destruction of any records relating, wholly or partly, to information obtained at such a time by the authorised conduct.

(7) No order shall be made under this section for the destruction of any records required for pending criminal or civil proceedings.

(8) Where an ordinary Surveillance Commissioner exercises a power conferred by this section, he shall, as soon as reasonably practicable, make a report of his exercise of that power, and of his reasons for doing so –

(a) to the most senior relevant person (within the meaning of section 36); and

(b) to the Chief Surveillance Commissioner.

(9) Where an order for the destruction of records is made under this section, the order shall not become operative until such time (if any) as –

(a) the period for appealing against the decision to make the order has expired; and

(b) any appeal brought within that period has been dismissed by the Chief Surveillance Commissioner.

(10) No notice shall be required to be given under section 35(1) in the case of a cancellation under subsection (3) of this section.

38 Appeals against decisions by Surveillance Commissioners

(1) Any senior authorising officer may appeal to the Chief Surveillance Commissioner against any of the following –

(a) any refusal of an ordinary Surveillance Commissioner to approve an authorisation for the carrying out of intrusive surveillance;

(b) any decision of such a Commissioner to quash or cancel such an authorisation;

(c) any decision of such a Commissioner to make an order under section 37 for the destruction of records.

(2) In the case of an authorisation granted by the designated deputy of a senior authorising office or by a person who for the purposes of section 34 is entitled to act for a senior authorising officer, that designated deputy or person shall also be entitled to appeal under this section.

(3) An appeal under this section must be brought within the period of seven days beginning with the day on which the refusal or decision appealed against is reported to the appellant.

(4) Subject to subsection (5), the Chief Surveillance Commissioner, on an appeal under this section, shall allow the appeal if –

(a) he is satisfied that there were reasonable grounds for believing that the requirements of section 32(2)(a) and (b) were satisfied in relation to the authorisation at the time in question; and

(b) he is not satisfied that the authorisation is one of which notice was given in accordance with section 35(3)(b) without there being any reasonable grounds for believing that the case was one of urgency.

(5) If, on an appeal falling within subsection (1)(b), the Chief Surveillance Commissioner –

(a) is satisfied that grounds exist which justify the quashing or cancellation under section 37 of the authorisation in question, but

(b) considers that the authorisation should have been quashed or cancelled from a different time from that from which it was quashed or cancelled by the ordinary Surveillance Commissioner against whose decision the appeal is brought,

he may modify that Commissioner's decision to quash or cancel the authorisation, and any related decision for the destruction of records, so as to give effect to the decision under section 37 that he considers should have been made.

(6) Where, on an appeal under this section against a decision to quash or cancel an authorisation, the Chief Surveillance Commissioner allows the appeal he shall also quash any related order for the destruction of records relating to information obtained by the authorised conduct.

(7) In this section 'designated deputy' has the same meaning as in section 34.

39 Appeals to the Chief Surveillance Commissioner: supplementary

(1) Where the Chief Surveillance Commissioner has determined an appeal under section 38, he shall give notice of his determination to both –

(a) the person by whom the appeal was brought; and

(b) the ordinary Surveillance Commissioner whose decision was appealed against.

(2) Where the determination of the Chief Surveillance Commissioner on an appeal under section 38 is a determination to dismiss the appeal, the Chief Surveillance Commissioner shall make a report of his findings –

(a) to the persons mentioned in subsection (1); and

(b) to the Prime Minister.

(3) Subsections (3) and (4) of section 107 of the Police Act 1997 (reports to be laid before Parliament and exclusion of matters from the report) apply in relation to any report to the Prime Minister under subsection (2) of this section as they apply in relation to any report under subsection (2) of that section.

(4) Subject to subsection (2) of this section, the Chief Surveillance Commissioner shall not give any reasons for any determination of his on an appeal under section 38.

40 Information to be provided to Surveillance Commissioners

It shall be the duty of –

(a) every member of a police force,

(b) every member of the National Criminal Intelligence Service,

(c) every member of the National Crime Squad,

(d) every customs officer, and

(e) every officer of the OFT,

to comply with any request of a Surveillance Commissioner for documents or information required by that Commissioner for the purpose of enabling him to carry out the functions of such a Commissioner under sections 35 to 39.

41 Secretary of State authorisations

(1) The Secretary of State shall not grant an authorisation for the carrying out of intrusive surveillance except on an application made by –

(a) a member of any of the intelligence services;

(b) an official of the Ministry of Defence;

(c) a member of Her Majesty's forces;

(d) an individual holding an office, rank or position with any such public authority as may be designated for the purposes of this section as an authority whose activities may require the carrying out of intrusive surveillance.

(2) Section 32 shall have effect in relation to the grant of an authorisation by the Secretary of State on the application of an official of the Ministry of Defence, or of a member of Her Majesty's forces, as if the only matters mentioned in subsection (3) of that section were –

(a) the interests of national security; and

(b) the purpose of preventing or detecting serious crime.

(3) The designation of any public authority for the purposes of this section shall be by order made by the Secretary of State.

(4) The Secretary of State may by order provide, in relation to any public authority, that an application for an authorisation for the carrying out of intrusive surveillance may be made by an individual holding an office, rank or position with that authority only where his office, rank or position is one prescribed by the order.

(5) The Secretary of State may by order impose restrictions –

(a) on the authorisations for the carrying out of intrusive surveillance that may be granted on the application of an individual holding an office, rank or position with any public authority designated for the purposes of this section; and

(b) on the circumstances in which, or the purposes for which, such authorisations may be granted on such an application.

(6) The Secretary of State shall not make a designation under subsection (3) unless a draft of the order containing the designation has been laid before Parliament and approved by a resolution of each House.

(7) References in this section to a member of Her Majesty's forces do not include references to any member of Her Majesty's forces who is a member of a police force by virtue of his service with the Royal Navy Regulating Branch, the Royal Military Police or the Royal Air Force Police.

42 Intelligence services authorisations

(1) The grant by the Secretary of State on the application of a member of one of the intelligence services of any authorisation under this Part must be made by the issue of a warrant.

(2) A single warrant issued by the Secretary of State may combine both –

(a) an authorisation under this Part; and

(b) an intelligence services warrant;

but the provisions of this Act or the Intelligence Services Act 1994 that are applicable in the case of the authorisation under this Part or the intelligence services warrant shall apply separately in relation to the part of the combined warrant to which they are applicable.

(3) Intrusive surveillance in relation to any premises or vehicle in the British Islands shall be capable of being authorised by a warrant issued under this Part

on the application of a member of the Secret Intelligence Service or GCHQ only if the authorisation contained in the warrant is one satisfying the requirements of section 32(2)(a) otherwise than in connection with any functions of that intelligence service in support of the prevention or detection of serious crime.

(4) Subject to subsection (5), the functions of the Security Service shall include acting on behalf of the Secret Intelligence Service or GCHQ in relation to –

(a) the application for and grant of any authorisation under this Part in connection with any matter within the functions of the Secret Intelligence Service or GCHQ; and

(b) the carrying out, in connection with any such matter, of any conduct authorised by such an authorisation.

(5) Nothing in subsection (4) shall authorise the doing of anything by one intelligence service on behalf of another unless –

(a) it is something which either the other service or a member of the other service has power to do; and

(b) it is done otherwise than in connection with functions of the other service in support of the prevention or detection of serious crime.

(6) In this section 'intelligence services warrant' means a warrant under section 5 of the Intelligence Services Act 1994.

43 General rules about grant, renewal and duration

(1) An authorisation under this Part –

(a) may be granted or renewed orally in any urgent case in which the entitlement to act of the person granting or renewing it is not confined to urgent cases; and

(b) in any other case, must be in writing.

(2) A single authorisation may combine two or more different authorisations under this Part; but the provisions of this Act that are applicable in the case of each of the authorisations shall apply separately in relation to the part of the combined authorisation to which they are applicable.

(3) Subject to subsections (4) and (8), an authorisation under this Part shall cease to have effect at the end of the following period –

(a) in the case of an authorisation which –

(i) has not been renewed and was granted either orally or by a person whose entitlement to act is confined to urgent cases, or

(ii) was last renewed either orally or by such a person,

the period of seventy–two hours beginning with the time when the grant of the authorisation or, as the case may be, its latest renewal takes effect;

(b) in a case not falling within paragraph (a) in which the authorisation is for the conduct or the use of a covert human intelligence source, the period of twelve months beginning with the day on which the grant of the authorisation or, as the case may be, its latest renewal takes effect; and

(c) in any case not falling within paragraph (a) or (b), the period of three months beginning with the day on which the grant of the authorisation or, as the case may be, its latest renewal takes effect.

(4) Subject to subsection (6), an authorisation under this Part may be renewed, at any time before the time at which it ceases to have effect, by any person who would be entitled to grant a new authorisation in the same terms.

(5) Sections 28 to 41 shall have effect in relation to the renewal of an authorisation under this Part as if references to the grant of an authorisation included references to its renewal.

(6) A person shall not renew an authorisation for the conduct or the use of a covert human intelligence source, unless he –

(a) is satisfied that a review has been carried out of the matters mentioned in subsection (7); and

(b) has, for the purpose of deciding whether he should renew the authorisation, considered the results of that review.

(7) The matters mentioned in subsection (6) are –

(a) the use made of the source in the period since the grant or, as the case may be, latest renewal of the authorisation; and

(b) the tasks given to the source during that period and the information obtained from the conduct or the use of the source.

(8) The Secretary of State may by order provide in relation to authorisations of such descriptions as may be specified in the order that subsection (3) is to have effect as if the period at the end of which an authorisation of a description so specified is to cease to have effect were such period shorter than that provided for by that subsection as may be fixed by or determined in accordance with that order.

(9) References in this section to the time at which, or the day on which, the grant or renewal of an authorisation takes effect are references –

(a) in the case of the grant of an authorisation to which paragraph (c) does not apply, to the time at which or, as the case may be, day on which the authorisation is granted;

(b) in the case of the renewal of an authorisation to which paragraph (c) does not apply, to the time at which or, as the case may be, day on which the authorisation would have ceased to have effect but for the renewal; and

(c) in the case of any grant or renewal that takes effect under subsection (2) of section 36 at a time or on a day later than that given by paragraph (a) or (b), to the time at which or, as the case may be, day on which the grant or renewal takes effect in accordance with that subsection.

(10) In relation to any authorisation granted by a member of any of the intelligence services, and in relation to any authorisation contained in a warrant issued by the

Secretary of State on the application of a member of any of the intelligence services, this section has effect subject to the provisions of section 44.

44 Special rules for intelligence services authorisations

(1) Subject to subsection (2), a warrant containing an authorisation for the carrying out of intrusive surveillance –

(a) shall not be issued on the application of a member of any of the intelligence services, and

(b) if so issued shall not be renewed,

except under the hand of the Secretary of State.

(2) In an urgent case in which –

(a) an application for a warrant containing an authorisation for the carrying out of intrusive surveillance has been made by a member of any of the intelligence services, and

(b) the Secretary of State has himself expressly authorised the issue of the warrant in that case,

the warrant may be issued (but not renewed) under the hand of a senior official.

(3) Subject to subsection (6), a warrant containing an authorisation for the carrying out of intrusive surveillance which –

(a) was issued, on the application of a member of any of the intelligence services, under the hand of a senior official, and

(b) has not been renewed under the hand of the Secretary of State,

shall cease to have effect at the end of the second working day following the day of the issue of the warrant, instead of at the time provided for by section 43(3).

(4) Subject to subsections (3) and (6), where any warrant for the carrying out of intrusive surveillance which is issued or was last renewed on the application of a member of any of the intelligence services, the warrant (unless renewed or, as the case may be, renewed again) shall cease to have effect at the following time, instead of at the time provided for by section 43(3), namely –

(a) in the case of a warrant that has not been renewed, at the end of the period of six months beginning with the day on which it was issued; and

(b) in any other case, at the end of the period of six months beginning with the day on which it would have ceased to have effect if not renewed again.

(5) Subject to subsection (6), where –

(a) an authorisation for the carrying out of directed surveillance is granted by a member of any of the intelligence services, and

(b) the authorisation is renewed by an instrument endorsed under the hand of the person renewing the authorisation with a statement that the renewal is believed to be necessary on grounds falling within section 32(3)(a) or (c), the authorisation (unless renewed again) shall cease to have effect at the end of the period of six months beginning with the day on which it would have ceased to have effect but for the renewal, instead of at the time provided for by section 43(3).

(6) The Secretary of State may by order provide in relation to authorisations of such descriptions as may be specified in the order that subsection (3), (4) or (5) is to have effect as if the period at the end of which an authorisation of a description so specified is to cease to have effect were such period shorter than that provided for by that subsection as may be fixed by or determined in accordance with that order.

(7) Notwithstanding anything in section 43(2), in a case in which there is a combined warrant containing both –

(a) an authorisation for the carrying out of intrusive surveillance, and

(b) an authorisation for the carrying out of directed surveillance,

the reference in subsection (4) of this section to a warrant for the carrying out of intrusive surveillance is a reference to the warrant so far as it confers both authorisations.

45 Cancellation of authorisations

(1) The person who granted or, as the case may be, last renewed an authorisation under this Part shall cancel it if –

(a) he is satisfied that the authorisation is one in relation to which the requirements of section 28(2)(a) and (b), 29(2)(a) and (b) or, as the case may be, 32(2)(a) and (b) are no longer satisfied; or

(b) in the case of an authorisation under section 29, he is satisfied that arrangements for the source's case that satisfy the requirements mentioned in subsection (2)(c) of that section no longer exist.

(2) Where an authorisation under this Part was granted or, as the case may be, last renewed –

(a) by a person entitled to act for any other person, or

(b) by the deputy of any other person,

that other person shall cancel the authorisation if he is satisfied as to either of the matters mentioned in subsection (1).

(3) Where an authorisation under this Part was granted or, as the case may be, last renewed by a person whose deputy had power to grant it, that deputy shall cancel the authorisation if he is satisfied as to either of the matters mentioned in subsection (1).

(4) The Secretary of State may by regulations provide for the person by whom any duty imposed by this section is to be performed in a case in which it would otherwise fall on a person who is no longer available to perform it.

(5) Regulations under subsection (4) may provide for the person on whom the duty is to fall to be a person appointed in accordance with the regulations.

(6) The references in this section to a person's deputy are references to the following –

(a) in relation to –

(i) a chief constable of a police force maintained under section 2 of the Police Act 1996,

(ii) the Commissioner of Police for the City of London, ...

to his designated deputy;

(b) in relation to the Commissioner of Police of the Metropolis, to an Assistant Commissioner of Police of the Metropolis; ...

(d) in relation to the Director General of the National Criminal Intelligence Service, to his designated deputy; and

(e) in relation to the Director General of the National Crime Squad, to any person designated by him for the purposes of section 32(6)(l) or to his designated deputy.

(7) In this section designated deputy has the same meaning as in section 34.

47 Power to extend or modify authorisation provisions

(1) The Secretary of State may by order do one or both of the following –

(a) apply this Part, with such modifications as he thinks fit, to any such surveillance that is neither directed nor intrusive as may be described in the order;

(b) provide for any description of directed surveillance to be treated for the purposes of this Part as intrusive surveillance.

(2) No order shall be made under this section unless a draft of it has been laid before Parliament and approved by a resolution of each House.

48 Interpretation of Part II

(1) In this Part –

'covert human intelligence source' shall be construed in accordance with section 26(8);

'directed' and 'intrusive', in relation to surveillance, shall be construed in accordance with section 26(2) to (6);

'OFT' means the Office of Fair Trading;

'private vehicle' means (subject to subsection (7)(a)) any vehicle which is used primarily for the private purposes of the person who owns it or of a person otherwise having the right to use it;

'residential premises' means (subject to subsection (7)(b)) so much of any premises as is for the time being occupied or used by any person, however temporarily, for residential purposes or otherwise as living accommodation (including hotel or prison accommodation that is so occupied or used);

'senior authorising officer' means a person who by virtue of subsection (6) of section 32 is a senior authorising officer for the purposes of that section;

'surveillance' shall be construed in accordance with subsections (2) to (4);

'surveillance device' means any apparatus designed or adapted for use in surveillance.

(2) Subject to subsection (3), in this Part 'surveillance' includes –

(a) monitoring, observing or listening to persons, their movements, their conversations or their other activities or communications;

(b) recording anything monitored, observed or listened to in the course of surveillance; and

(c) surveillance by or with the assistance of a surveillance device.

(3) References in this Part to surveillance do not include references to –

(a) any conduct of a covert human intelligence source for obtaining or recording (whether or not using a surveillance device) any information which is disclosed in the presence of the source;

(b) the use of a covert human intelligence source for so obtaining or recording information; or

(c) any such entry on or interference with property or with wireless telegraphy as would be unlawful unless authorised under –

(i) section 5 of the Intelligence Services Act 1994 (warrants for the intelligence services); or

(ii) Part III of the Police Act 1997 (powers of the police and of customs officers).

(4) References in this Part to surveillance include references to the interception of a communication in the course of its transmission by means of a postal service or telecommunication system if, and only if –

(a) the communication is one sent by or intended for a person who has consented to the interception of communications sent by or to him; and

(b) there is no interception warrant authorising the interception.

(5) References in this Part to an individual holding an office or position with a public authority include references to any member, official or employee of that authority.

(6) For the purposes of this Part the activities of a covert human intelligence source which are to be taken as activities for the benefit of a particular public authority include any conduct of his as such a source which is in response to inducements or requests made by or on behalf of that authority.

(7) In subsection (1) –

(a) the reference to a person having the right to use a vehicle does not, in relation to a motor vehicle, include a reference to a person whose right to use the vehicle derives only from his having paid, or undertaken to pay, for the use of the vehicle and its driver for a particular journey; and

(b) the reference to premises occupied or used by any person for residential purposes or otherwise as living accommodation does not include a reference to so much of any premises as constitutes any common area to which he has or is allowed access in connection with his use or occupation of any accommodation.

(8) In this section –

'premises' includes any vehicle or moveable structure and any other place whatever, whether or not occupied as land;

'vehicle' includes any vessel, aircraft or hovercraft.

NB For modifications of this Part, including the insertion of section 27A above, as to the carrying out of surveillance to detect whether a television receiver is being used in any residential or other premises, see the Regulation of Investigatory Powers (British Broadcasting Corporation) Order 2001.

PART IV

SCRUTINY, ETC OF INVESTIGATORY POWERS AND OF THE FUNCTIONS OF THE INTELLIGENCE SERVICES

57 Interception of Communications Commissioner

(1) The Prime Minister shall appoint a Commissioner to be known as the Interception of Communications Commissioner.

(2) Subject to subsection (4), the Interception of Communications Commissioner shall keep under review –

(a) the exercise and performance by the Secretary of State of the powers and duties conferred or imposed on him by or under sections 1 to 11; ...

(d) the adequacy of the arrangements by virtue of which –

(i) the duty which is imposed on the Secretary of State by section 15 ...

are sought to be discharged.

(3) The Interception of Communications Commissioner shall give the Tribunal all such assistance (including his opinion as to any issue falling to be determined by the Tribunal) as the Tribunal may require –

(a) in connection with the investigation of any matter by the Tribunal; or

(b) otherwise for the purposes of the Tribunal's consideration or determination of any matter.

(4) It shall not be the function of the Interception of Communications Commissioner to keep under review the exercise of any power of the Secretary of State to make, amend or revoke any subordinate legislation.

(5) A person shall not be appointed under this section as the Interception of

Communications Commissioner unless he holds or has held a high judicial office (within the meaning of the Appellate Jurisdiction Act 1876).

(6) The Interception of Communications Commissioner shall hold office in accordance with the terms of his appointment; and there shall be paid to him out of money provided by Parliament such allowances as the Treasury may determine.

(7) The Secretary of State, after consultation with the Interception of Communications Commissioner, shall –

(a) make such technical facilities available to the Commissioner, and

(b) subject to the approval of the Treasury as to numbers, provide the Commissioner with such staff,

as are sufficient to secure that the Commissioner is able properly to carry out his functions.

(8) On the coming into force of this section the Commissioner holding office as the Commissioner under section 8 of the Interception of Communications Act 1985 shall take and hold office as the Interception of Communications Commissioner as if appointed under this Act –

(a) for the unexpired period of his term of office under that Act; and

(b) otherwise, on the terms of his appointment under that Act.

58 Co-operation with and reports by s57 Commissioner

(1) It shall be the duty of –

(a) every person holding office under the Crown,

(b) every member of the National Criminal Intelligence Service,

(c) every member of the National Crime Squad,

(d) every person employed by or for the purposes of a police force,

(e) every person required for the purposes of section 11 to provide assistance with giving effect to an interception warrant,

(f) every person on whom an obligation to take any steps has been imposed under section 12, ...

(j) every person who is or has been employed for the purposes of any business of a person falling within paragraph (e), (f), (h) or (i),

to disclose or provide to the Interception of Communications Commissioner all such documents and information as he may require for the purpose of enabling him to carry out his functions under section 57.

(2) If it at any time appears to the Interception of Communications Commissioner –

(a) that there has been a contravention of the provisions of this Act in relation to any matter with which that Commissioner is concerned, and

(b) that the contravention has not been the subject of a report made to the Prime Minister by the Tribunal,

he shall make a report to the Prime Minister with respect to that contravention.

(3) If it at any time appears to the Interception of Communications Commissioner that any arrangements by reference to which the duties imposed by sections 15 and 55 have sought to be discharged have proved inadequate in relation to any matter with which the Commissioner is concerned, he shall make a report to the Prime Minister with respect to those arrangements.

(4) As soon as practicable after the end of each calendar year, the Interception of Communications Commissioner shall make a report to the Prime Minister with respect to the carrying out of that Commissioner's functions.

(5) The Interception of Communications Commissioner may also, at any time, make any such other report to the Prime Minister on any matter relating to the carrying out of the Commissioner's functions as the Commissioner thinks fit.

(6) The Prime Minister shall lay before each House of Parliament a copy of every annual report made by the Interception of Communications Commissioner under subsection (4), together with a statement as to whether any matter has been excluded from that copy in pursuance of subsection (7).

(7) If it appears to the Prime Minister, after consultation with the Interception of Communications Commissioner, that the publication of any matter in an annual report would be contrary to the public interest or prejudicial to –

(a) national security,

(b) the prevention or detection of serious crime,

(c) the economic well –being of the United Kingdom, or

(d) the continued discharge of the functions of any public authority whose activities include activities that are subject to review by that Commissioner,

the Prime Minister may exclude that matter from the copy of the report as laid before each House of Parliament.

59 Intelligence Services Commissioner

(1) The Prime Minister shall appoint a Commissioner to be known as the Intelligence Services Commissioner.

(2) Subject to subsection (4), the Intelligence Services Commissioner shall keep under review, so far as they are not required to be kept under review by the Interception of Communications Commissioner –

(a) the exercise by the Secretary of State of his powers under sections 5 to 7 of the Intelligence Services Act 1994 (warrants for interference with wireless telegraphy, entry and interference with property etc);

(b) the exercise and performance by the Secretary of State, in connection with or in relation to –

(i) the activities of the intelligence services, and

(ii) the activities in places other than Northern Ireland of the officials of the Ministry of Defence and of members of Her Majesty's forces, of the powers and duties conferred or imposed on him by Parts II and III of this Act;

(c) the exercise and performance by members of the intelligence services of the powers and duties conferred or imposed on them by or under Parts II and III of this Act;

(d) the exercise and performance in places other than Northern Ireland, by officials of the Ministry of Defence and by members of Her Majesty's forces, of the powers and duties conferred or imposed on such officials or members of Her Majesty's forces by or under Parts II and III; and

(e) the adequacy of the arrangements by virtue of which the duty imposed by section 55 is sought to be discharged –

(i) in relation to the members of the intelligence services; and

(ii) in connection with any of their activities in places other than Northern Ireland, in relation to officials of the Ministry of Defence and members of Her Majesty's forces.

(3) The Intelligence Services Commissioner shall give the Tribunal all such assistance (including his opinion as to any issue falling to be determined by the Tribunal) as the Tribunal may require –

(a) in connection with the investigation of any matter by the Tribunal; or

(b) otherwise for the purposes of the Tribunal's consideration or determination of any matter.

(4) It shall not be the function of the Intelligence Services Commissioner to keep under review the exercise of any power of the Secretary of State to make, amend or revoke any subordinate legislation.

(5) A person shall not be appointed under this section as the Intelligence Services Commissioner unless he holds or has held a high judicial office (within the meaning of the Appellate Jurisdiction Act 1876).

(6) The Intelligence Services Commissioner shall hold office in accordance with the terms of his appointment; and there shall be paid to him out of money provided by Parliament such allowances as the Treasury may determine.

(7) The Secretary of State shall, after consultation with the Intelligence Services Commissioner and subject to the approval of the Treasury as to numbers, provide him with such staff as the Secretary of State considers necessary for the carrying out of the Commissioner's functions. ...

(9) On the coming into force of this section the Commissioner holding office as the Commissioner under section 8 of the Intelligence Services Act 1994 shall take and hold office as the Intelligence Services Commissioner as if appointed under this Act –

(a) for the unexpired period of his term of office under that Act; and

(b) otherwise, on the terms of his appointment under that Act.

(10) Subsection (7) of section 41 shall apply for the purposes of this section as it applies for the purposes of that section.

60 Co-operation with and reports by s59 Commissioner

(1) It shall be the duty of –

(a) every member of an intelligence service,

(b) every official of the department of the Secretary of State, and

(c) every member of Her Majesty's forces,

to disclose or provide to the Intelligence Services Commissioner all such documents and information as he may require for the purpose of enabling him to carry out his functions under section 59.

(2) As soon as practicable after the end of each calendar year, the Intelligence Services Commissioner shall make a report to the Prime Minister with respect to the carrying out of that Commissioner's functions.

(3) The Intelligence Services Commissioner may also, at any time, make any such other report to the Prime Minister on any matter relating to the carrying out of the Commissioner's functions as the Commissioner thinks fit.

(4) The Prime Minister shall lay before each House of Parliament a copy of every annual report made by the Intelligence Services Commissioner under subsection (2), together with a statement as to whether any matter has been excluded from that copy in pursuance of subsection (5).

(5) If it appears to the Prime Minister, after consultation with the Intelligence Services Commissioner, that the publication of any matter in an annual report would be contrary to the public interest or prejudicial to –

(a) national security,

(b) the prevention or detection of serious crime,

(c) the economic well –being of the United Kingdom, or

(d) the continued discharge of the functions of any public authority whose activities include activities that are subject to review by that Commissioner,

the Prime Minister may exclude that matter from the copy of the report as laid before each House of Parliament.

(6) Subsection (7) of section 41 shall apply for the purposes of this section as it applies for the purposes of that section.

62 Additional functions of Chief Surveillance Commissioner

(1) The Chief Surveillance Commissioner shall (in addition to his functions under the Police Act 1997) keep under review, so far as they are not required to be kept under review by the Interception of Communications Commissioner, the Intelligence Services Commissioner ... –

(a) the exercise and performance, by the persons on whom they are conferred or imposed, of the powers and duties conferred or imposed by or under Part II; ...

(2) It shall not by virtue of this section be the function of the Chief Surveillance Commissioner to keep under review the exercise of any power of the Secretary of State to make, amend or revoke any subordinate legislation.

(3) In this section 'judicial authority' means –

(a) any judge of the High Court or of the Crown Court or any Circuit Judge; ...
(c) any justice of the peace; ...
(e) any person holding any such judicial office as entitles him to exercise the jurisdiction of a judge of the Crown Court or of a justice of the peace.

63 Assistant Surveillance Commissioners

(1) The Prime Minister may, after consultation with the Chief Surveillance Commissioner as to numbers, appoint as Assistant Surveillance Commissioners such number of persons as the Prime Minister considers necessary (in addition to the ordinary Surveillance Commissioners) for the purpose of providing the Chief Surveillance Commissioner with assistance under this section.

(2) A person shall not be appointed as an Assistant Surveillance Commissioner unless he holds or has held office as –

(a) a judge of the Crown Court or a Circuit judge; ...

(4) The assistance that may be provided under this section includes –

(a) the conduct on behalf of the Chief Surveillance Commissioner of the review of any matter; and
(b) the making of a report to the Chief Surveillance Commissioner about the matter reviewed.

(5) Subsections (3) to (8) of section 91 of the Police Act 1997 (Commissioners) apply in relation to a person appointed under this section as they apply in relation to a person appointed under that section.

64 Delegation of Commissioners' functions

(1) Anything authorised or required by or under any enactment ... to be done by a relevant Commissioner may be done by any member of the staff of that Commissioner who is authorised for the purpose (whether generally or specifically) by that Commissioner.

(2) In this section 'relevant Commissioner' means the Interception of Communications Commissioner, the Intelligence Services Commissioner, ... or any Surveillance Commissioner or Assistant Surveillance Commissioner.

65 The Tribunal

(1) There shall, for the purpose of exercising the jurisdiction conferred on them by

this section, be a tribunal consisting of such number of members as Her Majesty may by Letters Patent appoint.

(2) The jurisdiction of the Tribunal shall be –

(a) to be the only appropriate tribunal for the purposes of section 7 of the Human Rights Act 1998 in relation to any proceedings under subsection (1)(a) of that section (proceedings for actions incompatible with Convention rights) which fall within subsection (3) of this section;

(b) to consider and determine any complaints made to them which, in accordance with subsection (4), are complaints for which the Tribunal is the appropriate forum; ...

(3) Proceedings fall within this subsection if –

(a) they are proceedings against any of the intelligence services;

(b) they are proceedings against any other person in respect of any conduct, or proposed conduct, by or on behalf of any of those services; or ...

(d) they are proceedings relating to the taking place in any challengeable circumstances of any conduct falling within subsection (5).

(4) The Tribunal is the appropriate forum for any complaint if it is a complaint by a person who is aggrieved by any conduct falling within subsection (5) which he believes –

(a) to have taken place in relation to him, to any of his property, to any communications sent by or to him, or intended for him, or to his use of any postal service, telecommunications service or telecommunication system; and

(b) to have taken place in challengeable circumstances or to have been carried out by or on behalf of any of the intelligence services.

(5) Subject to subsection (6), conduct falls within this subsection if (whenever it occurred) it is –

(a) conduct by or on behalf of any of the intelligence services;

(b) conduct for or in connection with the interception of communications in the course of their transmission by means of a postal service or telecommunication system; ...

(ca) the carrying out of surveillance by a foreign police or customs officer (within the meaning of section 76A)

(d) other conduct to which Part II applies; ...

(f) any entry on or interference with property or any interference with wireless telegraphy.

(6) For the purposes only of subsection (3), nothing mentioned in paragraph (d) or (f) of subsection (5) shall be treated as falling within that subsection unless it is conduct by or on behalf of a person holding any office, rank or position with –

(a) any of the intelligence services;

(b) any of Her Majesty's forces;

(c) any police force;

(d) the National Criminal Intelligence Service;

(e) the National Crime Squad; or

(f) the Commissioners of Customs and Excise;

and section 48(5) applies for the purposes of this subsection as it applies for the purposes of Part II.

(7) For the purposes of this section conduct takes place in challengeable circumstances if –

(a) it takes place with the authority, or purported authority, of anything falling within subsection (8); or

(b) the circumstances are such that (whether or not there is such authority) it would not have been appropriate for the conduct to take place without it, or at least without proper consideration having been given to whether such authority should be sought;

but conduct does not take place in challengeable circumstances to the extent that it is authorised by, or takes place with the permission of, a judicial authority.

(7A) For the purposes of this section conduct also takes place in challengeable circumstances if it takes place, or purports to take place, under section 76A [Foreign surveillance operations].

(8) The following fall within this subsection –

(a) an interception warrant or a warrant under the Interception of Communications Act 1985; ...

(c) an authorisation under Part II of this Act; ... or

(f) an authorisation under section 93 of the Police Act 1997.

(9) Schedule 3 (which makes further provision in relation to the Tribunal) shall have effect. ...

(11) In this section 'judicial authority' means –

(a) any judge of the High Court or of the Crown Court or any Circuit Judge; ...

(c) any justice of the peace; ...

(e) any person holding any such judicial office as entitles him to exercise the jurisdiction of a judge of the Crown Court or of a justice of the peace.

67 Exercise of the Tribunal's jurisdiction

(1) Subject to subsections (4) and (5), it shall be the duty of the Tribunal –

(a) to hear and determine any proceedings brought before them by virtue of section 65(2)(a) or (d); and

(b) to consider and determine any complaint or reference made to them by virtue of section 65(2)(b) or (c).

(2) Where the Tribunal hear any proceedings by virtue of section 65(2)(a), they shall

apply the same principles for making their determination in those proceedings as would be applied by a court on an application for judicial review.

(3) Where the Tribunal consider a complaint made to them by virtue of section 65(2)(b), it shall be the duty of the Tribunal –

(a) to investigate whether the persons against whom any allegations are made in the complaint have engaged in relation to –

(i) the complainant,

(ii) any of his property,

(iii) any communications sent by or to him, or intended for him, or

(iv) his use of any postal service, telecommunications service or telecommunication system,

in any conduct falling within section 65(5);

(b) to investigate the authority (if any) for any conduct falling within section 65(5) which they find has been so engaged in; and

(c) in relation to the Tribunal's findings from their investigations, to determine the complaint by applying the same principles as would be applied by a court on an application for judicial review.

(4) The Tribunal shall not be under any duty to hear, consider or determine any proceedings, complaint or reference if it appears to them that the bringing of the proceedings or the making of the complaint or reference is frivolous or vexatious.

(5) Except where the Tribunal, having regard to all the circumstances, are satisfied that it is equitable to do so, they shall not consider or determine any complaint made by virtue of section 65(2)(b) if it is made more than one year after the taking place of the conduct to which it relates.

(6) Subject to any provision made by rules under section 69, where any proceedings have been brought before the Tribunal or any reference made to the Tribunal, they shall have power to make such interim orders, pending their final determination, as they think fit.

(7) Subject to any provision made by rules under section 69, the Tribunal on determining any proceedings, complaint or reference shall have power to make any such award of compensation or other order as they think fit; and, without prejudice to the power to make rules under section 69(2)(h), the other orders that may be made by the Tribunal include –

(a) an order quashing or cancelling any warrant or authorisation; and

(b) an order requiring the destruction of any records of information which –

(i) has been obtained in exercise of any power conferred by a warrant or authorisation; or

(ii) is held by any public authority in relation to any person.

(8) Except to such extent as the Secretary of State may by order otherwise provide, determinations, awards, orders and other decisions of the Tribunal (including

decisions as to whether they have jurisdiction) shall not be subject to appeal or be liable to be questioned in any court. ...

(10) The provision that may be contained in an order under subsection (8) may include –

(a) provision for the establishment and membership of a tribunal or body to hear appeals;

(b) the appointment of persons to that tribunal or body and provision about the remuneration and allowances to be payable to such persons and the expenses of the tribunal;

(c) the conferring of jurisdiction to hear appeals on any existing court or tribunal; and

(d) any such provision in relation to an appeal under the order as corresponds to provision that may be made by rules under section 69 in relation to proceedings before the Tribunal, or to complaints or references made to the Tribunal.

(11) The Secretary of State shall not make an order under subsection (8) unless a draft of the order has been laid before Parliament and approved by a resolution of each House. ...

70 Abolition of jurisdiction in relation to complaints

(1) The provisions set out in subsection (2) (which provide for the investigation etc of certain complaints) shall not apply in relation to any complaint made after the coming into force of this section.

(2) Those provisions are –

(a) section 5 of, and Schedules 1 and 2 to, the Security Service Act 1989 (investigation of complaints about the Security Service made to the Tribunal established under that Act);

(b) section 9 of, and Schedules 1 and 2 to, the Intelligence Services Act 1994 (investigation of complaints about the Secret Intelligence Service or GCHQ made to the Tribunal established under that Act); and

(c) section 102 of, and Schedule 7 to, the Police Act 1997 (investigation of complaints made to the Surveillance Commissioners).

71 Issue and revision of codes of practice

(1) The Secretary of State shall issue one or more codes of practice relating to the exercise and performance of the powers and duties mentioned in subsection (2).

(2) Those powers and duties are those (excluding any power to make subordinate legislation) that are conferred or imposed otherwise than on the Surveillance Commissioners by or under –

(a) Parts I to III of this Act;

(b) section 5 of the Intelligence Services Act 1994 (warrants for interference with property or wireless telegraphy for the purposes of the intelligence services); and

(c) Part III of the Police Act 1997 (authorisation by the police or customs and excise of interference with property or wireless telegraphy). ...

72 Effect of codes of practice

(1) A person exercising or performing any power or duty in relation to which provision may be made by a code of practice under section 71 shall, in doing so, have regard to the provisions (so far as they are applicable) of every code of practice for the time being in force under that section.

(2) A failure on the part of any person to comply with any provision of a code of practice for the time being in force under section 71 shall not of itself render him liable to any criminal or civil proceedings.

(3) A code of practice in force at any time under section 71 shall be admissible in evidence in any criminal or civil proceedings.

(4) If any provision of a code of practice issued or revised under section 71 appears to –

(a) the court or tribunal conducting any civil or criminal proceedings,

(b) the Tribunal,

(c) a relevant Commissioner carrying out any of his functions under this Act,

(d) a Surveillance Commissioner carrying out his functions under this Act or the Police Act 1997, or

(e) any Assistant Surveillance Commissioner carrying out any functions of his under section 63 of this Act,

to be relevant to any question arising in the proceedings, or in connection with the exercise of that jurisdiction or the carrying out of those functions, in relation to a time when it was in force, that provision of the code shall be taken into account in determining that question.

(5) In this section 'relevant Commissioner' means the Interception of Communications Commissioner, the Intelligence Services Commissioner ...

PART V

MISCELLANEOUS AND SUPPLEMENTAL

77 Ministerial expenditure, etc

There shall be paid out of money provided by Parliament –

(a) any expenditure incurred by the Secretary of State for or in connection with the carrying out of his functions under this Act; and

(b) any increase attributable to this Act in the sums which are payable out of money so provided under any other Act.

78 Orders, regulations and rules

(1) This section applies to any power of the Secretary of State to make any order, regulations or rules under any provision of this Act.

(2) The powers to which this section applies shall be exercisable by statutory instrument.

(3) A statutory instrument which contains any order made in exercise of a power to which this section applies (other than the power to appoint a day under section 83(2)) but which contains neither –

(a) an order a draft of which has been approved for the purposes of section 12(10), 13(3), 22(9), 25(5), 28(5), 29(6), 30(7), 35(5), 41(6), 47(2), 66(3), 67(11), 71(9) or 76A(9), nor

(b) the order to which section 35(7) applies,

shall be subject to annulment in pursuance of a resolution of either House of Parliament.

(4) A statutory instrument containing any regulations made in exercise of a power to which this section applies shall be subject to annulment in pursuance of a resolution of either House of Parliament.

(5) Any order, regulations or rules made in exercise of a power to which this section applies may –

(a) make different provisions for different cases;

(b) contain such incidental, supplemental, consequential and transitional provision as the Secretary of State thinks fit.

80 General saving for lawful conduct

Nothing in any of the provisions of this Act by virtue of which conduct of any description is or may be authorised by any warrant, authorisation or notice, or by virtue of which information may be obtained in any manner, shall be construed –

(a) as making it unlawful to engage in any conduct of that description which is not otherwise unlawful under this Act and would not be unlawful apart from this Act;

(b) as otherwise requiring –

(i) the issue, grant or giving of such a warrant, authorisation or notice, or

(ii) the taking of any step for or towards obtaining the authority of such a warrant, authorisation or notice,

before any such conduct of that description is engaged in; or

(c) as prejudicing any power to obtain information by any means not involving conduct that may be authorised under this Act.

81 General interpretation

(1) In this Act –

'apparatus' includes any equipment, machinery or device and any wire or cable;

'Assistant Commissioner of Police of the Metropolis' includes the Deputy Commissioner of Police of the Metropolis;

'Assistant Surveillance Commissioner' means any person holding office under section 63;

'civil proceedings' means any proceedings in or before any court or tribunal that are not criminal proceedings;

'communication' includes –

(a) (except in the definition of 'postal service' in section 2(1)) anything transmitted by means of a postal service;
(b) anything comprising speech, music, sounds, visual images or data of any description; and
(c) signals serving either for the impartation of anything between persons, between a person and a thing or between things or for the actuation or control of any apparatus;

'criminal', in relation to any proceedings or prosecution, shall be construed in accordance with subsection (4);

'customs officer' means an officer commissioned by the Commissioners of Customs and Excise under section 6(3) of the Customs and Excise Management Act 1979;

'document' includes a map, plan, design, drawing, picture or other image;

'enactment' includes –

(a) an enactment passed after the passing of this Act; and
(b) an enactment contained in Northern Ireland legislation;

'GCHQ' has the same meaning as in the Intelligence Services Act 1994;

'Her Majesty's forces' has the same meaning as in the Army Act 1955;

'intelligence service' means the Security Service, the Secret Intelligence Service or GCHQ;

'interception' and cognate expressions shall be construed (so far as it is applicable) in accordance with section 2;

'interception warrant' means a warrant under section 5; ...

'legal proceedings' means civil or criminal proceedings in or before any court or tribunal;

'modification' includes alterations, additions and omissions, and cognate expressions shall be construed accordingly;

'ordinary Surveillance Commissioner' means a Surveillance Commissioner other than the Chief Surveillance Commissioner;

'person' includes any organisation and any association or combination of persons;

'police force' means any of the following –

(a) any police force maintained under section 2 of the Police Act 1996 (police forces in England and Wales outside London);
(b) the metropolitan police force;
(c) the City of London police force; ...
(f) the Ministry of Defence Police;
(g) the Royal Navy Regulating Branch;
(h) the Royal Military Police;
(i) the Royal Air Force Police;
(j) the British Transport Police;

'postal service' and 'public postal service' have the meanings given by section 2(1);

'private telecommunication system', 'public telecommunications service' and 'public telecommunication system' have the meanings given by section 2(1);

'public authority' means any public authority within the meaning of section 6 of the Human Rights Act 1998 (acts of public authorities) other than a court or tribunal;

'senior official' means, subject to subsection (7), a member of the Senior Civil Service or a member of the Senior Management Structure of Her Majesty's Diplomatic Service;

'statutory', in relation to any power or duty, means conferred or imposed by or under any enactment or subordinate legislation;

'subordinate legislation' means any subordinate legislation (within the meaning of the Interpretation Act 1978) or any statutory rules (within the meaning of the Statutory Rules (Northern Ireland) Order 1979);

'Surveillance Commissioner' means a Commissioner holding office under section 91 of the Police Act 1997 and 'Chief Surveillance Commissioner' shall be construed accordingly;

'telecommunication system' and 'telecommunications service' have the meanings given by section 2(1);

'the Tribunal' means the tribunal established under section 65;

'wireless telegraphy' has the same meaning as in the Wireless Telegraphy Act 1949 and, in relation to wireless telegraphy, 'interfere' has the same meaning as in that Act;

'working day' means any day other than a Saturday, a Sunday, Christmas Day, Good Friday or a day which is a bank holiday under the Banking and Financial Dealings Act 1971 in any part of the United Kingdom.

(2) In this Act –

(a) references to crime are references to conduct which constitutes one or more criminal offences or is, or corresponds to, any conduct which, if it all took place in any one part of the United Kingdom would constitute one or more criminal offences; and

(b) references to serious crime are references to crime that satisfies the test in subsection (3)(a) or (b).

(3) Those tests are –

(a) that the offence or one of the offences that is or would be constituted by the conduct is an offence for which a person who has attained the age of twenty –one and has no previous convictions could reasonably be expected to be sentenced to imprisonment for a term of three years or more;

(b) that the conduct involves the use of violence, results in substantial financial gain or is conduct by a large number of persons in pursuit of a common purpose.

(4) In this Act 'criminal proceedings' includes –

(a) proceedings in the United Kingdom or elsewhere before –

(i) a court –martial constituted under the Army Act 1955, the Air Force Act 1955 or the Naval Discipline Act 1957;

(b) proceedings before the Courts –Martial Appeal Court; and

(c) proceedings before a Standing Civilian Court;

and references in this Act to criminal prosecutions shall be construed accordingly.

(5) For the purposes of this Act detecting crime shall be taken to include –

(a) establishing by whom, for what purpose, by what means and generally in what circumstances any crime was committed; and

(b) the apprehension of the person by whom any crime was committed;

and any reference in this Act to preventing or detecting serious crime shall be construed accordingly, except that, in Chapter I of Part I, it shall not include a reference to gathering evidence for use in any legal proceedings.

(6) In this Act –

(a) references to a person holding office under the Crown include references to any servant of the Crown and to any member of Her Majesty's forces; and

(b) references to a member of a police force, in relation to the Royal Navy Regulating Branch, the Royal Military Police or the Royal Air Force Police, do not include references to any member of that Branch or Force who is not for the time being attached to or serving either with the Branch or Force of which he is a member or with another of those police forces.

(7) If it appears to the Secretary of State that it is necessary to do so in consequence of any changes to the structure or grading of the home civil service or diplomatic service, he may by order make such amendments of the definition of 'senior official'

in subsection (1) as appear to him appropriate to preserve, so far as practicable, the effect of that definition.

82 Amendments, repeals and savings, etc ...

(3) For the avoidance of doubt it is hereby declared that nothing in this Act affects any power conferred on a postal operator (within the meaning of the Postal Services Act 2000) by or under any enactment to open, detain or delay and postal packet or to deliver any such packet to a person other than the person to whom it is addressed.

(4) Where any warrant under the Interception of Communications Act 1985 is in force under that Act at the time when the repeal by this Act of section 2 of that Act comes into force, the conduct authorised by that warrant shall be deemed for the period which –

(a) begins with that time, and

(b) ends with the time when that warrant would (without being renewed) have ceased to have effect under that Act,

as if it were conduct authorised by an interception warrant issued in accordance with the requirements of Chapter I of Part I of this Act.

(5) In relation to any such warrant, any certificate issued for the purposes of section 3(2) of the Interception of Communications Act 1985 shall have effect in relation to that period as if it were a certificate issued for the purposes of section 8(4) of this Act.

(6) Sections 15 and 16 of this Act shall have effect as if references to interception warrants and to section 8(4) certificates included references, respectively, to warrants under section 2 of the Interception of Communications Act 1985 and to certificates under section 3(2) of that Act; and references in sections 15 and 16 of this Act to intercepted or certified material shall be construed accordingly.

SCHEDULE 1

RELEVANT PUBLIC AUTHORITIES

PART I

RELEVANT AUTHORITIES FOR THE PURPOSES OF SS28 AND 29

Police forces etc

1. Any police force.

1A. The United Kingdom Atomic Energy Authority Constabulary.

2. The National Criminal Intelligence Service.

3. The National Crime Squad.

4. The Serious Fraud Office.

The intelligence services

5. Any of the intelligence services.

The armed forces

6. Any of Her Majesty's forces.

The revenue departments

7. The Commissioners of Customs and Excise.

8. The Commissioners of Inland Revenue.

Government departments

10. The Ministry of Defence.

12. The Department of Health.

13. The Home Office.

13A. The Northern Ireland Office.

15. The Department of Trade and Industry.

The Department for Environment, Food and Rural Affairs.

The Department for Transport.

The Office of the Deputy Prime Minister.

The Department for Work and Pensions.

The National Assembly for Wales

16. The National Assembly for Wales.

Local authorities

17. Any county council or district council in England, a London borough council, the Common Council of the City of London in its capacity as a local authority, the Council of the Isles of Scilly, and any county council or county borough council in Wales.

17A. Any fire authority within the meaning of the Fire Services Act 1947 (read with paragraph 2 of Schedule 11 to the Local Government Act 1985).

Other bodies

17B. The Charity Commission.

18. The Environment Agency.

19. The Financial Services Authority.

20. The Food Standards Agency.

20A. The Gaming Board for Great Britain.

20B. The Office of Fair Trading.

20C. The Office of the Police Ombudsman for Northern Ireland.

20D. The Postal Services Commission.

23. A universal service provider (within the meaning of the Postal Services Act 2000) acting in connection with the provision of a universal postal service (within the meaning of that Act).

23A. The Office of Communications. ...

PART II

RELEVANT AUTHORITIES FOR THE PURPOSES ONLY OF S28

The Health and Safety Executive

24. The Health and Safety Executive.

NHS bodies in England and Wales

25. A Health Authority established under section 8 of the National Health Service Act 1977.

26. A Special Health Authority established under section 11 of the National Health Service Act 1977.

27. A National Heath Service trust established under section 5 of the National Health Service and Community Care Act 1990.

27A. Local Health Boards in Wales established under section 6 of the National Health Service Reform and Health Care Professions Act 2002.

Her Majesty's Chief Inspector of Schools in England

27B. Her Majesty's Chief Inspector of Schools in England.

The Information Commissioner

27C. The Information Commissioner.

The Royal Parks Constabulary

27D. The Royal Parks Constabulary.

The Royal Pharmaceutical Society of Great Britain

28. The Royal Pharmaceutical Society of Great Britain. …

SCHEDULE 3

THE TRIBUNAL

1. – (1) A person shall not be appointed as a member of the Tribunal unless he is –

(a) a person who holds or has held a high judicial office (within the meaning of the Appellate Jurisdiction Act 1876);

(b) a person who has a ten year general qualification, within the meaning of section 71 of the Courts and Legal Services Act 1990;

(c) an advocate or solicitor in Scotland of at least ten years' standing; or

(d) a member of the Bar of Northern Ireland or solicitor of the Supreme Court of Northern Ireland of at least ten years' standing.

(2) Subject to the following provisions of this paragraph, the members of the Tribunal shall hold office during good behaviour.

(3) A member of the Tribunal shall vacate office at the end of the period of five years beginning with the day of his appointment, but shall be eligible for reappointment.

(4) A member of the Tribunal may be relieved of office by Her Majesty at his own request.

(5) A member of the Tribunal may be removed from office by Her Majesty on an Address presented to Her by both Houses of Parliament.

(6) If the Scottish Parliament passes a resolution calling for the removal of a member of the Tribunal, it shall be the duty of the Secretary of State to secure that a motion for the presentation of an Address to Her Majesty for the removal of that member, and the resolution of the Scottish Parliament, are considered by each House of Parliament.

2. – (1) Her Majesty may by Letters Patent appoint as President or Vice-President of the Tribunal a person who is, or by virtue of those Letters will be, a member of the Tribunal.

(2) A person shall not be appointed President of the Tribunal unless he holds or has held a high judicial office (within the meaning of the Appellate Jurisdiction Act 1876).

(3) If at any time –

(a) the President of the Tribunal is temporarily unable to carry out any functions conferred on him by this Schedule or any rules under section 69, or

(b) the office of President of the Tribunal is for the time being vacant,

the Vice-President shall carry out those functions.

(4) A person shall cease to be President or Vice-President of the Tribunal if he ceases to be a member of the Tribunal.

3. – (1) The President of the Tribunal shall designate one or more members of the Tribunal as the member or members having responsibilities in relation to matters involving the intelligence services.

(2) It shall be the duty of the President of the Tribunal, in exercising any power conferred on him by rules under section 69 to allocate the members of the Tribunal who are to consider or hear any complaint, proceedings, reference or preliminary or incidental matter, to exercise that power in a case in which the complaint, proceedings or reference relates to, or to a matter involving –

(a) an allegation against any of the intelligence services or any member of any of those services, or

(b) conduct by or on behalf of any of those services or any member of any of those services,

in such manner as secures that the allocated members consist of, or include, one or more of the members for the time being designated under sub-paragraph (1). ...

As amended by the Postal Services Act 2000 (Consequential Modifications No 1) Order 2001, arts 3(1), (2), 4(8), (11), Schedule 1, para 135(1)–(3); Regulation of Investigatory Powers (British Broadcasting Corporation) Order 2001, art 3; Armed Forces Act 2001, s38, Schedule 7, Pt 1; Enterprise Act 2002, s199(1)–(9), (11), 278(2), Schedule 26; Communications Act 2003, s406(1), (7), Schedule 17, para 161(1)–(3), Schedule 19(1); Crime (International Co-operation) Act 2003, s91(1), Schedule 5, paras 78–80. Detailed amendments were made to Schedule 1, above, by relevant statutory instruments.

POLITICAL PARTIES, ELECTIONS AND REFERENDUMS ACT 2000

(2000 c 41)

PART I

THE ELECTORAL COMMISSION

1 Establishment of the Electoral Commission

(1) There shall be a body corporate to be known as the Electoral Commission or, in Welsh, Comisiwn Etholiadol (in this Act referred to as 'the Commission').

(2) The Commission shall consist of members to be known as Electoral Commissioners.

(3) There shall be not less than five, but not more than nine, Electoral Commissioners.

(4) The Electoral Commissioners shall be appointed by Her Majesty (in accordance with section 3).

(5) Her Majesty shall (in accordance with section 3) appoint one of the Electoral Commissioners to be the chairman of the Commission.

(6) Schedule 1, which makes further provision in relation to the Commission, shall have effect.

2 Speaker's Committee

(1) There shall be a Committee (to be known as 'the Speaker's Committee') to perform the functions conferred on the Committee by this Act.

(2) The Speaker's Committee shall consist of the Speaker of the House of Commons, who shall be the chairman of the Committee, and the following other members, namely –

(a) the Member of the House of Commons who is for the time being the Chairman of the Home Affairs Select Committee of the House of Commons;

(b) the Lord Chancellor;

(c) a Member of the House of Commons who is a Minister of the Crown with responsibilities in relation to local government; and

(d) five Members of the House of Commons who are not Ministers of the Crown.

(3) The member of the Committee mentioned in subsection (2)(c) shall be appointed to membership of the Committee by the Prime Minister.

(4) The members of the Committee mentioned in subsection (2)(d) shall be appointed to membership of the Committee by the Speaker of the House of Commons.

(5) Schedule 2, which makes further provision in relation to the Speaker's Committee, shall have effect. ...

3 Appointment of Electoral Commissioners and Commission chairman

(1) The powers of Her Majesty under section 1(4) and (5) shall be exercisable on an Address from the House of Commons.

(2) No motion shall be made for such an Address except –

(a) with the agreement of the Speaker of the House of Commons; and

(b) after consultation with the registered leader of each registered party to which two or more Members of the House of Commons then belong.

(3) Such an Address shall specify the period (not exceeding 10 years) for which each proposed Electoral Commissioner to whom the Address relates is to hold office as such Commissioner or (as the case may be) the period for which the proposed chairman of the Commission is to hold office as such chairman.

(4) A person may not be appointed as an Electoral Commissioner if the person –

(a) is a member of a registered party;

(b) is an officer or employee of a registered party or of any accounting unit of such a party;

(c) holds a relevant elective office (within the meaning of Schedule 7); or

(d) has at any time within the last ten years –

(i) been such an officer or employee as is mentioned in paragraph (b), or

(ii) held such an office as is mentioned in paragraph (c), or

(iii) been named as a donor in the register of donations reported under Chapter III or V of Part IV.

(5) An Electoral Commissioner, or the chairman of the Commission, may be re-appointed (or further re-appointed). ...

4 Parliamentary Parties Panel

(1) There shall be a panel (to be known as 'the Parliamentary Parties Panel') which consists of representatives of qualifying parties appointed in accordance with this section.

(2) The function of the panel shall be to submit representations or information to the Commission about such matters affecting political parties as the panel think fit.

(3) Where the panel submit any such representations or information to the Commission, the Commission shall –

(a) consider the representations or information, and

(b) decide whether, and (if so) to what extent, they should act on the representations or information.

(4) Each qualifying party shall be entitled to be represented on the panel by a person appointed to the panel by the treasurer of the party.

(5) Subject to subsection (6), a person so appointed shall be a member of the panel for such period as the treasurer of the party may determine when making the appointment. ...

(9) In this section 'qualifying party' means a registered party –

(a) to which two or more Members of the House of Commons for the time being belong, who have made and subscribed to the oath required by the Parliamentary Oaths Act 1866 (or the corresponding affirmation) and are not disqualified from sitting or voting in the House; or

(b) to which two or more such Members belonged immediately after the most recent parliamentary general election.

5 Reports on elections and referendums

(1) The Commission shall, after –

(a) each election to which this section applies, and

(b) each referendum to which Part VII applies,

prepare and publish (in such manner as the Commission may determine) a report on the administration of the election or referendum.

(2) The elections to which this section applies are the following, namely –

(a) a parliamentary general election;

(b) a European Parliamentary general election;

(c) a Scottish Parliamentary general election;

(d) a National Assembly for Wales ordinary election;

(e) a Northern Ireland Assembly general election.

(3) After a poll held under section 36 of the Government of Wales Act 1998 the Commission shall, if requested to do so by the National Assembly for Wales, at the Assembly's expense prepare and publish (in such manner as the Commission may determine) a report on the administration of the poll.

6 Reviews of electoral and political matters

(1) The Commission shall keep under review, and from time to time submit reports to the Secretary of State on, the following matters, namely –

(a) such matters relating to elections to which this section applies as the Commission may determine from time to time;

(b) such matters relating to referendums to which this section applies as the Commission may so determine;

(c) the redistribution of seats at parliamentary elections;

(d) if any functions are transferred by an order under section 18(1), 19(1) or 20(1), the matters in relation to which those functions are exercisable;

(e) the registration of political parties and the regulation of their income and expenditure;

(f) political advertising in the broadcast and other electronic media;

(g) the law relating to the matters mentioned in each of paragraphs (a) to (f).

(2) At the request of the Secretary of State, and within such time as the Secretary of State may specify, the Commission shall –

(a) review, and

(b) submit a report to the Secretary of State on,

such matter or matters (whether or not falling within subsection (1)) as the Secretary of State may specify. ...

(5) Each report made by the Commission under this section shall be published by them in such manner as they may determine.

(6) The elections and referendums to which this section applies are –

(a) in the case of elections –

(i) the elections mentioned in section 5(2),

(ii) local government elections in England or Wales, and ...

(b) in the case of referendums, referendums to which Part VII applies and those under Part II of the Local Government Act 2000.

7 Commission to be consulted on changes to electoral law

(1) Before making an instrument to which this section applies, the authority making the instrument shall consult the Commission.

(2) This section applies to an instrument containing – ...

(c) an order under section 24(1)(c), (cc) or (e), 25(1)(b), 28(1)(b) or 35(2B) of the Representation of the People Act 1983 (designations of returning officers and acting returning officers); ...

(f) an order under section 11 or 36(4) or (5) of the Government of Wales Act 1998 (conduct of elections to the National Assembly for Wales and of polls held by the Assembly); ...

(i) an order under section 17A(3) of the Greater London Authority Act 1999 (free delivery of election addresses at elections to the Greater London Authority). ...

8 Powers with respect to elections exercisable only on Commission recommendation

(1) The function of giving directions under section 52(1) of the Representation of the People Act 1983 (directions as to discharge of registration duties) shall be exercisable only on, and in accordance with, a recommendation of the Commission. ...

10 Giving of advice and assistance

(1) The Commission may, at the request of any relevant body, provide the body with advice and assistance as respects any matter in which the Commission have skill and experience.

(2) The assistance which may be so provided includes (in particular) the secondment of members of the Commission's staff. ...

(6) In this section 'relevant body' means – ...

(c) the National assembly for Wales; ...

(f) any of the following local authorities –

(i) in England, the council of a county, district or London borough,

(ii) in Wales, the council of a county or county borough, ...

12 Policy development grants

(1) For the purposes of this section –

(a) 'a policy development grant' is a grant to a represented registered party to assist the party with the development of policies for inclusion in any manifesto on the basis of which –

(i) candidates authorised to stand by the party will seek to be elected at an election which is a relevant election for the purposes of Part II, or

(ii) the party itself will seek to be so elected (in the case of such an election for which the party itself may be nominated); and

(b) a registered party is 'represented' if there are at least two Members of the House of Commons belonging to the party who –

(i) have made and subscribed the oath required by the Parliamentary Oaths Act 1866 (or the corresponding affirmation), and

(ii) are not disqualified from sitting or voting in that House.

(2) The Commission shall submit recommendations to the Secretary of State for the terms of a scheme for the making by the Commission of policy development grants.

(3) Where the Secretary of State receives recommendations under subsection (2), he shall make an order setting out such a scheme in terms which, with any modifications he considers appropriate, give effect to the recommendations. ...

13 Education about electoral and democratic systems

(1) The Commission shall promote public awareness of –

(a) current electoral systems in the United Kingdom and any pending such systems, together with such matters connected with any such existing or pending systems as the Commission may determine;

(b) current systems of local government and national government in the United Kingdom and any pending such systems; and

(c) the institutions of the European Union. ...

(2) For the purposes of subsection (1) any system such as is mentioned in paragraph (a) or (b) of that subsection is pending at a time when arrangements for giving effect to it have been made by any enactment but the arrangements are not yet in force.

(3) Subsection (1) does not apply in relation to local government elections ... but in paragraph (b) of that subsection the reference to national government includes (in addition to the government of the United Kingdom) the government of parts of the United Kingdom for which there are devolved legislatures. ...

14 Boundary committees

(1) The Commission shall establish four Boundary Committees, one for each of England, Scotland, Wales and Northern Ireland.

(2) Each Boundary Committee shall consist of –

(a) a chairman, and

(b) not less than the appropriate number of other members,

appointed by the Commission.

(3) For the purposes of subsection (2) 'the appropriate number', in relation to a Boundary Committee, is –

(a) two, if no functions fall to be exercised by the Committee by virtue of section 18(1), section 19(1) or section 20(1) (as the case may be); and

(b) four, if any functions fall to be so exercised.

(4) Only an Electoral Commissioner or a deputy Electoral Commissioner may be appointed a member of a Boundary Committee; and only an Electoral Commissioner may be appointed chairman of a Boundary Committee.

(5) The Commission shall, where any functions fall to be exercised by a Boundary Committee as mentioned in subsection (3), so exercise their powers of appointment under this section and section 15 as to secure –

(a) that at least one of the members of the Committee is a person with experience of local government matters in England, Scotland or Wales (as the case may be); and

(b) that, in the case of the Boundary Committee for Wales, at least one of the members of the Committee is a person able to speak the Welsh language.

(6) The following persons shall be assessors to the Boundary Committees –

(a) in the case of each of the Boundary Committee for England and the Boundary Committee for Wales, the Registrar General for England and Wales and the Director General of Ordnance Survey; ...

15 Deputy Electoral Commissioners

(1) The Commission may appoint Deputy Electoral Commissioners.

(2) The number of Deputy Electoral Commissioners shall not exceed such number as the Commission, with the agreement of the Speaker's Committee, may determine.

(3) A person shall not be appointed as a Deputy Electoral Commissioner if he is a person who (by virtue of section 3(4)) may not be appointed as an Electoral Commissioner.

(4) The functions of a Deputy Electoral Commissioner are limited to serving as a member of any Boundary Committee to which he is appointed.

(5) Schedule 1 contains further provisions about Deputy Electoral Commissioners.

16 Transfer of functions of Boundary Commissions ...

(3) A Boundary Commission shall cease to exist at such time as the Secretary of State, being satisfied that they have no further functions to perform, by order directs. ...

18 Transfer of functions of Local Government Commission for England

(1) The Secretary of State may by order make provision for and in connection with transferring (to any extent) to –

(a) the Commission, or
(b) the Boundary Committee for England,

any of the functions of the Local Government Commission for England ...

20 Transfer of functions of Local Government Boundary Commission for Wales

(1) The National Assembly for Wales may by order make provision for and in connection with transferring (to any extent) to –

(a) the Commission, or
(b) the Boundary Committee for Wales,

any of the functions of the Local Government Boundary Commission for Wales ...

PART II
REGISTRATION OF POLITICAL PARTIES

22 Parties to be registered in order to field candidates at elections

(1) Subject to subsection (4), no nomination may be made in relation to a relevant election unless the nomination is in respect of –

(a) a person who stands for election in the name of a qualifying registered party; or

(b) a person who does not purport to represent any party; or

(c) a qualifying registered party, where the election is one for which registered parties may be nominated.

(2) For the purposes of subsection (1) a party (other than a minor party) is a 'qualifying registered party' in relation to a relevant election if –

(a) the constituency, local government area or electoral region in which the election is held –

(i) is in England, Scotland or Wales, or

(ii) is the electoral region of Scotland or Wales,

and the party was, on the last day for publication of notice of the election, registered in respect of that part of Great Britain in the Great Britain register maintained by the Commission under section 23 ...

(3) For the purposes of subsection (1) a person does not purport to represent any party if either –

(a) the description of the candidate given in his nomination paper, is –

(i) 'Independent', or

(ii) where the candidate is the Speaker of the House of Commons seeking re-election, 'The Speaker seeking re-election'; or

(b) no description of the candidate is given in his nomination paper.

(4) Subsection (1) does not apply in relation to any parish or community election.

(5) The following elections are relevant elections for the purposes of this Part –

(a) parliamentary elections,

(b) elections to the European Parliament,

(c) elections to the Scottish Parliament,

(d) elections to the National Assembly for Wales,

(e) elections to the Northern Ireland Assembly,

(f) local government elections, and

(g) local elections in Northern Ireland.

(6) For the purposes of this Act a person stands for election in the name of a

registered party if his nomination paper includes a description authorised by a certificate issued by or on behalf of the registered nominating officer of the party.

23 The new registers

(1) In place of the register of political parties maintained by the registrar of companies under the Registration of Political Parties Act 1998, there shall be the new registers of political parties mentioned in subsection (2) which –

(a) shall be maintained by the Commission, and

(b) (subject to the provisions of this section) shall be so maintained in such form as the Commission may determine.

(2) The new registers of political parties are –

(a) a register of parties that intend to contest relevant elections in one or more of England, Scotland and Wales (referred to in this Act as 'the Great Britain register'); and

(b) a register of parties that intend to contest relevant elections in Northern Ireland (referred to in this Act as 'the Northern Ireland register').

(3) Each party registered in the Great Britain register shall be so registered in respect of one or more of England, Scotland and Wales; and the entry for each party so registered shall be marked so as to indicate –

(a) the part or parts of Great Britain in respect of which it is registered; and

(b) if the party is a minor party, that it is such a party.

(4) A party may be registered under this Part in both of the new registers, but where a party is so registered –

(a) the party as registered in the Great Britain register, and

(b) the party as registered in the Northern Ireland register,

shall constitute two separate registered parties.

(5) In such a case –

(a) the party shall for the purposes of this Act be so organised and administered as to secure that the financial affairs of the party in Great Britain are conducted separately from those of the party in Northern Ireland ...

24 Office-holders to be registered

(1) For each registered party there shall be –

(a) a person registered as the party's leader;

(b) a person registered as the party's nominating officer; and

(c) a person registered as the party's treasurer;

but the person registered as leader may also be registered as nominating officer or treasurer (or both).

(2) The person registered as a party's leader must be –

(a) the overall leader of the party; or

(b) where there is no overall leader of the party, a person who is the leader of the party for some particular purpose.

(3) The person registered as a party's nominating officer must have responsibility for the arrangements for –

(a) the submission by representatives of the party of lists of candidates for the purpose of elections;

(b) the issuing of such certificates as are mentioned in section 22(6); and

(c) the approval of descriptions and emblems used on nomination and ballot papers at elections.

(4) The person registered as a party's treasurer shall be responsible for compliance on the part of the party –

(a) with the provisions of Parts III and IV (accounting requirements and control of donations), and

(b) unless a person is registered as the party's campaigns officer in accordance with section 25, with the provisions of Parts V to VII (campaign expenditure, third party expenditure and referendums) as well. ...

25 Parties with campaigns officers

(1) In the case of any registered party a person –

(a) may be registered as the party's campaigns officer, and

(b) may be so registered whether or not he is also registered as the party's leader or nominating officer (or both).

(2) The person registered as a party's campaign officer shall be responsible for compliance on the part of the party with the provisions of Parts V to VII. ...

26 Financial structure of registered party: adoption of scheme

(1) A party may not be registered unless it has adopted a scheme which –

(a) sets out the arrangements for regulating the financial affairs of the party for the purposes of this Act; and

(b) has been approved in writing by the Commission.

(2) The scheme must in particular determine for the purposes of this Act whether the party is to be taken to consist of –

(a) a single organisation with no division of responsibility for the financial affairs and transactions of the party for the purposes of Part III (accounting requirements), or

(b) a central organisation and one or more separate accounting units, that is to say constituent or affiliated organisations each of which is to be responsible for its own financial affairs and transactions for the purposes of that Part.

(3) In the latter case the scheme must –

(a) identify, by reference to organisations mentioned in the party's constitution, those which are to constitute the central organisation and the accounting units respectively; and

(b) give the name of each of those organisations.

(4) The scheme must in every case include such other information as may be prescribed by regulations made by the Commission. …

28 Registration of parties

(1) A party may apply to be registered under this Part by sending to the Commission an application which –

(a) complies with the requirements of Part I of Schedule 4, and

(b) is accompanied by a declaration falling within subsection (2).

(2) The declarations falling within this subsection are –

(a) a declaration that the party –

(i) intends to contest one or more relevant elections in Great Britain and one or more such elections in Northern Ireland, and

(ii) is accordingly applying to be registered (as two such separate parties as are mentioned in section 23(4)) in both the Great Britain register and the Northern Ireland register;

(b) a declaration that the party –

(i) intends to contest one or more relevant elections (which will not be confined to one or more parish or community elections) in Great Britain only, and

(ii) is accordingly applying to be registered in the Great Britain register only;

(c) a declaration that the party –

(i) intends to contest one or more relevant elections in Northern Ireland only, and

(ii) is accordingly applying to be registered in the Northern Ireland register only;

(d) a declaration that the party –

(i) intends only to contest one or more parish or community elections, and

(ii) is accordingly applying to be registered in the Great Britain register only.

…

(8) Where the Commission grant an application by a party under this section, they shall include in the party's entry in the register –

(a) the particulars, apart from home addresses, given in the application in accordance with paragraphs 2 to 4, 5(2) and 6 of Schedule 4;

(b) the date of registration. …

(9) Where the Commission refuse an application by a party under this section, they shall notify the party of their reasons for refusing the application. …

29 Emblems

(1) A party's application under section 28 may include a request for the registration of up to three emblems to be used by the party on ballot papers.

(2) Where a request is made by a party under this section in relation to an emblem, the Commission shall register the emblem as an emblem of the party unless in their opinion it –

(a) would either –

(i) be the same as a registered emblem of a party which is already registered in the register in which that party is applying to be registered, or

(ii) be likely to be confused by voters with a registered emblem of a party which is already registered in respect of the relevant part of the United Kingdom,

(b) is obscene or offensive,

(c) is of such a character that its publication would be likely to amount to the commission of an offence, or

(d) includes a word or expression prohibited [by order of the Secretary of State after consulting the Commission] by virtue of section 28(4)(f). …

31 Notification of changes in party's officers, etc

(1) If at any time any particulars in a party's entry in the register which relate to any relevant matter cease to be accurate, the person registered as treasurer of the party must give the Commission a notification under this section.

(2) For the purposes of this section 'relevant matter' means any of the following –

(a) the name of any registered officer of the party;

(b) the home address of any such officer;

(c) the address of the party's headquarters (or, if it has no headquarters, the address to which communications to the party may be sent);

(d) the name of the treasurer of any accounting unit of the party or of any officer of such a unit registered for the purposes of section 27(3);

(e) the name of any accounting unit of the party;

(f) the address of the headquarters of any accounting unit of the party (or, if it has no headquarters, the address to which communications to the accounting unit may be sent). …

32 Confirmation of registered particulars, etc

(1) The person registered as treasurer of a party must, at the time when the

statement of accounts for any financial year of the party is sent to the Commission under Part III, give a notification under this section to the Commission.

(2) A notification under this section must –

(a) state that the particulars in the party's entry in the register remain accurate and include any information prescribed under paragraph 6 of Schedule 4 since the relevant time, or

(b) so far as necessary to secure that such particulars will both be accurate and include any information so prescribed, contain one or more of the following, namely –

(i) an application under section 30,

(ii) a notification under section 31, or

(iii) any information so prescribed.

(3) A notification under this section must also give particulars of any change occurring in the party's constitution (within the meaning of section 26) since the relevant time.

(4) In subsections (2) and (3) 'the relevant time' means –

(a) the time when the party applied for registration, or

(b) if a notification has been previously given under this section in relation to the party, the time when the last such notification was given. …

33 Party ceasing to be registered

(1) Once a party is registered its entry may only be removed from the register in accordance with subsection (2).

(2) Where –

(a) a party applies to have its entry removed from the register, and

(b) the application includes a declaration on behalf of the party that it does not intend to have any candidates at any relevant election,

the Commission shall remove the party's entry from the register.

(3) On the removal of the party's entry from the register the party shall cease to be a registered party. …

34 Registration of minor parties

(1) This section applies to any party registered in the Great Britain register in pursuance of a declaration falling within section 28(2)(d) (referred to in this Act as a 'minor party').

(2) The following provisions do not apply to a minor party –

(a) any provisions of this Part so far as relating to the registration of a treasurer or campaigns officer for a registered party or otherwise referring to a registered treasurer or campaigns officer (or any deputy campaigns officer);

(b) sections 26 and 27; and

(c) section 36;

but this is subject to subsection (8)(a).

(3) The registered leader of a minor party must, in the case of each anniversary of the party's inclusion in the register, give a notification under this subsection to the Commission within the period beginning one month before the anniversary and ending three months after it.

(4) A notification under subsection (3) must –

(a) state that the particulars in the party's entry in the register remain accurate and include any information prescribed under paragraph 6 of Schedule 4 since the relevant time, or

(b) so far as necessary to secure that such particulars will both be accurate and include any information so prescribed, contain one or more of the following, namely –

(i) an application under section 30,

(ii) a notification under section 31, or

(iii) any information so prescribed. …

36 Assistance by Commission for existing registered parties

(1) The Commission may, in accordance with a scheme prepared by them for the purposes of this section, provide assistance for existing parties with a view to helping them to meet, or to reducing, the expenses falling to be initially incurred by them in order to comply with Parts III and IV.

(2) The assistance which may be so provided to an existing party may take the form of –

(a) a grant to the party, or

(b) the provision of non-financial benefits to the party (such as the provision of computer software free of charge),

or both, as the scheme may determine. …

(7) In this section 'existing party' means any party registered under the Registration of Political Parties Act 1998 at the commencement of this section.

37 Party political broadcasts

(1) A broadcaster shall not include in its broadcasting services any party political broadcast made on behalf of a party which is not a registered party.

(2) In this Act 'broadcaster' means –

(a) the holder of a licence under the Broadcasting Act 1990 or 1996 ,

(b) the British Broadcasting Corporation, or

(c) Sianel Pedwar Cymru. …

40 Interpretation of Part II

(1) In this Part –

'the appointed day' means the day appointed under section 163(2) for the coming into force of section 23;

'financial year', in relation to a registered party, shall be construed in accordance with section 41(6);

'parish or community election' means an election of councillors for a parish in England or a community in Wales;

'party' includes any organisation or person;

'the register' shall be construed in accordance with section 28(10);

'registered' (unless the context otherwise requires) means registered under this Part (whether in the Great Britain or the Northern Ireland register), and other references to registration shall be construed accordingly;

'the registrar of companies' means the registrar or other officer who performs the duty of registering companies under the Companies Act 1985;

'relevant election' shall be construed in accordance with section 22(5).

(2) For the purposes of this Part a registered party contests an election –

(a) by one or more candidates standing for election in the party's name at the election, or

(b) by the party itself standing nominated at the election. ...

41 Duty to keep accounting records

(1) The treasurer of a registered party must ensure that accounting records are kept with respect to the party which are sufficient to show and explain the party's transactions. ...

42 Annual statements of accounts

(1) The treasurer of a registered party shall prepare a statement of accounts in respect of each financial year of the party.

(2) A statement of accounts under this section must –

(a) comply with such requirements as to its form and contents as may be prescribed by regulations made by the Commission; and

(b) be approved –

(i) by the management committee of the party, if there is one, and

(ii) otherwise by the registered leader of the party. ...

43 Annual audits

(1) Where a registered party's gross income or total expenditure in any financial year exceeds £250,000, the accounts of the party for that year must be audited by a qualified auditor.

(2) Where –

(a) a registered party's gross income or total expenditure in any financial year does not exceed £250,000, but

(b) the Commission consider it desirable that the accounts of the party for that year should be audited,

the Commission may (at any time) give the treasurer of the party a direction requiring those accounts to be audited by a qualified auditor. …

44 Supplementary provisions about auditors

(1) An auditor appointed to carry out an audit under section 43 –

(a) has a right of access at all reasonable times to the party's books, documents and other records; and

(b) is entitled to require from the treasurer or any other officer of the party, or from any former treasurer or officer of the party, such information and explanations as he thinks necessary for the performance of his duty as auditor.

(2) If any person fails to provide an auditor with any access, information or explanation to which the auditor is entitled by virtue of subsection (1), the Commission may give that person such written directions as they consider appropriate for securing that the default is made good. …

45 Delivery of statements of accounts, etc to Commission

(1) The treasurer of a registered party shall, if the party's accounts for a financial year are not required to be audited by virtue of section 43(1) or (2), within 3 months of the end of that financial year deliver to the Commission –

(a) the statement of accounts prepared for that year under section 42; and

(b) the notification required to be sent with that statement by virtue of section 32(1).

(2) If a registered party's accounts for a financial year are required to be audited by virtue of section 43(1) or (2), the treasurer of the party shall, no later than 7 days after the end of the period allowed under section 43(3) for the audit of the accounts, deliver to the Commission –

(a) the documents mentioned in paragraphs (a) and (b) of subsection (1); and

(b) a copy of the auditor's report (unless the auditor was appointed by the Commission under section 43(4)). …

46 Public inspection of parties' statements of accounts

Where the Commission receive any statement of accounts under section 45, they shall –

(a) as soon as reasonably practicable after receiving the statement, make a copy of the statement available for public inspection; and

(b) keep any such copy available for public inspection for the period for which the statement is kept by them or, if they so determine, during such shorter period as they may specify.

48 Revision of defective statements of account

(1) If it appears to the treasurer of a registered party that any statement of accounts for any financial year of the party has not complied with any requirements of regulations under section 42(2)(a) ('the prescribed requirements'), he may prepare a revised statement of accounts. ...

PART IV

CONTROL OF DONATIONS TO REGISTERED PARTIES AND THEIR MEMBERS, ETC

CHAPTER I

DONATIONS TO REGISTERED PARTIES

50 Donations for purposes of Part IV

(1) The following provisions have effect for the purposes of this Part.

(2) 'Donation', in relation to a registered party, means (subject to section 52) –

(a) any gift to the party of money or other property;

(b) any sponsorship provided in relation to the party (as defined by section 51);

(c) any subscription or other fee paid for affiliation to, or membership of, the party;

(d) any money spent (otherwise than by or on behalf of the party) in paying any expenses incurred directly or indirectly by the party;

(e) any money lent to the party otherwise than on commercial terms;

(f) the provision otherwise than on commercial terms of any property, services or facilities for the use or benefit of the party (including the services of any person).

(3) Where –

(a) any money or other property is transferred to a registered party pursuant to any transaction or arrangement involving the provision by or on behalf of the party of any property, services or facilities or other consideration of monetary value, and

(b) the total value in monetary terms of the consideration so provided by or on behalf of the party is less than the value of the money or (as the case may be) the market value of the property transferred,

the transfer of the money or property shall (subject to subsection (5)) constitute a gift to the party for the purposes of subsection (2)(a).

(4) In determining –

(a) for the purposes of subsection (2)(e), whether any money lent to a registered party is so lent otherwise than on commercial terms, or

(b) for the purposes of subsection (2)(f), whether any property, services or facilities provided for the use or benefit of a registered party is or are so provided otherwise than on such terms,

regard shall be had to the total value in monetary terms of the consideration provided by or on behalf of the party in respect of the loan or the provision of the property, services or facilities.

(5) Where (apart from this subsection) anything would be a donation both by virtue of subsection (2)(b) and by virtue of any other provision of this section, subsection (2)(b) (together with section 51) shall apply in relation to it to the exclusion of the other provision of this section.

(6) Anything given or transferred to any officer, member, trustee or agent of a registered party in his capacity as such (and not for his own use or benefit) is to be regarded as given or transferred to the party (and references to donations received by a party accordingly include donations so given or transferred).

(7) Except so far as a contrary intention appears, references to a registered party in the context of –

(a) the making of donations to, or the receipt or acceptance of donations by, a registered party, or

(b) any provision having effect for or in connection with determining what constitutes a donation to such a party,

shall, in the case of a party with accounting units, be construed as references to the central organisation of the party or any of its accounting units.

(8) In this section –

(a) any reference to anything being given or transferred to a party or any person is a reference to its being so given or transferred either directly or indirectly through any third person;

(b) 'gift' includes bequest.

(9) Nothing in this Part applies in relation to donations received by a minor party.

51 Sponsorship

(1) For the purposes of this Part sponsorship is provided in relation to a registered party if –

(a) any money or other property is transferred to the party or to any person for the benefit of the party, and

(b) the purpose (or one of the purposes) of the transfer is (or must, having regard to all the circumstances, reasonably be assumed to be) –

(i) to help the party with meeting, or to meet, to any extent any defined expenses incurred or to be incurred by or on behalf of the party, or

(ii) to secure that to any extent any such expenses are not so incurred.

(2) In subsection (1) 'defined expenses' means expenses in connection with –

(a) any conference, meeting or other event organised by or on behalf of the party;

(b) the preparation, production or dissemination of any publication by or on behalf of the party; or

(c) any study or research organised by or on behalf of the party.

(3) The following do not, however, constitute sponsorship by virtue of subsection (1) –

(a) the making of any payment in respect of –

(i) any charge for admission to any conference, meeting or other event, or

(ii) the purchase price of, or any other charge for access to, any publication;

(b) the making of any payment in respect of the inclusion of an advertisement in any publication where the payment is made at the commercial rate payable for the inclusion of such an advertisement in any such publication;

and subsection (1) also has effect subject to section 52(3).

(4) The Secretary of State may by order made on the recommendation of the Commission amend subsection (2) or (3).

(5) In this section 'publication' means a publication made available in whatever form and by whatever means (whether or not to the public at large or any section of the public).

52 Payments, services, etc not to be regarded as donations

(1) For the purposes of this Part none of the following shall be regarded as a donation –

(a) any policy development grant (within the meaning of section 12);

(b) any grant under section 170 of the Criminal Justice and Public Order Act 1994 (security costs at party conferences);

(c) any payment made by or on behalf of the European Parliament for the purpose of assisting members of the Parliament to perform their functions as such members;

(d) the transmission by a broadcaster, free of charge, of a party political broadcast or a referendum campaign broadcast (within the meaning of section 127);

(e) any other facilities provided in pursuance of any right conferred on candidates or a party at an election or a referendum by any enactment;

(f) the provision of assistance by a person appointed under section 9 of the Local Government and Housing Act 1989;

(g) the provision by any individual of his own services which he provides voluntarily in his own time and free of charge;

(h) any interest accruing to a registered party in respect of any donation which is dealt with by the party in accordance with section 56(2)(a) or (b).

(2) For the purposes of this Part there shall be disregarded –

(a) any donation which (in accordance with any enactment) falls to be included in a return as to election expenses in respect of a candidate or candidates at a particular election; and

(b) except for the purposes of section 68, any donation whose value (as determined in accordance with section 53) is not more than £200.

(3) Nothing in section 50 or 51 shall have the result that a payment made in respect of the hire of a stand at a party conference organised by or on behalf of a registered party is to constitute a donation to the party for the purposes of this Part if or to the extent that the payment does not exceed such of the maximum rates which the Commission determine to be reasonable for the hire of stands at party conferences as is applicable to the hire of the stand in question.

53 Value of donations

(1) The value of any donation falling within section 50(2)(a) (other than money) shall be taken to be the market value of the property in question.

(2) Where, however, section 50(2)(a) applies by virtue of section 50(3), the value of the donation shall be taken to be the difference between –

(a) the value of the money, or the market value of the property, in question, and

(b) the total value in monetary terms of the consideration provided by or on behalf of the party.

(3) The value of any donation falling within section 50(2)(b) shall be taken to be the value of the money, or (as the case may be) the market value of the property, transferred as mentioned in section 51(1); and accordingly any value in monetary terms of any benefit conferred on the person providing the sponsorship in question shall be disregarded.

(4) The value of any donation falling within section 50(2)(e) or (f) shall be taken to be the amount representing the difference between –

(a) the total value in monetary terms of the consideration that would have had to be provided by or on behalf of the party in respect of the loan or the provision of the property, services or facilities if –

(i) the loan had been made, or

(ii) the property, services or facilities had been provided,

on commercial terms, and

(b) the total value in monetary terms of the consideration (if any) actually so provided by or on behalf of the party.

(5) Subsection (6) applies where a donation such as is mentioned in subsection (3) confers an enduring benefit on the party during the whole or part of –

(a) any period for which a report is to be prepared under this Part, or

(b) two or more such periods.

(6) In such a case, the amount to be recorded in any such report shall be so much of the total value of the donation (as determined in accordance with subsection (3)) as accrues during the whole or part of the period to which the report relates.

CHAPTER II

RESTRICTIONS ON DONATIONS TO REGISTERED PARTIES

54 Permissible donors

(1) A donation received by a registered party must not be accepted by the party if –

(a) the person by whom the donation would be made is not, at the time of its receipt by the party, a permissible donor; or

(b) the party is (whether because the donation is given anonymously or by reason of any deception or concealment or otherwise) unable to ascertain the identity of that person.

(2) For the purposes of this Part the following are permissible donors –

(a) an individual registered in an electoral register;

(b) a company –

(i) registered under the Companies Act 1985 or the Companies (Northern Ireland) Order 1986, and

(ii) incorporated within the United Kingdom or another member State,

which carries on business in the United Kingdom;

(c) a registered party ...;

(d) a trade union entered in the list kept under the Trade Union and Labour Relations (Consolidation) Act 1992 or the Industrial Relations (Northern Ireland) Order 1992;

(e) a building society (within the meaning of the Building Societies Act 1986);

(f) a limited liability partnership registered under the Limited Liability Partnerships Act 2000, or any corresponding enactment in force in Northern Ireland, which carries on business in the United Kingdom;

(g) a friendly society registered under the Friendly Societies Act 1974 or a society registered (or deemed to be registered) under the Industrial and

Provident Societies Act 1965 or the Industrial and Provident Societies Act (Northern Ireland) 1969; and

(h) any unincorporated association of two or more persons which does not fall within any of the preceding paragraphs but which carries on business or other activities wholly or mainly in the United Kingdom and whose main office is there. ...

(3) In relation to a donation in the form of a bequest subsection (2)(a) shall be read as referring to an individual who was, at any time within the period of five years ending with the date of his death, registered in an electoral register. ...

(4) Where any person ('the principal donor') causes an amount ('the principal donation') to be received by a registered party by way of a donation –

(a) on behalf of himself and one or more other persons, or

(b) on behalf of two or more other persons,

then for the purposes of this Part each individual contribution by a person falling within paragraph (a) or (b) of more than £200 shall be treated as if it were a separate donation received from that person. ...

55 Payments, etc which are (or are not) to be treated as donations by permissible donors

(1) The following provisions have effect for the purposes of this Part.

(2) Any payment out of public funds received by a registered party shall (subject to section 52(1)(a) and (b)) be regarded as a donation received by the party from a permissible donor.

(3) Any donation received by a registered party shall (if it would not otherwise fall to be so regarded) be regarded as a donation received by the party from a permissible donor if and to the extent that –

(a) the purpose of the donation is to meet qualifying costs incurred or to be incurred in connection with a visit by any member or officer of the party to a country or territory outside the United Kingdom, and

(b) the amount of the donation does not exceed a reasonable amount in respect of such costs.

(4) In subsection (3) 'qualifying costs', in relation to any member or officer of the party, means costs relating to that person in respect of –

(a) travelling between the United Kingdom and the country or territory in question, or

(b) travelling, accommodation or subsistence while within that country or territory.

(5) Any exempt trust donation received by a registered party shall be regarded as a donation received by the party from a permissible donor. ...

(6) But any donation received by a registered party from a trustee of any property (in his capacity as such) which is not –

(a) an exempt trust donation, or …

(b) a donation transmitted by the trustee to the party on behalf of beneficiaries under the trust who are –

(i) persons who at the time of its receipt by the party are permissible donors, or

(ii) the members of an unincorporated association which at that time is a permissible donor,

shall be regarded as a donation received by the party from a person who is not a permissible donor.

56 Acceptance or return of donations: general

(1) Where –

(a) a donation is received by a registered party, and

(b) it is not immediately decided that the party should (for whatever reason) refuse the donation,

all reasonable steps must be taken forthwith by or on behalf of the party to verify (or, so far as any of the following is not apparent, ascertain) the identity of the donor, whether he is a permissible donor, and (if that appears to be the case) all such details in respect of him as are required by virtue of paragraph 2 of Schedule 6 to be given in respect of the donor of a recordable donation.

(2) If a registered party receives a donation which it is prohibited from accepting by virtue of section 54(1), or which it is decided that the party should for any other reason refuse, then –

(a) unless the donation falls within section 54(1)(b), the donation, or a payment of an equivalent amount, must be sent back to the person who made the donation or any person appearing to be acting on his behalf,

(b) if the donation falls within that provision, the required steps (as defined by section 57(1)) must be taken in relation to the donation,

within the period of 30 days beginning with the date when the donation is received by the party.

(3) Where –

(a) subsection (2)(a) applies in relation to a donation, and

(b) the donation is not dealt with in accordance with that provision,

the party and the treasurer of the party are each guilty of an offence.

(4) Where –

(a) subsection (2)(b) applies in relation to a donation, and

(b) the donation is not dealt with in accordance with that provision,

the treasurer of the party is guilty of an offence.

(5) For the purposes of this Part a donation received by a registered party shall be taken to have been accepted by the party unless –

(a) the steps mentioned in paragraph (a) or (b) of subsection (2) are taken in relation to the donation within the period of 30 days mentioned in that subsection; and

(b) a record can be produced of the receipt of the donation and –

(i) of the return of the donation, or the equivalent amount, as mentioned in subsection (2)(a), or

(ii) of the required steps being taken in relation to the donation as mentioned in subsection (2)(b),

as the case may be.

(6) Where a donation is received by a registered party in the form of an amount paid into any account held by the party with a financial institution, it shall be taken for the purposes of this Part to have been received by the party at the time when the party is notified in the usual way of the payment into the account.

57 Return of donations where donor unidentifiable

(1) For the purposes of section 56(2)(b) the required steps are as follows –

(a) if the donation mentioned in that provision was transmitted by a person other than the donor, and the identity of that person is apparent, to return the donation to that person;

(b) if paragraph (a) does not apply but it is apparent that the donor has, in connection with the donation, used any facility provided by an identifiable financial institution, to return the donation to that institution; and

(c) in any other case, to send the donation to the Commission.

(2) In subsection (1) any reference to returning or sending a donation to any person or body includes a reference to sending a payment of an equivalent amount to that person or body.

(3) Any amount sent to the Commission in pursuance of subsection (1)(c) shall be paid by them into the Consolidated Fund.

58 Forfeiture of donations made by impermissible or unidentifiable donors

(1) This section applies to any donation received by a registered party –

(a) which, by virtue of section 54(1)(a) or (b), the party are prohibited from accepting, but

(b) which has been accepted by the party.

(2) The court may, on an application made by the Commission, order the forfeiture by the party of an amount equal to the value of the donation.

(3) The standard of proof in proceedings on an application under this section shall be that applicable to civil proceedings.

(4) An order may be made under this section whether or not proceedings are brought against any person for an offence connected with the donation.

(5) In this section 'the court' means –

(a) in relation to England and Wales, a magistrates' court; ...

and proceedings on an application under this section to the sheriff shall be civil proceedings.

59 Appeal against order under section 58

(1) Subsection (2) applies where an order ('the forfeiture order') is made under section 58 by a magistrates' court ...

(2) The registered party may, before the end of the period of 30 days beginning with the date on which the forfeiture order is made, appeal to the Crown Court ...

CHAPTER III

REPORTING OF DONATIONS TO REGISTERED PARTIES

62 Quarterly donation reports

(1) The treasurer of a registered party shall, in the case of each year, prepare a report under this subsection in respect of each of the following periods –

(a) January to March;
(b) April to June;
(c) July to September;
(d) October to December.

(2) In this section –

'donation report' means a report prepared under subsection (1);

'reporting period', in relation to such a report, means the period mentioned in any of paragraphs (a) to (d) of that subsection to which the report relates.

(3) The donation reports for any year shall, in the case of each permissible donor from whom any donation is accepted by the party during that year, comply with the following provisions of this section so far as they require any such donation to be recorded in a donation report; and in those provisions any such donation is referred to, in relation to the donor and that year, as a 'relevant donation'.

(4) Where no previous relevant donation or donations has or have been required to be recorded under this subsection, a relevant donation must be recorded –

(a) if it is a donation of more than £5,000, or

(b) if, when it is added to any other relevant donation or donations, the aggregate amount of the donations is more than £5,000. ...

(6) Where any previous relevant donation or donations has or have been required to be recorded under subsection (4), a relevant donation must be recorded at the point when there has or have been accepted –

(a) since the donation or donations required to be recorded under subsection (4), or

(b) if any relevant donation or donations has or have previously been required to be recorded under this subsection, since the donation or donations last required to be so recorded,

any relevant donation or donations of an amount or aggregate amount which is more than £1,000. ...

(9) A donation report must also record every donation falling within section 54(1)(a) or (b) and dealt with during the reporting period in accordance with section 56(2).

(10) If during any reporting period –

(a) no donations have been accepted by the party which, by virtue of the preceding provisions of this section, are required to be recorded in the donation report for that period, and

(b) no donations have been dealt with as mentioned in subsection (9),

the report shall contain a statement to that effect. ...

(13) Schedule 6 has effect with respect to the information to be given in donation reports.

63 Weekly donation reports during general election periods

(1) Subject to section 64, the treasurer of a registered party shall, in the case of any general election period, prepare a report under this section in respect of each of the following periods –

(a) the period of seven days beginning with the first day of the general election period;

(b) each succeeding period of seven days falling within the general election period; and

(c) any final period of less than seven days falling within that period. ...

(3) The weekly report for any reporting period shall record each donation of more than £5,000 received during that period ...

(a) by the party (if it is not a party with accounting units); or

(b) by the central organisation of the party (if it is a party with accounting units).

(4) If during any reporting period no donations falling within subsection (3) have

been received as mentioned in that subsection, the weekly report for that period shall contain a statement to that effect.

(5) Schedule 6 has effect with respect to the information to be given in weekly reports.

(6) In this section and section 64 'general election period' means the period –

(a) beginning with the date on which Her Majesty's intention to dissolve Parliament is announced in connection with a forthcoming parliamentary general election, and

(b) ending with the date of the poll.

64 Exemptions from section 63

(1) Section 63(1) shall not apply in relation to a registered party in respect of a general election period if the party has made an exemption declaration which covers the general election in question.

(2) A registered party shall be taken to have made an exemption declaration which covers a particular general election if a declaration that the party does not intend to have any candidates at that election –

(a) is signed by the responsible officers of the party; and

(b) is sent to the Commission within the period of seven days beginning with the date mentioned in section 63(6)(a). ...

65 Submission of donation reports to Commission

(1) A donation report under section 62 shall be delivered to the Commission by the treasurer of the party in question within the period of 30 days beginning with the end of the reporting period to which it relates.

(2) A donation report under section 63 shall be delivered to the Commission by the treasurer of the party in question –

(a) within the period of 7 days beginning with the end of the reporting period to which it relates; or

(b) (if that is not possible in the case of any party to which section 63(1) applies by virtue of section 64(5)) within the period of 7 days beginning with the first day on which the party has a candidate at the election in question. ...

66 Declaration by treasurer in donation report

(1) Each donation report under section 62 or 63 must, when delivered to the Commission, be accompanied by a declaration made by the treasurer which complies with subsection (2), (3) or (4).

(2) In the case of a report under section 62 (other than one making a nil return), the declaration must state that, to the best of the treasurer's knowledge and belief –

(a) all the donations recorded in the report as having been accepted by the party are from permissible donors, and

(b) during the reporting period –

(i) no other donations required to be recorded in the report have been accepted by the party, and

(ii) no donation from any person or body other than a permissible donor has been accepted by the party.

(3) For the purposes of subsection (2) a return under section 62 makes a nil return if it contains such a statement as is mentioned in subsection (10) of that section; and in the case of such a report the declaration must state that, to the best of the treasurer's knowledge and belief –

(a) that statement is accurate; and

(b) during the reporting period no donation from any person or body other than a permissible donor has been accepted by the party.

(4) In the case of a report under section 63, the declaration must state that, to the best of the treasurer's knowledge and belief, no donations have been received by the party, or (if section 63(3)(b) applies) by its central organisation, during the reporting period which –

(a) are required to be recorded in the report, but

(b) are not so recorded.

(5) A person commits an offence if he knowingly or recklessly makes a false declaration under this section.

68 Reporting of multiple small donations

(1) This section applies where a person ('the donor') has during the course of a calendar year made small donations to a registered party whose aggregate value is more than £5,000.

(2) The donor must make a report to the Commission in respect of the donations which gives the following details –

(a) the aggregate value of the donations and the year in which they were made;

(b) the name of the registered party to whom they were made; and

(c) the full name and address of the donor (if an individual) and (in any other case) such details in respect of the donor as are required by virtue of paragraph 2 of Schedule 6 to be given in respect of the donor of a recordable donation.

(3) The report must be delivered to the Commission by 31st January in the year following that in which the donations were made. …

(6) In this section –

(a) 'small donation' means a donation whose value is not more than £200; and

(b) 'specified' means specified in the report in question.

69 Register of recordable donations

(1) The Commission shall maintain a register of all donations reported to them under this Chapter. …

PART VII

REFERENDUMS

CHAPTER I

PRELIMINARY

101 Referendums to which this Part applies

(1) Subject to the following provisions of this section, this Part applies to any referendum held throughout –

(a) the United Kingdom;

(b) one or more of England, Scotland, Wales and Northern Ireland; or

(c) any region in England specified in Schedule 1 to the Regional Development Agencies Act 1998.

(2) In this Part –

(a) 'referendum' means a referendum or other poll held, in pursuance of any provision made by or under an Act of Parliament, on one or more questions specified in or in accordance with any such provision;

(b) 'question' includes proposition (and 'answer' accordingly includes response).

(3) A poll held under section 36 of the Government of Wales Act 1998 is not, however, to be taken to be a referendum falling within subsection (2). …

104 Referendum questions

(1) Subsection (2) applies where a Bill is introduced into Parliament which –

(a) provides for the holding of a poll that would be a referendum to which this Part applies, and

(b) specifies the wording of the referendum question.

(2) The Commission shall consider the wording of the referendum question, and shall publish a statement of any views of the Commission as to the intelligibility of that question –

(a) as soon as reasonably practicable after the Bill is introduced, and

(b) in such manner as they may determine.

(3) Subsections (4) and (5) apply where the wording of the referendum question in the case of any poll that would be a referendum to which this Part applies falls to be specified in subordinate legislation within the meaning of the Interpretation Act 1978.

(4) If a draft of the instrument in question is to be laid before Parliament for approval by each House, the Secretary of State –

(a) shall consult the Commission on the wording of the referendum question before any such draft is so laid, and

(b) shall, at the time when any such draft is so laid, lay before each House a report stating any views as to the intelligibility of that question which the Commission have expressed in response to that consultation.

(5) If the instrument in question is to be subject to annulment in pursuance of a resolution of either House of Parliament, the Secretary of State –

(a) shall consult the Commission on the wording of the referendum question before making the instrument; and

(b) shall, at the time when the instrument is laid before Parliament, lay before each House a report stating any views as to the intelligibility of that question which the Commission have expressed in response to that consultation.

(6) Where any Bill, draft instrument or instrument to which subsection (2), (4) or (5) applies specifies not only the referendum question but also any statement which is to precede that question on the ballot paper at the referendum, any reference in that subsection to the referendum question shall be read as a reference to that question and that statement taken together.

(7) In this section 'the referendum question' means the question or questions to be included in the ballot paper at the referendum.

105 Permitted participants

(1) In this Part 'permitted participant', in relation to a particular referendum to which this Part applies, means –

(a) a registered party by whom a declaration has been made under section 106 in relation to the referendum; or

(b) any of the following by whom a notification has been given under section 106 in relation to the referendum, namely –

(i) any individual resident in the United Kingdom or registered in an electoral register (as defined by section 54(8)), or

(ii) any body falling within any of paragraphs (b) and (d) to (h) of section 54(2).

(2) In this Part 'responsible person' means –

(a) if the permitted participant is a registered party –

(i) the treasurer of the party, or

(ii) in the case of a minor party, the person for the time being notified to the Commission by the party in accordance with section 106(2)(b);

(b) if the permitted participant is an individual, that individual; and

(c) otherwise, the person or officer for the time being notified to the Commission by the permitted participant in accordance with section 106(4)(b)(ii).

106 Declarations and notifications for purposes of section 105

(1) For the purposes of section 105(1) a registered party makes a declaration to the Commission under this section if the party makes a declaration to the Commission which identifies –

(a) the referendum to which it relates, and

(b) the outcome or outcomes for which the party proposes to campaign. ...

(3) For the purposes of section 105(1) an individual or body gives a notification to the Commission under this section if he or it gives the Commission a notification which identifies –

(a) the referendum to which it relates, and

(b) the outcome or outcomes for which the giver of the notification proposes to campaign. ...

107 Register of declarations and notifications for purposes of section 105

(1) The Commission shall maintain a register of –

(a) all declarations made to them under section 106; and

(b) all notifications given to them under that section.

(2) The register shall be maintained by the Commission in such form as they may determine and shall contain, in the case of each such declaration or notification, all of the information supplied to the Commission in connection with it in pursuance of section 106. ...

108 Designation of organisations to whom assistance is available

(1) The Commission may, in respect of any referendum to which this Part applies, designate permitted participants as organisations to whom assistance is available in accordance with section 110.

(2) Where there are only two possible outcomes in the case of a referendum to which this Part applies, the Commission –

(a) may, in relation to each of those outcomes, designate one permitted participant as representing those campaigning for the outcome in question; but

(b) otherwise shall not make any designation in respect of the referendum.

(3) Where there are more than two possible outcomes in the case of a referendum to which this Part applies, the Secretary of State may, after consulting the Commission, by order specify the possible outcomes in relation to which permitted participants may be designated in accordance with subsection (4).

(4) In such a case the Commission –

(a) may, in relation to each of two or more outcomes specified in any such order, designate one permitted participant as representing those campaigning for the outcome in question; but

(b) otherwise shall not make any designation in respect of the referendum.

109 Applications for designation under section 108

(1) A permitted participant seeking to be designated under section 108 must make an application for the purpose to the Commission. …

110 Assistance available to designated organisations

(1) Where the Commission have made any designations under section 108 in respect of a referendum, assistance shall be available to the designated organisations in accordance with this section.

(2) The Commission shall make to each designated organisation a grant of the same amount, which shall be an amount not exceeding £600,000 determined by the Commission.

(3) A grant under subsection (2) may be made subject to such conditions as the Commission consider appropriate.

(4) Each designated organisation (or, as the case may be, persons authorised by the organisation) shall have the rights conferred by or by virtue of Schedule 12, which makes provision as to –

(a) the sending of referendum addresses free of charge;

(b) the use of rooms free of charge for holding public meetings; and

(c) referendum campaign broadcasts.

(5) In this section and Schedule 12 'designated organisation', in relation to a referendum, means a person or body designated by the Commission under section 108 in respect of that referendum.

CHAPTER IV

CONDUCT OF REFERENDUMS

128 Chief Counting Officers, and counting officers, for referendums

(1) This section has effect in relation to any referendum to which this Part applies.

(2) There shall be a Chief Counting Officer for the referendum, who … shall be –

(a) the chairman of the Commission, or

(b) if the chairman of the Commission appoints some other person to act as Chief Counting Officer for the referendum, the person so appointed.

(3) The Chief Counting Officer for the referendum shall appoint a counting officer for each relevant area in Great Britain.

(4) The local authority in the case of each such area shall place the services of their officers at the disposal of the counting officer for the area for the purpose of assisting him in the discharge of his functions. ...

129 Orders regulating conduct of referendums

(1) The Secretary of State may by order make such provision as he considers expedient for or in connection with regulating the conduct of referendums to which this Part applies. ...

PART X

MISCELLANEOUS AND GENERAL

145 General function of Commission with respect to monitoring compliance with controls imposed by the Act, etc

(1) The Commission shall have the general function of monitoring compliance with –

(a) the restrictions and other requirements imposed by or by virtue of Parts III to VII; and

(b) the restrictions and other requirements imposed by other enactments in relation to –

(i) election expenses incurred by or on behalf of candidates at elections, or

(ii) donations to such candidates or their election agents. ...

(7) In this section and sections 146 and 148 –

'election' means a relevant election for the purposes of Part II;

'election agent' includes a sub-agent.

146 Supervisory powers of Commission

(1) The Commission may by notice require the relevant person in the case of any supervised organisation or individual (or former supervised organisation or individual) –

(a) to produce, for inspection by the Commission or a person authorised by the Commission, any such books, documents or other records relating to the income and expenditure of the organisation or individual as the Commission may reasonably require for the purposes of the carrying out by them of their functions, or

(b) to furnish the Commission, or a person authorised by the Commission, with such information or explanation relating to the income and expenditure of the organisation or individual as the Commission may reasonably so require,

and to do so within such reasonable time as is specified in the notice. ...

149 Inspection of Commission's registers, etc

(1) This section applies to any register kept by the Commission under –

(a) section 23;

(b) section 69;

(c) section 89 [notifications of third parties]; or

(d) section 107.

(2) The Commission shall make a copy of the register available for public inspection during ordinary office hours, either at the Commission's offices or at some convenient place appointed by them.

(3) The Commission may make other arrangements for members of the public to have access to the contents of the register.

(4) If requested to do so by any person, the Commission shall supply him with a copy of the register or any part of it.

(5) The Commission may charge such reasonable fee as they may determine in respect of –

(a) any inspection or access allowed under subsection (2) or (3); or

(b) any copy supplied under subsection (4). ...

157 Documents for purposes of the Act

(1) Any application, notice or notification required or authorised to be made or given under this Act must be in writing.

(2) Any document required or authorised to be given or sent under this Act may be sent by post.

159A Functions of the Lord Chancellor

In this Act, except –

(a) sections 9, 18(2) and (4) and 70, and

(b) paragraph 7 of Schedule 9,

'the Secretary of State' means the Secretary of State or the Lord Chancellor.

160 General interpretation

(1) In this Act – ...

'bequest' includes any form of testamentary disposition;

'body', without more, means a body corporate or any combination of persons or other unincorporated association;

'broadcaster' has the meaning given by section 37(2);

'business' includes every trade, profession and occupation; ...

'the Commission' means the Electoral Commission;

'document' means a document in whatever form it is kept; ...

'functions' includes powers and duties; ...

'market value', in relation to any property, means the price which might reasonably be expected to be paid for the property on a sale in the open market;

'minor party' means (in accordance with section 34(1)) a party registered in the Great Britain register in pursuance of a declaration falling within section 28(2)(d); ...

'organisation' includes any body corporate and any combination of persons or other unincorporated association;

'property' includes any description of property, and references to the provision of property accordingly include the supply of goods; ...

SCHEDULE 1

THE ELECTORAL COMMISSION

1. – (1) The Commission shall not be regarded –

(a) as the servant or agent of the Crown, or

(b) as enjoying any status, immunity or privilege of the Crown.

(2) The property of the Commission shall not be regarded as property of, or property held on behalf of, the Crown.

2. The Commission may do anything (except borrow money) which is calculated to facilitate, or is incidental or conducive to, the carrying out of any of their functions.

3. – (1) Subject to the provisions of this paragraph, an Electoral Commissioner shall hold office as such Commissioner –

(a) for the period for which he is appointed, and

(b) otherwise in accordance with the terms of his appointment.

(2) The period for which an Electoral Commissioner is appointed shall be the period specified in relation to him in the address pursuant to which he is appointed.

(3) An Electoral Commissioner shall cease to hold office on the occurrence of any of the following events –

(a) he consents to being nominated as a candidate at a relevant election (within the meaning of Part II) or to being included in a registered party's list of candidates at such an election;

(b) he takes up any office or employment in or with –

(i) a registered party or any accounting unit of such a party,

(ii) a recognised third party (within the meaning of Part VI), or

(iii) a permitted participant (within the meaning of Part VII);

(c) he is named as a donor in the register of donations reported under Chapter III or V of Part IV or in any statement of donations included in a return delivered to the Commission under section 98 or 122;

(d) he becomes a member of a registered party.

(4) An Electoral Commissioner may be removed from office by Her Majesty in pursuance of an Address from the House of Commons.

(5) No motion shall be made for such an Address unless the Speaker's Committee have presented a report to the House of Commons stating that the Committee are satisfied that one or more of the following grounds is made out in the case of the Electoral Commissioner in question –

(a) he has failed to discharge the functions of his office for a continuous period of at least 3 months;

(b) he has failed to comply with the terms of his appointment;

(c) he has been convicted of a criminal offence;

(d) he is an undischarged bankrupt or his estate has been sequestrated in Scotland and he has not been discharged;

(e) he has made an arrangement or composition contract with, or has granted a trust deed for, his creditors;

(f) he is otherwise unfit to hold his office or unable to carry out its functions.

(6) A motion for such an Address shall not be made on the ground mentioned in sub-paragraph (5)(a) if more than 3 months have elapsed since the end of the period in question.

(7) An Electoral Commissioner may be relieved of his office by Her Majesty at his own request.

(8) In this paragraph 'registered party' includes, in relation to times before the appointed day for the purposes of Part II of this Act, a party registered under the Registration of Political Parties Act 1998. ...

SCHEDULE 2

THE SPEAKER'S COMMITTEE

1. – (1) The Speaker's Committee shall, at least once in each year, make to the House of Commons a report on the exercise by the Committee of their functions.

(2) For the purposes of the law of defamation the publication of any matter by the Speaker's Committee in making such a report shall be absolutely privileged.

2. – (1) In this paragraph 'appointed member' means a member of the Speaker's Committee other than –

(a) the Speaker of the House of Commons;

(b) the member who is the Chairman of the Home Affairs Committee of the House of Commons; or

(c) the member who is the Lord Chancellor.

(2) An appointed member shall cease to be a member of the Speaker's Committee if –

(a) he ceases to be a Member of the House of Commons; or

(b) another person is appointed to be a member of the Committee in his place.

(3) An appointed member may resign from the Committee at any time by giving notice to the Speaker.

(4) Subject to sub-paragraphs (2) and (3), an appointed member shall be a member of the Committee for the duration of the Parliament in which he is appointed.

(5) An appointed member may be re-appointed (or further re-appointed) to membership of the Committee. …

NB At 1 February 2005, section 6(1)(c), above, was not in force and section 14, above, was in force in England only.

As amended by the Transfer of Functions (Transport, Local Government and the Regions) Order 2002, art 20, Schedule 2, para 25(1)–(4).

HOUSE OF COMMONS (REMOVAL OF CLERGY DISQUALIFICATION) ACT 2001

(2001 c 13)

1 Removal of disqualification of clergy

(1) A person is not disqualified from being or being elected as a member of the House of Commons merely because he has been ordained or is a minister of any religious denomination.

(2) But a person is disqualified from being or being elected as a member of that House if he is a Lord Spiritual. …

CRIMINAL JUSTICE AND POLICE ACT 2001

(2001 c 16)

PART 1

PROVISIONS FOR COMBATTING CRIME AND DISORDER

CHAPTER 1

ON THE SPOT PENALTIES FOR DISORDERLY BEHAVIOUR

1 Offences leading to penalties on the spot

(1) For the purposes of this Chapter 'penalty offence' means an offence committed under any of the provisions mentioned in the first column of the following Table and described, in general terms, in the second column:

Offence creating provision	*Description of offence*
Section 12 of the Licensing Act 1872 (c 94)	Being drunk in a highway, other public place or licensed premises
Section 80 of the Explosives Act 1875 (c 17)	Throwing fireworks in a thoroughfare
Section 31 of the Fire Services Act 1947 (c 41)	Knowingly giving a false alarm to a fire brigade
Section 55 of the British Transport Commission Act 1949 (c xxix)	Trespassing on a railway
Section 56 of the British Transport Commission Act 1949 (c xxix)	Throwing stones, etc at trains or other things on railways
Section 169C(3) of the Licensing Act 1964 (c 26)	Buying or attempting to buy alcohol for consumption in a bar in licensed premises by a person under 18
Section 91 of the Criminal Justice Act 1967 (c 80)	Disorderly behaviour while drunk in a public place

Section 5(2) of the Criminal Law Act 1967 (c 58)	Wasting police time or giving false report
Section 5 of the Public Order Act 1986 (c 64)	Behaviour likely to cause harassment, alarm or distress
Section 12 of this Act	Consumption of alcohol in designated public place
Section 127(2) of the Communications Act 2003	Using public electronic communications network in order to cause annoyance, inconvenience or needless anxiety

(2) The Secretary of State may by order amend an entry in the Table or add or remove an entry. ...

2 Penalty notices

(1) A constable who has reason to believe that a person aged 16 or over has committed a penalty offence may give him a penalty notice in respect of the offence.

(2) Unless the notice is given in a police station, the constable giving it must be in uniform.

(3) At a police station, a penalty notice may be given only by an authorised constable.

(4) In this Chapter 'penalty notice' means a notice offering the opportunity, by paying a penalty in accordance with this Chapter, to discharge any liability to be convicted of the offence to which the notice relates.

(5) 'Authorised constable' means a constable authorised, on behalf of the chief officer of police for the area in which the police station is situated, to give penalty notices.

(6) The Secretary of State may by order –

(a) amend subsection (1) by substituting for the age for the time being specified in that subsection a different age which is not lower than 10, and

(b) if that different age is lower than 16, make provision as follows –

(i) where a person whose age is lower than 16 is given a penalty notice, for a parent or guardian of that person to be notified of the giving of the notice, and

(ii) for that parent or guardian to be liable to pay the penalty under the notice.

(7) The provision which may be made by virtue of subsection (6)(b) includes provision amending, or applying (with or without modifications), this Chapter or any other enactment (whenever passed or made).

(8) The power conferred by subsection (6) is exercisable by statutory instrument.

(9) No order shall be made under subsection (6) unless a draft of the order has been laid before and approved by a resolution of each House of Parliament.

3 Amount of penalty and form of penalty notice

(1) The penalty payable in respect of a penalty offence is such amount as the Secretary of State may specify by order.

(1A) The Secretary of State may specify different amounts for persons of different ages.

(2) But the Secretary of State may not specify an amount which is more than a quarter of the amount of the maximum fine for which a person is liable on conviction of the offence.

(3) A penalty notice must –

(a) be in the prescribed form;

(b) state the alleged offence;

(c) give such particulars of the circumstances alleged to constitute the offence as are necessary to provide reasonable information about it;

(d) specify the suspended enforcement period (as to which see section 5) and explain its effect;

(e) state the amount of the penalty;

(f) state the justices' chief executive to whom, and the address at which, the penalty may be paid; and

(g) inform the person to whom it is given of his right to ask to be tried for the alleged offence and explain how that right may be exercised.

(4) 'Prescribed' means prescribed by regulations made by the Secretary of State. ...

4 Effect of penalty notice

(1) This section applies if a penalty notice is given to a person ('A') under section 2.

(2) If A asks to be tried for the alleged offence, proceedings may be brought against him.

(3) Such a request must be made by a notice given by A –

(a) in the manner specified in the penalty notice; and

(b) before the end of the period of suspended enforcement (as to which see section 5).

(4) A request which is made in accordance with subsection (3) is referred to in this Chapter as a 'request to be tried'.

(5) If, by the end of the suspended enforcement period –

(a) the penalty has not been paid in accordance with this Chapter, and

(b) A has not made a request to be tried,

a sum equal to one and a half times the amount of the penalty may be registered under section 8 for enforcement against A as a fine.

5 General restriction on proceedings

(1) Proceedings for the offence to which a penalty notice relates may not be brought until the end of the period of 21 days beginning with the date on which the notice was given ('the suspended enforcement period').

(2) If the penalty is paid before the end of the suspended enforcement period, no proceedings may be brought for the offence.

(3) Subsection (1) does not apply if the person to whom the penalty notice was given has made a request to be tried.

6 Secretary of State's guidance

The Secretary of State may issue guidance –

(a) about the exercise of the discretion given to constables by this Chapter;

(b) about the issuing of penalty notices;

(c) with a view to encouraging good practice in connection with the operation of provisions of this Chapter.

7 Payment of penalty

(1) If a person to whom a penalty notice is given decides to pay the penalty, he must pay it to the justices' chief executive specified in the notice.

(2) Payment of the penalty may be made by properly addressing, pre-paying and posting a letter containing the amount of the penalty (in cash or otherwise).

(3) Subsection (4) applies if a person –

(a) claims to have made payment by that method, and

(b) shows that his letter was posted.

(4) Unless the contrary is proved, payment is to be regarded as made at the time at which the letter would be delivered in the ordinary course of post.

(5) Subsection (2) is not to be read as preventing the payment of a penalty by other means.

(6) A letter is properly addressed for the purposes of subsection (2) if it is addressed in accordance with the requirements specified in the penalty notice.

8 Registration certificates

(1) The chief officer of police may, in respect of any registrable sum, issue a certificate (a 'registration certificate') stating that the sum is registrable for enforcement against the defaulter as a fine.

(2) If that officer issues a registration certificate, he must cause it to be sent to the justices' chief executive for the petty sessions area in which the defaulter appears to that officer to reside.

(3) A registration certificate must –

(a) give particulars of the offence to which the penalty notice relates, and

(b) state the name and last known address of the defaulter and the amount of the registrable sum.

(4) 'Registrable sum' means a sum that may be registered under this section as a result of section 4(5).

(5) 'Defaulter' means the person against whom that sum may be registered.

9 Registration of sums payable in default

(1) If the justices' chief executive for a petty sessions area receives a registration certificate, he must register the registrable sum for enforcement as a fine in that area by entering it in the register of a magistrates' court acting for that area.

(2) But if it appears to him that the defaulter does not reside in that area –

(a) subsection (1) does not apply to him; but

(b) he must cause the certificate to be sent to the person appearing to him to be the appropriate justices' chief executive.

(3) A justices' chief executive registering a sum under this section for enforcement as a fine, must give the defaulter notice of the registration.

(4) The notice must –

(a) specify the amount of the sum registered, and

(b) give the information with respect to the offence, and the authority for registration, which was included in the registration certificate under section 8.

(5) If a sum is registered in a magistrates' court as a result of this section, any enactment referring (in whatever terms) to a fine imposed, or other sum adjudged to be paid, on conviction by such a court applies as if the registered sum were a fine imposed by that court on the conviction of the defaulter on the date on which the sum was registered.

10 Enforcement of fines

(1) In this section –

'fine' means a sum which is enforceable as a fine as a result of section 9; and

'proceedings' means proceedings for enforcing a fine.

(2) Subsection (3) applies if, in any proceedings, the defaulter claims that he was not the person to whom the penalty notice concerned was issued.

(3) The court may adjourn the proceedings for a period of not more than 28 days for the purpose of allowing that claim to be investigated.

(4) On the resumption of proceedings that have been adjourned under subsection (3), the court must accept the defaulter's claim unless it is shown, on a balance of probabilities, that he was the recipient of the penalty notice.

(5) The court may set aside a fine in the interests of justice.

(6) If the court does set a fine aside it must –

(a) give such directions for further consideration of the case as it considers appropriate; or

(b) direct that no further action is to be taken in respect of the allegation that gave rise to the penalty notice concerned.

11 Interpretation of Chapter 1

In this Chapter –

'chief officer of police' includes the Chief Constable of the British Transport Police;

'defaulter' has the meaning given in section 8(5);

'penalty notice' has the meaning given in section 2(4);

'penalty offence' has the meaning given in section 1(1);

'registrable sum' has the meaning given in section 8(4).

CHAPTER 2

PROVISIONS FOR COMBATTING ALCOHOL-RELATED DISORDER

12 Alcohol consumption in designated public places

(1) Subsection (2) applies if a constable reasonably believes that a person is, or has been, consuming intoxicating liquor in a designated public place or intends to consume intoxicating liquor in such a place.

(2) The constable may require the person concerned –

(a) not to consume in that place anything which is, or which the constable reasonably believes to be, intoxicating liquor;

(b) to surrender anything in his possession which is, or which the constable reasonably believes to be, intoxicating liquor or a container for such liquor.

(3) A constable may dispose of anything surrendered to him under subsection (2) in such manner as he considers appropriate.

(4) A person who fails without reasonable excuse to comply with a requirement imposed on him under subsection (2) commits an offence and is liable on summary conviction to a fine not exceeding level 2 on the standard scale.

(5) A constable who imposes a requirement on a person under subsection (2) shall inform the person concerned that failing without reasonable excuse to comply with the requirement is an offence.

13 Designated public places

(1) A place is, subject to section 14, a designated public place if it is –

(a) a public place in the area of a local authority; and

(b) identified in an order made by that authority under subsection (2).

(2) A local authority may for the purposes of subsection (1) by order identify any public place in their area if they are satisfied that –

(a) nuisance or annoyance to members of the public or a section of the public; or

(b) disorder;

has been associated with the consumption of intoxicating liquor in that place. ...

14 Places which are not designated public places

(1) A place is not a designated public place or a part of such a place if it is –

(a) licensed premises or a registered club;

(b) a place within the curtilage of any licensed premises or registered club;

(c) a place where the sale of intoxicating liquor is for the time being authorised by an occasional permission or was so authorised within the last twenty minutes;

(d) a place where the sale of intoxicating liquor is not for the time being authorised by an occasional licence but was so authorised within the last twenty minutes;

(e) a place where facilities or activities relating to the sale or consumption of intoxicating liquor are for the time being permitted by virtue of a permission granted under section 115E of the Highways Act 1980 (c 66) (highway related uses).

(2) In subsection (1) –

'licensed premises', 'occasional licence' and 'registered club' have the same meaning as in the Licensing Act 1964 (c 26); and

'occasional permission' has the same meaning as in the Licensing (Occasional Permissions) Act 1983 (c 24).

15 Effect of sections 12 to 14 on byelaws

(1) Subsections (2) and (3) apply to any byelaw which –

(a) prohibits, by the creation of an offence, the consumption in a particular public place of intoxicating liquor (including any liquor of a similar nature which falls within the byelaw); or

(b) makes any incidental, supplementary or consequential provision (whether relating to the seizure or control of containers or otherwise).

(2) In so far as any byelaw to which this subsection applies would, apart from this subsection, have effect in relation to any designated public place, the byelaw –

(a) shall cease to have effect in relation to that place; or

(b) where it is made after the order under section 13(2), shall not have effect in relation to that place.

(3) In so far as any byelaw made by a local authority and to which this subsection applies still has effect at the end of the period of 5 years beginning with the day on which this subsection comes into force, it shall cease to have effect at the end of that period in relation to any public place.

16 Interpretation of sections 12 to 15

(1) In sections 12 to 15, unless the context otherwise requires –

'designated public place' has the meaning given by section 13(1);

'intoxicating liquor' has the same meaning as in the Licensing Act 1964; and

'public place' means any place to which the public or any section of the public has access, on payment or otherwise, as of right or by virtue of express or implied permission.

(2) In sections 12 to 15 'local authority' means –

(a) in relation to England –

(i) a unitary authority;
(ii) a district council so far as they are not a unitary authority;

(b) in relation to Wales, a county council or a county borough council.

(3) In subsection (2) 'unitary authority' means –

(a) the council of a county so far as they are the council for an area for which there are no district councils;
(b) the council of any district comprised in an area for which there is no county council;
(c) a London borough council;
(d) the Common Council of the City of London in its capacity as a local authority;
(e) the Council of the Isles of Scilly.

CHAPTER 3

OTHER PROVISIONS FOR COMBATTING CRIME AND DISORDER ...

42 Police directions stopping the harassment, etc of a person in his home

(1) Subject to the following provisions of this section, a constable who is at the scene may give a direction under this section to any person if –

(a) that person is present outside or in the vicinity of any premises that are used by any individual ('the resident') as his dwelling;

(b) that constable believes, on reasonable grounds, that that person is present there for the purpose (by his presence or otherwise) of representing to the resident or another individual (whether or not one who uses the premises as his dwelling), or of persuading the resident or such another individual –

(i) that he should not do something that he is entitled or required to do; or

(ii) that he should do something that he is not under any obligation to do; and

(c) that constable also believes, on reasonable grounds, that the presence of that person (either alone or together with that of any other persons who are also present) –

(i) amounts to, or is likely to result in, the harassment of the resident; or

(ii) is likely to cause alarm or distress to the resident.

(2) A direction under this section is a direction requiring the person to whom it is given to do all such things as the constable giving it may specify as the things he considers necessary to prevent one or both of the following –

(a) the harassment of the resident; or

(b) the causing of any alarm or distress to the resident.

(3) A direction under this section may be given orally; and where a constable is entitled to give a direction under this section to each of several persons outside, or in the vicinity of, any premises, he may give that direction to those persons by notifying them of his requirements either individually or all together.

(4) The requirements that may be imposed by a direction under this section include a requirement to leave the vicinity of the premises in question (either immediately or after a specified period of time).

(5) A direction under this section may make exceptions to any requirement imposed by the direction, and may make any such exception subject to such conditions as the constable giving the direction thinks fit; and those conditions may include –

(a) conditions as to the distance from the premises in question at which, or otherwise as to the location where, persons who do not leave their vicinity must remain; and

(b) conditions as to the number or identity of the persons who are authorised by the exception to remain in the vicinity of those premises.

(6) The power of a constable to give a direction under this section shall not include –

(a) any power to give a direction at any time when there is a more senior-ranking police officer at the scene; or

(b) any power to direct a person to refrain from conduct that is lawful under section 220 of the Trade Union and Labour Relations (Consolidation) Act 1992 (c 52) (right peacefully to picket a work place);

but it shall include power to vary or withdraw a direction previously given under this section.

(7) Any person who knowingly contravenes a direction given to him under this section shall be guilty of an offence and liable, on summary conviction, to imprisonment for a term not exceeding three months or to a fine not exceeding level 4 on the standard scale, or to both.

(8) A constable in uniform may arrest without warrant any person he reasonably suspects is committing an offence under this section.

(9) In this section 'dwelling' has the same meaning as in Part 1 of the Public Order Act 1986 (c 64).

PART 2

POWERS OF SEIZURE

50 Additional powers of seizure from premises

(1) Where –

(a) a person who is lawfully on any premises finds anything on those premises that he has reasonable grounds for believing may be or may contain something for which he is authorised to search on those premises,

(b) a power of seizure to which this section applies or the power conferred by subsection (2) would entitle him, if he found it, to seize whatever it is that he has grounds for believing that thing to be or to contain, and

(c) in all the circumstances, it is not reasonably practicable for it to be determined, on those premises –

(i) whether what he has found is something that he is entitled to seize, or

(ii) the extent to which what he has found contains something that he is entitled to seize,

that person's powers of seizure shall include power under this section to seize so much of what he has found as it is necessary to remove from the premises to enable that to be determined.

(2) Where –

(a) a person who is lawfully on any premises finds anything on those premises ('the seizable property') which he would be entitled to seize but for its being comprised in something else that he has (apart from this subsection) no power to seize,

(b) the power under which that person would have power to seize the seizable property is a power to which this section applies, and

(c) in all the circumstances it is not reasonably practicable for the seizable property to be separated, on those premises, from that in which it is comprised,

that person's powers of seizure shall include power under this section to seize both the seizable property and that from which it is not reasonably practicable to separate it.

(3) The factors to be taken into account in considering, for the purposes of this section, whether or not it is reasonably practicable on particular premises for something to be determined, or for something to be separated from something else, shall be confined to the following –

(a) how long it would take to carry out the determination or separation on those premises;

(b) the number of persons that would be required to carry out that determination or separation on those premises within a reasonable period;

(c) whether the determination or separation would (or would if carried out on those premises) involve damage to property;

(d) the apparatus or equipment that it would be necessary or appropriate to use for the carrying out of the determination or separation; and

(e) in the case of separation, whether the separation –

(i) would be likely, or

(ii) if carried out by the only means that are reasonably practicable on those premises, would be likely,

to prejudice the use of some or all of the separated seizable property for a purpose for which something seized under the power in question is capable of being used.

(4) Section 19(6) of the [Police and Criminal Evidence Act] 1984 (powers of seizure not to include power to seize anything that a person has reasonable grounds for believing is legally privileged) shall not apply to the power of seizure conferred by subsection (2).

(5) This section applies to each of the powers of seizure specified in Part 1 of Schedule 1. ...

51 Additional powers of seizure from the person

(1) Where –

(a) a person carrying out a lawful search of any person finds something that he has reasonable grounds for believing may be or may contain something for which he is authorised to search,

(b) a power of seizure to which this section applies or the power conferred by subsection (2) would entitle him, if he found it, to seize whatever it is that he has grounds for believing that thing to be or to contain, and

(c) in all the circumstances it is not reasonably practicable for it to be determined, at the time and place of the search –

(i) whether what he has found is something that he is entitled to seize, or

(ii) the extent to which what he has found contains something that he is entitled to seize, that person's powers of seizure shall include power under this section to seize so much of what he has found as it is necessary to remove from that place to enable that to be determined.

(2) Where –

(a) a person carrying out a lawful search of any person finds something ('the seizable property') which he would be entitled to seize but for its being comprised in something else that he has (apart from this subsection) no power to seize,

(b) the power under which that person would have power to seize the seizable property is a power to which this section applies, and

(c) in all the circumstances it is not reasonably practicable for the seizable property to be separated, at the time and place of the search, from that in which it is comprised,

that person's powers of seizure shall include power under this section to seize both the seizable property and that from which it is not reasonably practicable to separate it.

(3) The factors to be taken into account in considering, for the purposes of this section, whether or not it is reasonably practicable, at the time and place of a search, for something to be determined, or for something to be separated from something else, shall be confined to the following –

(a) how long it would take to carry out the determination or separation at that time and place;

(b) the number of persons that would be required to carry out that determination or separation at that time and place within a reasonable period;

(c) whether the determination or separation would (or would if carried out at that time and place) involve damage to property;

(d) the apparatus or equipment that it would be necessary or appropriate to use for the carrying out of the determination or separation; and

(e) in the case of separation, whether the separation –

(i) would be likely, or

(ii) if carried out by the only means that are reasonably practicable at that time and place, would be likely,

to prejudice the use of some or all of the separated seizable property for a purpose for which something seized under the power in question is capable of being used. ...

(4) Section 19(6) of the 1984 Act ... (powers of seizure not to include power to seize anything a person has reasonable grounds for believing is legally privileged) shall not apply to the power of seizure conferred by subsection (2).

(5) This section applies to each of the powers of seizure specified in Part 2 of Schedule 1.

52 Notice of exercise of power under s50 or 51

(1) Where a person exercises a power of seizure conferred by section 50, it shall (subject to subsections (2) and (3)) be his duty, on doing so, to give to the occupier of the premises a written notice –

(a) specifying what has been seized in reliance on the powers conferred by that section;

(b) specifying the grounds on which those powers have been exercised;

(c) setting out the effect of sections 59 to 61;

(d) specifying the name and address of the person to whom notice of an application under section 59(2) to the appropriate judicial authority in respect of any of the seized property must be given; and

(e) specifying the name and address of the person to whom an application may be made to be allowed to attend the initial examination required by any arrangements made for the purposes of section 53(2).

(2) Where it appears to the person exercising on any premises a power of seizure conferred by section 50 –

(a) that the occupier of the premises is not present on the premises at the time of the exercise of the power, but

(b) that there is some other person present on the premises who is in charge of the premises,

subsection (1) of this section shall have effect as if it required the notice under that subsection to be given to that other person.

(3) Where it appears to the person exercising a power of seizure conferred by section 50 that there is no one present on the premises to whom he may give a notice for the purposes of complying with subsection (1) of this section, he shall, before leaving the premises, instead of complying with that subsection, attach a notice such as is mentioned in that subsection in a prominent place to the premises.

(4) Where a person exercises a power of seizure conferred by section 51 it shall be his duty, on doing so, to give a written notice to the person from whom the seizure is made –

(a) specifying what has been seized in reliance on the powers conferred by that section;

(b) specifying the grounds on which those powers have been exercised;

(c) setting out the effect of sections 59 to 61;

(d) specifying the name and address of the person to whom notice of any application under section 59(2) to the appropriate judicial authority in respect of any of the seized property must be given; and

(e) specifying the name and address of the person to whom an application may be made to be allowed to attend the initial examination required by any arrangements made for the purposes of section 53(2). ...

53 Examination and return of property seized under s50 or 51

(1) This section applies where anything has been seized under a power conferred by section 50 or 51.

(2) It shall be the duty of the person for the time being in possession of the seized property in consequence of the exercise of that power to secure that there are arrangements in force which (subject to section 61) ensure –

(a) that an initial examination of the property is carried out as soon as reasonably practicable after the seizure;

(b) that that examination is confined to whatever is necessary for determining how much of the property falls within subsection (3);

(c) that anything which is found, on that examination, not to fall within subsection (3) is separated from the rest of the seized property and is returned as soon as reasonably practicable after the examination of all the seized property has been completed; and

(d) that, until the initial examination of all the seized property has been completed and anything which does not fall within subsection (3) has been returned, the seized property is kept separate from anything seized under any other power.

(3) The seized property falls within this subsection to the extent only –

(a) that it is property for which the person seizing it had power to search when he made the seizure but is not property the return of which is required by section 54;

(b) that it is property the retention of which is authorised by section 56; or

(c) that it is something which, in all the circumstances, it will not be reasonably practicable, following the examination, to separate from property falling within paragraph (a) or (b).

(4) In determining for the purposes of this section the earliest practicable time for the carrying out of an initial examination of the seized property, due regard shall be had to the desirability of allowing the person from whom it was seized, or a person with an interest in that property, an opportunity of being present or (if he chooses) of being represented at the examination.

(5) In this section, references to whether or not it is reasonably practicable to separate part of the seized property from the rest of it are references to whether or not it is reasonably practicable to do so without prejudicing the use of the rest of that property, or a part of it, for purposes for which (disregarding the part to be separated) the use of the whole or of a part of the rest of the property, if retained, would be lawful.

54 Obligation to return items subject to legal privilege

(1) If, at any time after a seizure of anything has been made in exercise of a power of seizure to which this section applies –

(a) it appears to the person for the time being having possession of the seized property in consequence of the seizure that the property –

(i) is an item subject to legal privilege, or

(ii) has such an item comprised in it,

and

(b) in a case where the item is comprised in something else which has been lawfully seized, it is not comprised in property falling within subsection (2),

it shall be the duty of that person to secure that the item is returned as soon as reasonably practicable after the seizure.

(2) Property in which an item subject to legal privilege is comprised falls within this subsection if –

(a) the whole or a part of the rest of the property is property falling within subsection (3) or property the retention of which is authorised by section 56; and

(b) in all the circumstances, it is not reasonably practicable for that item to be separated from the rest of that property (or, as the case may be, from that part of it) without prejudicing the use of the rest of that property, or that part of it, for purposes for which (disregarding that item) its use, if retained, would be lawful.

(3) Property falls within this subsection to the extent that it is property for which the person seizing it had power to search when he made the seizure, but is not property which is required to be returned under this section or section 55.

(4) This section applies –

(a) to the powers of seizure conferred by sections 50 and 51;

(b) to each of the powers of seizure specified in Parts 1 and 2 of Schedule 1; and

(c) to any power of seizure (not falling within paragraph (a) or (b)) conferred on a constable by or under any enactment, including an enactment passed after this Act.

55 Obligation to return excluded and special procedure material

(1) If, at any time after a seizure of anything has been made in exercise of a power to which this section applies –

(a) it appears to the person for the time being having possession of the seized property in consequence of the seizure that the property –

(i) is excluded material or special procedure material, or

(ii) has any excluded material or any special procedure material comprised in it,

(b) its retention is not authorised by section 56, and

(c) in a case where the material is comprised in something else which has been lawfully seized, it is not comprised in property falling within subsection (2) or (3),

it shall be the duty of that person to secure that the item is returned as soon as reasonably practicable after the seizure.

(2) Property in which any excluded material or special procedure material is comprised falls within this subsection if –

(a) the whole or a part of the rest of the property is property for which the person seizing it had power to search when he made the seizure but is not property the return of which is required by this section or section 54; and

(b) in all the circumstances, it is not reasonably practicable for that material to be separated from the rest of that property (or, as the case may be, from that part of it) without prejudicing the use of the rest of that property, or that part of it, for purposes for which (disregarding that material) its use, if retained, would be lawful.

(3) Property in which any excluded material or special procedure material is comprised falls within this subsection if –

(a) the whole or a part of the rest of the property is property the retention of which is authorised by section 56; and

(b) in all the circumstances, it is not reasonably practicable for that material to be separated from the rest of that property (or, as the case may be, from that part of it) without prejudicing the use of the rest of that property, or that part of it, for purposes for which (disregarding that material) its use, if retained, would be lawful.

(4) This section applies (subject to subsection (5)) to each of the powers of seizure specified in Part 3 of Schedule 1.

(5) In its application to the powers of seizure conferred by –

(b) section 56(5) of the Drug Trafficking Act 1994 (c 37), … and

(d) section 352(4) of the Proceeds of Crime Act 2002,

this section shall have effect with the omission of every reference to special procedure material.

(6) In this section, except in its application to –

(a) the power of seizure conferred by section 8(2) of the 1984 Act, …

'special procedure material' means special procedure material consisting of documents or records other than documents.

56 Property seized by constables, etc

(1) The retention of –

(a) property seized on any premises by a constable who was lawfully on the premises,

(b) property seized on any premises by a relevant person who was on the premises accompanied by a constable, and

(c) property seized by a constable carrying out a lawful search of any person,

is authorised by this section if the property falls within subsection (2) or (3).

(2) Property falls within this subsection to the extent that there are reasonable grounds for believing –

(a) that it is property obtained in consequence of the commission of an offence; and

(b) that it is necessary for it to be retained in order to prevent its being concealed, lost, damaged, altered or destroyed.

(3) Property falls within this subsection to the extent that there are reasonable grounds for believing –

(a) that it is evidence in relation to any offence; and

(b) that it is necessary for it to be retained in order to prevent its being concealed, lost, altered or destroyed.

(4) Nothing in this section authorises the retention (except in pursuance of section 54(2)) of anything at any time when its return is required by section 54.

(5) In subsection (1)(b) the reference to a relevant person's being on any premises accompanied by a constable is a reference only to a person who was so on the premises under the authority of –

(a) a warrant under section 448 of the Companies Act 1985 (c 6) authorising him to exercise together with a constable the powers conferred by subsection (3) of that section; ...

57 Retention of seized items

(1) This section has effect in relation to the following provisions (which are about the retention of items which have been seized and are referred to in this section as 'the relevant provisions') –

(a) section 22 of the 1984 Act; ...

(f) section 448(6) of the Companies Act 1985 (c 6);

(g) paragraph 4 of Schedule 8 to the Weights and Measures Act 1985 (c 72); ...

(k) section 40(4) of the Human Fertilisation and Embryology Act 1990 (c 37);

(m) paragraph 7(2) of Schedule 9 to the Data Protection Act 1998 (c 29);

(n) section 28(7) of the Competition Act 1998 (c 41);

(o) section 176(8) of the Financial Services and Markets Act 2000 (c 8);

(p) paragraph 7(2) of Schedule 3 to the Freedom of Information Act 2000 (c 36).

(2) The relevant provisions shall apply in relation to any property seized in exercise of a power conferred by section 50 or 51 as if the property had been seized under the power of seizure by reference to which the power under that section was exercised in relation to that property.

(3) Nothing in any of sections 53 to 56 authorises the retention of any property at any time when its retention would not (apart from the provisions of this Part) be authorised by the relevant provisions.

(4) Nothing in any of the relevant provisions authorises the retention of anything after an obligation to return it has arisen under this Part.

58 Person to whom seized property is to be returned

(1) Where –

(a) anything has been seized in exercise of any power of seizure, and

(b) there is an obligation under this Part for the whole or any part of the seized property to be returned,

the obligation to return it shall (subject to the following provisions of this section) be an obligation to return it to the person from whom it was seized.

(2) Where –

(a) any person is obliged under this Part to return anything that has been seized to the person from whom it was seized, and

(b) the person under that obligation is satisfied that some other person has a better right to that thing than the person from whom it was seized,

his duty to return it shall, instead, be a duty to return it to that other person or, as the case may be, to the person appearing to him to have the best right to the thing in question.

(3) Where different persons claim to be entitled to the return of anything that is required to be returned under this Part, that thing may be retained for as long as is reasonably necessary for the determination in accordance with subsection (2) of the person to whom it must be returned.

(4) References in this Part to the person from whom something has been seized, in relation to a case in which the power of seizure was exercisable by reason of that thing's having been found on any premises, are references to the occupier of the premises at the time of the seizure.

(5) References in this section to the occupier of any premises at the time of a seizure, in relation to a case in which –

(a) a notice in connection with the entry or search of the premises in question, or with the seizure, was given to a person appearing in the occupier's absence to be in charge of the premises, and

(b) it is practicable, for the purpose of returning something that has been seized, to identify that person but not to identify the occupier of the premises,

are references to that person.

59 Application to the appropriate judicial authority

(1) This section applies where anything has been seized in exercise, or purported exercise, of a relevant power of seizure.

(2) Any person with a relevant interest in the seized property may apply to the appropriate judicial authority, on one or more of the grounds mentioned in subsection (3), for the return of the whole or a part of the seized property.

(3) Those grounds are –

(a) that there was no power to make the seizure;

(b) that the seized property is or contains an item subject to legal privilege that is not comprised in property falling within section 54(2);

(c) that the seized property is or contains any excluded material or special procedure material which –

(i) has been seized under a power to which section 55 applies;

(ii) is not comprised in property falling within section 55(2) or (3); and

(iii) is not property the retention of which is authorised by section 56;

(d) that the seized property is or contains something seized under section 50 or 51 which does not fall within section 53(3);

and subsections (5) and (6) of section 55 shall apply for the purposes of paragraph (c) as they apply for the purposes of that section.

(4) Subject to subsection (6), the appropriate judicial authority, on an application under subsection (2), shall –

(a) if satisfied as to any of the matters mentioned in subsection (3), order the return of so much of the seized property as is property in relation to which the authority is so satisfied; and

(b) to the extent that that authority is not so satisfied, dismiss the application.

(5) The appropriate judicial authority –

(a) on an application under subsection (2),

(b) on an application made by the person for the time being having possession of anything in consequence of its seizure under a relevant power of seizure, or

(c) on an application made –

(i) by a person with a relevant interest in anything seized under section 50 or 51, and

(ii) on the grounds that the requirements of section 53(2) have not been or are not being complied with,

may give such directions as the authority thinks fit as to the examination, retention, separation or return of the whole or any part of the seized property.

(6) On any application under this section, the appropriate judicial authority may authorise the retention of any property which –

(a) has been seized in exercise, or purported exercise, of a relevant power of seizure, and

(b) would otherwise fall to be returned,

if that authority is satisfied that the retention of the property is justified on grounds falling within subsection (7).

(7) Those grounds are that (if the property were returned) it would immediately become appropriate –

(a) to issue, on the application of the person who is in possession of the property at the time of the application under this section, a warrant in pursuance of which, or of the exercise of which, it would be lawful to seize the property; or

(b) to make an order under –

(i) paragraph 4 of Schedule 1 to the 1984 Act, …

under which the property would fall to be delivered up or produced to the person mentioned in paragraph (a).

(8) Where any property which has been seized in exercise, or purported exercise, of a relevant power of seizure has parts ('part A' and 'part B') comprised in it such that –

(a) it would be inappropriate, if the property were returned, to take any action such as is mentioned in subsection (7) in relation to part A,

(b) it would (or would but for the facts mentioned in paragraph (a)) be appropriate, if the property were returned, to take such action in relation to part B, and

(c) in all the circumstances, it is not reasonably practicable to separate part A from part B without prejudicing the use of part B for purposes for which it is lawful to use property seized under the power in question,

the facts mentioned in paragraph (a) shall not be taken into account by the appropriate judicial authority in deciding whether the retention of the property is justified on grounds falling within subsection (7).

(9) If a person fails to comply with any order or direction made or given by a judge of the Crown Court in exercise of any jurisdiction under this section –

(a) the authority may deal with him as if he had committed a contempt of the Crown Court; and

(b) any enactment relating to contempt of the Crown Court shall have effect in relation to the failure as if it were such a contempt.

(10) The relevant powers of seizure for the purposes of this section are –

(a) the powers of seizure conferred by sections 50 and 51;

(b) each of the powers of seizure specified in Parts 1 and 2 of Schedule 1; and

(c) any power of seizure (not falling within paragraph (a) or (b)) conferred on a constable by or under any enactment, including an enactment passed after this Act.

(11) References in this section to a person with a relevant interest in seized property are references to –

(a) the person from whom it was seized;

b) any person with an interest in the property; or

(c) any person, not falling within paragraph (a) or (b), who had custody or control of the property immediately before the seizure.

(12) For the purposes of subsection (11)(b), the persons who have an interest in seized property shall, in the case of property which is or contains an item subject to legal privilege, be taken to include the person in whose favour that privilege is conferred.

60 Cases where duty to secure arises

(1) Where property has been seized in exercise, or purported exercise, of any power of seizure conferred by section 50 or 51, a duty to secure arises under section 61 in relation to the seized property if –

(a) a person entitled to do so makes an application under section 59 for the return of the property;

(b) in relation to England, Wales and Northern Ireland, at least one of the conditions set out in subsections (2) and (3) is satisfied; ... and

(d) notice of the application is given to a relevant person.

(2) The first condition is that the application is made on the grounds that the seized property is or contains an item subject to legal privilege that is not comprised in property falling within section 54(2).

(3) The second condition is that –

(a) the seized property was seized by a person who had, or purported to have, power under this Part to seize it by virtue only of one or more of the powers specified in subsection (6); and

(b) the application –

(i) is made on the ground that the seized property is or contains something which does not fall within section 53(3); and

(ii) states that the seized property is or contains special procedure material or excluded material.

(4) In relation to property seized by a person who had, or purported to have, power under this Part to seize it by virtue only of one or more of the powers of seizure conferred by –

(b) section 56(5) of the Drug Trafficking Act 1994 (c 37), ... or

(d) section 352(4) of the Proceeds of Crime Act 2002,

the second condition is satisfied only if the application states that the seized property is or contains excluded material.

(5) In relation to property seized by a person who had, or purported to have, power

under this Part to seize it by virtue only of one or more of the powers of seizure specified in Part 3 of Schedule 1 but not by virtue of –

(a) the power of seizure conferred by section 8(2) of the 1984 Act, …

the second condition is satisfied only if the application states that the seized property is or contains excluded material or special procedure material consisting of documents or records other than documents.

(6) The powers mentioned in subsection (3) are –

(a) the powers of seizure specified in Part 3 of Schedule 1;

(b) the powers of seizure conferred by the provisions of Parts 2 and 3 of the 1984 Act (except section 8(2) of that Act); …

(7) In this section 'a relevant person' means any one of the following –

(a) the person who made the seizure;

(b) the person for the time being having possession, in consequence of the seizure, of the seized property;

(c) the person named for the purposes of subsection (1)(d) or (4)(d) of section 52 in any notice given under that section with respect to the seizure.

61 The duty to secure

(1) The duty to secure that arises under this section is a duty of the person for the time being having possession, in consequence of the seizure, of the seized property to secure that arrangements are in force that ensure that the seized property (without being returned) is not, at any time after the giving of the notice of the application under section 60(1), either –

(a) examined or copied, or

(b) put to any use to which its seizure would, apart from this subsection, entitle it to be put,

except with the consent of the applicant or in accordance with the directions of the appropriate judicial authority.

(2) Subsection (1) shall not have effect in relation to any time after the withdrawal of the application to which the notice relates.

(3) Nothing in any arrangements for the purposes of this section shall be taken to prevent the giving of a notice under section 49 of the Regulation of Investigatory Powers Act 2000 (c 23) (notices for the disclosure of material protected by encryption etc.) in respect of any information contained in the seized material; but subsection (1) of this section shall apply to anything disclosed for the purpose of complying with such a notice as it applies to the seized material in which the information in question is contained.

(4) Subsection (9) of section 59 shall apply in relation to any jurisdiction conferred on the appropriate judicial authority by this section as it applies in relation to the jurisdiction conferred by that section.

62 Use of inextricably linked property

(1) This section applies to property, other than property which is for the time being required to be secured in pursuance of section 61, if –

(a) it has been seized under any power conferred by section 50 or 51 or specified in Part 1 or 2 of Schedule 1, and

(b) it is inextricably linked property.

(2) Subject to subsection (3), it shall be the duty of the person for the time being having possession, in consequence of the seizure, of the inextricably linked property to ensure that arrangements are in force which secure that that property (without being returned) is not at any time, except with the consent of the person from whom it was seized, either –

(a) examined or copied, or

(b) put to any other use.

(3) Subsection (2) does not require that arrangements under that subsection should prevent inextricably linked property from being put to any use falling within subsection (4).

(4) A use falls within this subsection to the extent that it is use which is necessary for facilitating the use, in any investigation or proceedings, of property in which the inextricably linked property is comprised.

(5) Property is inextricably linked property for the purposes of this section if it falls within any of subsections (6) to (8).

(6) Property falls within this subsection if –

(a) it has been seized under a power conferred by section 50 or 51; and

(b) but for subsection (3)(c) of section 53, arrangements under subsection (2) of that section in relation to the property would be required to ensure the return of the property as mentioned in subsection (2)(c) of that section.

(7) Property falls within this subsection if –

(a) it has been seized under a power to which section 54 applies; and

(b) but for paragraph (b) of subsection (1) of that section, the person for the time being having possession of the property would be under a duty to secure its return as mentioned in that subsection.

(8) Property falls within this subsection if –

(a) it has been seized under a power of seizure to which section 55 applies; and

(b) but for paragraph (c) of subsection (1) of that section, the person for the time being having possession of the property would be under a duty to secure its return as mentioned in that subsection.

63 Copies

(1) Subject to subsection (3) –

(a) in this Part, 'seize' includes 'take a copy of', and cognate expressions shall be construed accordingly;

(b) this Part shall apply as if any copy taken under any power to which any provision of this Part applies were the original of that of which it is a copy; and

(c) for the purposes of this Part, except sections 50 and 51, the powers mentioned in subsection (2) (which are powers to obtain hard copies etc. of information which is stored in electronic form) shall be treated as powers of seizure, and references to seizure and to seized property shall be construed accordingly.

(2) The powers mentioned in subsection (1)(c) are any powers which are conferred by –

(a) section 19(4) or 20 of the 1984 Act; ...

(3) Subsection (1) does not apply to section 50(6) or 57.

64 Meaning of 'appropriate judicial authority'

(1) Subject to subsection (2), in this Part 'appropriate judicial authority' means –

(a) in relation to England and Wales and Northern Ireland, a judge of the Crown Court; ...

(2) In this Part 'appropriate judicial authority', in relation to the seizure of items under any power mentioned in subsection (3) and in relation to items seized under any such power, means –

(a) in relation to England and Wales and Northern Ireland, the High Court; ...

(3) Those powers are –

(a) the powers of seizure conferred by –

(i) section 448(3) of the Companies Act 1985 (c 6); ...

(iii) section 28(2) of the Competition Act 1998;

(aa) the power of seizure conferred by section 352(4) of the Proceeds of Crime Act 2002, if the power is exercisable for the purposes of a civil recovery investigation (within the meaning of Part 8 of that Act); and

(b) any power of seizure conferred by section 50, so far as that power is exercisable by reference to any power mentioned in paragraph (a).

65 Meaning of 'legal privilege'

(1) Subject to the following provisions of this section, references in this Part to an item subject to legal privilege shall be construed –

(a) for the purposes of the application of this Part to England and Wales, in accordance with section 10 of the 1984 Act (meaning of 'legal privilege'); ...

(3A) In relation to property which has been seized in exercise, or purported exercise, of –

(a) the power of seizure conferred by section 352(4) of the Proceeds of Crime Act 2002, or

(b) so much of any power of seizure conferred by secion 50 as is exercisable by reference to that power,

references to this Part to an item subject to legal privilege shall be read as references to privileged material within the meaning of section 354(2) of that Act.

(4) An item which is, or is comprised in, property which has been seized in exercise, or purported exercise, of the power of seizure conferred by section 448(3) of the Companies Act 1985 (c 6) shall be taken for the purposes of this Part to be an item subject to legal privilege if, and only if, the seizure of that item was in contravention of section 452(2) of that Act (privileged information).

(7) An item which is, or is comprised in, property which has been seized in exercise, or purported exercise, of the power of seizure conferred by paragraph 1 of Schedule 9 to the Data Protection Act 1998 (c 29) shall be taken for the purposes of this Part to be an item subject to legal privilege if, and only if, the seizure of that item was in contravention of paragraph 9 of that Schedule (privileged communications).

(8) An item which is, or is comprised in, property which has been seized in exercise, or purported exercise, of the power of seizure conferred by paragraph 1 of Schedule 3 to the Freedom of Information Act 2000 (c 36) shall be taken for the purposes of this Part to be an item subject to legal privilege if, and only if, the seizure of that item was in contravention of paragraph 9 of that Schedule (privileged communications).

(9) An item which is, or is comprised in, property which has been seized in exercise, or purported exercise, of so much of any power of seizure conferred by section 50 as is exercisable by reference to a power of seizure conferred by –

(a) section 448(3) of the Companies Act 1985, ...

(d) paragraph 1 of Schedule 9 to the Data Protection Act 1998, or

(e) paragraph 1 of Schedule 3 to the Freedom of Information Act 2000,

shall be taken for the purposes of this Part to be an item subject to legal privilege if, and only if, the item would have been taken for the purposes of this Part to be an item subject to legal privilege had it been seized under the power of seizure by reference to which the power conferred by section 50 was exercised.

66 General interpretation of Part 2

(1) In this Part –

'appropriate judicial authority' has the meaning given by section 64;

'documents' includes information recorded in any form;

'item subject to legal privilege' shall be construed in accordance with section 65;

'premises' includes any vehicle, stall or moveable structure (including an offshore installation) and any other place whatever, whether or not occupied as land;

'offshore installation' has the same meaning as in the Mineral Workings (Offshore Installations) Act 1971 (c 61);

'return', in relation to seized property, shall be construed in accordance with section 58, and cognate expressions shall be construed accordingly;

'seize', and cognate expressions, shall be construed in accordance with section 63(1) and subsection (5) below;

'seized property', in relation to any exercise of a power of seizure, means (subject to subsection (5)) anything seized in exercise of that power; and

'vehicle' includes any vessel, aircraft or hovercraft.

(2) In this Part references, in relation to a time when seized property is in any person's possession in consequence of a seizure ('the relevant time'), to something for which the person making the seizure had power to search shall be construed –

(a) where the seizure was made on the occasion of a search carried out on the authority of a warrant, as including anything of the description of things the presence or suspected presence of which provided grounds for the issue of the warrant;

(b) where the property was seized in the course of a search on the occasion of which it would have been lawful for the person carrying out the search to seize anything which on that occasion was believed by him to be, or appeared to him to be, of a particular description, as including –

(i) anything which at the relevant time is believed by the person in possession of the seized property, or (as the case may be) appears to him, to be of that description; and

(ii) anything which is in fact of that description;

(c) where the property was seized in the course of a search on the occasion of which it would have been lawful for the person carrying out the search to seize anything which there were on that occasion reasonable grounds for believing was of a particular description, as including –

(i) anything which there are at the relevant time reasonable grounds for believing is of that description; and

(ii) anything which is in fact of that description;

(d) where the property was seized in the course of a search to which neither paragraph (b) nor paragraph (c) applies, as including anything which is of a description of things which, on the occasion of the search, it would have been lawful for the person carrying it out to seize otherwise than under section 50 and 51; ...

(3) For the purpose of determining in accordance with subsection (2), in relation to any time, whether or to what extent property seized on the occasion of a search authorised under section 9 of the Official Secrets Act 1911 (c 28) (seizure of evidence of offences under that Act having been or being about to be committed) is something for which the person making the seizure had power to search, subsection (1) of that section shall be construed –

(a) as if the reference in that subsection to evidence of an offence under that Act being about to be committed were a reference to evidence of such an offence having been, at the time of the seizure, about to be committed; and

(b) as if the reference in that subsection to reasonable ground for suspecting that such an offence is about to be committed were a reference to reasonable ground for suspecting that at the time of the seizure such an offence was about to be committed.

(4) References in subsection (2) to a search include references to any activities authorised by virtue of any of the following –

(b) section 29(1) of the Fair Trading Act 1973 (c 41) (power to enter premises and to inspect and seize goods and documents);

(d) section 162(1) of the Consumer Credit Act 1974 (c 39) (powers of entry and inspection); ...

(5) References in this Part to a power of seizure include references to each of the powers to take possession of items under – ...

(b) section 448(3) of the Companies Act 1985 (c 6); ...

(g) section 40(2) of the Human Fertilisation and Embryology Act 1990 (c 37);

(h) section 28(2)(c) of the Competition Act 1998 (c 41); ...

and references in this Part to seizure and to seized property shall be construed accordingly.

(6) In this Part, so far as it applies to England and Wales –

(a) references to excluded material shall be construed in accordance with section 11 of the 1984 Act (meaning of 'excluded material'); and

(b) references to special procedure material shall be construed in accordance with section 14 of that Act (meaning of 'special procedure material'). ...

(8) References in this Part to any item or material being comprised in other property include references to its being mixed with that other property. ...

SCHEDULE 1

POWERS OF SEIZURE

PART 1

POWERS TO WHICH SECTION 50 APPLIES

Police and Criminal Evidence Act 1984 (c 60)

1. Each of the powers of seizure conferred by the provisions of Part 2 or 3 of the 1984 Act (police powers of entry, search and seizure). ...

Official Secrets Act 1911 (c 28)

3. The power of seizure conferred by section 9(1) of the Official Secrets Act 1911 (seizure of evidence that an offence under that Act has been or is about to be committed). …

PART 2

POWERS TO WHICH SECTION 51 APPLIES

Police and Criminal Evidence Act 1984 (c 60)

74. Each of the powers of seizure conferred by the provisions of Part 3 of the 1984 Act (police powers of search and seizure on arrest). …

PART 3

POWERS TO WHICH SECTION 55 APPLIES

Police and Criminal Evidence Act 1984 (c 60)

84. The power of seizure conferred by section 8(2) of the 1984 Act (police power, on exercise of search warrant, to seize property searched for). …

As amended by the Financial Services and Markets Act 2000 (Consequential Amendments and Repeals) Order 2001, art 364(a)–(c); Criminal Justice and Police Act 2001 (Amendment) Order 2002; Police Reform Act 2002, s107(2), Schedule 8; Proceeds of Crime Act 2002, ss456, 457, Schedule 11, para 40, Schedule 12; Communications Act 2003, s406(1), (7), Schedule 17, para 169, Schedule 19(1); Anti-social Behaviour Act 2003, s87; Licensing Act 2003, ss155(2), 199, Schedule 7; Criminal Justice Act 2003, s12, Schedule 1, para 14.

ANTI-TERRORISM, CRIME AND SECURITY ACT 2001

(2001 c 24)

PART 4

IMMIGRATION AND ASYLUM

21 Suspected international terrorist: certification

(1) The Secretary of State may issue a certificate under this section in respect of a person if the Secretary of State reasonably –

(a) believes that the person's presence in the United Kingdom is a risk to national security, and

(b) suspects that the person is a terrorist.

(2) In subsection (1)(b) 'terrorist' means a person who –

(a) is or has been concerned in the commission, preparation or instigation of acts of international terrorism,

(b) is a member of or belongs to an international terrorist group, or

(c) has links with an international terrorist group.

(3) A group is an international terrorist group for the purposes of subsection (2)(b) and (c) if –

(a) it is subject to the control or influence of persons outside the United Kingdom, and

(b) the Secretary of State suspects that it is concerned in the commission, preparation or instigation of acts of international terrorism.

(4) For the purposes of subsection (2)(c) a person has links with an international terrorist group only if he supports or assists it.

(5) In this Part –

'terrorism' has the meaning given by section 1 of the Terrorism Act 2000 (c 11), and

'suspected international terrorist' means a person certified under subsection (1).

(6) Where the Secretary of State issues a certificate under subsection (1) he shall as soon as is reasonably practicable –

(a) take reasonable steps to notify the person certified, and

(b) send a copy of the certificate to the Special Immigration Appeals Commission.

(7) The Secretary of State may revoke a certificate issued under subsection (1).

(8) A decision of the Secretary of State in connection with certification under this section may be questioned in legal proceedings only under section 25 or 26.

(9) An action of the Secretary of State taken wholly or partly in reliance on a certificate under this section may be questioned in legal proceedings only by or in the course of proceedings under –

(a) section 25 or 26, or

(b) secton 2 of the Special Immigration Appeals Commission Act 1997 (c 68) (appeal).

22 Deportation, removal, etc

(1) An action of a kind specified in subsection (2) may be taken in respect of a suspected international terrorist despite the fact that (whether temporarily or indefinitely) the action cannot result in his removal from the United Kingdom because of –

(a) a point of law which wholly or partly relates to an international agreement, or

(b) a practical consideration.

(2) The actions mentioned in subsection (1) are –

(a) refusing leave to enter or remain in the United Kingdom in accordance with provision made by or by virtue of any of sections 3 to 3B of the Immigration Act 1971 (c 77) (control of entry to United Kingdom),

(b) varying a limited leave to enter or remain in the United Kingdom in accordance with provision made by or by virtue of any of those sections,

(c) recommending deportation in accordance with section 3(6) of that Act (recommendation by court),

(d) taking a decision to make a deportation order under section 5(1) of that Act (deportation by Secretary of State),

(e) making a deportation order under section 5(1) of that Act,

(f) refusing to revoke a deportation order,

(g) cancelling leave to enter the United Kingdom in accordance with paragraph 2A of Schedule 2 to that Act (person arriving with continuous leave),

(h) giving directions for a person's removal from the United Kingdom under any of paragraphs 8 to 10A or 12 to 14 of Schedule 2 to that Act (control of entry to United Kingdom),

(i) giving directions for a person's removal from the United Kingdom under section 10 of the Immigration and Asylum Act 1999 (c 33) (person unlawfully in United Kingdom), and

(j) giving notice to a person in accordance with regulations under section 105 of the Nationality, Immigration and Asylum Act 2002 of a decision to make a deportation order against him.

(3) Action of a kind specified in subsection (2) which has effect in respect of a suspected international terrorist at the time of his certification under section 21 shall be treated as taken again (in reliance on subsection (1) above) immediately after certification.

23 Detention

(1) A suspected international terrorist may be detained under a provision specified in subsection (2) despite the fact that his removal or departure from the United Kingdom is prevented (whether temporarily or indefinitely) by –

(a) a point of law which wholly or partly relates to an international agreement, or

(b) a practical consideration.

(2) The provisions mentioned in subsection (1) are –

(a) paragraph 16 of Schedule 2 to the Immigration Act 1971 (c 77) (detention of persons liable to examination or removal),

(b) paragraph 2 of Schedule 3 to that Act (detention pending deportation), and

(c) section 62 of the Nationality, Immigration and Asylum Act 2002 (detention by Secretary of State).

24 Bail

(1) A suspected international terrorist who is detained under a provision of the Immigration Act 1971, or under section 62 of the Nationality, Immigration and Asylum Act 2002 (detention by the Secretary of State), may be released on bail. ...

25 Certification: appeal

(1) A suspected international terrorist may appeal to the Special Immigration Appeals Commission against his certification under section 21.

(2) On an appeal the Commission must cancel the certificate if –

(a) it considers that there are no reasonable grounds for a belief or suspicion of the kind referred to in section 21(1)(a) or (b), or

(b) it considers that for some other reason the certificate should not have been issued.

(3) If the Commission determines not to cancel a certificate it must dismiss the appeal.

(4) Where a certificate is cancelled under subsection (2) it shall be treated as never having been issued.

(5) An appeal against certification may be commenced only –

(a) within the period of three months beginning with the date on which the certificate is issued, or

(b) with the leave of the Commission, after the end of that period but before the commencement of the first review under section 26.

26 Certification: review

(1) The Special Immigration Appeals Commission must hold a first review of each certificate issued under section 21 as soon as is reasonably practicable after the expiry of the period of six months beginning with the date on which the certificate is issued.

(2) But –

(a) in a case where before the first review would fall to be held in accordance with subsection (1) an appeal under section 25 is commenced (whether or not it is finally determined before that time) or leave to appeal is given under section 25(5)(b), the first review shall be held as soon as is reasonably practicable after the expiry of the period of six months beginning with the date on which the appeal is finally determined, and

(b) in a case where an application for leave under section 25(5)(b) has been commenced but not determined at the time when the first review would fall to be held in accordance with subsection (1), if leave is granted the first review shall be held as soon as is reasonably practicable after the expiry of the period of six months beginning with the date on which the appeal is finally determined.

(3) The Commission must review each certificate issued under section 21 as soon as is reasonably practicable after the expiry of the period of three months beginning with the date on which the first review or a review under this subsection is finally determined.

(4) The Commission may review a certificate during a period mentioned in subsection (1), (2) or (3) if –

(a) the person certified applies for a review, and

(b) the Commission considers that a review should be held because of a change in circumstance.

(5) On a review the Commission –

(a) must cancel the certificate if it considers that there are no reasonable grounds for a belief or suspicion of the kind referred to in section 21(1)(a) or (b), and

(b) otherwise, may not make any order (save as to leave to appeal).

(6) A certificate cancelled by order of the Commission under subsection (5) ceases to have effect at the end of the day on which the order is made.

(7) Where the Commission reviews a certificate under subsection (4), the period

for determining the next review of the certificate under subsection (3) shall begin with the date of the final determination of the review under subsection (4).

27 Appeal and review: supplementary

(1) The following provisions of the Special Immigration Appeals Commission Act 1997 (c 68) shall apply in relation to an appeal or review under section 25 or 26 as they apply in relation to an appeal under section 2 of that Act –

(a) section 6 (person to represent appellant's interests),
(b) section 7 (further appeal on point of law), and
(c) section 7A (pending appeal).

(2) The reference in subsection (1) to an appeal or review does not include a reference to a decision made or action taken on or in connection with –

(a) an application under section 25(5)(b) or 26(4)(a) of this Act, or
(b) subsection (8) below.

(3) Subsection (4) applies where –

(a) a further appeal is brought by virtue of subsection (1)(b) in connection with an appeal or review, and
(b) the Secretary of State notifies the Commission that in his opinion the further appeal is confined to calling into question one or more derogation matters within the meaning of section 30 of this Act.

(4) For the purpose of the application of section 26(2) and (3) of this Act the determination by the Commission of the appeal or review in connection with which the further appeal is brought shall be treated as a final determination.

(5) Rules under section 5 or 8 of the Special Immigration Appeals Commission Act 1997 (general procedure; and leave to appeal) may make provision about an appeal, review or application under section 24, 25 or 26 of this Act.

(6) Subject to any provision made by virtue of subsection (5), rules under section 5 or 8 of that Act shall apply in relation to an appeal, review or application under section 24, 25 or 26 of this Act with any modification which the Commission considers necessary.

(7) Subsection (8) applies where the Commission considers that an appeal or review under section 25 or 26 which relates to a person's certification under section 21 is likely to raise an issue which is also likely to be raised in other proceedings before the Commission which relate to the same person.

(8) The Commission shall so far as is reasonably practicable –

(a) deal with the two sets of proceedings together, and
(b) avoid or minimise delay to either set of proceedings as a result of compliance with paragraph (a).

(9) Cancellation by the Commission of a certificate issued under section 21 shall not

prevent the Secretary of State from issuing another certificate, whether on the grounds of a change of circumstance or otherwise.

(10) The reference in section 110 of the Nationality, Immigration and Asylum Act 2002 (international asylum appeal: grant to voluntary organisation) to persons who have rights of appeal under Part 5 of that Act shall be treated as including a reference to suspected international terrorists.

29 Duration of sections 21 to 23

(1) Sections 21 to 23 shall, subject to the following provisions of this section, expire at the end of the period of 15 months beginning with the day on which this Act is passed.

(2) The Secretary of State may by order –

(a) repeal sections 21 to 23;

(b) revive those sections for a period not exceeding one year;

(c) provide that those sections shall not expire in accordance with subsection (1) or an order under paragraph (b) or this paragraph, but shall continue in force for a period not exceeding one year. ...

(7) Sections 21 to 23 shall by virtue of this subsection cease to have effect at the end of 10th November 2006.

30 Legal proceedings: derogation

(1) In this section 'derogation matter' means –

(a) a derogation by the United Kingdom from Article 5(1) of the Convention on Human Rights which relates to the detention of a person where there is an intention to remove or deport him from the United Kingdom, or

(b) the designation under section 14(1) of the Human Rights Act 1998 (c 42) of a derogation within paragraph (a) above.

(2) A derogation matter may be questioned in legal proceedings only before the Special Immigration Appeals Commission; and the Commission –

(a) is the appropriate tribunal for the purpose of section 7 of the Human Rights Act 1998 in relation to proceedings all or part of which call a derogation matter into question; and

(b) may hear proceedings which could, but for this subsection, be brought in the High Court or the Court of Session.

(3) In relation to proceedings brought by virtue of subsection (2) –

(a) section 6 of the Special Immigration Appeals Commission Act 1997 (c 68) (person to represent appellant's interests) shall apply with the reference to the appellant being treated as a reference to any party to the proceedings,

(b) rules under section 5 or 8 of that Act (general procedure; and leave to appeal) shall apply with any modification which the Commission considers necessary, and

(c) in the case of proceedings brought by virtue of subsection (2)(b), the Commission may do anything which the High Court may do (in the case of proceedings which could have been brought in that court) or which the Court of Session may do (in the case of proceedings which could have been brought in that court).

(4) The Commission's power to award costs (or, in Scotland, expenses) by virtue of subsection (3)(c) may be exercised only in relation to such part of proceedings before it as calls a derogation matter into question.

(5) In relation to proceedings brought by virtue of subsection (2)(a) or (b) –

(a) an appeal may be brought to the appropriate appeal court (within the meaning of section 7 of the Special Immigration Appeals Commission Act 1997 (c 68)) with the leave of the Commission or, if that leave is refused, with the leave of the appropriate appeal court, and

(b) the appropriate appeal court may consider and do only those things which it could consider and do in an appeal brought from the High Court or the Court of Session in proceedings for judicial review.

(6) In relation to proceedings which are entertained by the Commission under subsection (2) but are not brought by virtue of subsection (2)(a) or (b), subsection (4) shall apply in so far as the proceedings call a derogation matter into question.

(7) In this section 'the Convention on Human Rights' has the meaning given to 'the Convention' by section 21(1) of the Human Rights Act 1998 (c 42).

31 Interpretation

A reference in section 22, 23 or 24 to a provision of the Immigration Act 1971 (c 77) includes a reference to that provision as applied by –

(a) another provision of that Act, or

(b) another Act.

33 Certificate that Convention does not apply

(1) This section applies to an asylum appeal before the Special Immigration Appeals Commission where the Secretary of State issues a certificate that –

(a) the appellant is not entitled to the protection of Article 33(1) of the Refugee Convention because Article 1(F) or 33(2) applies to him (whether or not he would be entitled to protection if that Article did not apply), and

(b) the removal of the appellant from the United Kingdom would be conducive to the public good.

(2) In this section –

'asylum appeal' means an appeal under section 2 of the Special Immigration

Appeals Commission Act 1997 (c 68) in which the appellant makes an asylum claim (within the meaning given by section 113(1) of the Nationality, Immigration and Asylum Act 2002), and

'the Refugee Convention' has the meaning given by that section.

(3) Where this section applies the Commission must begin its substantive deliberations on the asylum appeal by considering the statements in the Secretary of State's certificate.

(4) If the Commission agrees with those statements it must dismiss such part of the asylum appeal as amounts to an asylum claim (before considering any other aspect of the case).

(5) If the Commission does not agree with those statements it must quash the decision or action against which the asylum appeal is brought.

(6) Where a decision or action is quashed under subsection (5) –

(a) the quashing shall not prejudice any later decision or action, whether taken on the grounds of a change of circumstance or otherwise, and

(b) the asylum claim made in the course of the asylum appeal shall be treated for the purposes of section 77 of the Nationality, Immigration and Asylum Act 2002 (no removal while claim for asylum pending), as pending until it has been determined whether to take a new decision or action of the kind quashed.

(7) The Secretary of State may revoke a certificate issued under subsection (1).

(8) No court may entertain proceedings for questioning –

(a) a decision or action of the Secretary of State in connection with certification under subsection (1),

(b) a decision of the Secretary of State in connection with an asylum claim (within the meaning given by section 113(1) of the Nationality, Immigration and Asylum Act 2002) in a case in respect of which he issues a certificate under subsection (1) above, or

(c) a decision or action of the Secretary of State taken as a consequence of the dismissal of all or part of an asylum appeal in pursuance of subsection (4).

(9) Subsection (8) shall not prevent an appeal under section 7 of the Special Immigration Appeals Commission Act 1997 (appeal on point of law).

(10) Her Majesty may by Order in Council direct that this section shall extend, with such modifications as appear to Her Majesty to be appropriate, to any of the Channel Islands or the Isle of Man.

NB By virtue of the Anti-terrorism, Crime and Security Act 2001 (Continuation in force of sections 21 to 23) Order 2004, those sections continue in force for one year beginning 14 March 2004.

As amended by the Nationality, Immigration and Asylum Act 2002, ss62(15)(a), (b), (16), 114, Schedule 7, para 30; Nationality, Immigration and Asylum Act 2002 (Consequential and Incidental Provisions) Order 2003, art 3, Schedule, paras 14–16; Asylum and Immigration (Treatment of Claimants, etc) Act 2004, s32(2).

OFFICE OF COMMUNICATIONS ACT 2002

(2002 c 11)

1 The Office of Communications

(1) There shall be a body corporate to be known as the Office of Communications (in this Act referred to as 'OFCOM').

(2) OFCOM shall consist of such number of members as the Secretary of State may determine; but he shall not determine a membership for OFCOM of less than three or more than nine.

(3) The membership of OFCOM shall comprise –

(a) a chairman appointed by the Secretary of State;

(b) such number of other members appointed by the Secretary of State as he may determine; and

(c) the executive members.

(4) The executive members of OFCOM shall comprise –

(a) the chief executive of OFCOM; and

(b) such other persons (if any) as may be appointed to membership of OFCOM from amongst their employees.

(5) It shall be for the members of OFCOM mentioned in subsection (3)(a) and (b), after consulting the chief executive of OFCOM –

(a) to determine whether there should be any executive members falling within subsection (4)(b) and (subject to subsections (2) and (6)(a)) how many; and

(b) to make any appointments of executive members required for the purposes of any such determination.

(6) The Secretary of State –

(a) may, by a direction to OFCOM, set a maximum and a minimum number for the executive members of OFCOM; and

(b) shall exercise his powers under this section to secure that the number of executive members of OFCOM is, so far as practicable, at all times less than the number of other members.

(7) The Secretary of State may by order made by statutory instrument modify the numbers for the time being specified in subsection (2) as the maximum and minimum membership for OFCOM.

(8) A statutory instrument containing an order under subsection (7) shall be subject to annulment in pursuance of a resolution of either House of Parliament; and the power to make such an order shall include power to make such incidental, supplemental, consequential and transitional provision as the Secretary of State thinks fit.

(9) OFCOM shall not be treated for any purposes as a body exercising functions on behalf of the Crown; and, accordingly, no person shall be treated as a servant of the Crown by reason only of his membership of, or employment by, OFCOM.

(10) The Schedule (which makes provision in relation to OFCOM) shall have effect.

3 Management of OFCOM

OFCOM shall, in managing their affairs, have regard –

(a) to such general guidance concerning the management of the affairs of public bodies as OFCOM consider appropriate; and

(b) subject to any such guidance and only to the extent that they may reasonably be regarded as applicable in relation to a statutory corporation, to generally accepted principles of good corporate governance.

As amended by the Office of Communications (Membership) Order 2002.

EUROPEAN PARLIAMENTARY ELECTIONS ACT 2002

(2002 c 24)

1 Number of MEPs and electoral regions

(1) There shall be 78 members of the European Parliament ('MEPs') elected for the United Kingdom.

(2) For the purposes of electing those MEPs –

(a) the area of England and Gibraltar is divided into the nine electoral regions specified in Schedule 1; and

(b) Scotland, Wales and Northern Ireland are each single electoral regions.

(3) The number of MEPs to be elected for each electoral region is as follows –

East Midlands	6
Eastern	7
London	9
North East	3
North West	9
South East	10
South West	7
West Midlands	7
Yorkshire and the Humber	6
Scotland	7
Wales	4
Northern Ireland	3

1A Periodic reviews of distribution of MEPs

Schedule 1A (which provides for periodic reviews by the Electoral Commission of the distribution of MEPs between the electoral regions) has effect.

2 Voting system in Great Britain ...

(1) The system of election of MEPs in an electoral region other than Northern Ireland is to be a regional list system.

(2) The Secretary of State must by regulations –

(a) make provision for the nomination of registered parties in relation to an election in such a region, and

(b) require a nomination under paragraph (a) to be accompanied by a list of candidates numbering no more than the MEPs to be elected for the region.

(3) The system of election must comply with the following conditions.

(4) A vote may be cast for a registered party or an individual candidate named on the ballot paper.

(5) The first seat is to be allocated to the party or individual candidate with the greatest number of votes.

(6) The second and subsequent seats are to be allocated in the same way, except that the number of votes given to a party to which one or more seats have already been allocated are to be divided by the number of seats allocated plus one.

(7) In allocating the second or any subsequent seat there are to be disregarded any votes given to –

(a) a party to which there has already been allocated a number of seats equal to the number of names on the party's list of candidates, and

(b) an individual candidate to whom a seat has already been allocated.

(8) Seats allocated to a party are to be filled by the persons named on the party's list of candidates in the order in which they appear on that list.

(9) For the purposes of subsection (6) fractions are to be taken into account.

(10) In this section 'registered party' means a party registered under Part 2 of the Political Parties, Elections and Referendums Act 2000 (c 41).

8 Persons entitled to vote

(1) A person is entitled to vote as an elector at an election to the European Parliament in an electoral region if he is within any of subsections (2) to (5).

(2) A person is within this subsection if on the day of the poll he would be entitled to vote as an elector at a parliamentary election in a parliamentary constituency wholly or partly comprised in the electoral region, and –

(a) the address in respect of which he is registered in the relevant register of parliamentary electors is within the electoral region, or

(b) his registration in the relevant register of parliamentary electors results from an overseas elector's declaration which specifies an address within the electoral region.

(3) A person is within this subsection if –

(a) he is a peer who on the day of the poll would be entitled to vote at a local government election in an electoral area wholly or partly comprised in the electoral region, and

(b) the address in respect of which he is registered in the relevant register of local government electors is within the electoral region.

(4) A person is within this subsection if he is entitled to vote in the electoral region by virtue of section 3 of the Representation of the People Act 1985 (c 50) (peers resident outside the United Kingdom).

(5) A person is within this subsection if he is entitled to vote in the electoral region by virtue of the European Parliamentary Elections (Franchise of Relevant Citizens of the Union) Regulations 2001 (SI 2001/1184) (citizens of the European Union other than Commonwealth and Republic of Ireland citizens).

(6) Subsection (1) has effect subject to any provision of regulations made under this Act which provides for alterations made after a specified date in a register of electors to be disregarded.

(7) In subsection (3) 'local government election' includes a municipal election in the City of London (that is, an election to the office of mayor, alderman, common councilman or sheriff and also the election of any officer elected by the mayor, aldermen and liverymen in common hall). ...

10 Disqualification

(1) A person is disqualified for the office of MEP if –

(a) he is disqualified for membership of the House of Commons, or

(b) he is a Lord of Appeal in Ordinary.

(2) But a person is not disqualified for the office of MEP under subsection (1)(a) merely because –

(a) he is a peer,

(b) he is a Lord Spiritual,

(c) he holds an office mentioned in section 4 of the House of Commons Disqualification Act 1975 (c 24) (stewardship of Chiltern Hundreds etc), or

(d) he holds any of the offices described in Part 2 or 3 of Schedule 1 to that Act which are designated by order by the Secretary of State for the purposes of this section.

(3) A citizen of the European Union who is resident in the United Kingdom ... is not disqualified for the office of MEP under subsection (1)(a) merely because he is disqualified for membership of the House of Commons under section 3 of the Act of Settlement (12 & 13 Will 3 c 2) (disqualification of persons, other than Commonwealth and Republic of Ireland citizens, who are born outside Great Britain and Ireland and the dominions).

(4) A person is disqualified for the office of MEP for a particular electoral region if, under section 1(2) of the House of Commons Disqualification Act 1975 (c 24), he is disqualified for membership of the House of Commons for any parliamentary constituency wholly or partly comprised in that region. ...

(5) A person who –

(a) is a citizen of the European Union, and

(b) is not a Commonwealth citizen or a citizen of the Republic of Ireland,

is disqualified for the office of MEP if he is disqualified for that office through a criminal law or civil law decision under the law of the member state of which he is a national (and in this subsection 'criminal law or civil law decision' has the same meaning as in Council Directive 93/109/EC).

(6) If a person who is returned as an MEP for an electoral region under section 2, … or 5 –

(a) is disqualified under this section for the office of MEP, or

(b) is disqualified under this section for the office of MEP for that region,

his return is void and his seat vacant.

(7) If an MEP becomes disqualified under this section for the office of MEP or for the office of MEP for the electoral region for which he was returned, his seat is to be vacated.

(8) Subsection (1) is without prejudice to Article 7(1) and (2) of the Act annexed to Council Decision 76/787 (incompatibility of office of MEP with certain offices in or connected with Community institutions).

11 Judicial determination of disqualification

(1) Any person may apply to the appropriate court for a declaration … that a person who purports to be an MEP for a particular electoral region –

(a) is disqualified under section 10 (whether generally or for that region), or

(b) was so disqualified at the time when, or at some time since, he was returned as an MEP under section 2, … or 5 [Filling vacant seats].

(2) For the purposes of subsection (1), the appropriate court is –

(a) the High Court, if the electoral region concerned is an electoral region in England and Wales …

(3) The decision of the court on an application under this section is final. …

12 Ratification of treaties

(1) No treaty which provides for any increase in the powers of the European Parliament is to be ratified by the United Kingdom unless it has been approved by an Act of Parliament.

(2) In this section 'treaty' includes –

(a) any international agreement, and

(b) any protocol or annex to a treaty or international agreement.

17 Interpretation

In this Act – …

'the Act annexed to Council Decision 76/787' is the Act concerning the election of MEPs annexed to Council Decision 76/787/ECSC, EEC, Euratom of 20th September 1976;

'citizen of the European Union' is to be determined in accordance with Article 17.1 of the Treaty establishing the European Community. …

As amended by the European Parliament (Representation) Act 2003, ss1, 7(1); European Parliament (Number of MEPs) (United Kingdom and Gibraltar) Order 2004, art 2(1)–(3); European Parliamentary Elections (Combined Region and Campaign Expenditure) (United Kingdom and Gibraltar) Order 2004, art 3(1), (2), (3)(b), (5); European Parliamentary Elections (Common Electoral Principles) Regulations 2004, reg 2(1), (3).

POLICE REFORM ACT 2002

2002 (c 30)

PART 2

COMPLAINTS AND MISCONDUCT

9 The Independent Police Complaints Commission

(1) There shall be a body corporate to be known as the Independent Police Complaints Commission (in this Part referred to as 'the Commission').

(2) The Commission shall consist of –

(a) a chairman appointed by Her Majesty; and

(b) not less than ten other members appointed by the Secretary of State.

(3) A person shall not be appointed as the chairman of the Commission, or as another member of the Commission, if –

(a) he holds or has held office as a constable in any part of the United Kingdom;

(b) he is or has been under the direction and control of a chief officer or of any person holding an equivalent office in Scotland or Northern Ireland;

(c) he is a person in relation to whom a designation under section 39 is or has been in force;

(d) he is a person in relation to whom an accreditation under section 41 is or has been in force;

(e) he is or has been a member of the National Criminal Intelligence Service or the National Crime Squad; or

(f) he is or has at any time been a member of a body of constables which at the time of his membership is or was a body of constables in relation to which any procedures are or were in force by virtue of an agreement or order under –

(i) section 26 of this Act; or

(ii) section 78 of the 1996 Act or section 96 of the 1984 Act (which made provision corresponding to that made by section 26 of this Act).

(4) An appointment made in contravention of subsection (3) shall have no effect.

(5) The Commission shall not –

(a) be regarded as the servant or agent of the Crown; or

(b) enjoy any status, privilege or immunity of the Crown;

and the Commission's property shall not be regarded as property of, or property held on behalf of, the Crown.

(6) Schedule 2 (which makes further provision in relation to the Commission) shall have effect.

(7) The Police Complaints Authority shall cease to exist on such day as the Secretary of State may by order appoint.

10 General functions of the Commission

(1) The functions of the Commission shall be –

(a) to secure the maintenance by the Commission itself, and by police authorities and chief officers, of suitable arrangements with respect to the matters mentioned in subsection (2);

(b) to keep under review all arrangements maintained with respect to those matters;

(c) to secure that arrangements maintained with respect to those matters comply with the requirements of the following provisions of this Part, are efficient and effective and contain and manifest an appropriate degree of independence;

(d) to secure that public confidence is established and maintained in the existence of suitable arrangements with respect to those matters and with the operation of the arrangements that are in fact maintained with respect to those matters;

(e) to make such recommendations, and to give such advice, for the modification of the arrangements maintained with respect to those matters, and also of police practice in relation to other matters, as appear, from the carrying out by the Commission of its other functions, to be necessary or desirable; and

(f) to such extent as it may be required to do so by regulations made by the Secretary of State, to carry out functions in relation to the National Criminal Intelligence Service, the National Crime Squad and bodies of constables maintained otherwise than by police authorities which broadly correspond to those conferred on the Commission in relation to police forces by the preceding paragraphs of this subsection.

(2) Those matters are –

(a) the handling of complaints made about the conduct of persons serving with the police;

(b) the recording of matters from which it appears that there may have been conduct by such persons which constitutes or involves the commission of a criminal offence or behaviour justifying disciplinary proceedings;

(c) the manner in which any such complaints or any such matters as are mentioned in paragraph (b) are investigated or otherwise handled and dealt with.

(3) The Commission shall also have the functions which are conferred on it by –

(a) any regulations under section 39 or 83 of the 1997 Act (complaints etc against members of NCIS and NCS);

(b) any agreement or order under section 26 of this Act (other bodies of constables);

(c) any regulations under section 39 of this Act (police powers for contracted-out staff); or

(d) any regulations or arrangements relating to disciplinary or similar proceedings against persons serving with the police, or against members of the National Criminal Intelligence Service, the National Crime Squad or any body of constables maintained otherwise than by a police authority.

(4) It shall be the duty of the Commission –

(a) to exercise the powers and perform the duties conferred on it by the following provisions of this Part in the manner that it considers best calculated for the purpose of securing the proper carrying out of its functions under subsections (1) and (3); and

(b) to secure that arrangements exist which are conducive to, and facilitate, the reporting of misconduct by persons in relation to whose conduct the Commission has functions.

(5) It shall also be the duty of the Commission –

(a) to enter into arrangements with the chief inspector of constabulary for the purpose of securing co-operation, in the carrying out of their respective functions, between the Commission and the inspectors of constabulary; and

(b) to provide those inspectors with all such assistance and co-operation as may be required by those arrangements, or as otherwise appears to the Commission to be appropriate, for facilitating the carrying out by those inspectors of their functions.

(6) Subject to the other provisions of this Part, the Commission may do anything which appears to it to be calculated to facilitate, or is incidental or conducive to, the carrying out of its functions.

(7) The Commission may, in connection with the making of any recommendation or the giving of any advice to any person for the purpose of carrying out –

(a) its function under subsection (1)(e), or

(b) any corresponding function conferred on it by virtue of subsection (1)(f),

impose any such charge on that person for anything done by the Commission for the purposes of, or in connection with, the carrying out of that function as it thinks fit.

(8) Nothing in this Part shall confer any function on the Commission in relation to so much of any complaint or conduct matter as relates to the direction and control of a police force by –

(a) the chief officer of police of that force; or

(b) a person for the time being carrying out the functions of the chief officer of police of that force.

11 Reports to the Secretary of State

(1) As soon as practicable after the end of each of its financial years, the Commission shall make a report to the Secretary of State on the carrying out of its functions during that year.

(2) The Commission shall also make such reports to the Secretary of State about matters relating generally to the carrying out of its functions as he may, from time to time, require.

(3) The Commission may, from time to time, make such other reports to the Secretary of State as it considers appropriate for drawing his attention to matters which –

(a) have come to the Commission's notice; and

(b) are matters that it considers should be drawn to his attention by reason of their gravity or of other exceptional circumstances.

(4) The Commission shall prepare such reports containing advice and recommendations as it thinks appropriate for the purpose of carrying out –

(a) its function under subsection (1)(e) of section 10; or

(b) any corresponding function conferred on it by virtue of subsection (1)(f) of that section. ...

12 Complaints, matters and persons to which Part 2 applies

(1) In this Part references to a complaint are references (subject to the following provisions of this section) to any complaint about the conduct of a person serving with the police which is made (whether in writing or otherwise) by –

(a) a member of the public who claims to be the person in relation to whom the conduct took place;

(b) a member of the public not falling within paragraph (a) who claims to have been adversely affected by the conduct;

(c) a member of the public who claims to have witnessed the conduct;

(d) a person acting on behalf of a person falling within any of paragraphs (a) to (c).

(2) In this Part 'conduct matter' means (subject to the following provisions of this section, paragraph 2(4) of Schedule 3 and any regulations made by virtue of section 23(2)(d)) any matter which is not and has not been the subject of a complaint but in the case of which there is an indication (whether from the circumstances or otherwise) that a person serving with the police may have –

(a) committed a criminal offence; or

(b) behaved in a manner which would justify the bringing of disciplinary proceedings.

(3) The complaints that are complaints for the purposes of this Part by virtue of subsection (1)(b) do not, except in a case falling within subsection (4), include any

made by or on behalf of a person who claims to have been adversely affected as a consequence only of having seen or heard the conduct, or any of the alleged effects of the conduct.

(4) A case falls within this subsection if –

(a) it was only because the person in question was physically present, or sufficiently nearby, when the conduct took place or the effects occurred that he was able to see or hear the conduct or its effects; or

(b) the adverse effect is attributable to, or was aggravated by, the fact that the person in relation to whom the conduct took place was already known to the person claiming to have suffered the adverse effect.

(5) For the purposes of this section a person shall be taken to have witnessed conduct if, and only if –

(a) he acquired his knowledge of that conduct in a manner which would make him a competent witness capable of giving admissible evidence of that conduct in criminal proceedings; or

(b) he has in his possession or under his control anything which would in any such proceedings constitute admissible evidence of that conduct.

(6) For the purposes of this Part a person falling within subsection 1(a) to (c) to shall not be taken to have authorised another person to act on his behalf unless –

(a) that other person is for the time being designated for the purposes of this Part by the Commission as a person through whom complaints may be made, or he is of a description of persons so designated; or

(b) the other person has been given, and is able to produce, the written consent to his so acting of the person on whose behalf he acts.

(7) For the purposes of this Part, a person is serving with the police if –

(a) he is a member of a police force;

(b) he is an employee of a police authority who is under the direction and control of a chief officer; or

(c) he is a special constable who is under the direction and control of a chief officer.

13 Handling of complaints and conduct matters, etc

Schedule 3 (which makes provision for the handling of complaints and conduct matters and for the carrying out of investigations) shall have effect subject to section 14(1).

14 Direction and control matters

(1) Nothing in Schedule 3 shall have effect with respect to so much of any complaint as relates to the direction and control of a police force by –

(a) the chief officer of police of that force; or

(b) a person for the time being carrying out the functions of the chief officer of police of that force.

(2) The Secretary of State may issue guidance to chief officers and to police authorities about the handling of so much of any complaint as relates to the direction and control of a police force by such a person as is mentioned in subsection (1).

(3) It shall be the duty of a chief officer and of a police authority when handling any complaint relating to such a matter to have regard to any guidance issued under subsection (2).

15 General duties of police authorities, chief officers and inspectors

(1) It shall be the duty of –

(a) every police authority maintaining a police force,

(b) the chief officer of police of every police force, and

(c) every inspector of constabulary carrying out any of his functions in relation to a police force,

to ensure that it or he is kept informed, in relation to that force, about all matters falling within subsection (2).

(2) Those matters are –

(a) matters with respect to which any provision of this Part has effect;

(b) anything which is done under or for the purposes of any such provision; and

(c) any obligations to act or refrain from acting that have arisen by or under this Part but have not yet been complied with, or have been contravened.

(3) Where –

(a) a police authority maintaining any police force requires the chief officer of that force or of any other force to provide a member of his force for appointment under paragraph 16, 17 or 18 of Schedule 3,

(b) the chief officer of police of any police force requires the chief officer of police of any other police force to provide a member of that other force for appointment under any of those paragraphs, or

(c) a police authority or chief officer requires the Director General of the National Criminal Intelligence Service or the Director General of the National Crime Squad to provide a member of that Service or Squad for appointment under any of those paragraphs,

it shall be the duty of the chief officer or Director General to whom the requirement is addressed to comply with it.

(4) It shall be the duty of –

(a) every police authority maintaining a police force,

(b) the chief officer of police of every police force,

(c) the Service Authority for the National Criminal Intelligence Service and the Service Authority for the National Crime Squad, and

(d) the Directors General of that Service and of that Squad,

to provide the Commission and every member of the Commission's staff with all such assistance as the Commission or that member of staff may reasonably require for the purposes of, or in connection with, the carrying out of any investigation by the Commission under this Part.

(5) It shall be the duty of –

(a) every police authority maintaining a police force,

(b) the chief officer of every police force,

(c) the Service Authorities for the National Criminal Intelligence Service and of the National Crime Squad, and

(d) the Directors General of that Service and of that Squad,

to ensure that a person appointed under paragraph 16, 17 or 18 of Schedule 3 to carry out an investigation is given all such assistance and co-operation in the carrying out of that investigation as that person may reasonably require

(6) The duties imposed by subsections (4) and (5) on a police authority maintaining a police force and on the chief officer of such a force and on the Directors General of the National Criminal Intelligence Service and of the National Crime Squad have effect –

(a) irrespective of whether the investigation relates to the conduct of a person who is or has been a member of that force or of that Service or Squad; and

(b) irrespective of who has the person appointed to carry out the investigation under his direction and control;

but a chief officer of a third force may be required to give assistance and co-operation under subsection (5) only with the approval of the chief officer of the force to which the person who requires it belongs or, as the case may be, of the Director General of the Service or Squad to which that person belongs.

(7) In subsection (6) 'third force', in relation to an investigation, means a police force other than –

(a) the force to which the person carrying out the investigation belongs; or

(b) the force to which the person whose conduct is under investigation belonged at the time of the conduct;

and in this subsection references to a police force include references to the National Criminal Intelligence Service and the National Crime Squad.

17 Provision of information to the Commission

(1) It shall be the duty of –

(a) every police authority, and

(b) every chief officer,

at such times, in such circumstances and in accordance with such other requirements as may be set out in regulations made by the Secretary of State, to provide the Commission with all such information and documents as may be specified or described in regulations so made.

(2) It shall also be the duty of every police authority and of every chief officer –

(a) to provide the Commission with all such other information and documents specified or described in a notification given by the Commission to that authority or chief officer, and

(b) to produce or deliver up to the Commission all such evidence and other things so specified or described,

as appear to the Commission to be required by it for the purposes of the carrying out of any of its functions.

(3) Anything falling to be provided, produced or delivered up by any person in pursuance of a requirement imposed under subsection (2) must be provided, produced or delivered up in such form, in such manner and within such period as may be specified in –

(a) the notification imposing the requirement; or

(b) in any subsequent notification given by the Commission to that person for the purposes of this subsection.

(4) Nothing in this section shall require a police authority or chief officer –

(a) to provide the Commission with any information or document, or to produce or deliver up any other thing, before the earliest time at which it is practicable for that authority or chief officer to do so; or

(b) to provide, produce or deliver up anything at all in a case in which it never becomes practicable for that authority or chief officer to do so.

(5) A requirement imposed by any regulations or notification under this section may authorise or require information or documents to which it relates to be provided to the Commission electronically.

18 Inspections of police premises on behalf of the Commission

(1) Where –

(a) the Commission requires –

(i) a police authority maintaining any police force, or

(ii) the chief officer of police of any such force,

to allow a person nominated for the purpose by the Commission to have access to any premises occupied for the purposes of that force and to documents and other things on those premises, and

(b) the requirement is imposed for any of the purposes mentioned in subsection (2), it shall be the duty of the authority or, as the case may be, of the chief officer to secure that the required access is allowed to the nominated person.

(2) Those purposes are –

(a) the purposes of any examination by the Commission of the efficiency and effectiveness of the arrangements made by the force in question for handling complaints or dealing with recordable conduct matters;

(b) the purposes of any investigation by the Commission under this Part or of any investigation carried out under its supervision or management.

(3) A requirement imposed under this section for the purposes mentioned in subsection (2)(a) must be notified to the authority or chief officer at least 48 hours before the time at which access is required.

(4) Where –

(a) a requirement imposed under this section for the purposes mentioned in subsection (2)(a) requires access to any premises, document or thing to be allowed to any person, but

(b) there are reasonable grounds for not allowing that person to have the required access at the time at which he seeks to have it,

the obligation to secure that the required access is allowed shall have effect as an obligation to secure that the access is allowed to that person at the earliest practicable time after there cease to be any such grounds as that person may specify.

(5) The provisions of this section are in addition to, and without prejudice to –

(a) the rights of entry, search and seizure that are or may be conferred on –

(i) a person designated for the purposes of paragraph 19 of Schedule 3, or

(ii) any person who otherwise acts on behalf of the Commission,

in his capacity as a constable or as a person with the powers and privileges of a constable; or

(b) the obligations of police authorities and chief officers under sections 15 and 17.

19 Use of investigatory powers by or on behalf of the Commission

(1) The Secretary of State may by order make such provision as he thinks appropriate for the purpose of authorising –

(a) the use of directed and intrusive surveillance, and

(b) the conduct and use of covert human intelligence sources,

for the purposes of, or for purposes connected with, the carrying out of the Commission's functions.

(2) An order under this section may, for the purposes of or in connection with any such provision as is mentioned in subsection (1), provide for –

(a) Parts 2 and 4 the Regulation of Investigatory Powers Act 2000 (c 23) (surveillance and covert human intelligence sources and scrutiny of investigatory powers), and

(b) Part 3 of the 1997 Act (authorisations in respect of property),

to have effect with such modifications as may be specified in the order.

(3) The Secretary of State shall not make an order containing (with or without any other provision) any provision authorised by this section unless a draft of that order has been laid before Parliament and approved by a resolution of each House.

(4) Expressions used in this section and in Part 2 of the Regulation of Investigatory Powers Act 2000 have the same meanings in this section as in that Part.

20 Duty to keep the complainant informed

(1) In any case in which there is an investigation of a complaint in accordance with the provisions of Schedule 3 –

(a) by the Commission, or

(b) under its management,

it shall be the duty of the Commission to provide the complainant with all such information as will keep him properly informed, while the investigation is being carried out and subsequently, of all the matters mentioned in subsection (4).

(2) In any case in which there is an investigation of a complaint in accordance with the provisions of Schedule 3 –

(a) by the appropriate authority on its own behalf, or

(b) under the supervision of the Commission,

it shall be the duty of the appropriate authority to provide the complainant with all such information as will keep him properly informed, while the investigation is being carried out and subsequently, of all the matters mentioned in subsection (4).

(3) Where subsection (2) applies, it shall be the duty of the Commission to give the appropriate authority all such directions as it considers appropriate for securing that that authority complies with its duty under that subsection; and it shall be the duty of the appropriate authority to comply with any direction given to it under this subsection.

(4) The matters of which the complainant must be kept properly informed are –

(a) the progress of the investigation;

(b) any provisional findings of the person carrying out the investigation;

(c) whether any report has been submitted under paragraph 22 of Schedule 3;

(d) the action (if any) that is taken in respect of the matters dealt with in any such report; and

(e) the outcome of any such action.

(5) The duties imposed by this section on the Commission and the appropriate

authority in relation to any complaint shall be performed in such manner, and shall have effect subject to such exceptions, as may be provided for by regulations made by the Secretary of State.

(6) The Secretary of State shall not by regulations provide for any exceptions from the duties imposed by this section except so far as he considers it necessary to do so for the purpose of –

(a) preventing the premature or inappropriate disclosure of information that is relevant to, or may be used in, any actual or prospective criminal proceedings;

(b) preventing the disclosure of information in any circumstances in which it has been determined in accordance with the regulations that its non-disclosure –

(i) is in the interests of national security;

(ii) is for the purposes of the prevention or detection of crime, or the apprehension or prosecution of offenders;

(iii) is required on proportionality grounds; or

(iv) is otherwise necessary in the public interest.

(7) The non-disclosure of information is required on proportionality grounds if its disclosure would cause, directly or indirectly, an adverse effect which would be disproportionate to the benefits arising from its disclosure.

(8) Regulations under this section may include provision framed by reference to the opinion of, or a determination by, the Commission or any police authority or chief officer.

(9) It shall be the duty of a person appointed to carry out an investigation under this Part to provide the Commission or, as the case may be, the appropriate authority with all such information as the Commission or that authority may reasonably require for the purpose of performing its duty under this section.

21 Duty to provide information for other persons

(1) A person has an interest in being kept properly informed about the handling of a complaint or recordable conduct matter if –

(a) it appears to the Commission or to an appropriate authority that he is a person falling within subsection (2); and

(b) that person has indicated that he consents to the provision of information to him in accordance with this section and that consent has not been withdrawn.

(2) A person falls within this subsection if –

(a) he is a relative of a person whose death is the alleged result from the conduct complained of or to which the recordable conduct matter relates;

(b) he is a relative of a person whose serious injury is the alleged result from that conduct and that person is incapable of making a complaint;

(c) he himself has suffered serious injury as the alleged result of that conduct.

(3) A person who does not fall within subsection (2) has an interest in being kept properly informed about the handling of a complaint or recordable conduct matter if –

(a) the Commission or an appropriate authority considers that he has an interest in the handling of the complaint or recordable conduct matter which is sufficient to make it appropriate for information to be provided to him in accordance with this section; and

(b) he has indicated that he consents to the provision of information to him in accordance with this section.

(4) In relation to a complaint, this section confers no rights on the complainant.

(5) A person who has an interest in being kept properly informed about the handling of a complaint or conduct matter is referred to in this section as an 'interested person'.

(6) In any case in which there is an investigation of the complaint or recordable conduct matter in accordance with the provisions of Schedule 3 –

(a) by the Commission, or

(b) under its management,

it shall be the duty of the Commission to provide the interested person with all such information as will keep him properly informed, while the investigation is being carried out and subsequently, of all the matters mentioned in subsection (9).

(7) In any case in which there is an investigation of the complaint or recordable conduct matter in accordance with the provisions of Schedule 3 –

(a) by the appropriate authority on its own behalf, or

(b) under the supervision of the Commission,

it shall be the duty of the appropriate authority to provide the interested person with all such information as will keep him properly informed, while the investigation is being carried out and subsequently, of all the matters mentioned in subsection (9).

(8) Where subsection (7) applies, it shall be the duty of the Commission to give the appropriate authority all such directions as it considers appropriate for securing that that authority complies with its duty under that subsection; and it shall be the duty of the appropriate authority to comply with any direction given to it under this subsection.

(9) The matters of which the interested person must be kept properly informed are –

(a) the progress of the investigation;

(b) any provisional findings of the person carrying out the investigation;

(c) whether any report has been submitted under paragraph 22 of Schedule 3;

(d) the action (if any) that is taken in respect of the matters dealt with in any such report; and

(e) the outcome of any such action.

(10) The duties imposed by this section on the Commission and the appropriate authority in relation to any complaint or recordable conduct matter shall be performed in such manner, and shall have effect subject to such exceptions, as may be provided for by regulations made by the Secretary of State.

(11) Subsections (6) to (9) of section 20 apply for the purposes of this section as they apply for the purposes of that section.

(12) In this section 'relative' means a person of a description prescribed in regulations made by the Secretary of State.

22 Power of the Commission to issue guidance

(1) The Commission may issue guidance –

(a) to police authorities,

(b) to chief officers, and

(c) to persons who are serving with the police otherwise than as chief officers,

concerning the exercise or performance, by the persons to whom the guidance is issued, of any of the powers or duties specified in subsection (2).

(2) Those powers and duties are –

(a) those that are conferred or imposed by or under this Part; and

(b) those that are otherwise conferred or imposed but relate to –

(i) the handling of complaints;

(ii) the means by which recordable conduct matters are dealt with; or

(iii) the detection or deterrence of misconduct by persons serving with the police. …

(7) It shall be the duty of every person to whom any guidance under this section is issued to have regard to that guidance in exercising or performing the powers and duties to which the guidance relates.

(8) A failure by a person to whom guidance under this section is issued to have regard to the guidance shall be admissible in evidence in any disciplinary proceedings or on any appeal from a decision taken in any such proceedings.

23 Regulations

(1) The Secretary of State may make regulations as to the procedure to be followed under any provision of this Part. …

24 Consultation on regulations

Before making any regulations under this Part, the Secretary of State shall consult with –

(a) the Commission;

(b) persons whom he considers to represent the interests of police authorities;

(c) persons whom he considers to represent the interests of chief officers of police; and

(d) such other persons as he thinks fit.

27 Conduct of the Commission's staff

(1) The Secretary of State shall by regulations make provision for the manner in which the following cases are to be handled or dealt with –

(a) cases in which allegations of misconduct are made against members of the Commission's staff; and

(b) cases in which there is otherwise an indication that there may have been misconduct by a member of the Commission's staff.

(2) Regulations under this section may apply, with such modifications as the Secretary of State thinks fit, any provision made by or under this Part. …

29 Interpretation of Part 2

(1) In this Part –

'the appropriate authority', in relation to a person serving with the police or in relation to any complaint, matter or investigation relating to the conduct of such a person, means –

(a) if that person is a senior officer, the police authority for the area of the police force of which he is a member; and

(b) if he is not a senior officer, the chief officer under whose direction and control he is;

'chief officer' means the chief officer of police of any police force;

'the Commission' has the meaning given by section 9(1);

'complainant' shall be construed in accordance with subsection (2);

'complaint' has the meaning given by section 12;

'conduct' includes acts, omissions and statements (whether actual, alleged or inferred);

'conduct matter' has the meaning given by section 12;

'disciplinary proceedings' means –

(a) in relation to a member of a police force or a special constable, proceedings under any regulations made by virtue of section 50 or 51 of the 1996 Act and identified as disciplinary proceedings by those regulations; and

(b) in relation to a person serving with the police who is not a member of a police force or a special constable, proceedings identified as such by regulations made by the Secretary of State for the purposes of this Part;

'document' means anything in which information of any description is recorded;

'information' includes estimates and projections, and statistical analyses;

'local resolution', in relation to a complaint, means the handling of that complaint in accordance with a procedure which –

(a) does not involve a formal investigation; and

(b) is laid down by regulations under paragraph 8 of Schedule 3 for complaints which it has been decided, in accordance with paragraph 6 of that Schedule, to subject to local resolution;

'person complained against', in relation to a complaint, means the person whose conduct is the subject-matter of the complaint;

'recordable conduct matter' means (subject to any regulations under section 23(2)(d)) –

(a) a conduct matter that is required to be recorded by the appropriate authority under paragraph 10 or 11 of Schedule 3 or has been so recorded; or

(b) except in sub-paragraph (4) of paragraph 2 of Schedule 3, any matter brought to the attention of the appropriate authority under that sub-paragraph;

'relevant force', in relation to the appropriate authority, means –

(a) if that authority is a police authority, the police force maintained by it; and

(b) if that authority is the chief officer of police of a police force, his force;

'senior officer' means a member of a police force holding a rank above that of chief superintendent;

'serious injury' means a fracture, a deep cut, a deep laceration or an injury causing damage to an internal organ or the impairment of any bodily function;

'serving with the police', in relation to any person, shall be construed in accordance with section 12(7).

(2) References in this Part, in relation to anything which is or purports to be a complaint, to the complainant are references –

(a) except in the case of anything which is or purports to be a complaint falling within section 12(1)(d), to the person by whom the complaint or purported complaint was made; and

(b) in that case, to the person on whose behalf the complaint or purported complaint was made;

but where any person is acting on another's behalf for the purposes of any complaint or purported complaint, anything that is to be or may be done under this Part by or in relation to the complainant may be done, instead, by or in relation to the person acting on the complainant's behalf.

(3) Subject to subsection (4), references in this Part, in relation to any conduct or anything purporting to be a complaint about any conduct, to a member of the public include references to any person falling within any of the following paragraphs (whether at the time of the conduct or at any subsequent time) –

(a) a person serving with the police;

(b) a member of the National Criminal Intelligence Service or the National Crime Squad;

(c) a member of the staff of the Central Police Training and Development Authority; or

(d) a person engaged on relevant service, within the meaning of section 97(1)(a), (cc) or (d) of the 1996 Act (temporary service otherwise than with NCIS or NCS).

(4) In this Part references, in relation to any conduct or to anything purporting to be a complaint about any conduct, to a member of the public do not include references to –

(a) a person who, at the time when the conduct is supposed to have taken place, was under the direction and control of the same chief officer as the person whose conduct it was; or

(b) a person who –

(i) at the time when the conduct is supposed to have taken place, in relation to him, or

(ii) at the time when he is supposed to have been adversely affected by it, or to have witnessed it,

was on duty in his capacity as a person falling within subsection (3)(a) to (d).

(5) For the purposes of this Part a person is adversely affected if he suffers any form of loss or damage, distress or inconvenience, if he is put in danger or if he is otherwise unduly put at risk of being adversely affected.

(6) References in this Part to the investigation of any complaint or matter by the appropriate authority on its own behalf, under the supervision of the Commission, under the management of the Commission or by the Commission itself shall be construed as references to its investigation in accordance with paragraph 16, 17, 18 or, as the case may be, 19 of Schedule 3.

(7) The Commissioner of Police for the City of London shall be treated for the purposes of this Part as if he were a member of the City of London police force.

PART 4

POLICE POWERS, ETC

CHAPTER 1

EXERCISE OF POLICE POWERS, ETC BY CIVILIANS

38 Police powers for police authority employees

(1) The chief officer of police of any police force may designate any person who –

(a) is employed by the police authority maintaining that force, and

(b) is under the direction and control of that chief officer,

as an officer of one or more of the descriptions specified in subsection (2).

(2) The description of officers are as follows –

(a) community support officer;

(b) investigating officer;

(c) detention officer;

(d) escort officer. …

(3) A Director General may designate any person who –

(a) is an employee of his Service Authority, and

(b) is under the direction and control of that Director General,

as an investigating officer.

(4) A chief officer of police or a Director General shall not designate a person under this section unless he is satisfied that that person –

(a) is a suitable person to carry out the functions for the purposes of which he is designated;

(b) is capable of effectively carrying out those functions; and

(c) has received adequate training in the carrying out of those functions and in the exercise and performance of the powers and duties to be conferred on him by virtue of the designation.

(5) A person designated under this section shall have the powers and duties conferred or imposed on him by the designation.

(6) Powers and duties may be conferred or imposed on a designated person by means only of the application to him by his designation of provisions of the applicable Part of Schedule 4 that are to apply to the designated person; and for this purpose the applicable Part of that Schedule is –

(a) in the case of a person designated as a community support officer, Part 1;

(b) in the case of a person designated as an investigating officer, Part 2;

(c) in the case of a person designated as a detention officer, Part 3; and

(d) in the case of a person designated as an escort officer, Part 4.

(7) An employee of a police authority or of a Service Authority authorised or required to do anything by virtue of a designation under this section –

(a) shall not be authorised or required by virtue of that designation to engage in any conduct otherwise than in the course of that employment; and

(b) shall be so authorised or required subject to such restrictions and conditions (if any) as may be specified in his designation.

(8) Where any power exercisable by any person in reliance on his designation under this section is a power which, in the case of its exercise by a constable, includes or is supplemented by a power to use reasonable force, any person exercising that power

in reliance on that designation shall have the same entitlement as a constable to use reasonable force.

(9) Where any power exercisable by any person in reliance on his designation under this section includes power to use force to enter any premises, that power shall not be exercisable by that person except –

(a) in the company, and under the supervision, of a constable; or

(b) for the purpose of saving life or limb or preventing serious damage to property.

45 Code of practice relating to chief officers' powers under Chapter 1

(1) The Secretary of State shall issue a code of practice about the exercise and performance by chief officers of police and by Directors General of their powers and duties under this Chapter.

(2) The Secretary of State may from time to time revise the whole or any part of a code of practice issued under this section.

(3) Before issuing or revising a code of practice under this section, the Secretary of State shall consult with –

(a) the Service Authority for the National Criminal Intelligence Service;

(b) the Service Authority for the National Crime Squad;

(c) persons whom he considers to represent the interests of police authorities;

(d) the Director General of the National Criminal Intelligence Service;

(e) the Director General of the National Crime Squad;

(f) persons whom he considers to represent the interests of chief officers of police;

(g) persons whom he considers to represent the interests of local authorities;

(h) the Mayor of London; and

(i) such other persons as he thinks fit.

(4) The Secretary of State shall lay any code of practice issued by him under this section, and any revisions of any such code, before Parliament.

(5) In discharging any function to which a code of practice under this section relates, a chief officer of police or a Director General shall have regard to the code.

(6) For the purposes of subsection (3)(g), 'local authorities' means district councils, London borough councils, county councils in Wales, county borough councils, the Common Council of the City of London and the Council of the Isles of Scilly.

46 Offences against designated and accredited persons, etc

(1) Any person who assaults –

(a) a designated person in the execution of his duty,

(b) an accredited person in the execution of his duty, or

(c) a person assisting a designated or accredited person in the execution of his duty,

is guilty of an offence and shall be liable, on summary conviction, to imprisonment for a term not exceeding six months or to a fine not exceeding level 5 on the standard scale, or to both.

(2) Any person who resists or wilfully obstructs –

(a) a designated person in the execution of his duty,

(b) an accredited person in the execution of his duty, or

(c) a person assisting a designated or accredited person in the execution of his duty,

is guilty of an offence and shall be liable, on summary conviction, to imprisonment for a term not exceeding one month or to a fine not exceeding level 3 on the standard scale, or to both.

(3) Any person who, with intent to deceive –

(a) impersonates a designated person or an accredited person,

(b) makes any statement or does any act calculated falsely to suggest that he is a designated person or that he is an accredited person, or

(c) makes any statement or does any act calculated falsely to suggest that he has powers as a designated or accredited person that exceed the powers he actually has,

is guilty of an offence and shall be liable, on summary conviction, to imprisonment for a term not exceeding six months or to a fine not exceeding level 5 on the standard scale, or to both.

(4) In this section references to the execution by a designated person or accredited person of his duty are references to his exercising any power or performing any duty which is his by virtue of his designation or accreditation.

47 Interpretation of Chapter 1

(1) In this Chapter –

'accredited person' means a person in relation to whom an accreditation under section 41 is for the time being in force; ...

'conduct' includes omissions and statements;

'designated person' means a person in relation to whom a designation under section 38 or 39 is for the time being in force;

'Director General' means –

(a) the Director General of the National Criminal Intelligence Service; or

(b) the Director General of the National Crime Squad;

'Service Authority' means –

(a) in relation to employment with the National Criminal Intelligence Service or to its Director General, the Service Authority for the National Criminal Intelligence Service; and

(b) in relation to employment with the National Crime Squad or to its Director General, the Service Authority for the National Crime Squad.

(2) In this Chapter –

(a) references to carrying on business include references to carrying out functions under any enactment; and

(b) references to the employees of a person carrying on business include references to persons holding office under a person, and references to employers shall be construed accordingly.

CHAPTER 2

PROVISIONS MODIFYING AND SUPPLEMENTING POLICE POWERS ...

50 Persons acting in an anti-social manner

(1) If a constable in uniform has reason to believe that a person has been acting, or is acting, in an anti-social manner (within the meaning of section 1 of the Crime and Disorder Act 1998 (c 37) (anti-social behaviour orders)), he may require that person to give his name and address to the constable.

(2) Any person who –

(a) fails to give his name and address when required to do so under subsection (1), or

(b) gives a false or inaccurate name or address in response to a requirement under that subsection,

is guilty of an offence and shall be liable, on summary conviction, to a fine not exceeding level 3 on the standard scale.

SCHEDULE 4

POWERS EXERCISABLE BY POLICE CIVILIANS

PART 1

COMMUNITY SUPPORT OFFICERS

1. – (1) Where a designation applies this paragraph to any person, that person shall have the powers specified in sub-paragraph (2) in relation to any individual who he has reason to believe has committed a relevant fixed penalty offence at a place within the relevant police area.

(2) Those powers are the following powers so far as exercisable in respect of a relevant fixed penalty offence –

(a) the powers of a constable in uniform and of an authorised constable to give a penalty notice under Chapter 1 of Part 1 of the Criminal Justice and Police Act 2001 (c 16) (fixed penalty notices in respect of offences of disorder);

(b) the power of a constable in uniform to give a person a fixed penalty notice under section 54 of the Road Traffic Offenders Act 1988 (c 53) (fixed penalty notices) in respect of an offence under section 72 of the Highway Act 1835 (c 50) (riding on a footway) committed by cycling;

(c) the power of an authorised officer of a local authority to give a notice under section 4 of the Dogs (Fouling of Land) Act 1996 (c 20) (fixed penalty notices in respect of dog fouling); and

(d) the power of an authorised officer of a litter authority to give a notice under section 88 of the Environmental Protection Act 1990 (c 43) (fixed penalty notices in respect of litter).

(3) In this paragraph 'relevant fixed penalty offence', in relation to a designated person, means an offence which –

(a) is an offence by reference to which a notice may be given to a person in exercise of any of the powers mentioned in sub-paragraph 1(2)(a) to (d); and

(b) is specified or described in that person's designation as an offence he has been designated to enforce under this paragraph.

2. – (1) This paragraph applies if a designation applies it to any person.

(2) Where that person has reason to believe that another person has committed a relevant offence in the relevant police area, he may require that other person to give him his name and address.

(3) Where, in a case in which a requirement under sub-paragraph (2) has been imposed on another person –

(a) that other person fails to comply with the requirement, or

(b) the person who imposed the requirement has reasonable grounds for suspecting that the other person has given him a name or address that is false or inaccurate,

the person who imposed the requirement may require the other person to wait with him, for a period not exceeding thirty minutes, for the arrival of a constable.

(4) A person who has been required under sub-paragraph (3) to wait with a person to whom this Part of this Schedule applies may, if requested to do so, elect that (instead of waiting) he will accompany the person imposing the requirement to a police station in the relevant police area.

(5) A person who –

(a) fails to comply with a requirement under sub-paragraph (2),

(b) makes off while subject to a requirement under sub-paragraph (3), or

(c) makes off while accompanying a person to a police station in accordance with an election under sub-paragraph (4), is guilty of an offence and shall be liable, on summary conviction, to a fine not exceeding level 3 on the standard scale.

(6) In this paragraph 'relevant offence', in relation to a person to whom this paragraph applies, means any offence which is –

(a) a relevant fixed penalty offence for the purposes of the application of paragraph 1 to that person; or

(aa) an offence under section 32(2) of the Anti-social Behaviour Act 2003; or

(b) an offence the commission of which appears to that person to have caused –

(i) injury, alarm or distress to any other person; or

(ii) the loss of, or any damage to, any other person's property;

but a designation applying this paragraph to any person may provide that an offence is not to be treated as a relevant offence by virtue of paragraph (b) unless it satisfies such other conditions as may be specified in the designation.

3. – (1) Where a designation applies this paragraph to any person, that person shall, in the relevant police area, have the powers of a constable in uniform under section 50 to require a person whom he has reason to believe to have been acting, or to be acting, in an anti-social manner (within the meaning of section 1 of the Crime and Disorder Act 1998 (c 37) (anti-social behaviour orders)) to give his name and address.

(2) Sub-paragraphs (3) to (5) of paragraph 2 apply in the case of a requirement imposed by virtue of sub-paragraph (1) as they apply in the case of a requirement under sub-paragraph (2) of that paragraph.

4. – (1) This paragraph applies where a designation –

(a) applies this paragraph to a person to whom any or all of paragraphs 1 to 3 are also applied; and

(b) sets out the matters in respect of which that person has the power conferred by this paragraph.

(2) The matters that may be set out in a designation as the matters in respect of which a person has the power conferred by this paragraph shall be confined to –

(a) offences that are relevant penalty notice offences for the purposes of the application of paragraph 1 to the designated person;

(b) offences that are relevant offences for the purposes of the application of paragraph 2 to the designated person; and

(c) behaviour that constitutes acting in an anti-social manner (within the meaning of section 1 of the Crime and Disorder Act 1998 (c 37) (anti-social behaviour orders)).

(3) In any case in which a person to whom this paragraph applies has imposed a requirement on any other person under paragraph 2(2) or 3(1) in respect of anything appearing to him to be a matter set out in the designation, he may use reasonable force to prevent that other person from making off while he is either –

(a) subject to a requirement imposed in that case by the designated person under sub-paragraph (3) of paragraph 2; or

(b) accompanying the designated person to a police station in accordance with an election made in that case under sub-paragraph (4) of that paragraph. …

As amended by the Anti-social Behaviour Act 2003, s33(1), (2).

NATIONALITY, IMMIGRATION AND ASYLUM ACT 2002

(2002 c 41)

PART 4

DETENTION AND REMOVAL

62 Detention by Secretary of State

(1) A person may be detained under the authority of the Secretary of State pending –

(a) a decision by the Secretary of State whether to give directions in respect of the person under paragraph 10, 10A or 14 of Schedule 2 to the Immigration Act 1971 (c 77) (control of entry: removal), or

(b) removal of the person from the United Kingdom in pursuance of directions given by the Secretary of State under any of those paragraphs.

(2) Where the Secretary of State is empowered under section 3A of that Act (powers of Secretary of State) to examine a person or to give or refuse a person leave to enter the United Kingdom, the person may be detained under the authority of the Secretary of State pending –

(a) the person's examination by the Secretary of State,

(b) the Secretary of State's decision to give or refuse the person leave to enter,

(c) a decision by the Secretary of State whether to give directions in respect of the person under paragraph 8 or 9 of Schedule 2 to that Act (removal), or

(d) removal of the person in pursuance of directions given by the Secretary of State under either of those paragraphs.

(3) A provision of Schedule 2 to that Act about a person who is detained or liable to detention under that Schedule shall apply to a person who is detained or liable to detention under this section: and for that purpose –

(a) a reference to paragraph 16 of that Schedule shall be taken to include a reference to this section,

(b) a reference in paragraph 21 of that Schedule to an immigration officer shall be taken to include a reference to the Secretary of State, and

(c) a reference to detention under that Schedule or under a provision or Part of that Schedule shall be taken to include a reference to detention under this section.

(4) In the case of a restriction imposed under paragraph 21 of that Schedule by virtue of this section –

(a) a restriction imposed by an immigration officer may be varied by the Secretary of State, and

(b) a restriction imposed by the Secretary of State may be varied by an immigration officer.

(5) In subsection (1) the reference to paragraph 10 of that Schedule includes a reference to that paragraph as applied by virtue of section 10 of the Immigration and Asylum Act 1999 (c 33) (persons unlawfully in United Kingdom: removal). ...

67 Construction of reference to person liable to detention

(1) This section applies to the construction of a provision which –

(a) does not confer power to detain a person, but

(b) refers (in any terms) to a person who is liable to detention under a provision of the Immigration Acts.

(2) The reference shall be taken to include a person if the only reason why he cannot be detained under the provision is that –

(a) he cannot presently be removed from the United Kingdom, because of a legal impediment connected with the United Kingdom's obligations under an international agreement,

(b) practical difficulties are impeding or delaying the making of arrangements for his removal from the United Kingdom, or

(c) practical difficulties, or demands on administrative resources, are impeding or delaying the taking of a decision in respect of him.

(3) This section shall be treated as always having had effect.

68 Bail

(1) This section applies in a case where an immigration officer not below the rank of chief immigration officer has sole or shared power to release a person on bail in accordance with –

(a) a provision of Schedule 2 to the Immigration Act 1971 (c 77) (control of entry) (including a provision of that Schedule applied by a provision of that Act or by another enactment), or

(b) section 9A of the Asylum and Immigration Appeals Act 1993 (c 23) (pending appeal from Immigration Appeal Tribunal).

(2) In respect of an application for release on bail which is instituted after the expiry of the period of eight days beginning with the day on which detention commences, the power to release on bail –

(a) shall be exercisable by the Secretary of State (as well as by any person with whom the immigration officer's power is shared under the provision referred to in subsection (1)), and

(b) shall not be exercisable by an immigration officer (except where he acts on behalf of the Secretary of State).

(3) In relation to the exercise by the Secretary of State of a power to release a person on bail by virtue of subsection (2), a reference to an immigration officer shall be construed as a reference to the Secretary of State.

(4) The Secretary of State may by order amend or replace subsection (2) so as to make different provision for the circumstances in which the power to release on bail may be exercised by the Secretary of State and not by an immigration officer. ...

69 Reporting restriction: travel expenses

(1) The Secretary of State may make a payment to a person in respect of travelling expenses which the person has incurred or will incur for the purpose of complying with a reporting restriction. ...

70 Induction

(1) A residence restriction may be imposed on an asylum-seeker or a dependant of an asylum-seeker without regard to his personal circumstances if –

(a) it requires him to reside at a specified location for a period not exceeding 14 days, and

(b) the person imposing the residence restriction believes that a programme of induction will be made available to the asylum-seeker at or near the specified location. ...

71 Asylum-seeker: residence, etc restriction

(1) This section applies to –

(a) a person who makes a claim for asylum at a time when he has leave to enter or remain in the United Kingdom, and

(b) a dependant of a person within paragraph (a).

(2) The Secretary of State or an immigration officer may impose on a person to whom this section applies any restriction which may be imposed under paragraph 21 of Schedule 2 to the Immigration Act 1971 (c 77) (control of entry: residence, reporting and occupation restrictions) on a person liable to detention under paragraph 16 of that Schedule. ...

76 Revocation of leave to enter or remain

(1) The Secretary of State may revoke a person's indefinite leave to enter or remain in the United Kingdom if the person –

(a) is liable to deportation, but

(b) cannot be deported for legal reasons.

(2) The Secretary of State may revoke a person's indefinite leave to enter or remain in the United Kingdom if –

(a) the leave was obtained by deception,

(b) the person would be liable to removal because of the deception, but

(c) the person cannot be removed for legal or practical reasons.

(3) The Secretary of State may revoke a person's indefinite leave to enter or remain in the United Kingdom if the person, or someone of whom he is a dependant, ceases to be a refugee as a result of –

(a) voluntarily availing himself of the protection of his country of nationality,

(b) voluntarily re-acquiring a lost nationality,

(c) acquiring the nationality of a country other than the United Kingdom and availing himself of its protection, or

(d) voluntarily establishing himself in a country in respect of which he was a refugee. ...

77 No removal while claim for asylum pending

(1) While a person's claim for asylum is pending he may not be –

(a) removed from the United Kingdom in accordance with a provision of the Immigration Acts, or

(b) required to leave the United Kingdom in accordance with a provision of the Immigration Acts. ...

(4) Nothing in this section shall prevent any of the following while a claim for asylum is pending –

(a) the giving of a direction for the claimant's removal from the United Kingdom,

(b) the making of a deportation order in respect of the claimant, or

(c) the taking of any other interim or preparatory action. ...

78 No removal while appeal pending

(1) While a person's appeal under section 82(1) is pending he may not be –

(a) removed from the United Kingdom in accordance with a provision of the Immigration Acts, or

(b) required to leave the United Kingdom in accordance with a provision of the Immigration Acts.

(2) In this section 'pending' has the meaning given by section 104.

(3) Nothing in this section shall prevent any of the following while an appeal is pending –

(a) the giving of a direction for the appellant's removal from the United Kingdom,

(b) the making of a deportation order in respect of the appellant (subject to section 79), or

(c) the taking of any other interim or preparatory action.

(4) This section applies only to an appeal brought while the appellant is in the United Kingdom in accordance with section 92.

79 Deportation order: appeal

(1) A deportation order may not be made in respect of a person while an appeal under section 82(1) against the decision to make the order –

(a) could be brought (ignoring any possibility of an appeal out of time with permission), or

(b) is pending.

(2) In this section 'pending' has the meaning given by section 104.

PART 5

IMMIGRATION AND ASYLUM APPEALS

81 The Asylum and Immigration Tribunal

(1) There shall be a tribunal to be known as the Asylum and Immigration Tribunal

(2) Schedule 4 (which makes provision about the Tribunal) shall have effect.

(3) A reference in this Part to the Tribunal is a reference to the Asylum and Immigration Tribunal.

82 Right of appeal: general

(1) Where an immigration decision is made in respect of a person he may appeal to the Tribunal.

(2) In this Part 'immigration decision' means –

(a) refusal of leave to enter the United Kingdom,

(b) refusal of entry clearance,

(c) refusal of a certificate of entitlement under section 10 of this Act,

(d) refusal to vary a person's leave to enter or remain in the United Kingdom if the result of the refusal is that the person has no leave to enter or remain,

(e) variation of a person's leave to enter or remain in the United Kingdom if when the variation takes effect the person has no leave to enter or remain,

(f) revocation under section 76 of this Act of indefinite leave to enter or remain in the United Kingdom,

(g) a decision that a person is to be removed from the United Kingdom by way of directions under section 10(1)(a), (b) or (c) of the Immigration and Asylum Act 1999 (c 33) (removal of person unlawfully in United Kingdom),

(h) a decision that an illegal entrant is to be removed from the United Kingdom by way of directions under paragraphs 8 to 10 of Schedule 2 to the Immigration Act 1971 (c 77) (control of entry: removal),

(i) a decision that a person is to be removed from the United Kingdom by way of directions given by virtue of paragraph 10A of that Schedule (family),

(ia) a decision that a person is to be removed from the United Kingdom by way of directions under paragraph 12(2) of Schedule 2 to the Immigration Act 1971 (c 77) (seamen and aircrews),

(j) a decision to make a deportation order under section 5(1) of that Act, and

(k) refusal to revoke a deportation order under section 5(2) of that Act.

(3) A variation or revocation of the kind referred to in subsection (2)(e) or (f) shall not have effect while an appeal under subsection (1) against that variation or revocation –

(a) could be brought (ignoring any possibility of an appeal out of time with permission), or

(b) is pending.

(4) The right of appeal under subsection (1) is subject to the exceptions and limitations specified in this Part.

83 Appeal: asylum claim

(1) This section applies where a person has made an asylum claim and –

(a) his claim has been rejected by the Secretary of State, but

(b) he has been granted leave to enter or remain in the United Kingdom for a period exceeding one year (or for periods exceeding one year in aggregate).

(2) The person may appeal to the Tribunal against the rejection of his asylum claim.

84 Grounds of appeal

(1) An appeal under section 82(1) against an immigration decision must be brought on one or more of the following grounds –

(a) that the decision is not in accordance with immigration rules;

(b) that the decision is unlawful by virtue of section 19B of the Race Relations Act 1976 (c 74) ... (discrimination by public authorities);

(c) that the decision is unlawful under section 6 of the Human Rights Act 1998 (c 42) (public authority not to act contrary to Human Rights Convention) as being incompatible with the appellant's Convention rights;

(d) that the appellant is an EEA national or a member of the family of an EEA national and the decision breaches the appellant's rights under the Community Treaties in respect of entry to or residence in the United Kingdom;

(e) that the decision is otherwise not in accordance with the law;

(f) that the person taking the decision should have exercised differently a discretion conferred by immigration rules;

(g) that removal of the appellant from the United Kingdom in consequence of the immigration decision would breach the United Kingdom's obligations under the Refugee Convention or would be unlawful under section 6 of the Human Rights Act 1998 as being incompatible with the appellant's Convention rights.

(2) In subsection (1)(d) 'EEA national' means a national of a State which is a contracting party to the Agreement on the European Economic Area signed at Oporto on 2nd May 1992 (as it has effect from time to time).

(3) An appeal under section 83 must be brought on the grounds that removal of the appellant from the United Kingdom would breach the United Kingdom's obligations under the Refugee Convention.

85 Matters to be considered

(1) An appeal under section 82(1) against a decision shall be treated by the Tribunal as including an appeal against any decision in respect of which the appellant has a right of appeal under section 82(1).

(2) If an appellant under section 82(1) makes a statement under section 120, the Tribunal shall consider any matter raised in the statement which constitutes a ground of appeal of a kind listed in section 84(1) against the decision appealed against.

(3) Subsection (2) applies to a statement made under section 120 whether the statement was made before or after the appeal was commenced.

(4) On an appeal under section 82(1) or 83(2) against a decision the Tribunal may consider evidence about any matter which it thinks relevant to the substance of the decision, including evidence which concerns a matter arising after the date of the decision.

(5) But in relation to an appeal under section 82(1) against refusal of entry clearance or refusal of a certificate of entitlement under section 10 –

(a) subsection (4) shall not apply, and

(b) the Tribunal may consider only the circumstances appertaining at the time of the decision to refuse.

86 Determination of appeal

(1) This section applies on an appeal under section 82(1) or 83.

(2) The Tribunal must determine –

(a) any matter raised as a ground of appeal (whether or not by virtue of section 85(1)), and

(b) any matter which section 85 requires it to consider.

(3) The Tribunal must allow the appeal in so far as it thinks that –

(a) a decision against which the appeal is brought or is treated as being brought was not in accordance with the law (including immigration rules), or

(b) a discretion exercised in making a decision against which the appeal is brought or is treated as being brought should have been exercised differently.

(4) For the purposes of subsection (3) a decision that a person should be removed from the United Kingdom under a provision shall not be regarded as unlawful if it could have been lawfully made by reference to removal under another provision.

(5) In so far as subsection (3) does not apply, the Tribunal shall dismiss the appeal.

(6) Refusal to depart from or to authorise departure from immigration rules is not the exercise of a discretion for the purposes of subsection (3)(b).

87 Successful appeal: direction

(1) If the Tribunal allows an appeal under section 82 or 83 it may give a direction for the purpose of giving effect to its decision.

(2) A person responsible for making an immigration decision shall act in accordance with any relevant direction under subsection (1).

(3) But a direction under this section shall not have effect while –

(a) an application under section 103A(1) (other than an application out of time with permission) could be made or is awaiting determination,

(b) reconsideration of an appeal has been ordered under section 103A(1) and has not been completed,

(c) an appeal has been remitted to the Tribunal and is awaiting determination,

(d) an application under section 103B or 103E for permission to appeal (other than an application out of time with permission) could be made or is awaiting determination,

(e) an appeal under section 103B or 103E is awaiting determination, or

(f) a reference under section 103C is awaiting determination.

(4) A direction under subsection (1) shall be treated as part of the Tribunal's decision on the appeal for the purposes of section 103A.

88 Ineligibility

(1) This section applies to an immigration decision of a kind referred to in section 82(2)(a), (b), (d) or (e).

(2) A person may not appeal under section 82(1) against an immigration decision which is taken on the grounds that he or a person of whom he is a dependant –

(a) does not satisfy a requirement as to age, nationality or citizenship specified in immigration rules,

(b) does not have an immigration document of a particular kind (or any immigration document),

(c) is seeking to be in the United Kingdom for a period greater than that permitted in his case by immigration rules, or

(d) is seeking to enter or remain in the United Kingdom for a purpose other than one for which entry or remaining is permitted in accordance with immigration rules.

(3) In subsection (2)(b) 'immigration document' means –

(a) entry clearance,

(b) a passport,

(c) a work permit or other immigration employment document within the meaning of section 122, and

(d) a document which relates to a national of a country other than the United Kingdom and which is designed to serve the same purpose as a passport.

(4) Subsection (2) does not prevent the bringing of an appeal on any or all of the grounds referred to in section 84(1)(b), (c) and (g).

88A Ineligibility: entry clearance

(1) A person may not appeal under section 82(1) against refusal of entry clearance if the decision to refuse is taken on grounds which –

(a) relate to a provision of immigration rules, and

(b) are specified for the purpose of this section by order of the Secretary of State.

(2) Subsection (1) –

(a) does not prevent the bringing of an appeal on either or both of the grounds referred to in section 84(1)(b) and (c), and

(b) is without prejudice to the effect of section 88 in relation to an appeal under section 82(1) against refusal of entry clearance."

89 Visitor or student without entry clearance

(1) This section applies to a person who applies for leave to enter the United Kingdom –

(a) as a visitor,

(b) in order to follow a course of study for which he has been accepted and which will not last more than six months,

(c) in order to study but without having been accepted for a course, or

(d) as the dependant of a person who applies for leave to enter as a visitor or for a purpose described in paragraph (b) or (c).

(2) A person may not appeal under section 82(1) against refusal of leave to enter the United Kingdom if at the time of the refusal he does not have entry clearance.

(3) Subsection (2) does not prevent the bringing of an appeal on any or all of the grounds referred to in section 84(1)(b), (c) and (g).

90 Non-family visitor

(1) A person who applies for entry clearance for the purpose of entering the United Kingdom as a visitor may appeal under section 82(1) against refusal of entry clearance only if the application was made for the purpose of visiting a member of the applicant's family.

(2) In subsection (1) the reference to a member of the applicant's family shall be construed in accordance with regulations.

(3) Regulations under subsection (2) may, in particular, make provision wholly or partly by reference to the duration of two individuals' residence together.

(4) Subsection (1) does not prevent the bringing of an appeal on either or both of the grounds referred to in section 84(1)(b) and (c).

91 Student

(1) A person may not appeal under section 82(1) against refusal of entry clearance if he seeks it –

(a) in order to follow a course of study for which he has been accepted and which will not last more than six months,

(b) in order to study but without having been accepted for a course, or

(c) as the dependant of a person seeking entry clearance for a purpose described in paragraph (a) or (b).

(2) Subsection (1) does not prevent the bringing of an appeal on either or both of the grounds referred to in section 84(1)(b) and (c).

92 Appeal from within United Kingdom: general

(1) A person may not appeal under section 82(1) while he is in the United Kingdom unless his appeal is of a kind to which this section applies.

(2) This section applies to an appeal against an immigration decision of a kind specified in section 82(2)(c), (d), (e), (f) and (j).

(3) This section also applies to an appeal against refusal of leave to enter the United Kingdom if –

(a) at the time of the refusal the appellant is in the United Kingdom, and

(b) on his arrival in the United Kingdom the appellant had entry clearance.

(3A) But this section does not apply by virtue of subsection (3) if subsection (3B) or (3C) applies to the refusal of leave to enter.

(3B) This subsection applies to a refusal of leave to enter which is a deemed refusal under paragraph 2A(9) of Schedule 2 to the Immigration Act 1971 (c 77) resulting from cancellation of leave to enter by an immigration officer –

(a) under paragraph 2A(8) of that Schedule, and

(b) on the grounds specified in paragraph 2A(2A) of that Schedule.

(3C) This subsection applies to a refusal of leave to enter which specifies that the grounds for refusal are that the leave is sought for a purpose other than that specified in the entry clearance.

(3D) This section also applies to an appeal against refusal of leave to enter the United Kingdom if at the time of the refusal the appellant –

(a) is in the United Kingdom,

(b) has a work permit, and

(c) is any of the following (within the meaning of the British Nationality Act 1981 (c 61)) –

(i) a British overseas territories citizen,

(ii) a British Overseas citizen,

(iii) a British National (Overseas),

(iv) a British protected person, or

(v) a British subject.

(4) This section also applies to an appeal against an immigration decision if the appellant –

(a) has made an asylum claim, or a human rights claim, while in the United Kingdom, or

(b) is an EEA national or a member of the family of an EEA national and makes a claim to the Secretary of State that the decision breaches the appellant's rights under the Community Treaties in respect of entry to or residence in the United Kingdom.

94 Appeal from within United Kingdom: unfounded human rights or asylum claim

(1) This section applies to an appeal under section 82(1) where the appellant has made an asylum claim or a human rights claim (or both).

(1A) A person may not bring an appeal against an immigration decision of a kind specified in section 82(2)(c), (d) or (e) in reliance on section 92(2) if the Secretary of State certifies that the claim or claims mentioned in subsection (1) above is or are clearly unfounded.

(2) A person may not bring an appeal to which this section applies in reliance on section 92(4)(a) if the Secretary of State certifies that the claim or claims mentioned in subsection (1) is or are clearly unfounded.

(3) If the Secretary of State is satisfied that an asylum claimant or human rights claimant is entitled to reside in a State listed in subsection (4) he shall certify the claim under subsection (2) unless satisfied that it is not clearly unfounded.

(4) Those States are –

(k) the Republic of Albania,

(l) Bulgaria,

(m) Serbia and Montenegro,
(n) Jamaica,
(o) Macedonia,
(p) the Republic of Moldova,
(q) Romania,
(r) Bangladesh
(s) Bolivia,
(t) Brazil,
(u) Ecuador,
(v) Sri Lanka,
(w) South Africa, and
(x) Ukraine.

(5) The Secretary of State may by order add a State, or part of a State, to the list in subsection (4) if satisfied that –

(a) there is in general in that State or part no serious risk of persecution of persons entitled to reside in that State or part, and

(b) removal to that State or part of persons entitled to reside there will not in general contravene the United Kingdom's obligations under the Human Rights Convention.

(5A) If the Secretary of State is satisfied that the statements in subsection (5) (a) and (b) are true of a State or part of a State in relation to a description of person, an order under subsection (5) may add the State or part to the list in subsection (4) in respect of that description of person.

(5B) Where a State or part of a State is added to the list in subsection (4) in respect of a description of person, subsection (3) shall have effect in relation to a claimant only if the Secretary of State is satisfied that he is within that description (as well as being satisfied that he is entitled to reside in the State or part).

(5C) A description for the purposes of subsection (5A) may refer to –

(a) gender,
(b) language,
(c) race,
(d) religion,
(e) nationality,
(f) membership of a social or other group,
(g) political opinion, or
(h) any other attribute or circumstance that the Secretary of State thinks appropriate.'

(6) The Secretary of State may by order amend the list in subsection (4) so as to omit a State or part added under subsection (5); and the omission may be –

(a) general, or

(b) effected so that the State or part remains listed in respect of a description of person.

(6A) Subsection (3) shall not apply in relation to an asylum claimant or human rights claimant who –

(a) is the subject of a certificate under section 2 or 70 of the Extradition Act 2003 (c 41),

(b) is in custody pursuant to arrest under section 5 of that Act,

(c) is the subject of a provisional warrant under section 73 of that Act,

(d) is the subject of an authority to proceed under section 7 of the Extradition Act 1989 (c 33) or an order under paragraph 4(2) of Schedule 1 to that Act, or

(e) is the subject of a provisional warrant under section 8 of that Act or of a warrant under paragraph 5(1)(b) of Schedule 1 to that Act.

(7) A person may not bring an appeal to which this section applies in reliance on section 92(4) if the Secretary of State certifies that –

(a) it is proposed to remove the person to a country of which he is not a national or citizen, and

(b) there is no reason to believe that the person's rights under the Human Rights Convention will be breached in that country.

(8) In determining whether a person in relation to whom a certificate has been issued under subsection (7) may be removed from the United Kingdom, the country specified in the certificate is to be regarded as –

(a) a place where a person's life and liberty is not threatened by reason of his race, religion, nationality, membership of a particular social group, or political opinion, and

(b) a place from which a person will not be sent to another country otherwise than in accordance with the Refugee Convention.

(9) Where a person in relation to whom a certificate is issued under this section subsequently brings an appeal under section 82(1) while outside the United Kingdom, the appeal shall be considered as if he had not been removed from the United Kingdom.

95 Appeal from outside United Kingdom: removal

A person who is outside the United Kingdom may not appeal under section 82(1) on the ground specified in section 84(1)(g) (except in a case to which section 94(9) applies).

96 Earlier right of appeal

(1) An appeal under section 82(1) against an immigration decision ('the new decision') in respect of a person may not be brought if the Secretary of State or an immigration officer certifies –

(a) that the person was notified of a right of appeal under that section against another immigration decision ('the old decision') (whether or not an appeal was brought and whether or not any appeal brought has been determined),

(b) that the claim or application to which the new decision relates relies on a matter that could have been raised in an appeal against the old decision, and

(c) that, in the opinion of the Secretary of State or the immigration officer, there is no satisfactory reason for that matter not having been raised in an appeal against the old decision.

(2) An appeal under section 82(1) against an immigration decision ('the new decision') in respect of a person may not be brought if the Secretary of State or an immigration officer certifies –

(a) that the person received a notice under section 120 by virtue of an application other than that to which the new decision relates or by virtue of a decision other than the new decision,

(b) that the new decision relates to an application or claim which relies on a matter that should have been, but has not been, raised in a statement made in response to that notice, and

(c) that, in the opinion of the Secretary of State or the immigration officer, there is no satisfactory reason for that matter not having been raised in a statement made in response to that notice.

(4) In subsection (1) 'notified' means notified in accordance with regulations under section 105.

(5) Subsections (1) and (2) apply to prevent a person's right of appeal whether or not he has been outside the United Kingdom since an earlier right of appeal arose or since a requirement under section 120 was imposed.

(6) In this section a reference to an appeal under section 82(1) includes a reference to an appeal under section 2 of the Special Immigration Appeals Commission Act 1997 (c 68) which is or could be brought by reference to an appeal under section 82(1).

(7) A certificate under subsection (1) or (2) shall have no effect in relation to an appeal instituted before the certificate is issued.

97 National security, etc

(1) An appeal under section 82(1) or 83(2) against a decision in respect of a person may not be brought or continued if the Secretary of State certifies that the decision is or was taken –

(a) by the Secretary of State wholly or partly on a ground listed in subsection (2), or

(b) in accordance with a direction of the Secretary of State which identifies the person to whom the decision relates and which is given wholly or partly on a ground listed in subsection (2).

(2) The grounds mentioned in subsection (1) are that the person's exclusion or removal from the United Kingdom is –

(a) in the interests of national security, or

(b) in the interests of the relationship between the United Kingdom and another country.

(3) An appeal under section 82(1) or 83(2) against a decision may not be brought or continued if the Secretary of State certifies that the decision is or was taken wholly or partly in reliance on information which in his opinion should not be made public –

(a) in the interests of national security,

(b) in the interests of the relationship between the United Kingdom and another country, or

(c) otherwise in the public interest.

(4) In subsections (1)(a) and (b) and (3) a reference to the Secretary of State is to the Secretary of State acting in person.

98 Other grounds of public good

(1) This section applies to an immigration decision of a kind referred to in section 82(2)(a) or (b).

(2) An appeal under section 82(1) against an immigration decision may not be brought or continued if the Secretary of State certifies that the decision is or was taken –

(a) by the Secretary of State wholly or partly on the ground that the exclusion or removal from the United Kingdom of the person to whom the decision relates is conducive to the public good, or

(b) in accordance with a direction of the Secretary of State which identifies the person to whom the decision relates and which is given wholly or partly on that ground.

(3) In subsection (2)(a) and (b) a reference to the Secretary of State is to the Secretary of State acting in person.

(4) Subsection (2) does not prevent the bringing of an appeal on either or both of the grounds referred to in section 84(1)(b) and (c).

(5) Subsection (2) does not prevent the bringing of an appeal against an immigration decision of the kind referred to in section 82(2)(a) on the grounds referred to in section 84(1)(g).

99 Sections 96 to 98: appeal in progress

(1) This section applies where a certificate is issued under section 96(1) or (2), 97 or 98 in respect of a pending appeal.

(2) The appeal shall lapse.

103A Review of Tribunal's decision

(1) A party to an appeal under section 82 or 83 may apply to the appropriate court, on the grounds that the Tribunal made an error of law, for an order requiring the Tribunal to reconsider its decision on the appeal.

(2) The appropriate court may make an order under subsection (1) –

(a) only if it thinks that the Tribunal may have made an error of law, and

(b) only once in relation to an appeal.

(3) An application under subsection (1) must be made –

(a) in the case of an application by the appellant made while he is in the United Kingdom, within the period of 5 days beginning with the date on which he is treated, in accordance with rules under section 106, as receiving notice of the Tribunal's decision,

(b) in the case of an application by the appellant made while he is outside the United Kingdom, within the period of 28 days beginning with the date on which he is treated, in accordance with rules under section 106, as receiving notice of the Tribunal's decision, and

(c) in the case of an application brought by a party to the appeal other than the appellant, within the period of 5 days beginning with the date on which he is treated, in accordance with rules under section 106, as receiving notice of the Tribunal's decision.

(4) But –

(a) rules of court may specify days to be disregarded in applying subsection (3)(a), (b) or (c), and

(b) the appropriate court may permit an application under subsection (1) to be made outside the period specified in subsection (3) where it thinks that the application could not reasonably practicably have been made within that period.

(5) An application under subsection (1) shall be determined by reference only to –

(a) written submissions of the applicant, and

(b) where rules of court permit, other written submissions.

(6) A decision of the appropriate court on an application under subsection (1) shall be final.

(7) In this section a reference to the Tribunal's decision on an appeal does not include a reference to –

(a) a procedural, ancillary or preliminary decision, or

(b) a decision following remittal under section 103B, 103C or 103E.

(8) This section does not apply to a decision of the Tribunal where its jurisdiction is exercised by three or more legally qualified members.

(9) In this section 'the appropriate court' means –

(a) in relation to an appeal decided in England or Wales, the High Court, ...

103B Appeal from Tribunal following reconsideration

(1) Where an appeal to the Tribunal has been reconsidered, a party to the appeal may bring a further appeal on a point of law to the appropriate appellate court.

(2) In subsection (1) the reference to reconsideration is to reconsideration pursuant to –

(a) an order under section 103A(1), or

(b) remittal to the Tribunal under this section or under section 103C or 103E.

(3) An appeal under subsection (1) may be brought only with the permission of –

(a) the Tribunal, or

(b) if the Tribunal refuses permission, the appropriate appellate court.

(4) On an appeal under subsection (1) the appropriate appellate court may –

(a) affirm the Tribunal's decision;

(b) make any decision which the Tribunal could have made;

(c) remit the case to the Tribunal;

(d) affirm a direction under section 87;

(e) vary a direction under section 87;

(f) give a direction which the Tribunal could have given under section 87.

(5) In this section 'the appropriate appellate court' means –

(a) in relation to an appeal decided in England or Wales, the Court of Appeal, ...

103C Appeal from Tribunal instead of reconsideration

(1) On an application under section 103A in respect of an appeal the appropriate court, if it thinks the appeal raises a question of law of such importance that it should be decided by the appropriate appellate court, may refer the appeal to that court.

(2) On a reference under subsection (1) the appropriate appellate court may –

(a) affirm the Tribunal's decision;

(b) make any decision which the Tribunal could have made;

(c) remit the case to the Tribunal;

(d) affirm a direction under section 87;

(e) vary a direction under section 87;

(f) give a direction which the Tribunal could have given under section 87;

(g) restore the application under section 103A to the appropriate court.

(3) In this section –

'the appropriate court' has the same meaning as in section 103A, and

'the appropriate appellate court' has the same meaning as in section 103B. ...

103D Reconsideration: legal aid

(1) On the application of an appellant under section 103A, the appropriate court may order that the appellant's costs in respect of the application under section 103A shall be paid out of the Community Legal Service Fund established under section 5 of the Access to Justice Act 1999 (c. 22).

(2) Subsection (3) applies where the Tribunal has decided an appeal following reconsideration pursuant to an order made –

(a) under section 103A(1), and
(b) on the application of the appellant.

(3) The Tribunal may order that the appellant's costs –

(a) in respect of the application for reconsideration, and
(b) in respect of the reconsideration,

shall be paid out of that Fund.

(4) The Secretary of State may make regulations about the exercise of the powers in subsections (1) and (3). …

103E Appeal from Tribunal sitting as panel

(1) This section applies to a decision of the Tribunal on an appeal under section 82 or 83 where its jurisdiction is exercised by three or more legally qualified members.

(2) A party to the appeal may bring a further appeal on a point of law to the appropriate appellate court.

(3) An appeal under subsection (2) may be brought only with the permission of –

(a) the Tribunal, or
(b) if the Tribunal refuses permission, the appropriate appellate court.

(4) On an appeal under subsection (2) the appropriate appellate court may –

(a) affirm the Tribunal's decision;
(b) make any decision which the Tribunal could have made;
(c) remit the case to the Tribunal;
(d) affirm a direction under section 87;
(e) vary a direction under section 87;
(f) give a direction which the Tribunal could have given under section 87.

(5) In this section 'the appropriate appellate court' means –

(a) in relation to an appeal decided in England or Wales, the Court of Appeal, …

(7) In this section a reference to the Tribunal's decision on an appeal does not include a reference to –

(a) a procedural, ancillary or preliminary decision, or
(b) a decision following remittal under section 103B or 103C.'

109 European Union and European Economic Area

(1) Regulations may provide for, or make provision about, an appeal against an immigration decision taken in respect of a person who has or claims to have a right under any of the Community Treaties. ...

110 Grants

(1) The Secretary of State may make a grant to a voluntary organisation which provides –

(a) advice or assistance to persons who have a right of appeal under this Part;

(b) other services for the welfare of those persons.

(2) A grant under this section may be subject to terms or conditions (which may include conditions as to repayment).

111 Monitor of certification of claims as unfounded

(1) The Secretary of State shall appoint a person to monitor the use of the powers under sections 94(2) and 115(1).

(2) The person appointed under this section shall make a report to the Secretary of State –

(a) once in each calendar year, and

(b) on such occasions as the Secretary of State may request. ...

113 Interpretation

(1) In this Part, unless a contrary intention appears –

'asylum claim' means a claim made by a person to the Secretary of State at a place designated by the Secretary of State that to remove the person from or require him to leave the United Kingdom would breach the United Kingdom's obligations under the Refugee Convention,

'entry clearance' has the meaning given by section 33(1) of the Immigration Act 1971 (c 77) (interpretation),

'human rights claim' means a claim made by a person to the Secretary of State at a place designated by the Secretary of State that to remove the person from or require him to leave the United Kingdom would be unlawful under section 6 of the Human Rights Act 1998 (c 42) (public authority not to act contrary to Convention) as being incompatible with his Convention rights,

'the Human Rights Convention' has the same meaning as 'the Convention' in the Human Rights Act 1998 and 'Convention rights' shall be construed in accordance with section 1 of that Act,

'illegal entrant' has the meaning given by section 33(1) of the Immigration Act 1971, 'immigration rules' means rules under section 1(4) of that Act (general immigration rules),

'prescribed' means prescribed by regulations,

'the Refugee Convention' means the Convention relating to the Status of Refugees done at Geneva on 28th July 1951 and its Protocol,

'visitor' means a visitor in accordance with immigration rules, and

'work permit' has the meaning given by section 33(1) of the Immigration Act 1971 (c 77) (interpretation).

(2) A reference to varying leave to enter or remain in the United Kingdom does not include a reference to adding, varying or revoking a condition of leave.

115 Appeal from within United Kingdom: unfounded human rights or asylum claim: transitional provision

(1) A person may not bring an appeal under section 65 or 69 of the Immigration and Asylum Act 1999 (human rights and asylum) while in the United Kingdom if –

(a) the Secretary of State certifies that the appeal relates to a human rights claim or an asylum claim which is clearly unfounded, and

(b) the person does not have another right of appeal while in the United Kingdom under Part IV of that Act.

(2) A person while in the United Kingdom may not bring an appeal under section 69 of that Act, or raise a question which relates to the Human Rights Convention under section 77 of that Act, if the Secretary of State certifies that –

(a) it is proposed to remove the person to a country of which he is not a national or citizen, and

(b) there is no reason to believe that the person's rights under the Human Rights Convention will be breached in that country.

(3) A person while in the United Kingdom may not bring an appeal under section 65 of that Act (human rights) if the Secretary of State certifies that –

(a) it is proposed to remove the person to a country of which he is not a national or citizen, and

(b) there is no reason to believe that the person's rights under the Human Rights Convention will be breached in that country.

(4) In determining whether a person in relation to whom a certificate has been issued under subsection (2) or (3) may be removed from the United Kingdom, the country specified in the certificate is to be regarded as –

(a) a place where a person's life and liberty is not threatened by reason of his race, religion, nationality, membership of a particular social group, or political opinion, and

(b) a place from which a person will not be sent to another country otherwise than in accordance with the Refugee Convention.

(5) Where a person in relation to whom a certificate is issued under this section subsequently brings an appeal or raises a question under section 65, 69 or 77 of that Act while outside the United Kingdom, the appeal or question shall be considered as if he had not been removed from the United Kingdom.

(6) If the Secretary of State is satisfied that a person who makes a human rights claim or an asylum claim is entitled to reside in a State listed in subsection (7), he shall issue a certificate under subsection (1) unless satisfied that the claim is not clearly unfounded.

(7) Those States are –

(a) the Republic of Cyprus,
(b) the Czech Republic,
(c) the Republic of Estonia,
(d) the Republic of Hungary,
(e) the Republic of Latvia,
(f) the Republic of Lithuania,
(g) the Republic of Malta,
(h) the Republic of Poland,
(i) the Slovak Republic,
(j) the Republic of Slovenia,
(k) the Republic of Albania,
(l) Bulgaria,
(m) Serbia and Montenegro,
(n) Jamaica,
(o) Macedonia,
(p) the Republic of Moldova, and
(q) Romania.

(8) The Secretary of State may by order add a State, or part of a State, to the list in subsection (7) if satisfied that –

(a) there is in general in that State or part no serious risk of persecution of persons entitled to reside in that State or part, and

(b) removal to that State or part of persons entitled to reside there will not in general contravene the United Kingdom's obligations under the Human Rights Convention.

(9) The Secretary of State may by order remove from the list in subsection (7) a State or part added under subsection (8).

(10) In this section 'asylum claim' and 'human rights claim' have the meanings given by section 113 but –

(a) a reference to a claim in that section shall be treated as including a reference to an allegation, and

(b) a reference in that section to making a claim at a place designated by the Secretary of State shall be ignored.

SCHEDULE 4

THE ASYLUM AND IMMIGRATION TRIBUNAL

1. The Lord Chancellor shall appoint the members of the Asylum and Immigration Tribunal.

2. – (1) A person is eligible for appointment as a member of the Tribunal only if he –

(a) has a seven year general qualification within the meaning of section 71 of the Courts and Legal Services Act 1990 (c 41),

(b) is an advocate or solicitor in Scotland of at least seven years' standing,

(c) is a member of the Bar of Northern Ireland, or a solicitor of the Supreme Court of Northern Ireland, of at least seven years' standing,

(d) in the Lord Chancellor's opinion, has legal experience which makes him as suitable for appointment as if he satisfied paragraph (a), (b) or (c), or

(e) in the Lord Chancellor's opinion, has non-legal experience which makes him suitable for appointment.

(2) A person appointed under sub-paragraph (1)(a) to (d) shall be known as a legally qualified member of the Tribunal.

3. – (1) A member –

(a) may resign by notice in writing to the Lord Chancellor,

(b) shall cease to be a member on reaching the age of 70, and

(c) otherwise, shall hold and vacate office in accordance with the terms of his appointment (which may include provision –

(i) about the training, appraisal and mentoring of members of the Tribunal by other members, and

(ii) for removal).

(2) Sub-paragraph (1)(b) is subject to section 26(4) to (6) of the Judicial Pensions and Retirement Act 1993 (c 8) (extension to age 75).

4. The Lord Chancellor may by order make provision for the title of members of the Tribunal.

5. – (1) The Lord Chancellor shall appoint –

(a) a member of the Tribunal, who holds or has held high judicial office within the meaning of the Appellate Jurisdiction Act 1876 (c 59), as President of the Tribunal, and

(b) one or more members of the Tribunal as Deputy President.

(2) A Deputy President –

(a) may act for the President if the President is unable to act or unavailable, and

(b) shall perform such functions as the President may delegate or assign to him.

...

As amended by the Asylum (Designated States) Order 2003, arts 3, 4; Asylum (Designated States) (No 2) Order 2003, art 2; Asylum and Immigration (Treatment of Claimants, etc) Act 2004, ss26(1)–(7), 27(1)–(7), 28, 29(1), 30, 31, Schedule 1, Schedule 2, paras 16, 18, 19.

REGIONAL ASSEMBLIES (PREPARATIONS) ACT 2003

(2003 c 10)

PART 1

REFERENDUMS

1 Assembly referendums

(1) The Secretary of State may by order cause a referendum to be held in a region specified in the order about the establishment of an elected assembly for that region.

(2) The date of the referendum must be specified in the order.

(3) But the Secretary of State must not make an order under subsection (1) unless each of the following two conditions is satisfied in relation to the region.

(4) The first condition is that the Secretary of State has considered the level of interest in the region in the holding of such a referendum.

(5) The second condition is that the Boundary Committee for England have made recommendations in relation to the region in pursuance of section 13.

(6) The Secretary of State may make the order at any time during the period of two years starting with the date on which he gives a direction under section 13 in relation to the region so long as before he makes the order he has no cause to think that the level of interest has changed materially.

(7) A change in the level of interest is material if the changed level is one at which the Secretary of State (disregarding factors relating to any other region) thinks he would not have given a direction under section 13.

(8) If the Secretary of State has cause to think that the level of interest has changed materially as mentioned in subsection (6), that subsection does not apply but he must not make an order under subsection (1) unless for the purposes of subsection (4) he considers –

(a) views expressed and information and evidence provided to him;

(b) such published material as he thinks appropriate.

(9) The Secretary of State may by order vary or revoke an order under this section

if he thinks it is not appropriate for a referendum to be held on the date specified in the order.

2 Local government referendums

(1) This section applies if the Secretary of State makes an order under section 1 to cause a referendum to be held in a region about the establishment of an elected assembly for that region.

(2) The Secretary of State must by order cause a referendum to be held in each county area in the region about the government's proposals for the structure of local government in that area.

(3) A county area is an area in the region in relation to which both a county council and one or more district councils have functions.

(4) But if the government's proposals for a county area include an option providing for a local authority whose area includes any part of the area of more than one county area, the county area for the purposes of this section is the combined area of each of those county areas.

(5) The government's proposals for the structure of local government –

(a) are such of the recommendations of the Boundary Committee for England made in pursuance of a direction under section 13(1) or 16(4) as the Secretary of State thinks appropriate subject to such modifications (if any) as he proposes to make in pursuance of section 17(3);

(b) must include at least two options for structural change (within the meaning of Part 2 of the Local Government Act 1992 (c 19)) in relation to each county area in the region.

(6) The date of a referendum held in pursuance of an order under subsection (2) must be –

(a) specified in the order;

(b) the same date as the date specified in the order under section 1.

(7) An order under subsection (2) must not be made before the end of the period of six weeks starting with the day on which the Secretary of State receives the recommendations of the Boundary Committee in pursuance of a direction under section 13(1) or 16(4).

(8) The Secretary of State by order –

(a) may vary an order under subsection (2);

(b) must revoke such an order if he revokes the order under section 1.

(9) A Minister of the Crown may by order make such provision as he thinks appropriate in connection with a referendum held in pursuance of an order under subsection (2).

(10) An order under subsection (9) may –

(a) make provision for the creation of offences;

(b) apply or incorporate with or without modifications or exceptions any provision of any enactment (whenever passed or made and including this Act) relating to elections or referendums;

(c) modify any provision of Chapter 2 of Part 7 of the 2000 Act as it applies to a referendum held in pursuance of an order under section 1.

3 Referendum questions

(1) The question to be asked in a referendum held in pursuance of an order under section 1 is:

'Should there be an elected assembly for the (*insert name of region*) region?'

(2) The following statement (in as nearly as may be the following form) must precede the question on the ballot paper:

'You can help to decide whether there should be an elected assembly in the (*insert name of region*) region. If an elected assembly is to be established, it is intended that:

- the elected assembly would be responsible for a range of activities currently carried out mainly by central government bodies, including regional economic development; and
- local government would be reorganised into a single tier in those parts of the region that currently have both county and district councils.'

(3) The question to be asked in a referendum in pursuance of an order under section 2(2) is:

'Which of the following options for single tier local government do you prefer?

- *insert text of options set out in the order requiring the referendum to be held.*'

(4) If the same ballot paper is used for both a referendum held in pursuance of an order under section 1 and a referendum held in pursuance of an order under section 2(2), the following statement (in as nearly as may be the following form) must precede the question on the ballot paper used in any part of the region where a referendum is held in pursuance of an order under section 2(2):

'Your part of the region currently has both county and district councils. You can help to decide how local authorities in your part of the region will be reorganised into a single tier. There will be no such reorganisation if an elected assembly is not established.'

(5) If the same ballot paper is not used for both referendums as mentioned in subsection (4) the following statement (in as nearly as may be the following form) must precede the question on the ballot paper used for a referendum held in pursuance of an order under section 2(2):

'If an elected assembly is established for the (*insert name of region*) region, it is intended that local government will be reorganised into a single tier in those parts of the region that currently have both county and district councils.

Your part of the region currently has both county and district councils. You can help to decide how local authorities in your part of the region will be reorganised into a single tier. There will be no such reorganisation if an elected assembly is not established.'

(6) An order under section 2(2) must set out –

(a) the text of the options to be inserted in the question specified in subsection (3);

(b) such explanatory material relating to the options as will be made available for voters at the time they vote.

(7) Before an order under section 2(2) is laid before Parliament in pursuance of section 29(2) the Secretary of State must consult the Electoral Commission –

(a) on the wording of the text required to be inserted in pursuance of subsection (3);

(b) on the explanatory material.

(8) At the time when the order is so laid the Secretary of State must lay before each House a report stating any views which the Commission have expressed in response to the consultation as to –

(a) the intelligibility of the text mentioned in subsection (7);

(b) the explanatory material.

(9) Explanatory material does not include instructions to voters as to the conduct of the referendum.

4 Entitlement to vote

(1) A person is entitled to vote in a referendum held in a region in pursuance of an order under section 1 if on the date of the referendum he is entitled to vote at the election of councillors for any electoral area in the region.

(2) A person is entitled to vote in a referendum held in a county area of a region in pursuance of an order under section 2(2) if on the date of the referendum he is entitled to vote at the election of councillors for any electoral area in the county area.

(3) But subsections (1) and (2) are subject to provision made by the Secretary of State in regulations for disregarding alterations made after a specified date in a register of electors.

(4) The regulations may apply or incorporate with or without modifications or exceptions any provision of any enactment (whenever passed or made) relating to referendums or elections.

(5) An electoral area is any electoral division or ward (or in the case of a parish in

which there are no wards the parish) for which the election of councillors is held under the Local Government Act 1972 (c 70).

(6) County area must be construed in accordance with section 2.

5 Referendum period

For the purposes of Part 7 of the 2000 Act (referendums) the Secretary of State must by order determine the referendum period for a referendum held in pursuance of an order under section 1.

6 Further referendums

(1) Subsection (2) applies if –

(a) a referendum is held in a region in pursuance of an order under section 1, and

(b) a majority of the votes cast in the referendum is against there being an elected assembly for the region.

(2) No further order under section 1 may be made in relation to the region until the end of the period of seven years starting with the day on which the referendum was held.

(3) Any question as to the number of votes cast in a referendum in favour of an answer to a question is determined by the certificate of the Chief Counting Officer given under section 128 of the 2000 Act (functions of Chief Counting Officer).

(4) Subsection (5) applies if in any proceedings any certificate given by a person appointed for the purpose as to the number of votes cast in favour of any option in a referendum held in a county area in pursuance of an order under section 2(2) is declared or held to be invalid.

(5) The Secretary of State may by order cause a further referendum to be held in that county area as mentioned in that section and for that purpose the following provisions of section 2 apply as they apply for the purpose of an order made under section 2(2) –

(a) subsections (3) to (5);
(b) subsection (6)(a);
(c) subsections (9) and (10).

(6) If an order is made under subsection (5) any reference in this Act to a referendum held in pursuance of an order under section 2(2) or to the order must be construed as a reference to a referendum held in pursuance of an order under subsection (5) or to the order under that subsection (as the case may be).

(7) But subsection (6) applies to such a reference in section 3(7) and (8) only to the extent that the wording of the text mentioned in section 3(7)(a) or the explanatory material differs from that considered by the Electoral Commission for the purposes of the referendum held in pursuance of the order under section 2(2).

(8) For the purposes of a referendum held in pursuance of an order under subsection (5) the Secretary of State may by order vary the terms of the statement set out in section 3(5).

(9) Before an order under subsection (8) is laid before Parliament in pursuance of section 29(2) the Secretary of State must consult the Electoral Commission as to the wording of the statement as so varied.

(10) At the time when the order is so laid the Secretary of State must lay before each House a report stating any views which the Commission have expressed in response to the consultation as to the intelligibility of the statement as so varied.

(11) The Secretary of State may by order vary or revoke an order made under subsection (5) if he thinks that it is not appropriate for the referendum to be held on the date specified in the order.

(12) Explanatory material must be construed in accordance with section 3.

7 Combination of polls

(1) A Minister of the Crown may by order make provision for the combination of polls at a referendum held in pursuance of an order under section 1 or 2(2) with one another or with –

(a) polls at a referendum held under section 27 of the Local Government Act 2000 (c 22) or by virtue of regulations or an order under Part 2 of that Act;

(b) polls at any election.

(2) The order may –

(a) make provision in connection with the combination of polls;

(b) make provision for the creation of offences;

(c) apply or incorporate with or without modifications or exceptions any provision of any enactment (whenever passed or made) relating to elections or referendums.

8 Encouraging voting

The Electoral Commission may do anything they think necessary or expedient for the purpose of encouraging voting at referendums to be held in pursuance of an order under this Part.

9 Provision of information to voters

(1) Subsection (2) applies if –

(a) the Secretary of State makes an order under section 1 to cause a referendum to be held in a region about the establishment of an elected assembly for the region, and

(b) before the appropriate day the Electoral Commission have not designated (in relation to each possible outcome of the referendum) an organisation under section 108 of the 2000 Act (organisations to whom assistance is available under section 110 of that Act).

(2) The Electoral Commission may take such steps as they think appropriate to provide for persons entitled to vote in the referendum such information as the Commission think is likely to promote awareness among those persons about the arguments for and against each answer to the referendum question.

(3) The appropriate day is –

(a) the 43rd day of the referendum period if one or more applications under section 109 of the 2000 Act (applications for assistance under section 110 of that Act) is made before the 29th day of the referendum period in relation to each possible outcome of the referendum;

(b) the 29th day of the referendum period in any other case.

(4) But if a Minister of the Crown makes an order under section 109(6) of the 2000 Act the appropriate day is the day specified in the order for the purposes of this section.

(5) Subsection (6) applies if the Secretary of State makes an order under section 2(2) to cause a referendum to be held about the government's proposals for the structure of local government.

(6) The Electoral Commission may take such steps as they think appropriate to provide for persons entitled to vote in the referendum such information as the Commission think is likely to promote awareness among those persons about the arguments relating to the options in those proposals.

(7) Information provided in pursuance of this section must be provided by the means the Commission think is most likely to secure (in the most cost effective way) that the information comes to the notice of all persons entitled to vote in the referendum.

11 Legal challenge

(1) No court shall entertain any proceedings for questioning –

(a) the number of ballot papers or votes cast in a referendum held in pursuance of an order under section 1 as certified by the Chief Counting Officer for the referendum or by a counting officer;

(b) the number of ballot papers or votes cast in a referendum held in pursuance of an order under subsection (2) of section 2 as certified by a person appointed for the purpose in pursuance of an order under subsection (9) of that section,

unless the proceedings are brought in accordance with this section.

(2) The proceedings must be brought by a claim for judicial review.

(3) The court must not give permission for the claim unless the claim form is filed before the end of the period of six weeks starting with the certificate date.

(4) The certificate date is –

(a) the date on which a certificate as to the matters mentioned in subsection (1)(a) or (b) is given by the Chief Counting Officer, counting officer or other person mentioned in subsection (1)(b);

(b) if there is more than one such certificate in a referendum the date on which the last such certificate is given.

12 Supplementary

(1) This Part does not affect the power of a Minister of the Crown to make provision under section 129 of the 2000 Act (orders regulating the conduct of referendums) for or in connection with a referendum held in pursuance of an order under section 1 above.

(2) It is immaterial whether the power is exercised before or after the passing of this Act.

(3) Section 126 of the 2000 Act (identification of promoter and publisher of referendum materials) does not apply to any material published for the purposes of a referendum held in pursuance of an order under section 1 above if the publication is required under or by virtue of an order under section 129(1) of that Act or section 7 above.

(4) No order may be made under any of the following provisions unless the person making the order first consults the Electoral Commission –

(a) section 2(9);

(b) section 7(1);

(c) section 10(1).

(5) Expressions used in this Part and in Part 7 of the 2000 Act have the same meaning in this Part as they do in that Part.

(6) The 2000 Act is the Political Parties, Elections and Referendums Act 2000 (c 41).

(7) Subsection (5) –

(a) does not apply to references to the Secretary of State;

(b) is subject to section 28 below.

(8) This section applies for the purposes of this Part.

PART 2

LOCAL GOVERNMENT REVIEWS

13 Local government review

(1) If the Secretary of State is considering whether to cause a referendum to be held in a region about the establishment of an elected assembly for the region, he may direct the Boundary Committee for England –

(a) to carry out a local government review of the region;

(b) to make recommendations as to the matters considered by the review.

(2) But the Secretary of State must not give a direction unless he has considered the level of interest in the region in the holding of a referendum. …

14 Local government review: supplementary

(1) This section applies for the purposes of section 13.

(2) The number of people living in an area is taken to be the most recent estimate of that number published by the Office for National Statistics.

(3) A local government review is a review to consider –

(a) appropriate structural change for the region;

(b) whether any boundary changes should be made in the region in connection with or to facilitate the carrying out of the structural change.

(4) Relevant local authorities are the county council and district council for any area in the region in relation to which both councils have functions. …

(8) In carrying out their functions under this Part the Boundary Committee must –

(a) assume that there is an elected assembly for the region;

(b) recommend structural change for so much of the area of the region as is comprised of the areas of all of the relevant local authorities in the region;

(c) have regard to the need to reflect the identities and interests of local communities;

(d) have regard to the need to secure effective and convenient local government;

(e) have regard to guidance issued by the Secretary of State.

16 Boundary Committee recommendations

(1) This section applies in relation to recommendations made by the Boundary Committee in pursuance of section 13(1)(b).

(2) The recommendations must include at least two options for structural change in relation to each county area in the region.

(3) At any time after he receives the recommendations the Secretary of State may –

(a) direct the Boundary Committee to supply him with additional information or advice;

(b) reject one or more of the options.

(4) If the Secretary of State rejects one or more of the options he may direct the Boundary Committee either –

(a) to make different recommendations, or

(b) to carry out a further local government review of the region and to make further recommendations. …

17 Implementation of recommendations

(1) This section applies to a region if –

(a) a referendum has been held in the region in pursuance of an order under section 1, and

(b) the Secretary of State proposes that an elected assembly is established for the region.

(2) The Secretary of State may by order give effect to all or any of the recommendations of the Boundary Committee for England made to him in pursuance of a direction under section 13 or 16(4).

(3) Such an order may give effect to a recommendation with or without modifications. ...

PART 3

ADVICE OF ELECTORAL COMMISSION

21 Advice of the Electoral Commission

(1) This section applies in relation to a region if –

(a) a referendum has been held in the region in pursuance of an order under section 1, and

(b) the Secretary of State proposes that an elected assembly is established for the region.

(2) Not later than the end of the period of two years beginning with the day on which the referendum was held the Secretary of State must give the Electoral Commission a direction in respect of a region in relation to which this section applies.

(3) A direction under subsection (2) must require the Electoral Commission to give the Secretary of State advice as to such of the following matters as the Secretary of State thinks appropriate –

(a) the electoral areas into which the region is to be divided for the purposes of the election of members to any assembly established following the referendum;

(b) the number of electoral areas;

(c) the name by which each electoral area is to be known;

(d) the total number of members to be elected to the assembly.

(4) For the purposes of subsection (3) the direction –

(a) may specify maximum and minimum numbers or total numbers (as the case may be);

(b) may require the advice to be given in respect of a specified number of options.

(5) A direction given under this section may be varied (whether or not within the period of two years mentioned in subsection (2)) by a subsequent direction.

22 Preparation and submission of advice

(1) A direction given to the Electoral Commission under section 21 must specify the timetable in accordance with which any thing must be done in connection with the advice. ...

23 Electoral Commission exercise of functions

In carrying out their functions under this Part the Electoral Commission must have regard (in particular) to –

(a) the need to reflect the identities and interests of local communities;

(b) the need to secure that the number of electors for an electoral area for an assembly is as near as is reasonably practicable to the number of electors for the other electoral areas (taking account, where appropriate, of special geographical considerations);

(c) guidance given by the Secretary of State.

PART 5

GENERAL

26 Enactment establishing assemblies immaterial

For the purposes of this Act it is immaterial whether any enactment confers power on the Secretary of State to establish elected assemblies for regions.

28 Regions

In this Act a region is a region (except London) specified in Schedule 1 to the Regional Development Agencies Act 1998 (c 45).

ANTI-SOCIAL BEHAVIOUR ACT 2003

(2003 c 38)

PART 4

DISPERSAL OF GROUPS, ETC

30 Dispersal of groups and removal of persons under 16 to their place of residence

(1) This section applies where a relevant officer has reasonable grounds for believing –

(a) that any members of the public have been intimidated, harassed, alarmed or distressed as a result of the presence or behaviour of groups of two or more persons in public places in any locality in his police area (the 'relevant locality'), and

(b) that anti-social behaviour is a significant and persistent problem in the relevant locality.

(2) The relevant officer may give an authorisation that the powers conferred on a constable in uniform by subsections (3) to (6) are to be exercisable for a period specified in the authorisation which does not exceed 6 months.

(3) Subsection (4) applies if a constable in uniform has reasonable grounds for believing that the presence or behaviour of a group of two or more persons in any public place in the relevant locality has resulted, or is likely to result, in any members of the public being intimidated, harassed, alarmed or distressed.

(4) The constable may give one or more of the following directions, namely –

(a) a direction requiring the persons in the group to disperse (either immediately or by such time as he may specify and in such way as he may specify),

(b) a direction requiring any of those persons whose place of residence is not within the relevant locality to leave the relevant locality or any part of the relevant locality (either immediately or by such time as he may specify and in such way as he may specify), and

(c) a direction prohibiting any of those persons whose place of residence is not within the relevant locality from returning to the relevant locality or any part of the relevant locality for such period (not exceeding 24 hours) from the giving of the direction as he may specify;

but this subsection is subject to subsection (5).

(5) A direction under subsection (4) may not be given in respect of a group of persons –

(a) who are engaged in conduct which is lawful under section 220 of the Trade Union and Labour Relations (Consolidation) Act 1992 (c 52), or

(b) who are taking part in a public procession of the kind mentioned in section 11(1) of the Public Order Act 1986 (c 64) in respect of which –

(i) written notice has been given in accordance with section 11 of that Act, or

(ii) such notice is not required to be given as provided by subsections (1) and (2) of that section.

(6) If, between the hours of 9pm and 6am, a constable in uniform finds a person in any public place in the relevant locality who he has reasonable grounds for believing –

(a) is under the age of 16, and

(b) is not under the effective control of a parent or a responsible person aged 18 or over,

he may remove the person to the person's place of residence unless he has reasonable grounds for believing that the person would, if removed to that place, be likely to suffer significant harm.

(7) In this section any reference to the presence or behaviour of a group of persons is to be read as including a reference to the presence or behaviour of any one or more of the persons in the group.

31 Authorisations: supplemental

(1) An authorisation –

(a) must be in writing,

(b) must be signed by the relevant officer giving it, and

(c) must specify –

(i) the relevant locality,

(ii) the grounds on which the authorisation is given, and

(iii) the period during which the powers conferred by section 30(3) to (6) are exercisable.

(2) An authorisation may not be given without the consent of the local authority or each local authority whose area includes the whole or part of the relevant locality.

(3) Publicity must be given to an authorisation by either or both of the following methods –

(a) publishing an authorisation notice in a newspaper circulating in the relevant locality,

(b) posting an authorisation notice in some conspicuous place or places within the relevant locality.

(4) An 'authorisation notice' is a notice which –

(a) states the authorisation has been given,

(b) specifies the relevant locality, and

(c) specifies the period during which the powers conferred by section 30(3) to (6) are exercisable.

(5) Subsection (3) must be complied with before the beginning of the period mentioned in subsection (4)(c).

(6) An authorisation may be withdrawn by –

(a) the relevant officer who gave it, or

(b) any other relevant officer whose police area includes the relevant locality and whose rank is the same as or higher than that of the relevant officer mentioned in paragraph (a).

(7) Before the withdrawal of an authorisation, consultation must take place with any local authority whose area includes the whole or part of the relevant locality.

(8) The withdrawal of an authorisation does not affect the exercise of any power pursuant to that authorisation which occurred prior to its withdrawal.

(9) The giving or withdrawal of an authorisation does not prevent the giving of a further authorisation in respect of a locality which includes the whole or any part of the relevant locality to which the earlier authorisation relates.

(10) In this section 'authorisation' means an authorisation under section 30.

32 Powers under section 30: supplemental

(1) A direction under section 30(4) –

(a) may be given orally,

(b) may be given to any person individually or to two or more persons together, and

(c) may be withdrawn or varied by the person who gave it.

(2) A person who knowingly contravenes a direction given to him under section 30(4) commits an offence and is liable on summary conviction to –

(a) a fine not exceeding level 4 on the standard scale, or

(b) imprisonment for a term not exceeding 3 months,

or to both.

(3) A constable in uniform may arrest without warrant any person he reasonably suspects has committed an offence under subsection (2).

(4) Where the power under section 30(6) is exercised, any local authority whose area includes the whole or part of the relevant locality must be notified of that fact.

34 Code of practice

(1) The Secretary of State may issue a code of practice about –

(a) the giving or withdrawal of authorisations under section 30, and
(b) the exercise of the powers conferred by section 30(3) to (6).

(2) The Secretary of State may from time to time revise the whole or any part of a code of practice issued under this section.

(3) The Secretary of State must lay any code of practice issued by him under this section, and any revisions of such a code, before Parliament.

(4) In giving or withdrawing an authorisation under section 30, a relevant officer must have regard to any code of practice for the time being in force under this section.

(5) In exercising the powers conferred by section 30(3) to (6), a constable in uniform or community support officer must have regard to any code of practice for the time being in force under this section.

(6) A code of practice under this section may make different provision for different cases.

36 Interpretation

In this Part –

'anti-social behaviour' means behaviour by a person which causes or is likely to cause harassment, alarm or distress to one or more other persons not of the same household as the person,

'local authority' means –

(a) in relation to England, a district council, a county council that is the council for a county in which there are no district councils, a London borough council, the Common Council of the City of London or the Council of the Isles of Scilly,
(b) in relation to Wales, a county council or a county borough council,

'public place' means –

(a) any highway, and
(b) any place to which at the material time the public or any section of the public has access, on payment or otherwise, as of right or by virtue of express or implied permission,

'relevant locality' has the same meaning as in section 30,

'relevant officer' means a police officer of or above the rank of superintendent.

EUROPEAN PARLIAMENTARY AND LOCAL ELECTIONS (PILOTS) ACT 2004
(2004 c 2)

1 Piloting conduct at European and local elections

(1) An election to which this section applies (a pilot election) must be held –

(a) only by postal voting, and (for that purpose);

(b) in accordance with provision made by the Secretary of State by order (a pilot order).

(2) These are the elections to which this section applies –

(a) the European Parliamentary general election of 2004 in a pilot region;

(b) a local government election in England and Wales if the poll at such an election is combined with the poll at an election mentioned in paragraph (a).

(3) These are the pilot regions –

(a) North East;

(b) East Midlands;

(c) Yorkshire and the Humber;

(d) North West.

(4) Postal voting is voting where no polling station is used and a person entitled to vote in person or by proxy must deliver by post or by such other means as is specified in a pilot order –

(a) the ballot paper, and

(b) the completed declaration of identity form.

(5) The declaration of identity form is a form which is delivered along with the ballot paper and which is completed by being signed –

(a) by the person to whom the ballot paper is addressed, and

(b) by a witness to that signing whose name and address are clearly marked on the form.

(6) The declaration of identity must contain a statement advising the voter that the ballot paper should be completed by him –

(a) outside the presence of any other person, or

(b) in the case of a voter who requires assistance, in accordance with such advice as is provided for in the pilot order.

(7) A pilot order –

(a) may modify or disapply any provision made by or under a relevant enactment;
(b) may contain such consequential, incidental, supplementary or transitional provision or savings (including provision amending, replacing, suspending or revoking provision made by or under any enactment) as the Secretary of State thinks appropriate;
(c) may make different provision for different purposes.

4 Electoral Commission report

(1) After a pilot election has been held, the Electoral Commission must prepare a report in relation to it.

(2) For the purposes of subsection (1) the Electoral Commission must consult the council for every county and district in the region in which the pilot election was held.

(3) Every relevant local authority in the region must give the Commission such assistance as they may reasonably require in connection with the preparation of the report.

(4) The assistance may include –

(a) making arrangements for ascertaining the views of electors about the administration of the election;
(b) reporting to the Commission allegations of personation and of other electoral offences or malpractice.

(5) The report must include a copy of the pilot order.

(6) The report must also include an assessment of the extent to which postal voting and provision made by the pilot order –

(a) facilitated voting at the election;
(b) encouraged voting at the election;
(c) affected the incidence of personation or other electoral offences or malpractice;
(d) assisted the counting of votes at the election;
(e) provided opportunities for savings in the costs of administering the election or led to any increase in such costs.

(7) For the purposes of subsection (6)(a) the report must include a statement of the number of ballot papers which appear to the returning officer to have been delivered to him during the period of one week starting with the day after the date on which the poll closed.

(8) For the purposes of subsection (6)(c) the Commission must ascertain by such

means as it thinks appropriate and report on the views of electors as to whether postal voting and provision made by the pilot order –

(a) provided sufficient safeguards against fraud;

(b) provided appropriate protection for the secrecy of the ballot.

(9) The report must also include an assessment as to the following matters relating to the requirement by virtue of section 2 [Pilot order] to provide polling progress information –

(a) its effect on the campaigning of candidates and political parties;

(b) the use made by candidates and political parties of the information;

(c) the views of electors and political parties about the provision of the information (including views as to its effect on turnout of voters and use of the information by candidates and political parties);

(d) its effect on the conduct and administration of the election.

(10) The assessment must include a statement by the Electoral Commission as to whether in their opinion –

(a) the turnout of voters was higher than it would otherwise have been;

(b) electors found the procedures provided for their assistance easy to use.

(11) Not later than the end of the period of three months beginning with the date of the declaration of the result of the European Parliamentary general election in the region the Electoral Commission must –

(a) send a copy of the report to the Secretary of State, and

(b) publish the report in such manner as they think fit.

(12) The returning officer is the person who is described as such in the pilot order.

(13) This section does not affect the duty of the Electoral Commission to prepare and publish under section 5 of the Political Parties, Elections and Referendums Act 2000 (c 41) a report on the administration of the election.

APPENDIX

EUROPEAN CONVENTION FOR THE PROTECTION OF HUMAN RIGHTS AND FUNDAMENTAL FREEDOMS 1950

(Cmd 8969)

Article 1

The High Contracting Parties shall secure to everyone within their jurisdiction the rights and freedoms in Section 1 of this Convention [Articles 2 to 18].

SECTION I

Article 2

1 Everyone's right to life shall be protected by law. No one shall be deprived of his life intentionally save in the execution of a sentence of a court following his conviction of a crime for which this penalty is provided by law.

2 Deprivation of life shall not be regarded as inflicted in contravention of this Article when it results from the use of force which is no more than absolutely necessary:

(a) in defence of any person from unlawful violence;

(b) in order to effect a lawful arrest or to prevent the escape of a person lawfully detained;

(c) in action lawfully taken for the purpose of quelling a riot or insurrection.

Article 3

No one shall be subjected to torture or to inhuman or degrading treatment or punishment.

Article 4

1 No one shall be held in slavery or servitude.

2 No one shall be required to perform forced or compulsory labour.

3 For the purpose of this Article the term 'forced or compulsory labour' shall not include:

(a) any work required to be done in the ordinary course of detention imposed according to the provisions of Article 5 of this Convention or during conditional release from such detention;

(b) any service of a military character or, in case of conscientious objectors in countries where they are recognised, service exacted instead of compulsory military service;

(c) any service exacted in case of an emergency or calamity threatening the life or well-being of the community;

(d) any work or service which forms part of normal civil obligations.

Article 5

1 Everyone has the right to liberty and security of person. No one shall be deprived of his liberty save in the following cases and in accordance with a procedure prescribed by law:

(a) the lawful detention of a person after conviction by a competent court;

(b) the lawful arrest or detention of a person for non-compliance with the lawful order of a court or in order to secure the fulfilment of any obligation prescribed by law;

(c) the lawful arrest or detention of a person effected for the purpose of bringing him before the competent legal authority on reasonable suspicion of having committed an offence or when it is reasonably considered necessary to prevent his committing an offence or fleeing after having done so;

(d) the detention of a minor by lawful order for the purpose of educational supervision or his lawful detention for the purpose of bringing him before the competent legal authority;

(e) the lawful detention of persons for the prevention of the spreading of infectious diseases, of persons of unsound mind, alcoholics or drug addicts or vagrants;

(f) the lawful arrest or detention of a person to prevent his effecting an unauthorised entry into the country or of a person against whom action is being taken with a view to deportation or extradition.

2 Everyone who is arrested shall be informed promptly, in a language which he understands, of the reasons for his arrest and of any charge against him.

3 Everyone arrested or detained in accordance with the provisions of paragraph 1(c) of this Article shall be brought promptly before a judge or other officer authorised by law to exercise judicial power and shall be entitled to trial within a reasonable time or to release pending trial. Release may be conditioned by guarantees to appear for trial.

4 Everyone who is deprived of his liberty by arrest or detention shall be entitled to take proceedings by which the lawfulness of his detention shall be decided speedily by a court and his release ordered if the detention is not lawful.

5 Everyone who has been the victim of arrest or detention in contravention of the provisions of this Article shall have an enforceable right to compensation.

Article 6

1 In the determination of his civil rights and obligations or of any criminal charge against him, everyone is entitled to a fair and public hearing within a reasonable time by an independent and impartial tribunal established by law. Judgment shall be pronounced publicly but the press and public may be excluded from all or part of the trial in the interest of morals, public order or national security in a democratic society, where the interests of juveniles or the protection of the private life of the parties so require, or to the extent strictly necessary in the opinion of the court in special circumstances where publicity would prejudice the interests of justice.

2 Everyone charged with a criminal offence shall be presumed innocent until proved guilty according to law.

3 Everyone charged with a criminal offence has the following minimum rights:

(a) to be informed promptly, in a language which he understands and in detail, of the nature and cause of the accusation against him;

(b) to have adequate time and facilities for the preparation of his defence;

(c) to defend himself in person or through legal assistance of his own choosing or, if he has not sufficient means to pay for legal assistance, to be given it free when the interests of justice so require;

(d) to examine or have examined witnesses against him and to obtain the attendance and examination of witnesses on his behalf under the same conditions as witnesses against him;

(e) to have the free assistance of an interpreter if he cannot understand or speak the language used in court.

Article 7

1 No one shall be held guilty of any criminal offence on account of any act or omission which did not constitute a criminal offence under national or international law at the time when it was committed. Nor shall a heavier penalty be imposed than the one that was applicable at the time the criminal offence was committed.

2 This Article shall not prejudice the trial and punishment of any person for any act or omission which, at the time when it was committed, was criminal according to the general principles of law recognised by civilised nations.

Article 8

1 Everyone has the right to respect for his private and family life, his home and his correspondence.

2 There shall be no interference by a public authority with the exercise of this

right except such as is in accordance with the law and is necessary in a democratic society in the interests of national security, public safety or the economic well-being of the country, for the prevention of disorder or crime, for the protection of health or morals, or for the protection of the rights and freedoms of others.

Article 9

1 Everyone has the right to freedom of thought, conscience and religion; this right includes freedom to change his religion or beliefs and freedom, either alone or in community with others and in public or private, to manifest his religion or belief, in worship, teaching, practice and observance.

2 Freedom to manifest one's religion or beliefs shall be subject only to such limitations as are prescribed by law and are necessary in a democratic society in the interests of public safety, for the protection of public order, health or morals, or for the protection of the rights and freedoms of others.

Article 10

1 Everyone has the right to freedom of expression. This right shall include freedom to hold opinions and to receive and impart information and ideas without interference by public authority and regardless of frontiers. This Article shall not prevent States from requiring the licensing of broadcasting, television or cinema enterprises.

2 The exercise of these freedoms, since it carries with it duties and responsibilities, may be subject to such formalities, conditions, restrictions or penalties as are prescribed by law and are necessary in a democratic society, in the interests of national security, territorial integrity or public safety, for the prevention of disorder or crime, for the protection of health or morals, for the protection of the reputation or rights of others, for preventing the disclosure of information received in confidence, or for maintaining the authority and impartiality of the judiciary.

Article 11

1 Everyone has the right to freedom of peaceful assembly and to freedom of association with others, including the right to form and to join trade unions for the protection of his interests.

2 No restrictions shall be placed on the exercise of these rights other than such as are prescribed by law and are necessary in a democratic society in the interests of national security or public safety, for the prevention of disorder or crime, for the protection of health or morals or for the protection of the rights and freedoms of others. This Article shall not prevent the imposition of lawful restrictions on the exercise of these rights by members of the armed forces, of the police or of the administration of the State.

Article 12

Men and women of marriageable age have the right to marry and to found a family, according to the national laws governing the exercise of this right.

Article 13

Everyone whose rights and freedoms as set forth in this Convention are violated shall have an effective remedy before a national authority notwithstanding that the violation has been committed by persons acting in an official capacity.

Article 14

The enjoyment of the rights and freedoms set forth in this Convention shall be secured without discrimination on any ground such as sex, race, colour, language, religion, political or other opinion, national or social origin, association with a national minority, property, birth or other status.

Article 15

1 In time of war or other public emergency threatening the life of the nation any High Contracting Party may take measures derogating from its obligations under this Convention to the extent strictly required by the exigencies of the situation, provided that such measures are not inconsistent with its other obligations under international law.

2 No derogation from Article 2, except in respect of deaths resulting from lawful acts of war, or from Articles 3, 4 (paragraph 1) and 7 shall be made under this provision.

3 Any High Contracting Party availing itself of this right of derogation shall keep the Secretary-General of the Council of Europe fully informed of the measures which it has taken and the reasons therefor. It shall also inform the Secretary-General of the Council of Europe when such measures have ceased to operate and the provisions of the Convention are again fully executed.

Article 16

Nothing in Articles 10, 11 and 14 shall be regarded as preventing the High Contracting Parties from imposing restrictions on the political activity of aliens.

Article 17

Nothing in this Convention may be interpreted as implying for any State, group or person any right to engage in any activity or perform any act aimed at the destruction of any of the rights and freedoms set forth herein or at their limitation to a greater extent than is provided for in the Convention.

Article 18

The restrictions permitted under this Convention to the said rights and freedoms shall not be applied for any purpose other than those for which they have been prescribed. ...

INDEX

Old Bailey Press

The Old Bailey Press Integrated Student Law Library is tailor-made to help you at every stage of your studies, from the preliminaries of each subject through to the final examination. The series of Textbooks, Revision WorkBooks, 150 Leading Cases and Cracknell's Statutes are interrelated to provide you with a comprehensive set of study materials.

You can buy Old Bailey Press books from your University Bookshop, your local Bookshop, directly using this form, or you can order a free catalogue of our titles from the address shown overleaf.

The following subjects each have a Textbook, 150 Leading Cases, Revision WorkBook and Cracknell's Statutes unless otherwise stated.

Administrative Law
Commercial Law
Company Law
Conflict of Laws
Constitutional Law
Conveyancing (Textbook and 150 Leading Cases)
Criminal Law
Criminology (Textbook and Sourcebook)
Employment Law (Textbook and Cracknell's Statutes)
English and European Legal Systems
Equity and Trusts
Evidence
Family Law
Jurisprudence: The Philosophy of Law (Textbook, Sourcebook and Revision WorkBook)
Land: The Law of Real Property
Law of International Trade
Law of the European Union
Legal Skills and System (Textbook)
Obligations: Contract Law
Obligations: The Law of Tort
Public International Law
Revenue Law (Textbook, Revision WorkBook and Cracknell's Statutes)
Succession (Textbook, Revision WorkBook and Cracknell's Statutes)

Mail order prices:

Textbook	£15.95
150 Leading Cases	£12.95
Revision WorkBook	£10.95
Cracknell's Statutes	£11.95
Suggested Solutions 1999–2000	£6.95
Suggested Solutions 2000–2001	£6.95
Suggested Solutions 2001–2002	£6.95
101 Questions and Answers	£7.95
Law Update 2004	£10.95
Law Update 2005	£10.95

Please note details and prices are subject to alteration.

To complete your order, please fill in the form below:

Module	Books required	Quantity	Price	Cost
		Postage		
		TOTAL		

For the UK and Europe, add £4.95 for the first book ordered, then add £1.00 for each subsequent book ordered for postage and packing.
For the rest of the world, add 50% for airmail.

ORDERING

By telephone to Customer Services at 020 8317 6039, with your credit card to hand.

By fax to 020 8317 6004 (giving your credit card details).

Website: www.oldbaileypress.co.uk
E-Mail: customerservices@oldbaileypress.co.uk

By post to: Customer Services, Old Bailey Press at Holborn College, Woolwich Road, Charlton, London, SE7 8LN.

When ordering by post, please enclose full payment by cheque or banker's draft, or complete the credit card details below.You may also order a free catalogue of our complete range of titles from this address.

We aim to despatch your books within 3 working days of receiving your order. All parts of the form must be completed.

Name
Address

Postcode
E-Mail
Telephone

Total value of order, including postage: £

I enclose a cheque/banker's draft for the above sum, or

charge my ☐ Access/Mastercard ☐ Visa ☐ American Express

Cardholder: ....

Card number

☐☐☐☐ ☐☐☐☐ ☐☐☐☐ ☐☐☐☐

Expiry date ☐☐☐☐

Signature: .... Date: ....